The LONG DISCOURSES *of the* BUDDHA

THE TEACHINGS OF THE BUDDHA SERIES

The Connected Discourses of the Buddha:
A Translation of the Saṃyutta Nikāya

The Numerical Discourses of the Buddha:
A Translation of the Aṅguttara Nikāya

The Middle Length Discourses of the Buddha:
A Translation of the Majjhima Nikāya

In the Buddha's Words:
An Anthology of Discourses from the Pāli Canon

Great Disciples of the Buddha:
Their Lives, Their Works, Their Legacy

THE TEACHINGS OF THE BUDDHA

The *Long* Discourses *of the* Buddha

A Translation of the
Dīgha Nikāya

Translated from the Pāli

by

Maurice Walshe

Wisdom

Wisdom Publications
199 Elm Street
Somerville, MA 02144 USA
wisdompubs.org

First published in 1987 in paperback under the title of
Thus I Have Heard: The Long Discourses of the Buddha

Library of Congress Cataloging-in-Publication Data
Tipiṭaka. Suttapiṭaka. Dīghanikāya. English
The long discourses of the Buddha : a translation of the Dīgha Nikāya / by Maurice Walshe.
p. cm. — (Teachings of the Buddha)
Includes bibliographical references and index.
ISBN 0-86171-103-3 (alk. paper)
I. Walshe, Maurice O'C. (Maurice O'Connell) II. Title. III. Series.
BQ1292.E53W35 1996
294.3'823—dc20 95-1128

ISBN 978-0-86171-103-1
ebook ISBN 978-0-86171-979-2
20 19 18 17 16
13 12 11 10

Cover designed by L. J. Sawlit.
Set in DPalatino 10 pt. / 12.5 pt.

Wisdom Publications' books are printed on acid-free paper and meet the guidelines for permanence and durability of the Committee on Production Guidelines for Book Longevity of the Council on Library Resources.

Printed in the United States of America.

To the Sangha
East and West

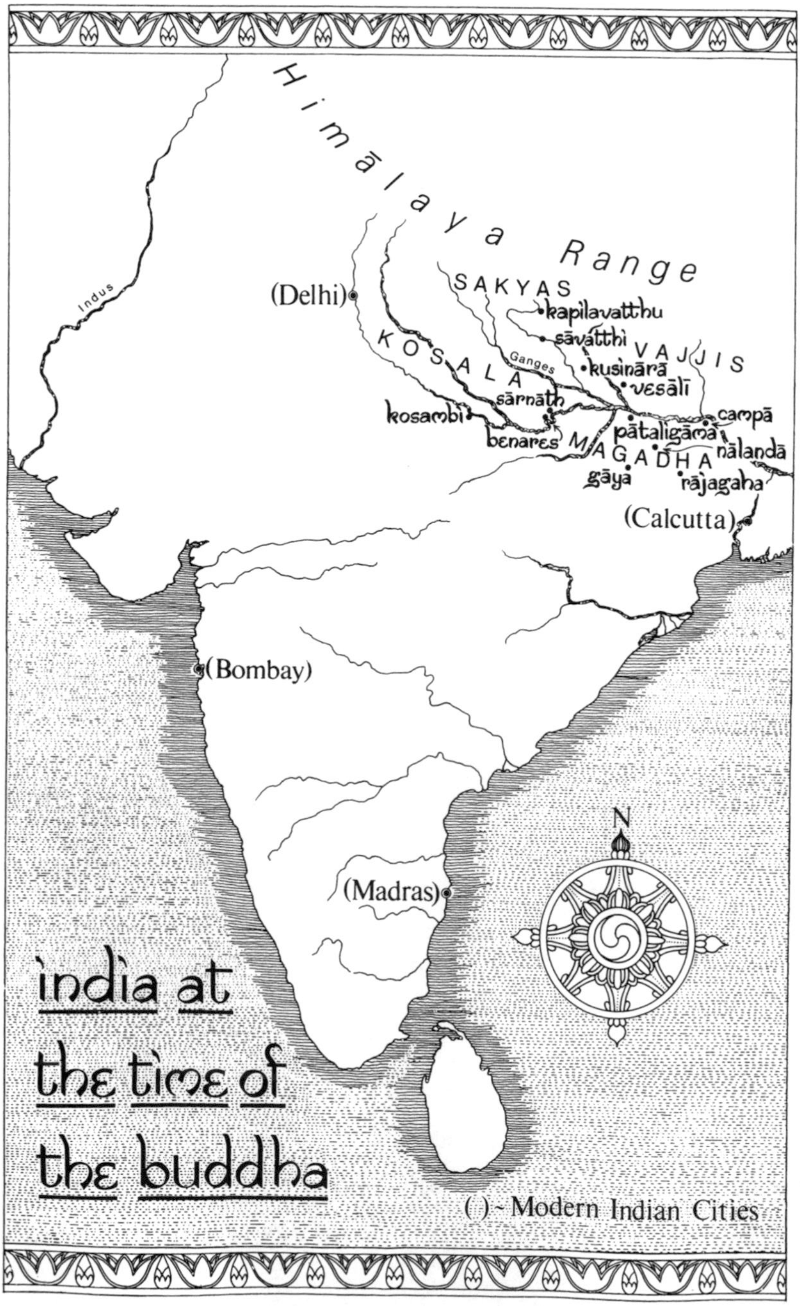
Himālaya Range
Indus
(Delhi)
SAKYAS
kapilavatthu
sāvatthi
VAJJIS
KOSALA
Ganges
kusinārā
vesālī
sārnāth
kosambi
campā
pātaligāma
benares
MAGADHA
nālandā
gāya
rājagaha
(Calcutta)
(Bombay)
(Madras)
N
india at the time of the buddha
( ) ~ Modern Indian Cities

Contents

List of Illustrations

Foreword

It is with much pleasure that I write this brief foreword to Mr Walshe's translation of the *Dīgha Nikāya*. The translator is a devout Buddhist whose Pali scholarship is backed up by personal practice of meditation. His translation work is therefore a most important contribution to the study of Buddhism.

Mr Walshe has been active in the Buddhist world of Great Britain for many years. Long before I came to Britain, his name was known to me through his essays in 'The Wheel' series of the Buddhist Publication Society of Sri Lanka. In 1977 my venerable teacher, Tan Ajahn Chah Subhatto and I arrived in London at the invitation of the English Sangha Trust of which Mr Walshe was one of the Trustees. This Trust had been established in 1956 in order to bring about a Western Sangha in Britain, and towards this end, Mr Walshe has consistently worked for nearly thirty years. At one time he combined this with the post of Vice-President of the Buddhist Society of Great Britain, his career at the Institute of Germanic Studies in London University (of which his translations of the sermons of Meister Eckhart are a testimonial), as well as studying Pali in his spare time.

Even though Pali scholars have produced quite accurate literal translations of the Pali Canon, one often feels the lack of profound insight into these remarkable scriptures. The Suttas need to be studied, reflected on, and practised in order to realise their true meaning. They are 'Dhamma discourses', or contemplations on the 'way things are'. They are not meant to be 'sacred scriptures' which tell us what to believe. One should read them, listen to them, think about them, contemplate them, and investigate the present reality, the present experience with them. Then, and only then, can one insightfully know the Truth beyond words.

In this new translation of the long discourses Mr Walshe has kindly offered us another opportunity to read and reflect on the Buddha's teachings.

May all those who read them, benefit and develop in their practice of the Dhamma.
May all beings be freed from all suffering.
May all beings be enlightened.

VENERABLE SUMEDHO THERA
Amaravati
Great Gaddesden
Hertfordshire
England
January 1986

Preface

The two main reasons for making this translation of some of the oldest Buddhist scriptures are: (1) The spread of Buddhism as a serious way of life in the Western world, and of even more widespread serious interest in it as a subject worthy of close study, and (2) the fact that English is now effectively the world language, the most widespread linguistic vehicle for all forms of communication. True, the Pali scriptures have already been translated in almost their entirety into English, mainly through the devoted efforts of the Pali Text Society, which has now entered into the second century of its activity. But existing translations are now dated stylistically as well as containing many errors and a modern version has therefore become necessary.

First, and foremost, the entire merit for this translation belongs to the Venerable Balangoda Ānandamaitreya Mahā Nāyaka Thera, Aggamahāpaṇḍita (though he has, of course, no need of such *puñña*) for having convinced me that I could, and therefore of course should, undertake this task. To me there remains merely the demerit of its many imperfections. Working on it has provided me with much joy, solace and illumination.

My particular thanks for help and encouragement are due, besides the illustrious and (in all senses) venerable gentleman just mentioned, to the Ven. Dr H. Saddhātissa, a friend of many years' standing from whom I have learnt so much, the Ven. Nyāṇaponika who inspired an earlier, more modest venture in translation, the Ven. Dr W. Rahula who guided my early, faltering steps in Pali, as well as the Ven. P. Vipassi and Messrs K.R. Norman and L.S. Cousins, whose collective brains I have picked on knotty points. It is fitting also to pay tribute here to the Ven. Achaan Cha (Bodhiñāṇa Thera) and his illustrious pupil Achaan Sumedho, whose efforts in establishing a flourishing branch of the Sangha in Britain have made such translation work all the more necessary; and – others please note! – much remains to be done in this field.

My principles of translation are briefly discussed in the Introduction. I am aware of a few trifling inconsistencies as well as a few repetitions in the notes. The former will, I think, cause no inconvenience: they were hard to avoid altogether in this, quite possibly the last, translation these scriptures will receive without benefit of electronic gadgetry. And as for the repetitions, these can perhaps be overlooked in connection with a text which is itself so repetitious.

My sincere thanks are due to Wisdom Publications for producing this book so splendidly, and to the Buddhist Society of Great Britain for a generous donation towards costs.

MAURICE WALSHE
St Albans
Hertfordshire
England
January 1986

Technical Notes

This book is in three parts: Division One, containing Suttas 1–13; Division Two, containing Suttas 14–23; Division Three, containing Suttas 24–34.

The Suttas are divided into verses and, in some cases, into sections as well. The verse and section numbers are based on Rhys Davids's system. Thus, Sutta 16, verse 2.25 denotes Sutta 16, chapter or section 2, verse 25. For the sake of brevity this appears in the notes as DN 16.2.25 and in the index as 16.2.25.

The numbers at the top of the page, for example i 123, refer to the volume and page number of the Pali Text Society's edition in Pali. Thus, i 123 refers to volume one, page 123 of the *Dīgha Nikāya*. The numbers in square brackets in the actual text also refer to these page numbers.

In this edition any passage can easily be looked up by either method.

PRONUNCIATION GUIDE

Pali texts printed in the West use a standard system of Roman spelling, with a few minor variations. Virtually the same system, with the addition of one or two extra letters, is used for Sanskrit. The Pali alphabet, like that of Sanskrit, is set out in a more logical order than the Roman

The vowels have their 'continental' values:

ā ī ū as in 'father', 'machine', 'rude'.

a i u as the corresponding short sounds.

e and o are always long as (approximately) in 'eh' and 'home', but without the southern English diphthongal glide.

Before two consonants e and o are also short.

ṁ (also printed ṃ and in some older works ŋ) is not really a vowel but a mark of nasalisation (probably originally rather as in French). Today it is read as ng in 'sing' (=ṅ).

Some consonants cause difficulty for the Western student. The difference between the consonants in the first (velar) row is this:

kh is like the normal English k in 'king', which we usually pronounce with a distinct puff of breath after it.

k is the same but without this puff of breath as in French 'kilo'. After s this pronunciation occurs in English too: compare 'kin' and 'skin'. In 'skin' the k is not the same as in 'kin'.

The Pali Alphabet

Vowels a ā i ī u ū e o ṁ(ṃ,ŋ)

Consonants	*Voiceless unaspirated*	*Voiceless aspirated*	*Voiced unaspirated*	*Voiced aspirated*	*Nasal*
Velar	k	kh	g	gh	ṅ
Palatal	c	ch	j	jh	ñ
Retroflex	ṭ	ṭh	ḍ	ḍh	ṇ
Dental	t	th	d	dh	n
Labial	p	ph	b	bh	m
Miscellaneous	y r l ḷ v s h				

g and gh differ in precisely the same way as k and kh, but it is difficult for English speakers to make this distinction.

ṅ is the corresponding nasal, that is, ng in 'sing'.

The same distinctions are made between the five columns for the palatal, retroflex, dental and labial rows. Thus c is almost like the English ch in 'church', or more exactly as in 'discharge'.

In the retroflex row (sometimes called 'cerebral') the tip of the tongue is turned back, whereas in the dental row it touches the upper front teeth. Most English speakers pronounce t and d somewhere between the two and can scarcely hear the difference between these two series.

Of the remaining consonants, y and s are always as in 'yes', ḷ is to l as ṭ is to t, and v is pronounced as English 'v' or 'w'.

Double consonants are pronounced double as in Italian: thus *mettā* is rather like 'met tar'. Note that kh, gh etc. are unitary consonants which only appear double in transcription. Each is represented by one letter in Oriental alphabets.

The Relationship Between Sanskrit and Pali

It is helpful to have some knowledge of the relationship between Pali and Sanskrit. Pali, as explained in the Introduction on page 48, is a kind of simplified Sanskrit.

Sanskrit in transcription has some extra consonants: ṛ (rarely ṝ), ḷ, ś, ṣ.

ṛ was originally syllabic r as in 'Brno', but is now usually pronounced *ri*.

ḷ was originally syllabic l as in 'Plzen' (or, almost, the second l in 'little'), but is now usually pronounced *li*. Note: Sanskrit ḷ is not the same as Pali ḷ, but both are so rare that there is no confusion.

ś is a thin sh sound as in 'shin'.

ṣ is a thick sh sound as might be heard in 'push' (exaggerating the difference from that in 'shin').

In Pali ṛ appears as a vowel, usually the same vowel as occurs near it: Sanskrit *kṛta* (done) > Pali *kata*; Sanskrit *ṛju* (straight) > Pali *uju*.

Both ś and ṣ appear in Pali as s, but are then subject to the usual rule of s̄ + consonant: Sanskrit s̄ + consonant becomes (the same) consonant + h: thus sp>ph, st>th, etc.

The above rules combine in the case of one key-word: Sanskrit *tṛṣṇā* (thirst, craving) > Pali *taṇhā*. Here ṛ>a, ṣ>s, and then sṇ>ṇh.

Sanskrit consonant clusters are simplified, producing one single or double consonant: Sanskrit *agni* (fire) > Pali *aggi*; Sanskrit *svarga* (heaven) > Pali *sagga*; Sanskrit *mārga* (path) > Pali *magga*; Sanskrit *ātman* (self) > Pali *attā*; Sanskrit *saṃjñā* (perception) Pali *saññā*; Sanskrit *sparśa* (contact) > Pali *phassa*; Sanskrit *alpa* (little) > Pali *appa* etc. Instead of *vv* we find *bb*, and instead of *dy*, *dhy* we find *jj*, *jh*: Sanskrit *nirvāṇa* > Pali *nibbāna*; Sanskrit *adya* (today) > Pali *ajja*; Sanskrit *dhyāna* (absorption) > Pali *jhāna*.

It follows that while the form of a Sanskrit word cannot be predicted from its Pali equivalent, the Pali form can usually be predicted from the Sanskrit, provided the word occurs. The meanings of Sanskrit and Pali words are also not quite always the same.

As regards grammatical simplification, it need perhaps only be mentioned here that the Sanskrit dative case has in most instances been replaced by the genitive in Pali. Thus in the phrase *Namo tassa Bhagavato Arahato Sammā-Sambuddhassa* (Homage to the Blessed One, the Arahant, fully-enlightened Buddha) the words *tassa* etc are originally genitive forms with dative meaning. However we do find the expression *namo Buddhāya* (homage to the Buddha) with a true dative form.

Those who wish to learn some Pali – which is to be encouraged! – should start with Johansson and proceed to Warder (see Bibliography). Sanskrit is a difficult language, but Michael Coulson's 'Teach Yourself' volume (1976) renders it as painless as possible.

Introduction

This translation is a 'substantive' translation because it is complete as to substance. Nothing has been omitted except the more wearisome of the very numerous repetitions which are such a striking feature of the original.

The Pali scriptures here translated are from the 'Triple Basket' (*Tipiṭaka*), a collection of the Buddha's teachings regarded as canonical by the Theravāda school of Buddhism, which is found today in Sri Lanka, Burma and Thailand, and was until recently equally strong in Laos and Cambodia. It is now also well established in Britain and other Western countries. The claim of this school is to have preserved the original teaching of the Buddha, and there are good grounds for at least considering that the doctrine as found in the Pali scriptures comes as close as we can get to what the Buddha actually taught. In any case the Pali *Tipiṭaka* is the only canon of an early school that is preserved complete. It is not, however, in the true spirit of Buddhism to adopt a 'fundamentalist' attitude towards the scriptures, and it is thus open to the reader, Buddhist as well as non-Buddhist, to regard the texts here translated with an open and critical mind.

THE LIFE OF THE BUDDHA

Siddhattha Gotama (in Sanskrit, Siddhārtha Gautama), who became the Buddha, the Enlightened One, may have lived from about 563-483 B.C., through many modern scholars suggest a later dating.[1] Oriental traditions offer a number of alternative datings, that favoured in Sri Lanka and south-east Asia being 623-543. It was on this basis that the 2500th anniversary of his passing into final Nibbāna was celebrated, as *Buddha Jayanti*, in the East in 1956–57. He belonged to the Sakya clan dwelling on the edge of the Himālayas, his actual birthplace being a few miles north of the present-day Indian border, in Nepal. His father, Suddhodana, was in fact an elected chief of the clan rather than the king he was later made out to be, though his title was *rājā*—a term which only partly corresponds to our word 'king'. Some of the states of North India at that time were kingdoms and others republics, and the Sakyan republic was subject to the powerful king of neighbouring Kosala, which lay to the south.

Disentangling the probable facts from the mass of legend surrounding Gotama's life, we may assume the following to be approximately correct. Though brought up to a life of luxury, the young prince was overcome by a sense of the essentially sorrowful aspect of life, and he decided to seek the cause and cure of this state which he termed *dukkha* (conventionally but inadequately rendered 'suffering' in English). At the age of twenty-nine he renounced the world, going forth 'from the household life into homelessness' in accordance with an already well-established tradition, thus joining the ranks of the wandering ascetics (*samaṇas*: see p. 22). He went successively to two teachers, Āḷāra Kālāma and Uddaka Rāmaputta, who taught him how to attain to high meditative states. Realising, however, that even the attainment of these states did not solve his problem, Gotama went off on his own and practised severe austerities for six years, gathering a little group of five ascetics around him. However, finding that even the most extreme forms of asceticism likewise did not lead to the goal, he abandoned these excesses, and sat down at the foot of a tree by the river Nerañjarā, at the place now known as Bodh Gaya, determined not to arise from the spot until enlightenment should dawn. During that night he passed beyond the meditative stages he had previously reached, and attained to complete liberation as the Buddha—the Enlightened or Awakened One. He spent the remaining forty-five years of his life wandering up and down the Ganges Valley, expounding the doctrine that he had found and establishing the Sangha or Order of Buddhist monks and nuns, which still exists today.

HISTORICAL AND PHILOSOPHICAL BACKGROUND TO THE BUDDHA'S TIMES

'Ascetics and Brahmins'

India in the Buddha's day did not yet suffer from the grinding poverty of the present time. The modern caste system had not fully developed, but we find its germ in the division of society into four groups or 'colours' (Pali *vaṇṇā*). The designation betrays the origin of the distinction, being based on the conquest of northern India in about 1600 B.C. by the comparatively light-skinned Aryans, who looked down on those of darker hue they found there. In the context of Buddhism, where this racial and aristocratic term (literally 'noble') is applied to the nobility of the spirit, we shall use the form Ariyan, based on Pali.

The Brahmins were the guardians of the religious cult brought into India by the Aryans. In later, non-Buddhist sources we always hear of the Brahmins as taking the leading place in society. Buddhist sources, however (Sutta 3, for example), assert the supremacy of the Khattiyas (Skt. *kṣatriya*), the Noble or Warrior class to which Gotama belonged. It appears that while further west the Brahmins had already established their supremacy, this was not yet the case in the Ganges valley. In the third place came the Vessas (Skt. *vaiśya*) or merchants, and finally the Suddas (Skt. *śudra*) or workers. Below these there were certainly some slaves (we even hear of a Sudda having a slave), and some unfortunates of the class who were later to become known as 'untouchables'. But in addition to these groupings, there were considerable numbers of people, including at least a few women, who had opted out of conventional society.

In the texts we frequently meet with the compound *samaṇa-brāhmaṇā*, which we render 'ascetics and Brahmins'. While the Pali Text Society dictionary correctly states that this compound expression denotes quite generally 'leaders in religious life', it is also true that the two groups were usually rivals.

The religious situation in northern India around 500 B.C. is very interesting, and was undoubtedly exceptionally favourable to the development of the Buddhist and other faiths.

Though the Brahmins formed an important and increasingly powerful hereditary priesthood, they were never, like their counterparts elsewhere, able to assert their undisputed authority by persecuting and perhaps exterminating other religious groups. It seems that some Brahmins would not have been averse to such a course, but it was not open to them. They were a caste set aside from other men (in reading about them in the Buddhist texts, one is insistently reminded of the New Testament picture of the Pharisees, though in both cases the picture presented is, to say the least, one-sided). They alone were learned in the Three Vedas, knew the mystic mantras, and could conduct the all-important, bloody and expensive sacrifices. In fact, not all Brahmins exercised their priestly functions; some had settled down to agriculture or even trade, while continuing to expect the deference which they regarded as their due.

The earlier (Dravidian?) inhabitants who had been overrun by the Aryans were the creators of the Indus Valley civilisation with the great cities of Harappā and Mohenjo Dāro, all now in Pakistan. And it is to this civilisation that we must look for the origins of the second stream of religious life, that of the *samaṇas* (Skt. *śramaṇas*). These have sometimes been absurdly called 'recluses', whereas the term really means the very opposite. True, a *samaṇa* might occasionally be a recluse, a hermit shut away from the world in a rocky cell, but the more usual type was a wanderer who had indeed 'abandoned the world' to lead a more or less ascetic life. He – or, rarely, she – was in fact, to use a modern expression, a drop-out from society, though differing from our modern drop-outs in at least one important respect: the *samaṇas* as a group received no less respect from all classes, even kings, than did the Brahmins (see Sutta 2, verse 25ff.). Their teachings were many and varied – some wise and some exceedingly foolish, some loftily spiritual and some crudely materialistic. The point is that they were completely free to teach whatever they pleased, and, so far from being persecuted as they might have been elsewhere, were received with honour wherever they went. We can distinguish several different groups of these people. There were in particular the self-mortifiers on the one hand, and the wanderers on the other, whose only austerity probably consisted in their detachment from family ties and, in theory at least, their observance of chastity. Many of the bizarre and often revolting practices of the first group are detailed in Sutta 8, verse 14. As pointed out in a note to that Sutta, the practice of extreme austerity (*tapas*) should not be called 'penance' because the motivation is entirely different from that of a Christian penitent, to whom such people might be superficially compared. The word *tapas*, which basically means 'heat', is used both for the austere practices indulged in and for the result they are intended to achieve, which is power, that is, the development of various paranormal powers. The belief was that these could be achieved by means of such practices and, in particular, by sexual restraint. Thus, so far from practising austerity like the Christian penitent, to atone for past sins, they undertook these practices in the hope of future powers, including, perhaps, those very joys that had been temporarily renounced.

The wanderers (*paribbājakas*), some of whom were Brahmins, wore clothes (unlike many of the others, who went completely naked), and they led a less uncomfortable life. They were 'philosophers' who propounded many different theories about the world and nature, and delighted in disputation. The Pali Canon introduces us to six well-known teachers of the time, all of whom were older than Gotama. They are Pūraṇa Kassapa, an amoralist, Makkhali Gosāla, a determinist, Ajita Kesakambali, a materialist, Pakudha Kaccāyana, a categorialist, the Nigaṇṭha Nātaputta (the Jain leader known to us as Mahāvīra), who was a relativist and eclectic, and Sañjaya Belaṭṭhaputta, an agnostic sceptic or positivist (I borrow most of the descriptive epithets from Jayatilleke). Their different views are quoted by King Ajātasattu in Sutta 2, verses 16–32.

Besides these there were the propounders of the originally secret teaching incorporated in the Upaniṣads which came to be grafted on to orthodox Brahmanism, and whose doctrines were later to form the core of the Vedānta system. For them, the impersonal Brahman is the supreme reality, and the goal of the teaching is the realisation that the individual human soul or self (*ātman*) is ultimately identical with the universal Self (*Ātman*), which is another term for Brahman (the capitalisation here is merely for clarity: the teaching was at first and for long oral, and even when written down in an Oriental alphabet, such a distinction could not be made, since capital letters do not exist in any Eastern script). These *aupaniṣadas* are not mentioned in the Pali Canon, though it is almost (but not, perhaps, quite) certain that Gotama was acquainted with their teachings.

It has been urged that 'at depth there is no contradiction between the greatest insights of the Upaniṣads and the Buddha's teaching' – a view that would be contested by many. We shall return very briefly to this point later (page 31). Suffice it to say here that any theory that the Buddha taught a doctrine of a supreme Self can only be said to fly in the face of the evidence. Nor is it true, as is sometimes said, that in ancient India everybody believed in karma (the law of moral cause and effect) and rebirth, or indeed in anything else. There were, as we have seen, materialists, sceptics and equivocators, and all sorts of fantastic theorists. Neither can we accept the statement that the Buddha was 'a Hindu who sought to reform the ancient religion'. Apart from the anachronistic use of the term 'Hindu', this is wrong because he rejected the claims of the Brahmins as religious authorities and, while not totally denying the existence of their gods, assigned to these a fundamentally unimportant role in the scheme of things. In so far as he belonged to any existing tradition, it was that of the *samaṇas*, and like them he taught as he saw fit. As a teacher he was not beholden to anyone: he agreed or disagreed with tradition or the views of others entirely in accordance with his sovereign perception of the truth. It is, however, correct to say that the situation in India in his time was particularly favourable to the spread of his teaching, while the Teacher's long life enabled this to become firmly established in his lifetime and under his direction.

MAIN POINTS OF THE TEACHING

The main points of the Buddha's teaching need only be briefly summarised here. In his first sermon (Saṁyutta Nikāya 56.11) the Buddha taught that there were two extremes to be avoided: over-indulgence in sensuality on the one hand, and self-torture on the other. He had had personal experience of both. Buddhism is thus the middle way between these extremes, and also between some other pairs of opposites, such as eternalism and annihilationism (see Sutta 1, verse 1.30ff. and verse 3.9ff.).

The Four Noble Truths

The most succinct formulation of the teaching is in the form of the Four Noble Truths:

1. Suffering (*dukkha*);
2. The Origin of Suffering (*dukkha-samudaya*), which is craving (*taṇhā*);
3. The Cessation of Suffering (*dukkha-nirodha*);
4. The Path Leading to the Cessation of Suffering (*dukkha-nirodha-gāminī-paṭipadā*), which is the Noble Eightfold Path (*ariya-aṭṭhangika-magga*). This consists of:

(1) Right View (*sammā-diṭṭhi*) (N.B. singular, not Right Views!)
(2) Right Thought (*sammā-sankappa*)
(3) Right Speech (*sammā-vācā*)
(4) Right Action (*sammā-kammanta*)
(5) Right Livelihood (*sammā-ājīva*)
(6) Right Effort (*sammā-vāyāma*)
(7) Right Mindfulness (*sammā-sati*)
(8) Right Concentration (*sammā-samādhi*).

For a full account of these, see Sutta 22, verses 18–22.

The eight steps can be subsumed under the three heads of I. Morality (*sīla*) (steps 3–5), II. Concentration (*samādhi*) (steps 6–8), and III. Wisdom (*paññā*) (steps 1–2). It will be noticed that in this arrangement the order is different. This is because, while some preliminary wisdom is needed to start on the path, the final flowering of the higher wisdom follows after development of morality and concentration (cf. Sutta 33, verse 3.3(6)).

Stages on the Path

Progress on the path leading to the cessation of suffering, and hence to Nibbāna, is described in many places, notably in Sutta 2, in a long passage which is repeated verbatim in the following Suttas.[2] The most fundamental meditative exercise is set forth in Sutta 22. The breakthrough to the transcendental is achieved in four stages, each of which is subdivided into two: path (*magga*) and fruition (*phala*). By attaining the first of these stages one ceases to be a mere 'worldling' (*puthujjana*) and becomes a noble person (*ariya-puggala*). The stages or 'path-moments' are designated in terms of the successive breaking of ten fetters. Standard descriptions of these stages are given at many places.

At the first stage, one 'enters the Stream' and thus becomes a Stream-Winner (*sotāpanna*) by an experience also referred to (for example, in Sutta 2, verse 102) as the 'opening of the Dhamma-eye'. The first path-moment is immediately followed by the fruition (*phala*), and likewise with the other three paths. At First Path, one is said to have 'glimpsed Nibbāna' (cf. *Visuddhimagga* 22.126), and thereby three of the five lower fetters are discarded for ever: 1. personality-belief (*sakkāya-diṭṭhi*), that is, belief in a self; 2. doubt (*vicikicchā*) and 3. attachment to rites and rituals (*sīlabbata-parāmāsa*). In other words, having had a glimpse of reality and perceived the falsity of the self-belief, one is unshakeable and no more dependent on external aids. One who has gained this state can, it is said, no longer be born in 'states of woe' and is assured of attaining Nibbāna after, at the most, seven more lives.

At the second stage, one becomes a Once-Returner (*sakadāgāmī*), in whom the fourth and fifth lower fetters are greatly weakened: 4. sensual desire (*kāma-rāga*) and 5. ill-will (*vyāpāda*). Such a person will attain to Nibbāna after at most one further human rebirth. It is interesting to note that sensuality and ill-will are so powerful that they persist, in however attenuated a form, for so long.

At the third stage, one becomes a Non-Returner (*anāgāmī*), in whom the fourth and fifth fetters are completely destroyed. In such a person all attachments to this world have ceased, and at death one will be reborn in a higher world, in one of the Pure Abodes (see *Cosmology* p. 42), and will attain Nibbāna from there without returning to this world. It may be mentioned that in Saṁyutta Nikāya 22.89 the Venerable Khemaka actually gives some account of what it feels like to be a Non-Returner.

Finally, at the fourth stage, one becomes an Arahant (Sanskrit

Arhat, literally 'worthy one'), by the destruction of the five higher fetters: 6. craving for existence in the Form World (*rūpa-rāga*), 7. craving for existence in the Formless World (*arūpa-rāga*) (see p. 42 for more about these), 8. conceit (*māna*), 9. restlessness (*uddhacca*), 10. ignorance (*avijjā*). For such a one, the task has been completed, and that person will attain final Nibbāna 'without remainder' at death.

It should perhaps be added that there are two different ideas that are widely circulated in the East. One is that in this degenerate age it is not possible to become an Arahant. The other, less pessimistic view is that while lay persons can attain to the first three paths, only monks can become Arahants. There is no scriptural authority for either idea. It should also be mentioned that the Arahant ideal is one that is perfectly valid for all schools of Buddhism. Likewise, the concept of the Bodhisattva, who renounces the enjoyment of Nirvāṇa in order to bring all beings to enlightenment, which is considered the hallmark of the Mahāyāna schools as opposed to the Hīnayāna,[3] in fact exists in Theravāda Buddhism as well. The difference of schools is one of emphasis, and does not constitute the unbridgeable gap imagined by some, chiefly in the West. But it cannot be our task to enter further into these matters here.

Nibbāna or Nirvāṇa

The Sanskrit form is better known in the West than the Pali *Nibbāna*. There are, not surprisingly, many misapprehensions about this. In fact it has been said by one witty scholar that all we have to go on is our misconception of Nirvāṇa, because until we have realised it we cannot know it as it really is. But if we cannot say much about what it *is*, we can at least say something about what it is *not*. Robert Caesar Childers, in his famous and still useful Pali dictionary (1875), devoted a whole long article, in fact a short treatise, to proving to his own satisfaction that Nibbāna implies total extinction, and this view, though certainly erroneous, is still to be met with among some Western scholars. And yet, it would be odd indeed if Buddhists were supposed to have to tread the entire path right up to the attainment of Arahantship merely in order to finish up with that total obliteration which the materialists, and many ordinary people today, assume to occur for all of us, good, bad and indifferent, at the end of our present life. It is true, some colour is given to this idea by the etymology of the term (*nir* + $\sqrt{}$*vā* = 'blowing out' as of a lamp). Contrasted with this, however, we find other very different descriptions of Nibbāna. Thus in Sutta 1.3.20 it is used for 'the highest happiness', defined as the indulgence in the pleasures of the five senses – obviously a non-Buddhist use of the word, though it is not otherwise attested in pre-Buddhist sources. We thus find two apparently contradictory meanings of Nibbāna: 1. 'extinction', 2. 'highest bliss'. And while these were wrongly used in the examples quoted, they both occur in authentic texts.

In considering this problem, it is as well to note the words of the Venerable Nyāṇatiloka in his *Buddhist Dictionary*:

> One cannot too often and too emphatically stress the fact that not only for the actual realization of the goal of Nibbāna, but also for a theoretical understanding of it, it is an indispensable preliminary condition to grasp fully the truth of Anattā, the egolessness and insubstantiality of all forms of existence. Without such an understanding, one will necessarily misconceive Nibbāna – according to one's either materialistic or metaphysical leanings – either as annihilation of an ego, or as an eternal state of existence into which an Ego or Self enters or with which it merges.

What this in effect means is that in order to 'understand' Nibbāna one should have 'entered the Stream' or gained First Path, and thus have got rid of the fetter of personality-belief. While scholars will continue to see it as part of their task to try to understand what the Buddha meant by Nibbāna, they should perhaps have sufficient humility to realise that this is something beyond the range of purely scholarly discussion. In the systematisation of the Abhidhamma (see p. 52), Nibbāna is simply included as the 'unconditioned element' (*asankhata-dhātu*), but with no attempt at definition. Nibbāna is indeed the extinction of the 'three fires' of greed, hatred and delusion, or the destruction of the 'corruptions' (*āsavā*) of sense-desire, becoming, wrong view and ignorance. Since the individual 'self' entity is not ultimately real, it cannot be said to be annihilated in Nibbāna, but the *illusion* of such a self is destroyed.

Very oddly, in the *Pali-English Dictionary*, it is said that Nibbāna is 'purely and simply an ethical state ... It is therefore not transcendental.' In fact it is precisely the one and only transcendental element in Buddhism, for which very reason no attempt is made to define it in terms of a personal god, a higher self, or the like. It is ineffable. It can, however, be realised, and its realisation is the aim of the Buddhist practice. While no description is possible, positive references to Nibbāna are not lacking: thus at Dhammapada 204 and elsewhere it is called 'the highest bliss' (*paramaṁ sukhaṁ*), and we may conclude this brief account with the famous quotation from Udāna 8.3:

> There is, monks, an Unborn, Unbecome, Unmade, Uncompounded (*ajātaṁ abhūtaṁ akataṁ asankhataṁ*). If there were not this Unborn ..., then there would be no deliverance here visible from that which is born, become, made, compounded. But since there *is* this Unborn, Unbecome, Unmade, Uncompounded, therefore a deliverance is visible from that which is born, become, made, compounded.

This is, at the same time, perhaps the best answer we can give concerning the Upaniṣadic *Ātman*. Buddhism teaches no such thing—nevertheless the above quotation could certainly be applied to the *Ātman* as understood in Vedānta, or indeed to the Christian conception of God. However, to the followers of those faiths it would be an insufficient description, and the additions they would make would for the most part be unacceptable to Buddhists. It can, however, be suggested that this statement represents the fundamental basis of all religions worthy of the name, as well as providing a criterion to distinguish true religion from such surrogates as Marxism, humanism and the like.

The Three Marks (tilakkhaṇa)

The formula of the three marks (also referred to as 'signs of being', 'signata', etc.) is found in many places (in expanded, versified form Dhammapada 277–9). It runs:

1. 'All *sankhāras*[4] (compounded things) are impermanent': *Sabbe sankhārā aniccā*
2. 'All *sankhāras* are unsatisfactory': *Sabbe sankhārā dukkhā*
3. 'All *dhammas* (all things including the unconditioned) are without self': *Sabbe dhammā anattā*

The first and second of these marks apply to all mundane things, everything that 'exists' (*sankhāra* in its widest sense). The third refers in addition to the unconditioned element (*a-sankhata*, that is, not a *sankhāra*, thus Nibbāna). This does not 'exist' (relatively), but IS.

Thus, nothing lasts for ever, all things being subject to change and disappearance. Nothing is completely satisfactory: *dukkha*, conventionally rendered 'suffering', has the wide meaning of not satisfying, frustrating, painful in whatever degree. Even pleasant things come to an end or cease to attract, and the painful aspect of life is too well-known and ubiquitous to need discussion.

The first two marks can perhaps be appreciated without too much effort, even though their profound penetration is more difficult. It is the third mark that has provoked much controversy and misunderstanding.

An-attā (Skt. *an-ātman*) is the negative of *attā/ātman* 'self'. So much is clear. In ordinary usage *attā* is a pronoun used for all persons and genders, singular and plural, meaning 'myself', 'herself', 'ourselves', 'themselves', etc. It has no metaphysical implications whatsoever. This, then, is the self of daily life, which has a purely relative and conventional reality if only because it is an almost indispensable expression in everyday speech. As a noun, *attā* to the Buddhist means an imaginary entity, a so-called 'self', which is not really there. The five *khandhas* or aggregates, the various parts that make up our empirical personality (see Sutta 22, verse 14), do not constitute a self, either individually or collectively. Our so-called 'self', then, is something bogus. It is, however, a concept that we cling to with great tenacity. See further, p. 32.

It was said earlier that any theory that the Buddha taught such a doctrine as the Upaniṣadic Higher Self can only be said to fly in the face of the evidence. This is borne out by the third mark: all *dhammas* are without self. The term *dhamma* here includes Nibbāna, the Buddhist ultimate. Thus this is expressly stated not to be any kind of 'Higher Self'. There are those who believe that what the Buddha taught and what the Upaniṣads taught must agree. Be that as it may at some deeper level, the expression is certainly different. It is arguable that the Buddha considered the term 'self', which to him was something evanescent, to be ludicrously inappropriate to the supreme reality, whatever its nature. To pursue such arguments as this any further is surely fruitless.

Levels of Truth

An important and often overlooked aspect of the Buddhist teaching concerns the levels of truth, failure to appreciate which has led to many errors (see n. 220). Very often the Buddha talks in the Suttas in terms of conventional or relative truth (*sammuti-* or *vohāra-sacca*), according to which people and things exist just as they appear to the naive understanding. Elsewhere, however, when addressing an audience capable of appreciating his meaning, he speaks in terms of ultimate truth (*paramattha-sacca*), according to which 'existence is a mere process of physical and mental phenomena within which, or beyond which, no real ego-entity nor any abiding substance can ever be found' (*Buddhist Dictionary* under *Paramattha*). In the Abhidhamma, the entire exposition is in terms of ultimate truth. It may also be observed that many 'Zen paradoxes' and the like really owe their puzzling character to their being put in terms of ultimate, not of relative truth. The full understanding of ultimate truth can, of course, only be gained by profound insight, but it is possible to become increasingly aware of the distinction. There would seem in fact to be a close parallel in modern times in the difference between our naive world-view and that of the physicist, both points of view having their use in their own sphere. Thus, conventionally speaking, or according to the naive world-view, there are solid objects such as tables and chairs, whereas according to physics the alleged solidity is seen to be an illusion, and whatever might turn out to be the ultimate nature of matter, it is certainly something very different from that which presents itself to our senses. However, when the physicist is off duty, he or she makes use of solid tables and chairs just like everyone else.

In the same way, all such expressions as 'I', 'self' and so on are always in accordance with conventional truth, and the Buddha never hesitated to use the word *attā* 'self' (and also with plural meaning: 'yourselves', etc.)[5] in its conventional and convenient sense. In fact, despite all that has been urged to the contrary, there is not the slightest evidence that he ever used it in any other sense except when critically quoting the views of others, as should clearly emerge from several of the Suttas here translated.

In point of fact, it should be stressed that conventional truth is sometimes extremely important. The whole doctrine of karma and rebirth has its validity only in the realm of conventional truth. That is why, by liberating ourselves from the viewpoint of conventional truth we cease to be subject to karmic law. Objections to the idea of rebirth in Buddhism, too, are sometimes based on a misunderstanding of the nature of the two truths. As long as we are unenlightened 'worldlings', our minds habitually operate in terms of 'me' and 'mine', even if in theory we know better. It is not until this tendency has been completely eradicated that full enlightenment can dawn. At Saṁyutta Nikāya 22.89 the Venerable Khemaka, who is a Non-Returner, explains how 'the subtle remnant of the 'I'-conceit, of the 'I'-desire, an unextirpated lurking tendency to think: 'I am'', still persists even at that advanced stage.

Probably the best account of the Buddha's attitude to truth is given by Jayatilleke in *The Early Buddhist Theory of Knowledge* (1963, 361ff.). It may be mentioned that for those who find this work hard going, his second, posthumous book, *The Message of the Buddha* (1975), makes for easier reading. Jayatilleke has been attacked for equating the philosophy of Buddhism too closely with the modern school of logical positivism. In this connection it is perhaps best to let him speak for himself:

> The Buddha, again, was the earliest thinker in history to recognise the fact that language tends to distort in certain respects the nature of reality and to stress the importance of not being misled by linguistic forms and conventions. In this respect, he foreshadowed the modern linguistic or analytical philosophers. (*The Message of the Buddha,* 33).

It seems hard to find any fault with that. Jayatilleke goes on:

> He was the first to distinguish meaningless questions and assertions from meaningful ones. As in science he recognised perception and inference as the twin sources of knowledge, but there was one difference. For perception, according to Buddhism, included extra-sensory forms as well, such as telepathy and clairvoyance. Science cannot ignore such phenomena and today there are Soviet as well as Western scientists, who have admitted the validity of extra-sensory perception in the light of experimental evidence.

Probably most readers will concede the possibility that the Buddha knew a few things which modern science is only now beginning to discover, or accept. We will leave it at that.

Kamma

The Sanskrit form of this word, *karma,* is more familiar to Westerners, but as its meaning in non-Buddhist contexts is not necessarily always the same as in Buddhism, there is some advantage in using the Pali form kamma here. The literal meaning of the word is 'action', and at Anguttara Nikāya 6.63 the Buddha defines it as volition (*cetanā*). It is therefore any deliberate act, good or bad (in Pali *kusala* 'skilful, wholesome' or *akusala* 'unskilful, unwholesome'). A good act will normally lead to pleasant results for the doer, and a bad act to unpleasant ones. The correct Pali (and Sanskrit) word for such results is *vipāka* ('ripening'), though karma/kamma tends in practice to be used loosely for the results as well as the deeds that produced them – even sometimes by those who really know better. But it is as well to be aware of the correct distinction.

The question is sometimes asked whether there is free-will in Buddhism. The answer should be clear: each karmic act is the exercise of a choice, good or bad. Thus though our actions are limited by conditions, they are not totally determined.

In this computerised age, it may be helpful to some to think of kamma as 'programming' our future. Thus the 'karma-formations' (*sankhāras*) mentioned below are the 'programme' which we have – through ignorance – made in past lives. The aim of the practice, of course, is to get beyond all kamma. An account of how to progress towards this aim is given in many Suttas, and especially in the first division of the Dīgha Nikāya.

The Twelve Links of the Chain of Dependent Origination

This famous formulation is found in many places in the Canon, and is also represented visually in Tibetan *thangkas* in the form of a twelve-spoked wheel. The Pali term *paṭicca-samuppāda* (Skt. *pratītya-samutpāda*) is usually rendered 'dependent origination', though Edward Conze preferred 'conditioned co-production'. It has been much debated by Western scholars, some of whom produced some strange theories on the subject. The usual formulation is as follows:

1. Ignorance conditions the 'Karma-formations' (*avijjā-paccayā sankhārā*)
2. The Karma-formations condition Consciousness (*sankhāra-paccayā viññāṇaṁ*)
3. Consciousness conditions Mind-and-Body (lit. 'Name-and-Form': *viññāṇa-paccayā nāma-rūpaṁ*)
4. Mind-and-Body conditions the Six Sense-Bases (*nāma-rūpa-paccayā saḷāyatanaṁ*)
5. The Six Sense-Bases condition Contact (*saḷāyatana-paccayā phasso*)
6. Contact conditions Feeling (*phassa-paccayā vedanā*)
7. Feeling conditions Craving (*vedanā-paccayā taṇhā*)

8. Craving conditions Clinging (*taṇhā-paccayā upādānaṁ*)
9. Clinging conditions Becoming (*upādāna-paccayā bhavo*)
10. Becoming conditions Birth (*bhava-paccayā jāti*)
11. Birth conditions (12) Ageing-and-Death (*jāti-paccayā jarā-maraṇaṁ*).

This is best understood if taken in reverse order. In Sutta 15, verse 2 the Buddha says to Ānanda: 'If you are asked: "Has ageing-and-death a condition for its existence?" you should answer: "Yes." If asked: "What conditions ageing-and-death?" you should answer: "Ageing-and-death is conditioned by birth"', and so on. Thus, if there were no birth, there could be no ageing-and-death: birth is a necessary condition for their arising.

According to the usual view, which is certainly correct but perhaps not the only way of regarding the matter, the twelve links (*nidānas*) are spread over three lives: 1–2 belonging to a past life, 3–10 to this present life, and 11–12 to a future life. Thus the development of our 'karma-formations' or behaviour patterns is due to past ignorance (that is, the fact that 'we' are not enlightened). These patterns condition the arising of a new consciousness in the womb, on the basis of which a new psycho-physical complex (*nāma-rūpa*) comes into being, equipped with the six sense-bases (of sight, hearing, smelling, tasting and touching, with mind as the sixth sense). Contact of any of these with a sense-object (sight, sound, etc.) produces feeling, which may be pleasant, unpleasant or neutral. On the basis of pleasant feeling, desire or craving arises. The links from consciousness to feeling are the results of past actions (*vipāka*), whereas craving, clinging and the process of becoming are volitional (that is, *kamma*), and will therefore have results for the future. In fact they set in train the same process of (re)birth (due to ignorance) that we witnessed before, and birth must inevitably lead to death. This is the continuous process in which we, as unenlightened beings, are caught up.

Curiously, in the Dīgha Nikāya we do not find the twelve links. The steps from feeling to ageing-and-death are mentioned in Sutta 1, verse 3.71, while in the two main expositions in this book, the process in reverse is traced back only to its starting-point in this life, that is, to consciousness and mind-and-body, which are said to condition each other mutually. Thus, in Sutta 14, we have a set of ten steps instead of the usual twelve, while in Sutta 15, still more remarkably, the six sense-bases are omitted, thus making a total of only nine links. In other parts of the Canon there are occasional expansions beyond the twelve links give here, but this is the standard formula. It seems that the repeaters (*bhāṇakā*) of the Dīgha had a tradition of their own to which they firmly adhered.

While we should certainly not make Ānanda's mistake (Sutta 15, verse 1) of thinking the whole thing easy to understand, we can get some general grasp of it, especially if we regard the links in reverse order, which is the way the Buddha explained it to Ānanda. At least we shall find that it is not so arbitrary or nonsensical as some Western scholars have supposed.

Rebirth

There are some people in the West who are attracted in many ways to Buddhism, but who find the idea of rebirth a stumbling-block, either because they find it distasteful and/or incredible in itself, or in some cases because they find it hard to reconcile with the 'non-self' idea. Some such considerations as any of these sometimes even lead people to declare that the Buddha did not actually teach rebirth at all, or that if he did so, this was only for popular consumption, because his hearers could not have accepted the truth. All such views are based on various kinds of misunderstanding.

It should be noted, incidentally, that Buddhists prefer to speak, not of reincarnation, but of rebirth. Reincarnation is the doctrine that there is a transmigrating soul or spirit that passes on from life to life. In the Buddhist view we may say, to begin with, that that is merely what appears to happen, though in reality no such soul or spirit passes on in this way. In Majjhima Nikāya 38 the monk Sāti was severely rebuked for declaring that 'this very consciousness' transmigrates, whereas in reality a new consciousness arises at rebirth *dependent* on the old. Nevertheless there is an illusion of continuity in much the same way as there is within this life. Rebirth from life to life is in principle scarcely different from the rebirth from moment to moment that goes on in this life. The point can be intellectually grasped, with a greater or less degree of difficulty, but it is only at the first path-moment, with the penetration of the spurious nature of what we call self, that it is clearly understood without a shadow of doubt remaining.

It cannot be the purpose of this book to argue in favour of a belief in rebirth, but sceptics might do well to read *Rebirth as Doctrine and Experience* by Francis Story (Buddhist Publication Society 1975), which has an introduction by Ian Stevenson, Carlson Professor of Psychiatry in the University of Virginia. This book contains some case-histories from Thailand and elsewhere which are difficult to explain except on the rebirth hypothesis, and Prof. Stevenson, too, has published several volumes of research-findings of a similar nature from various parts of the world. It may be that the excessive credulity which characterised some previous ages has, in the present time, given way to equally excessive scepticism.

Cosmology

If we even provisionally accept the idea of rebirth, this almost necessarily requires acceptance of some kind of spirit-world or worlds. In the Buddhist scriptures we find a scheme of post-mortem worlds which, while having much in common with general Indian ideas, is in many of its details unique. Here, there are no eternal heavens or hells, though some of both are said to be tremendously long-lasting; but all is in an eternal flux in which worlds and world-systems are born and perish, and living beings are continually born, die and are reborn according to their karmic deserts. It is a grandiose, but ultimately frightening and horrifying vision. Deliverance from it is only possible through the insight engendered by following the path taught by one of the Buddhas who occasionally arise on the scene. For those who fail to gain this insight there can be a happy rebirth for a long time in one of the temporary heaven-worlds, but no permanent deliverance from the perils of birth-and-death. This is *saṁsāra* or cyclic existence, the 'on-faring'.

All existence in the various realms of saṁsāra is in one of the three worlds: the World of Sense-Desires (*kāma-loka*), the World of Form (or the 'fine-material world': *rūpa-loka*) and the Formless (or 'immaterial') World (*arūpa-loka*), the latter two of which are inhabited by those who have attained, in this life, the corresponding mental absorptions (*jhānas*) frequently described in the texts. Beyond all this lies the realm of the Supramundane (*lokuttara*) or Nibbāna – the 'other shore', the only secure haven. And this, though it can be experienced, cannot be described.

There are thirty-one states in which, it is said, one can be reborn, distributed over the three worlds. The lowest of the three, the World of Sense-Desires, consists of the first eleven states, of which human rebirth is the fifth. Below this are the fourfold 'states of woe': hells, the world of asuras (sometimes rendered 'titans'), of hungry ghosts (*petas*), and of animals, while above it are the six lowest heavens. Above these are the sixteen heavens of the World of Form, and above these again the four heavens of the Formless World.

Special importance attaches to the human condition, since it is next to impossible to gain enlightenment from any other sphere than this: the realms below the human are too miserable, and those above it too happy and carefree for the necessary effort to be easily made.

The list as it stands show signs of late elaboration, but many of the spheres shown, or their inhabitants, are mentioned in the Suttas of this collection.

THE THIRTY-ONE ABODES

(*Reading from below*)

The Formless World	*Arūpa-loka*
31. Sphere of Neither-Perception-Nor-Non-Perception (devas of)	31. Nevasaññānâsaññâyatanūpagā devā
30. Sphere of No-Thingness (devas of)	30. Ākiñcaññâyatanūpagā devā
29. Sphere of Infinity of Consciousness (devas of)	29. Viññāṇañcâyatanūpagā devā
28. Sphere of Infinity of Space (devas of)	28. Ākāsānañcâyatanūpagā devā

The World of Form	*Rūpa-loka*
27. Peerless devas	27. Akaniṭṭhā devā
26. Clear-Sighted devas	26. Sudassī devā
25. Beautiful (*or* Clearly Visible) devas	25. Sudassā devā
24. Untroubled devas	24. Atappā devā
23. Devas not Falling Away	23. Avihā devā
22. Unconscious beings	22. Asaññasattā
21. Very Fruitful devas	21. Vehapphalā devā
20. Devas of Refulgent Glory	20. Subhakiṇṇā devā
19. Devas of Unbounded Glory	19. Appamāṇasubhā devā
18. Devas of Limited Glory	18. Parittasubhā devā
17. Devas of Streaming Radiance	17. Ābhassarā devā
16. Devas of Unbounded Radiance	16. Appamāṇabhā devā
15. Devas of Limited Radiance	15. Parittabhā devā
14. Great Brahmās	14. Mahā Brahmā
13. Ministers of Brahmā	13. Brahma-Purohitā devā
12. Retinue of Brahmā	12. Brahma-Parisajjā devā
The World of Sense-Desires	*Kāma-loka*
11. Devas Wielding Power over Others' Creations	11. Paranimmita-vasavattī devā
10. Devas Delighting in Creation	10. Nimmānaratī devā
9. Contented devas	9. Tusitā devā
8. Yāma devas	8. Yāmā devā
7. The Thirty-Three Gods	7. Tāvatiṁsa devā
6. Devas of the Four Great Kings	6. Catumahārājikā devā
5. THE HUMAN WORLD	5. MANUSSA LOKA
4. The animal world	4. Tiracchāna Yoni
3. The world of hungry ghosts	3. Peta Loka
2. The asuras ('titans')	2. Asurā
1. Hells	1. Niraya.

EXPLANATIONS OF THE THIRTY-ONE ABODES

The World of Sense Desires

1. *Hells.* The hell-states are often rendered 'purgatory' to indicate that they are not eternal. See n.244. Descriptions of the hells, their horrors and the length of time supposedly spent there, became increasingly lurid as time went on. In the Dīgha Nikāya there are no such descriptions, the kind and duration of suffering in such 'states of woe' being left quite vague. Jayatilleke (*The Message of the Buddha*, 251) quotes from the Saṁyutta Nikāya 36.4 (= S iv.206):

> When the average ignorant person makes an assertion that there is a Hell (*pātāla*) under the ocean, he is making a statement that is false and without basis. The word 'hell' is a term for painful bodily sensations.

This certainly deserves more credence as a saying of the Buddha than the late Suttas Majjhima Nikāya 129, 130. See also *Visuddhimagga* 13.93ff. for more on the first four abodes.

2. *Asuras.* See n.512. Rebirth among the asuras or titans is sometimes omitted from the list of separate destinations. In the Mahāyāna tradition they are often regarded more favourably than in the Pali Canon – perhaps a reminiscence of their earlier status as gods.

3. *Hungry ghosts.* These unhappy creatures are depicted with enormous bellies and tiny mouths. They wander about the world in great distress, which can, however, be alleviated by generous offerings. The Petavatthu, the seventh book of the Khuddaka Nikāya and one of the latest portions of the Canon, has many strange tales about them.

4. *The animal world.* The animal kingdom, together with the human realm, constitutes the only realm of beings normally visible to human sight and therefore indisputably existing (Ajita Kesakambali, like any modern rationalist, disbelieved in all the rest). There are those today in the West who object strongly to the idea that the Buddha taught that we can be reborn as animals, though at first sight the evidence is all against them. However, since *tiracchāna*, normally meaning

'animal', is used in Sutta 1 in the compounds *tiracchāna-kathā, tiracchāna-vijjā*, meaning 'low talk', 'base art', it is just possible that as a 'destination' for humans *tiracchāna-yoni* can be taken as a low rebirth. Some confirmation is provided by the case of Khorakkhattiya (Sutta 24, verse 9 and n.244).

5. *The human world.* Rebirth as a human being is regarded as a great opportunity which should be seized, since it may not easily recur, and it is almost impossible to 'enter the Stream' and so start on the path to Nibbāna from any other condition (but see n.600). Beings in the states below the human are too miserable, fearful and benighted, and those above it are too happy to make the necessary effort. In the human world we encounter both joy and sorrow, often very evenly balanced, and it is also possible to attain to a state of equanimity which is favourable to progress. Nevertheless, most human beings are very much under the sway of sense-desires, as indeed are the inhabitants of the worlds immediately above this one.

6. *The Realm of the Four Great Kings.* These kings are the guardians of the four quarters, and a lively account of existence on their plane is given in Sutta 20, to which reference should be made. The beings from here on are called devas, or in some cases alternatively Brahmās. Various kinds of non-human beings, not all of whom are beneficent, are supposed to be located in or associated with this realm, and are mentioned in Sutta 20. Since the inhabitants of this sphere (especially the gandhabbas, heavenly musicians and attendants on the kings and their followers) are still addicted to sense-pleasures, it is considered disgraceful for a monk to be reborn there. However, as we are told in Sutta 21, verse 11, it is possible for such to progress to a much higher plane if they make the effort.

7. *The Thirty-Three Gods.* Their heaven had once been the abode of the asuras, who had been expelled from it. No list of the thirty-three exists, but their chief is Sakka (Sankrit *Śakra*), who is either a reformed Indra or, as Rhys Davids considered, a Buddhist replacement for him. Many good people were reborn in this realm.

8. *Yāma devas.* These devas are usually only mentioned in passing. The name is said to mean 'those who have attained to divine bliss', but may also relate to Yama, king of the dead.

9. *Contented devas.* It is in their heaven that Bodhisattas reside before their last birth, and Once-Returners are also sometimes born here.

10, 11. *Devas Delighting in Creation; devas Wielding Power over Others' Creations.* The former can create any shape they like, the latter delight in things created by others, to get them in their power. These two are the highest in the World of Sense Desires.

The World of Form (Fine–Material World)

12. *The Retinue of Brahmā.* The inhabitants of abodes 12–21 are known as devas or Brahmas. Rebirth in these worlds is dependent on experience of the lower jhānas as well as moral behaviour. Those who live in them are free from sensual desire, though in most cases only by suppression through the jhānas, not by eradication.

13–14. *Ministers of Brahmā and Great Brahmās.* See below.

15–21. These are all worlds in which those who have experienced the lower jhānas may be reborn according to their development: thus the highest sphere, number 21, is inhabited by those who have had a strong experience of the fourth jhāna, and so on downwards.

22. *Unconscious beings.* See n.65.

23–27. These are the Pure Abodes in which Non-Returners are reborn, and whence they gain Nibbāna without returning to earth.

The Formless World (Immaterial World)

28–31. These correspond to the four higher jhānas of the Formless World, and rebirth in these realms depends on the attainment of these jhānas, as for numbers 12–21. Gotama attained to the Sphere of No-Thingness under his first teacher, Āḷārā Kālāma, and to the Sphere of Neither-Perception-Nor-Non-Perception under his second teacher Uddaka Rāmaputta. He thus reached the highest state attainable without breaking through to the Supramundane (*lokuttara*) which is 'beyond the Three Worlds'.

SOME NAMES AND DESIGNATIONS

Brahmā

In Buddhism there is not one Brahmā or Great Brahmā but many, and they are not immortal. The origin of the belief in Brahmā as creator of the world is given in Sutta 1, verse 2.2ff., and a satirical picture of the boastful Great Brahmā (who nevertheless is a true follower of the Buddha) is given in Sutta 11. But though not almighty or eternal, Brahmās are powerful and benevolent beings who are still believed, in Oriental Buddhist countries, to be able to bestow mundane favours (for example the Brahmā shrine outside the Erawan Hotel in Bangkok). One Great Brahmā, Sahampati, begged the newly-enlightened Buddha to teach those who had 'little dust on their eyes'.

There is no certain or even probable trace of the neuter Brahman in Pali scriptures. In Sutta 13 two young Brahmins consult the Buddha on how to attain to 'union with Brahmā' or more correctly 'fellowship with Brahmā'. Rhys Davids has been accused of mistranslating *sahavyatā* here as 'union', thus implying a mystical union rather than merely belonging to the company of Brahmā. But the Brahmins had explained to the Buddha that they were puzzled because different teachers interpreted the path to Brahmā in different ways. Thus both interpretations may well be implied here.

Buddha

This is of course a generic term, not a proper name: Gotama was 'the Buddha', not just 'Buddha' (the same should apply to Christ 'the Anointed', but usage is against this). It is a past participle form meaning 'awakened', thus 'enlightened'. Buddhas appear at vast intervals of time. Besides the fully-enlightened Buddha who teaches Dhamma to the world (*Sammā-Sambuddha*) there is the 'private Buddha' (*Pacceka-Buddha*), who is enlightened but does not teach. As time went on, a more and more elaborate Buddhology developed, the first beginnings of which can be seen here in Sutta 14. It was under the Buddha Dīpankara, vast ages ago, that the Brahmin

Sumedha first made the determination to become a Buddha, which he finally did as the historical Buddha Gotama. See especially Sutta 14.

Deva

This word is difficult to translate, and in general I have retained the Pali form, though in the case of the Thirty-Three Gods I have called them such, since they constitute something of a pantheon like that found in ancient Greece and elsewhere, even though few of them are individually named. As will be seen from the table, the term deva is applied to the inhabitants of all or any of the states above the human, though those in the World of Form can also be called Brahmā – a term which is probably better restricted to the inhabitants of realm No. 14. The etymological meaning of *deva* is 'bright, shining' (related to Latin *deus, dīvus*), but the word is popularly associated with the root *div* 'to play'.

Devas are said to be of three kinds: 1. Conventional, that is, kings and princes, who are addressed as 'Deva!' (hence the Indian idea of the 'god-king' – a title adopted by the kings of Cambodia but misapplied in modern times to the Dalai Lama!), 2. purified, that is, Buddhas and Arahants, and 3. spontaneously born (*uppattidevā*), that is, devas in the sense as used here. Besides the form *deva* (which is uncommon in the third sense in the singular), we find the abstract noun *devatā* used much like 'deity' in English. It should be noted that though this noun is grammatically feminine, it does not necessarily imply female sex. When it is wished to indicate the sex, the words *devaputta* 'deva's son' and *devadhītā* 'deva's daughter' may be used, though as most devas are spontaneously reborn this should not be taken literally (however, there are some indications of sexual reproduction occurring in the lowest heavens: we learn from Suttas 20 and 21 that the gandhabba chief Timbaru had a daughter).

Devas have all been human, and may be reborn again in human form, which in fact would be good fortune for them, as it is so much easier to gain enlightenment from the human state. In view of their former human state, it has been suggested that they are not unlike spirits (in the Spiritualist sense); another suggested translation is 'angels', but on the whole it seemed best (with one slight exception noted) to retain the Pali term for these beings. (The word *Devachan* used by Theosophists is not in fact derived from *deva*, but is the Tibetan word *bde-ba-can* 'land of bliss', rendering the Sanskrit *Sukhāvatī*.)

Gandhabbas

Celestial musicians (see Suttas 20, 21), subject to Dhataraṭṭha, the Great King of the East, they act as attendants on the devas, and are still much addicted to sense-pleasures.

It was formerly thought that gandhabbas also presided at conception, but this is due to a misunderstanding of a passage in Majjhima Nikāya 38 where it is stated that a 'gandhabba' must be present in addition to a man and a woman for conception to take place. The word here means, as the commentaries explain, 'being about to be born', that is the new consciousness arising dependent on that of a being who has died.

Garuḍās

These are giant birds, ever at war with the nāgas (except when, under the Buddha's influence, a truce is called: Sutta 20, verse 11). The garuḍā (*khruth*) is the royal badge of Thailand. In Indian legend, Viṣṇu rode on a garuḍā.

Nāgas

The most interesting and difficult of the various classes of non-human beings. Basically the term seems to apply to snakes, in particular the king cobra, but nāgas are also associated with elephants, probably on account of the snake- like trunk. They are very wise and powerful, though they suffer terribly from the attacks of the garuḍās. The term is often used for a great man, including the Buddha. But as Malalasekera writes (*Dictionary of Pali Proper Names* ii, 1355): 'In the accounts given of the nāgas, there is undoubtedly great confusion between the nāgas as supernatural (*sic*!) beings, as snakes, and as the name of certain non-Aryan tribes, but the confusion is too difficult to unravel.'

Tathāgata

The word generally used by the Buddha in referring to himself or to other Buddhas, though it seemingly can apply to any Arahant. Etymologically it means either — *tathā-āgata* 'thus come' or *tathā-gata* 'thus gone'. It would seem to be a way of indicating that 'he who stands before you' is not like other beings. For commentarial explanations, see Bhikkhu Bodhi's separate translation of Sutta 1 (see n.11). The Digha commentary (see p. 50) gives no fewer than eight different explanations, and the Mahāyāna schools have many more.

Yakkhas

Yakkhas, who are subject to Vessavaṇa, Great King of the North, are curiously ambivalent creatures, for reasons explained in Sutta 32, verse 2. Some are believers in the Buddha, but others, not wishing to keep the precepts, are hostile to the Dhamma, and they are in fact in the majority. Among the 'good yakkhas', however, we find (Sutta 19) Janavasabha, who had been King Bimbisāra of Magadha and a Stream-Winner! Later tradition insists more and more on the bad side of the yakkhas, who come to be regarded as ogres or demons pure and simple – with the female of the species being more deadly than the male.

THE PALI CANON

According to tradition, the text of the Pali Canon was settled at a Council held at Rājagaha immediately after the Teacher's passing, having been memorised by leading Elders, who were highly realised practitioners of the Dhamma. In fact it is clear that the collection as we have it originated over a longer period. The Canon was preserved in oral form until the first century B.C., when it became apparent that the sacred texts might vanish from the earth if they were not recorded in writing. They were accordingly written down under King Vaṭṭagāmanī at this time in Sri Lanka, though some portions may already have been committed to writing earlier. The feat of memory involved in preserving such an extensive body of text orally for so long may seem extraordinary to us, but was quite usual in ancient India. Writing was certainly known in India in the Buddha's time, but was not used for such purposes. It must, however, be remembered that in the course of forty-five years the Buddha preached, doubtless often in a standardised form (see p. 49), to many thousands of people, and that many of the monks and nuns had trained minds and memories, and will have known full well the meaning of what they were repeating.

From about the time of the Second Council, held at Vesālī a century after the Buddha's passing, we hear of divisions and the formation of sects within the Order. This led eventually to the rise of the Mahāyāna schools. An up-to-date account of these developments can be found in A.K. Warder's *Indian Buddhism*. Here we need merely note that the Theravāda type of Buddhism was carried early to Ceylon, and later to Burma, Thailand and other parts of south-east Asia, whereas the forms of Buddhism that spread to Tibet, China, Japan and other more northerly regions were of the developed, Mahāyāna type. Portions of the early scriptures of some of the schools that arose have been preserved, either in Sanskrit or, very often, in Chinese and/or Tibetan translations. The Sanskrit of these texts is often very bad, but the attempt was clearly made to lend dignity to the teaching by using the classical language. We thus find that Buddhist terms are found in both Pali and Sanskrit forms, and while the Pali terms are doubtless older, the Sanskrit forms are sometimes better known to the Western reader. Thus Sanskrit *karma* is more often used by Westerners than Pali *kamma*, Sanskrit *dharma* and *nirvāṇa* than Pali *dhamma* and *nibbāna*.

THE PALI LANGUAGE

Strictly speaking, the word *Pāḷi* means 'text'. But the expression *Pāḷibhāsā*, meaning 'language of the texts', was early taken to be the name of the language itself. Its use is practically confined to Buddhist subjects, and then only in the Theravāda school. Its exact origins are the subject of learned debate. While we cannot go too deeply into the matter here, it may be said that the traditional equation with the language of the ancient kingdom of Magadha, and the assertion that Pali is, literally and precisely, the language spoken by the Buddha himself, cannot be sustained. All the same, the language the Buddha actually spoke was in all probability not very different from Pali.

From the point of view of the non-specialist, we can think of Pali as a kind of simplified Sanskrit. Its development, like that of other early Indian dialects, can be thought of as similar to an early form of Italian just breaking away from Latin. A close parallel is found in the word for 'seven', where Latin *septem* has become Italian *sette*, the *pt* being simplified by assimilation to *tt*. The Sanskrit equivalent *sapta* is in Pali *satta*, and similar types of simplification are found in hundreds of words. The grammar, too, has been slightly simplified, though not nearly so much as that of Italian.[6] But the two languages are still so close that it is possible to convert whole passages of Sanskrit into Pali simply by making the necessary mechanical transpositions.[7] See p. 17 for more details about the relationship between Pali and Sanskrit.

THIS TRANSLATION

The text on which this translation is based is the Pali Text Society edition by T.W. Rhys Davids and J.E. Carpenter (3 volumes, 1890–1910).[8] I have made some slight use of the Thai translation as well as of Franke's German one, and have also made a few corrections following the Ven. Buddhadatta, Ñāṇamoli and others, as indicated at the appropriate places.

It must be pointed out that *any* translator of the Pali Canon is faced with peculiar difficulties, if only owing to the repetitiveness of the originals. Even the manuscripts contain numerous abridgements, and any translator must necessarily abridge a great deal more. I have dealt with repetitions in three ways. Long sections have been condensed into a few lines, which appear in italics and include the Sutta and verse numbers of the omitted passages. Where it is clear from the context what is being omitted I have simply used ellipses; where it is not clear I have used ellipses as well as the Sutta and verse number. In doing so I have ensured that nothing of substance has been omitted. I have made no excisions on account of real or alleged lateness or inauthenticity or the like: such matters are left to the reader's judgement, with an occasional note for guidance. I have as far as possible avoided the use of masculine nouns and pronouns where both sexes are implied. I have, however, always been guided by my understanding of the text, bearing in mind the many admonitions addressed specifically to monks, as well as the words of Brahmins and others who were undoubtedly 'sexist'. I have also kept the masculine gender in a few cases where to do otherwise would have produced intolerable awkwardness or (in verse) spoilt the scansion. I have tried to convey as much as possible the style of the original, rendering it into an English which is, I hope, neither too archaic nor too hypermodern.[9]

I have permitted myself a few syntactic abridgements. Phrases like *Bhagavatā saddhiṁ sammodi sammodanīyaṁ kathaṁ sārāṇīyaṁ vītisāretvā,* which Rhys Davids renders: 'He exchanged with the Blessed One the greetings and compliments of politeness and courtesy', have been cut down, in this case to 'exchanged courtesies with him'. As regards the designation *Bhagavā,* I have used 'the Lord' in narration, varied occasionally in quoted speech with 'the Blessed Lord'. Other translators have 'the Blessed One', 'the Exalted One', and so on.

The repetitions in the Canon have probably two distinct sources. It is extremely likely that the Buddha himself developed a standard form for sermons, which he doubtless uttered verbatim, or nearly so, many thousands of times during his forty-five years' ministry. He would seem to have gone on the principle which many teachers use and recommend to this day: 'First tell them what you are going to say, then say it, then tell them what you have said.' His disciples will then have extended this principle into a system of rigidly stereotyped phrases. The second source of repetition will have been inherent in the oral tradition itself, as is witnessed by oral literature all over the world. This is always characterised by long repetitive passages and stereotyped epithets and descriptions. This tendency will in the present instance have been reinforced by the wish to preserve the Master's words as accurately as possible. It should also be remembered that it was not all a mere matter of *mechanical* repetition, though this undoubtedly occurred occasionally too.

THE AUTHENTICITY OF THE PALI CANON

Certainly, not all parts of the Pali Canon are equally old or can be literally taken to be the Buddha's precise words. This is plain common sense and does not mean completely rejecting their authenticity. Recent research has gone far to vindicate the claim that the Pali Canon holds at least a prime place among our sources in the search for 'original' Buddhism, or, in fact, 'what the Buddha taught'. No attempt can be made here to go into any detail concerning questions of authenticity, or of the chronological stratification of the materials found in the Dīgha Nikāya. Some indications of scholarly opinion on this subject can be found, especially, in Pande, *Studies in the Origins of Buddhism* (1967), though not all his findings are equally acceptable. Personally I believe that all, or almost all *doctrinal* statements put directly into the mouth of the Buddha can be accepted as authentic, and this seems to me the most important point.[10]

THE COMMENTARIES

An invaluable aid to the understanding of the Pali Canon is provided by the old Commentaries (*Aṭṭhakathā*). These need to be used with caution, and they certainly contain numerous pious fabrications. Without them, however, our understanding of the Suttas would be woefully deficient. The two chief commentaries have been published in Pali by the Pali Text Society. The earliest is called *Sumangalavilāsinī* ('Effulgence of the Great Blessing'), but is usually known more prosaically as the Dīgha Nikāya Commentary (*Dīghanikāy-aṭṭhakathā* or DA, 3 volumes, 1886–1932, reprinted 1971). This is by the great Buddhaghosa, who lived in the 5th century C.E. The second, or Sub-Commentary (*ṭīkā*), called *Dīghanikāy-aṭṭhakathā-ṭīkā-Līnattha-*

vaṇṇanā 'Explanation of Obscurities in the Dīgha-Nikāya Commentary' or DAT for short (3 vols., ed. Lily de Silva, 1970), is a commentary on the commentary. Extensive extracts from these two commentaries on Suttas 1 and 15 (with further passages from a third, called the 'New Sub-Commentary') are given by Bhikkhu Bodhi in his separate translations of those Suttas, and similar extracts are given by Soma Thera in his version of Sutta 22. Some scanty comments are also quoted (sometimes without translation!) by Rhys Davids at intervals. I have added a few more extracts in my notes where it seemed necessary, besides occasionally clarifying or correcting Rhys Davids's notes.

Buddhaghosa was an Indian scholar-monk of amazing erudition who spent many years in Sri Lanka, where he wrote *The Path of Purification* (*Visuddhimagga*), a comprehensive guide to doctrine and meditation, splendidly translated into English by the Ven. Ñāṇamoli and published by the Buddhist Publication Society, Sri Lanka (1956+). His version is a great improvement on the older one published by the Pali Text Society as *The Path of Purity*. It appears that the old commentaries on the Pali Canon, some of which seem to have been very ancient, were translated into Sinhalese and the Pali originals lost, and that Buddhaghosa made from these a new Pali version. In general it is clear that he is recording traditional opinions and interpretations, holding back, except on rare occasions, from expressing a personal opinion with admirable self-effacement. It is to be expected that in due course the major commentaries will be translated into English from their rather difficult late Pali language.

THE DIVISIONS OF THE PALI CANON

The Pali Canon is divided into three main sections (*Tipiṭaka*: the Three Baskets).

1. *Vinaya Piṭaka*

This deals with monastic discipline, for monks and nuns. Translated by I.B. Horner as *The Book of Discipline* (6 volumes, PTS 1938–66).

2. *Sutta Piṭaka*

The 'Discourses' (*Suttas*): the portion of the Canon of most interest to lay Buddhists (see below).

3. *Abhidhamma Piṭaka*

The 'further doctrine', a highly schematised philosophical compendium in seven books, most of which have now been translated into English by the PTS.

The *Sutta Piṭaka* consists of five collections (*nikāyas*). The present translation is a new version of the first of these.

(1) *Dīgha Nikāya* ('long collection', i.e. collection of long discourses). Translated by T.W. and C.A.F. Rhys Davids (SBB, 3 volumes, 1899–1921) as 'Dialogues of the Buddha'. The Pali text (ed. T.W. Rhys Davids and J.E. Carpenter, PTS, 3 volumes, 1890–1910) is referred to here as D, the translation as RD (see Note on References).

(2) *Majjhima Nikāya* ('medium collection'). *The Teachings of the Buddha: The Middle Length Discourses of Buddha: A New Translation of the Majjhima Nikāya.* Original translation by Bhikkhu Ñāṇamoli, edited and revised by Bhikkhu Bodhi, Boston 1995. [MN]

(3) *Saṁyutta Nikāya* ('collection of groups', i.e. according to subject-matter). Translated by C.A.F. Rhys Davids and F.L. Woodward (PTS, 5 volumes, 1917–30) as 'Kindred Sayings'. [SN]

(4) *Anguttara Nikāya* ('collection of expanding groups', i.e. single things, twos, threes, and so on up to elevens). Translated by F.L. Woodward and E.M. Hare (PTS, 5 volumes, 1932–36) as 'Gradual Sayings'. [AN]

(5) *Khuddaka Nikāya* ('lesser collection'), a heterogeneous collection in 15 divisions of very varying interest to the modern reader:

(i) *Khuddaka Pātha* ('minor text'—used as a novice's handbook). Translated with its commentary by Ven. Ñāṇamoli (PTS 1960) as 'Minor Readings and Illustrator'. [Khp]

(ii) *Dhammapada* ('verses on Dhamma'), one of the most famous of Buddhist scriptures, an anthology in 26 chapters and

423 stanzas. Of the more than 30 English translations, the prose version by Nārada Thera (various editions, including one by Murray, London 1972) is recommended for the serious student. The Penguin translation by J. Mascaró, though very readable, is marred by serious errors of interpretation. [Dhp]

(iii) *Udāna* ('solemn utterances'), translated by F.L. Woodward (SBB 1935) as 'Verses of Uplift' (!). [Ud]

(iv) *Itivuttaka* ('thus it was said'), translated by Woodward together with (iii) as 'Thus It Was Said'. [It]

(v) *Sutta Nipāta* ('collection of suttas'), verse translation by E.M. Hare (SBB 1935) as 'Woven Cadences'; prose translation by K.R. Norman (PTS 1984) as 'The Group of Discourses' [Sn]

(vi) *Vimānavatthu* ('stories of the [heavenly] mansions'), translated by I.B. Horner (PTS 1974) as 'Stories of the Mansions'. [Vv]

(vii) *Petavatthu* ('stories of the departed' (or 'of hungry ghosts')), translated by H.S. Gehman as 'Stories of the Departed' and included with (vi). [Pv]

(viii) *Theragāthā* ('songs of the male elders', i.e. Arahants) [Thag] and (ix). *Therīgāthā* ('songs of the female elders', i.e. Arahants) [Thig]. Verse translation of (viii) and (ix) by C.A.F. Rhys Davids (PTS, 2 volumes, 1909, 1937) as 'Psalms of the Early Buddhists'; prose translation of (viii) and (ix) by K.R. Norman (PTS, 2 volumes, 1969, 1971) as 'The Elders' Verses'.

(x) *Jātaka* ('birth-stories', i.e. tales (547) of former lives of the Buddha). Much used as parables, otherwise mainly of interest as folklore. Translated (PTS 1895–1907, 1913 in 6 volumes, reprinted 1981 in 3 volumes) under editorship of E.B. Cowell [Ja]

(xi) *Niddesa* ('exposition'), an old commentary, ascribed to Sāriputta, to parts of (v). No English translation exists. [Nid]

(xii) *Paṭisambhidā Magga* ('path of discrimination'). Translation by the late Ven. Ñāṇamoli edited by A.K. Warder (PTS 1982). [Pṭs]

(xiii) *Apadāna* ('tradition', i.e. legend). Tales of Arahants similar to (x). No English translation exists. [Ap]

(xiv) *Buddhavaṁsa* ('chronicle of Buddhas') Translated by I.B. Horner (PTS 1975). [Bv]

(xv) *Cariyāpiṭaka* ('basket of conduct') Translated by I.B. Horner together with (xiv). [Cp]

A Summary of the Thirty-Four Suttas

DIVISION ONE: THE MORALITIES

1. *Brahmajāla Sutta*: The Supreme Net (What the Teaching is Not). The monks observe the wanderer Suppiya arguing with his pupil about the merits of the Buddha, his doctrine (*Dhamma*) and the order (*Sangha*). The Buddha tells them not to be affected by either praise or blame of the teaching, and declares that the 'worldling' will praise him for superficial reasons and not for the essence of his teaching. He lists sixty-two different types of wrong view, all of which are based on contact of the six sense-bases and their objects. Contact conditions craving, which in turn leads to clinging, to (re)becoming, to birth, to ageing and death and all manner of suffering. But the Tathāgata (the Buddha) has gone beyond these things, and all sixty-two wrong views are trapped in his net.

2. *Sāmaññaphala Sutta*: The Fruits of the Homeless Life. King Ajātasattu of Magadha, who gained the throne by parricide, comes to the Buddha with a question he has already posed in vain to six rival 'philosophers': What are the fruits, visible here and now (in this life) of the life of renunciation? The Buddha tells him, and then goes on to speak of the higher benefits, the various meditative states, and finally true liberation (this section recurs in the next eleven Suttas). The King, deeply impressed, declares himself a lay-follower. The Buddha later tells his disciples that but for his crime Ajātasattu would have become a Stream-winner by the 'opening of the Dhamma-eye'.

3. *Ambaṭṭha Sutta*: About Ambaṭṭha (Pride Humbled). Pokkharasāti, a famous Brahmin teacher, sends his pupil Ambaṭṭha (supposedly fully trained in Brahmin lore) to find out if the

'ascetic Gotama' is the great man he is alleged to be (and if, therefore, he bears the 'thirty-two marks of a Great Man'), Ambaṭṭha, proud of his Brahmin birth, behaves stupidly and arrogantly towards the Buddha, and thereupon learns a thing or two about his own ancestry, besides being made to realise that the Khattiyas (the warrior-noble caste) are superior to the Brahmins. Humbled, he returns to Pokkharasāti, who is furious at his conduct, hastens to see the Buddha, learns that he does indeed bear the thirty-two marks, and becomes a convert.

4. *Sonadaṇḍa Sutta*: About Sonadaṇḍa (Qualities of a True Brahmin). The Brahmin Sonadaṇḍa of Campā learns of the ascetic Gotama's arrival and goes to see him, against the advice of other Brahmins who think it beneath his dignity. The Buddha asks him about the qualities of a true Brahmin. He mentions five, but at the Buddha's instance admits that these can be reduced to two: wisdom and morality. He becomes a convert but does not experience the 'opening of the Dhamma-eye'.

5. *Kūṭadanta Sutta*: About Kūṭadanta (A Bloodless Sacrifice). The Brahmin Kūṭadanta wants to hold a great sacrifice with the slaughter of many hundreds of beasts. He appeals (improbably, as Rhys Davids points out!) to the Buddha for advice on how to do this. The Buddha tells him the story of an ancient king and his Brahmin chaplain, who performed a purely symbolic, bloodless sacrifice. Kūṭadanta sits in silence at the end of this narrative, having realised that the Buddha did not say: 'I have heard this', and the Buddha confirms that it is a story from one of his past lives, thus technically a 'birth-story' (*Jātaka*). The Buddha then tells of 'sacrifices more profitable', that is, the higher benefits as in Sutta 2. Kūṭadanta liberates the hundreds of animals he had destined for slaughter, saying: 'Let them be fed with green grass and given cool water to drink, and let cool breezes play upon them'. He becomes a lay-follower, and the 'pure and spotless Dhamma-eye' opens in him.

6. *Mahāli Sutta*: About Mahāli (Heavenly Sights, Soul and Body). Oṭṭhaddha (surnamed Mahāli) the Licchavi enquires of the Buddha about why some people cannot hear 'heavenly sounds' and so on, which the Buddha explains as due to their practice of 'one-sided samādhi'. In the latter part, the Buddha

tells how two ascetics, Maṇḍissa and Jāliya, had asked him whether the soul, or life principle, is the same as the body, or different (this is one of the 'unanswered questions' mentioned in Sutta 9). The Buddha says anyone who has attained to higher states of understanding will no longer be bothered by such questions.

7. *Jāliya Sutta*: About Jāliya merely repeats the last part of Sutta 6.

8. *Mahāsīhanāda Sutta*: The Great Lion's Roar is also called 'The Lion's Roar to Kassapa'. The naked ascetic Kassapa asks if it is true that the Buddha condemns all forms of austerity. The Buddha denies this, saying one must distinguish. Kassapa gives a list of standard practices (some of them rather revolting), and the Buddha says one may do any of these things but, if one's morality, heart and wisdom are not developed, one is still far from being an ascetic or a Brahmin (in the true sense). He himself has practised all possible austerities to perfection, and morality and wisdom as well. Kassapa requests ordination, and soon through diligent practice he becomes an Arahant.

9. *Poṭṭhapāda Sutta*: About Poṭṭhapāda (States of Consciousness). The ascetic Poṭṭhapāda tells the Buddha that he and his fellows have been debating about 'the higher extinction of consciousness', and seeks a ruling on the matter. The Buddha says those who think mental states arise and pass away by chance are quite wrong. He lists the various jhāna states, showing how perception can be 'controlled'. Poṭṭhapāda says he has never heard anything like all this before. The discussion moves to various kinds of possible self, all of which the Buddha refutes, and to the 'unanswered questions' and the reason for their not being answered. Citta, son of an elephant-trainer, joins in the discussion, and finally, while Poṭṭhapāda becomes a lay-follower, Citta becomes a bhikkhu and soon gains Arahantship. In this Sutta we first find the parable of the man who said he was in love with the most beautiful girl in the country, without knowing who she was or what she looked like.

10. *Subha Sutta*: About Subha (Morality, Concentration, Wisdom). Shortly after the Buddha's death, Ānanda explains the Ariyan morality, concentration and wisdom (as in Sutta 2) to the young Brahmin Subha, who becomes a lay-follower.

11. *Kevaddha Sutta*: About Kevaddha (What Brahmā Didn't Know). Kevaddha urges the Buddha to perform miracles to strengthen people's faith. The Buddha refuses, saying the only kind of miracle he approves of is the 'miracle of instruction'. He tells the story of the monk who wanted to know 'where the four great elements cease without remainder'. By psychic power he ascended into the heavens, but none there could tell him—not even the Great Brahmā, who referred him back to the Buddha for an answer.

12. *Lohicca Sutta*: About Lohicca (Good and Bad Teachers). Lohicca has the pernicious view that if anyone were to discover some new doctrine, he should keep it to himself. The Buddha puts him right and explains the difference between good and bad teachers.

13. *Tevijja Sutta*: The Threefold Knowledge (The Way to Brahmā). Two young Brahmins are puzzled because different teachers speak of different ways of attaining fellowship (or union) with Brahmā, which to them is the highest goal. The Buddha gets them to admit that none of their teachers, or even those from whom the tradition stems, have ever seen Brahmā face to face, then instructs them in the *Brahmavihāras*, which do lead to that goal—which is not, of course, the goal of Buddhism.

DIVISION TWO: THE GREAT DIVISION

14. *Mahâpadāna Sutta*: The Great Discourse on the Lineage. This refers to the last seven Buddhas, going back 'ninety-one aeons' in time. The life of the Buddha Vipassī at that remote period is told in terms similar to early versions of the life of Gotama. All Buddhas go through the same experiences in their last earthly life. The Buddha's realisation is equated with the understanding of dependent origination (see next Sutta).

15. *Mahānidāna Sutta*: The Great Discourse on Origination. Ānanda is rebuked for saying the law of dependent origination is 'as clear as clear' to him. The Buddha explains it in reverse order first, but going back only to mind-and-body and consciousness (that is, factors 4 and 3 of the usual list of 12), and also omitting the six sense-bases (No 5). The exposition ends

with a reference to the seven stages of consciousness and the two realms.

16. *Mahāparinibbāna Sutta*: The Great Passing (The Buddha's Last Days). The longest Sutta of all, telling (not without some legendary embroidery) the story of the Buddha's last days. King Ajātasattu, wishing to attack the Vajjians, sends to the Buddha to know what the outcome will be. The Buddha replies indirectly, pointing out the advantages of the Vajjian republican system, and later urges the monks to observe comparable rules for the Sangha. With Ānanda, he visits a series of places and gives discourses to monks and laity. At Pāṭaligāma he prophesies the place's future greatness (it became Asoka's capital Pāṭaliputra). At Vesāli the courtesan Ambapāli invites him to a meal, and gives her mango-grove to the order. He tells Ānanda that he will pass away within three months. At Pāvā Cunda the smith serves a meal including 'pig's delight' (*sūkara-maddava*) (pork, truffles?—opinions vary) which only the Buddha eats. Later he is taken very ill, but is careful to exonerate Cunda. At Kusināra the Buddha rests between twin *sāl*-trees. Ānanda begs him not to pass away in such an insignificant place, but he says it was once a famous capital (see Sutta 17). After giving last instructions to the Sangha (and refusing to appoint a successor), he utters the final admonition 'strive on untiringly' – *appamādena sampādetha* – and passes away. The Sutta concludes with an account of the funeral and distribution of the ashes in eight portions.

17. *Mahāsudassana Sutta*: The Great Splendour (A King's Renunciation). Much the same story recurs in Jātaka 95. King Mahāsudassana lived in fairy-tale splendour and possessed the seven treasures, but finally retired to his Dhamma palace (built by the gods) to lead a life of meditation.

18. *Janavasabha Sutta*: About Janavasabha (Brahmā Addresses the Gods). A yakkha (of the good variety) appears to the Buddha declaring that he is now called Janavasabha, but on earth was King Bimbisāra of Magadha, the Buddha's great supporter, killed by his son Ajātasattu. He tells of the assembly of the Thirty-Three Gods at which Brahmā declared how, since the Buddha's mission on earth, the ranks of the gods (devas) are increasing and those of their opponents the asuras, declining.

19. *Mahāgovinda Sutta*: The Great Steward (A Past Life of Gotama). The gandhabba Pañcasikha appears to the Buddha and reports, similarly to Sutta 18, on a meeting of the gods. Then follows the story of the Great Steward who conducted the affairs of seven kings and then retired into the homeless life, bringing many people to the Brahmā-world which is the highest people can reach in an age when there is no Buddha. At the end the Buddha tells Pañcasikha that he was that steward, but that the path he now teaches, as the Buddha, goes beyond what he was able to teach then.

20. *Mahāsamaya Sutta*: The Mighty Gathering (Devas Come to See the Buddha). A Sutta practically all in verse giving much mythological lore.

21. *Sakkapañha Sutta*: Sakka's Questions (A God Consults the Buddha). Sakka, king of the Thirty-Three Gods, approaches the Buddha through the aid of Pañcasikha, who sings a love-song (!) to him to attract his attention. Sakka puts various questions on the holy life to the Buddha. We also hear the story of the nun Gopikā who became a man, and as such rebuked three of the Buddha's monks who had been reborn in the lowest of the heavens, bidding them strive harder and rise higher, which two of them succeeded in doing. Sakka himself is put on the right path and rewards Pañcasikha (who is not so advanced!) with the hand of the gandhabba maiden he desired.

22. *Mahāsatipaṭṭhāna Sutta*: The Greater Discourse on the Foundations of Mindfulness. Very different in character from the Suttas immediately preceding, this is held by many to be the most important Sutta in the Canon. It recurs verbatim less verses 18–21, as No 10 in the Majjhima Nikāya. The 'one way' for the purification of beings, for the overcoming of sorrow and distress, for the gaining of Nibbāna is the four foundations of mindfulness: mindfulness of body, feelings, mind and mind-objects. Detailed instructions for mindful awareness of breathing, and so on, are given. Thus, under mind-objects, we read, for example: 'If sensual desire is present in himself, a monk knows that it is present. If sensual desire is absent in himself, a monk knows that it is absent. And he knows how unarisen sensual desire comes to arise, and he knows how the abandonment of arisen sensual desire comes about, and he knows how

the non-arising of the abandoned sensual desire in the future will come about.' ('Monk' here, according to the Commentary, means anyone who does the practice). The Sutta ends with an account of the Four Noble Truths.

23. *Pāyāsi Sutta*: About Pāyāsi (Debate with a Sceptic). Prince Pāyāsi does not believe in future lives, or in the rewards and penalties of good and bad deeds. The Ven. Kumāra-Kassapa convinces him of his error by means of a series of clever parables. Finally Pāyāsi, converted, establishes a charity for ascetics and the needy, but does so grudgingly. As a result he is reborn in the lowest of the heavens.

DIVISION THREE: THE 'PĀṬIKA' DIVISION

24. *Pāṭika Sutta*: About Pāṭikaputta (The Charlatan). The Buddha has an exceedingly stupid disciple Sunakkhatta, who eventually leaves him. Sunakkhatta is greatly impressed by some dubious 'holy men' whom he takes to be Arahants. The boastful naked ascetic Pāṭikaputta challenges the Buddha to a contest of miracles. The Buddha waits for him to appear, but – as the Buddha prophesied – he cannot even rise from his seat to meet the Buddha. The Sutta is not unamusing, but definitely substandard material. A final section on the 'Origin of Things' seems to have been tacked on.

25. *Udumbarika-Sīhanāda Sutta*: The Lion's Roar to the Udumbarikans. The wanderer Nigrodha, staying at the Udumbarika lodging, boasts that he can 'floor the ascetic Gotama' with a single question. He is of course defeated, and the Buddha shows a way beyond that of self-mortification – 'to reach the pith'.

26. *Cakkavatti-Sīhanāda Sutta*: The Lion's Roar on the Turning of the Wheel. At the beginning and end of the discourse, the Buddha exhorts his monks to 'keep to their own preserves' by the practice of mindfulness. Then he tells of a 'wheel-turning monarch' (a righteous ruler) who had the sacred Wheel-Treasure, which had to be carefully guarded. He was followed by a line of righteous kings, but eventually they degenerated, and society went from bad to worse, while the human life-span

sank to ten years and all sense of morality was lost. After a brief but dreadful 'sword-interval' things improved, and finally another Buddha, Metteyya (Sanskrit Maitreya) will appear.

27. *Aggañña Sutta*: On Knowledge of Beginnings. A somewhat similar fable, this time addressed to the Brahmins, whose pretensions the Buddha refutes. There is no difference between Brahmins and others if they behave badly. A somewhat fanciful account of the origin of castes is given.

28. *Sampasādanīya Sutta*: Serene Faith. Sāriputta explains his reasons for his complete faith in the Buddha.

29. *Pāsādika Sutta*: The Delightful Discourse. A discussion of good and bad teachers, and why the Buddha has not revealed certain points.

30. *Lakkhaṇa Sutta*: The Marks of a Great Man. Verses on the curious 'thirty-two marks of a Great Man' beloved of the Brahmins. These are in a variety of metres in the original.

31. *Sigālaka Sutta*: To Sigālaka (Advice to Lay People). Advice to the young layman Sigālaka on morality, related to the four quarters, zenith and nadir which, in memory of his father, he had been worshipping.

32. *Āṭānāṭiya Sutta*: The Āṭānāṭā Protective verses.

33. *Saṅgīti Sutta*: The Chanting Together (Lists of terms for recitation).

34. *Dasuttara Sutta*: Expanding Decades. Similar material to Sutta 33, arranged under ten heads.

The Long Discourses of the Buddha

Dīgha Nikāya

NAMO TASSA BHAGAVATO ARAHATO
SAMMĀSAMBUDDHASSA

HOMAGE TO THE BLESSED ONE, THE ARAHANT,
THE FULLY-ENLIGHTENED BUDDHA

Division One
The Moralities

1 *Brahmajāla Sutta: The Supreme Net*
What the Teaching Is Not

[1] 1.1. THUS HAVE I HEARD.[11] Once the Lord was travelling along the main road between Rājagaha and Nāḷandā[12] with a large company of some five hundred monks. And the wanderer Suppiya was also travelling on that road with his pupil the youth Brahmadatta. And Suppiya[13] was finding fault in all sorts of ways with the Buddha, the Dhamma and the Sangha, whereas his pupil Brahmadatta was speaking in various ways in their praise. And so these two, teacher and pupil, directly opposing each other's arguments, followed close behind the Lord and his order of monks.

1.2. Then the Lord stopped for one night with his monks at the royal park of Ambalaṭṭhikā. And Suppiya too stopped there for the night with his pupil Brahmadatta. And Suppiya went on abusing the Buddha, the Dhamma and the Sangha, while his [2] pupil Brahmadatta defended them. And thus disputing, they followed close behind the Buddha and his order of monks.

1.3. Now in the early morning a number of monks, having got up, gathered together and sat in the Round Pavilion, and this was the trend of their talk: 'It is wonderful, friends, it is marvellous how the Blessed Lord, the Arahant, the fully-enlightened Buddha knows, sees and clearly distinguishes the different inclinations of beings! For here is the wanderer Suppiya finding fault in all sorts of ways with the Buddha, the Dhamma and the Sangha, while his pupil Brahmadatta in various ways defends them. And, still disputing, they follow closely behind the Blessed Lord and his order of monks.'

1.4. Then the Lord, being aware of what those monks were saying, went to the Round Pavilion and sat down on the prepared seat. Then he said: 'Monks, what was the subject of your conversation just now? What talk have I interrupted?' And they told him.

1.5. 'Monks, if anyone should speak in disparagement of me, of the Dhamma or of the Sangha, [3] you should not be angry, resentful or upset on that account. If you were to be angry or displeased at such disparagement, that would only be a hindrance to you. For if others disparage me, the Dhamma or the Sangha, and you are angry or displeased, can you recognise whether what they say is right or not?' 'No, Lord.' 'If others disparage me, the Dhamma or the Sangha, then you must explain what is incorrect as being incorrect, saying: "That is incorrect, that is false, that is not our way,[14] that is not found among us."

1.6. 'But, monks, if others should speak in praise of me, of the Dhamma or of the Sangha, you should not on that account be pleased, happy or elated. If you were to be pleased, happy or elated at such praise, that would only be a hindrance to you. If others praise me, the Dhamma or the Sangha, you should acknowledge the truth of what is true, saying: "That is correct, that is right, that is our way, that is found among us."

1.7. 'It is, monks, for elementary, inferior matters of moral practice[15] that the worldling[16] would praise the Tathāgata.[17] And what are these elementary, inferior matters for which the worldling would praise him?'

[*Short Section on Morality*][18]

[4] 1.8. '"Abandoning the taking of life, the ascetic Gotama dwells refraining from taking life, without stick or sword, scrupulous, compassionate, trembling for the welfare of all living beings." Thus the worldling would praise the Tathāgata.[19] "Abandoning the taking of what is not given, the ascetic Gotama dwells refraining from taking what is not given, living purely, accepting what is given, awaiting what is given, without stealing. Abandoning unchastity, the ascetic Gotama lives far from it, aloof from the village-practice of sex.[20]

1.9. '"Abandoning false speech, the ascetic Gotama dwells refraining from false speech, a truth-speaker, one to be relied on, trustworthy, dependable, not a deceiver of the world. Abandoning malicious speech, he does not repeat there what he has heard here to the detriment of these, or repeat here what he has heard there to the detriment of those. Thus he is a reconciler of those at variance and an encourager of those at one, rejoicing in peace, loving it, delighting in it, one who speaks up for peace. Abandoning harsh speech, he refrains from it. He speaks whatever is blameless, pleasing to the ear, agreeable, reaching the heart, urbane, pleasing and attractive to the multitude. Abandoning idle chatter, he speaks at the right time, what is correct and to the point,[21] of Dhamma and discipline. He is a speaker whose words are to be treasured, seasonable, [5] reasoned, well-defined and connected with the goal."[22] Thus the worldling would praise the Tathāgata.

1.10. '"The ascetic Gotama is a refrainer from damaging seeds and crops. He eats once a day and not at night, refraining from eating at improper times.[23] He avoids watching dancing, singing, music and shows. He abstains from using garlands, perfumes, cosmetics, ornaments and adornments. He avoids using high or wide beds. He avoids accepting gold and silver.[24] He avoids accepting raw grain or raw flesh, he does not accept women and young girls, male or female slaves, sheep and goats, cocks and pigs, elephants, cattle, horses and mares, fields and plots;[25] he refrains from running errands, from buying and selling, from cheating with false weights and measures, from bribery and corruption, deception and insincerity, from wounding, killing, imprisoning, highway robbery, and taking food by force." Thus the worldling would praise the Tathāgata.'

[*Middle Section on Morality*]

1.11. '"Whereas, gentlemen, some ascetics and Brahmins, feeding on the food of the faithful, are addicted to the destruction of such seeds as are propagated from roots, from stems, from joints, from cuttings, from seeds, the ascetic Gotama refrains from such destruction." Thus the worldling would praise the Tathāgata. [6]

1.12. '"Whereas some ascetics and Brahmins, feeding on the

food of the faithful, remain addicted to the enjoyment of stored-up goods such as food, drink, clothing, carriages, beds, perfumes, meat, the ascetic Gotama refrains from such enjoyment.

1.13. '"Whereas some ascetics and Brahmins...remain addicted to attending such shows as dancing, singing, music, displays, recitations, hand-music, cymbals and drums, fairy-shows,[26] acrobatic and conjuring tricks,[27] combats of elephants, buffaloes, bulls, goats, rams, cocks and quail, fighting with staves, boxing, wrestling, sham-fights, parades, manoeuvres and military reviews, the ascetic Gotama refrains from attending such displays.

1.14. '"Whereas some ascetics and Brahmins remain addicted to such games and idle pursuits as eight- or ten-row chess,[28] 'chess in the air',[29] hopscotch, spillikins, dicing, hitting sticks, 'hand-pictures', ball-games, blowing through toy pipes, playing with toy ploughs, turning somersaults, playing with toy windmills, measures, carriages, [7] and bows, guessing letters,[30] guessing thoughts,[31] mimicking deformities, the ascetic Gotama refrains from such idle pursuits.

1.15. '"Whereas some ascetics and Brahmins remain addicted to high and wide beds and long chairs, couches adorned with animal figures,[32] fleecy or variegated coverlets, coverlets with hair on both sides or one side, silk coverlets, embroidered with gems or without, elephant-, horse- or chariot-rugs, choice spreads of antelope-hide, couches with awnings, or with red cushions at both ends, the ascetic Gotama refrains from such high and wide beds.

1.16. '"Whereas some ascetics and Brahmins remain addicted to such forms of self-adornment and embellishment as rubbing the body with perfumes, massaging, bathing in scented water, shampooing, using mirrors, ointments, garlands, scents, unguents, cosmetics, bracelets, headbands, fancy sticks, bottles, swords, sunshades, decorated sandals, turbans, gems, yak-tail fans, long-fringed white robes, the ascetic Gotama refrains from such self-adornment.

1.17. '"Whereas some ascetics and Brahmins remain addicted to such unedifying conversation[33] as about kings, robbers, ministers, armies, dangers, wars, food, drink, clothes, beds, garlands, perfumes, relatives, carriages, villages, towns and cities, countries, women, [8] heroes, street- and well-gossip, talk of the departed, desultory chat, speculations about land and sea,[34] talk about being and non-being,[35] the ascetic Gotama refrains from such conversation.

1.18. '"Whereas some ascetics and Brahmins remain addicted to disputation such as: 'You don't understand this doctrine and discipline – I do!' 'How could *you* understand this doctrine and discipline?' 'Your way is all wrong – mine is right!' 'I am consistent – you aren't!' 'You said last what you should have said first, and you said first what you should have said last!' 'What you took so long to think up has been refuted!' 'Your argument has been overthrown, you're defeated!' 'Go on, save your doctrine – get out of that if you can!' the ascetic Gotama refrains from such disputation.[36]

1.19. '"Whereas some ascetics and Brahmins remain addicted to such things as running errands and messages, such as for kings, ministers, nobles, Brahmins, householders and young men who say: 'Go here – go there! Take this there – bring that from there!' the ascetic Gotama refrains from such errand-running.

1.20. '"Whereas some ascetics and Brahmins remain addicted to deception, patter, hinting, belittling, and are always on the make for further gains, the ascetic Gotama refrains from such deception." Thus the worldling would praise the Tathāgata.'[37]

[*Large Section on Morality*]

1.21. '"Whereas some ascetics and Brahmins, feeding on the food of the faithful, make their living by such base arts, such wrong means of livelihood as palmistry,[38] divining by signs, portents, dreams, body-marks, mouse-gnawings, fire-oblations, oblations from a ladle, of husks, rice-powder, rice-grains, ghee or oil, from the mouth or of blood, reading the finger-tips, house- and garden-lore, skill in charms, ghost-lore, earth-house lore,[39] snake-lore, poison-lore, rat-lore, bird-lore, crow-lore, foretelling a person's life-span, charms against arrows, knowledge of animals' cries, the ascetic Gotama refrains from such base arts and wrong means of livelihood.

1.22. '"Whereas some ascetics and Brahmins make their living by such base arts as judging the marks of gems, sticks, clothes, swords, spears, arrows, weapons, women, men, boys, girls, male and female slaves, elephants, horses, buffaloes, bulls, cows, goats, rams, cocks, quail, iguanas, bamboo-rats,[40] tortoises, deer, the ascetic Gotama refrains from such base arts.

1.23. '"Whereas some ascetics and Brahmins make their living by such base arts as predicting: 'The chiefs[41] will march out – the chiefs will march back', 'Our chiefs [10] will advance and the other chiefs will retreat', 'Our chiefs will win and the other chiefs will lose', 'The other chiefs will win and ours will lose', 'Thus there will be victory for one side and defeat for the other', the ascetic Gotama refrains from such base arts.

1.24. '"Whereas some ascetics and Brahmins make their living by such base arts as predicting an eclipse of the moon, the sun, a star; that the sun and moon will go on their proper course – will go astray; that a star will go on its proper course – will go astray; that there will be a shower of meteors, a blaze in the sky, an earthquake, thunder; a rising, setting, darkening, brightening of the moon, the sun, the stars; and 'such will be the outcome of these things', the ascetic Gotama refrains from such base arts and wrong means of livelihood. [11]

1.25. '"Whereas some ascetics and Brahmins make their living by such base arts as predicting good or bad rainfall; a good or bad harvest; security, danger; disease, health; or accounting, computing, calculating, poetic composition, philosophising, the ascetic Gotama refrains from such base arts and wrong means of livelihood.

1.26. '"Whereas some ascetics and Brahmins make their living by such base arts as arranging the giving and taking in marriage, engagements and divorces; [declaring the time for] saving and spending, bringing good or bad luck, procuring abortions,[42] using spells to bind the tongue, binding the jaw, making the hands jerk, causing deafness, getting answers with a mirror, a girl-medium, a deva; worshipping the sun or Great Brahmā, breathing fire, invoking the goddess of luck, the ascetic Gotama refrains from such base arts and wrong means of livelihood.

1.27. '"Whereas some ascetics and Brahmins, feeding on the food of the faithful, make their living by such base arts, such wrong means of livelihood as appeasing the devas and redeeming vows to them, making earth-house spells, causing virility or impotence, preparing and consecrating building-sites, giving ritual rinsings and bathings, making sacrifices, giving emetics, purges, expectorants and phlegmagogues, giving ear-, eye-, nose-medicine, ointments and counter-ointments, eye-surgery, surgery, pediatry, using balms to counter the side-effects of previous remedies, the ascetic Gotama refrains from such base arts and wrong means of livelihood."[43] It is, monks, for such elementary, inferior matters of moral practice that the worldling would praise the Tathāgata.

[12] 1.28.'There are, monks, other matters, profound, hard to see, hard to understand, peaceful, excellent, beyond mere thought, subtle, to be experienced by the wise, which the Tathāgata, having realised them by his own super-knowledge, proclaims, and about which those who would truthfully praise the Tathāgata would rightly speak. And what are these matters?'

[*The Sixty-Two Kinds of Wrong Views*]

1.29. 'There are, monks, some ascetics and Brahmins who are speculators about the past, having fixed views about the past, and who put forward [13] various speculative theories about the past, in eighteen different ways. On what basis, on what grounds do they do so?

1.30. 'There are some ascetics and Brahmins who are Eternalists, who proclaim the eternity of the self and the world in four ways. On what grounds?

1.31. [Wrong view 1][44] 'Here, monks, a certain ascetic or Brahmin has by means of effort, exertion, application, earnestness and right attention attained to such a state of mental concentration that he thereby recalls past existences – one birth, two births, three, four, five, ten births, a hundred, a thousand, a hundred thousand births, several hundred, several thousand, several hundred thousand births. "There my name was so-and-so, my clan was so-and-so, my caste was so-and-so, my food was such-and-such, I experienced such-and-such pleasant and painful conditions, I lived for so long. Having passed away from there, I arose there. There my name was so-and-so...And having passed away from there, I arose here." Thus he remembers various past [14], lives, their conditions and details. And he says: "The self and the world are eternal, barren[45] like a mountain-peak, set firmly as a post. These beings rush round, circulate, pass away and re-arise, but this remains eternally. Why so? I have by means of effort, exertion, attained to such a state of mental concentration that I have thereby recalled various past existences...That is how I know the self and the world are eternal..." That is the first way in which some ascetics and Brahmins proclaim the eternity of the self and the world.

1.32. [Wrong view 2] 'And what is the second way? Here, monks, a certain ascetic or Brahmin has by means of effort, exertion...attained to such a state of mental concentration that he thereby recalls one period of contraction and expansion,[46] two such periods, three, four, five, ten periods of contraction and expansion..."There my name was so-and-so..." [15] That is the second way in which some ascetics and Brahmins proclaim the eternity of the self and the world.

1.33. [Wrong view 3] 'And what is the third way? Here, monks, a certain ascetic or Brahmin has by means of effort... attained to such a state of mental concentration that he recalls ten, twenty, thirty, forty periods of contraction and expansion. "There my name was so-and-so..." [16] That is the third way in which some ascetics and Brahmins proclaim the eternity of the self and the world.

1.34. [Wrong view 4] 'And what is the fourth way? Here a certain ascetic or Brahmin is a logician,[47] a reasoner. Hammering it out by reason, following his own line of thought, he argues: "The self and the world are eternal, barren like a mountain-peak, set firmly as a post. These beings rush round, circulate, pass away and re-arise, but this remains for ever."

That is the fourth way in which some ascetics and Brahmins proclaim the eternity of the self and the world.

1.35. 'These are the four ways in which these ascetics and Brahmins are Eternalists, and proclaim the eternity of the self and the world on four grounds. And whatever ascetics or Brahmins are Eternalists and proclaim the eternity of the self and the world, they do so on one or other of these four grounds. There is no other way.

1.36. 'This, monks, the Tathāgata understands: These viewpoints thus grasped and adhered to will lead to such-and-such destinations in another world. This the Tathāgata knows, and more, but he is not [17] attached to that knowledge. And being thus unattached he has experienced for himself perfect peace, and having truly understood the arising and passing away of feelings, their attraction and peril and the deliverance from them, the Tathāgata is liberated without remainder.

1.37. 'There are, monks, other matters, profound, hard to see, hard to understand, peaceful, excellent, beyond mere thought, subtle, to be experienced by the wise, which the Tathāgata, having realised them by his own super-knowledge, proclaims, and about which those who would truthfully praise the Tathāgata would rightly speak. And what are these matters?'

[*End of first recitation-section*]

2.1. 'There are, monks, some ascetics and Brahmins who are partly Eternalists and partly Non-Eternalists, who proclaim the partial eternity and the partial non-eternity of the self and the world in four ways. On what grounds?

2.2. 'There comes a time, monks, sooner or later after a long period, when this world contracts. At a time of contraction, beings are mostly reborn in the Ābhassara Brahmā[48] world. And there they dwell, mind-made,[49] feeding on delight,[50] self-luminous, moving through the air, glorious – and they stay like that for a very long time.

2.3. [Wrong view 5] 'But the time comes, sooner or later after a long period, when this world begins to expand. In this expanding world an empty palace of Brahmā[51] appears. And then one being, from exhaustion of his life-span or of his merits,[52] falls from the Ābhassara world and arises in the empty Brahmā-palace. And there he dwells, mind-made, feeding on delight, self-luminous, moving through the air, glorious – and he stays like that for a very long time.

2.4. 'Then in this being who has been alone for so long there arises unrest, discontent and worry, and he thinks: "Oh, if only some other beings would come here!" And other beings, [18] from exhaustion of their life-span or of their merits, fall from the Ābhassara world and arise in the Brahmā-palace as companions for this being. And there they dwell, mind-made,...and they stay like that for a very long time.

2.5. 'And then, monks, that being who first arose there thinks: "I am Brahmā, the Great Brahmā, the Conqueror, the Unconquered, the All-Seeing, the All-Powerful, the Lord, the Maker and Creator, Ruler, Appointer and Orderer, Father of All That Have Been and Shall Be. These beings were created by me. How so? Because I first had this thought: 'Oh, if only some other beings would come here!' That was my wish, and then these beings came into this existence!" But those beings who arose subsequently think: "This, friends, is Brahmā, Great Brahmā, the Conqueror, the Unconquered, the All-Seeing, the All-Powerful, the Lord, the Maker and Creator, Ruler, Appointer and Orderer, Father of All That Have Been and Shall Be. How so? We have seen that he was here first, and that we arose after him."

2.6. 'And this being that arose first is longer-lived, more beautiful and more powerful than they are. And it may happen that some being falls from that realm and arises in this world. Having arisen in this world, he goes forth from the household life into homelessness. Having gone forth, he by means of effort, exertion, application, earnestness and right attention attains to such a degree of mental concentration that he thereby recalls his last existence, but recalls none before that. And he thinks: "That Brahmā,...he made us, and he is permanent, stable, eternal, not subject to change, the same for ever and ever. But we who were [19] created by that Brahmā, we are impermanent, unstable, short-lived, fated to fall away, and we have come to this world." This is the first case whereby some ascetics and Brahmins are partly Eternalists and partly Non-Eternalists.

2.7. [Wrong view 6] 'And what is the second way? There are, monks, certain devas called Corrupted by Pleasure.[53] They spend an excessive amount of time addicted to merriment, play and enjoyment, so that their mindfulness is dissipated, and by the dissipation of mindfulness those beings fall from that state.

2.8. 'And it can happen that a being, having fallen from that state, arises in this world. Having arisen in this world, he goes forth from the household life into homelessness. Having gone forth, he by means of effort, exertion,...recalls his last existence, but recalls none before that.

2.9. 'He thinks: "Those reverend devas who are not corrupted by pleasure do not spend an excessive amount of time addicted to merriment, play and enjoyment. Thus their mindfulness is not dissipated, and so they do not fall from that state. They are permanent, stable, eternal, not subject to change, the same for ever and [20] ever. But we, who are corrupted by pleasure, spent an excessive amount of time addicted to merriment, play and enjoyment. Thus we, by the dissipation of mindfulness, have fallen from that state, we are impermanent, unstable, short-lived, fated to fall away, and we have come to this world." This is the second case.

2.10. [Wrong view 7] 'And what is the third way? There are, monks, certain devas called Corrupted in Mind.[54] They spend an excessive amount of time regarding each other with envy. By this means their minds are corrupted. On account of their corrupted minds they become weary in body and mind. And they fall from that place.

2.11. 'And it can happen that a being, having fallen from that state, arises in this world. He...recalls his last existence, but recalls none before that.

2.12. 'He thinks: "Those reverend devas who are not corrupted in mind do not spend an excessive amount of time regarding each other with envy...They do not become corrupted in mind, or weary in body and mind, and so they do not fall from that state. They are permanent, stable, eternal... [21] But we, who are corrupted in mind,...are impermanent, unstable, short-lived, fated to fall away, and we have come to this world." This is the third case.

2.13. [Wrong view 8] 'And what is the fourth way? Here, a certain ascetic or Brahmin is a logician, a reasoner. Hammering it out by reason, following his own line of thought, he argues: "Whatever is called eye or ear or nose or tongue or body, that is impermanent, unstable, non-eternal, liable to change. But what is called thought,[55] or mind or consciousness, that is a self that is permanent, stable, eternal, not subject to change, the same for ever and ever!" This is the fourth case.

2.14. 'These are the four ways in which these ascetics and Brahmins are partly Eternalists and partly Non-Eternalists... Whatever ascetics and Brahmins...proclaim the partial eternity and the partial non-eternity of the self and the world, they do so on one or other of these four grounds. There is no other way.

2.15. 'This, monks, the Tathāgata understands: These [22] viewpoints thus grasped and adhered to will lead to such-and-such destinations in another world. This the Tathāgata knows, and more, but he is not attached to that knowledge. And being thus unattached he has experienced for himself perfect peace, and having truly understood the arising and passing away of feelings, their attraction and peril and the deliverance from them, the Tathāgata is liberated without remainder.

'These, monks, are those other matters, profound, hard to see, hard to understand, peaceful, excellent, beyond mere thought, subtle, to be experienced by the wise, which the Tathāgata, having realised them by his own super-knowledge, proclaims, and about which those who would truthfully praise the Tathāgata would rightly speak.

2.16. 'There are, monks, some ascetics and Brahmins who are Finitists and Infinitists,[56] and who proclaim the finitude and infinitude of the world on four grounds. What are they?

2.17. [Wrong view 9] 'Here a certain ascetic or Brahmin has by means of effort...attained to such a state of concentration that he dwells perceiving the world as finite. He thinks: "This world is finite and bounded by a circle. How so? Because I have...attained to such a state of concentration that I dwell perceiving the world as finite. Therefore I know that this world is finite and bounded by a circle." This is the first case.

2.18. [Wrong view 10] 'And what is the second way? Here a certain ascetic or Brahmin has [23] attained to such a state of concentration that he dwells perceiving the world as infinite. He thinks: "This world is infinite and unbounded. Those ascetics and Brahmins who say it is finite and bounded are wrong. How so? Because I have attained to such a state of concentration that I dwell perceiving the world as infinite. Therefore I know that this world is infinite and unbounded." This is the second case.

2.19. [Wrong view 11] 'And what is the third way? Here a certain ascetic or Brahmin has attained to such a state of consciousness that he dwells perceiving the world as finite up-and-down, and infinite across. He thinks: "The world is finite and infinite. Those ascetics and Brahmins who say it is finite are wrong, and those who say it is infinite are wrong. How so? Because I have attained to such a state of concentration that I dwell perceiving the world as finite up-and-down, and infinite across. Therefore I know that the world is both finite and infinite." This is the third case.

2.20. [Wrong view 12] 'And what is the fourth case? Here a certain ascetic or Brahmin is a logician, a reasoner. Hammering it out by reason, he argues: "This world is neither finite nor infinite. Those who say it is finite are wrong, and so are those [24] who say it is infinite, and those who say it is finite *and* infinite. This world is neither finite nor infinite." This is the fourth case.[57]

2.21. 'These are the four ways in which these ascetics and Brahmins are Finitists and Infinitists, and proclaim the finitude and infinitude of the world on four grounds. There is no other way.

2.22. 'This, monks, the Tathāgata understands: These viewpoints thus grasped and adhered to will lead to such-and-such destinations in another world...(*as verse 15*).

'These, monks, are those other matters, profound, hard to

see, hard to understand, peaceful, excellent, beyond mere thought, subtle, to be experienced by the wise, which the Tathāgata, having realised them by his own super-knowledge, proclaims, and about which those who would truthfully praise the Tathāgata would rightly speak.

2.23. 'There are, monks, some ascetics and Brahmins who are Eel-Wrigglers.[58] When asked about this or that matter, they resort to evasive statements, and they wriggle like eels on four grounds. What are they?

2.24. [Wrong view 13] 'In this case there is an ascetic or Brahmin who does not in truth know whether a thing is good or bad. He thinks: "I do not in truth know whether this is good [25] or whether it is bad. Not knowing which is right, I might declare: 'That is good', or 'That is bad', and that might be a lie, and that would distress me. And if I were distressed, that would be a hindrance to me."[59] Thus fearing to lie, abhorring to lie,[60] he does not declare a thing to be good or bad, but when asked about this or that matter, he resorts to evasive statements and wriggles like an eel: "I don't say this, I don't say that. I don't say it is otherwise. I don't say it is not. I don't not say it is not." This is the first case.

2.25. [Wrong view 14] 'What is the second way? Here an ascetic or Brahmin does not in truth know whether a thing is good or bad. He thinks: "I might declare: 'That is good', or 'That is bad', and I might feel desire or lust or hatred or aversion. If I felt desire, lust, hatred or aversion, that would be attachment on my part. If I felt attachment, that would distress me, and if I were distressed, that would be a hindrance to me." [26] Thus, fearing attachment, abhorring attachment, he resorts to evasive statements...This is the second case.

2.26. [Wrong view 15] 'What is the third way? Here an ascetic or Brahmin does not in truth know whether a thing is good or bad. He thinks: "I might declare: 'That is good', or 'That is bad', but there are ascetics and Brahmins who are wise, skilful, practised debaters, like archers who can split hairs, who go around destroying others' views with their wisdom, and they might cross-examine me, demanding my reasons and arguing. And I might not be able to reply. Not being able to reply would distress me, and if I were distressed, that would be a hindrance to me." Thus, fearing debate, abhorring debate, he resorts to evasive statements. This is the third case. [27]

2.27. [Wrong view 16] 'What is the fourth way? Here, an ascetic or Brahmin is dull and stupid.[61] Because of his dullness and stupidity, when he is questioned he resorts to evasive statements and wriggles like an eel: "If you ask me whether there is another world – if I thought so, I would say there is another world. But I don't say so. And I don't say otherwise. And I don't say it is not, and I don't not say it is not." "Is there no other world?..." "Is there both another world and no other world?..." "Is there neither another world nor no other world?..."[62] "Are there spontaneously-born beings?..."[63] "Are there not...?" "Both...?" "Neither...?" "Does the Tathāgata exist after death? Does he not exist after death? Does he both exist and not exist after death? Does he neither exist nor not exist after death?..."[64] "If I thought so, I would say so...I don't say it is not." This is the fourth case.

2.28. 'These are the four ways [28] in which those ascetics and Brahmins who are Eel-Wrigglers resort to evasive statements...There is no other way.

2.29. 'This, monks, the Tathāgata understands: These viewpoints thus grasped and adhered to will lead to such-and-such destinations in another world...(*as verse 15*).

'These, monks, are those other matters, profound, hard to see...which the Tathāgata, having realised them by his own super-knowledge, proclaims, and about which those who would truthfully praise the Tathāgata would rightly speak.

2.30. 'There are, monks, some ascetics and Brahmins who are Chance-Originationists, and who proclaim the chance origin of the self and the world on two grounds. What are they?

2.31. [Wrong view 17] 'There are, monks, certain devas called Unconscious.[65] As soon as a perception arises in them, those devas fall from that realm. And it may happen that a being falls from that realm and arises in this world. He...recalls his last existence, but none [29] before that. He thinks: "The self and the world have arisen by chance. How so? Before this I did not exist. Now from not-being I have been brought to being." This is the first case.

2.32. [Wrong view 18] 'What is the second case? Here, an ascetic or Brahmin is a logician, a reasoner. He hammers out his own opinion and declares: "The self and the world have arisen by chance." This is the second case.

2.33. 'These are the two ways in which those ascetics and Brahmins who are Chance-Originists proclaim the chance origin of the self and the world. There is no other way.

2.34. 'This, monks, the Tathāgata understands...

'These, monks, are those other matters, profound, hard to see,...which the Tathāgata, having realised them by his own super-knowledge, proclaims, and about which those who [30] would truthfully praise the Tathāgata would rightly speak.

2.35. 'And these, monks, are the eighteen ways in which these ascetics and Brahmins are speculators about the past... There is no other way.

2.36. 'This, monks, the Tathāgata understands...

2.37. 'There are, monks, some ascetics and Brahmins who are speculators about the future, having fixed views about the future, and who put forward various speculative theories about the future in forty-four different ways. On what basis, on what grounds do they do so?

2.38. 'There are, monks, some ascetics and Brahmins who [31] proclaim a doctrine of Conscious Post-Mortem Survival, and do so in sixteen different ways. On what basis?

[Wrong views 19–34] 'They declare that the self after death is healthy and conscious and (1) material,[66] (2) immaterial,[67] (3) both material and immaterial, (4) neither material nor immaterial, (5) finite, (6) infinite, (7) both, (8) neither, (9) of uniform perception, (10) of varied perception, (11) of limited perception, (12) of unlimited perception, (13) wholly happy, (14) wholly miserable, (15) both, (16) neither.

2.39. 'These are the sixteen ways in which these ascetics and Brahmins proclaim a doctrine of conscious post-mortem survival. There is no other way.

2.40. 'This, monks, the Tathāgata understands...

'These, monks, are those other matters, profound, hard to

see,...which the Tathāgata, having realised them by his own super-knowledge, [32] proclaims, and about which those who would truthfully praise the Tathāgata would rightly speak.'

[*End of Second Recitation-Section*]

3.1. 'There are, monks, some ascetics and Brahmins who proclaim a doctrine of Unconscious Post-Mortem Survival, and they do so in eight ways. On what basis?

3.2. [Wrong views 35–42] 'They declare that the self after death is healthy and unconscious and (1) material, (2) immaterial, (3) both, (4) neither, (5) finite, (6) infinite, (7) both, (8) neither.[68]

3.3. 'These are the eight ways in which these ascetics and Brahmins proclaim a doctrine of Unconscious Post-Mortem Survival. There is no other way.

3.4. 'This, monks, the Tathāgata understands...These, monks, are those other matters, profound, hard to see,... which the Tathāgata, having realised them by his own super-knowledge, proclaims, [33] and about which those who would truthfully praise the Tathāgata would rightly speak.

3.5. 'There are some ascetics and Brahmins who declare a doctrine of Neither-Conscious-nor-Unconscious Post-Mortem Survival, and they do so in eight ways. On what basis?

3.6. [Wrong views 43–50] 'They declare that the self after death is healthy and neither conscious nor unconscious and (1) material, (2) immaterial, (3) both, (4) neither, (5) finite, (6) infinite, (7) both, (8) neither.[69]

3.7. 'These are the eight ways in which these ascetics and Brahmins proclaim a doctrine of Neither-Conscious-Nor-Un-Conscious Post-Mortem Survival. There is no other way.

3.8. 'This, monks, the Tathāgata understands...These, monks, are those other matters, profound, hard to see,... which the Tathāgata, having realised them by his own super-knowledge, proclaims, and about which those who would truthfully praise the Tathāgata would rightly speak. [34]

3.9. 'There are, monks, some ascetics and Brahmins who are Annihilationists, who proclaim the annihilation, destruction and non-existence of beings, and they do so in seven ways. On what basis?

3.10. [Wrong view 51] 'Here a certain ascetic or Brahmin declares and holds the view: "Since this self is material, composed of the four great elements,[70] the product of mother and father,[71] at the breaking-up of the body it is annihilated and perishes, and does not exist after death. This is the way in which this self is annihilated." That is how some proclaim the annihilation, destruction and non-existence of beings.

3.11. [Wrong view 52] 'Another says to him: "Sir, there is such a self as you say. I don't deny it. But that self is not wholly annihilated. For there is another self, divine,[72] material, belonging to the sense-sphere,[73] fed on real food.[74] You don't know it or see it, but I do. It is this self that at the breaking-up of the body perishes..."[75]

3.12. [Wrong view 53] 'Another says to him: "Sir, there is such a self as you say. I don't deny it. But that self is not wholly annihilated. For there is another self, divine, material, mind-made,[76] complete with all its parts, not defective in any sense-organ...It is this self that at the breaking-up of the body perishes..."

3.13. [Wrong view 54] 'Another says to him: "Sir, there is such a self as you say...There is another self which, by passing entirely beyond bodily sensations, by the disappearance of all sense of resistance and by non-attraction to the perception of diversity, seeing that space is infinite, has realised the Sphere of Infinite Space.[77] [35] It is this self that at the breaking-up of the body perishes..."

3.14. [Wrong view 55] 'Another says to him: "There is another self which, by passing entirely beyond the Sphere of Infinite Space, seeing that consciousness is infinite, has realised the Sphere of Infinite Consciousness. It is this self that at the breaking-up of the body perishes..."

3.15. [Wrong view 56] 'Another says to him: "There is another self which, by passing entirely beyond the Sphere of Infinite Consciousness, seeing that there is no thing, has realised the Sphere of No-Thingness. It is this self that at the breaking-up of the body perishes..."

3.16. [Wrong view 57] 'Another says to him: "Sir, there is

such a self as you say. I don't deny it. But that self is not wholly annihilated. For there is another self which, by passing entirely beyond the Sphere of No-Thingness and seeing: 'This is peaceful, this is sublime', has realised the Sphere of Neither-Perception-Nor-Non-Perception. You don't know it or see it, but I do. It is this self that at the breaking-up of the body is annihilated and perishes, and does not exist after death. This is the way in which the self is completely annihilated." That is how some proclaim the annihilation, destruction and non-existence of beings.

3.17. 'These are the seven ways in which these ascetics and Brahmins proclaim a doctrine of annihilation, destruction and non-existence of beings...[36] There is no other way.

3.18. 'This, monks, the Tathāgata understands...These, monks, are those other matters, profound, hard to see,... which the Tathāgata, having realised them by his own super-knowledge, proclaims, and about which those who would truthfully praise the Tathāgata would rightly speak.

3.19. 'There are, monks, some ascetics and Brahmins who are proclaimers of Nibbāna Here and Now, and who proclaim Nibbāna here and now for an existent being in five ways. On what grounds?

3.20. [Wrong view 58] 'Here a certain ascetic or Brahmin declares and holds the view: "In as far as this self, being furnished and endowed with the fivefold sense-pleasures, indulges in them, then that is when the self realises the highest Nibbāna here and now."[78] So some proclaim it.

3.21. [Wrong view 59] 'Another says to him: "Sir, there is such a self as you say. I don't deny it. But that is not where the self realises the highest Nibbāna here and now. Why so? Because, sir, sense-desires are impermanent, painful and subject to change, and from their change and transformation there arise sorrow, lamentation, pain, grief and distress. But [37] when this self, detached from sense-desires, detached from unwholesome states, enters and abides in the first jhāna,[79] which is accompanied by thinking and pondering,[80] and the delight[81] and happiness[82] born of detachment, that is when the self realises the highest Nibbāna here and now."

3.22. [Wrong view 60] 'Another says to him: "Sir, there is

such a self as you say. But that is not when the self attains Nibbāna. How so? Because on account of thinking and pondering, that state is considered gross. But when the self by the subsiding of thinking and pondering enters and abides in the second jhāna, with inner tranquillity and oneness of mind, which is free from thinking and pondering and is born of concentration,[83] and accompanied by delight and joy, that is when the self realises the highest Nibbāna here and now."

3.23. [Wrong view 61] 'Another says to him: "Sir, there is such a self as you say. But that is not when the self attains Nibbāna. How so? Because on account of the presence of delight there is mental exhilaration, and that state is considered gross. But when the self, with the waning of delight, dwells in equanimity,[84] mindful and clearly aware,[85] experiencing in his own body that joy of which the Noble Ones say: 'Happy dwells one who has equanimity and mindfulness', and so enters and abides in the third jhāna, that is when the self realises the highest Nibbāna here and now."

3.24. [Wrong view 62] 'Another says to him: "Sir, there is such a self as you say. I don't deny it. But that is not where the self experiences the highest Nibbāna here and now. Why so? Because the mind contains the idea of joy, and that state is considered gross. But when, with the abandonment of pleasure and pain, with the disappearance of previous joy and grief, [38] one enters and abides in a state beyond pleasure and pain in the fourth jhāna, which is purified by equanimity and mindfulness, that is where the self realises the highest Nibbāna here and now." That is how some proclaim the highest Nibbāna here and now for an existent being.

3.25. 'These are the five ways in which these ascetics and Brahmins proclaim a doctrine of Nibbāna here and now. There is no other way.

3.26. 'This, monks, the Tathāgata understands...

3.27. 'These are the forty-four ways in which those ascetics and Brahmins who are speculators about the future, having fixed ideas about the future, put forward various speculative views about the future. There is no other way.

3.28. 'This, monks, the Tathāgata understands...[39]

3.29. 'These are the sixty-two ways in which those ascetics and Brahmins who are speculators about the past, the future, or both, put forward views about these. There is no other way.

3.30. 'This, monks, the Tathāgata understands: These viewpoints thus grasped and adhered to will lead to such-and-such destinations in another world. This the Tathāgata knows, and more, but he is not attached to that knowledge. And being thus unattached he has experienced for himself perfect peace, and having truly understood the arising and passing away of feelings, their attraction and peril and the deliverance from them, the Tathāgata is liberated without remainder.

3.31. 'These, monks, are those other matters, profound, hard to see, hard to understand, peaceful, excellent, beyond mere thought, subtle, to be experienced by the wise, which the Tathāgata, having realised them by his own super-knowledge, proclaims, and about which those who would truthfully praise the Tathāgata would rightly speak.'

[*Conclusion*]

3.32. [Wrong views 1–4] 'Thus, monks, when those ascetics and Brahmins who are Eternalists proclaim the eternity of the self and the world in four [40] ways, that is merely the feeling of those who do not know and see, the worry and vacillation of those immersed in craving.

3.33. [Wrong views 5–8] 'When those who are partly Eternalists and partly Non-Eternalists proclaim the partial eternity and the partial non-eternity of the self and the world in four ways, that is merely the feeling of those who do not know and see...

3.34. [Wrong views 9–12] 'When those who are Finitists and Infinitists proclaim the finitude and infinitude of the world on four grounds, that is merely the feeling of those who do not know and see...

3.35. [Wrong views 13–16] 'When those who are Eel-Wrigglers resort to evasive statements, and wriggle like eels on four grounds, that is merely the feeling...

3.36. [Wrong views 17–18] 'When those who are Chance Originationists proclaim the chance origin of the self and the world on two grounds, this is merely the feeling...

3.37. [Wrong views 1–18] 'When those who are speculators about the past, having fixed views about the past, put forward various speculative theories about the past in eighteen different ways, this is merely the feeling of those who do not know and see, the worry and vacillation of those immersed in craving.

3.38. [Wrong views 19–34] 'When those who proclaim a doctrine of Conscious Post-Mortem Survival do so in sixteen different ways, that is merely the feeling...[41]

3.39. [Wrong views 35–42] 'When those who proclaim a doctrine of Unconscious Post-Mortem Survival do so in eight different ways, that is merely the feeling...

3.40. [Wrong views 43–50] 'When those who proclaim a doctrine of Neither-Conscious-nor-Unconscious Post-Mortem survival do so in eight ways, that is merely the feeling...

3.41. [Wrong views 51–57] 'When those who are Annihilationists proclaim the annihilation, destruction and non-existence of beings in seven ways, that is merely the feeling...

3.42. [Wrong views 58–62] 'When those who are proclaimers of Nibbāna Here and Now proclaim Nibbāna here and now for an existent being on five grounds, that is merely the feeling...

3.43. [Wrong views 19–62] 'When those who are speculators about the future in forty-four different ways...

3.44. [Wrong views 1–62] 'When those ascetics and Brahmins who are speculators about the past, the future, or both, having fixed views, put forward views in sixty-two different ways, that is merely the feeling of those who do not know and see, the worry and vacillation of those immersed in craving.

3.45. 'When those ascetics and Brahmins who are [42] Eternalists proclaim the eternity of the self and the world in four ways, that is conditioned by contact.[86]

3.46. 'When those who are partly Eternalists and partly Non-Eternalists...

3.47. 'When those who are Finitists and Infinitists...

3.48. 'When those who are Eel-Wrigglers...

3.49. 'When those who are Chance-Originationists...

3.50. 'When those who are speculators about the past in eighteen ways...

3.51. 'When those who proclaim a doctrine of Conscious Post-Mortem Survival...

3.52. 'When those who proclaim a doctrine of Unconscious Post-Mortem Survival...

3.53. 'When those who proclaim a doctrine of Neither-Conscious-Nor-Unconscious Post-Mortem Survival...

3.54. 'When those who are Annihilationists...

3.55. 'When those who are proclaimers of Nibbāna Here and Now...

3.56. 'When those who are speculators about the future... [43]

3.57. 'When those ascetics and Brahmins who are speculators about the past, the future, or both, having fixed views, put forward views in sixty-two different ways, that is conditioned by contact.

3.58–70. 'That all of these (*Eternalists and the rest*) should experience that feeling without contact is impossible. [44]

3.71. 'With regard to all of these..., [45] they experience these feelings by repeated contact through the six sense-bases;[87] feeling conditions craving; craving conditions clinging; clinging conditions becoming; becoming conditions birth; birth conditions ageing and death, sorrow, lamentation, sadness and distress.[88]

'When, monks, a monk understands as they really are the arising and passing away of the six bases of contact, their attraction and peril, and the deliverance from them, he knows that which goes beyond all these views.

3.72. 'Whatever ascetics and Brahmins who are speculators about the past or the future or both, having fixed views on the matter and put forth speculative views about it, these are all trapped in the net with its sixty-two divisions, and wherever they emerge and try to get out, they are caught and held in this net. Just as a skilled fisherman or his apprentice might cover a small piece of water with a fine-meshed net, thinking: "Whatever larger creatures there may be in this water, they are all trapped in the net, [46] caught, and held in the net", so it is with all these: they are trapped and caught in this net.

3.73. 'Monks, the body of the Tathāgata stands with the link that bound it to becoming cut.[89] As long as the body subsists, devas and humans will see him. But at the breaking-up of the body and the exhaustion of the life-span, devas and humans will see him no more. Monks, just as when the stalk of a bunch of mangoes has been cut, all the mangoes on it go with it, just so the Tathāgata's link with becoming has been cut. As long as the body subsists, devas and humans will see him. But at the breaking-up of the body and the exhaustion of the life-span, devas and humans will see him no more.'

3.74. At these words the Venerable Ānanda said to the Lord: 'It is marvellous, Lord, it is wonderful. What is the name of this exposition of Dhamma?'

'Ānanda, you may remember this exposition of Dhamma as the Net of Advantage,[90] the Net of Dhamma, the Supreme Net, the Net of Views, or as the Incomparable Victory in Battle.'

Thus the Lord spoke, and the monks rejoiced and were delighted at his words. And as this exposition was being proclaimed, the ten-thousand world-system shook.

2 *Sāmaññaphala Sutta: The Fruits of the Homeless Life*

[47] 1. THUS HAVE I HEARD. Once the Lord was staying at Rājagaha, in Jīvaka Komārabhacca's[91] mango-grove, together with a large company of some twelve hundred and fifty monks. And at that time King Ajātasattu Vedehiputta[92] of Magadha, having gone up to the roof of his palace, was sitting there surrounded by his ministers, on the fifteenth-day fast-day,[93] the full-moon of the fourth month,[94] called Komudi.[95] And King Ajātasattu, on that fast-day, gave vent to this solemn utterance: 'Delightful, friends, is this moonlight night! Charming is this moonlight night! Auspicious is this moonlight night! Can we not today visit some ascetic or Brahmin, to visit whom would bring peace to our heart?'[96]

2. Then one minister said to King Ajātasattu: 'Sire, there is Pūraṇa Kassapa, who has many followers, a teacher of many, who is well-known, renowned, the founder of a sect, highly honoured by the multitude, of long standing, long-since gone forth, aged and venerable. May Your Majesty visit this Pūraṇa Kassapa. He may well bring peace to Your Majesty's heart.' At these words King Ajātasattu was silent.

3. Another minister said: 'Sire, there is [48] Makkhali Gosāla, who has many followers...He may well bring peace to your Majesty's heart.' At these words King Ajātasattu was silent.

4. Another minister said: 'Sire, there is Ajita Kesakambalī ...' At these words King Ajātasattu was silent.

5. Another minister said: 'Sire, there is Pakudha Kaccāyana ...' At these words King Ajātasattu was silent.

6. Another minister said: 'Sire, there is Sañjaya Belaṭṭhaputta...' At these words King Ajātasattu was silent.

7. Another minister said: 'Sire, there is [49] the Nigaṇṭha

Nātaputta, who has many followers, a teacher of many, who is well-known,. . .aged and venerable. May Your Majesty visit the Nigaṇṭha Nātaputta. He may well bring peace to Your Majesty's heart.' At these words King Ajātasattu was silent.

8. All this time Jīvaka Komārabhacca was sitting silently near King Ajātasattu. The King said to him: 'You, friend Jīvaka, why are you silent?' 'Sire, there is this Blessed Lord, the Arahant, the fully-enlightened Buddha staying in my mango-grove with a large company of some twelve hundred and fifty monks. And concerning the Blessed Gotama this fair report has been spread about: "This Blessed Lord is an Arahant, a fully-enlightened Buddha, endowed with wisdom and conduct, the Well-Farer, Knower of the worlds, incomparable Trainer of men to be tamed,[97] Teacher of gods and humans, enlightened and blessed." May Your Majesty visit the Blessed Lord. He may well bring peace to Your Majesty's heart.' 'Then, Jīvaka, have the riding-elephants made ready.'

9. 'Very good, Sire', said Jīvaka, and he had five hundred she-elephants made ready, and for the King the royal tusker. Then he reported: 'Sire, the riding-elephants are ready. Now is the time to do as Your Majesty wishes.' And King Ajātasattu, having placed his wives each on one of the five hundred she-elephants, mounted the royal tusker and proceeded in royal state, accompanied by torch-bearers, from Rājagaha towards Jīvaka's mango-grove.

10. And when King Ajātasattu came near the mango-grove he felt fear and terror, and his hair stood on end. And feeling [50] this fear and the rising of the hairs, the King said to Jīvaka: 'Friend Jīvaka, you are not deceiving me? You are not tricking me? You are not delivering me up to an enemy? How is it that from this great number of twelve hundred and fifty monks not a sneeze, a cough or a shout is to be heard?'

'Have no fear, Your Majesty, I would not deceive you or trick you or deliver you up to an enemy. Approach, Sire, approach. There are the lights burning in the round pavilion.'

11. So King Ajātasattu, having ridden on his elephant as far as the ground would permit, alighted and continued on foot to the door of the round pavilion. Then he said: 'Jīvaka, where

is the Lord?' 'That is the Lord, Sire. That is the Lord sitting against the middle column with his order of monks in front of him.'

12. Then King Ajātasattu went up to the Lord and stood to one side, and standing there to one side the King observed how the order of monks continued in silence like a clear lake, and he exclaimed: 'If only Prince Udāyabhadda were possessed of such calm as this order of monks!'

'Do your thoughts go to the one you love, Your Majesty?' 'Lord, Prince Udāyabhadda[98] is very dear to me. If only he were possessed of the same calm as this order of monks!'

13. Then King Ajātasattu, having bowed down to the Lord and saluted the order of monks with [51] joined hands, sat down to one side and said: 'Lord, I would ask something, if the Lord would deign to answer me.' 'Ask, Your Majesty, anything you like.'

14. 'Lord, just as there are these various craftsmen, such as elephant-drivers, horse-drivers, chariot-fighters, archers, standard-bearers, adjutants, army caterers, champions and senior officers, scouts, heroes, brave fighters, cuirassiers, slaves' sons, cooks, barbers, bathmen, bakers, garland-makers, bleachers, weavers, basket-makers, potters, calculators and accountants – and whatever other skills there are: they enjoy here and now the visible fruits of their skills, they themselves are delighted and pleased with this, as are their parents, children and colleagues and friends, they maintain and support ascetics and Brahmins, thus assuring for themselves a heavenly, happy reward tending towards paradise. Can you, Lord, point to such a reward visible here and now as a fruit of the homeless life?'

15. 'Your Majesty, do you admit that you have put this question to other ascetics and Brahmins?' 'I admit it, Lord.'

'Would Your Majesty mind saying how they replied?' 'I do not mind telling the Lord, or one like him.' [52] 'Well then, Your Majesty, tell me.'

16. 'Once, Lord, I went to see Pūraṇa Kassapa.[99] Having exchanged courtesies, I sat down to one side and said: "Good Kassapa, just as there are these various craftsmen,. . . they en-

joy here and now the visible fruits of their skills...(*as verse 14*). Can you, Kassapa, point to such a reward visible here and now as a fruit of the homeless life?"

17. 'At this, Lord, Pūraṇa Kassapa said: "Your Majesty, by the doer or instigator of a thing, by one who cuts or causes to be cut, by one who burns or causes to be burnt, by one who causes grief and weariness, by one who agitates or causes agitation, who causes life to be taken or that which is not given to be taken, commits burglary, carries off booty, commits robbery, lies in ambush, commits adultery and tells lies, no evil is done. If with a razor-sharp wheel one were to make of this earth one single mass and heap of flesh, there would be no evil as a result of that, no evil would accrue. If one were to go along the south bank of the Ganges killing, slaying, cutting or causing to be cut, burning or causing to be burnt, there would be no evil as a result of that, no evil would accrue. Or if one were to go along the north bank of the Ganges giving and causing to be given, sacrificing and causing to be sacrificed, there would be no merit as a result of that, no merit would accrue. [53] In giving, self-control, abstinence and telling the truth, there is no merit, and no merit accrues."

18. 'Thus, Lord, Pūraṇa Kassapa, on being asked about the present fruits of the homeless life, explained non-action to me. Just as if on being asked about a mango he were to describe a breadfruit-tree, or on being asked about a breadfruit-tree he were to describe a mango, so Pūraṇa Kassapa, on being asked about the present fruits of the homeless life, explained non-action to me. And, Lord, I thought: "How should one like me think despitefully of any ascetic or Brahmin dwelling in my territory?"[100] so I neither applauded nor rejected Pūraṇa Kassapa's words but, though displeased, not expressing my displeasure, saying nothing, rejecting and scorning speech, I got up and left.

19. 'Once I visited Makkhali Gosāla,[101] and asked him the same question.

20. 'Makkahali Gosāla said: "Your Majesty, there is no cause or condition[102] for the defilement of beings, they are defiled without cause or condition. There is no cause or condition for the purification of beings, they are purified without cause or

condition. There is no self-power or other-power, there is no power in humans, no strength or force, no vigour or exertion. All beings, all living things, all creatures, all that lives is without control, without power or strength, they experience the fixed course of pleasure and pain through the six kinds of rebirth. There [54] are one million four hundred thousand principal sorts of birth, and six thousand others and again six hundred. There are five hundred kinds of kamma,[103] or five kinds,[104] and three kinds,[105] and half-kamma,[106] sixty-two paths, sixty-two intermediary aeons, six classes of humankind, eight stages of human progress, four thousand nine hundred occupations, four thousand nine hundred wanderers, four thousand nine hundred abodes of nāgas,[107] two thousand sentient existences, three thousand hells, thirty-six places of dust, seven classes of rebirth as conscious beings, seven as unconscious beings, and seven as beings 'freed from bonds',[108] seven grades of devas, men, goblins, seven lakes, seven great and seven small protuberances,[109] seven great and seven small abysses, seven great and seven small dreams, eight million four hundred thousand aeons during which fools and wise run on and circle round till they make an end of suffering.

'"Therefore there is no such thing as saying: 'By this discipline or practice or austerity or holy life I will bring my unripened kamma to fruition, or I will gradually make this ripened kamma go away.'[110] Neither of these things is possible, because pleasure and pain have been measured out with a measure limited by the round of birth-and-death, and there is neither increase nor decrease, neither excellence nor inferiority. Just as a ball of string when thrown runs till it is all unravelled, so fools and wise run on and circle round till they make an end of suffering."

21. 'Thus, Lord, Makkhali Gosāla, on being asked about the fruits of the homeless life, explained the purification of the round of birth-and-death to me... [55] So I neither applauded nor rejected Makkhali Gosāla's words but... got up and left.

22. 'Once I visited Ajita Kesakambalī,[111] and asked him the same question.

23. 'Ajita Kesakambalī said: "Your Majesty, there is nothing given, bestowed, offered in sacrifice, there is no fruit or result

of good or bad deeds, there is not this world or the next, there is no mother or father, there are no spontaneously arisen beings,[112] there are in the world no ascetics or Brahmins who have attained, who have perfectly practised, who proclaim this world and the next, having realised them by their own super-knowledge. This human being is composed of the four great elements, and when one dies the earth part reverts to earth, the water part to water, the fire part to fire, the air part to air, and the faculties pass away into space. They accompany the dead man with four bearers and the bier as fifth, their footsteps are heard as far as the cremation-ground. There the bones whiten, the sacrifice ends in ashes. It is the idea of a fool to give this gift: the talk of those who preach a doctrine of survival is vain and false. Fools and wise, at the breaking-up of the body, are destroyed and perish, they do not exist after death."

24. 'Thus, Lord, Ajita Kesakambalī, on being asked about the fruits of the homeless life, explained the doctrine of annihilation to me...[56]...I got up and left.

25. 'Once I visited Pakudha Kaccāyana,[113] and asked him the same question.

26. 'Pakudha Kaccāyana said: "Your Majesty, these seven things are not made or of a kind to be made, uncreated, unproductive, barren, false, stable as a column. They do not shake, do not change, obstruct one another, nor are they able to cause one another pleasure, pain, or both. What are the seven? The earth-body, the water-body, the fire-body, the air-body, pleasure and pain and the life-principle. These seven are not made...Thus there is neither slain nor slayer, neither hearer nor proclaimer, neither knower nor causer of knowing. And whoever cuts off a man's head with a sharp sword does not deprive anyone of life, he just inserts the blade in the intervening space between these seven bodies." [57]

27. 'Thus, Lord, Pakudha Kaccāyana, on being asked about the fruits of the homeless life, answered with something quite different...I got up and left.

28. 'I visited the Nigaṇṭha Nātaputta,[114] and asked him the same question.

29. 'The Nigaṇṭha Nātaputta said: "Your Majesty, here a

Nigaṇṭha is bound by a fourfold restraint. What four? He is curbed by all curbs, enclosed by all curbs, cleared by all curbs, and claimed by all curbs.[115] And as far as a Nigaṇṭha is bound by this fourfold restraint, thus the Nigaṇṭha is called self-perfected, self-controlled, self-established."

[58] 30. 'Thus, Lord, the Nigaṇṭha Nātaputta, on being asked about the fruits of the homeless life, explained the fourfold restraint to me...I got up and left.

31. 'Once I visited Sañjaya Belaṭṭhaputta, and asked him the same question.

32. 'Sañjaya Belaṭṭhaputta said: "If you ask me: 'Is there another world?' if I thought so, I would say so. But I don't think so. I don't say it is so, and I don't say otherwise. I don't say it is not, and I don't not say it is not. If you ask: 'Isn't there another world?'...'Both?'...'Neither?'...'Is there fruit and result of good and bad deeds?' 'Isn't there?'...'Both?'...'Neither?'...'Does the Tathāgata [59] exist after death?' 'Does he not?'...'Both?'...'Neither?'...I don't not say it is not."

33. 'Thus, Lord, Sañjaya Belaṭṭhaputta, on being asked about the fruits of the homeless life, replied by evasion. Just as if on being asked about a mango he were to describe a breadfruit-tree...And I thought: "Of all these ascetics and Brahmins, Sañjaya Belaṭṭhaputta is the most stupid and confused." So I neither applauded nor rejected his words, but go up and left.

34. 'And so, Lord, I now ask the Blessed Lord: Just as there are these various craftsmen,...who enjoy here and now the visible fruits of their skills,...assuring for themselves a heavenly, happy reward...[60] Can you, Lord, point to such a reward, visible here and now, as a fruit of the homeless life?'

'I can, Your Majesty. I will just ask a few questions in return and you, Sire, shall answer as you see fit.

35. 'What do you think, Sire? Suppose there were a man, a slave, a labourer, getting up before you and going to bed after you, willingly doing whatever has to be done, well-mannered, pleasant-spoken, working in your presence. And he might think: "It is strange, it is wonderful, the destiny and fruits of meritorious deeds![116] This King Ajātasattu Vedehiputta of Magadha is a man, and I too am a man. The King is addicted to and indulges in the fivefold sense-pleasures, just like a god,

whereas I am a slave...working in his presence. I ought to do something meritorious. Suppose I were to shave off my hair and beard, don yellow robes, and go forth from the household life into homelessness!" And before long he does so. And he, having thus gone forth might dwell, restrained in body, speech and thought, satisfied with the minimum of food and clothing, content, in solitude. And then if people were to announce to you: "Sire, you remember that slave who worked in your presence, and who shaved off his hair and beard and went forth into homelessness? He is living restrained in body, speech and thought,...in solitude" – would you then say: "That man must come back and be a slave and work for me as before"?'

36. 'No indeed, Lord. For we should pay homage to him, [61] we should rise and invite him and press him to receive from us robes, food, lodging, medicines for sickness and requisites, and make arrangements for his proper protection.'

'What do you think, Sire? Is that one fruit of the homeless life visible here and now?' 'Certainly, Lord.' 'Then that, Sire, is the first such fruit of the homeless life.'

37. 'But, Lord, can you show any other reward, visible here and now, as a fruit of the homeless life?'

'I can, Sire. I will just ask a few questions in return and you, Sire, shall answer as you see fit. What do you think, Sire? Suppose there were a man, a farmer, a householder, in your service, the steward of an estate. He might think: "It is strange, it is wonderful, the destiny and fruits of meritorious deeds! This King Ajātasattu is a man, and I too am a man. The King is addicted to and indulges in the fivefold sense-pleasures, just like a god, whereas I am a farmer,...the steward of an estate. I ought to do something meritorious. Suppose I were to...go forth from the household life into homelessness!" And before long he does so. And he, having thus gone forth might dwell...in solitude. And if people were to tell you this...[62] would you then say: "That man must come back and be a steward as before"?'

38. 'No indeed, Lord. For we should pay homage to him, we should rise and invite him and press him to receive from us robes, food, lodging, medicines for sickness and requisites, and make arrangements for his proper protection.'

'What do you think, Sire? Is that one fruit of the homeless life visible here and now?' 'Certainly, Lord.' 'Then that, Sire, is the second such fruit of the homeless life.'

39. 'But, Lord, can you show me any other reward, visible here and now, as a fruit of the homeless life that is more excellent and perfect than these?'

'I can, Sire. Please listen, Your Majesty, pay proper attention, and I will speak.' 'Yes, Lord', said King Ajātasattu, and the Lord went on:

40. 'Your Majesty, it happens that a Tathāgata arises in the world, an Arahant, fully-enlightened Buddha, endowed with wisdom and conduct, Well-Farer, Knower of the worlds, incomparable Trainer of men to be tamed, Teacher of gods and humans, enlightened and blessed. He, having realised it by his own super-knowledge, proclaims this world with its devas, māras[117] and Brahmās, its princes[118] and people. He preaches the Dhamma, which is lovely in its beginning, lovely in its middle, lovely in its ending, in the spirit and in the letter, and displays the fully-perfected and purified holy life.

41. 'This Dhamma is heard by a householder or a householder's son, or one reborn in some family or other. Having heard this Dhamma, [63] he gains faith in the Tathāgata. Having gained this faith, he reflects: "The household life is close and dusty, the homeless life is free as air. It is not easy, living the household life, to live the fully-perfected holy life, purified and polished like a conch-shell. Suppose I were to shave off my hair and beard, don yellow robes and go forth from the household life into homelessness!" And after some time, he abandons his property, small or great, leaves his circle of relatives, small or great, shaves off his hair and beard, dons yellow robes and goes forth into the homeless life.

42. 'And having gone forth, he dwells restrained by the restraint of the rules, persisting in right behaviour, seeing danger in the slightest faults, observing the commitments he has taken on regarding body, deed and word, devoted to the skilled and purified life, perfected in morality, with the sense-doors guarded, skilled in mindful awareness and content.

43.–62. 'And how, Sire, is a monk perfected in morality? Abandoning the taking of life, he dwells refraining from taking life, without stick or sword, scrupulous, compassionate, trembling for the welfare of all living beings. Thus he is accomplished in morality. Abandoning the taking of what is not given,. . . abandoning unchastity,. . . (*and so on through the three sections on morality as Sutta 1, verses 1.8–27*). A monk refrains from such base arts and wrong means of livelihood. Thus he is perfected in morality. [64–69]

63. 'And then, Sire, that monk who is perfected in morality sees no danger from any side owing to his being restrained by morality. Just as a duly-anointed Khattiya king, having conquered [70] his enemies, by that very fact sees no danger from any side, so the monk, on account of his morality, sees no danger anywhere. He experiences in himself the blameless bliss that comes from maintaining this Ariyan morality. In this way, Sire, he is perfected in morality.

64. 'And how, Sire, is he a guardian of the sense-doors? Here a monk, on seeing a visible object with the eye, does not grasp at its major signs or secondary characteristics. Because greed and sorrow, evil unskilled states, would overwhelm him if he dwelt leaving this eye-faculty unguarded, so he practises guarding it, he protects the eye-faculty, develops restraint of the eye-faculty. On hearing a sound with the ear,. . . on smelling an odour with the nose,. . . on tasting a flavour with the tongue,. . . on feeling an object with the body,. . . on thinking a thought with the mind, he does not grasp at its major signs or secondary characteristics,. . . he develops restraint of the mind-faculty. He experiences within himself the blameless bliss that comes from maintaining this Ariyan guarding of the faculties. In this way, Sire, a monk is a guardian of the sense-doors.

65. 'And how, Sire, is a monk accomplished in mindfulness and clear awareness? Here a monk acts with clear awareness in going forth and back, in looking ahead or behind him, in bending and stretching, in wearing his outer and inner robe and carrying his bowl, in eating, drinking, chewing and swallowing, in evacuating and urinating, in walking, standing, sitting, lying down, in waking, in speaking and in keeping silent he acts with clear awareness. In this way, [71] a monk is accomplished in mindfulness and clear awareness.

66. 'And how is a monk contented? Here, a monk is satisfied with a robe to protect his body, with alms to satisfy his stomach, and having accepted sufficient, he goes on his way. Just as a bird with wings flies hither and thither, burdened by nothing but its wings, so he is satisfied...In this way, Sire, a monk is contented.

67. 'Then he, equipped with this Ariyan morality, with this Ariyan restraint of the senses, with this Ariyan contentment, finds a solitary lodging, at the root of a forest tree, in a mountain cave or gorge, a charnel-ground, a jungle-thicket, or in the open air on a heap of straw. Then, having eaten after his return from the alms-round, he sits down cross-legged, holding his body erect, and concentrates on keeping mindfulness established before him.[119]

68. 'Abandoning worldly desires, he dwells with a mind freed from worldly desires, and his mind is purified of them. Abandoning ill-will and hatred...and by compassionate love for the welfare of all living beings, his mind is purified of ill-will and hatred. Abandoning sloth-and-torpor,...perceiving light,[120] mindful and clearly aware, his mind is purified of sloth-and-torpor. Abandoning worry-and-flurry...and with an inwardly calmed mind his heart is purified of worry-and-flurry. Abandoning doubt, he dwells with doubt left behind, without uncertainty as to what things are wholesome, his mind is purified of doubt.

69. 'Just as a man who had taken a loan to develop his business, and whose business had prospered, might pay off his old debts, and with what was left over could support a wife, might think: "Before this I developed my business by borrowing, [72] but now it has prospered...", and he would rejoice and be glad about that.

70. 'Just as a man who was ill, suffering, terribly sick, with no appetite and weak in body, might after a time recover, and regain his appetite and bodily strength, and he might think: "Before this I was ill...", and he would rejoice and be glad about that.

71. 'Just as a man might be bound in prison, and after a time he might be freed from his bonds without any loss, with

no deduction from his possessions. He might think: "Before this I was in prison...", and he would rejoice and be glad about that.

72. 'Just as a man might be a slave, not his own master, dependent on another, unable to go where he liked, and after some time he might be freed from slavery, able to go where he liked, might think: "Before this I was a slave..."[73] And he would rejoice and be glad about that.

73. 'Just as a man, laden with goods and wealth, might go on a long journey through the desert where food was scarce and danger abounded, and after a time he would get through the desert and arrive safe and sound at the edge of a village, might think: "Before this I was in danger, now I am safe at the edge of a village", and he would rejoice and be glad about that.

74. 'As long, Sire, as a monk does not perceive the disappearance of the five hindrances in himself,[121] he feels as if in debt, in sickness, in bonds, in slavery, on a desert journey. But when he perceives the disappearance of the five hindrances in himself, it is as if he were freed from debt, from sickness, from bonds, from slavery, from the perils of the desert.

75. 'And when he knows that these five hindrances have left him, gladness arises in him, from gladness comes delight, from the delight in his mind his body is tranquillised, with a tranquil body he feels joy, and with joy his mind is concentrated. Being thus detached from sense-desires, detached from unwholesome states, he enters and remains in the first jhāna, which is with thinking and pondering, born of detachment, filled with delight and joy. And with this delight and joy born of detachment, he so suffuses, drenches, fills and irradiates his body that there is no spot in his entire body that is untouched by this delight and joy born of detachment. [74]

76. 'Just as a skilled bathman or his assistant, kneading the soap-powder which he has sprinkled with water, forms from it, in a metal dish, a soft lump, so that the ball of soap-powder becomes one oleaginous mass, bound with oil so that nothing escapes – so this monk suffuses, drenches, fills and irradiates his body so that no spot remains untouched. This, Sire, is a

fruit of the homeless life, visible here and now, that is more excellent and perfect than the former ones.[122]

77. 'Again, a monk, with the subsiding of thinking and pondering, by gaining inner tranquillity and oneness of mind, enters and remains in the second jhāna, which is without thinking and pondering, born of concentration, filled with delight and joy. And with this delight and joy born of concentration he so suffuses his body that no spot remains untouched.

78. 'Just as a lake fed by a spring, with no inflow from east, west, north or south, where the rain-god sends moderate showers from time to time, the water welling up from below, mingling with cool water, would suffuse, fill and irradiate that cool water, so that no part of the pool was untouched by it – so, with this delight and joy born of concentration he so suffuses his body that no spot remains untouched. [75] This, Sire, is a fruit more excellent and perfect than the former ones.

79. 'Again, a monk with the fading away of delight remains imperturbable, mindful and clearly aware, and experiences in himself that joy of which the Noble Ones say: "Happy is he who dwells with equanimity and mindfulness", and he enters and remains in the third jhāna. And with this joy devoid of delight he so suffuses his body that no spot remains untouched.

80. 'Just as if, in a pond of blue, red or white lotuses[123] in which the flowers, born in the water, grown in the water, not growing out of the water, are fed from the water's depths, those blue, red or white lotuses would be suffused... with the cool water – so with this joy devoid of delight the monk so suffuses his body that no spot remains untouched. This is a fruit of the homeless life, more excellent and perfect than the former ones.

81. 'Again, a monk, having given up pleasure and pain, and with the disappearance of former gladness and sadness, enters and remains in the fourth jhāna which is beyond pleasure and pain, and purified by equanimity and mindfulness. And he sits suffusing his body with that mental purity and clarification [76] so that no part of his body is untouched by it.

82. 'Just as if a man were to sit wrapped from head to foot

in a white garment, so that no part of him was untouched by that garment – so his body is suffused... This is a fruit of the homeless life, more excellent and perfect than the former ones.

83. 'And so, with mind concentrated, purified and cleansed, unblemished, free from impurities,[124] malleable, workable, established, and having gained imperturbability, he directs and inclines his mind towards knowing and seeing. And he knows: "This my body is material, made up from the four great elements, born of mother and father, fed on rice and gruel, impermanent, liable to be injured and abraded, broken and destroyed, and this is my consciousness which is bound to it and dependent on it."[125]

84. 'It is just as if there were a gem, a beryl,[126] pure, excellent, well cut into eight facets, clear, bright, unflawed, perfect in every respect, strung on a blue, yellow, red, white or orange cord. A man with good eyesight, taking it in his hand and inspecting it, would describe it as such. In the same way, Sire, a monk with mind concentrated, purified and cleansed, ...directs his mind towards knowing and seeing. And he knows: "This my body is material, made up of the four great elements,...[77] and this is my consciousness which is bound to it and dependent on it." This is a fruit of the homeless life, more excellent and perfect than the former ones.

85. 'And he, with mind concentrated,...having gained imperturbability, applies and directs his mind to the production of a mind-made body. And out of this body he produces another body, having a form,[127] mind-made, complete in all its limbs and faculties.

86. 'It is just as if a man were to draw out a reed from its sheath. He might think: "This is the reed, this is the sheath, reed and sheath are different. Now the reed has been pulled from the sheath." Or as if a man were to draw a sword from the scabbard. He might think: "This is the sword, this is the scabbard, sword and scabbard are different. Now the sword has been drawn from the scabbard." Or as if a man were to draw a snake from its [old] skin. He might think: "This is the snake, this is the skin, snake and skin are different. Now the snake has been drawn from its skin." In the same way a monk with mind concentrated...directs his mind to the production

of a mind-made body. He draws that body out of this body, having form, mind-made, complete with all its limbs and faculties. This is a fruit of the homeless life more excellent and perfect than the former ones.

87. 'And he, with mind concentrated,...applies and directs his mind [78] to the various supernormal powers.[128] He then enjoys different powers: being one, he becomes many – being many, he becomes one; he appears and disappears; he passes through fences, walls and mountains unhindered as if through air; he sinks into the ground and emerges from it as if it were water; he walks on the water without breaking the surface as if on land; he flies cross-legged through the sky like a bird with wings; he even touches and strokes with his hand the sun and moon, mighty and powerful as they are;[129] and he travels in the body as far as the Brahmā world.

88. 'Just as a skilled potter or his assistant can make from well-prepared clay whatever kind of bowl he likes, or just as a skilled ivory-carver or his assistant can produce from well-prepared ivory any object he likes, or just as a skilled goldsmith or his assistant can make any gold article he likes – so the monk with mind concentrated...enjoys various supernormal powers...[79] This is a fruit of the homeless life...

89. 'And he, with mind concentrated,...applies and directs his mind to the divine ear.[130] With the divine ear, purified and surpassing that of human beings, he hears sounds both divine and human, whether far or near.

90. 'Just as a man going on a long journey might hear the sound of a big drum, a small drum, a conch, cymbals or a kettle-drum, and he might think: "That is a big drum,...a kettle-drum", so the monk with mind concentrated...hears sounds, divine or human, far or near. This is a fruit of the homeless life, more excellent and perfect than the former ones.

91. 'And he, with mind concentrated,...applies and directs his mind to the knowledge of others' minds. He knows and distinguishes with his mind the minds of other beings or other persons. He knows the mind with passion to be with passion; he knows the mind without passion to be without passion.[131] [80] He knows the mind with hate to be with hate; he knows the mind without hate to be without hate. He

knows the deluded mind to be deluded; he knows the undeluded mind to be undeluded. He knows the narrow mind to be narrow; he knows the broad mind to be broad. He knows the expanded mind to be expanded; he knows the unexpanded mind to be unexpanded. He knows the surpassed mind to be surpassed; he knows the unsurpassed mind to be unsurpassed. He knows the concentrated mind to be concentrated; he knows the unconcentrated mind to be unconcentrated. He knows the liberated mind to be liberated; he knows the unliberated mind to be unliberated.

92. 'Just as a woman, or a man or young boy, fond of his appearance, might examine his face in a brightly polished mirror or in water, and by examination would know whether there was a spot there or not, so the monk, with mind concentrated,...directs his mind to the knowledge of others' minds...(*as verse 91*). [81] This is a fruit of the homeless life...

93. 'And he, with mind concentrated,...applies and directs his mind to the knowledge of previous existences. He remembers many previous existences: one birth, two, three, four, five births, ten, twenty, thirty, forty, fifty births, a hundred, a thousand, a hundred thousand births, several periods of contraction, of expansion, of both contraction and expansion. "There my name was so-and-so, my clan was so-and-so, my caste was so-and-so, my food was such-and-such, I experienced such-and-such pleasant and painful conditions, I lived for so long. Having passed away from there, I arose there. There my name was so-and-so...And having passed away from there, I arose here." Thus he remembers various past births, their conditions and details.

94. 'It is just as if a man were to go from his village to another, from that to yet another, and thence return to his home village. He might think: "I came from my own village to that other one where I stood, sat, spoke or remained silent like this, and from that one I went to another, where I stood, sat, spoke or remained silent like this, and from there [82] I have just returned to my own village."[132] Just so the monk with mind concentrated...remembers past births...This is a fruit of the homeless life...

95. 'And he, with mind concentrated,...applies and directs his mind to the knowledge of the passing-away and arising of beings. With the divine eye,[133] purified and surpassing that of humans, he sees beings passing away and arising: base and noble, well-favoured and ill-favoured, to happy and unhappy destinations as kamma directs them, and he knows: "These beings, on account of misconduct of body, speech or thought, or disparaging the Noble Ones, have wrong view and will suffer the kammic fate of wrong view. At the breaking-up of the body after death they are reborn in a lower world, a bad destination, a state of suffering, hell. But these beings, on account of good conduct of body, speech or thought, of praising the Noble Ones, have right view and will reap the kammic reward of right view. At the breaking-up of the body after death they are reborn in a good destination, a heavenly world." Thus with the divine eye...[83] he sees beings passing away and rearising...

96. 'It is just as if there were a lofty building at a crossroads, and a man with good eyesight standing there might see people entering or leaving a house, walking in the street, or sitting in the middle of the crossroads. And he might think: "These are entering a house..." Just so, with the divine eye, ...he sees beings passing away and rearising...This is a fruit of the homeless life...

97. 'And he with mind concentrated, purified and cleansed, unblemished, free from impurities, malleable, workable, established and having gained imperturbability, applies and directs his mind to the knowledge of the destruction of the corruptions.[134] He knows as it really is: "This is suffering", [84] he knows as it really is: "This is the origin of suffering", he knows as it really is: "This is the cessation of suffering", he knows as it really is: "This is the path leading to the cessation of suffering." And he knows as it really is: "These are the corruptions", "This is the origin of the corruptions", "This is the cessation of the corruptions", "This is the path leading to the cessation of the corruptions." And through his knowing and seeing his mind is delivered from the corruption of sense-desire, from the corruption of becoming, from the corruption

of ignorance, and the knowledge arises in him: "This is deliverance!", and he knows: "Birth is finished, the holy life has been led, done is what had to be done, there is nothing further here."[135]

98. 'Just as if, Sire, in the midst of the mountains there were a pond, clear as a polished mirror, where a man with good eyesight standing on the bank could see oyster-shells, gravel-banks, and shoals of fish, on the move or stationary. And he might think: "This pond is clear,. . . there are oyster-shells. . .", just so, with mind concentrated,. . . he knows: "Birth is finished, the holy life has been led, done is what had to be done, there is nothing further here." [85] This, Sire, is a fruit of the homeless life, visible here and now, which is more excellent and perfect than the previous fruits. And, Sire, there is no fruit of the homeless life, visible here and now, that is more excellent and perfect than this.'[136]

99. At this King Ajātasattu exclaimed: 'Excellent, Lord, excellent! It is as if someone were to set up what had been knocked down, or to point out the way to one who had got lost, or to bring an oil-lamp into a dark place, so that those with eyes could see what was there. Just so the Blessed Lord has expounded the Dhamma in various ways. And I, Lord, go for refuge to the Blessed Lord, to the Dhamma, and to the Sangha. May the Blessed Lord accept me from this day forth as a lay-follower as long as life shall last! Transgression[137] overcame me, Lord, foolish, erring and wicked as I was, in that I for the sake of the throne deprived my father, that good man and just king, of his life. May the Blessed Lord accept my confession of my evil deed that I may restrain myself in future!'[138]

100. 'Indeed, Sire, transgression overcame you when you deprived your father, that good man and just king, of his life. But since you have acknowledged the transgression and confessed it as is right, we will accept it. For he who acknowledges his transgression as such and confesses it for betterment in future, will grow in the Ariyan discipline.'

101. At this, King Ajātasattu said: 'Lord, permit me to depart now. I am busy and have much to do.' 'Do now, Your Majesty, as you think fit.'

Then King Ajātasattu, rejoicing and delighting at these words, rose from his seat, saluted the Lord, and departed with his right side towards him.

102. As soon as the King had gone, [86] the Lord said: 'The King is done for, his fate is sealed, monks![139] But if the King had not deprived his father, that good man and just king, of his life, then as he sat here the pure and spotless Dhamma-eye[140] would have arisen in him.'

Thus the Lord spoke, and the monks, delighted, rejoiced at his words.

3 *Ambaṭṭha Sutta: About Ambaṭṭha*
Pride Humbled

[87] 1.1 THUS HAVE I HEARD. Once the Lord was touring Kosala with a large number of monks, some five hundred, and he came to a Kosalan Brahmin village called Icchānankala. And he stayed in the dense jungle of Icchānankala. At that time the Brahmin Pokkharasāti was living at Ukkhaṭṭha, a populous place, full of grass, timber, water and corn, which had been given to him by King Pasenadi of Kosala as a royal gift and with royal powers.[141]

1.2. And Pokkharasāti heard say: 'The ascetic Gotama, son of the Sakyans, who has gone forth from the Sakya clan,. . .is staying in the dense jungle of Icchānankala. And concerning that Blessed Lord a good report has been spread about: "This Blessed Lord is an Arahant, a fully-enlightened Buddha, perfected in knowledge and conduct, a Well-Farer, Knower of the worlds, unequalled Trainer of men to be tamed, Teacher of gods and humans, a Buddha, a Blessed Lord." He proclaims this world with its gods, māras, Brahmās, the world of ascetics and Brahmins with its princes and people, having come to know it by his own knowledge. He teaches a Dhamma that is lovely in its beginning, lovely in its middle, and lovely in its ending, in the spirit and in the letter, and he displays the fully-perfected, thoroughly purified [88] holy life. And indeed it is good to see such Arahants.'

1.3. Now at that time Pokkharasāti had a pupil, the youth Ambaṭṭha, who was a student of the Vedas, who knew the mantras, perfected in the Three Vedas, a skilled expounder of the rules and rituals, the lore of sounds and meanings and, fifthly, oral tradition, complete in philosophy[142] and in the marks[143] of a Great Man, admitted and accepted by his master in the Three Vedas with the words: 'What I know, you know; what you know, I know.'

1.4. And Pokkharasāti said to Ambaṭṭha: 'Ambaṭṭha, my son, the ascetic Gotama...is staying in the dense jungle of Icchānankala. And concerning that Blessed Lord a good report has been spread about...Now you go to see the ascetic Gotama and find out whether this report is correct or not, and whether the Reverend Gotama is as they say or not. In that way we shall put the Reverend Gotama to the test.'

1.5. 'Sir, how shall I find out whether the report is true, or whether the Reverend Gotama is as they say or not?' 'According to the tradition of our mantras, Ambaṭṭha, the great man who is possessed of the thirty-two marks of a Great Man has only two courses open to him. If he lives the household life he will become a ruler, a wheel-turning righteous monarch of the law,[144] conqueror of the four quarters, who has established the security of his realm and is possessed of the [89] seven treasures.[145] These are: the Wheel-Treasure, the Elephant-Treasure, the Horse-Treasure, the Jewel-Treasure, the Woman-Treasure, the Householder-Treasure, and, as seventh, the Counsellor-Treasure. He has more than a thousand sons who are heroes, of heroic stature, conquerors of the hostile army. He dwells having conquered this sea-girt land without stick or sword, by the law. But if he goes forth from the household life into homelessness, then he will become an Arahant, a fully-enlightened Buddha, one who draws back the veil from the world.[146] And, Ambaṭṭha, I am the passer-on of the mantras, and you are the receiver.'

1.6. 'Very good, sir', said Ambaṭṭha at Pokkharasāti's words, and he got up, passed by Pokkharasāti with his right side, got into his chariot drawn by a mare and, accompanied by a number of young men, headed for the dense jungle of Icchānankala. He drove as far as the carriage would go, then alighted and continued on foot.

1.7. At that time a number of monks were walking up and down in the open air. Ambaṭṭha approached them and said: 'Where is the Reverend Gotama to be found just now? We have come to see the Reverend Gotama.'

1.8. The monks thought: 'This is Ambaṭṭha, a youth of good

family and a pupil of the distinguished Brahmin Pokkharasāti. The Lord would not mind having a conversation with such a young man.' And they said to Ambaṭṭha: 'That is his dwelling, with the door closed. Go quietly up to it, go on to the verandah without haste, cough, and knock on the bolt. The Lord will open the door to you.'

1.9. Ambaṭṭha went up to the dwelling and on to the verandah, coughed, and knocked. The Lord opened the door, and Ambaṭṭha went in. The young men entered, exchanged courtesies with the Lord, and sat down to one side. But Ambaṭṭha walked up and down while the Lord sat there, [90] uttered some vague words of politeness, and then stood so speaking before the seated Lord.

1.10. And the Lord said to Ambaṭṭha: 'Well now, Ambaṭṭha, would you behave like this if you were talking to venerable and learned Brahmins, teachers of teachers, as you do with me, walking and standing while I am sitting, and uttering vague words of politeness?' 'No, Reverend Gotama. A Brahmin should walk with a walking Brahmin, stand with a standing Brahmin, sit with a sitting Brahmin, and lie down with a Brahmin who is lying down. But as for those shaven little ascetics, menials, black scourings from Brahmā's foot, with them it is fitting to speak just as I do with the Reverend Gotama.'

1.11. 'But, Ambaṭṭha, you came here seeking something. Whatever it was you came for, you should listen attentively to hear about it. Ambaṭṭha, you have not perfected your training. Your conceit of being trained is due to nothing but inexperience.'

1.12. But Ambaṭṭha was angry and displeased at being called untrained, and he turned on the Lord with curses and insults. Thinking: 'The ascetic Gotama bears me ill-will', he said: 'Reverend Gotama, the Sakyans are fierce, rough-spoken, touchy [91] and violent. Being of menial origin, being menials, they do not honour, respect, esteem, revere or pay homage to Brahmins. With regard to this it is not proper...that they do not pay homage to Brahmins.' This was the first time Ambaṭṭha accused the Sakyans of being menials.

1.13. 'But, Ambaṭṭha, what have the Sakyans done to you?'

'Reverend Gotama, once I went to Kapilavatthu on some business for my teacher, the Brahmin Pokkharasāti, and I came to the Sakyans' meeting-hall. And at that time a lot of Sakyans were sitting on high seats in their meeting-hall, poking each other with their fingers, laughing and playing about together, and it seemed to me that they were just making fun of me, and no one offered me a seat. With regard to this, it is not proper that they do not pay homage to the Brahmins.' This was the second time Ambaṭṭha accused the Sakyans of being menials.

1.14. 'But Ambaṭṭha, even the quail, that little bird, can talk as she likes on her own nest. Kapilavatthu is the Sakyans' home, Ambaṭṭha. They do not deserve censure for such a trifle.'

'Reverend Gotama, there are four castes:[147] the Khattiyas, the Brahmins, the merchants and the artisans. And of these four castes three – the Khattiyas, the merchants and the artisans – are entirely subservient to the Brahmins. With regard to this, [92] it is not proper that they should not pay homage to the Brahmins.' This was the third time Ambaṭṭha accused the Sakyans of being menials.

1.15. Then the Lord thought: 'This young man goes too far in abusing the Sakyans. Suppose I were to ask after his clan-name?' So he said: 'Ambaṭṭha, what is your clan?' 'I am a Kaṇhāyan, Reverend Gotama.'

'Ambaṭṭha, in former days, according to those who remember the ancestral lineage, the Sakyans were the masters, and you are descended from a slave-girl of the Sakyans. For the Sakyans regard King Okkāka as their ancestor. At one time King Okkāka, to whom his queen was dear and beloved, wishing to transfer the kingdom to her son, banished his elder brothers from the kingdom – Okkāmukha, Karaṇḍu, Hatthinīya and Sīnipura. And these, being banished, made their home on the flank of the Himālayas beside a lotus-pond where there was a big grove of teak-trees.[148] And for fear of contaminating the stock they cohabited with their own sisters. Then King Okkāka asked his ministers and counsellors: "Where are the princes living now?" and they told him. At this King Okkāha exclaimed: [93] "They are strong as teak (*sāka*), these princes, they are real Sakyans!"[149] And that is how the Sakyans got their well-known name. And the King was the ancestor of the Sakyans.

1.16. 'Now King Okkāka had a slave-girl called Disā, who gave birth to a black child. The black thing, when it was born, exclaimed: "Wash me, mother! Bath me, mother! Deliver me from this dirt, and I will bring you profit!" Because, Ambaṭṭha, just as people today use the term hobgoblin (*pisāca*) as a term of abuse, so in those days they said black (*kaṇha*). And they said: "As soon as he was born, he spoke. He is born a Kaṇha, a hobgoblin!" That is how in former days...the Sakyans were the masters, and you are descended from a slave-girl of the Sakyans.'

1.17. On hearing this, the young men said: 'Reverend Gotama, do not humiliate Ambaṭṭha too much with talk of his being descended from a slave-girl: Ambaṭṭha is well-born, of a good family, he is very learned, he is well-spoken, a scholar, well able to hold his own in this discussion with the Reverend Gotama!'

1.18. Then the Lord said to the young men: 'If you consider that Ambaṭṭha is ill-born, not of a good family, unlearned, [94] ill-spoken, no scholar, unable to hold his own in this discussion with the ascetic Gotama, then let Ambaṭṭha be silent, and you conduct this discussion with me. But if you think he is... able to hold his own, then you be quiet, and let him discuss with me.'

1.19. 'Ambaṭṭha is well-born, Reverend Gotama...We will be silent, he shall continue.'

1.20. Then the Lord said to Ambaṭṭha: 'Ambaṭṭha, I have a fundamental question for you, which you will not like to answer. If you don't answer, or evade the issue, if you keep silent or go away, your head will split into seven pieces. What do you think, Ambaṭṭha? Have you heard from old and venerable Brahmins, teachers of teachers, where the Kaṇhāyans came from, or who was their ancestor?' At this, Ambaṭṭha remained silent. The Lord asked him a second time. [95] Again Ambaṭṭha remained silent, and the Lord said: 'Answer me now, Ambaṭṭha, this is not a time for silence. Whoever, Ambaṭṭha, does not answer a fundamental question put to him by a Tathāgata by the third asking has his head split into seven pieces.'[150]

1.21. And at that moment Vajirapāni the yakkha,[151] holding a huge iron club, flaming, ablaze and glowing, up in the sky just above Ambaṭṭha, was thinking: 'If this young man Ambaṭṭha does not answer a proper question put to him by the Blessed Lord by the third time of asking, I'll split his head into seven pieces!' The Lord saw Vajirapāni, and so did Ambaṭṭha. And at the sight, Ambaṭṭha was terrified and unnerved, his hairs stood on end, and he sought protection, shelter and safety from the Lord. Crouching down close to the Lord, he said: 'What did the Reverend Gotama say? May the Reverend Gotama repeat what he said!' 'What do you think, Ambaṭṭha? Have you heard who was the ancestor of the Kaṇhāyans?' 'Yes, I have heard it just as the Reverend Gotama said, that is where the Kaṇhāyans came from, he was their ancestor.'

1.22. Hearing this, the young men made a loud noise and clamour: 'So Ambaṭṭha is ill-born, not of a good family, born of a slave-girl of the Sakyans, and the Sakyans are Ambaṭṭha's masters! We disparaged the ascetic Gotama, thinking he was not speaking the truth!'

1.23. Then the Lord thought: 'It is too much, [96] the way these young men humiliate Ambaṭṭha for being the son of a slave-girl. I must get him out of this.' So he said to the young men: 'Don't disparage Ambaṭṭha too much for being the son of a slave-girl! That Kaṇha was a mighty sage.[152] He went to the south country,[153] learnt the mantras of the Brahmins there, and then went to King Okkāka and asked for his daughter Maddarūpī. And King Okkāka, furiously angry, exclaimed: "So this fellow, the son of a slave-girl, wants my daughter!", and put an arrow to his bow. But he was unable either to shoot the arrow or to withdraw it.[154] Then the ministers and counsellors came to the sage Kaṇha and said: "Spare the king, Reverend Sir, spare the king!"

'"The king will be safe, but if he looses the arrow downwards, the earth will quake as far as his kingdom extends."

'"Reverend Sir, spare the king, spare the land!"

'"The king and the land will be safe, but if he looses the

arrow upwards, as far as his realm extends the god will not let it rain for seven years."[155]

'"Reverend Sir, spare the king and the land, and may the god let it rains!"

'"The king and the land will be safe, and the god will let it rain, but if the king points the arrow at the crown prince, the prince will be completely safe."

'Then the ministers exclaimed: "Let King Okkāka point the arrow at the crown prince, the prince will be perfectly safe!" The king did so, and the prince was unharmed. Then King Okkāka, terrified and fearful of divine punishment,[156] [97] gave away his daughter Maddarūpī. So, young men, do not disparage Ambaṭṭha too much for being the son of a slave-girl. That Kaṇha was a mighty sage.'

1.24. Then the Lord said: 'Ambaṭṭha, what do you think? Suppose a Khattiya youth were to wed a Brahmin maiden, and there was a son of the union. Would that son of a Khattiya youth and a Brahmin maiden receive a seat and water from the Brahmins?' 'He would, Reverend Gotama.'

'Would they allow him to eat at funeral-rites, at rice-offerings, at sacrifices or as a guest?' 'They would, Reverend Gotama.'

'Would they teach him mantras or not?' 'They would, Reverend Gotama.'

'Would they keep their women covered or uncovered?' 'Uncovered, Reverend Gotama.'

'But would the Khattiyas sprinkle him with the Khattiya consecration?' 'No, Reverend Gotama.'

'Why not?' 'Because, Reverend Gotama, he is not well-born on his mother's side.'

1.25. 'What do you think, Ambaṭṭha? Suppose a Brahmin youth were to wed a Khattiya maiden, and there was a son of the union. Would that son of a Khattiya youth and a Brahmin maiden receive a seat and water from the Brahmins?' 'He would, Reverend Gotama.' ...(*as verse 24*) [98] But would the Khattiyas sprinkle him with the Khattiya consecration?' 'No, Reverend Gotama.'

'Why not?' 'Because, Reverend Gotama, he is not well-born on his father's side.'

1.26. 'So, Ambaṭṭha, the Khattiyas, through a man taking a woman or a woman taking a man, are senior to the Brahmins. What do you think, Ambaṭṭha? Take the case of a Brahmin who, for some reason, has had his head shaved by the Brahmins, has been punished with a bag of ashes and banished from the country or the city. Would he receive a seat and water from the Brahmins?' 'No, Reverend Gotama.'

'Would they allow him to eat...as a guest?' 'No, Reverend Gotama.'

'Would they teach him mantras, or not?' 'They would not, Reverend Gotama.'

'Would they keep their women covered or uncovered?' 'Covered, Reverend Gotama.'

1.27. 'What do you think, Ambaṭṭha? Take the case of a Khattiya who...had his head shaved by the Khattiyas,...and has been banished from the country or the city. Would he receive a seat and water from the Brahmins?' 'He would, Reverend Gotama.' ...(*as verse 24*) 'Would they keep their women covered or uncovered?' 'Uncovered, Reverend Gotama.'

'But that Khattiya has so far reached the extreme of humiliation [99] that he has...been banished from the country or the city. So even if a Khattiya has suffered extreme humiliation, he is superior and the Brahmins inferior.

1.28. 'Ambaṭṭha, this verse was pronounced by Brahmā Sanankumāra:

> "The Khattiya's best among those who value clan;
> He with knowledge and conduct is best of gods and men."

'This verse was rightly sung, not wrongly, rightly spoken, not wrongly, connected with profit, not unconnected. And, Ambaṭṭha, I too say this:

> "The Khattiya's best among those who value clan:
> He with knowledge and conduct is best of gods and men."'

[*End of first recitation-section*]

2.1. 'But, Reverend Gotama, what is this conduct, what is this knowledge?'

'Ambaṭṭha, it is not from the standpoint of the attainment of unexcelled knowledge-and-conduct that reputation based on birth and clan is declared, nor on the conceit which says: "You are worthy of me, you are not worthy of me!" For wherever there is a giving, a taking, or a giving and taking in marriage, there is always this talk and this conceit. . . But those who are enslaved by such things are far from the attainment of the unexcelled knowledge-and-conduct, [100] which is attained by abandoning all such things!'

2.2 'But, Reverend Gotama, what is this conduct, what is this knowledge?'

'Ambaṭṭha, a Tathāgata arises in this world an Arahant, fully-enlightened Buddha, endowed with wisdom and conduct, Well-Farer, Knower of the worlds, incomparable Trainer of men to be tamed, Teacher of gods and humans, enlightened and blessed. He, having realised it by his own super-knowledge, proclaims this world with its devas, māras and Brahmās, its princes and people. He preaches the Dhamma which is lovely in its beginning, lovely in its middle, lovely in its ending, in the spirit and in the letter, and displays the fully-perfected and purified holy life.[157] *A disciple goes forth and practises the moralities (Sutta 2, verse 41–62); he guards the sense-doors, etc. (Sutta 2, verse 64–75); attains the four jhānas (Sutta 2, verse 75–82).* Thus he develops conduct. *He attains various insights (Sutta 2, verse 83–95), and the cessation of the corruptions (Sutta 2, verse 97). . .* And beyond this there is no further development of knowledge and conduct that is higher or more perfect.

2.3. 'But, Ambaṭṭha, in the pursuit of this unexcelled attainment of knowledge and conduct [101] there are four paths of failure.[158] What are they? In the first place, an ascetic or Brahmin who has not managed to gain[159] this unexcelled attainment, takes his carrying-pole[160] and plunges into the depths of the forest thinking: "I will live on windfalls." But in this way he only becomes an attendant on one who has attained. This is the first path of failure. Again, an ascetic or Brahmin . . ., being unable to live on windfalls, takes a spade and basket, thinking: "I will live on tubers and roots."[161]... This is the second path of failure. Again, an ascetic or Brahmin, being unable to live on tubers and roots, makes a fire-hearth at the edge of a village or small town and sits tending the flame[162]...This is the third path of failure. Again, an ascetic or Brahmin, being unable to tend the flame, [102] erects a house with four doors at the crossroads thinking: "Whatever ascetic or Brahmin arrives from the four quarters, I will honour to the best of my strength and ability." But in this way he only becomes an attendant on one who has attained to unexcelled knowledge and conduct. This is the fourth path of failure.

2.4. 'What do you think, Ambaṭṭha? Do you and your teacher live in accordance with this unexcelled knowledge and conduct?' 'No indeed, Reverend Gotama! Who are my teacher and I in comparison? We are far from it!'

'Well then, Ambaṭṭha, could you and your teacher, being unable to gain this..., go with your carrying-poles into the depths of the forest, intending to live on windfalls?' 'No indeed, Reverend Gotama.'

'Well then, Ambaṭṭha, could you and your teacher, being unable to gain this..., live on tubers and roots,...sit tending the flame, [103]...erect a house...?' 'No indeed, Reverend Gotama.'

2.5. 'And so, Ambaṭṭha, not only are you and your teacher incapable of attaining this unexcelled knowledge and conduct, but even the four paths of failure are beyond you. And yet you and your teacher the Brahmin Pokkharasāti utter these words: "These shaven little ascetics, menials, black scrapings from Brahmā's foot, what converse can they have with Brahmins learned in the Three Vedas?" – even though you can't even manage the duties of one who has failed. See, Ambaṭṭha, how your teacher has let you down!

2.6. 'Ambaṭṭha, the Brahmin Pokkharasāti lives by the grace and favour of King Pasenadi of Kosala. And yet the King does not allow him to have audience face to face. When he confers with the King it is through a curtain. Why should the King not grant audience face to face to one on whom he has bestowed a proper and blameless source of revenue? See how your teacher has let you down!

2.7. 'What do you think, Ambaṭṭha? Suppose King Pasenadi was sitting on the neck of an elephant or on horseback, or was standing on the chariot-mat, conferring with his ministers and princes about something. [104] And suppose he were to step aside and some workman or workman's servant were to come along and stand in his place. And standing there he might say: "This is what King Pasenadi of Kosala says!" Would he be speaking the King's words, as if he were the King's equal?' 'No indeed, Reverend Gotama.'

2.8. 'Well then, Ambaṭṭha, it is just the same thing. Those who were, as you say, the first sages of the Brahmins, the makers and expounders of the mantras, whose ancient verses are chanted, pronounced and collected by the Brahmins of today – Aṭṭhaka, Vāmaka, Vāmadeva, Vessāmitta, Yamataggi, Angirasa, Bhāradvāja, Vāseṭṭha, Kassapa, Bhagu[163] – whose mantras are said to be passed on to you and your teacher: yet you do not thereby become a sage or one practised in the way of a sage – such a thing is not possible.

2.9. 'What do you think, Ambaṭṭha? What have you heard said by Brahmins who are venerable, aged, the teachers of teachers? Those first sages..., Aṭṭhaka,...Bhagu – did they enjoy themselves, well-bathed, perfumed, their hair and beards trimmed, adorned with garlands and wreaths, dressed in white clothes, indulging in the pleasures of the five senses and addicted to them, as you and your teacher do now?' [105] 'No, Reverend Gotama.'

2.10. 'Or did they eat special fine rice with the black spots removed, with various soups and curries, as you and your teacher do now?' 'No, Reverend Gotama.'

'Or did they amuse themselves with women dressed up in flounces and furbelows, as you and your teacher do now?' 'No, Reverend Gotama.'

'Or did they ride around in chariots drawn by mares with braided tails, that they urged on with long goad-sticks?' 'No, Reverend Gotama.'

'Or did they have themselves guarded in fortified towns with palisades and barricades, by men with long swords...?' 'No, Reverend Gotama.'

'So, Ambaṭṭha, neither you nor your teacher are a sage or one trained in the way of a sage. And now, as for your doubts and perplexities concerning me, we will clarify these by your asking me, and by my answering your questions.'

2.11 Then, descending from his lodging, the Lord started to walk up and down, and Ambaṭṭha did likewise. And as he walked along with the Lord, Ambaṭṭha looked out for the thirty-two marks of a Great Man on the Lord's body. And he could see all of them except [106] for two. He was in doubt and perplexity about two of these marks: he could not make up his mind or be certain about the sheathed genitals or the large tongue.

2.12. And the Lord, being aware of his doubts, effected by his psychic power that Ambaṭṭha could see his sheathed genitals, and then, sticking out his tongue, he reached out to lick both ears and both nostrils, and then covered the whole circle of his forehead with his tongue. Then Ambaṭṭha thought: 'The ascetic Gotama is equipped with all the thirty-two marks of a Great Man, complete and with none missing.' Then he said to the Lord: 'Reverend Gotama, may I go now? I have much business, much to do.' 'Ambaṭṭha, do what you now think fit.' So Ambaṭṭha got back into his chariot drawn by mares and departed.

2.13. Meanwhile the Brahmin Pokkharasāti had gone outside and was sitting in his park with a large number of Brahmins, just waiting for Ambaṭṭha. Then Ambaṭṭha came to the park. He rode in the chariot as far as it would go, and then continued on foot to where Pokkharasāti was, saluted him, and sat down to one side. Then Pokkharasāti said:

2.14. 'Well, dear boy, did you see the Reverend Gotama?' 'I did, sir.'

'And was the Reverend Gotama such [107] as he is reported to be, and not otherwise? And is he of such nature, and not otherwise?' 'Sir, he is as he is reported to be, and he is of such nature and not otherwise. He is possessed of the thirty-two marks of a Great Man, all complete, with none missing.'

'But was there any conversation between you and the ascetic Gotama?' 'There was, sir.'

'And what was this conversation about?' So Ambaṭṭha told Pokkharasāti all that had passed between the Lord and himself.

2.15. At this Pokkharasāti exclaimed: 'Well, you're a fine little scholar, a fine wise man, a fine expert in the Three Vedas! Anyone going about his business like that ought when he dies, at the breaking-up of the body, to go to the downfall, to the evil path, to ruin, to hell! You have heaped insults on the Reverend Gotama, as a result of which he has brought up more and more things against us! You're a fine little scholar . . .!' He was so angry and enraged that he kicked Ambaṭṭha over, and wanted to start out at once to see the Lord. [108]

2.16. But the Brahmins said: 'It is far too late, sir, to go to see the ascetic Gotama today. The Reverend Pokkharasāti should go to see him tomorrow.'

Then Pokkharasāti, having had fine hard and soft food prepared in his own home, set out by the light of torches from Ukkaṭṭha for the jungle of Icchānankala. He went by chariot as far as possible, then continued on foot to where the Lord was. Having exchanged courtesies with the Lord, he sat down to one side and said:

2.17. 'Venerable Gotama, did not our pupil Ambaṭṭha come to see you?' 'He did, Brahmin.' 'And was there any conversation between you?' 'There was.' 'And what was this conversation about?'

Then the Lord told Pokkharasāti all that had passed between him and Ambaṭṭha. At this, Pokkharasāti said to the Lord: 'Reverend Gotama, Ambaṭṭha is a young fool. May the Reverend Gotama pardon him.' 'Brahmin, may Ambaṭṭha be happy.' [109]

2.18–19. Then Pokkharasāti looked out for the thirty-two marks of a Great Man on the Lord's body and he could see all of them except for two: *the sheathed genitals and the large tongue; but the Lord set his mind at rest about these* (*as verse 11–12*). And Pokkharasāti said to the Lord: 'May the Reverend Gotama accept a meal from me today together with his order of monks!' And the Lord consented by silence.

2.20. Seeing his acceptance, Pokkharasāti said to the Lord: 'It is time, Reverend Gotama, the meal is ready.' And the Lord, having dressed in the early morning and taken his robe and bowl,[164] went with his order of monks to Pokkharasāti's residence, and sat down on the prepared seat. Then Pokkharasāti personally served the Lord with choice hard and soft food, and the young men served the monks. And when the Lord had taken his hand from the bowl, Pokkharasāti sat down to one side on a low stool.

2.21 And as Pokkharasāti sat there, [110] the Lord delivered a graduated discourse on generosity, on morality and on heaven, showing the danger, degradation and corruption of sense-desires, and the profit of renunciation. And when the Lord knew that Pokkharasāti's mind was ready, pliable, free from the hindrances, joyful and calm, then he preached a sermon on Dhamma in brief: on suffering, its origin, its cessation, and the path. And just as a clean cloth from which all stains have been removed receives the dye perfectly, so in the Brahmin Pokkharasāti, as he sat there, there arose the pure and spotless Dhamma-eye, and he knew: 'Whatever things have an origin must come to cessation.'[165]

2.22. And Pokkharasāti, having seen, attained, experienced and penetrated the Dhamma, having passed beyond doubt, transcended uncertainty, having gained perfect confidence in the Teacher's doctrine without relying on others, said: 'Excellent, Lord, excellent! It is as if someone were to set up what had been knocked down, or to point out the way to one who had got lost, or to bring an oil-lamp into a dark place, so that those with eyes could see what was there. Just so the Blessed Lord has expounded the Dhamma in various ways...I go with my son, my wife, my ministers and counsellors for refuge to the Reverend Gotama, to the Dhamma and to the Sangha.[166] May the Reverend Gotama accept me as a lay-follower who has taken refuge from this day forth as long as life shall last! And whenever the Reverend Gotama visits other families or lay-followers in Ukkaṭṭha, may he also visit the family of Pokkharasāti! Whatever young men and maidens are there will revere the Reverend Gotama and rise before him, will give him a seat and water and will be glad at heart, and that will be for their welfare and happiness for a long time.'

'Well said, Brahmin!'

4 *Soṇadaṇḍa Sutta: About Soṇadaṇḍa*
The Qualities of a True Brahmin

[111] 1. THUS HAVE I HEARD. Once the Lord was travelling among the Angas with a large company of some five hundred monks, and he arrived at Campā. At Campā he stayed by Gaggarā's lotus-pond. At that time the Brahmin Soṇadaṇḍa was living at Campā, a populous place, full of grass, timber, water and corn, which had been given to him by King Seniya Bimbisāra of Magadha as a royal gift and with royal powers.

2. And the Brahmins and householders of Campā heard say: 'The ascetic Gotama of the Sakyans, who has gone forth from the Sakya clan is travelling among the Angas...and is staying by Gaggarā's lotus-pool. And concerning that Blessed Lord Gotama a good report has been spread about: "This Blessed Lord is an Arahant, a fully-enlightened Buddha, perfected in knowledge and conduct, a Well-Farer, Knower of the worlds, unequalled Trainer of men to be tamed, Teacher of gods and humans, a Buddha, a Blessed Lord." He proclaims this world with its gods, māras, Brahmās, the world of ascetics and Brahmins with its princes and people, having come to know it by his own knowledge. He teaches a Dhamma that is lovely in its beginning, lovely in its middle and lovely in its ending, in the spirit and in the letter, and he displays the fully-perfected, thoroughly purified holy life. And indeed it is good to see such Arahants.' [112] Thereupon the Brahmins and householders of Campā, leaving Campā in great crowds, in vast numbers, went to Gaggarā's lotus-pond.

3. Just then, the Brahmin Soṇadaṇḍa had gone up to his verandah for his midday rest. Seeing all the Brahmins and householders making for Gaggarā's lotus-pond, he asked his steward the reason.

'Sir, it is the ascetic Gotama of the Sakyans...That is why they are going to see him.'

'Well then, steward, go to the Brahmins and householders of Campā and say to them: "Please wait, gentlemen, the Brahmin Soṇadaṇḍa will come to see the ascetic Gotama."'

And the steward conveyed this message to [113] the Brahmins and householders of Campā.

4. Now at that time some five hundred Brahmins from various provinces were in Campā on some business, and they heard that Soṇadaṇḍa intended to visit the ascetic Gotama. So they called upon him and asked if this were true. 'So it is, gentlemen, I am going to visit the ascetic Gotama.'

5. 'Sir, do not visit the ascetic Gotama, it is not fitting that you should do so! If the Reverend Soṇadaṇḍa goes to visit the ascetic Gotama, his reputation will decrease, and that of the ascetic Gotama will increase. This being so, it is not right that the Reverend Soṇadaṇḍa should visit the ascetic Gotama, but rather the ascetic Gotama should visit him.

'The Reverend Soṇadaṇḍa is well-born on both the mother's and the father's side, of pure descent to the seventh generation, unbroken, of irreproachable birth, and therefore he should not call on the ascetic Gotama, but rather the ascetic Gotama should call on him. The Reverend Soṇadaṇḍa is possessed of great wealth and resources...[114] The Reverend Soṇadaṇḍa is a scholar, versed in the mantras, accomplished in the Three Vedas, a skilled expounder of the rules and rituals, the lore of sounds and meanings and, fifthly, oral tradition – an expounder, fully versed in natural philosophy and the marks of a Great Man. The Reverend Soṇadaṇḍa is handsome, good-looking, pleasing, of the most beautiful complexion, in form and countenance like Brahmā, of no mean appearance. He is virtuous, of increasing virtue, endowed with increasing virtue. He is well-spoken, of pleasing address, polite, of pure and clear enunciation, speaking to the point. He is the teacher's teacher of many, teaching the mantras to three hundred youths, and many young men come from different districts and regions seeking to learn the mantras in his presence, desirous to learn them from him. He is aged, grown old, venerable, advanced in years, long past his youth, whereas the ascetic Gotama is youthful and newly gone forth as a wanderer. The Reverend Soṇadaṇḍa is esteemed, made much of, honoured, revered, worshipped by King Seniya Bimbisāra and by the Brahmin Pokkharasāti. He lives at Campā, a populous place, full of grass, timber, water and corn, which has been given to him by King Seniya Bimbisāra of Magadha as a royal gift, and with royal powers. This being so, it is not proper that he should visit the ascetic Gotama, but rather the ascetic Gotama should visit him.'[167]

6. At this Soṇadaṇḍa replied: [115] 'Now listen, gentlemen, as to why it is fitting for us to visit the Reverend Gotama, and why it is not fitting for him to visit us. The ascetic Gotama is well-born on both sides of pure descent to the seventh generation, unbroken, of it reproachable birth... (*as verse 5*). Therefore it is fitting for us to visit him. He went forth, leaving a great body of kinsmen. In fact he gave up much gold and wealth to go forth, both hidden away and openly displayed. The ascetic Gotama, while youthful, a black-haired youth, in the prime of his young days, in the first stage of life went forth from the household life into homelessness. Leaving his grieving parents weeping with tear-stained faces, having cut off his hair and beard and put on yellow robes, he went forth into homelessness. He is handsome,... virtuous,... well-spoken,... the teacher's teacher of many. He has abandoned sensuality and dispelled vanity. He teaches action and the results of action, honouring the blameless Brahmin way of life. He is a wanderer of high birth, of a leading Khattiya family. He is a wanderer from a wealthy family, of great wealth and possessions. [116] People come to consult him from foreign kingdoms and foreign lands. Many thousands of devas have taken refuge with him.

'This good report has been spread about him: "This Blessed Lord is an Arahant, a fully-enlightened Buddha, perfected in knowledge and conduct..." (*as verse 2*). He bears the thirty-two marks of a Great Man. He is welcoming, kindly of speech, courteous, genial, clear and ready of speech. He is attended by four assemblies, revered, honoured, esteemed and worshipped by them. Many devas and humans are devoted to him. Whenever he stays in any town or village, that place is not troubled by non-human beings. He has a crowd, a multitude of followers, is a teacher of many, he is consulted by the chief of the various leaders of sects. It is not the way with the ascetic Gotama's reputation, as it is with that of some ascetics and Brahmins, about whom this or that is reported – the ascetic Gotama's fame is based on his achievement of unsurpassed wisdom and conduct. Indeed King Seniya Bimbisāra of Magadha has gone for refuge to him together with his son, his wife, his followers and his ministers. So have King Pasenadi of Kosala and the Brahmin Pokkharasāti. He is revered, honoured, esteemed and worshipped by them. [117]

'The ascetic Gotama has arrived in Campā and is staying by Gaggarā's lotus-pond. And whatever ascetics and Brahmins come to our territory are our guests. And we should revere, honour, esteem and worship guests. Having come to Gaggarā's lotus-pond, the ascetic Gotama is such a guest, and should be treated as such. Therefore it is not proper that he should come to us, but rather we should go to him. However much I might praise the ascetic Gotama, that praise is insufficient, he is beyond all praise.'

7. On hearing this, the Brahmins said to Soṇadaṇḍa: 'Sir, since you praise the ascetic Gotama so much, then even if he were to live a hundred yojanas from here, it would be fitting for a believing clansman to go with a shoulder-bag to visit him. And so, sir, we shall all go to visit the ascetic Gotama.' And so Soṇadaṇḍa went with a large company of Brahmins to Gaggarā's lotus-pond.

8. But when Soṇadaṇḍa had traversed the jungle-thickets, he thought: 'If I ask the ascetic Gotama a question, he might say to me: "That, Brahmin, is not a fitting question, it is not at all a fitting question", and then the company might despise me, saying: "Soṇadaṇḍa is a fool, he has no sense, [118] he can't put a proper question to the ascetic Gotama." And if anyone were despised by this company, his reputation would suffer, and then his income would suffer, for our income depends on the gaining of a reputation. Or if the ascetic Gotama were to ask me a question, my answer might not satisfy him, and he might say: "That is not the right way to answer this question." And then the company might despise me...And if,

having come into the presence of the ascetic Gotama, I were to turn away without showing myself, this company might despise me...'

9. Then Soṇadaṇḍa approached the Lord, exchanged courtesies with him, and sat down to one side. Some of the Brahmins and householders made obeisance to the Lord, some exchanged courtesies with him, some saluted him with joined palms, some announced their name and clan, and some sat down to one side in silence. [119]

10. So Soṇadaṇḍa took his seat with many thoughts going through his mind: 'If I ask the ascetic Gotama a question, he might say to me: "That, Brahmin, is not a fitting question..." If only the ascetic Gotama would ask me a question from my own field of the Three Vedas! Then I could give him an answer that would satisfy him!'

11. And the Lord, reading his mind, thought: 'This Soṇadaṇḍa is worried. Suppose I were to ask him a question from his own field as a teacher of the Three Vedas!' So he said to Soṇadaṇḍa: 'By how many qualities do Brahmins recognise a Brahmin? How would one declare truthfully and without falling into falsehood: "I am a Brahmin"?'

12. Then Soṇadaṇḍa thought: [120] 'Now what I wanted, hoped for, desired and longed for has happened...Now I can give him an answer that will satisfy him.'

13. Straightening up, and looking round the assembly, he said: 'Reverend Gotama, there are five such qualities...What are they? A Brahmin is well-born on both the mother's and the father's side, of pure descent to the seventh generation,... he is a scholar versed in the mantras,...he is handsome, pleasing,...he is virtuous,...he is learned and wise, and is the first or second to hold the sacrificial ladle. These are the five qualities of a true Brahmin.'

14. 'But if one of these five qualities were omitted, could not one be recognised as a true Brahmin, being possessed of four of these qualities?'

'It is possible, Gotama. We could leave out appearance, for what does that matter? If a Brahmin had the other four qualities [121] he could be recognised as a true Brahmin.'

15. 'But could not one of these four qualities be omitted,

leaving three whereby one could be recognised as a true Brahmin?'

'It is possible, Gotama. We could leave out the mantras, for what do they matter? If he had the other three qualities he could be recognised as a true Brahmin.'

16. 'But could not one of these three qualities be omitted . . .?'

'It is possible, Gotama. We could leave out birth, for what does that matter? If a Brahmin is virtuous, of increasing virtue, . . . and if he is learned and wise, and is the first or second to hold the sacrificial ladle – then he can be recognised as a true Brahmin and truthfully claim to be so.' [122]

17. At this the Brahmins said to Soṇadaṇḍa: 'Don't say that, Soṇadaṇḍa don't say it! The Reverend Soṇadaṇḍa is decrying appearance, the mantras and birth, he is actually adopting the ascetic Gotama's own words!'

18. Then the Lord said to the Brahmins: 'If you think the Brahmin Soṇadaṇḍa is not concentrating on his task, is using wrong words, is lacking in wisdom, and is not fit to converse with the ascetic Gotama, then let him cease, and you talk to me. But if you think he is learned, speaks properly, is wise and fit to converse with the ascetic Gotama, then you cease and let him speak.'

19. Then Soṇadaṇḍa said to the Lord: 'Let that be, Reverend Gotama, and be silent. I will answer in this matter.' To the Brahmins he said: 'Do not say the Reverend Soṇadaṇḍa is decrying appearance . . . and adopting the ascetic Gotama's own words! [123] I do not decry appearance, mantras, or birth.'

20. Now at that time Soṇadaṇḍa's nephew, a young man called Angaka, was sitting in the assembly, and Soṇadaṇḍa said: 'Gentlemen, do you see my nephew Angaka?' 'Yes, sir.'

'Angaka is handsome, good-looking, pleasing, of supremely fair complexion, in form and countenance like Brahmā, of no mean appearance, and there is none in this assembly his equal except the ascetic Gotama. He is a scholar . . . I was his mantra-teacher. He is well-born on both sides . . . I know his parents. But if Angaka were to take life, take what is not given, commit adultery, tell lies and drink strong drink – what would good looks, or mantras, or birth profit him? But it is because a Brahmin is virtuous,...because he is wise...: on account of these two points that he can truthfully declare: "I am a Brahmin."'

21. 'But, Brahmin, if one were to omit one of these two points, could one truthfully declare: "I am a Brahmin"?' [124] 'No, Gotama. For wisdom is purified by morality, and morality is purified by wisdom: where one is, the other is, the moral man has wisdom and the wise man has morality, and the combination of morality and wisdom is called the highest thing in the world. Just as one hand washes the other, or one foot the other, so wisdom is purified by morality and this combination is called the highest thing in the world.'

22. 'So it is, Brahmin. Wisdom is purified by morality, and morality is purified by wisdom: where one is, the other is, the moral man has wisdom and the wise man has morality, and the combination of morality and wisdom is called the highest thing in the world. But, Brahmin, what is this morality and what is this wisdom?'

'We only know this much, Gotama. It would be well if the Reverend Gotama were to explain the meaning of this.'

23. 'Then listen, Brahmin, pay proper attention, and I will tell you.' 'Yes, sir', said Soṇadaṇḍa in reply, and the Lord said:

'Brahmin, a Tathāgata arises in this world, an Arahant, fully-enlightened Buddha, endowed with wisdom and conduct, Well-Farer, Knower of the worlds, incomparable Trainer of men to be tamed, Teacher of gods and humans, enlightened and blessed. He, having realised it by his own super-knowledge, proclaims this world with its devas, māras and Brahmās, its princes and people. He preaches the Dhamma which is lovely in its beginning, lovely in its middle, lovely in its ending, in the spirit and in the letter, and displays the fully-perfected and purified holy life. *A disciple goes forth and practises the moralities* (*Sutta 2, verses 41–63*); *he guards the sense-doors, etc.* (*Sutta 2, verses 64–74*). That, Brahmin, is morality.[168] *He attains the four jhānas* (*Sutta 2, verses 75–82*); *he attains various insights* (*Sutta 2, verses 83–95*), *and the cessation of the corruptions* (*Sutta 2, verse 97*). Thus he develops wisdom. That, Brahmin, is wisdom.'

24. At these words Soṇadaṇḍa said: 'Excellent, Lord, excellent! It is as if someone were to set up what had been knocked down, or to point out the way to one who had got lost, or to bring an oil-lamp into a dark place, so that those with eyes could see what was there. Just so the Blessed Lord has expounded the Dhamma in various ways. And I go for refuge to the Blessed Lord Gotama, to the Dhamma and to the Sangha. May the Reverend Gotama accept me from this day forth as a lay-follower as long as life shall last! And may the Reverend Gotama and his order of monks accept a meal from me tomorrow!'

The Lord assented by silence. Then Soṇadaṇḍa, seeing his assent, rose, saluted the Lord, passed by to his right and departed. As day was breaking, he caused hard and soft food to be prepared in his own home, and when it was ready he announced: 'Reverend Gotama, it is time; the meal is ready.'

25. And the Lord, having risen early, went with robe and bowl and attended by his monks to Soṇadaṇḍa's residence and sat down on the prepared seat. And Soṇadaṇḍa served the Buddha and his monks with the finest foods with his own hands until they were satisfied. And when the Lord had eaten and taken his hand away from the bowl, Soṇadaṇḍa took a low stool and sat down to one side. Then he said to the Lord:

26. 'Reverend Gotama, if when I have gone into the assembly I were to rise and salute the Lord, the company would despise me. In that case my reputation would suffer, and if a man's reputation suffers, his income suffers...So if, on entering the assembly, I should join my palms in greeting, may the Reverend Gotama take it as if I had risen from my seat. And if [126] on entering the assembly I should take off my turban, may you take it as if I had bowed at your feet. Or if, when riding in my carriage, I were to alight to salute the Lord, the company would despise me...So if, when I am riding in my carriage, I raise my goad, may you take it as if I had alighted from my carriage, and if I lower my hand, may you take it as if I had bowed my head at your feet.'[169]

27. Then the Lord, having instructed Soṇadaṇḍa with a talk on Dhamma, inspired him, fired him with enthusiasm and delighted him, rose from his seat and departed.

5 *Kūṭadanta Sutta: About Kūṭadanta*
A Bloodless Sacrifice

[127] 1. THUS HAVE I HEARD. Once the Lord was travelling through Magadha with a large company of some five hundred monks, and he arrived at a Brahmin village called Khānumata. And there he stayed at the Ambalaṭṭhikā park.[170] Now at that time the Brahmin Kūṭadanta was living at Khānumata, a populous place, full of grass, timber, water and corn, which had been given to him by King Seniya Bimbisāra of Magadha as a royal gift and with royal powers.

And Kūṭadanta planned a great sacrifice: seven hundred bulls, seven hundred bullocks, seven hundred heifers, seven hundred he-goats and seven hundred rams were all tied up to the sacrificial posts.[171]

2. And the Brahmins and householders of Khānumata heard say: 'The ascetic Gotama...is staying at Ambalaṭṭhikā. And concerning that Blessed Lord Gotama a good report has been spread about: "This Blessed Lord is an Arahant, a fully-enlightened Buddha, perfected in knowledge and conduct, a Well-Farer, Knower of the worlds, unequalled Trainer of men to be tamed, Teacher of gods and humans, a Buddha, a Blessed Lord." [128] He proclaims this world with its gods, māras and Brahmās, the world of ascetics and Brahmins with its princes and people, having come to know it by his own knowledge. He teaches a Dhamma that is lovely in its beginning, lovely in its middle and lovely in its ending, in the spirit and in the letter, and he displays the fully-perfected, thoroughly purified holy life. And indeed it is good to see such Arahants.' And at that the Brahmins and householders, leaving Khānumata in great numbers, went to Ambalaṭṭhikā.

3. Just then, Kūṭadanta had gone up to his verandah for his

midday rest. Seeing all the Brahmins and householders making for Ambalaṭṭhikā, he asked his steward the reason. The steward replied: 'Sir, it is the ascetic Gotama, concerning whom a good report has been spread about: "This Blessed Lord is an Arahant,...a Buddha, a Blessed Lord". That is why they are going to see him.'

4. Then Kūṭadanta thought: 'I have heard that the ascetic Gotama understands how to conduct successfully the triple sacrifice with its sixteen requisites. Now I do not understand all this, but I want to make a big sacrifice. Suppose [129] I were to go to the ascetic Gotama and ask him about the matter.' So he sent his steward to the Brahmins and householders of Khānumata to ask them to wait for him.

5. And at that time several hundred Brahmins were staying at Khānumata intending to take part in Kūṭadanta's sacrifice. Hearing of his intention to visit the ascetic Gotama, they went and asked him if this were true. 'So it is, gentlemen, I am going to visit the ascetic Gotama.'

6. 'Sir, do not visit the ascetic Gotama...(*exactly the same arguments as at Sutta 4, verse 5*). [130–131] This being so, it is not proper that the Reverend Kūṭadanta should visit the ascetic Gotama, but rather the ascetic Gotama should visit him.'

7. Then Kūṭadanta said to the Brahmins: 'Now listen, gentlemen, as to why it is fitting for us to visit the Reverend Gotama, and why it is not fitting for him to visit us...(*exactly the same as Sutta 4, verse 6*). [132–133] The ascetic Gotama has arrived in Khānumata and is staying at Ambalaṭṭhikā. And whatever ascetics or Brahmins come to our territory are our guests...He is beyond all praise.'

8. On hearing this, the Brahmins said: 'Sir, since you praise the ascetic Gotama so much, then even if he were to live a hundred yojanas from here, it would be fitting for a believing clansman to go with a shoulder-bag to visit him. And, sir, we shall all go to visit the ascetic Gotama.' And so Kūṭadanta went with a large company of Brahmins to Ambalaṭṭhikā. He approached the Lord, [134] exchanged courtesies with him, and sat down to one side. Some of the Brahmins and householders of Khānumata made obeisance to the Lord, some exchanged courtesies with him, some saluted him with joined

palms, some announced their name and clan, and some sat down to one side in silence.

9. Sitting to one side, Kūṭadanta addressed the Lord: 'Reverend Gotama, I have heard that you understand how to conduct successfully the triple sacrifice with its sixteen requisites. Now I do not understand all this, but I want to make a big sacrifice. It would be well if the ascetic Gotama were to explain this to me.' 'Then listen, Brahmin, pay proper attention, and I will explain.' 'Yes, sir', said Kūṭadanta, and the Lord said:

10. 'Brahmin, once upon a time there was a king called Mahāvijita.[172] He was rich, of great wealth and resources, with an abundance of gold and silver, of possessions and requisites, of money and money's worth, with a full treasury and granary. And when King Mahāvijita was musing in private, the thought came to him: "I have acquired extensive wealth in human terms, I occupy a wide extent of land which I have conquered. Suppose now I were to make a great sacrifice which would be to my benefit and happiness for a long time?" And calling his minister-chaplain,[173] he told him his thought. [135] "I want to make a big sacrifice. Instruct me, Reverend Sir, how this may be to my lasting benefit and happiness."

11. 'The chaplain replied: "Your Majesty's country is beset by thieves, it is ravaged, villages and towns are being destroyed, the countryside is infested with brigands. If Your Majesty were to tax this region, that would be the wrong thing to do. Suppose Your Majesty were to think: 'I will get rid of this plague of robbers by executions and imprisonment, or by confiscation, threats and banishment', the plague would not be properly ended. Those who survived would later harm Your Majesty's realm. However, with this plan you can completely eliminate the plague. To those in the kingdom who are engaged in cultivating crops and raising cattle, let Your Majesty distribute grain and fodder; to those in trade, give capital; to those in government service assign proper living wages. Then those people, being intent on their own occupations, will not harm the kingdom. Your Majesty's revenues will be great, the land will be tranquil and not beset by thieves, and the people,

with joy in their hearts, will play with their children, and will dwell in open houses."

'And saying: "So be it!", the king accepted the chaplain's advice: he gave grain and fodder, capital to those in trade,... proper living wages...and the people with joy in their hearts ...dwelt in open houses.

12. 'Then King Mahāvijita sent for the chaplain and said: "I have got rid of the plague of robbers; following your plan my revenue has grown, the land is tranquil and not beset by thieves, and the people with joy in their hearts play with their children and dwell in open houses. Now I wish to make a great sacrifice. Instruct me as to how this may be done to my lasting benefit and happiness." "For this, Sire, you should send for your Khattiyas from town and country, your advisers and counsellors, the most influential Brahmins and the wealthy householders of your realm, and say to them: 'I wish to make a great sacrifice. Assist me in this, gentlemen, that it may be to my lasting benefit and happiness.'"

'The King agreed, and [137] did so. "Sire, let the sacrifice begin, now is the time, Your Majesty. These four assenting groups[174] will be the accessories for the sacrifice.

13. '"King Mahāvijita is endowed with eight things. He is well-born on both sides,...(*as Sutta 4, verse 5*) of irreproachable birth. He is handsome,...of no mean appearance. He is rich...with a full treasury and granary. He is powerful, having a four-branched army[175] that is loyal, dependable, making bright his reputation among his enemies. He is a faithful giver and host, not shutting his door against ascetics, Brahmins and wayfarers, beggars and the needy – a fountain of goodness. He is very learned in what should be learnt. He knows the meaning of whatever is said, saying: 'This is what that means.' He is a scholar, accomplished, wise, competent to perceive advantage in the past, the future or the present.[176] King Mahāvijita is endowed with these eight things. These constitute the accessories for the sacrifice.

[138] 14. '"The Brahmin chaplain is endowed with four things. He is well-born...He is a scholar, versed in the mantras...He is virtuous, of increasing virtue, endowed with increasing virtue. He is learned, accomplished and wise, and is the

first or second to hold the sacrificial ladle. He has these four qualities. These constitute the accessories to the sacrifice."

15. 'Then, prior to the sacrifice, the Brahmin chaplain taught the King the three modes. "It might be that Your Majesty might have some regrets about the intended sacrifice: 'I am going to lose a lot of wealth', or during the sacrifice: 'I am losing a lot of wealth', or after the sacrifice: 'I have lost a lot of wealth.' In such cases, Your Majesty should not entertain such regrets."

16. 'Then, prior to the sacrifice, the chaplain dispelled the King's qualms with ten conditions for the recipient: "Sire, there will come to the sacrifice those who take life and those who abstain from taking life. To those who take life, so will it be to them; but those who abstain from taking life will have a successful sacrifice and will rejoice in it, and their hearts may be calmed within. There will come those who take what is not given and those who refrain..., those who indulge in sexual misconduct and those who refrain..., those who tell lies..., indulge in calumny, harsh and frivolous speech..., [139] those who are covetous and those who are not, those who harbour ill-will and those who do not, those who have wrong views and those who have right views. To those who have wrong views it will turn out accordingly, but those who have right views will have a successful sacrifice and will rejoice in it, and their hearts may be calmed within." So the chaplain dispelled the King's doubts with ten conditions.

17. 'So the chaplain instructed the King who was making the great sacrifice with sixteen reasons, urged him, inspired him and gladdened his heart. "Someone might say: 'King Mahāvijita is making a great sacrifice, but he has not invited his Khattiyas..., his advisers and counsellors, the most influential Brahmins and wealthy householders...' But such words would not be in accordance with the truth, since the King has invited them. Thus the King may know that he will have a successful sacrifice and rejoice in it, and his heart will be calmed within. Or someone might say: 'King Mahāvijita is making a great sacrifice, but he is not well-born on both sides...'[140] But such words would not be in accordance with the truth...Or someone might say: 'His chaplain is not

well-born...' [141] But such words would not be in accordance with the truth." Thus the chaplain instructed the King with sixteen reasons...

18. 'In this sacrifice, Brahmin, no bulls were slain, no goats or sheep, no cocks and pigs, nor were various living beings subjected to slaughter, nor were trees cut down for sacrificial posts, nor were grasses mown for the sacrificial grass, and those who are called slaves or servants or workmen did not perform their tasks for fear of blows or threats, weeping and in tears. But those who wanted to do something did it, those who did not wish to did not: they did what they wanted to do, and not what they did not want to do. The sacrifice was carried out with ghee, oil, butter, curds, honey and molasses. [142]

19. 'Then, Brahmin, the Khattiyas..., the ministers and counsellors, the influential Brahmins, the wealthy householders of town and country, having received a sufficient income, came to King Mahāvijita and said: "We have brought sufficient wealth, Your Majesty, please accept it." "But, gentlemen, I have collected together sufficient wealth. Whatever is left over, you take away."

'At the King's refusal, they went away to one side and consulted together: "It is not right for us to take this wealth back to our own homes. The King is making a great sacrifice. Let us follow his example."

20. 'Then the Khattiyas put their gifts to the east of the sacrificial pit, the advisers and counsellors set out theirs to the south, the Brahmins to the west and the wealthy householders to the north. And in this sacrifice no bulls were slain,... nor were living beings subjected to slaughter...Those who wanted to do something did it, those who did not wish to did not... The sacrifice was carried out with ghee, oil, butter, curds, honey and molasses. [143] Thus there were the four assenting groups, and King Mahāvijita was endowed with eight things, and the chaplain with four things in three modes. This, Brahmin, is called the sixteenfold successful sacrifice in three modes.'

21. At this the Brahmins shouted loudly and noisily: 'What a splendid sacrifice! What a splendid way to perform a sacrifice!' But Kūṭadanta sat in silence. And the Brahmins asked

him why he did not applaud the ascetic Gotama's fine words. He replied: 'It is not that I do not applaud them. My head would split open if I did not.[177] But it strikes me that the ascetic Gotama does not say: "I have heard this", or "It must have been like this", but he says: "It was like this or like that at the time." And so, gentlemen, it seems to me that the ascetic Gotama must have been at that time either King Mahāvijita, the lord of the sacrifice, or else the Brahmin chaplain who conducted the sacrifice for him. Does the Reverend Gotama acknowledge that he performed, or caused to be performed, such a sacrifice, and that in consequence at death, after the breaking-up of the body, he was reborn in a good sphere, a heavenly state?' 'I do, Brahmin. I was the Brahmin chaplain who conducted that sacrifice.'

22. 'And, Reverend Gotama, is there any other sacrifice that is simpler, less difficult, more fruitful and profitable than this threefold sacrifice with its sixteen attributes?' [144] 'There is, Brahmin.'

'What is it, Reverend Gotama?' 'Wherever regular family gifts are given to virtuous ascetics, these constitute a sacrifice more fruitful and profitable than that.'

23. 'Why, Reverend Gotama, and for what reason is this better?'

'Brahmin, no Arahants or those who have attained the Arahant path will attend such a sacrifice. Why? Because there they see beatings and throttlings, so they do not attend. But they will attend the sacrifice at which regular family gifts are given to virtuous ascetics, because there there are no beatings or throttlings. That is why this kind of sacrifice is more fruitful and profitable.'

24. 'But, Reverend Gotama, is there any other sacrifice that is more profitable than [145] either of these?' 'There is, Brahmin.'

'What is it, Reverend Gotama?' 'Brahmin, if anyone provides shelter for the Sangha coming from the four quarters, that constitutes a more profitable sacrifice.'

25. 'But, Reverend Gotama, is there any sacrifice that is more profitable than these three?' 'There is, Brahmin.'

'What is it, Reverend Gotama?' 'Brahmin, if anyone with a pure heart goes for refuge to the Buddha, the Dhamma and the Sangha, that constitutes a sacrifice more profitable than [146] any of these three.'

26. 'But, Reverend Gotama, is there any sacrifice that is more profitable than these four?' 'There is, Brahmin.'

'What is it, Reverend Gotama?' 'Brahmin, if anyone with a pure heart undertakes the precepts – to refrain from taking life, from taking what is not given, from sexual immorality, from lying speech and from taking strong drink and sloth-producing drugs – that constitutes a sacrifice more profitable than any of these four.'

27. 'But, Reverend Gotama, is there any sacrifice that is more profitable than these five?' 'There is, Brahmin.' [147]

'What is it, Reverend Gotama?' 'Brahmin, a Tathāgata arises in this world, an Arahant, fully-enlightened Buddha, endowed with wisdom and conduct, Well-Farer, Knower of the worlds, incomparable Trainer of men to be tamed, Teacher of gods and humans, enlightened and blessed. He, having realised it by his own super-knowledge, proclaims this world with its devas, māras and Brahmās, its princes and people. He preaches the Dhamma which is lovely in its beginning, lovely in its middle, lovely in its ending, in the spirit and in the letter, and displays the fully-perfected and purified holy life. *A disciple goes forth and practises the moralities, etc.* (*Sutta 2, verses 41–74*). Thus a monk is perfected in morality. *He attains the four jhānas* (*Sutta 2, verses 75–82*). That, Brahmin, is a sacrifice . . . more profitable. *He attains various insights* (*Sutta 2, verse 83–95*), *and the cessation of the corruptions* (*Sutta 2, verse 97*). He knows: "There is nothing further in this world." That, Brahmin, is a sacrifice that is simpler, less difficult, more fruitful and more profitable than all the others. And beyond this there is no sacrifice that is greater and more perfect.'

28. 'Excellent, Reverend Gotama, excellent! It is as if someone were to set up what had been knocked down, or to point out the way to one who had got lost, or to bring an oil-lamp into a dark place, so that those with eyes could see what was there. Just so the Reverend Gotama has expounded the Dhamma in various ways, May the Reverend Gotama accept me as a lay-follower from this day forth as long as life shall last! And, [148] Reverend Gotama, I set free the seven hundred bulls,

seven hundred bullocks, seven hundred heifers, seven hundred he-goats and seven hundred rams. I grant them life, let them be fed with green grass and given cool water to drink, and let cool breezes play upon them.'

29. Then the Lord delivered a graduated discourse to Kūṭadanta, on generosity, on morality and on heaven, showing the danger, degradation and corruption of sense-desires, and the profit of renunciation. And when the Lord knew that Kūṭadanta's mind was ready, pliable, free from the hindrances, joyful and calm, then he preached a sermon on Dhamma in brief: on suffering, its origin, its cessation, and the path. And just as a clean cloth from which all stains have been removed receives the dye perfectly, so in the Brahmin Kūṭadanta, as he sat there, there arose the pure and spotless Dhamma-eye, and he knew: 'Whatever things have an origin must come to cessation.'

30. Then Kūṭadanta, having seen, attained, experienced and penetrated the Dhamma, having passed beyond doubt, transcended uncertainty, having gained perfect confidence in the Teacher's doctrine without relying on others, said: 'May the Reverend Gotama and his order of monks accept a meal from me tomorrow!'

The Lord assented by silence. Then Kūṭadanta, seeing his consent, rose, saluted the Lord, passed by to his right and departed. As day was breaking, he caused hard and soft food to be prepared at his place of sacrifice, and when it was ready he announced: 'Reverend Gotama, it is time; the meal is ready.'

And the Lord, having risen early, went with robe and bowl and attended by his monks to Kūṭadanta's place of sacrifice and sat down on the prepared seat. And Kūṭadanta [149] served the Buddha and his monks with the finest foods with his own hands until they were satisfied. And when the Lord had eaten and taken his hand away from the bowl, Kūṭadanta took a low stool and sat down to one side.

Then the Lord, having instructed Kūṭadanta with a talk on Dhamma, inspired him, fired him with enthusiasm and delighted him, rose from his seat and departed.[178]

6 *Mahāli Sutta: About Mahāli* Heavenly Sights, Soul and Body

[150] 1. THUS HAVE I HEARD. Once the Lord was staying at Vesālī, at the Gabled Hall in the Great Forest. And at that time a large number of Brahmin emissaries from Kosala and Magadha were staying at Vesālī on some business. And they heard say: 'The ascetic Gotama, son of the Sakyans, who has gone forth from the Sakya clan, is staying at Vesālī, at the Gabled Hall in the Great Forest. And concerning that Blessed Lord a good report has been spread about: "This Blessed Lord is an Arahant, a fully-enlightened Buddha, perfected in knowledge and conduct, a Well-Farer, Knower of the worlds, unequalled Trainer of men to be tamed, Teacher of gods and humans, a Buddha, a Blessed Lord." He proclaims this world with its gods, māras and Brahmās, the world of ascetics and Brahmins with its princes and peoples, having come to know it by his own knowledge. He teaches a Dhamma that is lovely in its beginning, lovely in its middle and lovely in its ending, in the spirit and in the letter, and he displays the fully-perfected, thoroughly purified holy life. And indeed it is good to see such Arahants.'

2. And so these Brahmin emissaries from Kosala and Magadha went to the Great Forest, to the Gabled Hall. At that time the Venerable Nāgita was the Lord's personal attendant. So they approached the Venerable Nāgita and said: 'Reverend Nāgita, where is the Reverend Gotama now staying? We would like to see him.' [151]

'Friends, it is not the right time to see the Lord. He is in solitary meditation.' But the Brahmins just sat down to one side and said: 'When we have seen the Lord Gotama, we will go.'

3. Just then Oṭṭhaddha the Licchavi came to the Gabled Hall

with a large company, saluted the Venerable Nāgita and stood aside, saying: 'Where is the Blessed Lord staying, the Arahant, the fully-enlightened Buddha? We would like to see him.' 'Mahāli,[179] it is not the right time to see the Lord, He is in solitary meditation.' But Oṭṭhaddha just sat down to one side, and said: 'When I have seen the Blessed Lord, the Arahant, the fully-enlightened Buddha, I will go.'

4. Then the novice Sīha[180] came to the Venerable Nāgita, stood aside and said: 'Venerable Kassapa,[181] these many Brahmin emissaries from Kosala and Magadha have come here to see the Lord, and Oṭṭhaddha the Licchavi, too, has come with a large company to see the Lord. It would be well, Venerable Kassapa, to allow these people to see him.' 'Well then, Sīha, you announce them to the Lord.' 'Yes, Venerable Sir', said Sīha. Then he went to the Lord, saluted him, stood aside and said: 'Lord, these Brahmin emissaries from Kosala and Magadha have come here to see the Lord, and Oṭṭhaddha the Licchavi likewise with a large [152] company. It would be well if the Lord were to let these people see him.' 'Then, Sīha, prepare a seat in the shade of this dwelling.' 'Yes, Lord', said Sīha, and did so. Then the Lord came out of his dwelling-place and sat down on the prepared seat.

5. The Brahmins approached the Lord. Having exchanged courtesies with him, they sat down to one side. But Oṭṭhaddha did obeisance to the Lord, and then sat down to one side, saying: 'Lord, not long ago Sunakkhatta the Licchavi[182] came to me and said: "Soon I shall have been a follower of the Lord for three years. I have seen heavenly sights, pleasant, delightful, enticing, but I have not heard any heavenly sounds that were pleasant, delightful, enticing." Lord, are there any such heavenly sounds, which Sunakkhatta cannot hear, or are there not?' 'There are such sounds, Mahāli.'

6. 'Then, Lord, what is the reason, what is the cause why Sunakkahtta cannot hear them?' [153] 'Mahāli, in one case a monk, facing east, goes into one-sided samādhi[183] and sees heavenly sights, pleasant, delightful, enticing...but does not hear heavenly sounds. By means of this one-sided samādhi he sees heavenly sights but does not hear heavenly sounds. Why

is this? Because this samādhi only leads to the seeing of heavenly sights, but not to the hearing of heavenly sounds.

7. 'Again, a monk facing south, west, north goes into a one-sided samādhi and facing upwards, downwards or across sees heavenly sights [in that direction], but does not hear heavenly sounds. Why is this? Because this samādhi only leads to the seeing of heavenly sights, but not to the hearing of heavenly sounds. [154]

8. 'In another case, Mahāli, a monk facing east...hears heavenly sounds but does not see heavenly sights...

9. 'Again, a monk facing south, west, north, facing upwards, downwards or across hears heavenly sounds, but does not see heavenly sights...

10. 'In another case, Mahāli, a monk facing east goes into two-sided samādhi and both sees heavenly sights, pleasant, delightful, enticing [155] and hears heavenly sounds. Why is this? Because this two-sided samādhi leads to both the seeing of heavenly sights and the hearing of heavenly sounds.

11. 'Again, a monk facing south, west, north, facing upwards, downwards or across sees heavenly sights and hears heavenly sounds...And that is the reason why Sunakkhatta comes to see heavenly sights but not to hear heavenly sounds.'[184]

12. 'Well, Lord, is it for the realisation of such samādhi-states that monks lead the holy life under the Blessed Lord?' 'No, Mahāli, there are other things, higher and more perfect than these, for the sake of which monks lead the holy life under me.'

[156] 13. 'What are they, Lord?' 'Mahāli, in one case a monk, having abandoned three fetters, becomes a Stream-Winner, not liable to states of woe, firmly set on the path to enlightenment. Again, a monk who has abandoned the three fetters, and has reduced his greed, hatred and delusion, becomes a Once-Returner who, having returned to this world once more, will make an end of suffering. Again, a monk who has abandoned the five lower fetters takes a spontaneous rebirth[185] [in a higher sphere] and, without returning from that world, gains enlightenment. Again, a monk through the extinction of

the corruptions reaches in this very life the uncorrupted deliverance of mind, the deliverance through wisdom, which he has realised by his own insight. That is another thing higher and more perfect than these, for the sake of which monks lead the holy life under me.'

14. 'Lord, is there a path, is there a method for the realisation of these things?' 'There is a path, Mahāli, there is a method.' [157] 'And, Lord, what is this path, what is this method?'

'It is the Noble Eightfold Path, namely Right View, Right Thought; Right Speech, Right Action, Right Livelihood; Right Effort, Right Mindfulness and Right Concentration. This is the path, this is the way to the realisation of these things.'

15. 'Once, Mahāli, I was staying at Kosambī, in the Ghosita Park. And two wanderers, Maṇḍissa and Jāliya, the pupil of the wooden-bowl ascetic, came to me, exchanged courtesies with me, and sat down to one side. Then they said: "How is it, friend Gotama, is the soul[186] the same as the body, or is the soul one thing and the body another?" "Well now, friends, you listen, pay proper attention, and I will explain." "Yes, friend", they said, and I went on:

16. '"Friends, a Tathāgata arises in the world, an Arahant, fully-enlightened Buddha, endowed with wisdom and conduct, Well-Farer, Knower of the worlds, incomparable Trainer of men to be tamed, Teacher of gods and humans, enlightened and blessed. He, having realised it by his own super-knowledge, proclaims this world with its devas, māras and Brahmās, its princes and people. He preaches the Dhamma which is lovely in its beginning, lovely in its middle, lovely in its ending, in the spirit and in the letter, and displays the fully-perfected and purified holy life.

'"*A disciple goes forth and practises the moralities* (*Sutta 2, verses 41–63*). On account of his morality, he sees no danger anywhere. He experiences in himself the blameless bliss that comes from maintaining this Ariyan morality. In this way, he is perfected in morality. (*as Sutta 2, verses 64–74*) . . . It is as if he were freed from debt, from sickness, from bonds, from slavery, from the perils of the desert. . . Being thus detached from sense-desires, detached from unwholesome states, he enters and remains in the first jhāna . . . and so suffuses, drenches, fills and irradiates his body, that there is no spot in his entire body that is untouched by this delight and joy born of detachment. Now of one who thus knows and thus sees, is it proper to say: 'The soul is the same as the body', or 'The soul is different from the body'?" "It is not, friend."[187] "But I thus know and see, and I do not say that the soul is either the same as, or different from the body."

17. '"And the same with the second . . . , the third . . . , [158] the fourth jhāna (*as Sutta 2, verses 77–82*).

18. '"The mind bends and tends towards knowledge and vision. Now, of one who thus knows and thus sees, is it proper to say: 'The soul is the same as the body', or 'The soul is different from the body'?" "It is not, friend."

19. '"He knows: 'There is nothing further here.' Now of one who thus knows and thus sees, is it proper to say: 'The soul is the same as the body', or 'The soul is different from the body'?" "It is not, friend." "But I thus know and see, and I do not say that the soul is either the same as, or different from the body."'

Thus the Lord spoke, and Oṭṭhaddha the Licchavi rejoiced at his words.

7 *Jāliya Sutta: About Jāliya*

[159] 1. THUS HAVE I HEARD.[188] Once the Lord was staying at Kosambī, in the Ghosita Park. And two wanderers, Maṇḍissa and Jāliya, the pupil of the wooden-bowl ascetic, came to him, exchanged courtesies with him and sat down to one side... (*verses 1–5 = Sutta 6, verses 15–19*). [160]

Thus the Lord spoke, and the two wanderers rejoiced at his words.

8 *Mahāsīhanāda Sutta: The Great Lion's Roar*[189]

[161] 1. THUS HAVE I HEARD. Once the Lord was staying at Ujuññāya in the deer-park of Kaṇṇakatthale.[190] There the naked ascetic Kassapa came to him, exchanged courtesies with him, and stood to one side. Then he said:

2. 'Friend Gotama, I have heard it said: "The ascetic Gotama disapproves of all austerities, and censures and blames all those who lead a harsh life of self-mortification.[191] Now are those who say this telling the truth, and do they not slander the Lord Gotama with lies? Do they explain the truth about his Dhamma and what pertains to it, or does some fellow-teacher of a different sect deserve to be blamed for this statement? We would like to see the Lord Gotama refute this charge."

3. 'Kassapa, those who say this are not telling the truth, they slander me with lies. The situation occurs, Kassapa, that I see one practiser of mortification, and with the divine [162] eye[192] which is purified beyond the sight of humans I see him arising after death, at the breaking-up of the body, in a place of woe, a baleful state, a place of destruction, in hell. Again, I see one practiser of mortification...arising after death in a good place, a heavenly state. Again, I see one who practises little austerity...arising in a state of woe...Again, I see one who practises little austerity...arising after death in a good place, a heavenly state. Since I can see as it is the arising, the destiny, the death and re-arising of those ascetics, how could I disapprove of all austerities, and censure and blame all those who lead a harsh life of self-mortification?

4. 'Kassapa, there are some ascetics and Brahmins who are wise, skilled, practised in disputation, splitters of hairs, acute,

who walk cleverly along the paths of views. Sometimes their views accord with mine, sometimes they do not. What they sometimes applaud, we sometimes applaud. What they sometimes do not applaud, we sometimes do not applaud; what they sometimes applaud, we sometimes do not applaud, and what they sometimes do not applaud, we sometimes applaud. What we sometimes applaud, they sometimes applaud, what we sometimes do not applaud, they sometimes do not applaud. [163] What we sometimes applaud, they sometimes do not applaud, and what we sometimes do not applaud, they sometimes applaud.

5. 'On approaching them I say: "In these things there is no agreement, let us leave them aside. In these things there is agreement: there let the wise take up, cross-question and criticise these matters with the teachers or with their followers, saying: 'Of those things that are unskilful[193] and reckoned as such, censurable, to be refrained from, unbefitting a Noble One, black, and reckoned as such – who is there who has completely abandoned such things and is free from them: the ascetic Gotama, or some other venerable teachers?'"

6. 'It may be that the wise...say: "Of those things that are unskilled...the ascetic Gotama has completely freed himself, but the other reverend teachers only in part." In this case the wise give us the greatest share of praise.

7. 'Or the wise may say: "Of those things that are skilled and reckoned as such, blameless, to be practised, fitting for a Noble One, bright and reckoned as such, who is there who has completely mastered them – the ascetic Gotama, or some other reverend teachers?"

8. 'Or the wise may [164] say: "Of these things...the ascetic Gotama has completely mastered them, but the other reverend teachers only in part." In this case the wise give us the greatest share of praise.

9–12 (*As verses 5–8 but*: 'the order of the ascetic Gotama's disciples, or that of the other reverend teachers.') [165]

13. 'Kassapa, there is a path, there is a course of training, whereby one who has followed it will know and see for himself: "The ascetic Gotama speaks at the proper time, what is true, to the point[194] – the Dhamma and the discipline." What

is this path and this course of training? It is the Noble Eightfold Path, namely Right View, Right Thought; Right Speech, Right Action, Right Livelihood; Right Effort, Right Mindfulness, Right Concentration. This is the path whereby one may know and see for oneself: "The ascetic Gotama speaks at the proper time, what is true, to the point – the Dhamma and the discipline."'

14. At this, Kassapa said to the Lord: 'Gotama, these ascetic practices of certain practisers of self-mortification [166] are considered proper to them: a naked ascetic uses no polite restraints,[195] licks his hands, does not come or stand still when requested. He does not accept food offered or prepared for him, or an invitation to a meal. He does not accept food out of the pot or pan, nor on the threshold, among the firewood or the rice-pounders, nor where two people are eating, from a pregnant or nursing woman or from one living with a man, nor from gleanings, from where a dog is standing or where flies are swarming. He eats no fish or meat and drinks no rum or spirits or fermented rice-gruel.[196] He is a one-house man[197] or a one-piece man,[198] a two-house man, a seven-piece man or a seven-house man. He exists on one, two or seven little offerings, eats only once a day, once in two days, once in seven days. He takes to eating rice only twice a month. These are considered proper practices.

'Or a man becomes a herb-eater, a millet-eater, a raw-rice-eater, a wild-rice-eater, an eater of water-plants, of rice-husk-powder, of rice-scum, of the flowers of oil-seeds, grass or cow-dung, of forest roots and fruits, eating windfalls. He wears coarse hemp or mixed material, shrouds from corpses, rags from the dust-heap, garments of bark-fibre, [167] antelope-skins, grass, bark, shavings, blankets of human hair[199] or horse-hair, the wings of owls. He is a plucker-out of hair and beard, devoted to this practice; he is a covered-thorn man, making his bed on them, sleeping alone in a garment of wet mud, living in the open air, accepting whatever seat is offered, living on filth and addicted to the practice, one who drinks no water[200] and is addicted to the practice, or he dwells intent on the practice of going to bathe three times before evening.'[201]

15. 'Kassapa, a practiser of self-mortification may do all these

things, but if his morality, his heart and his wisdom are not developed and brought to realisation, then indeed he is still far from being an ascetic or a Brahmin. But, Kassapa, when a monk develops non-enmity, non-ill-will and a heart full of loving-kindness and, abandoning the corruptions, realises and dwells in the uncorrupted deliverance of mind, the deliverance through wisdom, having realised it in this very life by his own insight, then, Kassapa, that monk is termed an ascetic and a Brahmin.'[202] [168]

16. At this Kassapa said to the Lord: 'Reverend Gotama, it is hard to be an ascetic, it is hard to be a Brahmin.'

'So they say in the world, Kassapa: "It is hard to be an ascetic, it is hard to be a Brahmin." If a naked ascetic were to do all these things...(*as verse 14*), and if this were the measure and practice of the difficulty, the great difficulty, of being an ascetic or Brahmin, it would not be right to say: "It is hard to be an ascetic, it is hard to be a Brahmin", because any householder or householder's son – even the slave-girl who draws water – could do this saying: "Well, I will go naked..." (*as verse 14*). But, Kassapa, because there is a very different kind of asceticism beside this, therefore it is right to say: "It is hard to be an ascetic, it is hard to be a Brahmin." [169] But, Kassapa, when a monk develops non-enmity, non-ill-will and a heart full of loving kindness...(*as verse 15*), then that monk is called an ascetic and a Brahmin.' [170]

17. At this Kassapa said to the Lord: 'Reverend Gotama, it is hard to understand an ascetic, it is hard to understand a Brahmin.'

'So they say in the world, Kassapa: "It is hard to understand an ascetic, it is hard to understand a Brahmin." If a naked ascetic were to do all these things, and if this were the measure and practice of the difficulty, the great difficulty, of understanding an ascetic or Brahmin, it would not be right to say that, because any householder...could understand it. [171] But, Kassapa, because there is a very different kind of asceticism and Brahmanism beside this, it is right to say: "It is hard to understand an ascetic or a Brahmin." But, Kassapa, when a monk develops non-enmity, non-ill-will and a heart full of loving-kindness and, abandoning the corruptions, realises and dwells in the uncorrupted deliverance of mind, the deliverance through wisdom, having realised it in this very life by his own insight, then, Kassapa, that monk is called an ascetic and a Brahmin.'

18–20. Then Kassapa said to the Lord: 'Reverend Gotama, what then is the development of morality, of the heart, and of wisdom?'

'Kassapa, a Tathāgata arises in the world an Arahant, fully-enlightened Buddha, endowed with wisdom and conduct, Well-Farer, Knower of the worlds, incomparable Trainer of men to be tamed, Teacher of gods and humans, enlightened and blessed. He, having realised it by his own super-knowledge, proclaims this world with its devas, māras and Brahmās, its princes and people. He preaches the Dhamma which is lovely in its beginning, lovely in its middle, lovely in its ending, in the spirit and in the letter, and displays the fully-perfected and purified holy life. *A disciple goes forth and practises the moralities (Sutta 2, verses 41–63).* [172] That is the perfection of morality. *He guards the sense-doors, etc. and attains the four jhānas (Sutta 2 verses 64–82).* [173–4] That is the perfection of the heart. *He attains various insights and the cessation of the corruptions (Sutta 2, verses 83–98).* That is the perfection of wisdom. And, Kassapa, there is nothing further or more perfect than this perfection of morality, of the heart and of wisdom.

21. 'Kassapa, there are some ascetics and Brahmins who preach morality. They praise morality in various ways. But as regards the highest Ariyan morality, Kassapa, I do not see any who have surpassed me in this. I am supreme in this regard, in super-morality. There are some ascetics and Brahmins who preach self-mortification and scrupulous austerity, which they praise in various ways. But as regards the highest Ariyan self-mortification and austerity, Kassapa, I do not see any who have surpassed me in this. I am supreme in this regard, in super-austerity. There are some ascetics and Brahmins who preach wisdom. They praise wisdom in various ways. But as regards the highest Ariyan wisdom, Kassapa, I do not see any who have surpassed me in this. I am supreme in this regard, in super-wisdom. There are some ascetics and Brahmins who preach liberation. They praise liberation in various ways. But

as regards the highest Ariyan liberation, Kassapa, I do not see any who have surpassed me in this. I am supreme in this regard, in super-liberation. [175]

22. 'Kassapa, it may be that wanderers of other sects will say: "The ascetic Gotama roars his lion's roar, but only in empty places, not in company." They should be told that this is not true: "The ascetic Gotama roars his lion's roar, and he roars it in company." Or they may say: "The ascetic Gotama roars his lion's roar, and in company, but he does so without confidence." They should be told that this is not true: "The ascetic Gotama roars his lion's roar, in company and confidently." Or they may say: "The ascetic Gotama roars his lion's roar, and in company, and confidently, but they do not question him." They should be told that this is not true: "The ascetic Gotama roars his lion's roar...and they question him." Or they may say: "...and they question him, but he does not answer." ...Or they may say: "...he answers, but he does not win them over with his answers." ...Or they may say: "...but they don't find it pleasing." ...Or they may say: "...but they are not satisfied with what they have heard." ...Or they may say: "...but they don't behave as if they were satisfied." ...Or they may say: "...but they are not on the path of truth." ...Or they may say: "...but they are not satisfied with the practice." They should be told that this is not true: "The ascetic Gotama roars his lion's roar, in company and confidently, they question him and he answers, he wins them over with his answers, they find it pleasing and are satisfied with what they have heard, they behave as if they were satisfied, they are on the path of truth, and they are satisfied with the practice." That, Kassapa, is what they should be told.

23. 'Once, Kassapa, I was staying at Rājagaha at the Vultures' Peak. And a certain practiser of mortification [176] called Nigrodha consulted me about the practice of austerity.[203] And he was delighted with my explanation beyond all measure.'

'Lord, who on hearing Dhamma from you would fail to be delighted beyond all measure? I am delighted beyond all measure. Excellent, Lord, excellent! It is as if someone were to set up what had been knocked down, or to point out the way to one who had got lost, or to bring an oil-lamp into a dark place, so that those with eyes could see what was there. Just so the Blessed Lord has expounded the Dhamma in various ways. Lord, may I receive the going-forth at the Lord's hands, may I receive ordination!'

24. 'Kassapa, whoever has formerly belonged to another sect and wishes for the going-forth or ordination in this Dhamma and discipline must wait four months, and at the end of four months' probation, the monks who are established in mind will give him the going-forth and the monastic ordination. But there can be a distinction of persons in this.' 'Lord, if such is the case, I will even wait four years, and at the end of that time let the monks give me the going-forth and the monastic ordination.'

Then Kassapa received the going-[177]-forth from the Lord himself, and the monastic ordination. And the newly-ordained Venerable Kassapa, alone, secluded, unwearying, zealous and resolute, in a short time attained that for which young men of good birth go forth from the household life into homelessness, that unexcelled culmination of the holy life, having realised it here and now by his own super-knowledge and dwelt therein knowing: 'Birth is destroyed, the holy life has been lived, what had to be done has been done, there is nothing further here.'

And the Venerable Kassapa became another of the Arahants.

9 *Poṭṭhapāda Sutta: About Poṭṭhapāda*
States of Consciousness

[178] 1. THUS HAVE I HEARD. Once the Lord was staying at Sāvatthi, in Jeta's grove, in Anāthapiṇḍika's park. And at that time the wanderer Poṭṭhapāda was at the debating-hall near the Tinduka tree, in the single-halled park of Queen Mallikā,[204] with a large crowd of about three hundred wanderers.

2. Then the Lord, rising early, took his robe and bowl and went to Sāvatthi for alms. But it occurred to him: 'It is too early to go to Sāvatthi for alms. Suppose I were to go to the debating-hall to see the wanderer Poṭṭhapāda?' And he did so.

3. There Poṭṭhapāda was sitting with his crowd of wanderers, all shouting and making a great commotion, indulging in various kinds of unedifying conversation, such as about kings, robbers, ministers, armies, dangers, wars, food, drink, clothes, beds, garlands, perfumes, relatives, carriages, villages, towns and cities, [179] countries, women, heroes, street- and well-gossip, talk of the departed, desultory chat, speculations about land and sea, talk of being and non-being.

4. But Poṭṭhapāda saw the Lord coming from a distance, and so he called his followers to order, saying: 'Be quiet, gentlemen, don't make a noise, gentlemen! That ascetic Gotama is coming, and he likes quiet and speaks in praise of quiet. If he sees that this company is quiet, he will most likely want to come and visit us.' At this the wanderers fell silent.

5. Then the Lord came to Poṭṭhapāda, who said: 'Come, reverend Lord, welcome, reverend Lord! At last the reverend Lord has gone out of his way to come here. Be seated, Lord, a seat is prepared.'

The Lord sat down on the prepared seat, and Poṭṭhapāda took a low stool and sat down to one side. The Lord said:

'Poṭṭhapāda, what were you all talking about? What conversation have I interrupted?'

6. Poṭṭhapāda replied: 'Lord, never mind the conversation we were having just now, it will not be difficult for the Lord to hear about that later. In the past few days, Lord, the discussion among the ascetics and Brahmins of various schools, sitting together and meeting in the debating-hall, has concerned [180] the higher extinction of consciousness,[205] and how this takes place. Some said: "One's perceptions arise and cease without cause or condition. When they arise, one is conscious, when they cease, then one is unconscious." That is how they explained it. But somebody else said: "No, that is not how it is. Perceptions[206] are a person's self, which comes and goes. When it comes, one is conscious, when it goes, one is unconscious." Another said: "That is not how it is. There are ascetics and Brahmins of great powers, of great influence. They draw down consciousness into a man and withdraw it. When they draw it down into him, he is conscious, when they withdraw it, he is unconscious."[207] And another said: "No, that is not how it is. There are deities of great powers, of great influence. They draw down consciousness into a man and withdraw it. When they draw it down into him, he is conscious, when they withdraw it, he is unconscious."[208] It was in this connection that I thought of the Lord: "Ah, surely, the Blessed Lord, the Well-Farer, he is supremely skilled[209] about these matters! The Blessed Lord well understands the higher extinction of consciousness." What then, Lord, is this higher extinction of consciousness?'

7. 'In this matter, Poṭṭhapāda, those ascetics and Brahmins who say one's perceptions arise and cease without cause or condition are totally wrong. Why is that? One's perceptions arise and cease [181] owing to a cause and conditions. Some perceptions arise through training, and some pass away through training.' 'What is this training?', the Lord said. 'Poṭṭhapāda, a Tathāgata arises in this world an Arahant, fully-enlightened Buddha, endowed with wisdom and conduct, Well-Farer, Knower of the worlds, incomparable Trainer of men to be tamed, Teacher of gods and humans, enlightened and blessed. He, having realised it by his own super-know-

ledge, proclaims this world with its devas, māras and Brahmās, its princes and people. He preaches the Dhamma which is lovely in its beginning, lovely in its middle, lovely in its ending, in the spirit and in the letter, and displays the fully-perfected and purified holy life. *A disciple goes forth and practises the moralities* (*Sutta 2, verses 41–62*). That for him is morality.

8. 'And then, Poṭṭhapāda, that monk who is perfected in morality sees no danger from any side... (*as Sutta 2, verse 63*). In this way he is perfected in morality.

9–10. *He guards the sense-doors, etc.* (*Sutta 2, verses 64–75*). [182] Having reached the first jhāna, he remains in it. And whatever sensations of lust that he previously had disappear. At that time there is present a true but subtle perception of delight and happiness,[210] born of detachment, and he becomes one who is conscious of this delight and happiness. In this way some perceptions arise through training, and some pass away through training. And this is that training', said the Lord.

11. 'Again, a monk, with the subsiding of thinking and pondering, by gaining inner tranquillity and unity of mind, reaches and remains in the second jhāna, which is free from thinking and pondering, born of concentration, filled with delight and happiness. His former true but subtle perception of delight and happiness born of detachment vanishes. At that time there arises a true but subtle perception [183] of delight and happiness born of concentration, and he becomes one who is conscious of this delight and happiness. In this way some perceptions arise through training, and some pass away through training.

12. 'Again, after the fading away of delight he dwells in equanimity, mindful and clearly aware, and he experiences in his body that pleasant feeling of which the Noble Ones say: "Happy dwells the man of equanimity and mindfulness", and he reaches and remains in the third jhāna. His former true but subtle sense of delight and happiness born of concentration vanishes, and there arises at that time a true but subtle sense of equanimity and happiness, and he becomes one who is conscious of this true but subtle sense of equanimity and

happiness. In this way some perceptions arise through training, and some pass away through training.

13. 'Again, with the abandonment of pleasure and pain, and with the disappearance of previous joy and grief, he reaches and remains in the fourth jhāna, a state beyond pleasure and pain, purified by equanimity and mindfulness. His former true but subtle sense of equanimity and happiness vanishes, and there arises a true but subtle sense of neither happiness nor unhappiness, and he becomes one who is conscious of this true but subtle sense of neither happiness nor unhappiness. In this way some perceptions arise through training, and some pass away through training.

14. 'Again, by passing entirely beyond bodily sensations, by the disappearance of all sense of resistance and by non-attraction to the perception of diversity, seeing that space is infinite, he reaches and remains in the Sphere of Infinite Space. In this way some perceptions arise through training, and some pass away through training.

15. 'Again, by passing entirely beyond [184] the Sphere of Infinite Space, seeing that consciousness is infinite, he reaches and remains in the Sphere of Infinite Consciousness. In this way some perceptions arise through training, and some pass away through training.

16. 'Again, by passing entirely beyond the Sphere of Infinite Consciousness, seeing that there is no thing, he reaches and remains in the Sphere of No-Thingness, and he becomes one who is conscious of this true but subtle perception of the Sphere of No-Thingness. In this way some perceptions arise through training, and some pass away through training. And this is that training', said the Lord.

17. 'Poṭṭhapāda, from the moment when a monk has gained this controlled perception,[211] he proceeds from stage to stage till he reaches the limit of perception. When he has reached the limit of perception it occurs to him: "Mental activity is worse for me, lack of mental activity is better. If I were to think and imagine,[212] these perceptions [that I have attained] would cease, and coarser perceptions would arise in me. Suppose I were not to think or imagine?" So he neither thinks nor imagines. And then, in him, just these perceptions arise, but

other, coarser perceptions do not arise. He attains cessation. And that, Poṭṭhapāda, is the way in which the cessation of perception is brought about by successive steps.

18. 'What do you think, Poṭṭhapāda? Have you heard of this before?' 'No, Lord. As I understand it, the Lord has said: "Poṭṭhapāda, from the moment when a monk has gained this controlled perception, he proceeds from stage to stage until he reaches the limit of perception...He attains cessation [185]... and that is the way in which the cessation of perception is brought about by successive steps."' 'That is right, Poṭṭhapāda.'

19. 'Lord, do you teach that the summit of perception is just one, or that it is many?' 'I teach it as both one and many.' 'Lord, how is it one, and how is it many?' 'According as he attains successively to the cessation of each perception, so I teach the summit of that perception: thus I teach both one summit of perception, and I also teach many.'

20. 'Lord, does perception arise before knowledge, or knowledge arise before perception, or do both arise simultaneously?' 'Perception arises first, Poṭṭhapāda, then knowledge, and from the arising of perception comes the arising of knowledge. And one knows: "Thus conditioned, knowledge arises." In this way you can see how perception arises first, and then knowledge, and that from the arising of perception comes the arising of knowledge.'[213]

21. 'Lord, is perception a person's self, or is perception one thing, and self another?'[214] 'Well, Poṭṭhapāda, do you postulate[215] a self?' [186] 'Lord, I postulate a gross self, material, composed of the four elements, and feeding on solid food.' 'But with such a gross self, Poṭṭhapāda, perception would be one thing, and the self another. You can see that in this way. Given such a gross self, certain perceptions would arise in a person, and others pass away. In this way you can see that perception must be one thing, the self another.'[216]

22. 'Lord, I postulate a mind-made self complete with all its parts, not defective in any sense-organ.'[217] 'But with such a mind-made self, perception would be one thing, and the self another...' [187]

23. 'Lord, I assume a formless self, made up of percep-

tion.'[218] 'But with such a formless self, perception would be one thing, and self another...'

24. 'But Lord, is it possible for me to know whether perception is a person's self, or whether perception is one thing, and self another?' 'Poṭṭhāpada, it is difficult for one of different views, a different faith, under different influences, with different pursuits and a different training to know whether these are two different things or not.'

25. 'Well, Lord, if this question of self and perceptions is difficult for one like me – tell me: Is the world eternal?[219] Is only this true and the opposite false?' 'Poṭṭhapāda, I have not declared that the world is eternal and that the opposite view is false.' 'Well, Lord, is the world not eternal?' 'I have not declared that the world is not eternal...' 'Well, Lord, is the world infinite,...not infinite?...' [188] 'I have not declared that the world is not infinite and that the opposite view is false.'

26. 'Well, Lord, is the soul the same as the body,...is the soul one thing and the body another?' 'I have not declared that the soul is one thing and the body another.'

27. 'Well, Lord, does the Tathāgata exist after death? Is only this true and all else false?' 'I have not declared that the Tathāgata exists after death.' 'Well, Lord, does the Tathāgata not exist after death,...both exist and not exist after death? ...neither exist nor not exist after death?' 'I have not declared that the Tathāgata neither exists nor does not exist after death, and that all else is false.'

28. 'But, Lord, why has the Lord not declared these things?' 'Poṭṭhāpada, that is not conducive to the purpose, not conducive to Dhamma, [189] not the way to embark on the holy life; it does not lead to disenchantment, to dispassion, to cessation, to calm, to higher knowledge, to enlightenment, to Nibbāna. That is why I have not declared it.'

29. 'But, Lord, what has the Lord declared?' 'Poṭṭhapāda, I have declared: "This is suffering, this is the origin of suffering, this is the cessation of suffering, and this is the path leading to the cessation of suffering."'

30. 'But, Lord, why has the Lord declared this?' 'Because, Poṭṭhapāda, this is conducive to the purpose, conducive to

Dhamma, the way to embark on the holy life; it leads to disenchantment, to dispassion, to cessation, to calm, to higher knowledge, to enlightenment, to Nibbāna. That is why I have declared it.'

'So it is, Lord, so it is, Well-Farer. And now is the time for the Blessed Lord to do as he sees fit.' Then the Lord rose from his seat and went away.

31. Then the wanderers, as soon as the Lord had left, reproached, sneered and jeered at Poṭṭhapāda from all sides, saying: 'Whatever the ascetic Gotama says, Poṭṭhapāda agrees with him: "So it is, Lord, so it is, Well-Farer!" *We* don't understand a word of the ascetic Gotama's whole discourse: "Is the world eternal or not? – Is it finite or infinite? – Is the soul the same as the body or different? – Does the Tathāgata exist after death or not, [190] or both, or neither?"'

Poṭṭhapāda replied: 'I don't understand either about whether the world is eternal or not...or whether the Tathāgata exists after death or not, or both, or neither. But the ascetic Gotama teaches a true and real way of practice which is consonant with Dhamma and grounded in Dhamma. And why should not a man like me express approval of such a true and real practice, so well taught by the ascetic Gotama?'

32. Two or three days later, Citta, the son of the elephant-trainer, went with Poṭṭhāpada to see the Lord. Citta prostrated himself before the Lord and sat down to one side. Poṭṭhapāda exchanged courtesies with the Lord, sat down to one side, and told him what had happened. [191]

33. 'Poṭṭhapāda, all those wanderers are blind and sightless, you alone among them are sighted. Some things I have taught and pointed out, Poṭṭhāpada, as being certain, others as being uncertain. Which are the things I have pointed out as uncertain? "The world is eternal" I have declared to be uncertain... "The Tathāgata exists after death..." Why? Because they are not conducive...to Nibbāna. That is why I have declared them as uncertain.

'But what things have I pointed out as certain? "This is suffering, [192] this is the origin of suffering, this is the cessation of suffering, this is the path leading to the cessation of suffering." Why? Because they are conducive to the purpose, conducive to Dhamma, the way to embark on the holy life; they lead to disenchantment, to dispassion, to cessation, to calm, to higher knowledge, to enlightenment, to Nibbāna. That is why I have declared them as certain.

34. 'Poṭṭhapāda, there are some ascetics and Brahmins who declare and believe that after death the self is entirely happy and free from disease. I approached them and asked if this was indeed what they declared and believed, and they replied: "Yes." Then I said: "Do you, friends, living in the world, know and see it as an entirely happy place?" and they replied: "No." I said: "Have you ever experienced a single night or day, or half a night or day, that was entirely happy?" and they replied: "No." I said: "Do you know a path or a practice whereby an entirely happy world might be brought about?" and they replied: "No." I said: "Have you heard the voices of deities who have been reborn in an entirely happy world, saying: 'The attainment of an entirely happy world has been well and rightly gained, and we, gentlemen, [193] have been reborn in such a realm'?" and they replied: "No." What do you think, Poṭṭhapāda? Such being the case, does not the talk of those ascetics and Brahmins turn out to be stupid?

35. 'It is just as if a man were to say: "I am going to seek out and love the most beautiful girl in the country." They might say to him: "Well, as to this most beautiful girl in the country, do you know whether she belongs to the Khattiya, the Brahmin, the merchant or the artisan class?" and he would say: "No." Then they might say: "Well, do you know her name, her clan, whether she is tall or short or of medium height, whether she is dark or light-complexioned or sallow-skinned, or what village or town or city she comes from?" and he would say: "No." And they might say: "Well then, you don't know or see the one you seek for and desire?" and he would say: "No." Does not the talk of that man turn out to be stupid?' 'Certainly, Lord.'

36. 'And so it is with those ascetics and Brahmins who declare and believe that after death the self is entirely happy and free from disease... [194] Does not their talk turn out to be stupid?' 'Certainly, Lord.'

37. 'It is just as if a man were to build a staircase for a palace

at a crossroads. People might say to him: "Well now, this staircase for a palace that you are building – do you know whether the palace will face east, or west, or north or south, or whether it will be high, low or of medium height?" and he would say: "No." And they might say: "Well then, you don't know or see what kind of a palace you are building the staircase for?" and he would say: "No." Don't you think that man's talk would turn out to be stupid?' 'Certainly, Lord.'

38. (*as verse 34*) [195]

39. 'Poṭṭhapāda, there are three kinds of "acquired self":[220] the gross acquired self, the mind-made acquired self, the formless acquired self. What is the gross acquired self? It has form, is composed of the four great elements, nourished by material food. What is the mind-made self? It has form, complete with all its parts, not defective in any sense-organ. What is the formless acquired self? It is without form, and made up of perception.

40. 'But I teach a doctrine for getting rid of the gross acquired self, whereby defiling mental states disappear and states tending to purification grow strong, and one gains and remains in the purity and perfection of wisdom here [196] and now, having realised and attained it by one's own super-knowledge. Now, Poṭṭhāpada, you might think: "Perhaps these defiling mental states might disappear..., and one might still be unhappy."[221] That is not how it should be regarded. If defiling states disappear..., nothing but happiness and delight develops, tranquillity, mindfulness and clear awareness – and that is a happy state.

41. 'I also teach a doctrine for getting rid of the mind-made acquired self...(*as verse 40*).

42. 'I also teach a doctrine for getting rid of the formless acquired self...(*as verse 40*). [197]

43. 'Poṭṭhapāda, if others ask us: "What, friend, is this gross acquired self whose abandonment you preach...?" being so asked, we should reply: "This *is*[222] that gross acquired self for the getting rid of which we teach a doctrine..."

44. 'If others ask us: "What is this mind-made acquired self ...?" (*as verse 43*). [198]

45. 'If others ask us: "What is this formless acquired self

. . . ?" (*as verse 43*). What do you think, Poṭṭhapāda? Does not that statement turn out to be well-founded?' 'Certainly, Lord.'

46. 'It is just as if a man were to build a staircase for a palace, which was below that palace. They might say to him: "Well now, this staircase for a palace that you are building, do you know whether the palace will face east or west, or north or south, or whether it will be high, low or of medium height?" and he would say: "This staircase is right under the palace." Don't you think that man's statement would be well-founded?' 'Certainly, Lord.' [199]

47. 'In just the same way, Poṭṭhapāda, if others ask us: "What is this gross acquired self. . . ?" "What is this mind-made acquired self. . . ?" "What is this formless acquired self . . . ?" we reply: "This *is* this [gross, mind-made, formless] acquired self for the getting rid of which we teach a doctrine, whereby defiling mental states disappear and states tending to purification grow strong, and one gains and remains in the purity and perfection of wisdom here and now, having realised and attained it by one's own super-knowledge." Don't you think that statement is well-founded?' 'Certainly, Lord.'

48. At this, Citta, son of the elephant-trainer, said to the Lord: 'Lord, whenever the gross acquired self is present, would it be wrong to assume the existence of the mind-made acquired self, or of the formless acquired self? Does only the gross acquired self truly exist then? And similarly with the mind-made acquired self, and the formless acquired self?'

49. 'Citta, whenever the gross acquired self is present, we do not at that time speak of a mind-made acquired self, [200] we do not speak of a formless acquired self. We speak only of a gross acquired self.[223] Whenever the mind-made acquired self is present, we speak only of a mind-made acquired self, and whenever the formless acquired self is present, we speak only of a formless acquired self.

'Citta, suppose they were to ask you: "Did you exist in the past or didn't you, will you exist in the future or won't you, do you exist now or don't you?" how would you answer?'

'Lord, if I were asked such a question, I would say: "I did exist in the past, I did not not exist; I shall exist in the future, I shall not not exist; I do exist now, I do not not exist." That, Lord, would be my answer.'

50. 'But, Citta, if they asked: "The past acquired self that you had, is that your only true acquired self, and are the future and present ones false? Or is the one you will have in the future the only true one, and are the past and present ones false? Or is your present acquired self the only true one, and are the past and future ones false?" how would you reply?'

'Lord, if they asked me these things, [201] I would reply: "My past acquired self was at the time my only true one, the future and present ones were false. My future acquired self will then be the only true one, the past and present ones will be false. My present acquired self is now the only true one, the past and future ones are false." That is how I would reply.'

51. 'In just the same way, Citta, whenever the gross acquired self is present, we do not at that time speak of a mind-made acquired self...[or] of a formless acquired self.

52. 'In just the same way, Citta, from the cow we get milk, from the milk curds, from the curds butter, from the butter ghee, and from the ghee cream of ghee. And when there is milk we don't speak of curds, of butter, of ghee or of cream of ghee, we speak of milk; when there are curds we don't speak of butter...; when there is cream of ghee...we speak of cream of ghee. [202]

53. 'So too, whenever the gross acquired self is present, we do not speak of the mind-made or formless acquired self; whenever the mind-made acquired self is present, we do not speak of the gross or formless acquired self; whenever the formless acquired self is present, we do not speak of the gross acquired self or the mind-made acquired self, we speak of the formless acquired self. But, Citta, these are merely names, expressions, turns of speech, designations in common use in the world, which the Tathāgata uses without misapprehending them.'[224]

54. And at these words Poṭṭhapāda the wanderer said to the Lord: 'Excellent, Lord, excellent! It is as if someone were to set up what had been knocked down, or to point out the way to one who had got lost, or to bring an oil-lamp into a dark

place, so that those with eyes could see what was there. Just so the Blessed Lord has expounded the Dhamma in various ways. Lord, I go for refuge to the Lord, the Dhamma and the Sangha. May the Lord accept me as a lay-follower who has taken refuge in him from this day forth as long as life shall last!'

55. But Citta, son of the elephant-trainer, said to the Lord: 'Excellent, Lord, excellent! It is as if someone were to set up what had been knocked down, or to point out the way to one who had got lost, or to bring an oil-lamp into a dark place, so that those with eyes could see what was there. Just so the Blessed Lord has expounded the Dhamma in various ways. Lord, I go for refuge to the Lord, the Dhamma and the Sangha. May I, Lord, receive the going-forth at the Lord's hands, may I receive ordination!'

56. And Citta, son of the elephant-trainer, received the going-forth at the Lord's hands, and the ordination. And the newly-ordained Venerable Citta, alone, secluded, unwearying, zealous and resolute, in a short time attained to that for the sake of which young men of good birth go forth from the household life into [203] homelessness, that unexcelled culmination of the holy life, having realised it here and now by his own super-knowledge and dwelt therein, knowing: 'Birth is destroyed, the holy life has been lived, what had to be done has been done, there is nothing further here.'

And the Venerable Citta, son of the elephant-trainer, became another of the Arahants.

10 *Subha Sutta: About Subha* Morality, Concentration, Wisdom

[204] 1.1. THUS HAVE I HEARD.[225] Once the Venerable Ānanda was staying at Sāvatthi, in Jeta's grove, in Anāthapiṇḍika's park, shortly after the Lord's final passing.[226] And at that time the youth Subha, Todeyya's son,[227] was staying at Sāvatthi on some business.

1.2. And Subha said to a certain young man: 'Go, my lad, to where the ascetic Ānanda is, ask him in my name if he is in good health, free from fatigue, strong, vigorous and dwelling in comfort, and say: "It would be good if the Reverend Ānanda would, out of compassion, visit the dwelling of Subha the son of Todeyya."'

1.3 'Very good, sir', replied the young man. Then he went to the Venerable Ānanda, exchanged courtesies with him, and sat down to one side. Then he delivered [205] the message.

1.4. The Venerable Ānanda replied: 'It is not the right time, young man. Today I have taken some medicine. Perhaps it will be possible to come tomorrow when the time and the occasion are suitable.' And the young man rose, returned to Subha and reported what had passed between him and the Venerable Ānanda, adding: 'My mission has been thus far accomplished, that the Reverend Ānanda will probably take the opportunity to come tomorrow.'

1.5. And indeed, as that night was ending, the Venerable Ānanda dressed in the early morning, took his robe and bowl and, accompanied by the Venerable Cetaka,[228] came to Subha's dwelling, and sat down on the prepared seat. Then Subha approached the Venerable Ānanda, exchanged courtesies with him, and sat down to one side. Then he said: [206] 'The Reverend Ānanda was for a long time the Reverend Gotama's personal attendant, dwelling in his presence and near him. You, Reverend Ānanda, would know what things the Reverend Gotama praised, and with which he aroused, exhorted and established people. Which, Reverend Ānanda, were those things?'

1.6. 'Subha, there were three divisions of things which the Lord praised, and with which he aroused, exhorted and established people. Which three? The division of Ariyan morality,[229] the division of Ariyan concentration, and the division of Ariyan wisdom. These were the three divisions of things which the Lord praised...'

'Well, Reverend Ānanda, what is the division of Ariyan morality which the Reverend Gotama praised...?'

1.7–29. 'Young sir, a Tathāgata arises in the world, an Arahant, fully-enlightened Buddha, endowed with wisdom and conduct, Well-Farer, Knower of the worlds, incomparable Trainer of men to be tamed, Teacher of gods and humans, enlightened and blessed. He, having realised it by his own super-knowledge, proclaims this world with its devas, māras and Brahmās, its princes and people. He preaches the Dhamma which is lovely in its beginning, lovely in its middle, lovely in its ending, in the spirit and in the letter, and displays the fully-perfected and purified holy life. *A disciple goes forth and practises the moralities, etc.* (*Sutta 2, verses 41–63*). Thus a monk is perfected in morality.

1.30. 'That is the division of Ariyan morality which the Lord praised...But something more remains to be done.' 'It is wonderful, Reverend Ānanda, it is marvellous! This division of Ariyan morality is perfectly fulfilled, not left incomplete. And I do not see this division of Ariyan morality [207] fulfilled thus anywhere among the ascetics and Brahmins of other schools. And if any of them were to have found this perfection in themselves, they would have been so delighted that they would have said: "We've done enough! The goal of our asceticism has been reached! There's nothing more to be done!" And yet the Reverend Ānanda declares that there is more to be done!'

[*End of first recitation-section*]

2.1. 'Reverend Ānanda, what is the division of Ariyan concentration which the Reverend Gotama praised...?'

2.2–18. 'And how is a monk guardian of the sense-doors? *He guards the sense-doors and attains the four jhānas* (*Sutta 2, verses 64–82*). This comes to him through concentration. [208]

2.19. 'That is the division of Ariyan concentration which the Lord praised...But something more remains to be done.' 'It is wonderful, Reverend Ānanda, it is marvellous! This division of Ariyan concentration is perfectly fulfilled, not left incomplete. And I do not see this division of Ariyan concentration fulfilled thus anywhere among the ascetics and Brahmins of other schools. And if any of them were to have found this perfection in themselves, they would have been so delighted that they would have said: "We've done enough! The goal of our asceticism has been reached! There's nothing more to be done!" And yet the Reverend Ānanda declares that there is more to be done!'

2.20. 'Reverend Ānanda, what is the division of Ariyan wisdom which the Reverend Gotama praised?'

2.21–22. 'And so, with mind concentrated *he attains various insights* (*Sutta 2, verses 83–84*). That is known to him by wisdom.

2.23–36. *'He realises the Four Noble Truths, the path and the cessation of the corruptions* (*Sutta 2, verses 85–97*). And he knows: "...There is nothing further here."

2.37. 'That is the division of Ariyan wisdom which the Lord praised, with which he aroused, exhorted and established people. Beyond that there is nothing to be done.' [210]

'It is wonderful, Reverend Ānanda, it is marvellous! This division of Ariyan wisdom is perfectly fulfilled, not left incomplete. And I do not see this division of Ariyan wisdom fulfilled thus anywhere among the ascetics and Brahmins of other schools. And there is nothing further to be done! Excellent, Reverend Ānanda, excellent! It is as if someone were to set up what had been knocked down, or to point out the way to one who had got lost, or to bring an oil-lamp into a dark place, so that those with eyes could see what was there. Just so the Reverend Ānanda has expounded the Dhamma in various ways.

'Reverend Ānanda, I go for refuge to the Lord Gotama, the Dhamma and the Sangha. May the Reverend Ānanda accept me as a lay-follower who has taken refuge from this day forth as long as life shall last!'

11 *Kevaddha Sutta: About Kevaddha*
What Brahma Didn't Know

[211] 1. THUS HAVE I HEARD. Once the Lord was staying at Nāḷandā, in Pāvārika's mango grove. And the householder Kevaddha[230] came to the Lord, prostrated himself before him, and sat down to one side. He then said: 'Lord, this Nāḷandā is rich, prosperous, populous, and full of people who have faith in the Lord. It would be well if the Lord were to cause some monk to perform superhuman feats and miracles. In this way Nāḷandā would come to have even more faith in the Lord.'

The Lord replied: 'Kevaddha, this is not the way I teach Dhamma to the monks, by saying: "Go, monks, and perform superhuman feats and miracles for the white-clothed lay-people!'

2. For a second time Kevaddha said: 'Lord, I would not be importunate, but I still say: "This Nāḷandā is rich, prosperous ... [212] and would come to have even more faith in the Lord."' And the Lord replied as before.

3. When Kevaddha repeated his request for a third time, the Lord said: 'Kevaddha, there are three kinds of miracle that I have declared, having realised them by my own insight. Which three? The miracle of psychic power,[231] the miracle of telepathy,[232] the miracle of instruction.[233]

4. 'What is the miracle of psychic power? Here, Kevaddha, a monk displays various psychic powers in different ways. Being one he becomes many, being many he becomes one... (*as Sutta 2, verse 87*) [213] and he travels in the body as far as the Brahma world. Then someone who has faith and trust sees him doing these things.

5. 'He tells this to someone else who is sceptical and un-

believing, saying: "It is wonderful, sir, it is marvellous, the great power and skill of that ascetic..." And that man might say: "Sir, there is something called the Gandhāra charm.[234] It is by means of this that that monk becomes many..." What do you think, Kevaddha, would not a sceptic say that to a believer?' 'He would, Lord.' 'And that is why, Kevaddha, seeing the danger of such miracles, I dislike, reject and despise them.

6. 'And what is the miracle of telepathy? Here, a monk reads the minds of other beings, of other people, reads their mental states, their thoughts and ponderings, and says: "That is how your mind is, that is how it inclines, that is in your heart." Then someone who has faith and trust sees him doing these things.

7. 'He tells this to someone else who is sceptical and unbelieving, saying: "It is [214] wonderful, sir, it is marvellous, the great power and skill of that ascetic..." And that man might say: "Sir, there is something called the Maṇika charm.[235] It is by means of this that that monk can read the minds of others ..." And that is why, seeing the danger of such miracles, I... despise them.

8. 'And what is the miracle of instruction? Here, Kevaddha, a monk gives instruction as follows: "Consider in this way, don't consider in that, direct your mind this way, not that way, give up that, gain this and persevere in it." That, Kevaddha, is called the miracle of instruction.

9–66. 'Again, Kevaddha, a Tathāgata arises in the world, an Arahant, fully-enlightened Buddha, endowed with wisdom and conduct, Well-Farer, Knower of the worlds, incomparable Trainer of men to be tamed, Teacher of gods and humans, enlightened and blessed. He, having realised it by his own super-knowledge, proclaims this world with its devas, māras and Brahmās, its princes and people. He preaches the Dhamma which is lovely in its beginning, lovely in its middle, lovely in its ending, in the spirit and in the letter, and displays the fully-perfected and purified holy life. *A disciple goes forth and practises the moralities* (*Sutta 2, verses 41–63*). *He guards the sense-doors and attains the four jhānas* (*Sutta 2, verses 64–82*);

he attains various insights (Sutta 2, verses 83–84); he realises the Four Noble Truths, the path and the cessation of the corruptions (Sutta 2, verses 85–97),[236] and he knows: "...There is nothing further here." That, Kevaddha, is called the miracle of instruction.

67. 'And I, Kevaddha, have experienced these three miracles by my own super-knowledge. Once, Kevaddha, in this order of monks the thought occurred to a certain monk: "I wonder where the four great elements – the earth element, the water element, the fire element, the air element – cease without remainder." And that monk attained to such a state of mental concentration that the way to the deva-realms appeared before him.

68. 'Then, coming to the Realm of the devas of the Four Great Kings,[237] he asked those devas: "Friends, where do the four great elements – earth, water, fire and air – cease without remainder?" At this question the devas of the Four Great Kings [216] said to him: "Monk, we don't know where the four great elements cease without remainder. But the Four Great Kings are loftier and wiser than we are. They may know where the four great elements cease..."

69. 'So that monk went to the Four Great Kings and asked the same question, but they replied: "We don't know, but the Thirty-Three Gods may know..."

70. 'So that monk went to the Thirty-Three Gods, who said: "We don't know, but Sakka, lord of the gods, may know..." [217]

71. 'Sakka, lord of the gods, said: "The Yāma devas may know..."

72. 'The Yāma devas said: "Suyāma, son of the devas,[238] may know..."

73. 'Suyāma said: "The Tusita [218] devas may know..."

74. 'The Tusita devas said: "Santusita, son of the devas, may know..."

75. 'Santusita said: "The Nimmānarati devas may know..."

76. [219] 'The Nimmānarati devas said: "Sunimmita, son of the devas, may know..."

77. 'Sunimitta said: "The Paranimmita-Vasavatti devas may know..."

78. 'The Paranimmita-Vasavatti devas said: "Vasavatti, son of the devas, may know..."

79. [220] 'Vasavatti said: "The devas of Brahmā's retinue may know..."

80. 'Then that monk, by the appropriate concentration, made the way to the Brahmā world appear before him. He went to the devas of Brahmā's retinue and asked them. They said: "We don't know. But there is Brahmā, Great Brahmā, the Conqueror, the Unconquered, the All-Seeing, All-Powerful, the Lord, the Maker and Creator, the Ruler, Appointer and Orderer, Father of All That Have Been and Shall Be. He is loftier and wiser than we are. He would know where the four great elements cease without remainder." "And where, friends, is this Great Brahmā now?" "Monk, we do not know when, how and where Brahmā will appear. But when the signs are seen – when a light appears and a radiance shines forth – then Brahmā will appear. Such signs are an indication that he will appear."

81. 'Then it was not long before the Great Brahmā [221] appeared. And that monk went up to him and said: "Friend, where do the four great elements – earth, water, fire, air – cease without remainder?" to which the Great Brahmā replied: "Monk, I am Brahmā, Great Brahmā, the Conqueror, the Unconquered, the All-Seeing, All-Powerful, the Lord, the Maker and Creator, the Ruler, Appointer and Orderer, Father of All That Have Been and Shall Be."

82. 'A second time the monk said: "Friend, I did not ask if you are Brahmā, Great Brahmā...I asked you where the four great elements cease without remainder." And a second time the Great Brahmā replied as before.

83. 'And a third time the monk said: "Friend, I did not ask you that, I asked where the four great elements – earth, water, fire, air – cease without remainder." Then, Kevaddha, the Great Brahmā took that monk by the arm, led him aside and [222] said: "Monk, these devas believe there is nothing Brahmā does not see, there is nothing he does not know, there is nothing he is unaware of. That is why I did not speak in front of them. But, monk, I don't know where the four great ele-

ments cease without remainder. And therefore, monk, you have acted wrongly, you have acted incorrectly by going beyond the Blessed Lord and going in search of an answer to this question elsewhere. Now, monk, you just go to the Blessed Lord and put this question to him, and whatever answer he gives, accept it."

84. 'So that monk, as swiftly as a strong man might flex or unflex his arm, vanished from the Brahmā world and appeared in my presence. He prostrated himself before me, then sat down to one side and said: "Lord, where do the four great elements – the earth element, the water element, the fire element and the air element – cease without remainder?"

85. 'I replied: "Monk, once upon a time seafaring merchants, when they set sail on the ocean, took in their ship a land-sighting bird. When they could not see the land themselves, they released this bird. The bird flew to the east, to the south, to the west, to the north, it flew to the zenith and to the intermediate points of the compass. If it saw land anywhere, it flew there. But if it saw no land, it returned to the ship. In the same way, monk, you have been [223] as far as the Brahmā world searching for an answer to your question and not finding it, and now you come back to me. But, monk, you should not ask your question in this way: 'Where do the four great elements – the earth element, the water element, the fire element, the air element – cease without remainder?' Instead, this is how the question should have been put:

> 'Where do earth, water, fire and air no footing find?
> Where are long and short, small and great, fair and
> foul –
> Where are "name-and-form" wholly destroyed?'[239]

And the answer is:

> 'Where consciousness is signless,[240] boundless, all-
> luminous,[241]
> That's where earth, water, fire and air find no footing,
> *There* both long and short, small and great, fair and
> foul –

There "name-and-form" are wholly destroyed.
With the cessation of consciousness this is all destroyed.'"'[242]

Thus the Lord spoke, and the householder Kevaddha, delighted, rejoiced at his words.

12 *Lohicca Sutta: About Lohicca*
Good and Bad Teachers

[224] 1. THUS HAVE I HEARD. Once the Lord was touring Kosala with a large company of some five hundred monks, and, coming to Sālavatikā, he stayed there. And at that time the Brahmin Lohicca was living at Sālavatikā, a populous place, full of grass, timber, water and corn, which had been given to him by King Pasenadi of Kosala as a royal gift and with royal powers.

2. Just then this evil line of reasoning occurred to Lohicca: 'Suppose an ascetic or Brahmin were to discover some good doctrine,[243] having done so, he ought not to declare it to anyone else; for what can one man do for another? It is just as if a man, having cut through an old fetter, were to make a new one. I declare that such a thing is an evil deed rooted in attachment, for what can one man do for another?'

3. Then Lohicca heard it said that the ascetic Gotama had arrived at Sālavatikā, and that concerning the Blessed Lord Gotama a good report had been spread about...(*as Sutta 4, verse 2*). [225] 'And indeed it is good to see such Arahants.'

4. And Lohicca said to Bhesika the barber: 'Friend Bhesika, go to the ascetic Gotama, ask in my name after his health and then say: "May the Reverend Gotama consent to take tomorrow's meal, with his order of monks, from the Brahmin Lohicca!"'

5. 'Very good, sir', said Bhesika, and carried out the errand. The Lord signified his acceptance by silence.

6. Then Bhesika, understanding the Lord's acceptance, rose from his seat and passed by with his right side to the Lord. He returned to Lohicca and told him [226] of the Lord's acceptance.

7. And Lohicca, as the night was ending, had choice hard and soft foods prepared at his own home. Then he sent Bhesika to tell the Lord that the meal was ready. And the Lord, having risen early and taken his robe and bowl, went with his order of monks to Sālavatikā.

8. And Bhesika the barber followed the Lord close at hand. And he said: 'Lord, this evil thought has occurred to the Brahmin Lohicca... Truly, Lord, this is what the Brahmin Lohicca has been thinking.' 'It may well be so, Bhesika, it may well be so.'

9. So the Lord came to Lohicca's dwelling, and sat down on [227] the prepared seat. Lohicca personally served the Buddha and his order of monks with choice hard and soft food till they were contented and satisfied. When the Lord had taken his hand from the bowl, Lohicca took a low stool and sat down to one side. Then the Lord said to him: 'Lohicca, is it true that an evil line of reasoning has occurred to you... (*as verse 2*)?' 'Yes, Reverend Gotama.'

10. 'What do you think, Lohicca? Don't you reside at Sālavatikā?' 'Yes, Reverend Gotama.' 'Well now, if anyone should say: "The Brahmin Lohicca resides at Sālavatikā, and he should enjoy the entire fruits and revenues of Sālavatikā, not giving anything away to others" – would not anyone who spoke like that be a source of danger to your tenants?' 'He would be a source of danger, Reverend Gotama.'

'And as such, would he be solicitous for their welfare or not?' 'He would not, Reverend Gotama.'

'And, by not being solicitous for their welfare, would he have a heart full of love for them, or of hatred?' 'Of hatred, Reverend Gotama.'

'And in a heart full of hatred, is there wrong view or right view?' 'Wrong view, Reverend Gotama,' [228]

'But Lohicca, I declare that wrong view leads to one of two destinies – hell or an animal rebirth.[244]

11. 'What do you think, Lohicca? Does King Pasenadi of Kosala reside at Kāsi-Kosala?' 'He does, Reverend Gotama.' 'Well, if anyone should say: "King Pasenadi of Kosala resides at Kāsi-Kosala, and he should enjoy the entire fruits and revenues of Kosala, not giving anything away to others" – would

not anyone who spoke like that be a source of danger to his tenants?...Would he not have a heart full of hatred...and would that not be wrong view?' 'It would, Reverend Gotama.'

12. 'Then surely, if anyone were to say the same of the Brahmin Lohicca...that would be wrong view.

13. 'In the same way, Lohicca, if anyone should say: "Suppose an ascetic or Brahmin were to discover some good doctrine and thought he ought not to declare it to anyone else, [229] for what can one man do for another?" he would be a source of danger to those young men of good family who, following the Dhamma and discipline taught by the Tathāgata, attain to such excellent distinction as to realise the fruit of Stream-Entry, of Once-Returning, of Non-Returning, of Arahantship – and to all who ripen the seeds of a rebirth in the deva-world.[245] Being a source of danger to them, he is uncompassionate, and his heart is grounded in hostility, and that constitutes wrong view, which leads to...hell or an animal rebirth.

14. 'And if anyone were to speak thus of King Pasenadi, he would be a source of danger to the King's tenants, yourself and others...

15. (*as verse 13*) [230]

16. 'Lohicca, these three kinds of teachers in the world are blameworthy, and if anyone blames such teachers, his blame is proper, true, in accordance with reality and faultless. Which three? Here, Lohicca, is a teacher who has gone forth from the household life into homelessness, but who has not gained the goal of asceticism. And without having gained this goal, he teaches his disciples a doctrine,[246] saying: "This is for your good, this is for your happiness." But his pupils don't wish to hear, they don't listen, the don't arouse the thought of enlightenment, and the teacher's instructions are flouted. He should be blamed, saying: "This venerable one has gone forth ..., his instructions are flouted. It is just as if a man were to persist in making advances to a woman who rejected him, and to embrace her though she turned away." This I declare to be an evil doctrine based on attachment, for what can one man do for another?[247] This is the first teacher who is blameworthy...

17. 'Again, there is a teacher who has gone forth...but who has not gained the goal of asceticism. Without having gained this goal, he teaches his disciples a doctrine, saying: "This is for your good, this is for your happiness." His pupils wish to hear, they listen, [231] they rouse the thought of enlightenment, and the teacher's instructions are not flouted. He should be blamed, saying: "This venerable one has gone forth..." It is as if, leaving his own field, he should think another's field in need of weeding. I declare this to be an evil doctrine rooted in attachment...This is the second teacher who is blameworthy...

18. 'Again, there is a teacher who has gone forth...and who has gained the goal of asceticism. Having gone forth, he teaches...But his pupils don't wish to hear him,...his instructions are flouted. He too should be blamed...Just as if, having cut through an old fetter, one were to make a new one, I declare that this is an evil doctrine rooted in attachment, for what can one man do for another? This is the third teacher who is blameworthy...[232] And these are the three kinds of teacher that I spoke of as blameworthy.'

19. Then Lohicca said: 'Reverend Gotama, are there any teachers in the world who are not blameworthy?'

20–55. 'Here, Lohicca, a Tathāgata arises in the world, an Arahant, fully-enlightened Buddha, endowed with wisdom and conduct, Well-Farer, Knower of the worlds, incomparable Trainer of men to be tamed, Teacher of gods and humans, enlightened and blessed. He, having realised it by his own super-knowledge, proclaims this world with its devas, māras and Brahmās, its princes and people. He preaches the Dhamma which is lovely in its beginning, lovely in its middle, lovely in its ending, in the spirit and in the letter, and displays the fully-perfected and purified holy life. *A disciple goes forth and practises the moralities, guards the sense-doors, attains the first jhāna* (*Sutta 2, verses 41–76*). [233] And whenever the pupil of a teacher attains to such excellent distinction, that is a teacher who is not to be blamed in the world. And if anyone blames that teacher, his blame is improper, untrue, not in accordance with reality, and faulty.

56–62. *'He attains the other three jhānas* (*as Sutta 2, verses 77–*

82) and various insights (Sutta 2, verses 83–84). Whenever the pupil of a teacher attains to such excellent distinction, that is a teacher who is not to be blamed in the world...

63–77. *'He realises the Four Noble Truths, the path, and the cessation of the corruptions...(as Sutta 2, verses 85–97).*

'Whenever the pupil of a teacher attains to such excellent distinction, that is a teacher who [234] is not to be blamed in the world. And if anyone blames that teacher, his blame is improper, untrue, not in accordance with reality, and faulty.'

78. At this the Brahmin Lohicca said to the Lord: 'Reverend Gotama, it is as if a man were to seize someone by the hair who had stumbled and was falling into a pit,[248] and to set him on firm ground – just so, I, who was falling into the pit, have been saved by the Reverend Gotama! Excellent, Reverend Gotama, excellent! It is as if someone were to set up what had been knocked down, or to point out the way to one who had got lost, or to bring an oil-lamp into a dark place, so that those with eyes could see what was there. Just so the Reverend Gotama has expounded the Dhamma in various ways.'

'I go for refuge to the Lord Gotama, the Dhamma and the Sangha. May the Reverend Gotama accept me as a lay-follower who has taken refuge from this day forth for as long as life shall last!'

13 *Tevijja Sutta: The Threefold Knowledge*
The Way to Brahmā

[235] 1. THUS HAVE I HEARD. Once the Lord was touring Kosala with a large company of some five hundred monks. He came to a Kosalan Brahmin village called Manasākaṭa, and stayed to the north of the village in a mango-grove on the bank of the River Aciravatī.

2. And at that time many very well-known and prosperous Brahmins were staying at Manasākaṭa, including Cankī, Tārukkha, Pokkharasāti, Jāṇussoni, and Todeyya.

3. And Vāseṭṭha and Bhāradvāja went strolling along the road, and as they did so, an argument broke out between them on the subject of right and wrong paths.

4. The young Brahmin Vāseṭṭha said: 'This is the only straight path, this is the direct path, the path of salvation that leads one who follows it to union with Brahmā, as is taught by the Brahmin Pokkharasāti!'[249]

5. And the young Brahmin Bhāradvāja said: '*This* is the only straight path. . . [236] as taught by the Brahmin Tārukkha!'

6. And Vāseṭṭha could not convince Bhāradvāja, nor could Bhāradvāja convince Vāseṭṭha.

7. Then Vāseṭṭha said to Bhāradvāja: 'This ascetic Gotama is staying to the north of the village, and concerning this Blessed Lord a good report has been spread about. . . (*as Sutta 4, verse 2*). Let us go to the ascetic Gotama and ask him, and whatever he tells us, we shall accept.' And Bhāradvāja agreed.

8. So the two of them went to see the Lord. Having exchanged courtesies with him, they sat down to one side, and Vāseṭṭha said: 'Reverend Gotama, as we were strolling along the road, we got to discussing right and wrong paths. I said: "This is the only straight path. . . as is taught by the Brahmin

Pokkharasāti", and Bhāradvāja said: "*This* is the only straight path...as is taught by the Brahmin Tārukkha." This is our dispute, our quarrel, our difference.' [237]

9. 'So, Vāseṭṭha, you say that the way to union with Brahmā is that taught by the Brahmin Pokkharasāti, and Bhāradvāja says it is that taught by the Brahmin Tārukha. What is the dispute, the quarrel, the difference all about?'

10. 'Right and wrong paths, Reverend Gotama. There are so many kinds of Brahmins who teach different paths: the Addhariya, the Tittiriya, the Chandoka, the Chandāva, the Brāhmacariya[250] Brahmins – do all these ways lead to union with Brahmā? Just as if there were near a town or village many different paths – do all these come together at that place? And likewise, do the ways of the various Brahmins...lead the one who follows them to union with Brahmā?'

11. 'You say: "They lead", Vāseṭṭha?' 'I say: "They lead", Reverend Gotama.'

'You say: "They lead", Vāseṭṭha?' 'I say: "They lead", Reverend Gotama.'

'You say: "They lead", Vāseṭṭha?' 'I say: "They lead", Reverend Gotama.' [238]

12. 'But, Vāseṭṭha, is there then a single one of these Brahmins learned in the Three Vedas who has seen Brahmā face to face?' 'No, Reverend Gotama.'

'Then has the teacher's teacher of any one of them seen Brahmā face to face?' 'No, Reverend Gotama.'

'Then has the ancestor seven generations back of the teacher of one of them seen Brahmā face to face?' 'No, Reverend Gotama.'

13. 'Well then, Vāseṭṭha, what about the early sages of those Brahmins learned in the Three Vedas, the makers of the mantras, the expounders of the mantras, whose ancient verses are chanted, pronounced and collected by the Brahmins of today, and sung and spoken about – such as Aṭṭhaka, Vāmaka, Vāmadeva, Vessāmitta, Yamataggi, Angirasa, Bhāradvāja, Vāseṭṭha, Kassapa, Bhagu[251] – did they ever say: "We know and see when, how and where Brahmā appears"?'[252] 'No, Reverend Gotama.'

14. 'So, Vāseṭṭha, not one of these Brahmins learned in the

Three Vedas has seen Brahmā face to face, nor has one of their teachers, or teacher's teachers, [239] nor even the ancestor seven generations back of one of their teachers. Nor could any of the early sages say: "We know and see when, how and where Brahmā appears." So what these Brahmins learned in the Three Vedas are saying is: "We teach this path to union with Brahmā that we do not know or see, this is the only straight path...leading to union with Brahmā." What do you think, Vāseṭṭha? Such being the case, does not what these Brahmins declare turn out to be ill-founded?' 'Yes indeed, Reverend Gotama.'

15. 'Well, Vāseṭṭha, when these Brahmins learned in the Three Vedas teach a path that they do not know or see, saying: "This is the only straight path...",this cannot possibly be right. Just as a file of blind men go on, clinging to each other, and the first one sees nothing, the middle one sees nothing, and the last one sees nothing[253] – so it is with the talk of these Brahmins learned in the Three Vedas: the first one [240] sees nothing, the middle one sees nothing, the last one sees nothing. The talk of these Brahmins learned in the Three Vedas turns out to be laughable, mere words, empty and vain.

16. 'What do you think, Vāseṭṭha? Do these Brahmins learned in the Three Vedas see the sun and moon just as other people do, and when the sun and moon rise and set do they pray, sing praises and worship with clasped hands?' 'They do, Reverend Gotama.'

17. 'What do you think, Vāseṭṭha? These Brahmins learned in the Three Vedas, who can see the sun and moon just as other people do,...can they point out a way to union with the sun and moon, saying: "This is the only straight path... that leads to union with the sun and moon"?' 'No, Reverend Gotama.'

18. 'So, Vāseṭṭha, these Brahmins learned in the Three Vedas cannot point out a way to union with the sun and moon, which they have seen. And, too, none of them has seen Brahmā face to face,...[241] nor has even the ancestor seven generations back of one of their teachers. Nor could any of the early sages say: "We know and see when, how and where

Brahmā appears." Does not what these Brahmins declare turn out to be ill-founded?' 'Yes indeed, Reverend Gotama.'

19. 'Vāseṭṭha, it is just as if a man were to say: "I am going to seek out and love the most beautiful girl in the country." They might say to him: "...Do you know what caste she belongs to?" "No." "Well, do you know her [242] name, her clan, whether she is tall or short..., dark or light-complexioned..., or where she comes from?" "No." And they might say: "Well then, you don't know or see the one you seek for and desire?" and he would say: "No." Does not the talk of that man turn out to be stupid?' 'Certainly, Reverend Gotama.'

20. 'Then, Vāseṭṭha, it is like this: not one of these Brahmins ...has seen Brahmā face to face, nor has one of their teachers ...' 'Yes indeed, Reverend Gotama.'

'That is right, Vāseṭṭha. When these Brahmins learned in the Three Vedas [243] teach a path that they do not know and see, this cannot possibly be right.

21. 'Vāseṭṭha, it is just as if a man were to build a staircase for a palace at a crossroads. People might say: "This staircase for a palace – do you know whether the palace will face east or west, north or south, or whether it will be high, low or of medium height?" and he would say: "No." And they might say: "Well then, you don't know or see what kind of a palace you are building the staircase for?" and he would say: "No." Does not the talk of that man turn out to be stupid?' 'Certainly, Reverend Gotama.'

22–23. (*as verse 20*) [244]

24. 'Vāseṭṭha, it is just as if this River Aciravatī were brimful of water so that a crow could drink out of it, and a man should come along wishing to cross over, to get to the other side, to get across, and, standing on this bank, were to call out: "Come here, other bank, come here!" What do you think, Vāseṭṭha? Would the other bank of the River Aciravatī come over to this side on account of that man's calling, begging, requesting or wheedling?' 'No, Reverend Gotama.'

25. 'Well now, Vāseṭṭha, those Brahmins learned in the Three Vedas who persistently neglect what a Brahmin should do, and persistently do what a Brahmin should not do, declare:

"We call on Indra, Soma, Varuṇa, Isāna, Pajāpati, Brahmā, Mahiddhi, Yama." But that such Brahmins who persistently [245] neglect what a Brahmin should do,...will, as a consequence of their calling, begging, requesting or wheedling, attain after death, at the breaking-up of the body, to union with Brahmā – that is just not possible.

26. 'Vāseṭṭha, it is just as if this River Aciravatī were brimful of water so that a crow could drink out of it, and a man should come wishing to cross over,...but he was bound and pinioned on this side by a strong chain, with his hands behind his back. What do you think, Vāseṭṭha? Would that man be able to get to the other side?' 'No, Reverend Gotama.'

27. 'In just the same way, Vāseṭṭha, in the Ariyan discipline these five strands of sense-desire are called bonds and fetters. Which five? Forms seen by the eye which are agreeable, loved, charming, attractive, pleasurable, arousing desire; sounds heard by the ear...; smells smelt by the nose...; tastes savoured by the tongue...; contacts felt by the body which are agreeable,...arousing desire. These five in the Ariyan discipline are called bonds and fetters. And, Vāseṭṭha, those Brahmins learned in the Three Vedas are enslaved, infatuated by these five strands of sense-desire, which they enjoy guiltily, unaware of danger, knowing no way out.

28. 'But that such Brahmins learned in the Three Vedas, who persistently neglect what a Brahmin should do,...[246] who are enslaved by these five strands of sense-desire,... knowing no way out, should attain after death, at the breaking-up of the body, to union with Brahmā – that is just not possible.

29. 'It is just as if this River Aciravatī were brimful of water so that a crow could drink out of it, and a man should come along wishing to cross over...and were to lie down on this bank, covering his head with a shawl. What do you think, Vāseṭṭha? Would that man be able to get to the other side?' 'No, Reverend Gotama.'

30. 'In the same way, Vāseṭṭha, in the Ariyan discipline these five hindrances are called obstacles, hindrances, coverings-up, envelopings. Which five? The hindrance of sensuality, of ill-will, of sloth-and-torpor, of worry-and-flurry, of doubt.

These five are called obstacles, hindrances, coverings-up, envelopings. And these Brahmins learned in the Three Vedas are caught up, hemmed in, obstructed, entangled in these five hindrances. But that such Brahmins learned in the Three Vedas, who persistently neglect what a Brahmin should do... and who are caught up,...entangled in these five hindrances, should attain after death, at the breaking-up of the body, [247] to union with Brahmā – that is just not possible.

31. 'What do you think, Vāseṭṭha? What have you heard said by Brahmins who are venerable, aged, the teachers of teachers? Is Brahmā encumbered with wives and wealth,[254] or unencumbered?' 'Unencumbered, Reverend Gotama.'

'Is he full of hate or without hate?' 'Without hate, Reverend Gotama.'

'Is he full of ill-will or without ill-will?' 'Without ill-will, Reverend Gotama.'

'Is he impure or pure?' 'Pure, Reverend Gotama.'

'Is he disciplined[255] or undisciplined?' 'Disciplined, Reverend Gotama.'

32. 'And what do you think, Vāseṭṭha? Are the Brahmins learned in the Three Vedas encumbered with wives and wealth, or unencumbered?' 'Encumbered, Reverend Gotama.'

'Are they full of hate or without hate?' 'Full of hate, Reverend Gotama.'

'Are they full of ill-will or without ill-will?' 'Full of ill-will, Reverend Gotama.'

'Are they impure or pure?' 'Impure, Reverend Gotama.'

'Are they disciplined or undisciplined?' 'Undisciplined, Reverend Gotama.'

33. 'So, Vāseṭṭha, the Brahmins learned in the Three Vedas are encumbered with wives and wealth, and Brahmā is unencumbered. Is there any communion, anything in common between these encumbered Brahmins and the unencumbered Brahmā?' 'No, Reverend Gotama.'

34. 'That is right, Vāseṭṭha. That these encumbered Brahmins, learned in the Three Vedas, should after death, at the breaking-up of the body, [248] be united with the unencumbered Brahmā – that is just not possible.

35. 'Likewise, do these Brahmins learned in the Three Vedas

and full of hate..., full of ill-will..., impure..., undisciplined, have any communion, anything in common with the disciplined Brahmā?' 'No, Reverend Gotama.'

36. 'That is right, Vāseṭṭha. That these undisciplined Brahmins should after death be united with Brahmā is just not possible. But these Brahmins learned in the Three Vedas, having sat down on the bank, sink down despairingly, thinking maybe to find a dry way across. Therefore their threefold knowledge is called the threefold desert, the threefold wilderness, the threefold destruction.'

37. At these words Vāseṭṭha said: 'Reverend Gotama, I have heard them say: "The ascetic Gotama knows the way to union with Brahmā."'

'What do you think, Vāseṭṭha? Suppose there were a man here born and brought up in Manasākaṭa, and somebody who had come from Manasākaṭa and [249] and had missed the road should ask him the way. Would that man, born and bred in Manasākaṭa, be in a state of confusion or perplexity?' 'No, Reverend Gotama. And why not? Because such a man would know all the paths.'

38. 'Vāseṭṭha, it might be said that such a man on being asked the way might be confused or perplexed – but the Tathāgata, on being asked about the Brahmā world and the way to get there, would certainly not be confused or perplexed. For, Vāseṭṭha, I know Brahmā and the world of Brahmā, and the way to the world of Brahmā, and the path of practice whereby the world of Brahmā may be gained.'

39. At this Vāseṭṭha said: 'Reverend Gotama, I have heard them say: "The ascetic Gotama teaches the way to union with Brahmā." It would be good if the Reverend Gotama were to teach us the way to union with Brahmā, may the Reverend Gotama help the people of Brahmā!'

'Then, Vāseṭṭha, listen, pay proper attention, and I will tell you.' 'Very good, Reverend Sir', said Vāseṭṭha. The Lord said:

40–75. 'Vāseṭṭha, a Tathāgata arises in the world, an Arahant, fully-enlightened Buddha, endowed with wisdom and conduct, Well-Farer, Knower of the worlds, incomparable Trainer of men to be tamed, Teacher of gods and humans, enlightened and blessed. He, having realised it by his own super-knowledge, proclaims this world with its devas, māras and Brahmās, its princes and people. He preaches the Dhamma which is lovely in its beginning, lovely in its middle, lovely in its ending, in the spirit and in the letter, and displays the fully-perfected and purified holy life. [250] *A disciple goes forth, practises the moralities, attains the first jhāna (as Sutta 2, verses 43–75).*

76. 'Then, with his heart filled with loving-kindness, he dwells suffusing one quarter, [251] the second, the third, the fourth. Thus he dwells suffusing the whole world, upwards, downwards, across, everywhere, always with a heart filled with loving-kindness, abundant, unbounded,[256] without hate or ill-will.

77. 'Just as if a mighty trumpeter were with little difficulty to make a proclamation to the four quarters, so by this meditation, Vāseṭṭha, by this liberation of the heart through loving-kindness he leaves nothing untouched, nothing unaffected in the sensuous sphere.[257] This, Vāseṭṭha, is the way to union with Brahmā.

78. 'Then with his heart filled with compassion,...with sympathetic joy, with equanimity he dwells suffusing one quarter, the second, the third, the fourth. Thus he dwells suffusing the whole world, upwards, downwards, across, everywhere, always with a heart filled with equanimity, abundant, unbounded, without hate or ill-will.

79. 'Just as if a mighty trumpeter were with little difficulty to make a proclamation to the four quarters, so by this meditation, Vāseṭṭha, by this liberation of the heart through compassion,...through sympathetic joy,...through equanimity, he leaves nothing untouched, nothing unaffected in the sensuous sphere. This, Vāseṭṭha, is the way to union with Brahmā.

80. 'What do you think, Vāseṭṭha? Is a monk dwelling thus encumbered with wives and wealth or unencumbered?' 'Unencumbered, Reverend Gotama. He is without hate..., without ill-will..., pure and disciplined, Reverend Gotama.' [252]

81. 'Then, Vāseṭṭha, the monk is unencumbered, and Brahmā is unencumbered. Has that unencumbered monk anything in common with the unencumbered Brahmā?' 'Yes indeed, Reverend Gotama.'

'That is right, Vāseṭṭha. Then that an unencumbered monk, after death, at the breaking-up of the body, should attain to union with the unencumbered Brahmā – that is possible. Likewise a monk without hate..., without ill-will..., pure..., disciplined...Then that a disciplined monk, after death, at the breaking-up of the body, should attain to union with Brahmā – that is possible.'

82. At this the young Brahmins Vāseṭṭha and Bhāradvāja said to the Lord: 'Excellent, Reverend Gotama, excellent! It is as if someone were to set up what had been knocked down, or to point out the way to one who had got lost, or to bring an oil-lamp into a dark place, so that those with eyes could see what was there. Just so the Reverend Gotama has expounded the Dhamma in various ways.'

'We take refuge in the Reverend Gotama, in the Dhamma, and in the Sangha. May the Reverend Gotama accept us as lay-followers having taken refuge from this day forth as long as life shall last!'[258]

Division Two
The Great Division

14 *Mahâpadāna Sutta: The Great Discourse on the Lineage*

[1] 1.1. THUS HAVE I HEARD.[259] Once the Lord was staying at Sāvatthi, in Anāthapiṇḍika's park in the Jeta grove, in the Kareri hutment. And among a number of monks who had gathered together after their meal, after the alms-round, sitting in the Kareri pavilion, there arose a serious discussion on former lives, as they said: 'This is how it was in a former life', or 'That was how it was.'

1.2. And the Lord, with the purified divine-ear faculty surpassing the powers of humans, heard what they were talking about. Getting up from his seat, he went to the Kareri pavilion, sat down on the prepared seat, and said: 'Monks, what was your conversation as you sat together? What discussion did I interrupt?' And they told him. [2]

1.3. 'Well, monks, would you like to hear a proper discourse on past lives?' 'Lord, it is time for that! Well-Farer, it is time for that! If the Lord were to give a proper discourse on past lives, the monks would listen and remember it!' 'Well then, monks, listen, pay close attention, and I will speak.'

'Yes, Lord', the monks replied, and the Lord said:

1.4. 'Monks, ninety-one aeons ago the Lord, the Arahant, the fully-enlightened Buddha Vipassī arose in the world. Thirty-one aeons ago the Lord Buddha Sikhī arose; in the same thirty-first aeon before this Lord Buddha Vessabhū arose. And in this present fortunate aeon[260] the Lords Buddhas Kakusandha, Konāgamana and Kassapa arose in the world. And, monks, in this present fortunate aeon I too have now arisen in the world as a fully-enlightened Buddha.

1.5. 'The Lord Buddha Vipassī was born of Khattiya race, and arose in a Khattiya family; the Lord Buddha Sikhī likewise; [3] the Lord Buddha Vessabhū likewise; the Lord Buddha Kakusandha was born of Brahmin race, and arose in a Brahmin family; the Lord Buddha Konāgamana likewise; the Lord Buddha Kassapa likewise; and I, monks, who am now the Arahant and fully-enlightened Buddha, was born of Khattiya race, and arose in a Khattiya family.

1.6. 'The Lord Buddha Vipassī was of the Kondañña clan; the Lord Buddah Sikhī likewise; the Lord Buddah Vessabhū likewise; the Lord Buddha Kakusandha was of the Kassapa clan; the Lord Buddha Konagāmana likewise; the Lord Buddha Kassapa likwise; I who am now the Arahant and fully-enlightened Buddha, am of the Gotama clan.

1.7. 'In the time of the Lord Buddha Vipassī the life-span was eighty thousand years; in the time of the Lord Buddha Sikhī seventy thousand; in the time of the Lord Buddha Vessabhū sixty thousand; in the time of the Lord Buddha Kakusandhu forty thousand; in the time of the Lord Buddha Konāgamana thirty thousand; [4] in the time of the Lord Buddha Kassapa it wạs twenty thousand years. In my time the life-span is short, limited and quick to pass: it is seldom that anybody lives to be a hundred.

1.8. 'The Lord Buddha Vipassī gained his full enlightenment at the foot of a trumpet-flower tree; the Lord Buddha Sikhī under a white-mango tree; the Lord Buddha Vessabhū under a *sāl*-tree; the Lord Buddha Kakusandha under an acacia-tree; the Lord Buddha Konāgamana under a fig-tree; the Lord Buddha Kassapa under a banyan-tree; and I became fully enlightened at the foot of an *assattha*-tree.[261]

1.9. 'The Lord Buddha Vipassī had the pair of noble disciples Khaṇḍa and Tissa; the Lord Buddha Sikhī had Abhibhū and Sambhava; the Lord Buddha Vessabhū had Soṇa and Uttara; the Lord Buddha Kakusandha had Vidhūra and Sañjīva; the Lord Buddha Konāgamana had Bhiyyosa and Uttara; [5] the Lord Buddha Kassapa had Tissa and Bhāradvāja; I myself now have the pair of noble disciples Sāriputta and Moggallāna.

1.10. 'The Lord Buddha Vipassī had three assemblies of disciples: one of six million eight hundred thousand, one of a hundred thousand, and one of eighty thousand monks, and of these three assemblies all were Arahants; the Lord Buddha

Sikhī had three assemblies of disciples: one of a hundred thousand, one of eighty thousand, and one of seventy thousand monks – all Arahants; the Lord Buddha Vessabhū had three assemblies: one of eighty thousand, one of seventy thousand, and one of sixty thousand monks – all Arahants; the Lord Buddha Kakusandha had one assembly: forty thousand monks – all Arahants; the Lord Buddha Konāgamana [6] had one assembly: thirty thousand monks – all Arahants; the Lord Buddha Kassapa had one assembly: twenty thousand monks – all Arahants; I, monks, have one assembly of disciples, one thousand two hundred and fifty monks, and this one assembly consists only of Arahants.

1.11. 'The Lord Buddha Vipassī's personal attendant was the monk Asoka; the Lord Buddha Sikhī's was Khemankara; the Lord Buddha Vessabhū's was Upasannaka; the Lord Buddha Kakusandhu's was Vuḍḍhija; the Lord Buddha Konāgamana's was Sotthija; the Lord Buddha Kassapa's was Sabbamitta; my chief personal attendant now is Ānanda.

1.12. 'The Lord Buddha Vipassī's father was King Bandhumā, [7] his mother was Queen Bandhumatī, and King Bandhumā's royal capital was Bandhumatī. The Lord Buddha Sikhī's father was King Aruṇa, his mother was Queen Pabhāvatī; King Aruṇa's capital was Aruṇavatī. The Lord Buddha Vessabhū's father was King Suppatīta, his mother was Queen Yasavatī; King Suppatīta's capital was Anopama. The Lord Buddha Kakusandha's father was the Brahmin Aggidatta, his mother was the Brahmin lady Visākhā. The king at that time was called Khema; his capital was Khemavatī. The Lord Buddha Konāgamana's father was the Brahmin Yaññadatta, his mother was the Brahmin lady Uttarā. The king at that time was Sobha; his capital was Sobhavatī. The Lord Buddha Kassapa's father was the Brahmin Brahmadatta, his mother was the Brahmin lady Dhanavatī. The king at that time was Kikī; his capital was Vārāṇasī. And now, monks, my father was King Suddhodana, my mother was Queen Māyā, and the royal capital was Kapilavatthu.'

Thus the Lord spoke, and the Well-Farer then rose from his seat and went to his lodging. [8]

1.13. Soon after the Lord had gone, another discussion arose among the monks:[262] 'It is marvellous, friends, it is wonderful, the Tathāgata's great power and ability – the way he recalls past Buddhas who have gained Parinibbāna, having cut away the hindrances, cut off the road [of craving], put an end to the round of becoming, overcome all suffering. He recalls their birth, their name, their clan, their life-span, the disciples and assemblies connected with him: "Being born thus, these Blessed Lords were such-and-such, such were their names, their clans, their discipline, their Dhamma, their wisdom, their liberation." Well now, friends, how did the Tathāgata come by the penetrative knowledge through which he remembers all this ...? Did some deva reveal this knowledge to [9] him?' This was the conversation of those monks which came to be interrupted.

1.14. Then the Lord, rising from the seclusion of the rest-period, went to the Kareri pavilion and sat down on the prepared seat. He said: 'Monks, what was your conversation as you sat together? What discussion did I interrupt?' And the monks [10] told him.

1.15. 'The Tathāgata understands these things...by his own penetration of the principles of Dhamma; and devas, too, have told him. Well, monks, do you wish to hear still more [11] about past lives?' 'Lord, it is time for that! Well-Farer, it is time for that! If the Lord were to give a proper discourse on past lives, the monks would listen and remember it.' 'Well then, monks, listen, pay close attention, and I will speak.' 'Yes, Lord', the monks replied, and the Lord said:

1.16. 'Monks, ninety-one aeons ago the Lord, the Arahant, the fully-enlightened Buddha Vipassī arose in the world. He was born of Khattiya race, and arose in a Khattiya family. He was of the Koṇḍañña clan. The span of his life was eighty thousand years. He gained his full enlightenment at the foot of a trumpet-flower tree. He had the pair of noble disciples Khaṇḍa and Tissa as his chief followers. He had three assemblies of disciples: one of six million eight hundred thousand, one of a hundred thousand, and one of eighty thousand monks, all Arahants. His chief personal attendant was the monk Asoka. His father was King Bandhumā, [12] his mother was Queen Bandhumatī. The king's capital was Bandhumatī.

1.17. [263]'And so, monks, the Bodhisatta Vipassī descended from the Tusita heaven, mindful and clearly aware, into his mother's womb. This, monks, is the rule.[264]

'It is the rule, monks, that when a Bodhisatta descends from the Tusita heaven into his mother's womb, there appears in this world with its devas, māras and Brahmās, its ascetics and Brahmins, princes and people an immeasurable, splendid light surpassing the glory of the most powerful devas. And whatever dark spaces lie beyond the world's end, chaotic, blind and black, such that they are not even reached by the mighty rays of sun and moon, are yet illumined by this immeasurable splendid light surpassing the glory of the most powerful devas. And those beings that have been reborn there[265] recognise each other by this light and know: "Other beings, too, have been born here!" And this ten-thousandfold world-system trembles and quakes and is convulsed. And this immeasurable light shines forth. That is the rule.

'It is the rule that when a Bodhisatta has entered his mother's womb, four devas[266] come to protect him from the four quarters, saying: "Let no man, no non-human being, no thing whatever harm this Bodhisatta or this Bodhisatta's mother!" That is the rule.

1.18. 'It is the rule that when a Bodhisatta has entered his mother's womb, his mother becomes by nature virtuous, refraining from taking life, from taking what is not given, from sexual [13] misconduct, from lying speech, or from strong drink and sloth-producing drugs. That is the rule.

1.19. 'It is the rule that when a Bodhisatta has entered his mother's womb, she has no sensual thoughts connected with a man, and she cannot be overcome by any man with lustful thoughts. That is the rule.

1.20. 'It is the rule that when a Bodhisatta has entered his mother's womb, she enjoys the fivefold pleasures of the senses and takes delight, being endowed and possessed of them. That is the rule.

1.21. 'It is the rule that when a Bodhisatta has entered his mother's womb, she has no sickness of any kind, she is at ease and without fatigue of body, and she can see the Bodhisatta inside her womb, complete with all his members and faculties. Monks, it is as if a gem, a beryl, pure, excellent, well cut into eight facets, clear, bright, flawless and perfect in every respect, were strung on a blue, yellow, red, white or orange cord. And a man with good eyesight, taking it in his hand, would describe it as such. Thus does the Bodhisatta's mother, with no sickness, [14] see him, complete with all his members and faculties. That is the rule.

1.22. 'It is the rule that the Bodhisatta's mother dies seven days after his birth and is reborn in the Tusita heaven. That is the rule.

1.23. 'It is the rule that whereas other women carry the child in their womb for nine or ten months before giving birth, it is not so with the Bodhisatta's mother, who carries him for exactly ten months before giving birth. That is the rule.

1.24. 'It is the rule that whereas other women give birth sitting or lying down, it is not so with the Bodhisatta's mother, who gives birth standing up. That is the rule.

1.25. 'It is the rule that when the Bodhisatta issues from his mother's womb, devas welcome him first, and then humans. That is the rule.

1.26. 'It is the rule that when the Bodhisatta issues from his mother's womb, he does not touch the earth. Four devas[267] receive him and place him before his mother, saying: "Rejoice, Your Majesty, a mighty son has been born to you!" That is the rule.

1.27. 'It is the rule that when the Bodhisatta issues from his mother's womb he issues forth stainless, not defiled by water, mucus, blood or any impurity, pure and spotless. Just as when a jewel is laid on muslin from Kāsī,[268] the jewel does not stain the muslin, or the muslin the jewel. Why not? Because of the purity of both. In the same way the Bodhisatta issues forth stainless...[15] That is the rule.

1.28. 'It is the rule that when the Bodhisatta issues forth from his mother's womb, two streams of water appear from the sky, one cold, the other warm, with which they ritually wash the Bodhisatta and his mother. That is the rule.

1.29. 'It is the rule that as soon as he is born the Bodhisatta takes a firm stance on both feet facing north, then takes seven strides and, under a white sunshade,[269] he scans the four quarters and then declares with a bull-like voice: "I am chief in the world, supreme in the world, eldest in the world. This is my last birth, there will be no more re-becoming."[270] That is the rule.

1.30. 'It is the rule that when the Bodhisatta issues from his mother's womb there appears in this world...an immeasurable, splendid light...(*as verse 17*). This is the rule.[271] [16]

1.31. 'Monks, when Prince Vipassī was born, they showed him to King Bandhumā and said: "Your Majesty, a son has been born to you. Deign, Sire, to look at him." The king looked at the prince and then said to the Brahmins skilled in signs: "You gentlemen are skilled in signs, examine the prince." The Brahmins examined the prince, and said to King Bandhumā: "Sire, rejoice, for a mighty son has been born to you. It is a gain for you, Sire, it is a great profit for you, Sire, that such a son has been born into your family. Sire, this prince is endowed with the thirty-two marks of a Great Man. To such, only two courses are open. If he lives the household life he will become a ruler, a wheel-turning righteous monarch of the law, conqueror of the four quarters, who has established the security of his realm and is possessed of the seven treasures. These are: the Wheel Treasure, the Elephant Treasure, the Horse Treasure, the Jewel Treasure, the Woman Treasure, the Householder Treasure, and, as seventh, the Counsellor Treasure. He has more than a thousand sons who are heroes, of heroic stature, conquerors of the hostile army. He dwells having conquered this sea-girt land without stick or sword, by the law. But if he goes forth from the household life into homelessness, then he will become an Arahant, a fully-enlightened Buddha, one who draws back the veil from the world."

1.32. '"And what, Sire, are these thirty-two marks...?[272] [17] (1) He has feet with level tread. (2) On the soles of his feet are wheels with a thousand spokes. (3) He has projecting heels. (4) He has long fingers and toes. (5) He has soft and tender hands and feet. (6) His hands and feet are net-like. (7) He has high-raised ankles. (8) His legs are like an antelope's. (9) Standing and without bending, he can touch and rub his knees with either hand. (10) His male organs are enclosed in a sheath. (11)

His complexion is bright, the colour of gold. (12) His skin is delicate and so smooth that no [18] dust adheres to it. (13) His body-hairs are separate, one to each pore. (14) They grow upwards, bluish-black like collyrium, growing in rings to the right. (15) His body is divinely straight. (16) He has the seven convex surfaces. (17) The front part of his body is like a lion's. (18) There is no hollow between his shoulders. (19) He is proportioned like a banyan-tree: his height is as the span of his arms. (20) His bust is evenly rounded. (21) He has a perfect sense of taste. (22) He has jaws like a lion's. (23) He has forty teeth. (24) His teeth are even. (25) There are no spaces between his teeth. (26) His canine teeth are very bright. (27) His tongue is very long. (28) He has a Brahmā-like voice, like that of the *karavīka*-bird. (29) His eyes are deep blue. (30) He has eyelashes like a cow's. (31) The hair between his eyebrows is white, and soft like [19] cotton-down. (32) His head is like a royal turban."

1.33. '"Sire, this prince is endowed with the thirty-two marks of a Great Man. To such, only two courses are open. If he lives the household life he will become a ruler, a wheel-turning righteous monarch of the law...But if he goes forth from the household life into homelessness, then he will become an Arahant, a fully-enlightened Buddha, one who draws back the veil from the world."

'Then King Bandhumā, having clothed those Brahmins in fresh clothes, satisfied all their wishes.

1.34. 'And King Bandhumā appointed nurses for Prince Vipassī. Some suckled him, some bathed him, some carried him, some dandled him. A white umbrella was held over him night and day, that he might not be harmed by cold or heat or grass or dust. And Prince Vipassī was much beloved of the people. Just as everybody loves a blue, [20] yellow or white lotus, so they all loved Prince Vipassī. Thus he was borne from lap to lap.

1.35. 'And Prince Vipassī had a sweet voice, a beautiful voice, charming and delightful. Just as in the Himālaya mountains the *karavīka*-bird has a voice sweeter, more beautiful, charming and delightful than all other birds, so too was Prince Vipassī's voice the finest of all.

1.36. 'And owing to the results of past kamma, the divine eye was present to Prince Vipassī, with which he could see for a league day and night alike.

1.37. 'And Prince Vipassī was unblinkingly watchful, like the Thirty-Three Gods. And because it was said that he was unblinkingly watchful, the prince came to be called "Vipassī".[273] When King Bandhumā was trying a case, he took Prince Vipassī on his knee and instructed him [21] in the case. Then, putting him down from his knee, his father would carefully explain the issues to him. And for this reason he was all the more called Vipassī.

1.38. 'Then King Bandhumā caused three palaces to be built for Prince Vipassī, one for the rainy season, one for the cold season, and one for the hot season, to cater for all the fivefold sense-pleasures. There Prince Vipassī stayed in the rainy-season palace for the four months of the rainy season, with no male attendants, surrounded by female musicians, and he never left that palace.'

[*End of first recitation-section* (*the birth-section*)]

2.1. 'Then, monks, after many years, many hundreds and thousands of years had passed,[274] Prince Vipassī said to his charioteer: "Harness some fine carriages, charioteer! We will go to the pleasure-park to inspect it." The charioteer did so, then reported to the prince: "Your Royal Highness, the fine carriages are harnessed, it is time to do as you wish." And Prince Vipassī mounted a carriage and drove in procession to the pleasure-park.

2.2 'And as he was being driven to the pleasure-park, Prince Vipassī saw [22] an aged man, bent like a roof-beam, broken, leaning on a stick, tottering, sick, his youth all vanished. At the sight he said to the charioteer: "Charioteer, what is the matter with this man? His hair is not like other men's, his body is not like other men's."

'"Prince, that is what is called an old man." "But why is he called an old man?"

'"He is called old, Prince, because he has not long to live."

'"But am I liable to become old, and not exempt from old age?" "Both you and I, Prince, are liable to become old, and are not exempt from old age."

'"Well then, charioteer, that will do for today with the pleasure-park. Return now to the palace." "Very good, Prince", said the charioteer, and brought Prince Vipassī back to the palace.[275] Arrived there, Prince Vipassī was overcome with grief and dejection, crying: "Shame on this thing birth, since to him who is born old age must manifest itself!"

2.3. 'Then King Bandhumā sent for the charioteer and said: "Well, did not the prince enjoy himself at the pleasure-park? Wasn't he happy there?" "Your Majesty, the prince did not enjoy himself, he was not happy there." "What did he see on the way there?" [23] So the charioteer told the King all that had happened.

2.4. 'Then King Bandhumā thought: "Prince Vipassī must not renounce the throne, he must not go forth from the household life into homelessness – the words of the Brahmins learned in signs must not come true!" So the King provided for Prince Vipassī to have even more enjoyment of the fivefold sense-pleasures, in order that he should rule the kingdom and not go forth from the household life into homelessness... Thus the prince continued to live indulging in, and addicted to the fivefold sense-pleasures.

2.5 *'After many hundreds of thousands of years Prince Vipassī ordered his charioteer to drive to the pleasure-park* (*as verse 2.1*). [24]

2.6. 'And as he was being driven to the pleasure-park, Prince Vipassī saw a sick man, suffering, very ill, fallen in his own urine and excrement, and some people were picking him up, and others putting him to bed. At the sight he said to the charioteer: "What is the matter with this man? His eyes are not like other men's, his head[276] is not like other men's."

'"Prince, that is what is called a sick man." "But why is he called a sick man?"

'"Prince, he is so called because he can hardly recover from his illness."

'"But am I liable to become sick, and not exempt from sickness?" "Both you and I, Prince, are liable to become sick, and not exempt from sickness."

'"Well then, charioteer, return now to the palace." Arrived there, Prince Vipassī was overcome with grief and dejection, crying: "Shame on this thing birth, since he who is born must experience sickness!"

2.7. 'Then King Bandhumā sent for the charioteer, who told him what had happened. [25]

2.8. 'The king provided Prince Vipassī with even more sense-pleasures, in order that he should rule the kingdom and not go forth from the household life into homelessness...

2.9 *'After many hundreds of thousands of years Prince Vipassī ordered his charioteer to drive to the pleasure-park.*

2.10. 'And as he was being driven to the pleasure-park, Prince Vipassī saw a large crowd collecting, clad in many colours, and carrying a bier. At the sight he said to the charioteer: "Why are those people doing that?" [26] "Prince, that is what they call a dead man." "Drive me over to where the dead man is." "Very good, Prince, said the charioteer, and did so. And Prince Vipassī gazed at the corpse of the dead man. Then he said to the charioteer: "Why is he called a dead man?"

'"Prince, he is called a dead man because now his parents and other relatives will not see him again, nor he them."

'"But am I subject to dying, not exempt from dying?" "Both you and I, Prince, are subject to dying, not exempt from it."

'"Well then, charioteer, that will do for today with the pleasure-park. Return now to the palace...Arrived there, Prince Vipassī was overcome with grief and dejection, crying: "Shame on this thing birth, since to him who is born death must manifest itself!"

2.11. 'Then King Bandhumā sent for the charioteer, who told him what had happened. [27]

2.12. 'The king provided Prince Vipassī with even more sense-pleasures...[28]

2.13 *'After many hundreds of thousands of years Prince Vipassī ordered his charioteer to drive to the pleasure-park.*

2.14. 'And as he was being driven to the pleasure-park, Prince Vipassī saw a shaven-headed man, one who had gone forth,[277] wearing a yellow robe. And he said to the charioteer: "What is the matter with that man? His head is not like other men's, and his clothes are not like other men's."

'"Prince, he is called one who has gone forth." "Why is he called one who has gone forth?"

'"Prince, by one who has gone forth we mean one who truly follows Dhamma,[278] who truly lives in serenity, does good actions, performs meritorious deeds, is harmless and truly has compassion for living beings."

'"Charioteer, he is well called one who has gone forth... [29] Drive the carriage over to where he is." "Very good, Prince", said the charioteer, and did so. And Prince Vipassī questioned the man who had gone forth.

'"Prince, as one who has gone forth I truly follow Dhamma, ...and have compassion for living beings." "You are well called one who has gone forth..."

2.15. 'Then Prince Vipassī said to the charioteer: "You take the carriage and drive back to the palace. But I shall stay here and shave off my hair and beard, put on yellow robes, and go forth from the household life into homelessness." "Very good, Prince", said the charioteer, and returned to the palace. And Prince Vipassī, shaving off his hair and beard and putting on yellow robes, went forth from the household life into homelessness.

2.16. 'And a great crowd from the royal capital city, Bandhumatī, eighty-four thousand people,[279] heard that [30] Prince Vipassī had gone forth into homelessness. And they thought: "This is certainly no common teaching and discipline, no common going-forth, for which Prince Vipassī has shaved off hair and beard, donned yellow robes and gone forth into homelessness. If the Prince has done so, why should not we?" And so, monks, a great crowd of eighty-four thousand, having shaved off their hair and beards and donned yellow robes, followed the Bodhisatta Vipassī[280] into homelessness. And with this following the Bodhisatta went on his rounds through villages, towns and royal cities.

2.17. 'Then the Bodhisatta Vipassī, having retired to a secluded spot, had this thought: "It is not proper for me to live with a crowd like this. I must live alone, withdrawn from this crowd." So after a while he left the crowd and dwelt alone. The eighty-four thousand went one way, the Bodhisatta another.

2.18. 'Then, when the Bodhisatta had entered his dwelling

alone, in a secluded spot, he thought: "This world, alas, is in a sorry state: there is birth and decay,[281] there is death and falling into other states and being reborn. And no one knows [31] any way of escape from this suffering, this ageing and death. When will deliverance be found from this suffering, this ageing and death?"

'And then, monks, the Bodhisatta thought: "With what being present, does ageing-and-death occur? What conditions ageing-and-death?" And then, monks, as a result of the wisdom born of profound consideration[282] the realisation dawned on him: "*Birth* being present, ageing-and-death occurs, birth conditions ageing-and-death."[283]

'Then he thought: "What conditions birth?" And the realisation dawned on him: "Becoming[284] conditions birth"..."What conditions becoming?"..."Clinging conditions becoming"... "Craving conditions clinging"..."Feeling conditions craving" ...[32] "Contact[285] conditions feeling"..."The six sense-bases condition contact"..."Mind-and-body conditions the six sense-bases"..."Consciousness conditions mind-and-body." And then the Bodhisatta Vipassī thought: "With what being present, does consciousness occur. What conditions consciousness?" And then, as a result of the wisdom born of profound consideration, the realisation dawned on him: "Mind-and-body conditions consciousness."

2.19. 'Then, monks, the Bodhisatta Vipassī thought: "This consciousness turns back at mind-and-body, it does not go any further.[286] To this extent there is birth and decay, there is death and falling into other states and being reborn, namely: Mind-and-body conditions consciousness and consciousness conditions mind-and-body, mind-and-body conditions the six sense-bases, the six sense-bases-condition contact, contact conditions feeling, feeling conditions [33] craving, craving conditions clinging, clinging conditions becoming, becoming conditions birth, birth conditions ageing and death, sorrow, lamentation, pain, grief and distress. And thus this whole mass of suffering takes its origin." And at the thought: "Origin, origin", there arose in the Bodhisatta Vipassī, with insight into things never realised before, knowledge, wisdom, awareness, and light.

2.20. 'Then he thought: "What now being absent, does ageing-and-death not occur? With the cessation of what comes the cessation of ageing-and-death?" And then, as a result of the wisdom born of profound consideration, the realisation dawned on him: "Birth being absent, ageing-and-death does not occur. With the cessation of birth comes the cessation of ageing-and-death"..."With the cessation of what comes the cessation of birth?"..."With the cessation of becoming comes the cessation of birth"..."With the cessation of clinging comes the cessation of becoming"..."With the cessation of craving comes the cessation of clinging"...[34] "With the cessation of feeling comes the cessation of craving"..."With the cessation of contact comes the cessation of feeling"..."With the cessation of the six sense-bases comes the cessation of contact"... "With the cessation of mind-and-body comes the cessation of the six sense-bases"..."With the cessation of consciousness comes the cessation of mind-and-body"..."With the cessation of mind-and-body comes the cessation of consciousness."

2.21. 'Then the Bodhisatta Vipassī thought: "I have found the insight (*vipassanā*) way[287] to enlightenment, [35] namely:

'"By the cessation of mind-and-body consciousness ceases, by the cessation of consciousness, mind-and-body ceases; by the cessation of mind-and-body the six sense-bases cease; by the cessation of the six sense-bases contact ceases; by the cessation of contact feeling ceases; by the cessation of feeling craving ceases; by the cessation of craving clinging ceases; by the cessation of clinging becoming ceases; by the cessation of becoming birth ceases; by the cessation of birth ageing and death, sorrow, lamentation, pain, grief and distress cease. And thus this whole mass of suffering ceases." And at the thought: "Cessation, cessation", there arose in the Bodhisatta Vipassī, with insight into things never realised before, knowledge, vision, awareness, and light.

2.22. 'Then, monks, at another time the Bodhisatta Vipassī dwelt contemplating the rise and fall of the five aggregates of clinging: "Such is the body, such its arising, such its passing away; such is feeling...; such is perception...; such are the mental formations...; such is consciousness, such its arising, such its passing away." And as he remained contemplating the rise and fall of the five aggregates of clinging, before long his mind was freed from the corruptions without remainder.'[288]

[*End of second recitation-section*]

3.1. 'Then, monks, the Blessed Lord, the Arahant, the fully-enlightened Buddha Vipassī thought: "Suppose now I were to teach Dhamma?" And then he thought: [36] "I have attained to this Dhamma which is profound, hard to see, hard to grasp, peaceful, excellent, beyond reasoning,[289] subtle, to be apprehended by the wise. But this generation delights in clinging,[290] rejoices in it and revels in it. But for those who so delight, rejoice and revel in clinging this matter is hard to see, namely the conditioned nature of things,[291] or dependent origination.[292] Equally hard to see would be the calming of all the mental formations,[293] the abandonment of all the substrates of rebirth,[294] the waning of craving, dispassion, cessation and Nibbāna. And if I were to teach Dhamma to others and they did not understand me, that would be a weariness and a trouble to me."

3.2. 'And to the Lord Buddha Vipassī there occurred spontaneously this verse, never previously heard:

"This that I've attained, why should I proclaim?
Those full of lust and hate can never grasp it.
Leading upstream this Dhamma, subtle, deep,
Hard to see, no passion-blinded folk can see it."

'As the Lord Buddha Vipassī pondered thus, his mind was inclined to inaction rather than to teaching the Dhamma. And, monks, the Lord Buddha Vipassī's reasoning became mentally known to a certain Great Brahmā.[295] And [37] he thought: "Alas, the world is perishing, it will be destroyed because the mind of Vipassī, the Blessed Lord, the Arahant, the fully-enlightened Buddha is inclined to inaction rather than to teaching the Dhamma!"

3.3. 'So this Great Brahmā, as swiftly as a strong man might stretch his flexed arm, or flex it again, disappeared from the Brahmā world and reappeared before the Lord Buddha Vipassī. Arranging his upper robe over one shoulder and kneeling on his right knee, he saluted the Lord Buddha Vipassī with joined hands and said: "Lord, may the Blessed Lord teach Dhamma, may the Well-Farer teach Dhamma! There are beings with little dust on their eyes who are perishing through not hearing Dhamma: they will become knowers of Dhamma!"[296]

3.4. *'Then the Lord Buddha Vipassī explained (as verses 1–2 above)* [38] *why he inclined to inaction rather than to teaching the Dhamma.*

3.5.–6. 'And the Great Brahmā appealed a second and a third time to the Lord Buddha Vipassī to teach... Then the Lord Buddha Vipassī, recognising Brahmā's appeal and moved by compassion for beings, surveyed the world with his Buddha-eye.[297] And he saw beings with little dust on their eyes and with much dust, with faculties sharp and dull, of good and bad disposition, easy and hard to teach, and few of them living in fear of transgression and of the next world. And just as in a pool of blue, red or white lotuses some are born in the water, grow in the water, and, not leaving the water, thrive in the water; some are born in the water and reach the surface; while some are born in the water and, having reached the surface, grow out of the water and are not polluted by it, [39] in the same way, monks, the Lord Buddha Vipassī, surveying the world with his Buddha-eye, saw some beings with little dust on their eyes...

3.7. 'Then, knowing his thought, the Great Brahmā addressed the Lord Buddha Vipassī in these verses:

"As on a mountain-peak a watcher sees the folk below,
So, Man of Wisdom,[298] seeing all, look down from Dhamma's heights!
Free from woe, look on those who are sunk in grief, oppressed with birth and age.
Arise, hero, victor in battle, leader of the caravan, traverse the world!
Teach, O Lord, the Dhamma, and they will understand."

And the Lord Buddha Vipassī replied to the Great Brahmā in verse:

> "Open to them are the doors of the Deathless!
> Let those that hear now put forth faith.[299]
> For fear of trouble I did not preach at first
> The excellent Dhamma for men, Brahmā!"

Then that Great Brahmā, thinking: "I have been the cause of the Lord Buddha Vipassī's preaching Dhamma", [40] made obeisance to the Lord Buddha, and, passing by to his right, vanished there and then.

3.8. 'Then the Lord Buddha Vipassī thought: "To whom should I first teach this Dhamma? Who would understand it quickly?" Then he thought: "There are Khaṇḍa the King's son[300] and Tissa the chaplain's[301] son, living in the capital city of Bandhumatī. They are wise, learned, experienced, and for a long time have had little dust on their eyes. If now I teach Dhamma first to Khaṇḍa and Tissa, they will understand it quickly." And so the Lord Buddha Vipassī, as swiftly as a strong man might stretch out his flexed arm, or flex it again, vanished there and then from the root of that tree of enlightenment, and reappeared in the royal capital of Bandhumatī, in the deer-park of Khema.

3.9. 'And the Lord Buddha Vipassī said to the park-keeper: "Keeper, go to Bandhumatī and say to Prince Khaṇḍa and the chaplain's son Tissa: 'My lords, Vipassī the Blessed Lord, the Arahant, the fully-enlightened Buddha, has come to Bandhumatī and is staying in the deer-park of Khema. He wishes to see you.'"

'"Very good, Lord", said the park-keeper, and went and delivered the message.

3.10. 'Then Khaṇḍa and Tissa, [41] having harnessed some fine carriages, drove out of Bandhumatī making for the deer-park of Khema. They took the carriages as far as they would go, then alighted and continued on foot till they came to the Lord Buddha Vipassī. When they reached him, they made obeisance to him and sat down to one side.

3.11. 'And the Lord Buddha Vipassī delivered to them a graduated discourse on generosity, on morality, and on heaven,[302] showing the danger, degradation and corruption of sense-desires, and the profit of renunciation. And when the Lord Buddha Vipassī knew that the minds of Khaṇḍa and Tissa were ready, pliable, free from the hindrances, joyful and calm, then he preached the Buddhas' special sermon in brief: on suffering, its origin, its cessation, and the path. And just as a clean cloth from which all stains have been removed receives the dye perfectly, so in Prince Khaṇḍa and Tissa the chaplain's son, as they sat there, there arose the pure and spotless Dhamma-Eye, and they knew: "Whatever things have an origin must come to cessation."

3.12. 'And they, having seen, attained, experienced and penetrated the Dhamma, having passed beyond doubt, having gained perfect confidence in the Teacher's doctrine without relying on others, said: "Excellent, Lord, excellent! It is as if someone were to set up what had been knocked down, or to point out the way to one who had got lost, or to bring an oil-lamp into a dark place, so that those with eyes could see what was there. Just so the Blessed Lord has expounded the Dhamma in various ways. We go [42] for refuge to the Lord, and to the Dhamma. May we receive the going-forth at the Lord's hands, may we receive ordination!"

3.13. 'And so Prince Khaṇḍa and Tissa the chaplain's son received the going-forth at the hands of the Lord Buddha Vipassī, and they received ordination. Then the Lord Buddha Vipassī instructed them with a discourse on Dhamma, inspired them, fired them and delighted them, showing the danger, degradation and corruption of conditioned things[303] and the profit of Nibbāna.[304] And through their being inspired, fired and delighted with this discourse, it was not long before their minds were freed from the corruptions without remainder.

3.14. 'And a great crowd of eighty-four thousand people from Bandhumatī heard that the Lord Buddha Vipassī was staying in the deer-park of Khema, and that Khaṇḍa and Tissa had shaved off their hair and beards, donned yellow robes, and gone forth from the household life into homelessness. And they thought: "This is certainly no common teaching and discipline. . . for which Prince Khaṇḍa and Tissa the chaplain's son have gone forth into homelessness. If they can do this in the presence of the Lord Buddha Vipassī, why should not we?" And so this great crowd of eighty-four thousand left Bandhumatī for the deer-park of Khema where the Lord Buddha [43] Vipassī was. When they came to him they made obeisance to him and sat down to one side.

3.15. 'And the Lord Buddha Vipassī delivered to them a graduated discourse on generosity, on morality, and on heaven, showing the danger, degradation and corruption of sense-desires, and the profit of renunciation. And just as a clean cloth. . . receives the dye perfectly, so in those eighty-four thousand, as they sat there, there arose the pure and spotless Dhamma-eye, and they knew: "Whatever things have an origin must come to cessation."

3.16. (*as verse 12*)

3.17. 'And those eighty-four thousand received the going-forth at the hands of the Lord Buddha Vipassī, and they received ordination. And the Lord Buddha Vipassī instructed them with a discourse on Dhamma. . . (*as verse 13*) [44] and it was not long before their minds were freed from the corruptions without remainder.

3.18. 'Then the first eighty-four thousand who had gone forth heard: "The Lord Buddha Vipassī has come to Bandhumatī and is staying in the Khema deer-park, teaching Dhamma."

3.19.—21. 'And all happened as before. . . [45] And it was not long before their minds were freed from the corruptions without remainder.

3.22. 'And at that time, in the royal capital of Bandhumatī, there was a vast gathering of six million, eight hundred thousand[305] monks. And when the Lord Buddha Vipassī had withdrawn into seclusion, he thought: "There is now this great gathering of monks here in the capital. Suppose I were to give them permission: 'Wander abroad, monks, for the good of the many, for the happiness of the many, out of compassion for the world, for the welfare and happiness of devas and humans. Do not go two together, monks, [46] but teach the Dhamma that is lovely in its beginning, lovely in its middle, and lovely in its ending, both in the letter and in the spirit, and display the holy life fully complete and perfect. There are beings with little dust on their eyes who are perishing through not hearing Dhamma: they will become knowers of Dhamma. But at the end of six years precisely you are to come together to the royal capital of Bandhumatī to recite the disciplinary code.'"

3.23. 'Then a certain Great Brahmā, having divined the Lord Buddha Vipassī's thought, as swiftly as a strong man might stretch his flexed arm, or flex it again, vanished from the Brahmā world and appeared before the Lord Buddha Vipassī. Arranging his robe over one shoulder and saluting the Lord with joined palms, he said: "Just so, O Lord, just so, O Well-Farer! Let the Lord give permission to this great gathering to wander abroad for the good of the many,. . .out of compassion for the world. . .There are beings with little dust on their eyes, who are perishing through not hearing Dhamma: they will become knowers of Dhamma. And we too will do the same as the monks: at the end of six years we will come together to the royal capital of Bandhumatī to recite the disciplinary code."

'Having spoken thus, [47] that Brahmā made obeisance to the Lord Buddha and, passing by to his right, vanished there and then.

3.24.–25. 'So the Lord Buddha Vipassī, emerging from the seclusion of his rest-period, told the monks what had occurred occurred. [48]

3.26. '"I allow you, monks, to wander abroad for the good of the many, for the welfare and happiness of devas and humans. Do not go two together, monks, but teach the Dhamma that is lovely in its beginning, lovely in its middle, and lovely in its ending, both in the letter and in the spirit, and display the holy life fully complete and perfect. There are beings with little dust on their eyes who are perishing through not hearing Dhamma: they will become knowers of Dhamma. But at the end of six years precisely you are to come together to the royal capital of Bandhumatī to recite the disciplinary code." And the majority of those monks left that very day to wander about the country.

3.27. 'And at that time there were eighty-four thousand religious residences in Jambudīpa.[306] And at the end of one year the devas would proclaim: "Gentlemen, one year has passed, five remain. At the end of five years you are to return to Bandhumatī to recite the disciplinary code", and similarly at the end of two, [49] three, four, five years. And when six years had passed, the devas announced: "Gentlemen, six years have passed, it is now time to go to the royal capital of Bandhumatī to recite the disciplinary code!" And those monks, some by their own psychic powers and some by that of the devas, all in one day came to Bandhumatī to recite the disciplinary code.

3.28. 'And then the Lord Buddha Vipassī gave to the assembled monks the following precepts:

"Patient forbearance is the highest sacrifice,
Supreme is Nibbāna, so say the Buddhas.
He's not 'one gone forth' who hurts others,
No ascetic he who harms another.[307]

Not to do any evil, but cultivate the good,
To purify one's mind, this the Buddhas teach.[308]

Not insulting, not harming, restraint according to
  rule, [50]
Moderation in food, seclusion of dwelling,
Devotion to high thinking, this the Buddhas teach."[309]

3.29. 'Once, monks, I was staying at Ukkaṭṭhā[310] in the Subhaga grove at the foot of a great *sāl*-tree. And as I dwelt there in seclusion it occurred to me: "There is no abode of beings easily accessible that has not been visited by me for so long as that of the devas of the Pure Abodes.[311] Suppose I were to visit them now?" And then, as swiftly as a strong man might stretch his flexed arm, or flex it again, I vanished from Ukkaṭṭhā and appeared among the Aviha devas. And many thousands of them came to me, saluted me and stood to one side. Then they said: "Sir,[312] it is ninety-one aeons since the Lord Buddha Vipassī appeared in the world.

'"The Lord Buddha Vipassī was born of Khattiya race, and arose in a Khattiya family; he was of the Koṇḍañña clan; in his time the life-span was eighty thousand years; he gained his full enlightenment under a trumpet-flower tree; he had the pair of noble disciples Khaṇḍa and Tissa; [51] he had three assemblies of disciples, one of six million eight hundred thousand, one of a hundred thousand, and one of eighty thousand monks, all of whom were Arahants; his chief personal attendant was the monk Asoka, his father was King Bandhumā, his mother was Queen Bandhumatī, and his father's royal capital was Bandhumatī. The Lord Buddha Vipassī's renunciation was like this, his going-forth like this, his striving like this, his full enlightenment like this; his turning of the wheel like this.

'"And we, sir, who lived the holy life under the Lord Buddha Vipassī, having freed ourselves from sense-desires, have arisen here."[313]

3.30. 'In the same way many thousands of devas came... (*referring similarly to Sikhī and other Buddhas as verse 1.12*). They said: "Sir, in this fortunate aeon now the Lord Buddha has arisen in the world. He was born of Khattiya race...; he is of the Gotama clan; [52] in his time the life-span is short, limited and quick to pass: it is seldom that anybody lives to be a hundred. He gained his full enlightenment under an *assattha*-tree; he has a pair of noble disciples Sāriputta and Moggallāna; he has one assembly of disciples, one thousand two hundred and fifty monks who are all Arahants; his chief personal attendant is Ānanda; his father is King Suddhodana, his mother was Queen Māyā, and his royal capital is Kapilavatthu. Such was the Lord's renunciation, such his going-forth, such his striving, such his full enlightenment, such his turning of the wheel. And we, sir, who have lived the holy life under the Lord, having freed ourselves from sense-desires, have arisen here."

3.31.–32. 'Then I went with the Aviha devas to see the Atappa devas, and with these to see the Sudassa devas, and with these to see the Sudassī devas, and with all of these to see the Akaniṭṭha devas. [53] And there many thousands of devas came, saluted me and stood to one side, saying: "Sir, it is ninety-one aeons since the Lord Buddha Vipassī appeared in the world..." (*as verses 29–30*).

3.33. 'And so it is, monks, that by his penetration of the fundamentals of Dhamma[314] the Tathāgata remembers the past Buddhas who have attained final Nibbāna, cutting through multiplicity,[315] blazing a trail, have exhausted the round,[316] have passed by all suffering; he recalls their births, their names, their clan, [54] their life-span, their twin-disciples, their assemblies of disciples: "These Blessed Lords were born thus, were called thus, thus was their clan, thus was their morality, their Dhamma, their wisdom, their dwelling, thus was their liberation.'"[317]

Thus the Lord spoke, and the monks, delighted, rejoiced at his words.

15 *Mahānidāna Sutta: The Great Discourse on Origination*

[55] 1. THUS HAVE I HEARD.[318] Once the Lord was staying among the Kurus. There is a market town there called Kammāsa-dhamma.[319] And the Venerable Ānanda came to the Lord, saluted him, sat down to one side, and said: 'It is wonderful, Lord, it is marvellous how profound this dependent origination is, and how profound it appears! And yet it appears to me as clear as clear!'

'Do not say that, Ānanda, do not say that! This dependent origination is profound and appears profound. It is through not understanding, not penetrating this doctrine that this generation has become like a tangled ball of string, covered as with a blight,[320] tangled like coarse grass, unable to pass beyond states of woe, the ill destiny, ruin and the round of birth-and-death.[321]

2. 'If, Ānanda, you are asked: "Has ageing-and-death a condition for its existence?"[322] you should answer: "Yes." If asked: "What conditions ageing-and-death?" you should answer: "Ageing-and-death is conditioned by birth."...[56] "What conditions birth?"..."Becoming conditions birth."..."Clinging conditions becoming."..."Craving conditions clinging."... "Feeling conditions craving."..."Contact conditions feeling." ..."Mind-and-body conditions contact."[323]..."Consciousness conditions mind-and-body."...If asked: "Has consciousness a condition for its existence?" you should answer: "Yes." If asked: "What conditions consciousness?" you should answer: "Mind-and-body conditions consciousness."[324]

3. 'Thus, Ānanda, mind-and-body conditions consciousness and consciousness conditions mind-and-body, mind-and-body conditions contact, contact conditions feeling, feeling condi-

tions craving, craving conditions clinging, clinging conditions becoming, becoming conditions birth, birth conditions ageing-and-death, sorrow, [57] lamentation, pain, grief and distress.[325] Thus this whole mass of suffering comes into existence.

4. 'I have said: "Birth conditions ageing-and-death", and this is the way that should be understood. If, Ānanda, there were no birth at all, anywhere, of anybody or anything: of devas to the deva-state, of gandhabbas..., of yakkhas..., of ghosts...,[326] of humans..., of quadrupeds..., of birds..., of reptiles to the reptile state, if there were absolutely no birth at all of all these beings, then, with the absence of all birth, the cessation of birth, could ageing-and-death appear?' 'No, Lord.' 'Therefore, Ānanda, just this is the root, the cause, the origin, the condition for ageing-and-death – namely birth.

5. 'I have said: "Becoming conditions birth."...If there were absolutely no becoming: in the World of Sense-Desires, of Form or the Formless World...could birth appear?'

'No, Lord.' 'Therefore just this is the condition of birth – namely becoming.

6. '"Clinging conditions becoming."...If there were absolutely no clinging: sensuous [58] clinging, clinging to views, to rite-and-ritual, to personality-belief..., could becoming appear?

7. '"Craving conditions clinging."...If there were absolutely no craving: for sights, sounds, smells, tastes, tangibles, mind-objects..., could clinging appear?

8. '"Feeling conditions craving."...If there were absolutely no feeling: feeling born of eye-contact, ear-contact, nose-contact, tongue-contact, body-contact, mind-contact – in the absence of all feeling, with the cessation of feeling, could craving appear?'

'No, Lord.' 'Therefore, Ānanda, just this is the root, the cause, the origin, the condition for craving – namely feeling.

9. 'And so, Ānanda, feeling conditions craving, craving conditions seeking,[327] seeking conditions acquisition,[328] acquisition conditions decision-making,[329] decision-making conditions lustful desire,[330] lustful desire conditions attachment,[331] attachment conditions appropriation,[332] appropriation conditions avarice,[333] avarice [59] conditions guarding of possessions,[334] and because of the guarding of possessions there

arise the taking up of stick and sword, quarrels, disputes, arguments, strife, abuse, lying and other evil unskilled states.

10. 'I have said: "All these evil unskilled states arise because of the guarding of possessions." For if there were absolutely no guarding of possessions...would there be the taking up of stick or sword...?' 'No, Lord.' 'Therefore, Ānanda, the guarding of possessions is the root, the cause, the origin, the condition for all these evil unskilled states.

11. 'I have said: "Avarice conditions the guarding of possessions..."

12–17. '"Appropriation conditions avarice,...[60] attachment conditions appropriation,...lustful desire conditions attachment,...decision-making conditions lustful desire,... acquisition conditions decision-making,...seeking conditions acquisition..." [61]

18. 'I have said: "Craving conditions seeking."...If there were no craving for sensual pleasures, existence, annihilation,... would there be any seeking?' 'No, Lord.' 'Therefore, Ānanda, craving is the root, the cause, the origin, the condition for all seeking. Thus these two things become united in one by feeling.[335] [62]

19. 'I have said: "Contact conditions feeling."...Therefore contact is the root, the cause, the origin, the condition for feeling.

20. '"Mind-and-body conditions contact." By whatever properties, features, signs or indications the mind-factor[336] is conceived of, would there, in the absence of such properties... pertaining to the mind-factor, be manifest any grasping at the idea of the body-factor?'[337] 'No, Lord.'

'Or in the absence of any such properties pertaining to the body-factor, would there be any grasping at sensory reaction on the part of the mind-factor?' 'No, Lord.'

'By whatever properties the mind-factor and the body-factor are designated – in their absence is there manifested any grasping at the idea, or at sensory reaction?' 'No, Lord.'

'By whatever properties, features, signs or indications the mind-factor is conceived of, in the absence of these is there any contact to be found?' 'No, Lord.'

'Then, Ānanda, just this, namely mind-and-body, is the root, the cause, the origin, the condition for all contact.

21. 'I have said: "Consciousness conditions mind-and-body." ...[63] If consciousness were not to come into the mother's womb, would mind-and-body develop there?' 'No, Lord.'

'Or if consciousness, having entered the mother's womb, were to be deflected, would mind-and-body come to birth in this life?' 'No, Lord.' 'And if the consciousness of such a tender young being, boy or girl, were thus cut off, would mind-and-body grow, develop and mature?' 'No, Lord.' 'Therefore, Ānanda, just this, namely consciousness, is the root, the cause, the origin, the condition of mind-and-body.

22. 'I have said: "Mind-and-body conditions consciousness." ...If consciousness did not find a resting-place in mind-and-body, would there subsequently be an arising and coming-to-be of birth, ageing, death and suffering?' 'No, Lord.' 'Therefore, Ānanda, just this, namely mind-and-body, is the root, the cause, the origin, the condition of consciousness. Thus far then, Ānanda, we can trace[338] birth and decay, death and falling into other states and being reborn,[339] thus far extends the way of designation, of concepts, thus far is the sphere of understanding, thus far the round goes [64] as far as can be discerned in this life,[340] namely to mind-and-body together with consciousness.

23. 'In what ways, Ānanda, do people explain the nature of the self? Some declare the self to be material and limited,[341] saying: "My self is material and limited"; some declare it to be material and unlimited...; some declare it to be immaterial and limited...; some declare it to be immaterial and unlimited, saying: "My self is immaterial and unlimited."

24. 'Whoever declares the self to be material and limited, considers it to be so either now, or in the next world, thinking: "Though it is not so now, I shall acquire it there."[342] That being so, that is all we need say about the view that the self is material and limited, and the same applies to the other [65] theories. So much, Ānanda, for those who proffer an explanation of the self.

25.–26. 'How is it with those who do not explain the nature of the self?...(*as verses 23–24 but negated*). [66]

27. 'In what ways, Ānanda, do people regard the self? They equate the self with feeling: "Feeling is my self",[343] or: "Feel-

ing is not my self, my self is impercipient",[344] or: "Feeling is not my self, but my self is not impercipient, it is of a nature to feel."[345]

28. 'Now, Ānanda, one who says: "Feeling is my self" should be told: "There are three kinds of feeling, friend: pleasant, painful, and neutral. Which of the three do you consider to be your self?" When a pleasant feeling is felt, no painful or neutral feeling is felt, but only pleasant feeling. When a painful feeling is felt, no pleasant or neutral feeling is felt, but only painful feeling. And when a neutral feeling is felt, no pleasant or painful feeling is felt, but only neutral feeling.

29. 'Pleasant feeling is impermanent, conditioned,[346] dependently-arisen, bound to decay, to vanish, to fade away, to cease – and so too are painful feeling [67] and neutral feeling. So anyone who, on experiencing a pleasant feeling, thinks: "This is my self", must, at the cessation of that pleasant feeling, think: "My self has gone!" and the same with painful and neutral feelings. Thus whoever thinks: "Feeling is my self" is contemplating something in this present life that is impermanent, a mixture of happiness and unhappiness, subject to arising and passing away. Therefore it is not fitting to maintain: "Feeling is my self."

30. 'But anyone who says: "Feeling is not my self, my self is impercipient" should be asked: "If, friend, no feelings at all were to be experienced, would there be the thought: 'I am'?" [to which he would have to reply:] "No, Lord."[347] Therefore it is not fitting to maintain: "Feeling is not my self, my self is impercipient."

31. 'And anyone who says: "Feeling is not my self, but my self is not impercipient, my self is of a nature to feel" should be asked: "Well, friend, if all feelings absolutely and totally ceased, could there be the thought: 'I am this?'"[348] [to which he would have to reply:] "No, Lord." Therefore it is not fitting to maintain: [68] "Feeling is not my self, but my self is not impercipient, my self is of a nature to feel."

32. 'From the time, Ānanda, when a monk no longer regards feeling as the self, or the self as being impercipient, or as being percipient and of a nature to feel, by not so regarding, he clings to nothing in the world; not clinging, he is not ex-

cited by anything, and not being excited he gains personal liberation,[349] and he knows: "Birth is finished, the holy life has been led, done was what had to be done, there is nothing more here."

'And if anyone were to say to a monk whose mind was thus freed: "The Tathāgata exists after death",[350] that would be [seen by him as] a wrong opinion and unfitting, likewise: "The Tathāgata does not exist..., both exists and does not exist..., neither exists nor does not exist after death." Why so? As far, Ānanda, as designation and the range of designation reaches, as far as language and the range of language reaches, as far as concepts and the range of concepts reaches, as far as understanding and the range of understanding reaches, as far as the cycle reaches and revolves – that monk is liberated from all that by super-knowledge,[351] and to maintain that such a liberated monk does not know and see would be a wrong view and incorrect.

33. 'Ānanda, there are seven stations of consciousness[352] and two realms.[353] Which are the seven? There are beings different in [69] body and different in perception, such as human beings, some devas and some in states of woe. That is the first station of consciousness. There are beings different in body and alike in perception, such as the devas of Brahmā's retinue, born there [on account of having attained] the first jhāna. That is the second station. There are beings alike in body and different in perception, such as the Ābhassara devas.[354] That is the third station. There are beings alike in body and alike in perception, such as the Subhakiṇṇa devas. That is the fourth station. There are beings who have completely transcended all perception of matter, by the vanishing of the perception of sense-reactions and by non-attention to the perception of variety; thinking: "Space is infinite", they have attained to the Sphere of Infinite Space. That is the fifth station. There are beings who, by transcending the Sphere of Infinite Space, thinking: "Consciousness is infinite", have attained to the Sphere of Infinite Consciousness. That is the sixth station. There are beings who, having transcended the Sphere of Infinite Consciousness, thinking: "There is no thing", have attained to the Sphere of No-Thingness. That is the

seventh station of consciousness. [The two realms are:] The Realm of Unconscious Beings and, secondly, the Realm of Neither-Perception-Nor-Non-Perception.

34. 'Now, Ānanda, as regards this first station of consciousness, with difference of body and difference of perception, as in the case of human beings and so on, if anyone were to understand it, its origin, its cessation, its attraction and its peril, and the deliverance from it, would it be fitting for him to take pleasure in it?' [70] 'No, Lord.' 'And as regards the other stations, and the two spheres likewise?' 'No, Lord.'

'Ānanda, insofar as a monk, having known as they really are these seven stations of consciousness and these two spheres, their origin and cessation, their attraction and peril, is freed without attachment, that monk, Ānanda, is called one who is liberated by wisdom.[355]

35. 'There are, Ānanda, these eight liberations.[356] What are they?

'(1) Possessing form, one sees forms.[357] That is the first liberation. (2) Not perceiving material forms in oneself, one sees them outside.[358] That is the second liberation. [71] (3) Thinking: "It is beautiful", one becomes intent on it.[359] That is the third. (4) By completely transcending all perception of matter, by the vanishing of the perception of sense-reactions and by non-attention to the perception of variety, thinking: "Space is infinite", one enters and abides in the Sphere of Infinite Space. That is the fourth. (5) By transcending the Sphere of Infinite Space, thinking: "Consciousness is infinite", one enters and abides in the Sphere of Infinite Consciousness. That is the fifth. (6) By transcending the Sphere of Infinite Consciousness, thinking: "There is no thing", one enters and abides in the Sphere of No-Thingness. That is the sixth. (7) By transcending the Sphere of No-Thingness, one reaches and abides in the Sphere of Neither-Perception-Nor-Non-Perception. That is the seventh. (8) By transcending the Sphere of Neither-Perception-Nor-Non-Perception one enters and abides in the Cessation of Perception and Feeling.[360] That is the eighth liberation.

36. 'Ānanda, when once a monk attains these eight liberations in forward order, in reverse order, and in forward-and-reverse order, entering them and emerging from them as and

when, and for as long as he wishes, and has gained by his own super-knowledge here and now both the destruction of the corruptions and the uncorrupted liberation of heart and liberation by wisdom,[361] that monk is called "both-ways-liberated",[362] and, Ānanda, there is no other way of "both-ways-liberation" that is more excellent or perfect than this.'

Thus the Lord spoke. And the Venerable Ānanda rejoiced and was delighted at his words.

16 *Mahāparinibbāna Sutta: The Great Passing*
The Buddha's Last Days

[72] 1.1. THUS HAVE I HEARD.[363] Once the Lord was staying at Rājagaha on the mountain called Vultures' Peak.[364] Now just then King Ajātasattu Vedehiputta[365] of Magadha wanted to attack the Vajjians.[366] He said: 'I will strike the Vajjians who are so powerful and strong, I will cut them off and destroy them, I will bring them to ruin and destruction!'

1.2. And King Ajātasattu said to his chief minister the Brahmin Vassakāra: 'Brahmin, go to the Blessed Lord, worship him with your head to his feet in my name, ask if he is free from sickness or disease, if he is living at ease, vigorously and comfortably, and then say: "Lord, King Ajātasattu Vedehiputta of Magadha wishes to attack the Vajjians and says: 'I will strike the Vajjians. . . ,bring them to ruin and [73] destruction!' " And whatever the Lord declares to you, report that faithfully back to me, for Tathāgatas never lie.'

1.3. 'Very good, Sire', said Vassakāra and, having had the state carriages harnessed, he mounted one of them and drove in state from Rājagaha to Vultures' Peak, riding as far as the ground would allow, then continuing on foot to where the Lord was. He exchanged courtesies with the Lord, then sat down to one side and delivered the King's message.

1.4. Now the Venerable Ānanda was standing behind the Lord, fanning him. And the Lord said: 'Ānanda, have you heard that the Vajjians hold regular and frequent assemblies?' 'I have heard, Lord, that they do.'

'Ānanda, as long as the Vajjians hold regular and frequent assemblies, they may be expected to prosper and not decline. Have you heard [74] that the Vajjians meet in harmony, break up in harmony, and carry on their business in harmony?' 'I have heard, Lord, that they do.'

'Ānanda, as long as the Vajjians meet in harmony, break up in harmony, and carry on their business in harmony, they may be expected to prosper and not decline. Have you heard that the Vajjians do not authorise what has not been authorised already, and do not abolish what has been authorised, but proceed according to what has been authorised by their ancient tradition?' 'I have, Lord.'...'Have you heard that they honour, respect, revere and salute the elders among them, and consider them worth listening to?...that they do not forcibly abduct others' wives and daughters and compel them to live with them?...that they honour, respect, revere and salute the Vajjian shrines at home and abroad, not withdrawing the proper support made and given before?...[75] that proper provision is made for the safety of Arahants, so that such Arahants may come in future to live there, and those already there may dwell in comfort?' 'I have, Lord.'

'Ānanda, so long as such proper provision is made,...the Vajjians may be expected to prosper and not decline.'

1.5. Then the Lord said to the Brahmin Vassakāra: 'Once, Brahmin, when I was at the Sārandada Shrine in Vesālī, I taught the Vajjians these seven principles for preventing decline, and as long as they keep to these seven principles, as long as these principles remain in force, the Vajjians may be expected to prosper and not decline.'

At this, Vassakāra replied: 'Reverend Gotama, if the Vajjians keep to even one of these principles, they may be expected to prosper and not [76] decline – far less all seven. Certainly the Vajjians will never be conquered by King Ajātasattu by force of arms, but only by means of propaganda[367] and setting them against one another. And now, Reverend Gotama, may I depart? I am busy and have much to do.' 'Brahmin, do as you think fit.' Then Vassakāra, rejoicing and delighted at the Lord's words, rose from his seat and departed.

1.6. Soon after Vassakāra had gone, the Lord said: 'Ānanda, go to whatever monks there are round about Rājagaha, and summon them to the assembly hall.' 'Very good, Lord', said Ānanda, and did so. Then he came to the Lord, saluted him, stood to one side and said: 'Lord, the order of monks is assembled. Now is the time for the Lord to do as he sees fit.' Then the Lord rose from his seat, went to the assembly hall, sat down on the prepared seat, and said: 'Monks, I will teach you seven things that are conducive to welfare.[368] Listen, pay careful attention, and I will speak.' 'Yes, Lord', said the monks, and the Lord said:

'As long as the monks hold regular and frequent assemblies, they may be expected to prosper and not decline. As long as they meet in harmony, break up in harmony, and carry on their [77] business in harmony, they may be expected to prosper and not decline. As long as they do not authorise what has not been authorised already, and do not abolish what has been authorised, but proceed according to what has been authorised by the rules of training...; as long as they honour, respect, revere and salute the elders of long standing who are long ordained, fathers and leaders of the order...; as long as they do not fall prey to desires which arise in them and lead to rebirth...; as long as they are devoted to forest-lodgings...; as long as they preserve their personal mindfulness, so that in future the good among their companions will come to them, and those who have already come will feel at ease with them ...; as long as the monks hold to these seven things and are seen to do so, they may be expected to prosper and not decline.

1.7. 'I will tell you another seven things conducive to welfare...As long as monks do not rejoice, delight and become absorbed in works,[369]...in chattering,...in sleeping,...in company,...in evil desires,...in mixing and associating with evil friends,...as long as they do not rest content with partial achievements[370]...; as long as the monks hold to these seven things and are seen to do so, they may be expected to prosper and not decline.

1.8. 'I will tell you another seven things conducive to welfare...As long as monks continue with faith, with modesty, with fear of doing wrong, with learning, [79] with aroused vigour, with established mindfulness, with wisdom...

1.9. 'I will tell you another seven things...As long as monks develop the enlightenment-factors of mindfulness, of investigation of phenomena, of energy, of delight, of tranquillity, of concentration, of equanimity...

1.10. 'I will tell you another seven things...As long as monks develop the perception of impermanence, of non-self, of impurity, of danger, of overcoming, of dispassion, of cessation, ...[80] they may be expected to prosper and not decline.

1.11. 'Monks, I will tell you six things that are conducive to communal living...As long as monks both in public and in private show loving-kindness to their fellows in acts of body, speech and thought,...share with their virtuous fellows whatever they receive as a rightful gift, including the contents of their alms-bowls, which they do not keep to themselves,... keep consistently, unbroken and unaltered those rules of conduct that are spotless, leading to liberation, praised by the wise, unstained and conducive to concentration, and persist therein with their fellows both in public and in private,... continue in that noble view that leads to liberation, to the utter destruction of suffering, remaining in such awareness with their fellows both in public and in private...[81] As long as monks hold to these six things and are seen to do so, they may be expected to prosper and not decline.'

1.12. And then the Lord, while staying at Vultures' Peak, gave a comprehensive discourse: 'This is morality, this is concentration, this is wisdom. Concentration, when imbued with morality, brings great fruit and profit. Wisdom, when imbued with concentration, brings great fruit and profit. The mind imbued with wisdom becomes completely free from the corruptions, that is, from the corruption of sensuality, of becoming, of false views and of ignorance.'

1.13. And when the Lord had stayed at Rājagaha as long as he wished, he said to the Venerable Ānanda: 'Come, Ānanda, let us go to Ambalaṭṭhikā.' 'Very good, Lord', said Ānanda, and the Lord went there with a large company of monks.

1.14. And the Lord stayed in the royal park at Ambalaṭṭhikā,[371] and there he delivered a comprehensive discourse: 'This is morality, this is concentration, this is wisdom...'

1.15. Having stayed at Ambalaṭṭhikā as long as he wished, the Lord said to Ānanda: 'Let us go to Nāḷandā', and they did so. At Nāḷandā the Lord stayed in Pāvārika's mango-grove.

1.16. Then the Venerable Sāriputta came to see the Lord, saluted him, [82] sat down to one side, and said: 'It is clear to me, Lord, that there never has been, will be or is now another ascetic or Brahmin who is better or more enlightened than the Lord.'

'You have spoken boldly with a bull's voice, Sāriputta, you have roared the lion's roar of certainty! How is this? Have all the Arahant Buddhas of the past appeared to you, and were the minds of all those Lords open to you, so as to say: "These Lords were of such virtue, such was their teaching, such their wisdom, such their way, such their liberation"?' 'No, Lord.'

'And have you perceived all the Arahant Buddhas who will appear in the future...?' 'No, Lord.'

'Well then, Sāriputta, you know me as the Arahant Buddha, and do you know: "The Lord is of such virtue, such is his teaching, such his wisdom, such his way, such his liberation"?' 'No, Lord.'

'So, Sāriputta, you do not have knowledge of the minds of the Buddhas of the past, the future or the present. Thus, Sāriputta, [83] have you not spoken boldly with a bull's voice and roared the lion's roar of certainty with your declaration?'

1.17. 'Lord, the minds of the Arahant Buddhas of the past, future and present are not open to me. But I know the drift of the Dhamma.[372] Lord, it is as if there were a royal frontier city, with mighty bastions and a mighty encircling wall in which was a single gate, at which was a gatekeeper, wise, skilled and clever, who kept out strangers and let in those he knew. And he, constantly patrolling and following along a path, might not see the joins and clefts in the bastion, even such as a cat might creep through. But whatever larger creatures entered or left the city, must all go through this very gate. And it seems to me, Lord, that the drift of the Dhamma is the same. All those Arahant Buddhas of the past attained to supreme enlightenment by abandoning the five hindrances, defilements of mind that weaken the understanding, having firmly established the four foundations of mindfulness in their minds, and realised the seven factors of enlightenment as they really are. All the Arahant Buddhas of the future will do likewise, and you, Lord, who are now the Arahant, fully-enlightened Buddha, have done the same.'

1.18. Then, while staying at Nāḷandā, [84] in Pāvārika's mango-grove, the Lord gave a comprehensive discourse to the monks.

'This is morality, this is concentration, this is wisdom...' (*as verse 12*).

1.19. And having stayed at Nāḷandā as long as he wished, the Lord said to Ānanda: 'Let us go to Pāṭaligāma.' And they did so.

1.20. At Pāṭaligāma they heard say: 'The Lord has arrived here'. And the lay-followers of Pāṭaligāma came to the Lord, saluted him, sat down to one side, and said: 'May the Lord consent to stay at our rest-house!' And the Lord consented by silence.

1.21. Understanding his consent, they rose from their seats, saluted the Lord and, passing him by to the right, went to the rest-house and strewed the floor, prepared seats, provided a water-pot and filled the oil-lamp. Then they went to the Lord, saluted him, stood to one side and said: 'All is ready at the rest-house, Lord. Now is the time to do as the Lord wishes.' [85]

1.22. Then the Lord dressed, took his robe and bowl, and went with his monks to the rest-house, where he washed his feet, went in and sat down facing east, with his back against the central pillar. And the monks, having washed their feet, went in and sat down with their backs to the west wall, facing east, and with the Lord sitting in front of them. And the lay-followers of Pāṭaligāma, having washed their feet, went in and sat down with their backs to the east wall, facing west and with the Lord before them.

1.23. Then the Lord addressed the lay-followers of Pāṭaligāma: 'Householders, there are these five perils to one of bad morality, of failure in morality. What are they? In the first place, he suffers great loss of property through neglecting his affairs. In the second place, he gets a bad reputation for immorality and misconduct. In the third place, whatever assembly he approaches, whether of Khattiyas, Brahmins, householders or ascetics, he does so diffidently and shyly. In the fourth place, he dies confused. In the fifth place, after death, at the breaking-up of the body, he arises in an evil state, a bad fate, in suffering and hell. These are the five perils to one of bad morality.

[86] 1.24. 'And, householders, there are these five advantages

to one of good morality and of success in morality. What are they? In the first place, through careful attention to his affairs he gains much wealth. In the second place, he gets a good reputation for morality and good conduct. In the third place, whatever assembly he approaches, whether of Khattiyas, Brahmins, householders or ascetics, he does so with confidence and assurance. In the fourth place, he dies unconfused. In the fifth place, after death, at the breaking-up of the body, he arises in a good place, a heavenly world. These are the five advantages to one of good morality, and of success in morality.'

1.25. Then the Lord instructed, inspired, fired and delighted the lay-followers of Pāṭaligāma with talk on Dhamma until far into the night. Then he dismissed them, saying: 'Householders, the night is nearly over. Now it is time for you to do as you think fit.' 'Very good, Lord', they said and, rising and saluting the Lord, they passed him by to the right and departed. And the Lord spent the remainder of the night in the rest-house left empty by their departure.

1.26. Now at this time Sunidha and Vassakāra, the Magadhan ministers, were building a fortress in Pāṭaligāma as a defence against the Vajjians. And at that time a multitude of [87] thousands of devas were taking up lodging in Pāṭaligāma. And in the parts where powerful devas settled, they caused the minds of the most powerful royal officials to pick those sites for their dwellings, and where middle and lower-ranking devas settled, so too they caused the minds of royal officials of corresponding grade to pick those sites for their dwellings.

1.27. And the Lord, with his divine eye surpassing that of humans, saw the thousands of devas taking up residence in Pāṭaligāma. And, getting up at break of day, he said to the Venerable Ānanda: 'Ānanda, who is building a fortress at Pāṭaligāma?' 'Lord, Sunidha and Vassakāra, the Magadhan ministers, are building a fortress against the Vajjians.'

1.28. 'Ānanda, just as if they had taken counsel with the Thirty-Three Gods, Sunidha and Vassakāra are building a fortress at Pāṭaligāma. I have seen with my divine eye how thousands of devas were taking up lodging there...(*as verse* 26). Ānanda, as far as the Ariyan realm extends, as far as its trade extends, this will be the chief city, Pāṭaliputta, scattering its seeds far and [88] wide. And Pāṭaliputta will face three perils: from fire, from water and from internal dissension.'

1.29. Then Sunidha and Vassakāra called on the Lord and, having exchanged courtesies, stood to one side and said: 'May the Reverend Gotama accept a meal from us tomorrow with his order of monks!' And the Lord consented by silence.

1.30. Understanding his consent, Sunidha and Vassakāra went home and there had a fine meal of hard and soft food prepared. When it was ready, they reported to the Lord: 'Reverend Gotama, the meal is ready.' Then the Lord, having dressed in the morning, took his robe and bowl, went with the order of monks to the residence of Sunidha and Vassakāra, and sat down on the prepared seat. Then Sunidha and Vassakāra served the Buddha and his order of monks with choice soft and hard foods till they were satisfied. And when the Lord took his hand away from the bowl they sat down on low stools to one side.

1.31. And as they sat there, the Lord thanked them with these verses:

> 'In whatever realm the wise man makes his home,
> He should feed the virtuous leaders of the holy life.
>
> Whatever devas there are who report this offering,
> They will pay him respect and honour for this. [89]
>
> They tremble for him as a mother for her son,
> And he for whom devas tremble ever happy is.'

Then the Lord rose from his seat and took his departure.

1.32. Sunidha and Vassakāra followed closely behind the Lord, saying: 'Whichever gate the ascetic Gotama goes out by today, that shall be called the Gotama gate; and whichever ford he uses to cross the Ganges, that shall be called the Gotama ford.' And so the gate by which the Lord went out was called the Gotama Gate.

1.33. And then the Lord came to the River Ganges. And just then, the river was so full that a crow could drink out of it. And some people were looking for a boat, and some were looking for a raft, and some were binding together a raft of reeds to get to the other side. But the Lord, as swiftly as a strong man might stretch out his flexed arm or flex it again, vanished from this side of the Ganges and reappeared with his order of monks on the other shore.

1.34. And the Lord saw those people who were looking for a boat, looking for a raft, and binding together a raft of reeds to get to the other side. And seeing their intentions, he uttered this verse on the spot:

> 'When they want to cross the sea, the lake or pond,
> People make a bridge or raft – the wise have crossed already.'

[*End of first recitation-section*]

[90] 2.1. The Lord said to Ānanda: 'Let us go to Koṭigāma.' 'Very good, Lord', said Ānanda, and the Lord went with a large company of monks to Koṭigāma, and stayed there.

2.2. Then the Lord addressed the monks thus: 'Monks, it is through not understanding, not penetrating the Four Noble Truths that I as well as you have for a long time run on and gone round the cycle of birth-and-death. What are they? By not understanding the Noble Truth of Suffering we have fared on, by not understanding the Noble Truth of the Origin of Suffering, of the Cessation of Suffering, and of the Path Leading to the Cessation of Suffering we have fared on round the cycle of birth-and-death. And by the understanding, the penetration of the same Noble Truth of Suffering, of the Origin of Suffering, of the Cessation of Suffering and of the Path Leading to the Cessation of Suffering, the craving for becoming has been cut off, the support of becoming has been destroyed, there is no more re-becoming.'

2.3. The Lord having said this, the Well-Farer having spoken, the Teacher said: [91]

> 'Not seeing the Four Noble Truths as they are,
> Having long traversed the round from life to life,
> These being seen, becoming's supports pulled up,
> Sorrow's root cut off, rebirth is done.'

2.4. Then the Lord, while staying at Koṭigāma, gave a comprehensive discourse: 'This is morality, this is concentration, this is wisdom. Concentration, when imbued with morality, brings great fruit and profit. Wisdom, when imbued with concentration, brings great fruit and profit. The mind imbued with wisdom becomes completely free from the corruptions, that is, from the corruption of sensuality, of becoming, of false views and of ignorance.'

2.5. When the Lord had stayed at Koṭigāma as long as he wished, he said: 'Ānanda, let us go to Nādikā.' 'Very good, Lord', said Ānanda, and the Lord went with a large company of monks to Nādikā, where he stayed at the Brick House.[373]

2.6. And the Venerable Ānanda came to the Lord, saluted him, sat down to one side, and said: 'Lord, the monk Sāḷha and the nun Nandā have died at Nādikā. What rebirth have they taken after death? [92] The lay-follower Sudatta and the laywoman-follower Sujātā, the lay-followers Kakudha, Kālinga, Nikaṭa, Kaṭissabha, Tuṭṭha, Santuṭṭha, Bhadda and Subhadda have all died in Nādikā. What rebirths have they taken?'

2.7. 'Ānanda, the monk Sāḷha, by the destruction of the corruptions, attained in this life, through his own super-knowledge, the uncorrupted liberation of mind, the liberation by wisdom. The nun Nandā, by the destruction of the five lower fetters, has been spontaneously reborn,[374] and will gain Nibbāna from that state without returning to this world. The lay-follower Sudatta, by the destruction of three fetters and the reduction of greed, hatred and delusion, is a Once-Returner who will come back once more to this world, and then make an end of suffering. The laywoman-follower Sujātā, by the destruction of three fetters, is a Stream-Winner, incapable of falling into states of woe, certain of attaining Nibbāna. The lay-follower Kakudha, by the destruction of the five lower fetters, has been spontaneously reborn, and will gain Nibbāna from that state without returning to this world. Likewise Kālinga, Nikaṭa, Kaṭissabha, Tuṭṭha, Santuṭṭha, Bhadda and Subhadda. [93] Ānanda, in Nādikā more than fifty lay-followers have by the destruction of the five lower fetters been spontaneously reborn, and will gain Nibbāna from that state without returning to this world. Rather more than ninety, by the destruction of three fetters and the reduction of greed, hatred and delusion, are Once-Returners who will come back once more to this world and then make an end of suffering. And well over five hundred, by the destruction of three fetters, are Stream-Winners, incapable of falling into states of woe, certain of attaining Nibbāna.

2.8. 'Ānanda, it is not remarkable that that which has come to be as a man should die. But that you should come to the Tathāgata to ask the fate of each of those who have died, that is a weariness to him.[375] Therefore, Ānanda, I will teach you a way of knowing Dhamma, called the Mirror of Dhamma,[376] whereby the Ariyan disciple, if he so wishes, can discern of himself: "I have destroyed hell, animal-rebirth, the realm of ghosts, all downfall, evil fates and sorry states. I am a Stream-Winner, incapable of falling into states of woe, certain of attaining Nibbāna."

2.9. 'And what is this Mirror of Dhamma by which he can know this? Here, Ānanda, this Ariyan disciple is possessed of unwavering confidence[377] in the Buddha, thus: "This Blessed Lord is an Arahant, a fully-enlightened Buddha, endowed with wisdom and conduct, the Well-Farer, Knower of the worlds, incomparable Trainer of men to be tamed, Teacher of gods and humans, enlightened and blessed." He is possessed of unwavering faith in the Dhamma, thus: "Well-proclaimed by the Lord is the Dhamma, visible here and now, timeless, inviting inspection, leading onward, to be comprehended by the wise each one for himself." He is possessed of unwavering confidence in the Sangha, thus: "Well-directed is the Sangha of the Lord's disciples, of upright conduct, on the right [94] path, on the perfect path; that is to say the four pairs of persons,[378] the eight kinds of humans. The Sangha of the Lord's disciples is worthy of offerings, worthy of hospitality, worthy of gifts, worthy of veneration, an unsurpassed field of merit in the world. And he[379] is possessed of morality dear to the Noble Ones, unbroken, without defect, unspotted, without inconsistency,[380] liberating, uncorrupted, and conducive to concentration.

'This, Ānanda, is the Mirror of Dhamma, whereby the

Aryan disciple... can discern of himself: "I have destroyed hell, ...I am a Stream-Winner,... certain of attaining Nibbāna."' (*as verse 8*)

2.10. Then the Lord, staying at Nādikā in the Brick House, gave a comprehensive discourse to the monks: 'This is morality, this is concentration, this is wisdom...' (*as verse 2.4*).

2.11. And when the Lord had stayed at Nādikā as long as he wished,... he went with a large company of monks to Vesālī, where he stayed at Ambapālī's grove.

2.12. And there the Lord addressed the monks: 'Monks, a monk should be mindful and clearly aware, this is our charge to you!

'And how is a monk mindful?[381] Here, a monk abides contemplating the body as body,[382] earnestly, clearly aware, [95] mindful and having put away all hankering and fretting for the world, and likewise with regard to feelings, mind and mind-objects. That is how a monk is mindful.

2.13. 'And how is a monk clearly aware? Here, a monk, when going forward or backward, is aware of what he is doing; in looking forward or back he is aware of what he is doing; in bending and stretching he is aware of what he is doing; in carry-ing his inner and outer robe and bowl he is aware of what he is doing; in eating, drinking, chewing and savouring he is aware of what he is doing; in passing excrement or urine he is aware of what he is doing; in walking, standing, sitting or lying down, in keeping awake, in speaking or in staying silent, he is aware of what he is doing. That is how a monk is clearly aware. A monk should be mindful and clearly aware, this is our charge to you!'

2.14. Now Ambapālī the courtesan[383] heard that the Lord had arrived at Vesālī and was staying at her grove. She had the best carriages made ready and drove from Vesālī to her park. She drove as far as the ground would allow, then alighted and went on foot to where the Lord was. She saluted the Lord and sat down to one side, and as she sat, the Lord instructed, inspired, fired and delighted her with a talk on Dhamma. And being thus delighted, Ambapālī said: 'Lord, may the Lord consent to take a meal from me tomorrow with his order of monks!' The Lord consented by silence, and Ambapālī, understanding his acceptance, rose from her seat, saluted the Lord and, passing him by to the right, departed.

2.15. And the Licchavis of Vesālī heard that the Lord [96] had arrived at Vesālī and was staying at Ambapālī's grove. So they had the best carriages made ready and drove out of Vesālī. And some of the young Licchavis were all in blue,[384] with blue make-up,[385] blue clothes and blue adornment, while some were in yellow, some in red, some in white, with white make-up, white clothes and white adornment.

2.16. And Ambapālī met the young Licchavis axle to axle, wheel to wheel, yoke to yoke. And they said to her: 'Ambapālī, why do you drive up against us like that?' 'Because, young sirs, the Blessed Lord has been invited by me for a meal with his order of monks.'

'Ambapālī, give up this meal for a hundred thousand pieces!' 'Young sirs, if you were to give me all Vesālī with its revenues[386] I would not give up such an important meal!'

Then the Licchavis snapped their fingers, saying: 'We've been beaten by the mango-woman,[387] we've been cheated by the mango-woman!' And they set out for Ambapālī's grove.

2.17. And the Lord, having seen the Licchavis from afar, said: 'Monks, any of you who have not seen the Thirty-Three Gods, just look at this troop of Licchavis! Take a good look at them, [97] and you will get an idea of the Thirty-Three Gods!'

2.18. Then the Licchavis drove in their carriages as far as the ground would allow, then they alighted and went on foot to where the Lord was, saluted him and sat down to one side. And as they sat, the Lord instructed, inspired, fired and delighted them with a talk on Dhamma. And being thus delighted, they said: 'Lord, may the Lord consent to take a meal from us tomorrow with his order of monks!' 'But, Licchavis, I have already accepted a meal for tomorrow from the courtesan Ambapālī!'

And the Licchavis snapped their fingers, saying: 'We've been beaten by the mango-woman, we've been cheated by the mango-woman!' Then, having rejoiced and delighted in his talk, they rose from their seats, saluted the Lord and, passing him by on the right, departed.

2.19. And Ambapālī, when night was nearly over, having had choice hard and soft food prepared at her home, announced to the Lord that the meal was ready. Having dressed and taken robe and bowl, the Lord went with the order of monks to Ambapālī's residence and sat down on the prepared seat. And she served the Buddha and his monks with choice hard and soft food till they were satisfied. And when the Lord had taken his hand from the bowl, Ambapālī took a low stool and [98] sat down to one side. So seated, she said: 'Lord, I give this park to the order of monks with the Buddha as its head.' The Lord accepted the park, and then he instructed, inspired, fired and delighted her with a talk on Dhamma, after which he rose from his seat and departed.

2.20. Then, while staying at Vesālī, the Lord delivered a comprehensive discourse to the monks: 'This is morality, this is concentration, this is wisdom...' (*as verse 2.4*).

2.21. And when the Lord had stayed at Ambapālī's grove as long as he wished,...he went with a large company of monks to the little village of Beluva, where he stayed.

2.22. There the Lord said to the monks: 'You, monks, should go to anywhere in Vesālī where you have friends or acquaintances or supporters, and spend the Rains there. I shall spend the Rains here in Beluva.' 'Very good, Lord', replied the monks, and [99] they did so, but the Lord spent the Rains in Beluva.

2.23. And during the Rains the Lord was attacked by a severe sickness, with sharp pains as if he were about to die. But he endured all this mindfully, clearly aware and without complaining. He thought: 'It is not fitting that I should attain final Nibbāna without addressing my followers and taking leave of the order of monks. I must hold this disease in check by energy and apply myself to the force of life.' He did so, and the disease abated.

2.24. Then the Lord, having recovered from his sickness, as soon as he felt better, went outside and sat on a prepared seat in front of his dwelling. Then the Venerable Ānanda came to him, saluted him, sat down to one side and said: 'Lord, I have seen the Lord in comfort, and I have seen the Lord's patient enduring. And, Lord, my body was like a drunkard's. I lost my bearings and things were unclear to me because of the

Lord's sickness. The only thing that was some comfort to me was the thought: "The Lord will not attain final Nibbāna until he has made some statement about the order of monks."' [100]

2.25. 'But, Ānanda, what does the order of monks expect of me? I have taught the Dhamma, Ānanda, making no "inner" and "outer":[388] the Tathāgata has no "teacher's fist" in respect of doctrines. If there is anyone who thinks: "I shall take charge of the order",[389] or "The order should refer to me", let him make some statement about the order, but the Tathāgata does not think in such terms. So why should the Tathāgata make a statement about the order?

'Ānanda, I am now old, worn out, venerable, one who has traversed life's path, I have reached the term of life, which is eighty.[390] Just as an old cart is made to go by being held together with straps,[391] so the Tathāgata's body is kept going by being strapped up. It is only when the Tathāgata withdraws his attention from outward signs,[392] and by the cessation of certain feelings,[393] enters into the signless concentration of mind,[394] that his body knows comfort.

2.26. 'Therefore, Ānanda, you should live as islands[395] unto yourselves, being your own refuge, with no one else as your refuge, with the Dhamma as an island, with the Dhamma as your refuge, with no other refuge. And how does a monk live as an island unto himself, . . . with no other refuge? Here, Ānan-da, a monk abides contemplating the body as body, earnestly, clearly aware, mindful and having put away all hankering and fretting for the world, and likewise with regard to feelings, mind and mind-objects. That, Ānanda, is how a monk lives as an island unto himself, . . . with no other refuge. [101] And those who now in my time or afterwards live thus, they will become the highest,[396] if they are desirous of learning.'

[*End of second recitation-section*]

[102] 3.1 Then the Lord, rising early, dressed, took his robe and bowl, and entered Vesālī for alms. Having eaten on his return from the alms-round, he said to the Venerable Ānanda: 'Bring a mat, Ānanda. We will go to the Cāpāla Shrine for the

siesta.' 'Very good, Lord', said Ānanda, and, getting a mat, he followed behind.

3.2. Then the Lord came to the Cāpāla Shrine, and sat down on the prepared seat. Ānanda saluted the Lord and sat down to one side, and the Lord said: 'Ānanda, Vesālī is delightful, the Udena Shrine is delightful, the Gotamaka Shrine is delightful, the Sattambaka[397] Shrine is delightful, the Bahuputta[398] Shrine is delightful, the Cāpāla Shrine is delightful. [103]

3.3. 'Ānanda, whoever has developed the four roads to power,[399] practised them frequently, made them his vehicle, made them his base, established them, become familiar with them and properly undertaken them, could undoubtedly live for a century,[400] or the remainder of one. The Tathāgata has developed these powers,...properly undertaken them. And he could, Ānanda, undoubtedly live for a century, or the remainder of one.'

3.4. But the Venerable Ānanda, failing to grasp this broad hint, this clear sign, did not beg the Lord: 'Lord, may the Blessed Lord stay for a century, may the Well-Farer stay for a century for the benefit and happiness of the multitude, out of compassion for the world, for the benefit and happiness of devas and humans', so much was his mind possessed by Māra.[401]

3.5. And a second time..., and a third time...(*as verses 3–4*). [104]

3.6. Then the Lord said: 'Ānanda, go now and do what seems fitting to you.' 'Very good, Lord', said Ānanda and, rising from his seat, he saluted the Lord, passed by on the right and sat down under a tree some distance away.

3.7. Soon after Ānanda had left, Māra the Evil One came to the Lord, stood to one side, and said: 'Lord, may the Blessed Lord now attain final Nibbāna, may the Well-Farer now attain final Nibbāna. Now is the time for the Blessed Lord's final Nibbāna. Because the Blessed Lord has said this: "Evil One, I will not take final Nibbāna till I have monks and disciples who are accomplished, trained, skilled, learned, knowers of the Dhamma, trained in conformity with the Dhamma, correctly trained and walking in the path of the Dhamma, who will pass on what they have gained from their Teacher, teach it, declare it, establish it, expound it, analyse it, make it clear; till they shall be able by means of the Dhamma to refute false teachings that have arisen, and teach the Dhamma of wondrous effect."[402]

3.8. 'And now, Lord, the Blessed Lord has such monks and disciples. May the Blessed Lord now attain final Nibbāna, may the Well-Farer now attain final Nibbāna. Now is the time for the Blessed Lord's final Nibbāna. And the Blessed Lord has said: "I will not take final Nibbāna till I have nuns and female disciples who are accomplished,...till I have laymen-followers,...till I have laywomen-followers..." (*as verse 7*). [106] May the Blessed Lord now take final Nibbāna...And the Blessed Lord has said: "Evil One, I will not take final Nibbāna till this holy life has been successfully established and flourishes, is widespread, well-known far and wide, well-proclaimed among mankind everywhere." And all this has come about. May the Blessed Lord now attain final Nibbāna, may the Well-Farer now attain final Nibbāna. Now is the time for the Blessed Lord's final Nibbāna.'

3.9. At this the Lord said to Māra: 'You need not worry, Evil One. The Tathāgata's final passing will not be long delayed. Three months from now, the Tathāgata will take final Nibbāna.'

3.10. So the Lord, at the Cāpāla Shrine, mindfully and in full awareness renounced the life-principle, and when this occurred there was a great earthquake, terrible, hair-raising and accompanied by thunder. And when the Lord [107] saw this he uttered this verse:

> 'Gross or fine, things become the sage abjured.
> Calm, composed, he burst becoming's shell.'[403]

3.11. And the Venerable Ānanda thought: 'It is marvellous, it is wonderful how this great earthquake arises, this terrible earthquake, so dreadful and hair-raising, accompanied by thunder! Whatever can have caused it?'

3.12. He went to the Lord, saluted him, sat down to one side, and asked him that question.

3.13. 'Ānanda, there are eight reasons, eight causes for the appearance of a great earthquake. This great earth is established on water, the water on the wind, the wind on space. And when a mighty wind blows, this stirs up the water, and through the stirring-up of the water the earth quakes. That [108] is the first reason.

3.14. 'In the second place there is an ascetic or Brahmin who has developed psychic powers, or a mighty and powerful deva whose earth-consciousness is weakly developed and his water-consciousness is immeasurable,[404] and he makes the earth shudder and shake and violently quake. That is the second reason.

3.15. 'Again, when a Bodhisatta descends from the Tusita Heaven, mindful and clearly aware, into his mother's womb, then the earth shudders and shakes and violently quakes. That is the third reason.

3.16. 'Again, when the Bodhisatta emerges from his mother's womb, mindful and clearly aware, then the earth shudders and shakes and violently quakes. That is the fourth reason.

3.17. 'Again, when the Tathāgata gains unsurpassed enlightenment, then the earth shudders and shakes and violently quakes. That is the fifth reason.

3.18. 'Again, when the Tathāgata sets in motion the Wheel of the Dhamma, then the earth shudders and shakes and violently quakes. That is the sixth reason.

3.19. 'Again, when the Tathāgata, mindful and clearly aware, renounces the life-principle, then the earth shudders and shakes and violently quakes.

3.20. 'Again, when the Tathāgata [109] gains the Nibbāna-element without remainder,[405] then the earth shudders and shakes and violently quakes. That is the eighth reason. These, Ānanda, are the eight reasons, the eight causes for the appearance of a great earthquake.

3.21. 'Ānanda, these eight [kinds of] assemblies. What are they? They are the assembly of Khattiyas, the assembly of Brahmins, the assembly of householders, the assembly of ascetics, the assembly of devas of the Realm of the Four Great Kings, the assembly of the Thirty-Three Gods, the assembly of māras, the assembly of Brahmās.

3.22. 'I remember well, Ānanda, many hundreds of assemblies of Khattiyas[406] that I have attended; and before I sat down with them, spoke to them or joined in their conversation, I adopted their appearance and speech, whatever it might be. And I instructed, inspired, fired and delighted them with a discourse on Dhamma. And as I spoke with them they did not know me and wondered: "Who is it that speaks like this – a deva or a man?" And having thus instructed them, I disappeared, and still they did not know: "He who has just disappeared – was he a deva or a man?"

3.23. 'I remember well many hundreds of assemblies of Brahmins, of householders, of ascetics, of devas of the Realm of the Four Great Kings, of the Thirty-Three Gods, of māras, of Brahmās...,[110] and still they did not know: "He who has just disappeared – was he a deva or a man?" Those, Ānanda, are the eight assemblies.

3.24. 'Ānanda, there are eight stages of mastery.[407] What are they?

3.25. 'Perceiving forms internally,[408] one sees external forms, limited and beautiful or ugly, and in mastering these, one is aware that one knows and sees them. That is the first stage.

3.26. 'Perceiving forms internally, one sees external forms, unlimited and beautiful or ugly...(*as verse 25*). That is the second stage.

3.27. 'Not perceiving forms internally, one sees external forms, limited and beautiful or ugly...(*as verse 25*). That is the third stage.

3.28. 'Not perceiving forms internally, one sees external forms, unlimited and beautiful or ugly, and in mastering these, one is aware that one knows and sees them. That is the fourth stage.

3.29. 'Not perceiving forms internally, one sees external forms that are blue, of blue colour, of blue lustre. Just as a flax flower which is blue, of blue colour, of blue lustre, or a Benares cloth smoothed on both sides that is blue,...so one perceives external forms that are blue,...and in mastering these, one is aware that one knows and sees them. That is the fifth stage.

[111] 3.30. 'Not perceiving forms internally, one sees external forms that are yellow...Just as a *kaṇṇikāra*[409] flower which is yellow,...or a Benares cloth that is yellow, so one perceives external forms that are yellow...That is the sixth stage.

3.31. 'Not perceiving forms internally, one sees external forms that are red...Just as a hibiscus flower which is red,...or a Benares cloth which is red,...so one perceives external forms that are red...That is the seventh stage.

3.32. 'Not perceiving forms internally, one sees external forms that are white, of white colour, of white lustre, just as the morning-star Osadhi[410] is white,...or a Benares cloth smoothed on both sides that is white,...so not perceiving forms internally, one sees external forms that are white,...and in mastering these, one is aware that one knows and sees them. That is the eighth stage of mastery. These, Ānanda, are the eight stages of mastery.

3.33. 'There are, Ānanda, these eight liberations. What are they? Possessing form, one sees forms. That is the first. [112] Not perceiving material forms in oneself, one sees them outside. That is the second. Thinking: "It is beautiful", one becomes intent on it. That is the third. By completely transcending all perception of matter,...thinking: "Space is infinite", one enters and abides in the Sphere of Infinite Space. That is the fourth. By transcending the Sphere of Infinite Space, thinking: "Consciousness is infinite", one enters and abides in the Sphere of Infinite Consciousness. That is the fifth. By transcending the Sphere of Infinite Consciousness, thinking: "There is no thing", one enters and abides in the Sphere of No-Thingness. That is the sixth. By transcending the Sphere of No-Thingness, one reaches and abides in the Sphere of Neither-Perception-Nor-Non-Perception. That is the seventh. By transcending the Sphere of Neither-Perception-Nor-Non-Perception, one enters and abides in the Cessation of Perception and Feeling. That is the eighth liberation (*as Sutta 15, verse 35*).

3.34. 'Ānanda, once I was staying at Uruvelā on the bank of the River Nerañjarā, under the Goatherd's Banyan-tree, when I had just attained supreme enlightenment. And Māra the Evil One came to me, stood to one side and said: "May the Blessed Lord now attain final Nibbāna, may the Well-Farer now attain final Nibbāna. Now is the time for the Blessed Lord's final Nibbāna."

3.35. 'At this I said to Māra: "Evil One, I will not take final Nibbāna till I have monks and disciples who are accomplished, trained, skilled, learned, knowers of the Dhamma,...(*as verse 7*), [113] till I have nuns..., laymen-followers, lay-women-followers who will...teach the Dhamma of wondrous effect. I will not take final Nibbāna till this holy life has been successfully established and flourishes, is widespread, well-known far and wide, well-proclaimed among mankind every-where."

3.36. 'And just now, today, Ānanda, at the Cāpāla Shrine, Māra came to me, stood to one, side and said: "Lord, may the Blessed Lord now attain final Nibbāna...Now is the time for the Blessed Lord's final Nibbāna."

[114] 3.37. 'And I said: "You need not worry, Evil One. Three months from now the Tathāgata will take final Nibbāna." So now, today, Ānanda, at the Cāpāla Shrine, the Tathāgata has mindfully and in full awareness renounced the life-principle.' [115]

3.38. At this the Venerable Ānanda said: 'Lord, may the Blessed Lord stay for a century, may the Well-Farer stay for a century for the benefit and happiness of the multitude, out of compassion for the world, for the benefit and happiness of devas and humans!' 'Enough, Ānanda! Do not beg the Tathā-gata, it is not the right time for that!'

3.39. And a second and a third time the Venerable Ānanda made the same request.

'Ānanda, have you faith in the Tathāgata's enlightenment?' 'Yes, Lord.'

'Then why do you bother the Tathāgata with your request up to three times?'

3.40. 'But Lord, I have heard from the Lord's own lips, I have understood from the Lord's own lips: "Whoever has developed the four roads to power...could undoubtedly live for a century, or for the remainder of one."'

'Have you faith, Ānanda?' 'Yes, Lord.'

'Then, Ānanda, yours is the fault, yours is the failure that, having been given such a broad hint, such a clear sign by the Tathāgata, you did not understand and did not beg the Tathā-gata to stay for a century...If, Ānanda, you had begged him, the Tathāgata would twice have refused you, but the third time he would have consented. Therefore, Ānanda, yours is the fault, yours is the failure.

3.41. 'Once, Ānanda, I was staying at Rājagaha, at the Vultures' Peak. And there I said: [116] "Ānanda, Rājagaha is delightful, the Vultures' Peak is delightful. Whoever has developed the four roads to power...could undoubtedly live for a century..."(*as verse 3*). But you, Ānanda, in spite of such a broad hint did not understand and did not beg the Tathāgata to stay for a century...

3.42. 'Once I was staying at Rājagaha in the Banyan Park..., at Robbers' Cliff..., at the Satapaṇṇi Cave on the side of Mount Vebhāra..., at the Black Rock on the slope of Mount Isigili..., at the slope by the Snakes' Pool in Cool Wood..., at the Tapodā Park..., at the Squirrels' Feeding-Ground in Veḷuvana..., in Jīvaka's mango-grove..., and also at Rājagaha in the Maddakucchi deer-park.

3.43. 'At all these places I said to you: "Ānanda, this place is delightful..." [117]

3.44. '"Whoever has developed the four roads to power... could undoubtedly live for a century..."(*as verse 3*).

3.45. 'Once I was at Vesālī at the Udena Shrine...[118]

3.46. 'Once I was at Vesālī at the Gotamaka Shrine..., at the Sattambaka Shrine..., at the Bahuputta Shrine..., at the Sārandada Shrine...

3.47. 'And now today at the Cāpāla Shrine I said: "These places are delightful. Ānanda, whoever has developed the four roads to power...could undoubtedly live for a century, or the remainder of one. The Tathāgata has developed these powers...and he could, Ānanda, undoubtedly live for a century, or the remainder of one."

'But you, Ānanda, failing to grasp this broad hint, this clear sign, did not beg the Tathāgata to stay for a century. If, Ānanda, you had begged him, the Tathāgata would twice have refused you, but the third time he would have consented.

3.48. 'Ānanda, have I not told you before: All those things that are dear and pleasant to us must suffer change, separation and alteration? So how could this be possible? Whatever is born, become, compounded, is liable to decay – that it should not decay is impossible. And that has been renounced, given up, rejected, abandoned, forsaken: the Tathāgata has renounced the life-principle. The Tathāgata has said once for all: "The Tathāgata's final passing [119] will not be long delayed. Three months from now the Tathāgata will take final Nibbāna." That the Tathāgata should withdraw such a declaration in order to live on, is not possible.[411] Now come, Ānanda, we will go to the Gabled Hall in the Great Forest.' 'Very good, Lord.'

3.49. And the Lord went with the Venerable Ānanda to the Gabled Hall in the Great Forest. When he got there, he said: 'Ānanda, go and gather together all the monks living in the vicinity of Vesālī, and get them to come to the assembly hall.' 'Very good, Lord', said Ānanda, and did so. He then returned to the Lord, saluted him, stood to one side and said: 'Lord, the order of monks is gathered together. Now is the time for the Lord to do as he wishes.'

3.50. Then the Lord entered the assembly hall and sat down on the prepared seat. Then he said to the monks: 'Monks, for this reason those matters which I have discovered and proclaimed should be thoroughly learnt by you, practised, developed and cultivated, so that this holy life may endure for a long time, that it may be for the benefit and happiness of the multitude, out of compassion for the world, for the benefit and happiness of devas and humans. And what are those matters...? [120] They are: The four foundations of mindfulness, the four right efforts, the four roads to power, the five spiritual faculties,[412] the five mental powers,[413] the seven factors of enlightenment, the Noble Eightfold Path.'[414]

3.51. Then the Lord said to the monks: 'And now, monks, I declare to you – all conditioned things are of a nature to decay – strive on untiringly. The Tathāgata's final passing will not be long delayed. Three months from now the Tathāgata will take his final Nibbāna.'

Thus the Lord spoke. The Well-Farer having thus spoken, the Teacher said this:

'Ripe I am in years. My life-span's determined.
Now I go from you, having made myself my refuge.

Monks, be untiring, mindful, disciplined,
Guarding your minds with well-collected thought.
[121]
He who, tireless, keeps to law and discipline,
Leaving birth behind will put an end to woe.'

[*End of third recitation-section*]

[122] 4.1. Then the Lord, having risen early and dressed, took his robe and bowl and went into Vesālī for alms. Having returned from the alms-round and eaten, he looked back at Vesālī with his 'elephant-look'[415] and said: 'Ānanda, this is the last time the Tathāgata will look upon Vesālī. Now we will go to Bhaṇḍagāma.' 'Very good, Lord', said Ānanda, and the Lord proceeded with a large company of monks to Bhaṇḍagāma, and stayed there.

4.2. And there the Lord addressed the monks: 'It is, monks, through not understanding, not penetrating four things that I as well as you have for a long time fared on round the cycle of rebirths. What are the four? Through not understanding the Ariyan morality, through not understanding the Ariyan concentration, through not understanding the Ariyan wisdom, through not understanding the Ariyan liberation,[416] I as well as you have for a long time fared on round the cycle of rebirths. And it is by understanding [123] and penetrating the Ariyan morality, the Ariyan concentration, the Ariyan wisdom and the Ariyan liberation that the craving for becoming has been cut off, the tendency towards becoming has been exhausted, and there will be no more rebirth.'

4.3. Thus the Lord spoke. The Well-Farer having thus spoken, the Teacher said this:

'Morality, samādhi, wisdom and final release,
These glorious things Gotama came to know.
The Dhamma he'd discerned he taught his monks:
He whose vision ended woe to Nibbāna's gone.'

4.4. Then the Lord, while staying at Bhaṇḍagāma, delivered a comprehensive discourse: 'This is morality, this is concentration, this is wisdom. Concentration, when imbued with morality, brings great fruit and profit. Wisdom, when imbued with concentration, brings great fruit and profit. The mind imbued with wisdom becomes completely free from the corruptions, that is, from the corruption of sensuality, of becoming, of false views and of ignorance.'

4.5. And when the Lord had stayed at Bhaṇḍagāma for as long as he wished, he said: 'Ānanda, let us go to Hatthigāma ..., to Ambagāma..., to Jambugāma...' giving the same discourse at each place. Then he said: 'Ānanda, let us go to Bhoganagara.'

4.6. 'Very good, Lord', said Ānanda, and the Lord went with a large company of monks to Bhoganagara.

4.7. At Bhoganagara the Lord stayed at the Ānanda Shrine. And here he said to the monks: 'Monks, I will teach you four criteria. Listen, pay close attention, and I will speak.' [124] 'Yes, Lord', replied the monks.

4.8. 'Suppose a monk were to say: "Friends, I heard and received this from the Lord's own lips: this is the Dhamma, this is the discipline, this is the Master's teaching", then, monks, you should neither approve nor disapprove his words. Then, without approving or disapproving, his words and expressions should be carefully noted and compared with the Suttas and reviewed in the light of the discipline. If they, on such comparison and review, are found not to conform to the Suttas or the discipline, the conclusion must be: "Assuredly this is not the word of the Buddha, it has been wrongly understood by this monk", and the matter is to be rejected. But where on such comparison and review they are found to conform to the Suttas or the discipline, the conclusion must be: "Assuredly this is the word of the Buddha, it has been rightly understood by this monk." This is the first criterion.

4.9. 'Suppose a monk were to say: "In such and such a place there is a community with elders and distinguished teachers. I have heard and received this from that community", then, monks, you should neither approve nor disapprove his words ...(*as verse 4.8*). [125] That is the second criterion.

4.10. 'Suppose a monk were to say: "In such and such a place there are many elders who are learned, bearers of the tradition, who know the Dhamma, the discipline, the code of rules..." (*as verse 4.8*). This is the third criterion.

4.11. 'Suppose a monk were to say: "In such and such a place there is one elder who is learned...I have heard and received this from that elder..." (*as verse 4.8*). But where on such comparison and review they are found to conform to the Suttas and the discipline, then the conclusion must be: [126] 'Assuredly this is the word of the Buddha, it has been rightly understood by this monk.'

4.12. Then the Lord, while staying at Bhoganagara, delivered a comprehensive discourse: 'This is morality, this is concentration, this is wisdom...'

4.13. And when the Lord had stayed at Bhoganagara for as long as he wished, he said: 'Ānanda, let us go to Pāvā.' 'Very good, Lord', said Ānanda, and the Lord went with a large company of monks to Pāvā, where he stayed at the mango-grove of Cunda the smith.

4.14. And Cunda heard that the Lord had arrived at Pāvā and was staying at his mango-grove. So he went to the Lord, saluted him and sat down to one side, and the Lord instructed, inspired, fired and delighted him with a talk on Dhamma.

4.15. Then Cunda said: 'May the Lord accept a meal from me tomorrow with his order of monks!' And the Lord consented by silence.

4.16. And Cunda, understanding his consent, rose from his seat, saluted the Lord [127] and, passing by to the right, departed.

4.17. And as the night was ending Cunda had a fine meal of hard and soft food prepared with an abundance of 'pig's delight',[417] and when it was ready he reported to the Lord: 'Lord, the meal is ready.'

4.18. Then the Lord, having dressed in the morning, took his robe and bowl and went with his order of monks to Cunda's dwelling, where he sat down on the prepared seat and said: 'Serve the "pig's delight" that has been prepared to me, and serve the remaining hard and soft food to the order of monks.' 'Very good, Lord', said Cunda, and did so.

4.19. Then the Lord said to Cunda: 'Whatever is left over of the "pig's delight" you should bury in a pit, because, Cunda,

I can see none in this world with its devas, māras and Brahmās, in this generation with its ascetics and Brahmins, its princes and people who, if they were to eat it, could thoroughly digest it except the Tathāgata.'[418] 'Very good, Lord', said Cunda and, having buried the remains of the 'pig's delight' in a pit, he came to the Lord, saluted him and sat down to one side. Then the Lord, having instructed, inspired, fired and delighted him with a talk on Dhamma, rose from his seat and departed.

4.20. And after having eaten the meal provided by Cunda, the Lord was attacked by a severe sickness with bloody diarrhoea, and with sharp pains as if he were about to die. [128] But he endured all this mindfully and clearly aware, and without complaint. Then the Lord said: 'Ānanda, let us go to Kusināra.' 'Very good, Lord', said Ānanda.

> Having eaten Cunda's meal (this I've heard),
> He suffered a grave illness, painful, deathly;
> From eating a meal of 'pig's delight'
> Grave sickness assailed the Teacher.
> Having purged, the Lord then said:
> 'Now I'll go to Kusinārā town.'[419]

4.21. Then turning aside from the road, the Lord went to the foot of a tree and said: 'Come, Ānanda, fold a robe in four for me: I am tired and want to sit down.' 'Very good, Lord', said Ānanda, and did so.

4.22. The Lord sat down on the prepared seat and said: 'Ānanda, bring me some water: I am thirsty and want to drink.' Ānanda replied: 'Lord, five hundred carts have passed this way. The water is churned up by their wheels and is not good, it is dirty and disturbed. But, Lord, the River Kakutthā nearby has clean water, [129] pleasant, cool, pure, with beautiful banks, delightful. There the Lord shall drink the water and cool his limbs.'

4.23. A second time the Lord said: 'Ānanda, bring me some water...', and Ānanda replied as before.

4.24. A third time the Lord said: 'Ānanda, bring me some water: I am thirsty and want to drink.' 'Very good, Lord', said Ānanda and, taking his bowl, he went to the stream. And that stream whose water had been churned up by the wheels and was not good, dirty and disturbed, as Ānanda approached it began to flow pure, bright and unsullied.

4.25. And the Venerable Ānanda thought: 'Wonderful, marvellous are the Tathāgata's great and mighty powers! This water was churned up by wheels..., and at my approach it flows pure, bright and unsullied!' He took water in his bowl, brought it to the Lord and told him of his thought, saying: 'May the Lord drink the water, may the Well-Farer drink!' And the Lord drank the water. [130]

4.26. At that moment Pukkusa the Malla, a pupil of Āḷāra Kālāma,[420] was going along the main road from Kusinārā to Pāvā. Seeing the Lord sitting under a tree, he went over, saluted him and sat down to one side. Then he said: 'It is wonderful, Lord, it is marvellous how calm these wanderers are!

4.27. 'Once, Lord, Āḷāra Kālāma was going along the main road and, turning aside, he went and sat down under a nearby tree to take his siesta. And five hundred carts went rumbling by very close to him. A man who was walking along behind them came to Āḷāra Kālāma and said: "Lord, did you not see five hundred carts go by?" "No, friend, I did not." "But didn't you hear them, Lord?" "No, friend, I did not." "Well, were you asleep, Lord?" "No, friend, I was not asleep." "Then, Lord, were you conscious?" "Yes, friend". "So, Lord, being conscious and awake you neither saw nor heard five hundred carts passing close by you, even though your outer robe was bespattered with dust?" "That is so, friend."

'And that man thought: "It is wonderful, it is marvellous! These wanderers are so calm that though conscious [131] and awake, a man neither saw nor heard five hundred carts passing close by him!" And he went away praising Āḷāra Kālāma's lofty powers.'

4.28. 'Well, Pukkusa, what do you think? What do you consider is more difficult to do or attain to – while conscious and awake not to see or hear five hundred carts passing nearby or, while conscious and awake, not to see or hear anything when the rain-god streams and splashes, when lightning flashes and thunder crashes?'

4.29. 'Lord, how can one compare not seeing or hearing five hundred carts with that – or even six, seven, eight, nine or ten hundred, or hundreds of thousands of carts to that? To see or hear nothing when such a storm rages is more difficult...'

4.30. 'Once, Pukkusa, when I was staying at Ātumā, at the threshing-floor, the rain-god streamed and splashed, lightning flashed and thunder crashed, and two farmers, brothers, and four oxen were killed. And a lot of people went out of Ātumā to where the two brothers and the four oxen were killed.

4.31. 'And, Pukkusa, I had at that time gone out of the door of the threshing-floor and was walking up and down outside. And a man from the crowd came to me, saluted me and stood to one side. And I said to him:

4.32. '"Friend, why are all these people gathered here?" [132] "Lord, there has been a great storm and two farmers, brothers, and four oxen have been killed. But you, Lord, where have you been?" "I have been right here, friend." "But what did you see, Lord?" "I saw nothing, friend." "Or what did you hear, Lord?" "I heard nothing, friend." "Were you sleeping, Lord?" "I was not sleeping, friend." "Then, Lord, were you conscious?" "Yes, friend." "So, Lord, being conscious and awake you neither saw nor heard the great rainfall and floods and the thunder and lightning?" "That is so, friend."

4.33. 'And, Pukkusa, that man thought: "It is wonderful, it is marvellous! These wanderers are so calm that they neither see nor hear when the rain-god streams and splashes, lightning flashes and thunder crashes!" Proclaiming my lofty powers, he saluted me, passed by to the right and departed.'

4.34. At this, Pukkusa the Malla said: 'Lord, I reject the lofty powers of Āḷāra Kālāma as if they were blown away by a mighty wind or carried off by a swift stream or river! Excellent, Lord, excellent! It is as if someone were to set up what had been knocked down, or to point out the way to one who had got lost, or to bring an oil lamp into a dark place, so that those with eyes could see what was there. Just so the Blessed Lord has expounded the Dhamma in various ways. [133] And I, Lord, go for refuge to the Blessed Lord, the Dhamma and the Sangha. May the Blessed Lord accept me from this day forth as a lay-follower as long as life shall last!'

4.35. Then Pukkusa said to one man: 'Go and fetch me two fine sets of robes of cloth-of-gold, burnished and ready to wear.' 'Yes, Lord', the man replied, and did so. And Pukkusa offered the robes to the Lord, saying: 'Here, Lord, are two fine sets of robes of cloth-of-gold. May the Blessed Lord be graciously pleased to accept them!' 'Well then, Pukkusa, clothe me in one set and Ānanda in the other.' 'Very good, Lord', said Pukkusa, and did so.[421]

4.36. Then the Lord instructed, inspired, fired and delighted Pukkusa the Malla with a talk on Dhamma. Then Pukkusa rose from his seat, saluted the Lord, passed by to the right, and departed.

4.37. Soon after Pukkusa had gone, Ānanda, having arranged one set of the golden robes on the body of the Lord, observed that against the Lord's body it appeared dulled. And he said: 'It is wonderful, Lord, it is marvellous how clear and bright the Lord's skin appears! It looks even brighter than the golden [134] robes in which it is clothed.' 'Just so, Ānanda. There are two occasions on which the Tathāgata's skin appears especially clear and bright. Which are they? One is the night in which the Tathāgata gains supreme enlightenment, the other is the night when he attains the Nibbāna-element without remainder at his final passing. On these two occasions the Tathāgata's skin appears especially clear and bright.

4.38. 'Tonight, Ānanda, in the last watch, in the *sāl*-grove of the Mallas near Kusinārā, between two *sāl*-trees, the Tathāgata's final passing will take place. And now, Ānanda, let us go to the River Kakutthā.' 'Very good, Lord', said Ānanda.[422]

Two golden robes were Pukkusa's offering:
Brighter shone the Teacher's body than its dress.

4.39. Then the Lord went with a large number of monks to the River Kakutthā. He entered the water, bathed and drank and, emerging, went to the mango grove, where he said to the Venerable Cundaka: 'Come, Cundaka, fold a robe in four for me. I am tired and want to lie down.' 'Very good, Lord', said Cundaka, and did so.

4.40. Then the Lord adopted the lion-posture, lying on his

right side, placing one foot on the other, mindfully and with clear awareness [135] bearing in mind the time of awakening. And the Venerable Cundaka sat down in front of the Lord.

4.41. The Buddha having gone to Kakutthā the river
With its clear, bright and pleasant waters,
Therein the Teacher plunged his weary body.
Tathāgata – without an equal in the world.
Surrounded by the monks whose head he was.
The Teacher and Lord, Preserver of Dhamma,
To the Mango Grove the great Sage went,
And to Cundaka the monk he said:
'On a fourfold robe I'll lie down.'
And thus adjured by the great Adept,
Cundaka placed the fourfold robe.
The Teacher laid his weary limbs to rest
While Cundaka kept watch beside him.

4.42. Then the Lord said to the Venerable Ānanda: 'It might happen, Ānanda, that Cunda the smith should feel remorse, thinking: "It is your fault, friend Cunda, it is by your misdeed that the Tathāgata gained final Nibbāna after taking his last meal from you!" But Cunda's remorse should be expelled in this way: "That is your merit, Cunda, that is your good deed, that the Tathāgata gained final Nibbāna after taking his last meal from you! For, friend Cunda, I have heard and understood from the Lord's own lips that these two alms-givings are of very great [136] fruit, of very great result, more fruitful and advantageous than any other. Which two? The one is the alms-giving after eating which the Tathāgata attains supreme enlightenment, the other that after which he attains the Nibbāna-element without remainder at his final passing. These two alms-givings are more fruitful and profitable than all others. Cunda's deed is conducive to long life, to good looks, to happiness, to fame, to heaven and to lordship." In this way, Ānanda, Cunda's remorse is to be expelled.'

4.43. Then the Lord, having settled this matter, at that time uttered this verse:

'By giving, merit grows, by restraint, hatred's checked.
He who's skilled abandons evil things.
As greed, hate and folly wane, Nibbāna's gained.'

[*End of the fourth recitation-section, concerning Āḷāra*]

[137] 5.1. The Lord said: 'Ānanda, let us cross the Hiraññavatī River and go to the Mallas' *sāl*-grove in the vicinity of Kusinārā.'[423] 'Very good, Lord', said Ānanda, and the Lord, with a large company of monks, crossed the river and went to the *sāl*-grove. There the Lord said: 'Ānanda, prepare me a bed between these twin *sāl*-trees with my head to the north. I am tired and want to lie down.' 'Very good, Lord', said Ānanda, and did so. Then the Lord lay down on his right side in the lion-posture, placing one foot on the other, mindful and clearly aware.

5.2. And those twin *sāl*-trees burst forth into an abundance of untimely blossoms, which fell upon the Tathāgata's body, sprinkling it and covering it in homage. Divine coral-tree flowers fell from the sky, divine sandal-wood powder fell from the sky, sprinkling and covering the Tathāgata's body [138] in homage. Divine music and song sounded from the sky in homage to the Tathāgata.

5.3. And the Lord said: 'Ānanda, these *sāl*-trees have burst forth into an abundance of untimely blossoms...Divine music and song sound from the sky in homage to the Tathāgata. Never before has the Tathāgata been so honoured, revered, esteemed, worshipped and adored. And yet, Ānanda, whatever monk, nun, male or female lay-follower dwells practising the Dhamma properly, and perfectly fulfils the Dhamma-way, he or she honours the Tathāgata, reveres and esteems him and pays him the supreme homage. Therefore, Ānanda, "We will dwell practising the Dhamma properly and perfectly fulfil the Dhamma-way" – this must be your watchword.'

5.4. Just then the Venerable Upavāṇa was standing in front of the Lord, fanning him. And the Lord told him to move: 'Move aside, monk, do not stand in front of me.' And the Venerable Ānanda thought: 'This Venerable [139] Upavāṇa has for long been the Lord's attendant, keeping close at hand, at his beck and call. And now in his last hour the Lord tells him to stand aside and not stand in front of him. Why ever does he do that?'

5.5. And he asked the Lord about this. 'Ānanda, the devas from ten world-spheres have gathered to see the Tathāgata. For a distance of twelve yojanas around the Mallas' *sāl*-grove near Kusinārā there is not a space you could touch with the point of a hair that is not filled with mighty devas, and they are grumbling: "We have come a long way to see the Tathāgata. It is rare for a Tathāgata, a fully-enlightened Buddha, to arise in the world, and tonight in the last watch the Tathāgata will attain final Nibbāna, and this mighty monk is standing in front of the Lord, preventing us from getting a last glimpse of the Tathāgata!"'

5.6. 'But, Lord, what kind of devas can the Lord perceive?' 'Ānanda, there are sky-devas whose minds are earth-bound, they are weeping and tearing their hair, raising their arms, [140] throwing themselves down and twisting and turning, crying: "All too soon the Blessed Lord is passing away, all too soon the Well-Farer is passing away, all too soon the Eye of the World is disappearing!" And there are earth-devas whose minds are earth-bound, who do likewise. But those devas who are free from craving endure patiently, saying: "All compounded things are impermanent – what is the use of this?"[424]

5.7. 'Lord, formerly monks who had spent the Rains in various places used to come to see the Tathāgata, and we used to welcome them so that such well-trained monks might see you and pay their respects. But with the Lord's passing, we shall no longer have a chance to do this.'

5.8. 'Ānanda, there are four places the sight of which should arouse emotion[425] in the faithful. Which are they? "Here the Tathāgata was born" is the first.[426] "Here the Tathāgata attained supreme enlightenment" is the second.[427] "Here the Tathāgata set in motion the Wheel of Dhamma" is the third.[428] "Here the Tathāgata attained the Nibbāna-element without remainder" is the fourth.[429] [141] And, Ānanda, the faithful monks and nuns, male and female lay-followers will visit those places. And any who die while making the pilgrimage to these shrines with a devout heart will, at the breaking-up of the body after death, be reborn in a heavenly world.

5.9. 'Lord, how should we act towards women?' 'Do not see them, Ānanda.' 'But if we see them, how should we behave, Lord?' 'Do not speak to them, Ānanda.' 'But if they speak to us, Lord, how should we behave?' 'Practise mindfulness, Ānanda.'[430]

5.10. 'Lord, what shall we do with the Tathāgata's remains?' 'Do not worry yourselves about the funeral arrangements, Ānanda. You should strive for the highest goal,[431] devote yourselves to the highest goal, and dwell with your minds tirelessly, zealously devoted to the highest goal. There are wise Khattiyas, Brahmins and householders who are devoted to the Tathāgata: they will take care of the funeral.'

5.11. 'But, Lord, what are we to do with the Tathāgata's remains?' 'Ānanda, they should be dealt with like the remains of a wheel-turning monarch.' 'And how is that, Lord?' 'Ānanda, the remains of a wheel-turning monarch are wrapped in a new linen-cloth. This they wrap in teased cotton wool, and this in a [142] new cloth. Having done this five hundred times each, they enclose the king's body in an oil-vat of iron,[432] which is covered with another iron pot. Then having made a funeral-pyre of all manner of perfumes they cremate the king's body, and they raise a stupa at a crossroads. That, Ānanda, is what they do with the remains of a wheel-turning monarch, and they should deal with the Tathāgata's body in the same way. A stupa should be erected at the crossroads for the Tathāgata. And whoever lays wreaths or puts sweet perfumes and colours[433] there with a devout heart, will reap benefit and happiness for a long time.

5.12. 'Ānanda, there are four persons worthy of a stupa. Who are they? A Tathāgata, Arahant, fully-enlightened Buddha is one, a Pacceka Buddha[434] is one, a disciple of the Tathāgata is one, and a wheel-turning monarch is one. And why is each of these worthy of a stupa? Because, Ānanda, at the thought: "This is the stupa of a Tathāgata, of a Pacceka Buddha, [143] of a disciple of the Tathāgata, of a wheel-turning monarch", people's hearts are made peaceful, and then, at the breaking-up of tne body after death they go to a good destiny and rearise in a heavenly world. That is the reason, and those are the four who are worthy of a stupa.'

5.13. And the Venerable Ānanda went into his lodging[435] and stood lamenting, leaning on the door-post:[436] 'Alas, I am still a learner with much to do! And the Teacher is passing away, who was so compassionate to me!'

Then the Lord enquired of the monks where Ānanda was, and they told him. So he said to a certain monk: 'Go, monk, and say to Ānanda from me: "Friend Ānanda, the Teacher summons you."' [144] 'Very good, Lord', said the monk, and did so. 'Very good, friend', Ānanda replied to that monk, and he went to the Lord, saluted him and sat down to one side.

5.14. And the Lord said: 'Enough, Ānanda, do not weep and wail! Have I not already told you that all things that are pleasant and delightful are changeable, subject to separation and becoming other? So how could it be, Ānanda – since whatever is born, become, compounded is subject to decay – how could it be that it should not pass away? For a long time, Ānanda, you have been in the Tathāgata's presence, showing loving-kindness in act of body, speech and mind, beneficially, blessedly, whole-heartedly and unstintingly. You have achieved much merit, Ānanda. Make the effort, and in a short time you will be free of the corruptions.'[437]

5.15. Then the Lord addressed the monks: 'Monks, all those who were Arahant fully-enlightened Buddhas in the past have had just such a chief attendant as Ānanda, and so too will those Blessed Lords who come in the future. Monks, Ānanda is wise. He knows when it is the right time for monks to come to see the Tathāgata, when it is the right time for nuns, for male lay-followers, [145] for female lay-followers, for kings, for royal ministers, for leaders of other schools, and for their pupils.

5.16. 'Ānanda has four remarkable and wonderful qualities. What are they? If a company of monks comes to see Ānanda, they are pleased at the sight of him, and when Ānanda talks Dhamma to them they are pleased, and when he is silent they are disappointed. And so it is, too, with nuns, with male and female lay-followers.[438] And these four qualities apply to a wheel-turning monarch: if he is visited by a company of Khattiyas, of Brahmins, of householders, or of ascetics, they are pleased at the sight of him and when he talks to them, and when he is silent they are disappointed. [146] And so too it is with Ānanda.'

5.17. After this the Venerable Ānanda said: 'Lord, may the Blessed Lord not pass away in this miserable little town of wattle-and-daub, right in the jungle in the back of beyond! Lord, there are other great cities such as Campā, Rājagaha, Sāvatthi, Sāketa, Kosambī or Vārāṇasī. In those places there are wealthy Khattiyas, Brahmins and householders who are devoted to the Tathāgata, and they will provide for the Tathāgata's funeral in proper style.'

'Ānanda, don't call it a miserable little town of wattle-and-daub, right in the jungle in the back of beyond!

5.18. 'Once upon a time, Ānanda, King Mahāsudassana was a wheel-turning monarch, a rightful and righteous king, who had conquered the land in four directions and ensured the security of his realm, and who possessed the seven treasures. And, Ānanda, this King Mahāsudassana had this very Kusinārā, under the name of Kusāvatī, for his capital. And it was twelve yojanas long from east to west, and seven yojanas wide from north to south. Kusāvatī was rich, prosperous [147] and well-populated, crowded with people and well-stocked with food. Just as the deva-city of Āḷakamandā[439] is rich, prosperous and well-populated, crowded with yakkhas and well-stocked with food, so was the royal city of Kusāvatī. And the city of Kusāvatī was never free of ten sounds by day or night: the sound of elephants, horses, carriages, kettle-drums, side-drums, lutes, singing, cymbals and gongs, with cries of "Eat, drink and be merry!" as tenth.[440]

5.19. 'And now, Ānanda, go to Kusinārā and announce to the Mallas of Kusinārā: "Tonight, Vāseṭṭhas,[441] in the last watch, the Tathāgata will attain final Nibbāna. Approach him, Vāseṭṭhas, approach him, lest later you should regret it, saying: 'The Tathāgata passed away in our parish, and we did not take the opportunity to see him for the last time!'"' 'Very good, Lord', said Ānanda and, taking robe and bowl, he went with a companion to Kusinārā.

5.20. Just then the Mallas of Kusinārā were assembled in their meeting-hall on some business. And Ānanda came to them and delivered the Lord's words. [148]

5.21. And when they heard Ānanda's words, the Mallas, with their sons, daughters-in-law and wives were struck with anguish and sorrow, their minds were overcome with grief so that they were all weeping and tearing their hair...Then they all went to the *sāl*-grove where the Venerable Ānanda was.

5.22. And Ānanda thought: 'If I allow the Mallas of Kusinārā to salute the Lord individually, the night will have passed before they have all paid homage. I had better let them pay homage family by family, saying: "Lord, the Malla so-and-so with his children, his wife, his servants and his friends pays homage at the Lord's feet."' And so he presented them in that way, and thus allowed all the Mallas of Kusinārā to pay homage to the Lord in the first watch.

5.23. And at that time a wanderer called Subhadda was in Kusinārā, and he heard that the ascetic Gotama was to attain final Nibbāna in the final watch of that night. [149] He thought: 'I have heard from venerable wanderers, advanced in years, teachers of teachers, that a Tathāgata, a fully-enlightened Buddha, only rarely arises in the world. And tonight in the last watch the ascetic Gotama will attain final Nibbāna. Now a doubt has arisen in my mind, and I feel sure that the ascetic Gotama can teach me a doctrine to dispel that doubt.'

5.24. So Subhadda went to the Mallas' *sāl*-grove, to where the Venerable Ānanda was, and told him what he had thought: 'Reverend Ānanda, may I be permitted to see the ascetic Gotama?' But Ānanda replied: 'Enough, friend Subhadda, do not disturb the Tathāgata, the Lord is weary.' And Subhadda made his request a second and a third time, but still Ānanda [150] refused it.

5.25. But the Lord overheard this conversation between Ānanda and Subhadda, and he called to Ānanda: 'Enough, Ānanda, do not hinder Subhadda, let him see the Tathāgata. For whatever Subhadda asks me he will ask in quest of enlightenment[442] and not to annoy me, and what I say in reply to his questions he will quickly understand.' Then Ānanda said: 'Go in, friend Subhadda, the Lord gives you leave.'

5.26. Then Subhadda approached the Lord, exchanged courtesies with him, and sat down to one side, saying: 'Venerable Gotama, all those ascetics and Brahmins who have orders and followings, who are teachers, well-known and famous as founders of schools, and popularly regarded as saints, like Pūraṇa Kassapa, Makkhali Gosāla, Ajita Kesakambalī, Pakudha Kaccāyana, Sañjaya Belaṭṭhaputta and the Nigaṇṭha Nātaputta – have they all realised the truth as they all make out, or have none [151] of them realised it, or have some realised it and some not?' 'Enough, Subhadda, never mind whether all, or none, or some of them have realised the truth. I will teach you Dhamma, Subhadda. Listen, pay close attention, and I will speak.' 'Yes, Lord', said Subhadda, and the Lord said:

5.27. 'In whatever Dhamma and discipline the Noble Eightfold Path is not found, no ascetic is found of the first, the second, the third or the fourth grade.[443] But such ascetics can be found, of the first, second, third and fourth grade in a Dhamma and discipline where the Noble Eightfold Path is found. Now, Subhadda, in this Dhamma and discipline the Noble Eightfold Path *is* found, and in it are to be found ascetics of the first, second, third and fourth grade. Those other schools are devoid of [true] ascetics; but if in this one the monks were to live the life to perfection, the world would not lack for Arahants.

Twenty-nine years of age I was
When I went forth to seek the Good.
Now over fifty years have passed
Since the day that I went forth
To roam the realm of wisdom's law
Outside of which no ascetic is [152]
[First, second, third or fourth degree].
Other schools of such are bare,
But if here monks live perfectly,
The world won't lack for Arahants.'[444]

5.28. At this the wanderer Subhadda said: 'Excellent, Lord, excellent! It is as if someone were to set up what had been knocked down, or to point out the way to one who had got lost, or to bring an oil lamp into a dark place, so that those with eyes could see what was there. Just so the Blessed Lord has expounded the Dhamma in various ways. And I, Lord, go for refuge to the Blessed Lord, the Dhamma and the Sangha. May I receive the going-forth in the Lord's presence! May I receive ordination!'

5.29. 'Subhadda, whoever, coming from another school, seeks the going-forth and ordination in this Dhamma and discipline, must wait four months on probation. And at the end of four months, those monks who are established in mind[445] may let him go forth and give him ordination to the status of a monk. However, there can be a distinction of persons.'

'Lord, if those coming from other schools must wait four months on probation,...I will wait four years, and then let them give me the going-forth and the ordination!' But the Lord said to Ānanda: 'Let Subhadda go forth!' 'Very good, Lord', said Ānanda.

5.30. And Subhadda said to the Venerable Ānanda: 'Friend Ānanda, it is a great gain for you all, it is very profitable for you, that you have obtained the consecration of discipleship in the Teacher's presence.' [153]

Then Subhadda received the going-forth in the Lord's presence, and the ordination. And from the moment of his ordination the Venerable Subhadda, alone, secluded, unwearying, zealous and resolute, in a short time attained to that for which young men of good family go forth from the household life into homelessness, that unexcelled culmination of the holy life, having realised it here and now by his own insight, and dwelt therein: 'Birth is destroyed, the holy life has been lived, what had to be done has been done, there is nothing further here.' And the Venerable Subhadda became another of the Arahants. He was the last personal disciple of the Lord.[446]

[*End of the fifth recitation-section* (*Hiraññavatī*)]

[154] 6.1. And the Lord said to Ānanda: 'Ānanda, it may be that you will think: "The Teacher's instruction has ceased, now we have no teacher!" It should not be seen like this,

Ānanda, for what I have taught and explained to you as Dhamma and discipline will, at my passing, be your teacher.

6.2. 'And whereas the monks are in the habit of addressing one another as "friend", this custom is to be abrogated after my passing. Senior monks shall address more junior monks by their name, their clan or as "friend",[447] whereas more junior monks are to address their seniors either as "Lord"[448] or as "Venerable Sir".[449]

6.3. 'If they wish, the order may abolish the minor rules after my passing.[450]

6.4. 'After my passing, the monk Channa is to receive the Brahma-penalty.'[451] 'But, Lord, what is the Brahma-penalty?' 'Whatever the monk Channa wants or says, he is not to be spoken to, admonished or instructed by the monks.'

6.5. Then the Lord addressed the monks, saying: 'It may be, monks, that some monk has doubts or uncertainty about the Buddha, the Dhamma, the Sangha, or about the path or the practice. Ask, monks! Do not afterwards [155] feel remorse, thinking: "The Teacher was there before us, and we failed to ask the Lord face to face!"' At these words the monks were silent. The Lord repeated his words a second and a third time, and still the monks were silent. Then the Lord said: 'Perhaps, monks, you do not ask out of respect for the Teacher. Then, monks, let one friend tell it to another.' But still they were silent.

6.6. And the Venerable Ānanda said: 'It is wonderful, Lord, it is marvellous! I clearly perceive that in this assembly there is not one monk who has doubts or uncertainty...' 'You, Ānanda, speak from faith.[452] But the Tathāgata knows that in this assembly there is not one monk who has doubts or uncertainty about the Buddha, the Dhamma or the Sangha or about the path or the practice. Ānanda, the least one of these five hundred monks is a Stream-Winner, incapable of falling into states of woe, certain of Nibbāna.'

6.7. Then the Lord said to the monks: [156] 'Now, monks, I declare to you: all conditioned things are of a nature to decay – strive on untiringly.'[453] These were the Tathāgata's last words.

6.8. Then the Lord entered the first jhāna. And leaving that he entered the second, the third, the fourth jhāna. Then leaving the fourth jhāna he entered the Sphere of Infinite Space, then the Sphere of Infinite Consciousness, then the Sphere of No-Thingness, then the Sphere of Neither-Perception-Nor-Non-Perception, and leaving that he attained the Cessation of Feeling and Perception.[454]

Then the Venerable Ānanda said to the Venerable Anuruddha: 'Venerable Anuruddha, the Lord has passed away.' 'No, friend Ānanda,[455] the Lord has not passed away, he has attained the Cessation of Feeling and Perception.'

6.9. Then the Lord, leaving the attainment of the Cessation of Feeling and Perception, entered the Sphere of Neither-Perception-Nor-Non-Perception, from that he entered the Sphere of No-Thingness, the Sphere of Infinite Consciousness, the Sphere of Infinite Space. From the Sphere of Infinite Space he entered the fourth jhāna, from there the third, the second and the first jhāna. Leaving the first jhāna, he entered the second, the third, the fourth jhāna. And, leaving the fourth jhāna, the Lord finally passed away.

6.10. And at the Blessed Lord's final passing there was a great earthquake, terrible and hair-raising, accompanied by thunder. [157] And Brahmā Sahampati[456] uttered this verse:

'All beings in the world, all bodies must break up:
Even the Teacher, peerless in the human world,
The mighty Lord and perfect Buddha's passed away.'

And Sakka, ruler of the devas, uttered this verse:

'Impermanent are compounded things, prone to rise
and fall,
Having risen, they're destroyed, their passing truest
bliss.'[457]

And the Venerable Anuruddha uttered this verse:

'No breathing in and out – just with steadfast heart
The Sage who's free from lust has passed away to
peace.
With mind unshaken he endured all pains:
By Nibbāna the Illumined's mind is freed.'

And the Venerable Ānanda uttered this verse:

> 'Terrible was the quaking, men's hair stood on end,
> When the all-accomplished Buddha passed away.'

And those monks who had not yet overcome their passions wept and tore their hair, raising their arms, throwing themselves down and twisting and turning, crying: 'All too soon [158] the Blessed Lord has passed away, all too soon the Well-Farer has passed away, all too soon the Eye of the World has disappeared!' But those monks who were free from craving endured mindfully and clearly aware, saying: 'All compounded things are impermanent – what is the use of this?'

6.11. Then the Venerable Anuruddha said: 'Friends, enough of your weeping and wailing! Has not the Lord already told you that all things that are pleasant and delightful are changeable, subject to separation and to becoming other? So why all this, friends? Whatever is born, become, compounded is subject to decay, it cannot be that it does not decay. The devas, friends, are grumbling.'

'Venerable Anuruddha, what kind of devas are you aware of?' 'Friend Ānanda, there are sky-devas whose minds are earth-bound they are weeping and tearing their hair...And there are earth-devas whose minds are earth-bound, they do likewise. But those devas who are free from craving endure patiently, saying: "All compounded things are impermanent. What is the use of this?"'

6.12. Then the Venerable Anuruddha and the Venerable Ānanda spent the rest of the night in conversation on Dhamma. And the Venerable Anuruddha said: 'Now go, friend Ānanda, to Kusinārā and announce to the Mallas: "Vāseṭṭhas, the Lord has passed away. Now is the time to do as you think fit." "Yes, Lord", said Ānanda, and having dressed in the morning and taken his robe and bowl, he went with a companion to Kusinārā. [159] At that time the Mallas of Kusinārā were assembled in their meeting-hall on some business. And the Venerable Ānanda came to them and delivered the Venerable Anuruddha's message. And when they heard the Venerable Ānanda's words, the Mallas...were struck with anguish and sorrow, their minds were overcome with grief so that they were all tearing their hair...

6.13. Then the Mallas ordered their men to bring perfume and wreaths, and gather all the musicians together. And with the perfumes and wreaths, and all the musicians, and with five hundred sets of garments they went to the *sāl*-grove where the Lord's body was lying. And there they honoured, paid respects, worshipped and adored the Lord's body with dance and song and music, with garlands and scents, making awnings and circular tents in order to spend the day there. And they thought: 'It is too late to cremate the Lord's body today. We shall do so tomorrow.' And so, paying homage in the same way, they waited for a second, a third, a fourth, a fifth, a sixth day.

6.14. And on the seventh day the Mallas of Kusinārā thought: [160] 'We have paid sufficient honour with song and dance... to the Lord's body, now we shall burn his body after carrying him out by the south gate.' Then eight Malla chiefs, having washed their heads and put on new clothes, declared: 'Now we will lift up the Lord's body', but found they were unable to do so. So they went to the Venerable Anuruddha and told him what had happened: 'Why can't we lift up the Lord's body?' 'Vāseṭṭhas, your intention is one thing, but the intention of the devas is another.'

6.15. 'Lord, what is the intention of the devas?' 'Vāseṭṭhas, your intention is, having paid homage to the Lord's body with dance and song..., to burn his body after carrying him out by the south gate. But the devas' intention is, having paid homage to the Lord's body with heavenly dance and song..., to carry him to the north of the city, bring him in through the north gate and bear him through the middle of the city and out through the eastern gate to the Mallas' shrine of Makuṭa-Bandhana, and there to burn the body.' 'Lord, if that is the devas' intention, so be it!'

6.16. At that time even the sewers and rubbish-heaps of Kusinārā were covered knee-high with coral-tree flowers. And the devas as well as the Mallas of Kusinārā honoured the Lord's body with divine and human [161] dancing, song...; and they carried the body to the north of the city, brought it in through the north gate, through the middle of the city and out through the eastern gate to the Mallas' shrine of Makuṭa-Bandhana, where they set the body down.

6.17. Then they asked the Venerable Ānanda: 'Lord, how should we deal with the body of the Tathāgata?' 'Vāseṭṭhas, you should deal with the Tathāgata's body as you would that of a wheel-turning monarch.' 'And how do they deal with that, Lord?'

'Vāseṭṭhas, the remains are wrapped in a new linen-cloth. This they wrap in teased cotton-wool...; then having made a funeral-pyre of all manner of perfumes, they cremate the king's body and they raise a stupa at a cross roads...'

6.18. Then the Mallas ordered their men to bring their teased cotton-wool. And they dealt with the Tathāgata's body accordingly...[162]

6.19. Now just then the Venerable Kassapa the Great[458] was travelling along the main road from Pāvā to Kusinārā with a large company of about five hundred monks. And leaving the road, the Venerable Kassapa the Great sat down under a tree. And a certain Ājīvika[459] chanced to be coming along the main road towards Pāvā, and he had picked a coral-tree flower in Kusinārā. The Venerable Kassapa saw him coming from afar, and said to him: 'Friend, do you know our Teacher?' 'Yes, friend, I do. The ascetic Gotama passed away a week ago. I picked this coral-tree flower there.' And those monks who had not yet overcome their passions wept and tore their hair... But those monks who were free from craving endured mindfully and clearly aware, saying: 'All compounded things are impermanent – what is the use of this?'

6.20. And sitting in the group was one Subhadda,[460] who had gone forth late in life, and he said to those monks: 'Enough, friends, do not weep and wail! We are well rid of the Great Ascetic. We were always bothered by his saying: "It is fitting for you to do this, it is not fitting for you to do that!" Now we can do what we like, and not do what we don't like!'

But the Venerable Kassapa the Great said to the monks: 'Friends, enough of your weeping and wailing! [163] Has not the Lord already told you that all things that are pleasant and delightful are changeable, subject to separation and becoming other? So why all this, friends? Whatever is born, become, compounded is subject to decay, it cannot be that it does not decay.'

6.21. Meanwhile four Malla chiefs, having washed their heads and put on new clothes, said: 'We will light the Lord's funeral pyre', but they were unable to do so. They went to the Venerable Anuruddha and asked him why this was. 'Vāseṭṭhas, your intention is one thing, but that of the devas is another.' 'Well, Lord, what is the intention of the devas?' 'Vāseṭṭhas, the devas' intention is this: "The Venerable Kassapa the Great is coming along the main road from Pāvā to Kusinārā with a large company of five hundred monks. The Lord's funeral pyre will not be lit until the Venerable Kassapa the Great has paid homage with his head to the Lord's feet."' 'Lord, if that is the devas' intention, so be it!'

6.22. Then the Venerable Kassapa the Great went to the Mallas' shrine at Makuṭa-Bandhana to the Lord's funeral pyre and, covering one shoulder with his robe, joined his hands in salutation, circumambulated the pyre three times and, uncovering the Lord's feet, paid homage with his head to them, and the five hundred monks did likewise. [164] And when this was done, the Lord's funeral pyre ignited of itself.

6.23. And when the Lord's body was burnt, what had been skin, under-skin, flesh, sinew, or joint-fluid, all that vanished and not even ashes or dust remained, only the bones[461] remained. Just as when butter or oil is burnt, no ashes or dust remain, so it was with the Lord's body..., only the bones were left. And all the five hundred garments, even the innermost and the outermost cloth, were burnt up. And when the Lord's body was burnt up, a shower of water from the sky, and another which burst forth from the *sāl*-trees[462] extinguished the funeral pyre. And the Mallas of Kusinārā poured perfumed water over it for the same purpose. Then the Mallas honoured the relics for a week in their assembly hall, having made a lattice-work of spears and an encircling wall of bows, with dancing, singing, garlands and music.

6.24. And King Ajātasattu Vedehiputta of Magadha heard that the Lord had passed away at Kusinārā. And he sent a message to the Mallas of Kusinārā: 'The Lord was a Khattiya and I am a Khattiya. I am worthy to receive a share of the Lord's remains. I will make a great stupa for them.' The Licchavis of Vesālī heard, and they sent a message: 'The Lord was a Khattiya and we are Khattiyas. We are worthy to [165] receive a share of the Lord's remains, and we will make a great stupa for them.' The Sakyas of Kapilavatthu heard, and they sent a message: 'The Lord was the chief of our clan. We are worthy to receive a share of the Lord's remains, and we will make a great stupa for them.' 'The Bulayas of Allakappa and the Koliyas of Rāmagāma replied similarly. The Brahmin of Veṭhadīpa heard, and he sent a message: 'The Lord was a Khattiya, I am a Brahmin...', and the Mallas of Pāvā sent a message: 'The Lord was a Khattiya, we are Khattiyas. We are worthy to receive a share of the Lord's remains, and we will make a great stupa for them.'

6.25. On hearing all this, the Mallas of Kusinārā addressed the crowd, saying: [166] 'The Lord passed away in our parish. We will not give away any share of the Lord's remains.' At this the Brahmin Doṇa addressed the crowd in this verse:

'Listen, lords, to my proposal.
Forbearance is the Buddha's teaching.
It is not right that strife should come
From sharing out the best of men's remains.
Let's all be joined in harmony and peace,
In friendship sharing out portions eight:
Let stupas far and wide be put up,
That all may see – and gain in faith!'

'Well then, Brahmin, you divide up the remains of the Lord in the best and fairest way!' 'Very good, friends', said Doṇa. And he made a good and fair division into eight portions, and then said to the assembly: 'Gentlemen, please give me the urn, and I will erect a great stupa for it.' So they gave Doṇa the urn.

6.26. Now the Moriyas of Pipphalavana heard of the Lord's passing, and they sent a message: 'The Lord was a Khattiya and we are Khattiyas. We are worthy to receive a portion of the Lord's remains, and we will make a great stupa for them.'

'There is not a portion of the Lord's remains left, they have all been divided up. So you must take the embers.' And so they took the embers.

6.27. Then King Ajātasattu of Magadha built a great stupa

for the Lord's relics at Rājagaha. [167] The Licchavis of Vesālī built one at Vesālī, the Sakyans of Kapilavatthu built one at Kapilavatthu, the Bulayas of Allakappa built one at Allakappa, the Koliyas of Rāmagāma built one at Rāmagāma, the Brahmin of Veṭhadīpa built one at Veṭhadīpa, the Mallas of Pāvā built one at Pāvā, the Mallas of Kusinārā built a great stupa for the Lord's relics at Kusinārā, the Brahmin Doṇa built a great stupa for the urn, and the Moriyas of Pipphalavana built a great stupa for the embers at Pipphalavana. Thus, eight stupas were built for the relics, a ninth for the urn, and a tenth for the embers. That is how it was in the old days.[463]

6.28. Eight portions of relics there were of him,
The All-Seeing One. Of these, seven remained
In Jambudīpa with honour. The eighth
In Rāmagāma's kept by nāga kings.
One tooth the Thirty Gods have kept,
Kalinga's kings have one, the nāgas too.
They shed their glory o'er the fruitful earth.
Thus the Seer's honoured by the honoured. [168]
Gods and nāgas, kings, the noblest men
Clasp their hands in homage, for hard it is
To find another such for countless aeons.[464]

17 *Mahāsudassana Sutta: The Great Splendour* A King's Renunciation

[169] 1.1. Thus have I heard.[465] Once the Lord was staying at Kusinārā in the Mallas' *sāl*-grove shortly before his final Nibbāna between the twin *sāl*-trees.

1.2. The Venerable Ānanda came to the Lord, saluted him, sat down to one side and said: 'Lord, may the Blessed Lord not pass away in this miserable little town of wattle-and-daub, right in the jungle in the back of beyond! Lord, there are other great cities such as Campā, Rājagaha, Sāvatthi, Sāketa, Kosambī or Vārāṇasī. In those places there are wealthy Khattiyas, Brahmins and householders who are devoted to the Tathāgata and they will provide for the Tathāgata's funeral in proper style.'

1.3. 'Ānanda, don't call it a miserable little town of wattle-and-daub, right in the jungle in the back of beyond! Once upon a time, Ānanda, King Mahāsudassana[466] was a wheel-turning monarch, a rightful and righteous king, who had conquered the land in four directions and ensured the security of his realm. [170] And this King Mahāsudassana had this very Kusinārā, under the name of Kusāvatī, for his capital. And it was twelve yojanas long from east to west, and seven yojanas wide from north to south. Kusāvatī was rich, prosperous and well-populated, crowded with people and well-stocked with food. Just as the deva-city of Āḷakamandā is rich... (*as Sutta 16, verse 5.18*), so was the royal city of Kusavatī. And the city of Kusavatī was never free of ten sounds by day or night: the sound of elephants, horses, carriages, kettle-drums, side-drums, lutes, singing, cymbals and gongs, with cries of "Eat, drink and be merry" as tenth.

1.4. 'The royal city of Kusāvatī was surrounded by seven

encircling walls. One was of gold, one silver, one beryl, one crystal, one ruby, one emerald, and one of all sorts of gems.

1.5. 'And the gates of Kusāvatī were of four colours: one gold, one silver, one beryl, one crystal. [171] And before each gate were set seven pillars, three or four times a man's height. One was of gold, one silver, one beryl, one crystal, one ruby, one emerald, and one of all sorts of gems.

1.6. 'Kusāvatī was surrounded by seven rows of palm-trees, of the same materials. The gold trees had gold trunks with silver leaves and fruit, the silver trees had silver trunks with gold leaves and fruit. The beryl trees had beryl trunks with crystal leaves and fruit, the crystal trees had crystal trunks with beryl leaves and fruit. The ruby trees had ruby trunks and emerald leaves and fruit, the emerald trees had emerald trunks and ruby leaves and fruit, while the trees of all sorts of gems were the same as regards trunks, leaves and fruit. The sound of the leaves stirred by the wind was lovely, delightful, sweet and intoxicating, just like that of the five kinds of musical instruments[467] played in concert by well-trained and skilful players. [172] And, Ānanda, those who were libertines and drunkards in Kusāvatī had their desires assuaged by the sound of the leaves in the wind.[468]

1.7. 'King Mahāsudassana was endowed with the seven treasures and the four properties. What are the seven? Once, on a fast-day of the fifteenth,[469] when the King had washed his head and gone up to the verandah on top of his palace to observe the fast-day, the divine Wheel-Treasure[470] appeared to him, thousand-spoked, complete with felloe, hub and all appurtenances. On seeing it, King Mahāsudassana thought: "I have heard that when a duly anointed Khattiya king sees such a wheel on the fast-day of the fifteenth, he will become a wheel-turning monarch. May I become such a monarch!"

1.8. 'Then, rising from his seat, covering one shoulder with his robe, the King took a gold vessel in his left hand, sprinkled the Wheel with his right hand, and said: "May the noble Wheel-Treasure turn, may the noble Wheel-Treasure conquer!" The Wheel turned to the east, and King Mahāsudassana followed it with his fourfold army.[471] And in whatever country [173] the Wheel stopped, the King took up residence with his fourfold army.

1.9. 'And those kings who faced him in the eastern region came and said: "Come, Your Majesty, welcome! We are yours, Your Majesty. Rule us, Your Majesty!" And the King said: "Do not take life. Do not take what is not given. Do not commit sexual misconduct. Do not tell lies. Do not drink strong drink. Be moderate in eating."[472] And those who had faced him in the eastern region became his subjects.

1.10. 'And when the Wheel had plunged into the eastern sea, it emerged and turned south, and King Mahāsudassana followed it with his fourfold army. And those Kings... become his subjects. Having plunged into the southern sea it turned west..., having plunged into the western sea it turned north, and King Mahāsudassana followed it with his fourfold army ...[174] and those who had faced him in the northern region became his subjects.

1.11. 'Then the Wheel-Treasure, having conquered the lands from sea to sea, returned to the royal capital of Kusāvatī and stopped before the King's palace as he was trying a case,[473] as if to adorn the royal palace. And this is how the Wheel-Treasure appeared to King Mahāsudassana.

1.12. 'Then the Elephant-Treasure appeared to King Mahāsudassana, pure white,[474] of sevenfold strength, with the wonderful power of travelling through the air, a royal tusker called Uposatha.[475] Seeing him, the King thought: "What a wonderful riding-elephant, if only he could be brought under control!" And this Elephant-Treasure submitted to control just like a thoroughbred that had been trained for a long time. And once the King, to try him, mounted the Elephant-Treasure at crack of dawn and rode him from sea to sea, returning to Kusāvatī in time for breakfast. And that is how the Elephant-Treasure appeared to King Mahāsudassana.

1.13. 'Then the Horse-Treasure appeared to King Mahāsudassana, with a crow's head,[476] dark-maned, with the wondrous power of travelling through the air, a royal stallion called Valāhaka.[477] And the King thought: "What a wonderful mount, if only he could be brought under control!" And [175] this Horse-Treasure submitted to control just like a thoroughbred that had been trained for a long time... And that is how the Horse-Treasure appeared to King Mahāsudassana.

1.14. 'Then the Jewel-Treasure appeared to King Mahāsudassana. It was a beryl, pure, excellent, well-cut into eight facets, clear, bright, unflawed, perfect in every respect. The lustre of this Jewel-Treasure radiated for an entire yojana round about. And once the King, to try it, went on night-manoeuvres on a dark night with his four-fold army, with the Jewel-Treasure fixed to the top of his standard. And all who lived in the villages round about started their daily work, thinking it was daylight. And that is how the Jewel-Treasure appeared to King Mahāsudassana.

1.15. 'Then the Woman-Treasure appeared to King Mahāsudassana, lovely, fair to see, charming, with a lotus-like complexion, not too tall or too short, not too thin or too fat, not too dark or too fair, of more than human, deva-like beauty. And the touch of the skin of the Woman-Treasure was like cotton or silk, and her limbs were cool when it was hot, and warm when it was cold. Her body smelt of sandal-wood and her lips of lotus. This Woman-Treasure rose before the King [176] and retired later, and was always willing to do his pleasure, and she was pleasant of speech. And this Woman-Treasure was not unfaithful to the King even in thought, much less in deed. And that is how the Woman-Treasure appeared to King Mahāsudassana.[478]

1.16. 'Then the Householder-Treasure appeared to King Mahāsudassana. With the divine eye which, as the result of kamma, he possessed,[479] he saw where treasure, owned and ownerless, was hidden. He came to the King and said: "Have no fear, Your Majesty, I will look after your wealth properly." And once, the King, to try him, went on board a ship and had it taken to the current in the middle of the Ganges. Then he said to the Householder-Treasure: "Householder, I want some gold coin!" "Well then, Sire, let the ship be brought to one bank." "I want the gold coins here!" Then the householder touched the water with both hands and drew out a vessel full of gold coins, saying: "Is that enough, Sire? Will that do, Sire?" and the King said: "That is enough, householder, that will do, you have served me enough." [177] And that is how the Householder-Treasurer appeared to King Mahāsudassana.

1.17. 'Then the Counsellor-Treasure appeared to King Mahāsudassana. He was wise, experienced, clever and competent to advise the King on how to proceed with what should be proceeded with, and to withdraw from what should be withdrawn from, and to overlook what should be overlooked.[480] He came to the King and said: "Have no fear, Your Majesty, I shall advise you." And that is how the Counsellor-Treasure appeared to King Mahāsudassana, and how he was equipped with all the seven treasures.

1.18. 'Again, Ānanda, King Mahāsudassana was endowed with the four properties.[481] What are they? Firstly, the King was handsome, good to look at, pleasing, with a complexion like the finest lotus, surpassing other men.

1.19. 'Secondly, he was long-lived, outliving other men.

1.20. 'Thirdly, he was free from illness, free from sickness, with a healthy digestion, less subject to cold and heat than that of other men.[482] [178]

1.21. 'Fourthly, he was beloved and popular with Brahmins and householders. Just as a father is beloved by his children, so he was with Brahmins and householders. And they were beloved by the King as children are beloved by their father. Once the King set out for the pleasure-park with his fourfold army, and the Brahmins and householders came to him and said: "Pass slowly by, Sire, that we may see you as long as possible!" And the King said to the charioteer: "Drive the chariot slowly so that I can see these Brahmins and householders as long as possible." Thus King Mahāsudassana was endowed with these four properties.

1.22. 'Then King Mahāsudassana thought: "Suppose I were to construct lotus-ponds between the palm-trees, a hundred bow-lengths[483] apart." And he did so. The lotus-ponds were lined with four-coloured tiles, gold, silver, beryl and crystal, each pond being approached by four staircases, one gold, one silver, one beryl and one crystal. And the gold staircase had gold posts [179] with silver railings and banisters, the silver had silver posts with gold railings and banisters, and so on. And the lotus-ponds were provided with two kinds of parapet, gold and silver – the gold parapets having gold posts, silver railings and banisters, and the silver parapets having silver posts, gold railings and banisters.

1.23. 'Then the King thought: "Suppose I were to provide

each pond with suitable [flowers for] garlands[484] – blue, yellow, red and white lotuses which will last through all seasons without fading?" And he did so. Then he thought: "Suppose I were to place bathmen on the banks of these ponds, to bathe those who come there?" And he did so. Then he thought: "Suppose I were to establish charitable posts on the banks of these ponds, so that those who want food can get it, those who want drink can get it, those who want clothes can get it, those who want transport can get it, those who want a sleeping-place can get it, those who want a wife can get one, and those who want gold coin can get it?" [180] And he did so.

1.24. 'Then the Brahmins and householders took great wealth and went to the King, saying: "Sire, here is wealth that we have gathered together especially for Your Majesty, please accept it!" "Thank you, friends, but I have enough wealth from legitimate revenues. Let this be yours, and take away more besides!" Being thus refused by the King, they withdrew to one side and considered: "It would not be right for us to take this wealth back home again. Suppose we were to build a dwelling for King Mahāsudassana." So they went to the King and said: "Sire, we would build you a dwelling", and the King accepted by silence.

1.25. 'Then Sakka, ruler of the gods, knowing in his mind King Mahāsudassana's thought, said to the attendant-deva Vissakamma:[485] "Come, friend Vissakamma, and build a dwelling for King Mahāsudassana, a palace called Dhamma." "Very good, Lord", Vissakamma [181] replied and, as swiftly as a strong man might stretch his flexed arm or flex it again, he at once vanished from the Heaven of the Thirty-Three and appeared before King Mahāsudassana, and said to him: "Sire, I shall build you a dwelling, a palace called Dhamma." The King assented by silence, and Vissakamma built him the Palace of Dhamma.

1.26. 'The Palace of Dhamma, Ānanda, was a yojana in length from east to west, and half a yojana wide from north to south. The whole palace was faced up to three times a man's height with tiles of four colours, gold, silver, beryl and crystal, and it contained eighty-four thousand columns of the same four colours. It had twenty-four staircases of the same four colours, and the gold staircases had gold posts with silver railings and banisters... (*as verse 23*). [182] It also had eighty-four thousand chambers of the same colours. In the gold chamber was a silver couch, in the silver chamber a gold couch, in the beryl chamber an ivory couch, and in the crystal chamber a sandalwood couch. On the door of the gold chamber a silver palm-tree was figured, with silver stem, gold leaves and fruit...On the door of the silver chamber a golden palm-tree was figured, with golden trunk, leaves and fruit, on the door of the beryl chamber a crystal palm-tree was figured, with crystal trunk and beryl leaves and fruit, on the door of the crystal chamber a beryl palm-tree was figured, with crystal leaves and fruit.

1.27. 'Then the King thought: "Suppose I were to make a grove of palm-trees all of gold by the door of the great gabled chamber where I sit in the daytime?" and he did so.

1.28. 'Surrounding the Dhamma Palace were two parapets, [183] one of gold, one of silver. The gold one had gold posts, silver railings and banisters, and the silver one had silver posts, gold railings and banisters.

1.29. 'The Dhamma Palace was surrounded by two nets of tinkling bells. One net was gold with silver bells, the other silver with gold bells. And when these nets of bells were stirred by the wind their sound was lovely, delightful, sweet and intoxicating, just like that of the five kinds of musical instruments played in concert by well-trained and skilful players. And those who were libertines and drunkards in Kusāvatī had their desires assuaged by the sound of those nets of bells.

1.30. 'And when the Dhamma Palace was finished, it was hard to look at, dazzling to the eyes, just as in the last month of the Rains, in autumn, when there is a clear and cloudless sky, the sun breaking through the mists is hard to look at, [184] so was the Dhamma Palace when it was finished.

1.31. 'Then the King thought: "Suppose I were to make a lotus-lake called Dhamma in front of the Dhamma Palace?" so he did so. This lake was a yojana long from east to west, and half a yojana wide from north to south, and lined with four kinds of tiles, gold, silver, beryl and crystal. There were twenty-four staircases to it of four different kinds: gold, silver, beryl and crystal. The gold staircases had gold posts with silver railings and banisters, the silver had gold railings and banisters...(*and so on, as verse 22*).

1.32. 'The Dhamma Lake was surrounded by seven kinds of palm-trees. The sound of the leaves stirred by the wind was lovely, delightful, sweet and intoxicating, just like that of the five kinds of musical instruments played in concert by well-trained and skilful players. And, Ānanda, those who were libertines and drunkards in Kusāvatī had their desires assuaged by the sound of the leaves in the wind. [185]

1.33. 'When the Dhamma Palace and the Dhamma Lake were finished, King Mahāsudassana, having satisfied every wish of those who at the time were ascetics or Brahmins, or revered as such, ascended into the Dhamma Palace.'

[*End of first recitation-section*]

2.1. 'Then King Mahāsudassana thought: "Of what kamma is it the fruit, of what kamma is it the result, that I am now so mighty and powerful?" [186] Then he thought: "It is the fruit, the result of three kinds of kamma: of giving, self-control, and abstinence."[486]

2.2. 'Then the King went to the great gabled chamber and, standing at the door, exclaimed: "May the thought of lust cease! May the thought of ill-will cease! May the thought of cruelty cease! Thus far and no further the thought of lust, of ill-will, of cruelty!"

2.3. 'Then the King went into the great gabled chamber, sat down cross-legged on the golden couch and, detached from all sense-desires, detached from unwholesome mental states, entered and remained in the first jhāna, which is with thinking and pondering, born of detachment, filled with delight and joy. And with the subsiding of thinking and pondering, by gaining inner tranquillity and oneness of mind, he entered and remained in the second jhāna, which is without thinking and pondering, born of concentration, filled with delight and joy. And with the fading away of delight, remaining imperturbable, mindful and clearly aware, he experienced in himself that joy of which the Noble Ones say: "Happy is he who dwells with equanimity and mindfulness", he entered and remained in the third jhāna. And, having given up pleasure and pain, and with the disappearance of former gladness and sadness, he entered and remained in the fourth jhāna which is beyond pleasure and pain, and purified by equanimity and mindfulness.

2.4. 'Then the King, emerging from the great gabled chamber, went to the golden gabled chamber and, seated cross-legged on the silver couch, stayed pervading first one quarter, then the second, the third and the fourth quarter with a mind filled with loving-kindness. Thus he stayed, spreading the thought of loving-kindness above, below and across, everywhere, always with a mind filled with loving-kindness, abundant, magnified, unbounded, without hatred or ill-will. And he did likewise with compassion, sympathetic joy, and [187] equanimity.[487]

2.5. 'Of King Mahāsudassana's eighty-four thousand cities,[488] his capital Kusāvatī was the chief; of his eighty-four thousand palaces Dhamma was the chief; of his eighty-four thousand gabled halls the great gabled chamber was the chief; his eighty-four thousand couches were of gold, silver, ivory, sandal-wood, covered with fleece, wool, spread with *kadali*-deer hide, with head-covers, with red cushions at both ends; of his eighty-four thousand elephants adorned with gold ornaments, with gold banners and spread with gold nets, Uposatha the royal tusker was chief; of his eighty-four thousand carriages, covered with lion-skins, tiger-skins, leopard-skins or with orange-coloured cloth, adorned with gold ornaments, gold banners and spread with gold nets, the chariot Vejayanta[489] was the chief; of his eighty-four thousand jewels the Jewel-Treasure was the chief; of his eighty-four thousand wives Queen Subhaddā[490] was the chief; [188] of his eighty-four thousand householders the Householder-Treasure was the chief; of his eighty-four thousand Khattiya retainers the Counsellor-Treasure was the chief; his eighty-four thousand cows had tethers of fine jute and milk-pails (?) of silver;[491] his eighty-four thousand bales of clothing were of the finest linen, cotton, silk and wool; his eighty-four thousand rice-offerings were there for the taking by those in need, evening and morning.

2.6. 'And at that time, King Mahāsudassana's eighty-four thousand elephants waited on him evening and morning. And he thought: "These eighty-four thousand elephants wait on me evening and morning. How if, at the end of each century, forty-two thousand elephants were to wait on me, turn and turn about?" And he gave instructions accordingly to his Counsellor-Treasure, [189] and so it was done.

2.7. 'And, Ānanda, after many hundred, many hundred thousand years, Queen Subhaddā thought: "It is a long time since I saw King Mahāsudassana. Suppose I were to go and see him?" So she said to her women: "Come now, wash your heads and put on clean clothes. It is long since we saw King Mahāsudassana. We shall go to see him." "Yes, Your Majesty", they said, and prepared themselves as ordered, then returned to the Queen. And Queen Subhaddā said to the Counsellor-Treasure: "Friend Counsellor, draw up the fourfold army. It is long since we saw King Mahāsudassana. We shall go and see him." "Very good, Your Majesty", said the Counsellor-Treasure and, having drawn up the fourfold army, he reported to the Queen: "Now is the time to do as Your Majesty wishes." [190]

2.8. 'Then Queen Subhaddā went with the fourfold army and her womenfolk to the Dhamma Palace and, entering, went to the great gabled chamber and stood leaning against the door-post. And King Mahāsudassana, thinking: "What is this great noise, as of a crowd of people?" came out of the door and saw Queen Subhaddā leaning against the door-post. And he said: "Stay there, Queen! Do not enter!"

2.9. 'Then King Mahāsudassana said to a certain man: "Here, fellow, go to the great gabled chamber, bring the gold couch out and lay it down among the gold palm-trees." "Very good, Sire", said the man, and did so. Then King Mahāsudassana adopted the lion-posture on his right side with one foot on the other, mindful and clearly aware.[492]

2.10. 'Then Queen Subhaddā thought: "King Mahāsudassana's faculties are purified, his complexion is clear and bright, oh – I hope he is not dead!"[493] So she said to him: "Sire, of your eighty-four thousand cities, Kusāvatī is the chief. Make a wish, arouse the desire to live there!" *Thus, reminding him of all his royal possessions (as verse 5) she exhorted him to wish to stay alive.* [191] [192]

2.11. 'At this, King Mahāsudassana said to the Queen: "For a long time, Queen, you spoke pleasing, delightful, attractive words to me, but now at this last time your words have been unpleasing, undelightful, unattractive to me." "Sire, how then am I to speak to you?"

'This is how you should speak: "All things that are pleasing and attractive are liable to change, to vanish, to become otherwise. Do not, Sire, die filled with longing. To die filled with longing is painful and blameworthy. Of your eighty-four thousand cities, Kusāvatī is the chief: abandon desire, abandon the longing to live with them...Of your eighty-four thousand palaces, Dhamma is the chief: abandon desire, abandon the longing to live there..." (*and so on throughout, as verse 5*). [193] [194]

2.12. 'At this, Queen Subhaddā cried out and burst into tears. Then, wiping away her tears, she said: "Sire, all things that are pleasing and attractive are liable to change...Do not, Sire, die filled with longing...'[195]

2.13. 'Soon after this, King Mahāsudassana died; and just as a householder or his son might feel drowsy after a good meal, so he felt the sensation [196] of passing away, and he had a favourable rebirth in the Brahmā-world.

'King Mahāsudassana indulged in boyish sports for eighty-four thousand years, for eighty-four thousand years he exercised the viceroyalty, for eighty-four thousand years he ruled as King, and for eighty-four thousand years, as a layman, he lived the holy life in the Dhamma Palace.[494] And, having practised the four divine abidings, at the breaking-up of the body he was reborn in the Brahmā-world.[495]

2.14. 'Now, Ānanda, you might think King Mahāsudassana at that time was somebody else. But you should not regard it so, for I was King Mahāsudassana then. Those eighty-four thousand cities of which Kusāvatī was the chief were mine,... [197] the eighty-four thousand rice-offerings...were mine.

2.15. 'And of those eighty-four thousand cities I dwelt in

just one, Kusāvatī,... [198] of the eighty-four thousand wives I had, just one looked after me, and she was called Khattiyāni or Velāmikāni;[496] of the eighty-four thousand bales of cloth I had just one...; of the eighty-four thousand rice-offerings there was just one measure of choice curry that I ate.

2.16. 'See, Ānanda, how all those conditioned states of the past have vanished and changed! Thus, Ānanda, conditioned states are impermanent, they are unstable, they can bring us no comfort, and such being the case, Ānanda, we should not rejoice in conditioned states, we should cease to take an interest in them, and be liberated from them.

2.17. 'Six times, Ānanda, I recall discarding the body in this place, and at the seventh time I discarded it as a wheel-turning monarch, a righteous king who had conquered the four quarters and established a firm rule, and who possessed the seven treasures. But, Ānanda, I do not see any place in this world with its devas [199] and māras and Brahmās, or in this generation with its ascetics and Brahmins, princes and people, where the Tathāgata will for an eighth time discard the body.'

So the Lord spoke. The Well-Farer having said this, the Teacher said:

> 'Impermanent are compounded things, prone to rise and fall,
> Having risen, they're destroyed, their passing truest bliss.'

18 *Janavasabha Sutta: About Janavasabha*
Brahmā Addresses the Gods

[200] 1. THUS HAVE I HEARD. Once the Lord was staying at Nādikā at the Brick House.[497] And at that time the Lord was explaining the rebirths of various devotees up and down the country who had died and passed away: Kāsis and Kosalans, Vajjians and Mallas, Cetis and Vaṁsas, Kurus and Pañcālas, Macchas and Sūrasenas, saying: 'This one was reborn there, and that one there.'[498] More than fifty Nādikan devotees, having abandoned the five lower fetters, were reborn spontaneously and would attain Nibbāna without returning to this world; over ninety of them, having abandoned three fetters and weakened greed, hatred and delusion, were Once-Returners, who would return to this world once more and then make an end of suffering; and more than five hundred, having abandoned three fetters, were Stream-Winners, incapable of falling into states of woe, certain of Nibbāna. [201]

2. This news reached the ears of the devotees in Nādikā, and they were pleased, delighted and filled with joy to hear the Lord's replies.

3. And the Venerable Ānanda heard of the Lord's report[499] and the Nādikans' delight.

4. And he thought: [202] 'There were also Magadhan disciples of long standing who have died and passed away. One would think Anga and Magadha contained no Magadhan disciples who had died. Yet they too were devoted to the Buddha, the Dhamma and the Sangha, and they observed the discipline perfectly. The Lord has not stated their destiny. It would be good to have a declaration about this: it would make the multitude have faith and so attain a good rebirth.

'Now King Seniya Bimbisāra of Magadha was a righteous

and lawful king, a friend of Brahmins, householders, town and country-dwellers, so that his fame is spread abroad: "That righteous king of ours is dead[500] who gave us so much happiness. Life was easy for us who dwelt under his righteous rule."[501] And he was devoted to the Buddha, the Dhamma and the Sangha, and observed the discipline perfectly. Thus people say: "King Bimbisāra, who praised the Lord to his dying day, is dead!" The Lord has not declared his destiny, and it would be good to have a declaration... Besides, it was in Magadha that the Lord gained his enlightenment. Since the Lord gained his enlightenment in Magadha, why does he not declare the destinies of those who have died there? For the Lord not to make such a declaration would cause unhappiness to the Magadhans. [203] Such being the case, why does not the Lord make such a declaration?'

5. And after thus reflecting in solitude on behalf of the Magadhan devotees, the Venerable Ānanda rose at the crack of dawn, went to the Lord and saluted him. Then, sitting down to one side, he said: 'Lord, I have heard what has been declared concerning the inhabitants of Nādikā.' (*as verse 1–2*)

6. 'These were all devoted to the Buddha, the Dhamma and the Sangha, and they observed the discipline perfectly. The Lord has not stated their destiny...(*as verse 4*). [204] Why does not the Lord make such a declaration?' Then, having thus spoken to the Lord on behalf of the Magadhan devotees, he rose from his seat, saluted the Lord, passed him by to the right, and departed.

7. As soon as Ānanda had gone, the Lord took his robe and bowl and went into Nādikā for alms. Later, on his return, after his meal, he went to the Brick House and, having washed his feet, he went in and, having thought over, considered and given his whole mind to the question of the Magadhan devotees, he sat down on the prepared seat, saying: 'I shall know their destiny and future lot, whatever it is.'[502] And then he perceived the destiny and fate of [205] each one of them. And in the evening, emerging from meditative seclusion, the Lord came out of the Brick House and sat down on the prepared seat in the shade of his lodging.

8. Then the Venerable Ānanda came to the Lord, saluted

him, sat down to one side and said: 'Lord, the Lord's countenance looks bright and shining, showing that the Lord's mind is at ease. Has the Lord been satisfied with today's lodging?'

9. 'Ānanda, after you spoke to me about the devotees of Magadha, I took my robe and bowl and went into Nādikā for alms. Later on...I went to the Brick House and considered the question of the Magadhan devotees... And I perceived the destiny and fate of each one of them. Then the voice of a yakkha[503] who had passed over cried out: "I am Janavasabha, Lord! I am Janavasabha, Well-Farer!" Well, Ānanda, do you know anyone who formerly bore the name of Janavasabha?' 'I must admit, Lord, that I have never heard such a name; and yet, on hearing the name "Janavasabha"[504] my hairs stood on end, and I thought: "He [206] whose name is Janavasabha will not be such a low-ranking yakkha!"'

10. 'Ānanda, immediately after I heard this voice, the yakkha appeared before me as a noble vision, and uttered a second cry: "I am Bimbisāra, Lord! I am Bimbisāra, Well-Farer! I have now for the seventh time been reborn into the entourage of the Lord Vessavaṇa.[505] Thus having passed away as a king of humans, I have now become among the devas a king of non-human beings.

Seven states here and seven there, fourteen births,
That's the tally of lives I can recall.

For a long time, Lord, I have known myself to be exempt from states of woe,[506] and now the desire arises in me to become a Once-Returner." I said: "It is amazing, it is astonishing that the reverend yakkha Janavasabha should say this. On what grounds can he know of such an august specific attainment?"

11. '"Not otherwise, Lord, not otherwise, Well-Farer, than through your teaching! From the time when I became fully committed and gained complete faith, from then on, Lord, for a long time [207] I have known myself to be exempt from states of woe, and the desire has arisen in me to become a Once-Returner. And here, Lord, having been sent by King Vessavaṇa on some business to King Virūḷhaka,[507] I saw the Lord entering the Brick House and sitting down and considering

the question of the Magadhan devotees...And since I had only just heard King Vessavaṇa announce to his assembly what those folk's fates were, it is no wonder that I thought: 'I will go and see the Lord and report this to him.' And these, Lord, are the two reasons[508] why I came to see the Lord." (*Janavasabha continued:*)

12. '"Lord, in earlier days, long ago, on the fast-day of the fifteenth at the beginning of the Rains,[509] in the full-moon night all the Thirty-Three Gods were seated in the Sudhammā Hall[510] – a great congregation of divine beings, and the Four Great Kings from the four quarters were there. There was the Great King Dhataraṭṭha[511] from the east at the head of his followers, facing west; the Great King Virūḷhaka from the south...facing north; the Great King Virūpakkha from the west...facing east; and the Great King Vessavaṇa from the north...facing south. [208]

'"On such occasions that is the order in which they are seated, and after that came our seats. And those devas who, having lived the holy life under the Lord, had recently appeared in the Heaven of the Thirty-Three, outshone the other devas in brightness and glory. And for that reason the Thirty-Three Gods were pleased, happy, filled with delight and joy, saying: 'The devas' hosts are growing, the asuras' hosts are declining!'[512]

13. '"Then, Lord, Sakka, ruler of the gods, seeing the satisfaction of the Thirty-Three, uttered these verses of rejoicing:

> 'The gods of Thirty-Three rejoice, their leader too,
> Praising the Tathāgata, and Dhamma's truth,
> Seeing new-come devas, fair and glorious
> Who've lived the holy life, now well reborn.
> Outshining all the rest in fame and splendour,
> The mighty Sage's pupils singled out.
> Seeing this, the Thirty-Three rejoice, their leader too,
> Praising the Tathāgata, and Dhamma's truth.' [209]

At this the Thirty-Three Gods rejoiced still more, saying: 'The devas' hosts are growing, the asuras' hosts are declining!'

14. '"And then they consulted and deliberated together about

the matter concerning which they had assembled in the Sudhammā Hall, and the Four Great Kings were advised and admonished on this matter as they stood by their seats unmoving.[513]

> The Kings, instructed, marked the words they spoke,
> Standing calm, serene, beside their seats.

15. '"And then, Lord, a glorious radiance shone forth from the north, and a splendour was seen greater than the sheen of the devas. And Sakka said to the Thirty-Three Gods: 'Gentlemen, when such signs are seen, such light is seen and such radiance shines forth, Brahmā will appear.[514] The appearance of such radiance is the first sign of Brahmā's approaching manifestation.'

> When they see these signs, Brahmā will soon appear:
> This is Brahmā's sign, radiance vast and great.

16. '"Then the Thirty-Three Gods sat down each in his proper place, saying: 'Let us find out what comes[515] of this radiance, and having found the truth of it, we will go towards it.' The Four Great Kings, sitting down in their places, said [210] the same. Thus they were all agreed.

17. '"Lord, whenever Brahmā Sanankumāra[516] appears to the Thirty-Three Gods, he appears having assumed a grosser form, because his natural appearance is not such as to be perceptible to their eyes.[517] When he appears to the Thirty-Three Gods, he outshines other devas in radiance and glory, just as a figure made of gold outshines the human figure. And, Lord, when Brahmā Sanankumāra appears to the Thirty-Three Gods, not one of them salutes him, or rises, or offers him a seat. They all sit silently with palms together,[518] cross-legged,[519] thinking he will sit down on the couch[520] of that god from whom he wants something. And the one on whose couch he sits down is as thrilled and delighted as a duly-anointed Khattiya king on assuming his royal office. [211]

18. '"Then, Lord, Brahmā Sanankumāra, having assumed a grosser form, appeared to the Thirty-Three Gods in the shape of the youth Pañcasikha.[521] Rising up in the air, he appeared floating cross-legged, just as a strong man might sit down on

a properly-spread couch or on the ground. And seeing the delight of the Thirty-Three Gods, he uttered these verses of rejoicing:

'The gods of Thirty-Three rejoice, their leader too,
Praising the Tathāgata, and Dhamma's truth,
Seeing new-come devas, fair and glorious
Who've lived the holy life, now well reborn.
Outshining all the rest in fame and splendour,
The mighty Sage's pupils singled out.
Seeing this, the Thirty-Three rejoice, their leader too,
Praising the Tathāgata, and Dhamma's truth.'

19. '"Now to the matter of Brahmā Sanankumāra's speech, and as for the manner of his speech, his voice had eight qualities: it was distinct, intelligible, pleasant, attractive, compact, concise, deep and resonant. And when he spoke in that voice to the assembly, its sound did not carry outside. Whoever has such a voice as that is said to have the voice of Brahmā.

20. '"And Brahmā Sanankumāra, multiplying his shape by thirty-three, [212] sat down cross-legged on each individual couch of the Thirty-Three, and said: 'What do my lords the Thirty-Three think? Since the Lord, out of compassion for the world and for the benefit and happiness of the many, has acted to the advantage of devas and mankind, those, whoever they may be, who have taken refuge in the Buddha, the Dhamma and the Sangha and have observed the moral precepts[522] have, at death and the breaking-up of the body, arisen in the company of the Parinimmita-Vasavatti devas,[523] or the Nimmānaratti devas, or the Tusita devas, or the Yāma devas, or in the retinue of the Thirty-Three Gods, or of the Four Great Kings – or at the very least in the company of the gandhabbas.'[524]

21. '"This was the burden of Brahmā Sanankumāra's speech. And every one of the gods he spoke to thought: 'He is sitting on my couch, he is speaking to me alone.'

All the forms assumed with one voice speak,
And having spoken, all at once are silent.

And so the Thirty-Three, their leader too,
Each thinks: 'He speaks to me alone.'

22. '"Then Brahmā Sanankumāra assumed a single form;[525] then he sat down on [213] the couch of Sakka and said: 'What do my lords the Thirty-Three think? This Lord, the Arahant supreme Buddha has known and seen the four roads to power,[526] and how to develop, perfect and practise them. What four? Here a monk develops concentration of intention accompanied by effort of will, concentration of energy..., concentration of consciousness..., and concentration of investigation accompanied by effort of will. These are the four roads to power... And whatever ascetics or Brahmins have in the past realised such powers in different ways, they have all developed and strongly practised these four ways, and the same applies to all who may in the future, or who do now realise such powers. Do my lords the Thirty-Three observe such powers in me?' 'Yes, Brahmā.' 'Well, I too have developed and strongly practised [214] these four ways.'

23. '"This was the burden of Brahmā Sanankumāra's speech. He went on: 'What do my lords of the Thirty-Three think? There are three gateways to the bliss proclaimed by the Lord who knows and sees. What are they? In the first place someone dwells in association with sense-desires, with unwholesome conditions. At some time he hears the Ariyan Dhamma, he pays close attention and practises in conformity with it. By so doing he comes to live dissociated from such sense-desires and unwholesome conditions. As a result of this dissociation, pleasant feeling[527] arises, and what is more, gladness.[528] Just as pleasure might give birth to rejoicing, so from pleasant feeling he experiences gladness.

24. '"'In the second place there is someone in whom the gross tendencies[529] of body, speech and thought are not allayed. At some time he hears the Ariyan Dhamma,...and his gross tendencies of body, speech and [215] thought are allayed. As a result of this allaying, pleasant feeling arises, and what is more, gladness...

25. '"'In the third place there is someone who really does not know what is right and what is wrong, what is blameworthy

and what is not, what is to be practised and what is not, what is base and what is noble, and what is foul, fair or mixed in quality. At some time he hears the Ariyan Dhamma, he pays close attention and practises in conformity with it. As a result, he comes to know in reality what is right and wrong, what is blameworthy and what is not, what is to be practised and what is not, what is base and what is noble, and what is foul, fair or mixed in quality. In him who knows and sees thus, ignorance is dispelled and knowledge arises. With the waning of ignorance and the arising of knowledge, pleasant feeling arises, and what is more, gladness. Just as pleasure might give birth to rejoicing, so from pleasant feeling he experiences gladness. [216] These are the three gateways to the bliss proclaimed by the Lord who knows and sees.'

26. '"This was the burden of Brahmā Sanankumāra's speech. He went on: 'What do my lords of the Thirty-Three think? How well has the Lord Buddha who knows and sees pointed out the four foundations of mindfulness[530] for the attainment of that which is good! What are they? Here a monk abides contemplating the body as body, earnestly, clearly aware, mindful and having put away all hankering and fretting for the world. As he thus dwells contemplating his own body as body, he becomes perfectly concentrated and perfectly serene. Being thus calm and serene, he gains knowledge and vision externally of the bodies of others.[531] He abides contemplating his own feelings as feelings,...he abides contemplating his own mind as mind,...he abides contemplating his own mind-objects as mind-objects, earnestly, clearly aware, mindful and having put away all hankering and fretting for the world. As he thus dwells contemplating his own mind-objects as mind-objects, he becomes perfectly concentrated and perfectly serene. Being thus calm and serene, he gains knowledge and vision externally of the mind-objects of others. These are the four foundations of mindfulness well pointed out by the Lord Buddha who knows and sees, for the attainment of that which is good.'

27. '"This was the burden of Brahmā Sanankumāra's speech. He went on: 'What do my lords of the Thirty-Three think? How well has the Lord Buddha who knows and sees pointed

out the seven requisites of concentration, for the development of perfect concentration and the perfection of concentration! What are they? They are right view, right thought, right speech, right action, right [217] livelihood, right effort, right mindfulness.[532] That one-pointedness of mind that is produced by these seven factors is called the Ariyan right concentration with its bases and requisites. From right view arises right thought, from right thought arises right speech, from right speech arises right action, from right action arises right livelihood, from right livelihood arises right effort, from right effort arises right mindfulness, from right mindfulness arises right concentration, from right concentration arises right knowledge,[533] from right knowledge arises right liberation.[534] If anyone truthfully declaring: "Well-proclaimed by the Lord is the Dhamma, visible here and now, timeless, inviting inspection, leading onward, to be comprehended by the wise each one for himself", were to say: "Open are the doors of the Deathless!"[535] he would be speaking in accordance with the highest truth. For indeed, my lords, the Dhamma is well-proclaimed by the Lord, visible here and now, timeless, inviting inspection, leading onward, to be comprehended by the wise, each one for him or herself, and, too, the doors to the Deathless are open!

'"'Those who have unshakeable faith in the Buddha, the Dhamma and the Sangha, and are endowed with the virtues pleasing to the Noble Ones, [218] those beings who have arisen here on account of their Dhamma-training, amounting to more than twenty-four hundred Magadhan followers who have passed over, have by the destruction of three fetters become Stream-Winners, incapable of falling into states of woe and certain of enlightenment, and indeed there are Once-Returners here too.

But of that other race indeed
Of greater merit still, my mind
Can make no reckoning at all,
For fear that I should speak untruth.'[536]

28. '"This was the burden of Brahmā Sanankumāra's speech. And in connection with this the Great King Vessavaṇa reflect-

ed in his mind: 'It is marvellous, it is wonderful, that such a glorious Teacher should arise, that there should be such a glorious proclamation of Dhamma, and that such glorious paths to the sublime should be made known!' Then Brahmā Sanankumāra, reading King Vessavaṇa's mind, said to him: 'What do you think, King Vessavaṇa? There has been such a glorious Teacher in the past, and such a proclamation, and such paths made known, and there will be again in the future.'"'

29. Such was the burden of what Brahmā Sanankumāra proclaimed to the Thirty-Three Gods. And the Great King Vessavaṇa, [219] having heard and received it in person, related it to his followers. And the yakkha Janavasabha, having heard it himself, related it to the Lord. And the Lord, having heard it himself and also come to know it by his own super-knowledge, related it to the Venerable Ānanda, who in turn related it to the monks and nuns, the male and female lay-followers.

And so the holy life waxed mighty and prospered and spread widely as it was proclaimed among mankind.

19 *Mahāgovinda Sutta: The Great Steward*
A Past Life of Gotama

[220] 1. THUS HAVE I HEARD.[537] Once the Lord was staying at Rājagaha, on Vultures' Peak. And when the night was nearly over, Pañcasikha of the gandhabbas,[538] lighting up the entire Vultures' Peak with a splendid radiance,[539] approached the Lord, saluted him, stood to one side and said: 'Lord, I wish to report to you what I have personally seen and observed when I was in the presence of the Thirty-Three Gods.' 'Tell me then, Pañcasikha', said the Lord.

2.–3. 'Lord, in earlier days, long ago, on the fast-day of the fifteenth at the end of the Rains *the Thirty-Three Gods assembled and rejoiced that the devas' hosts were growing, the asuras' hosts declining (as Sutta 18, verse 12).* [221] *Then Sakka uttered the verse:*

> "The gods of Thirty-Three rejoice, their leader too,
> Praising the Tathāgata, and Dhamma's truth,
> Seeing new-come devas, fair and glorious
> Who've lived the holy life, now well reborn.
> Outshining all the rest in fame and splendour,
> The mighty Sage's pupils singled out.
> Seeing this, the Thirty-Three rejoice, their leader too,
> Praising the Tathāgata, and Dhamma's truth." [222]

At this, Lord, the Thirty-Three Gods rejoiced still more, saying: "The devas' hosts are growing, the asuras' hosts are declining!"

4. [Pañcasikha continued:] 'Then Sakka, seeing their satisfaction, said to the Thirty-Three Gods: "Would you like, gentlemen, to hear eight truthful statements in praise of the Lord?" and on receiving their assent, he declared:

5. '"What do you think, my lords of the Thirty-Three? As regards the way in which the Lord has striven for the welfare

of the many, for the happiness of the many, out of compassion for the world, for the welfare and happiness of devas and humans – we can find no teacher endowed with such qualities, whether we consider the past or the present, other than the Lord.

6. '"Well-proclaimed, truly, is this Lord's Teaching, visible here and now, timeless, inviting inspection, leading onward, to be realised by the wise each one for himself – and we can find no proclaimer of such an onward-leading doctrine, either in the past or in the present, other than the Lord.

7. '"The Lord has well explained what is right and what is wrong, what [223] is blameworthy and what is blameless, what is to be followed and what is not to be followed, what is base and what is noble, what is foul, fair and mixed in quality.[540] And we can find none who is a proclaimer of such things... other than the Lord.

8. '"Again, the Lord has well explained to his disciples the path leading to Nibbāna,[541] and they coalesce, Nibbāna and the path, just as the waters of the Ganges and the Yamunā coalesce and flow on together. And we can find no proclaimer of the path leading to Nibbāna...other than the Lord.

9. '"And the Lord has gained companions, both learners[542] and those who, having lived the life, have abolished the corruptions,[543] and the Lord dwells together with them, all rejoicing in the one thing. And we can find no such teacher ...other than the Lord.

10. '"The gifts given to the Lord are well-bestowed, his fame is well established, so much so that, I think, the Khattiyas will continue to be attached to him, yet the Lord takes his food-offering without conceit. And we can find no teacher who does this...[224] other than the Lord.

11. '"And the Lord acts as he speaks, and speaks as he acts. And we can find no teacher who does likewise, in every detail of doctrine...other than the Lord.

12. '"The Lord has transcended doubt,[544] passed beyond all 'how' and 'why', he has accomplished his aim in regard to his goal and the supreme holy life. And we can find no teacher who has done the like, whether we consider the past or the present, other than the Lord."

'And when Sakka had thus proclaimed these eight truthful statements in praise of the Lord, the Thirty-Three Gods were even more pleased, overjoyed and filled with delight and happiness at what they had heard in the Lord's praise.

13. 'Then certain gods exclaimed: "Oh, if only four fully-enlightened Buddhas were to arise in the world and teach Dhamma just like the Blessed Lord! That would be for the benefit and happiness of the many, out of compassion for the world, for the benefit and happiness of devas and humans!" And some said: "Never mind four fully-enlightened Buddhas – three would suffice!" and others said: "Never mind three – two would suffice!" [225]

14. 'At this Sakka said: "It is impossible, gentlemen, it cannot happen that two fully-enlightened Buddhas should arise simultaneously in a single world-system. That cannot be. May this Blessed Lord continue to live long, for many years to come, free from sickness and disease! That would be for the benefit and happiness of the many, out of compassion for the world it would be for the benefit and happiness of devas and humans!"

'Then the Thirty-Three Gods consulted and deliberated together about the matter concerning which they had assembled in the Sudhammā Hall, and the Four Great Kings were advised and admonished on this matter as they stood by their seats unmoving:

> The Kings, instructed, marked the words they spoke,
> Standing calm, serene, beside their seats.

15–16. *'A great radiance was seen, heralding the approach of Brahmā. All took their proper seats (as Sutta 18, verses 15–17), each hoping Brahmā would sit on his couch.* [226–7]

17. 'Then Brahmā Sanankumāra, having descended from his heaven, and seeing their pleasure, uttered these verses:

> "The gods of Thirty-Three rejoice, their leader too
> . . ." (*as above*).

18. *'Brahmā Sanankumāra's voice had eight qualities (as Sutta 18, verse 19).*

19. 'Then the Thirty-Three Gods said to Brahmā Sananku-

māra: "It is well, Brahmā! We rejoice at what we have heard. [228] Sakka, lord of the devas, has also declared eight truthful statements to us about the Lord, at which we also rejoice." Then Brahmā said to Sakka: "It is well, Lord of the devas. And we too would like to hear those eight truthful statements about the Lord." "Very well, Great Brahmā", said Sakka, and he repeated those eight statements:

20.–27. '"What do you think, Lord Brahmā...?" (*as verses 5–12*). [229] [230] And Brahmā Sanankumāra was pleased, overjoyed and filled with delight and happiness at what he had heard in the Lord's praise.

28. '*Brahmā Sanankumāra assumed a grosser form and appeared in the shape of Pañcasikha (as Sutta 18, verse 18).*[545] And sitting thus cross-legged, he said to the Thirty-Three Gods: "For how long has the Blessed Lord been one of mighty wisdom?

29. '"Once upon a time there was a king called Disampatī. His chaplain[546] was a Brahmin called the Steward.[547] The King's son was a youth called Reṇu, and the Steward's son was called Jotipāla. Prince Reṇu and Jotipāla, together with six other Khattiyas, formed a band of eight friends. [231] In the course of time the Steward died, and King Disampati mourned him, saying: 'Alas, at the very moment when we had entrusted all our responsibilities to the Steward, and were abandoning ourselves to the pleasures of the five senses, the Steward has passed away!'

'"Hearing this, Prince Reṇu said: 'Sire, do not mourn the Steward's death overmuch! His son Jotipāla[548] is cleverer than his father was and has a better eye for what is advantageous. You should let Jotipāla manage all the business you entrusted to his father.' 'Is that so, my boy?' 'Yes, Sire.'

30. '"Then the King called a man and said: 'Come here, my good man, go to the youth Jotipāla and say: "May the Reverend Jotipāla be well! King Disampati sends for you, he would like to see you."' 'Very good, Your Majesty', said the man, and delivered the message. [232] On receiving the message, Jotipāla said: 'Very good, sir', and went to see the King. On entering the royal presence, he exchanged courtesies with the King, then sat down to one side. The King said: 'We wish the Reverend Jotipāla to manage our affairs. Do not refuse. I will

install you in your father's place and consecrate[549] you as Steward.' 'Very good, Lord', replied Jotipāla.

31. '"So King Disampatı appointed Jotipāla as steward in his father's place. And once installed, Jotipāla carried out the business his father had carried out, not doing any business his father had not done. He accomplished all the tasks his father had accomplished, and no others. And people said: 'This Brahmin is truly a steward! Indeed he is a great steward!' And that is how the young Brahmin Jotipāla came to be known as the Great Steward.

32. '"And one day the Great Steward went to the group of six nobles and said: 'King Disampati is aged, decrepit, [233] stricken with age. His life is near its end and he cannot last much longer. Who can tell how long people will live? When King Disampati dies, the king-makers[550] are bound to anoint Prince Reṇu as King. You should go, gentlemen, to Prince Reṇu and say: "We are the beloved, dear and favoured friends of the Lord Reṇu, sharing his joys and his sorrows. Our Lord King Disampati is aged...When he dies, the king-makers are bound to anoint the Lord Reṇu as King. If the Lord Reṇu should gain the kingship, let him share it with us."'

33. '"'Very good, sir', said the six nobles, and they went to Prince Reṇu and spoke to him as the Great Steward had proposed. 'Well, gentlemen, who, apart from myself, ought to prosper but you? If, gentlemen, I gain the kingship, I will share it with you.' [234]

34. '"In due course King Disampati died, and the king-makers anointed Prince Reṇu King in his place. And having been made King, Reṇu abandoned himself to the pleasures of the five senses. Then the Great Steward went to the six nobles and said: 'Gentlemen, now King Disampati is dead the Lord Reṇu, who has been anointed in his place, has abandoned himself to the pleasures of the five senses. Who knows what will come of this? The sense-pleasures are intoxicating. You should go to him and say: "King Disampati is dead and the Lord Reṇu has been anointed King. Do you remember your word, Lord?"'

'"They did so, and the King said: 'Gentlemen, I remember my word. Who is there who can divide this mighty realm of earth, so broad in the north and so [narrow] like the front of a cart[551] in the south, into seven equal parts?' 'Who indeed, Lord, if not the Great Steward?'

35. '"So King Reṇu sent a man to the Great Steward to say: 'My lord, the King sends for you.' [235] The man went, and the Great Steward came to the King, exchanged courtesies with him, and sat down to one side. Then the King said: 'My Lord Steward, go and divide this mighty realm of earth, so broad in the north and so narrow like the front of a cart in the south, into seven equal parts.' 'Very good, Sire', said the Great Steward, and he did so.

36. '"And King Reṇu's country was in the centre:

> Dantapura to the Kālingas, Potaka to the Assakas,
> Mahissati to the Avantis, Roruka to the Sovīras.
>
> Mithilā to the Videhas, Campā to the Angas goes,
> Benares to the Kāsī, thus did the Steward dispose. [236]

The six nobles were delighted with their respective gains and at the success of the plan: 'What we wanted, desired, aimed at and strove for, we have got!'

> Sattabhū, Brahmadatta, Vessabhū and Bharata,
> Reṇu and two Dhataraṭṭhas, these are the seven Bhārat kings."'[552]

[*End of first recitation-section*]

37. '"Then the six nobles came to the Great Steward and said: 'Reverend Steward, just as you were a beloved, dear and faithful friend to King Reṇu, so you have been to us. Please manage our affairs for us! We trust you will not refuse.' So he administered the realms of seven anointed kings,[553] and he also taught the mantras to seven distinguished Brahmins and seven hundred advanced pupils.[554] [237]

38. '"In course of time good reports were spread about concerning the Great Steward: 'The Great Steward can see Brahmā with his own eyes, talks with him face to face and consults with him!'[555] And he thought: 'Now this good report is being

spread about concerning me, that I can see Brahmā with my own eyes,...but it is not true. However, I have heard it said by aged and respectable Brahmins, the teachers of teachers, that anyone who withdraws into meditation for the four months of the Rains, developing the absorption on compassion, *can* see Brahmā with his own eyes, talk with him face to face and consult with him. Suppose I were to do this!'[556]

39. '"So the Great Steward went to King Reṇu and told him of the report, and of his wish to go into retreat and develop the absorption on compassion. 'And nobody is to come near me except to bring me food.' 'Reverend Steward, do as you think fit.' [238]

40. '"The six nobles likewise replied: 'Reverend Steward, do as you think fit.'

41. '"He went to the seven Brahmins and the seven hundred pupils and told them of his intentions, adding: 'So, gentlemen, you carry on with reciting the mantras you have heard and learnt, and teach them to each other.' 'Reverend Steward, do as you think fit', they replied. [239]

42. '"Then he went to his forty equal-ranking wives, and they said: 'Reverend Steward, do as you think fit.'

43. '"So the Great Steward erected a new lodging to the east of the city and withdrew there for the four months of the Rains, developing the absorption on compassion, and nobody came near him except to bring him food. But at the end of four months he felt nothing but dissatisfaction and weariness as he thought: 'I heard it said...that anyone who withdraws into meditation for the four months of the Rains, developing the absorption on compassion, can see Brahmā with his own eyes...But I cannot see Brahmā with my own eyes, and cannot talk, discuss or consult with him!'

44. '"Now Brahmā Sanankumāra read his thoughts and, [240] as swiftly as a strong man might stretch out his flexed arm or flex it again, he disappeared from the Brahmā world and appeared before the Great Steward. And the Great Steward felt fear and trembling, and his hair stood on end at such a sight as he had never seen before. And thus fearful, trembling, with hair standing on end, he addressed Brahmā Sanankumāra in these verses:

'O splendid vision, glorious and divine,
Who are you, Lord? I fain would know your name.'

'In highest heaven I am known by all:
Brahmā Sanankumāra – know me thus.'

'A seat, and water for the feet, and cakes
Are fitting for a Brahmā. Let the Lord
Decide what hospitality he would.'[557]

'We accept the gift that's offered: now declare
What it is you wish from us – a boon
Of profit in this very life, or in the next.
Say, Lord Steward, what it is you'd have.'

45. '"Then the Great Steward thought: 'Brahmā Sanankumāra offers me a boon. What shall I choose – benefits in this life, or in that to come?' [241] Then he thought: 'I am an expert in matters of advantage in this life, and others consult me about this. Suppose I were to ask Brahmā Sanankumāra for something of benefit in the life to come?' And he addressed Brahmā in these verses:

'I ask Brahmā Sanankumāra this,
Doubting, him who has no doubts I ask
(For others too I ask): By doing what
Can mortals reach the deathless Brahmā world?'

'That man who spurns all possessive thoughts,
Alone, intent, compassion-filled,
Aloof from stench, free from lust –
Established thus, and training thus,
Can mortals reach the deathless Brahmā world.'[558]

46. '"'I understand "Spurning possessive thoughts". This means that one renounces one's possessions, small or great, leaves one's relatives, few or many, and, shaving off hair and beard, goes forth from the household life into homelessness. This is how I understand "Spurning possessive thoughts". [242] I understand "Alone, intent". That means that one goes off on one's own and chooses a lodging in the forest, at the foot of a tree, in a mountain glen, in a rocky cave, a charnel-ground,

in the jungle or on a heap of grass in the open...I understand "Compassion-filled". That means that one dwells suffusing one quarter with a mind filled with compassion, then a second, then a third and a fourth quarter. Thus one abides suffusing the whole world, up, down and across, everywhere, all around, with a mind filled with compassion, expanded, immeasurable, free from hatred and ill-will. That is how I understand "Compassion-filled". But the Lord's words about "Aloof from stench" I do not understand:

> What do you mean, Brahmā, by "stench" among men?
> Pray lighten my ignorance, O wise one, on this.
> What hindrance causes man to stink and fester,
> Heading for hell, from Brahmā-realm cut off?' [243]

> 'Anger, lying, fraud and cheating,
> Avarice, pride and jealousy,
> Coveting, doubt and harming others,
> Greed and hate, stupor and delusion:
> The loathsome stench that these give off
> Heads man for hell, from Brahmā-realm cut off.'

'As I understand the Lord's words about the stench, these things are not easy to overcome if one lives the household life. I will therefore go forth from the household life into the homeless state.' 'Reverend Steward, do as you think fit.'

47. '"So the Great Steward went to King Reṇu and said: 'My Lord, please appoint another minister[559] to manage your affairs. I wish to go forth from the household life into homelessness. After what Brahmā has told me about the stench of the world, which cannot easily be overcome by one living the household life, I am going forth into homelessness:

> King Reṇu, lord of this realm, I declare,
> You yourself must rule, I'll counsel you no more!'

> 'If anything you lack, I'll make it good,
> If any hurt you, my royal arms shall guard you.
> You my father, I your son, Steward, stay!'

> 'I lack nothing, none there is who harms me;
> No human voice I heard — at home I cannot stay.' [244]

'"Non-human" – what's he like who calls, that you
At once abandon home and all of us?'

'Before I went on this retreat I thought of sacrifice,
Lighting the sacred fire, strewing *kusa*-grass.
But now – eternal Brahmā[560] from Brahmā-realm's
appeared.
I asked, he answered: I now can stay no more.'

'Reverend Steward, in your words I trust. Such words
Once heard, you had no other course.
We will follow: Steward, be our Master.
Like a beryl-gem, clear, of finest water,
So purified, we'll follow in your wake.

If the Reverend Steward goes forth from the household life into homelessness, I will do the same. Wherever you go, we will follow.'

48. '"Then the Great Steward went to the six nobles and said to them: 'My lords, please appoint another minister to manage your affairs. I wish to go forth from the household life into homelessness...' And the six nobles went aside [245] and consulted together: 'These Brahmins are greedy for money. Perhaps we can win the Great Steward round with money.' So they came back to him and said: 'Sir, there is plenty of wealth in these seven kingdoms. Take as much as you like.' 'Enough, gentlemen, I have received plenty of wealth from my lords already. That is the very thing that I am renouncing in order to go forth from the household life into homelessness, as I have explained.'

49. '"Then the six nobles went aside again and consulted together: 'These Brahmins are greedy for women. Perhaps we can win the Great Steward round with women.' So they came to him and said: 'Sir, there are plenty of women in these seven kingdoms. Take your pick!' 'Enough, gentlemen, I already have forty equal wives, and I am leaving them in order to go forth from the household life into homelessness, as I have explained.' [246]

50. '"'If the Reverend Steward goes forth from the household life into homelessness, we will do likewise. Wherever you go, we will follow:

"If you renounce those lusts that bind most men,[561]
Exert yourselves, be strong and patiently endure!
This is the path that's straight, the peerless path,
The path of truth, guarded by the good, to Brahmā's realm."

51. '"'And so, Lord Steward, just wait seven years, and then we too will go forth into homelessness. Wherever you go, we will follow.'

'"'Gentlemen, seven years is far too long, I cannot wait for seven years! Who can tell how long people will live? We have to go on into the next world, we must learn by means of wisdom,[562] we must do what is right and live the holy life, for nothing that is born is immortal. Now I am going forth as I have explained.'

52. '"'Well, Reverend Steward, just wait six years,...five year,...four years,...three years,...two years,...one year, and then we too will go forth into homelessness. Wherever you go, we will follow.'

53. '"'Gentlemen, one year is far too long...' 'Then wait seven months...'

54. '"'Gentlemen, seven months is far too long...' 'Then wait six months,...five months,...four months,...three months,...two months,...one month,...half a month...'

55. '"'Gentlemen, half a month is far too long...' [248] 'Then, Reverend Steward, just wait seven days while we make over our kingdoms to our sons and brothers. At the end of seven days we will go forth into homelessness. Wherever you go, we will follow.' 'Seven is not long, gentlemen. I agree, my lords, to seven days.'

56. '"Then the Great Steward went to the seven Brahmins and their seven hundred advanced pupils, and said to them: 'Now, Your Reverences, you must seek another teacher to teach you the mantras. I mean to go forth from the household life into homelessness. After what Brahmā has told me about the stench of the world, which cannot be easily overcome by one living the household life, I am going forth into homelessness.' 'Reverend Steward, do not do so! There is little power and profit in the homeless life, and much power and profit in the life of a Brahmin!'[563] 'Do not say such things, gentlemen!

Besides, who has greater power and profit than I have? I have been like a king to kings, like Brahmā to the Brahmins, like a deity to householders, and I am giving all this up in order to go forth from the household life into homelessness, as I have [249] explained.' 'If the Reverend Steward goes forth from the household life into homelessness, we will do likewise. Wherever you go, we will follow.'

57. '"Then the Great Steward went to his forty equal wives and said: 'Whichever of you ladies wishes to may go back to her own family and seek another husband. I mean to go forth into homelessness...' 'You alone are the kinsman we could wish for, the only husband we want. If the Reverend Steward goes forth into homelessness, we will do likewise. Wherever you go, we will follow.'

58. '"And so the Great Steward, at the end of the seven days, shaved off his hair and beard, donned yellow robes and went forth from the household life into homelessness. And with him went the seven anointed Khattiya kings, the seven wealthy and distinguished Brahmins with their seven hundred advanced pupils, his forty equal wives, several thousand Khattiyas, several thousand Brahmins, several thousand householders, even some harem-women.

'"And so, followed by this company, the Great Steward wandered through villages, towns and royal [250] cities. And whenever he came to a village or town, he was like a king to kings, like Brahmā to the Brahmins, like a deity to householders. And in those days, whenever anyone sneezed or stumbled, they used to say: 'Praise be to the Great Steward! Praise be to the Minister of Seven!'

59. '"And the Great Steward dwelt suffusing one quarter with a mind filled with loving-kindness, then a second, then a third and a fourth quarter. He dwelt suffusing the whole world, up, down and across, everywhere, all around, with a mind filled with compassion,...with a mind filled with sympathetic joy,...with a mind filled with equanimity,...free from hatred and ill-will. And thus he taught his disciples the way to union with the Brahmā-world.

60. '"And all those who had at that time been the Great Steward's pupils and had fully mastered his teaching, were after death at the breaking-up of the body reborn in a happy

sphere, in the Brahmā-world. And those who had not fully mastered his teaching were reborn either among the Paranimmita-Vasavatti devas, among the Nimmānarati devas, among the Tusita devas, among the Yāma devas, [251] among the devas of the Thirty-Three Gods, or among the devas of the Four Great Kings. And the very lowest realm that any of them attained was that of the gandhabbas. Thus the going-forth of all those people was not fruitless or barren, but productive of fruit and profit."

61. 'Do you remember this, Lord?' 'I do, Pañcasikha. At that time I was the Brahmin, the Great Steward, and I taught those disciples the path to union with the Brahmā-world.

'However, Pañcasikha, *that* holy life does not lead to disenchantment, to dispassion, to cessation, to peace, to super-knowledge, to enlightenment, to Nibbāna, but only to birth in the Brahmā-world, whereas my holy life leads unfailingly to disenchantment, to dispassion, to cessation, to peace, to super-knowledge, to enlightenment, to Nibbāna. That is the Noble Eightfold Path, namely Right View, Right Thought, Right Speech, Right Action, Right Livelihood, Right Effort, Right Mindfulness, Right Concentration.

62. 'And, Pañcasikha, those of my disciples who have fully mastered my teaching have by their own super-knowledge realised, [252] by the destruction of the corruptions in this very life, the uncorrupted freedom of heart and mind. And of those who have not fully mastered it, some by the destruction of the five lower fetters will be reborn spontaneously, attaining thence to Nibbāna without returning to this world; some by the destruction of three fetters and the reduction of greed, hatred and delusion will become Once-Returners, who will return once more to this world before making an end of suffering; and some by the destruction of three fetters will become Stream-Winners, incapable of falling into states of woe, assured of enlightenment. Thus the going-forth of all these people was not fruitless or barren, but productive of fruit and profit.'

Thus the Lord spoke, and Pañcasikha of the gandhabbas was delighted and rejoiced at the Lord's words. And, having saluted him, he passed him by on the right and vanished from the spot.

20 *Mahāsamaya Sutta: The Mighty Gathering* Devas Come to See the Buddha

[253] 1. Thus have I heard.[564] Once the Lord was staying among the Sakyans in the Great Forest at Kapilavatthu, with a large company of some five hundred monks, all Arahants. And devas from ten world-systems[565] frequently came there to visit the Lord and his order of monks.

2. And it occurred to four devas of the Pure Abodes:[566] 'The Blessed Lord is staying at Kapilavatthu, with a large company of some five hundred monks, all Arahants. What if we were to approach him, and each recite a verse?'

3. Then those devas, as swiftly as a strong man might stretch his flexed arm, or flex it again, [254] vanished from the Pure Abodes and appeared before the Lord. Then they saluted him and stood to one side, and one of them recited this verse:

> 'Great the assembly in the forest here, the devas have
>   met
> And we are here to see the unconquered
>   brotherhood.'

Another said:

> 'The monks with concentrated minds are straight:
> They guard their senses as the driver does his reins.'

Another said:

> 'Bars and barriers broken, the threshold-stone of lust
>   torn up,
> Unstained the spotless seers go, like well-trained
>   elephants.' [255]

And another said:

'Who takes refuge in the Buddha, no downward path
will go:
Having left the body he'll join the deva hosts.'

4. Then the Lord said to his monks: 'Monks, it has often happened that the devas from ten world-systems have come to see the Tathāgata and his order of monks. So it has been with the supreme Buddhas of the past, and so it will be with those of the future, as it is with me now. I will detail for you the names of the groups of devas, announce them and teach them to you. Pay close attention, and I will speak.'

'Yes, Lord', said the monks, and the Lord said:

5. 'I'll tell you them in verse: to which realm each
belongs.
But those who dwell composed and resolute
Like lions in mountain-caves, have overcome
Hair-raising fear and dread, their minds
White and pure, unstained and calm.'[567] [256]

In Kapilavatthu's wood the Lord perceived
Five hundred of his Arahants and more,
Lovers of his word. To them he said:
'Monks, observe the deva-host approach!'
And the monks strove eagerly to see.

6. With superhuman vision thus arising,
Some saw a hundred gods, a thousand some.
While some saw seventy thousand, others saw
Gods innumerable, all around.
And He-Who-Knows-with-Insight was aware
Of all that they could see and understand.

And to the lovers of his word the Lord,
Turning said: 'The deva-hosts approach.
Look and seek to know them, monks, in turn,
As I declare their names to you in verse!'[568]

7. 'Seven thousand yakkhas of Kapila's realm,
Well-endowed with power and mighty skills,

Fair to see, with splendid train have come
Rejoicing to this wood to see such monks.

And six thousand yakkhas from Himālaya,
Of varied hue, and well-endowed with powers,
Fair to see, with splendid train have come
Rejoicing to this wood to see such monks.

From Sāta's Mount three thousand yakkhas more
Of varied hue...

The sum is sixteen thousand yakkhas all,
Of varied hue...[257]

8. Of Vessāmitta's host five hundred more
Of varied hue...

Kumbhīra too from Rājagaha comes
(Whose dwelling-place is on Vepulla's slopes):
A hundred thousand yakkhas follow him.

9. King Dhataraṭṭha,[569] ruler of the East,
The gandhabbas' Lord, a mighty king,
Has come with retinue. Many sons
Are his, who all bear Indra's name,
All well-endowed with mighty skills...

King Virūḷha, ruler of the South,
The Kumbaṇḍhas' lord, a mighty king...

Virūpakkha, ruler of the West,
Lord of nāgas and a mighty king...

King Kuvera, ruler of the North,
Lord of yakkhas and a mighty king...[258]

From the East King Dhataraṭṭha shone,
From South Virūḷhaka, and from the West
Virūpakkha, Kuvera from the North:
Thus ranged in Kapilavatthu's wood
The Four Great Kings in all their splendour stood.'

10. With them came their vassals versed in guile,
Skilled deceivers all: Kuṭeṇḍu first,

Then Veṭeṇḍu, Viṭu and Viṭucca,
Candana and Kāmaseṭṭha next,
Kinnughaṇḍu and Nighaṇḍu, these,
Panāda, Opamañña, Mātali
(Who was the devas' charioteer), Naḷa,
Cittasena of the gandhabbas,
Rājā, Janesabha, Pañcasikha,
Timbarū with Suriyavaccasā
His daughter – these, and more, rejoicing came
To that wood to see the Buddha's monks.

11. From Nabhasa, Vesāli, Tacchaka
Came Nāgas, Kambalas, Assataras,
Payāgas with their kin. From Yamunā
Dhataraṭṭha came with splendid host,
Erāvana too, the mighty nāga chief[570]
To the forest meeting-place has come.

And the twice-born,[571] winged and clear of sight,
Fierce garuḍa birds (the nāgas' foes) have
come [259]
Flying here – Citrā and Supaṇṇā.
But here the nāga kings are safe: the Lord
Has imposed a truce. With gentle speech
They and the nāgas share the Buddha's peace.

12. Asuras too, whom Indra's hand[572] once struck,
Ocean-dwellers now, in magic skilled,
Vāsava's replendent brothers came,
The Kālakañjas, terrible to see,
Dānaveghasas, Vepacitti,
Sucitti and Pahārādha too,
Fell Namucī, and Bali's hundred sons
(Who all were called Veroca) with a band
Of warriors who joined their master Rāhu,
Who had come to wish their meeting well.

13. Gods of water, earth, and fire, and wind,
The Varuṇas and their retainers. Soma
And Yasa too. Devas born of love
And compassion, with a splendid train,

These ten, with tenfold varied hosts,
Endowed with mighty powers, and fair to see,
Rejoicing came to see the Buddha's monks.

14. Veṇhu[573] too with his Sahalis came,
The Asamas, the Yama twins, and those
Devas who attend on moon and sun,
Constellation-gods, sprites of clouds, [260]
Sakka the Vasus' lord, ancient giver,[574]
These ten, with tenfold varied hosts...

15. The Sahabhus, radiant, bright, came next,
Fiery-crested. The Ariṭṭhakas,
The Rojas, cornflower-blue, with Varuṇā
And Sahadhammā, Accutā, Anejakā,
Sūleyya, Rucirā, the Vāsavanesis,
These ten, with tenfold varied hosts...

16. The Samānas and Mahā-Samānas both,
Beings manlike and more than manlike came,
The 'Pleasure-corrupted' and 'Mind-corrupted' gods,[575]
Green devas, and the red ones too,
Pāragas, Mahā-Pāragas with train,
These ten, with tenfold varied hosts...

17. Sukkas, Karumhas, Aruṇas, Veghanasas,
Follow in the Odātagayhas' wake.
Vicakkhaṇas, Sadāmattas, Harāgajas,
Those gods called 'Mixed in Splendour', and Pajunna
The Thunderer, who also causes rain,
These ten, with tenfold varied hosts...[261]

18. The Khemiyas, the Tusitas and Yāmas,
The Kaṭṭhakas with train, Lambītakas,
The Lāma chiefs, and the gods of flame
(The Āsavas), those who delight in shapes
They've made, and those who seize on others' work,[576]
These ten, with tenfold varied hosts...

19. These sixty deva-hosts, of varied kinds,
All came arranged in order of their groups,
And others too, in due array. They said:
'He who's transcended birth, he for whom
No obstacle remains, who's crossed the flood,
Him, cankerless, we'll see, the Mighty One,
Traversing free without transgression, as
It were the moon that passes through the clouds.'

20. Subrahmā next, and with him Paramatta,
Sanankumāra, Tissa, who were sons
Of the Mighty One, these also came.
Mahā-Brahmā, who ruled a thousand worlds,
In the Brahmā-world supreme, arisen there,
Shining bright, and terrible to see,
With all his train. Ten lords of his who each
Rule a Brahmā-world, and in their midst
Hārita, who ruled a hundred thousand.

21. And when all these had come in vast array,
With Indra and the hosts of Brahmā too,
Then too came Māra's hosts, and now observe
That Black One's folly.[577] [262] For he said:
'Come on, seize and bind them all! With lust
We'll catch them all! Surround them all about,
Let none escape, whoever he may be!'
Thus the war-lord urged his murky troops.
With his palm he struck the ground, and made
A horrid din, as when a storm-cloud bursts
With thunder, lightning and with heavy rain –
And then – shrank back, enraged, but powerless!

22. And He-Who-Knows-by-Insight saw all this
And grasped its meaning. To his monks he said:
'The hosts of Māra come, monks – pay good heed!'
They heard the Buddha's words, and stayed alert.

And Māra's hosts drew back from those on whom
Neither lust nor fear could gain a hold.

'Victorious, transcending fear, they've won:
His followers rejoice with all the world!'[578]

21 *Sakkapañha Sutta: Sakka's Questions*
A God Consults the Buddha

[263] 1.1. THUS HAVE I HEARD.[579] Once the Lord was staying in Magadha, to the east of Rājagaha, by a Brahmin village called Ambasaṇḍā, to the north of the village on Mount Vediya, in the Indasāla Cave.[580] And at that time Sakka, lord of the gods,[581] felt a strong desire to see the Lord. And Sakka thought: 'Where is the Blessed Lord, the fully-enlightened Buddha, now staying?' Then, perceiving where the Lord was, Sakka said to the Thirty-Three Gods: 'Gentlemen, the Blessed Lord is staying in Magadha...in the Indasāla Cave. How would it be if we were to go and visit the Lord?' 'Very good, Lord, and may good fortune go with you', replied the Thirty-Three Gods.

1.2. Then Sakka said to Pañcasikha of the gandhabbas: [264] 'The Blessed Lord is staying in Magadha...in the Indasāla Cave. I propose to go to visit him.' 'Very good, Lord', said Pañcasikha and, taking his yellow *beluva*-wood lute,[582] he followed in attendance on Sakka. And, just as swiftly as a strong man might stretch forth his flexed arm, or flex it again, Sakka, surrounded by the Thirty-Three Gods and attended by Pañcasikha, vanished from the heaven of the Thirty-Three and appeared in Magadha...on Mount Vediya.

1.3. Then a tremendous light shone over Mount Vediya, illuminating the village of Ambasaṇḍā – so great was the power of the gods – so that in the surrounding villages they were saying: 'Look, Mount Vediya is on fire today – it's burning – it's in flames! What is the matter, that Mount Vediya and Ambasaṇḍā are lit up like this?' and they were so terrified that their hair stood on end.

1.4. Then Sakka said: 'Pañcasikha, [265] it is hard for the

likes of us to get near the Tathāgatas when they are enjoying the bliss of meditation,[583] and therefore withdrawn. But if you, Pañcasikha, were first to attract[584] the ear of the Blessed Lord, then we might afterwards be able to approach and see the Blessed Lord, the fully-enlightened Buddha.' 'Very good, Lord', said Pañcasikha and, taking his yellow *beluva*-wood lute, he approached the Indasāla Cave. Thinking: 'As far as this is neither too far nor too near to the Lord, and he will hear my voice', he stood to one side. Then, to the strains of his lute, he sang these verses extolling the Buddha, the Dhamma, the Arahants, and love:[585]

1.5. 'Lady, your father Timbarū greet,
Oh Sunshine[586] fair, I give him honour due,
By whom was sired a maid as fair as you
Who are the cause of all my heart's delight.

Delightful as the breeze to one who sweats,
Or as a cooling draught to one who thirsts,
Your radiant beauty is to me as dear
As the Dhamma is to Arahants. [266]

Just as medicine to him who's ill,
Or nourishment to one who's starving still,
Bring me, gracious lady, sweet release
With water cool from my consuming flames.

The elephant, oppressed by summer heat,[587]
Seeks out a lotus-pool upon which float
Petals and pollen of that flower,
So into your bosom sweet I'd plunge.

As an elephant, urged by the goad,
Pays no heed to pricks of lance and spear,
So I, unheeding, know not what I do,
Intoxicated by your beauteous form.

By you my heart is tightly bound in bonds,
All my thoughts are quite transformed, and I
Can no longer find my former course:
I'm like a fish that's caught on baited hook.

Come, embrace me, maiden fair of thighs,[588]
Seize and hold me with your lovely eyes,
Take me in your arms, it's all I ask!
My desire was slight at first, O maid
Of waving tresses, but it grew apace,
As grow the gifts that Arahants receive.

Whatever merit I have gained by gifts
To those Noble Ones, may my reward
When it ripens, be your love, most fair! [267]

As the Sakyans' Son in jhāna rapt
Intent and mindful, seeks the deathless goal,
Thus intent I seek your love, my Sun!

Just as that Sage would be rejoiced, if he
Were to gain supreme enlightenment,
So I'd rejoice to be made one with you.[589]

If Sakka, Lord of Three-and-Thirty Gods
Were perchance to grant a boon to me,
It's you I'd crave, my love for you's so strong.

Your father, maid so wise, I venerate
Like a *sāl*-tree fairly blossoming,
For his offspring's sake, so sweet and fair.'

1.6. When he heard this, the Lord said: 'Pañcasikha, the sound of your strings blends so well with your song, and your song with the strings, that neither prevails excessively over the other.[590] When did you compose these verses on the Buddha, the Dhamma, the Arahants, and love?' 'Lord, it was when the Blessed Lord was staying on the bank of the River Nerañjarā, under the goatherd's *banyan* tree [268] prior to his enlightenment. At that time I fell in love with the lady Bhaddā, bright as the sun, the daughter of King Timbarū of the gandhabbas. But the lady was in love with somebody else. It was Sikhaddi, the son of Mātali the charioteer, whom she favoured. And when I found that I could not win the lady by any manner of means, I took my yellow *beluva*-wood lute and went to the home of King Timbarū of the gandhabbas, and there I sang these verses:

1.7. (*Verses as 5*). 'And, Lord, having heard the verses the lady Bhaddā Suriyavaccasā said to me: "Sir, I have not personally seen that Blessed Lord, though I heard of him when I went to the Sudhammā Hall of the Thirty-Three Gods to dance. And since, sir, you praise that Blessed Lord so highly, let us meet today." [269] And so, Lord, I met the lady, not then but later.'

1.8. Then Sakka thought: 'Pañcasikha and the Lord are in friendly conversation', so he called to Pañcasikha: 'My dear Pañcasikha, salute the Blessed Lord from me, saying: "Lord, Sakka, king of the gods, together with his ministers and followers, pays homage at the feet of the Blessed Lord."' 'Very good, Lord', said Pañcasikha, and did so.

'Pañcasikha, may Sakka, king of the gods, his ministers and followers be happy, for they all desire happiness: devas, humans, asuras, nāgas, gandhabbas, and whatever other groups of beings there are!' for that is the way the Tathāgatas greet such mighty beings. After this greeting, Sakka entered the Indasāla Cave, saluted the Lord, and stood to one side, and the Thirty-Three Gods, with Pañcasikha, did the same.

1.9. Then in the Indasāla Cave the rough passages became smooth, the narrow parts became wide, and in the pitch-dark cavern it became bright, owing to the [270] power of the devas. Then the Lord said to Sakka: 'It is wonderful, it is marvellous that the Venerable Kosiya,[591] with so much, so many things to do, should come here!' 'Lord, I have long wished to visit the Blessed Lord, but I have always been so busy on behalf of the Thirty-Three that I was unable to come. Once the Blessed Lord was staying at Sāvatthi in the Salaḷa hut, and I went to Sāvatthi to see the Lord.

1.10. 'At that time the Blessed Lord was seated in some form of meditation, and King Vessavaṇa's wife Bhuñjatī was waiting on him, venerating him with palms together. I said to her: "Lady, please salute the Blessed Lord for me and say: 'Sakka, the king of the gods, with his ministers and followers, pays homage at the Lord's feet'. But she said: "Sir, it is not the right time to see the Blessed Lord, he is in retreat." [271] "Well then, lady, when the Blessed Lord rises from his meditation, please tell him what I have said." Lord, did the lady salute you on my behalf, and does the Lord remember what she said?' 'She did salute me, King of the Gods, and I remember what she said. I also remember that it was the sound of Your Reverence's chariot-wheels that roused me from my meditation.'[592]

1.11. 'Lord, those gods who arose in the heaven of the Thirty-Three before I did have told me and assured me that whenever a Tathāgata, a fully-enlightened Arahant Buddha arises in the world, the ranks of devas increase, and those of the asuras decline in numbers. In fact I have witnessed this myself. There was, Lord, right here in Kapilavatthu a Sakyan girl called Gopikā who had faith in the Buddha, the Dhamma and the Sangha, and who observed the precepts scrupulously. She rejected the status of a woman and developed the thought of becoming a man. Then, after her death, at the breaking-up of the body, she went to a happy destination, being reborn in a heaven-state among the Thirty-Three Gods, as one of our sons, becoming known as Gopaka the devas' son.[593] Also, there were three monks who, having observed the holy life under the Blessed Lord, had been reborn in the inferior condition of gandhabbas. They lived indulging in the pleasures of the five senses, as our attendants and servants. At this, Gopaka [272] rebuked them, saying: "What were you about, sirs, that you did not listen to the Blessed Lord's teaching? I was a woman who had faith in the Buddha...I rejected the status of a woman...and was reborn among the Thirty-Three Gods and am known as Gopaka the devas' son. But you, after having observed the holy life under the Blessed Lord, have been reborn in the inferior condition of gandhabbas! It is a sorry sight for us to see our fellows in the Dhamma reborn in the inferior condition of gandhabbas!" And being thus rebuked, two of those devas immediately developed mindfulness,[594] and so attained to the Realm of the Retinue of Brahma.[595] But one of them remained addicted to sensual pleasures.

1.12 [Gopaka spoke:]

'"Disciple once of Him-Who-Sees,
The name I bore then Gopikā.

In Buddha, Dhamma firmly trusting
I served the Sangha cheerfully.
For loyal service paid to him
See me now, a Sakka-son,
Mighty, in the Threefold Heaven,[596]
Resplendent; Gopaka my name.
Then former monks I saw, who'd reached
No higher than gandhabba's rank,
Who before had human birth
And led the life the Buddha taught.
We supplied their food and drink
And waited on them in our homes.[597] [273]
Had they no ears, that they thus blest
Still could not grasp the Buddha's law?
Each for himself must understand
That Dhamma taught by Him-Who-Sees,
And well-proclaimed. I, serving you,
Heard the Noble Ones' good words,
And so I'm born, a Sakka-son,
Mighty, in the Threefold Heaven,
And resplendent, whereas you,
Though you served the Prince of Men
And led the matchless life he taught,
Have reappeared in humble state,
And not attained your proper rank,
A sorry sight it is to see
One's Dhamma-fellows sunk so low
That, gandhabba-spirits, you
But come to wait upon the gods,
While as for me — I am transformed!
From household life, and female, I
Am now reborn a male, a god,
Rejoicing in celestial bliss!"

When thus rebuked by Gopaka,
Disciple true of Gotama,
In sore distress they all replied:
"Alas, let's go, and strive amain,
And be no longer others' slaves!" [274]

And of the three, two struggled hard,
And bore in mind the Teacher's word.
They purified their hearts of lust,
Perceiving peril in desires,
And like the elephant that bursts
All restraining bonds, they broke
The fetters and the bonds of lust,
Those fetters of the evil one
So hard to overcome – and thus
The very gods, the Thirty-Three,
With Indra and Pajāpati,
Who sat enthroned in Council Hall,
These two heroes, passions purged,
Outstripped, and left them far behind.

On seeing which, Vāsava,[598] dismayed,
Chief amidst that throng of gods,
Cried: "See how these of lesser rank
Outstrip the gods, the Thirty-Three!"
Then hearing of his ruler's fears,
Gopaka said to Vāsava:
"Lord Indra, in the world of men
A Buddha, called the Sakyan Sage,[599]
Has gained the mastery of lust,
And these his pupils, who had failed
In mindfulness when claimed by death,
Have now regained it with my help. [275]
Though one of them is left behind
And still among gandhabbas dwells,
These two, on highest wisdom set,
In deep absorption spurn the gods!
Let no disciple ever doubt
That truth may yet be realised
By those who dwell in these abodes.[600]
To him who's crossed the flood and made
An end of doubts, our homage due,
The Buddha, Victor, Lord, we give."

Even here, they gained the truth, and so
Have passed beyond to greater eminence.

Those two have gained a higher place than this
In Realms of Brahmā's Retinue. And we
Have come, O Lord, in hope that we may gain
That truth, and, if the Lord will give us leave,
To put our questions to the Blessed Lord.'

1.13. Then the Lord thought: 'Sakka has lived a pure life for a long time. Whatever questions he may ask will be to the point and not frivolous, and he will be quick to understand my answers.' So the Blessed Lord replied to Sakka in this verse:

'Ask me, Sakka, all that you desire!
On what you ask, I'll put your mind at rest.'

[*End of first recitation-section*] [276]

2.1. Being thus invited, Sakka, ruler of the gods, put his first question to the Lord: 'By what fetters, sir,[601] are beings bound – gods, humans, asuras, nāgas, gandhabbas and whatever other kinds there may be – whereby, although they wish to live without hate, harming, hostility or malignity, and in peace, they yet live in hate, harming one another, hostile and malign?' This was Sakka's first question to the Lord, and the Lord replied: 'Ruler of the Gods, it is the bonds of jealousy and avarice[602] that bind beings so that, though they wish to live without hate,...they yet live in hate, harming one another, hostile and malign.' This was the Lord's reply, and Sakka, delighted, exclaimed: 'So it is, Lord, so it is, Well-Farer! Through the Lord's answer I have overcome my doubt and got rid of uncertainty!'

2.2. Then Sakka, having [277] expressed his appreciation, asked another question: 'But sir, what gives rise to jealousy and avarice, what is their origin, how are they born, how do they arise? Owing to the presence of what do they arise, owing to the absence of what do they not arise?' 'Jealousy and avarice, Ruler of the Gods, take rise from like and dislike,[603] this is their origin, this is how they are born, how they arise. When these are present, they arise; when these are absent, they do not arise.' 'But, sir, what gives rise to like and dislike?...Owing to the presence of what do they arise, owing to the absence of what do they not arise?' 'They arise, Ruler of the Gods, from desire[604]...Owing to the presence of desire they arise, owing to the absence of desire they do not arise.' 'But, sir, what gives rise to desire?...' 'Desire, Ruler of the Gods, arises from thinking[605]...When the mind thinks about something, desire arises; when the mind thinks about nothing, desire does not arise.' 'But, sir, what gives rise to thinking? ...' 'Thinking, Ruler of the Gods, arises from the tendency to proliferation[606]...When this tendency is present, thinking arises; when it is absent, thinking does not arise.'

2.3. 'Well, sir, what practice has that monk undertaken,[607] who has reached the right way which is needful and leading to the cessation of the tendency to proliferation?' [278]

'Ruler of the Gods, I declare that there are two kinds of happiness:[608] the kind to be pursued, and the kind to be avoided. The same applies to unhappiness[609] and equanimity.[610] Why have I declared this in regard to happiness? This is how I understood happiness: When I observed that in the pursuit of such happiness, unwholesome factors increased and wholesome factors decreased, then that happiness was to be avoided. And when I observed that in the pursuit of such happiness unwholesome factors decreased and wholesome ones increased, then that happiness was to be sought after. Now, of such happiness as is accompanied by thinking and pondering,[611] and of that which is not so accompanied, the latter is the more excellent. The same applies to unhappiness, and [279] to equanimity. And this, Ruler of the Gods, is the practice that monk has undertaken who has reached the right way...leading to the cessation of the tendency to proliferation.' And Sakka expressed his delight at the Lord's answer.

2.4. Then Sakka, having expressed his appreciation, asked another question: 'Well, sir, what practice has that monk undertaken who has acquired the restraint required by the rules?'[612]

'Ruler of the Gods, I declare that there are two kinds of bodily conduct: the kind to be pursued, and the kind to be avoided. The same applies to conduct of speech and to the pursuit of goals. [280] Why have I declared this in regard to bodily conduct? This is how I understood bodily conduct: When I observed that by the performance of certain actions, unwholesome factors increased and wholesome factors decreased, then that form of bodily action was to be avoided. And when I observed that by the performance of such actions unwholesome factors decreased and wholesome ones increased, then such bodily action was to be followed. That is why I make this distinction. The same applies to conduct of speech and the pursuit of goals. [281] And this, Ruler of the Gods, is the practice that monk has undertaken who has acquired the restraint required by the rules.' And Sakka expressed his delight at the Lord's answer.

2.5. Then Sakka asked another question: 'Well, sir, what practice has that monk undertaken who has acquired control of his sense-faculties?'

'Ruler of the Gods, I declare that things perceived by the eye are of two kinds: the kind to be pursued, and the kind to be avoided. The same applies to things perceived by the ear, the nose, the tongue, the body and the mind.' At this, Sakka said: 'Lord, I understand in full the true meaning of what the Blessed Lord has outlined in brief. Lord, whatever object perceived by the eye, if its pursuit leads to the increase of unwholesome factors and the decrease of wholesome ones, that is not to be sought after; if its pursuit leads to the decrease of unwholesome factors and the increase of wholesome ones, such an object is [282] to be sought after. And the same applies to things perceived by the ear, the nose, the tongue, the body and the mind. Thus I understand in full the true meaning of what the Blessed Lord has outlined in brief, and thus through the Lord's answer I have overcome my doubt and got rid of uncertainty.'

2.6. Then Sakka asked another question: 'Sir, do all ascetics and Brahmins teach the same doctrine, practise the same discipline, want the same thing[613] and pursue the same goal?' 'No, Ruler of the Gods, they do not.' 'But why, sir, do they not do so?' 'The world, Ruler of the Gods, is made up of many and various elements. Such being the case, beings adhere to one or other of these various things, and whatever they adhere to they become powerfully addicted to, and declare: 'This alone is the truth, everything else is false!' Therefore they do not all teach the same doctrine, practise the same discipline, want the same thing, pursue the same goal.'

'Sir, are all ascetics and Brahmins fully [283] proficient, freed from bonds, perfect in the holy life, have they perfectly reached the goal?' 'No, Ruler of the Gods.' 'Why is that, sir?' 'Only those, Ruler of the Gods, who are liberated by the destruction of craving are fully proficient, freed from the bonds, perfect in the holy life, and have perfectly reached the goal.' And Sakka rejoiced at the answer as before.

2.7. Then Sakka said: 'Passion,[614] sir, is a disease, a boil, a dart. It seduces a man, drawing him into this or that state of becoming, so that he is reborn in high states or low. Whereas other ascetics and Brahmins of differing viewpoints gave me no chance to ask these questions, the Lord has instructed me at length, and thus removed the dart of doubt and uncertainty from me.' [284] 'Ruler of the Gods, do you admit to having asked the same question of other ascetics and Brahmins?' 'Yes, Lord.' 'Then, if you don't mind, please tell me what they said.' 'I do not mind telling the Blessed Lord, or one like him.'[615] 'Then tell me, Ruler of the Gods.'

'Lord, I went to those I considered to be ascetics and Brahmins because of their solitary life in the woods, and I put these questions to them. But instead of giving me a proper answer,[616] they asked me in return: "Who are you, Venerable Sir?" I replied that I was Sakka, ruler of the gods, and they asked me what had brought me there. Then I taught them the Dhamma as far as I had heard it and practised it. But they were very pleased with even that much, and they said: "We have seen Sakka, the ruler of the gods, and he has answered the questions we put to him!" And they became my pupils instead of my becoming theirs. But I, Lord, am a disciple of the Blessed Lord, a Stream-Winner, not subject to rebirth in states of woe, firmly established and destined for full enlightenment.'[617] 'Ruler of the Gods, do you admit to having ever previously experienced rejoicing and happiness such as you experience now?' [285] 'Yes, Lord.' 'And what was that about?' 'In the past, Lord, war had broken out between the gods and the asuras, and the gods had defeated the asuras. And after the battle, as victor, I thought: "Whatever is now the food of the gods,[618] and what is the food of the asuras, henceforth we shall enjoy both." But, Lord, such happiness and satisfaction, which was due to blows and wounds, does not conduce to dispassion, detachment, cessation, peace, higher knowledge, enlightenment, Nibbāna. But that happiness and satisfaction that is obtained by hearing the Dhamma from the Blessed Lord, which is not due to blows and wounds, does conduce to dispassion, detachment, cessation, peace, higher knowledge, enlightenment, Nibbāna.'

2.8. 'And, Ruler of the Gods, what things do you call to mind when you admit to experiencing such satisfaction and happiness as this?' 'Lord, at such a time, six things come to mind at which I rejoice:

> "I who merely as a god exist, have gained
> The chance, by kamma, of another earthly life."[619]

That, Lord, is the first thing that occurs to me. [286]

> "Leaving this non-human realm of gods behind,
> Unerringly I'll seek the womb I wish to find."

That, Lord, is the second thing...

> "My problems solved, I'll gladly live by Buddha's law,
> Controlled and mindful, and with clear awareness filled."

That, Lord, is the third thing...

> "And should thereby enlightenment arise in me,
> As one-who-knows I'll dwell, and there await my end."

That, Lord, is the fourth thing...

> "Then when I leave the human world again, I'll be
> Once more a god, and one of highest rank."

That, Lord, is the fifth thing...

> "More glorious than devas are the Peerless Gods,[620]
> Among whom dwelling I shall make my final
> home." [287]

That, Lord, is the sixth thing that occurs to me, and these are the six things at which I rejoice.

2.9. 'Long I wandered, unfulfilled, in doubt,
In quest of the Tathāgata. I thought
Hermits who live secluded and austere
Must surely be enlightened: I'll seek them.
"What must I do to gain success, and what
Course but leads to failure?" – but, thus asked,
They could not tell me how to tread the path.
Instead, when they found out that I am king
Of gods, they asked me why I'd come to them,
And I it was who taught them what I knew
Of Dhamma, and at that, rejoicing, they
Cried: "It's Vāsava, the Lord, we've seen!"
But now – I've seen the Buddha, and my doubts
Are all dispelled, my fears are allayed,
And now to the Enlightened One I pay
Homage due, to him who's drawn the dart
Of craving, to the Buddha, peerless Lord,
Mighty hero, kinsman of the Sun![621] [288]
Just as Brahmā's worshipped by the gods,
So likewise today we worship you,
Enlightened One, and Teacher unsurpassed,
Whom none can equal in the human world,
Or in the heavens, dwelling of the gods!'

2.10. Then Sakka, ruler of the gods, said to Pañcasikha of the gandhabbas: 'My dear Pañcasikha, you have been of great help to me for gaining the ear of the Blessed Lord. For it was through your gaining his ear that we were admitted to the presence of the Blessed Lord, the Arahant, the supremely enlightened Buddha. I will be a father to you, you shall be king of the gandhabbas, and I will give you Bhaddā Suriya-vaccasā, whom you desired.'

And then Sakka, ruler of the gods, touched the earth with his hand and called out three times:

> 'Homage to the Blessed One, the Arahant, the
> supremely enlightened Buddha!
> Homage to the Blessed One, the Arahant, the
> supremely enlightened Buddha!
> Homage to the Blessed One, the Arahant, the
> supremely enlightened Buddha!'

And while he had been speaking in this dialogue,[622] the pure and spotless Dhamma-Eye arose within Sakka, ruler of the gods, and he knew: 'Whatever things have an origin must come to cessation.' And the same thing happened to eighty [289] thousand devas as well.

Such were the questions which Sakka, ruler of the gods, was desirous to ask,[623] and which the Lord answered for him. Therefore this discourse is called 'Sakka's Questions.'

22 *Mahāsatipaṭṭhāna Sutta: The Greater Discourse on the Foundations of Mindfulness*

[290] 1. THUS HAVE I HEARD.[624] Once the Lord was staying among the Kurus. There is a market-town of theirs called Kammāsadhamma.[625] And there the Lord addressed the monks: 'Monks!' 'Lord', they replied, and the Lord said:

'There is, monks, this one way[626] to the purification of beings, for the overcoming of sorrow and distress, for the disappearance of pain and sadness,[627] for the gaining of the right path,[628] for the realisation of Nibbāna: – that is to say the four foundations of mindfulness.[629]

'What are the four? Here, monks, a monk[630] abides contemplating body as body,[631] ardent, clearly aware and mindful, having put aside hankering and fretting for the world;[632] he abides contemplating feelings as feelings[633] . . . ; he abides contemplating mind as mind[634] . . . ; he abides contemplating mind-objects as mind-objects,[635] ardent, clearly aware and mindful, having put aside hankering and fretting for the world.' [291]

(CONTEMPLATION OF THE BODY)

(1. *Mindfulness of Breathing*)

2. 'And how, monks, does a monk abide contemplating the body as body? Here a monk, having gone into the forest, or to the root of a tree, or to an empty place,[636] sits down cross-legged, holding his body erect, having established mindfulness before him.[637] Mindfully he breathes in, mindfully he breathes out.[638] Breathing in a long breath, he knows that he breathes in a long breath,[639] and breathing out a long breath, he knows that he breathes out a long breath. Breathing in a short breath, he knows that he breathes in a short breath, and

breathing out a short breath, he knows that he breathes out a short breath. He trains himself, thinking: "I will breathe in, conscious of the whole body."[640] He trains himself, thinking: "I will breathe out, conscious of the whole body." He trains himself, thinking: "I will breathe in, calming the whole bodily process."[641] He trains himself, thinking: "I will breathe out, calming the whole bodily process." Just as a skilled turner, or his assistant, in making a long turn, knows that he is making a long turn, or in making a short turn, knows that he is making a short turn, so too a monk, in breathing in a long breath, knows that he breathes in a long breath...and so trains himself, thinking: "I will breathe out, calming the whole bodily process."'[292]

(INSIGHT)

'So he abides contemplating body as body internally,[642] contemplating body as body externally, contemplating body as body both internally and externally. He abides contemplating arising phenomena[643] in the body, he abides contemplating vanishing phenomena[644] in the body, he abides contemplating both arising and vanishing phenomena in the body. Or else, mindfulness that "there is body" is present to him just to the extent necessary for knowledge and awareness.[645] And he abides independent, not clinging to anything in the world. And that, monks, is how a monk abides contemplating body as body.'

(2. *The Four Postures*)

3. 'Again, a monk, when walking, knows that he is walking, when standing, knows that he is standing, when sitting, knows that he is sitting, when lying down, knows that he is lying down. In whatever way his body is disposed, he knows that that is how it is.

'So he abides contemplating body as body internally, externally, and both internally and externally...And he abides independent, not clinging to anything in the world. And that, monks, is how a monk abides contemplating body as body.'

(3. *Clear Awareness*)

4. 'Again, a monk, when going forward or back, is clearly aware of what he is doing,[646] in looking forward or back he is clearly aware of what he is doing, in bending and stretching he is clearly aware of what he is doing, in carrying his inner and outer robe and his bowl he is clearly aware of what he is doing, in eating, drinking, chewing and savouring he is clearly aware of what he is doing, in passing excrement or urine he is clearly aware of what he is doing, in walking, standing, sitting, falling asleep and waking up, in speaking or in staying silent, he is clearly aware of what he is doing. [293]

'So he abides contemplating body as body internally, externally, and both internally and externally...And he abides independent, not clinging to anything in the world. And that, monks, is how a monk abides contemplating body as body.'

(4. *Reflection on the Repulsive: Parts of the Body*)

5. 'Again, a monk reviews[647] this very body from the soles of the feet upwards and from the scalp downwards, enclosed by the skin and full of manifold impurities: "In this body there are head-hairs, body-hairs, nails, teeth, skin,[648] flesh, sinews, bones, bone-marrow, kidneys, heart, liver, pleura, spleen, lungs, mesentery, bowels, stomach, excrement, bile, phlegm, pus, blood, sweat, fat, tears, tallow, saliva, snot, synovic fluid, urine."[649] Just as if there were a bag, open at both ends, full of various kinds of grain such as hill-rice, paddy, green gram,[650] kidney-beans, sesame, husked rice, and a man with good eyesight were to open the bag and examine them, saying: "This is hill-rice, this is paddy, this is green gram, these are kidney-beans, this is sesame, this is husked rice", so too a monk reviews this very body: "In this body there are head-hairs,...[294] urine."

'So he abides contemplating body as body internally, externally, and both internally and externally...And he abides independent, not clinging to anything in the world. And that, monks, is how a monk abides contemplating body as body.'

(5. *The Four Elements*)

6. 'Again, a monk reviews this body, however it may be placed or disposed, in terms of the elements: "There are in this body the earth-element, the water-element, the fire-element, the air-element."[651] Just as if a skilled butcher or his assistant, having slaughtered a cow,[652] were to sit at a cross-roads with the carcass divided into portions, so a monk reviews this very body...in terms of the elements: "There are in this body the earth-element, the water-element, the fire-element, the air-element."

'So he abides contemplating body as body internally...[295] And he abides independent, not clinging to anything in the world. And that, monks, is how a monk abides contemplating body as body.'

(6. *The Nine Charnel-Ground Contemplations*)

7. 'Again, a monk, as if he were to see a corpse thrown aside in a charnel-ground,[653] one, two or three days dead, bloated, discoloured, festering, compares this body with that, thinking: "This body is of the same nature, it will become like that, it is not exempt from that fate."

'So he abides contemplating body as body internally, externally, and both internally and externally. And he abides independent, not clinging to anything in the world. And that, monks, is how a monk abides contemplating body as body.

8. 'Again, a monk, as if he were to see a corpse in a charnel-ground, thrown aside, eaten by crows, hawks or vultures, by dogs or jackals, or various other creatures, compares this body with that, thinking: "This body is of the same nature, it will become like that, it is not exempt from that fate." [296]

9. 'Again, a monk, as if he were to see a corpse in a charnel-ground, thrown aside, a skeleton with flesh and blood, connected by sinews,...a fleshless skeleton smeared with blood, connected by sinews,...a skeleton detached from the flesh and blood, connected by sinews,...randomly connected bones, scattered in all directions, a hand-bone here, a foot-

bone there, a shin-bone here, a thigh-bone there, a hip-bone here, [297] a spine here, a skull there, compares this body with that...

10. 'Again, a monk, as if he were to see a corpse in a charnel-ground, thrown aside, the bones whitened, looking like shells..., the bones piled up, a year old..., the bones rotted away to a powder, compares this body with that, thinking: "This body is of the same nature, will become like that, is not exempt from that fate."'

(INSIGHT)

'So he abides contemplating body as body internally, contemplating body as body externally, abides contemplating body [298] as body both internally and externally. He abides contemplating arising phenomena in the body, contemplating vanishing phenomena in the body, he abides contemplating both arising and vanishing phenomena in the body. Or else, mindfulness that "there is body" is present to him just to the extent necessary for knowledge and awareness. And he abides independent, not clinging to anything in the world. And that, monks, is how a monk abides contemplating body as body.'

(CONTEMPLATION OF FEELINGS)

11. 'And how, monks, does a monk abide contemplating feelings as feelings?[654] Here, a monk feeling a pleasant feeling knows that he feels a pleasant feeling;[655] feeling a painful feeling he knows that he feels a painful feeling;[656] feeling a feeling that is neither-painful-nor-pleasant he knows that he feels a feeling that is neither-painful-nor-pleasant;[657] feeling a pleasant sensual feeling he knows that he feels a pleasant sensual feeling;[658] feeling a pleasant non-sensual feeling he knows that he feels a pleasant non-sensual feeling;[659] feeling a painful sensual feeling...; feeling a painful non-sensual feeling...; feeling a sensual feeling that is neither-painful-nor-pleasant...; feeling a non-sensual feeling that is neither-pain-

ful-nor-pleasant, he knows that he feels a non-sensual feeling that is neither painful-nor-pleasant.'

(INSIGHT)

'So he abides contemplating feelings as feelings internally. He abides contemplating feelings as feelings externally[660]... He abides contemplating arising phenomena in the feelings, vanishing phenomena and both arising and vanishing phenomena in the feelings. [299] Or else, mindfulness that "there is feeling" is present to him just to the extent necessary for knowledge and awareness. And he abides independent, not clinging to anything in the world. And that, monks, is how a monk abides contemplating feelings as feelings.'

(CONTEMPLATION OF MIND)

12. 'And how, monks, does a monk abide contemplating mind as mind?[661] Here, a monk knows a lustful mind as lustful, a mind free from lust as free from lust; a hating mind as hating, a mind free from hate as free from hate; a deluded mind as deluded, an undeluded mind as undeluded; a contracted mind as contracted,[662] a distracted mind as distracted;[663] a developed mind as developed,[664] an undeveloped mind as undeveloped;[665] a surpassed mind as surpassed,[666] an unsurpassed mind as unsurpassed;[667] a concentrated mind as concentrated,[668] an unconcentrated mind as unconcentrated;[669] a liberated mind as liberated,[670] an unliberated mind as unliberated.'

(INSIGHT)

'So he abides contemplating mind as mind internally. He abides contemplating mind as mind externally[671]... He abides contemplating arising phenomena in the mind... Or else, mindfulness that "there is mind" is present [300] just to the extent necessary for knowledge and awareness. And he abides detached, not grasping at anything in the world. And that, monks, is how a monk abides contemplating mind as mind.'

(CONTEMPLATION OF MIND-OBJECTS)

13. 'And how, monks, does a monk abide contemplating mind-objects as mind-objects?'[672]

(1. *The Five Hindrances*)

'Here, a monk abides contemplating mind-objects as mind-objects in respect of the five hindrances. How does he do so? Here, monks, if sensual desire[673] is present in himself, a monk knows that it is present. If sensual desire is absent in himself, a monk knows that it is absent. And he knows how unarisen sensual desire comes to arise, and he knows how the abandonment of arisen sensual desire comes about, and he knows how the non-arising of the abandoned sensual desire in the future will come about.[674]

'If ill-will[675] is present in himself, a monk knows that it is present...And he knows how the non-arising of the abandoned ill-will in the future will come about.

'If sloth-and-torpor[676] is present in himself, a monk knows that it is present...And he knows how the non-arising of the abandoned sloth-and-torpor in the future will come about.

'If worry-and-flurry[677] is present in himself, a [301] monk knows that it is present...And he knows how the non-arising of the abandoned worry-and-flurry in the future will come about.

'If doubt[678] is present in himself, a monk knows that it is present. If doubt is absent in himself, he knows that it is absent. And he knows how unarisen doubt comes to arise, and he knows how the abandonment of arisen doubt comes about, and he knows how the non-arising of the abandoned doubt in the future will come about.'

(INSIGHT)

'So he abides contemplating mind-objects as mind-objects internally...He abides contemplating arising phenomena in mind-objects[679]...Or else, mindfulness that "there are mind-objects" is present just to the extent necessary for knowledge and awareness. And he abides detached, not grasping at anything in the world. And that, monks, is how a monk abides contemplating mind-objects as mind-objects in respect of the five hindrances.'

(2. *The Five Aggregates*)

14. 'Again, monks, a monk abides contemplating mind-objects as mind-objects in respect of the five aggregates of grasping.[680] How does he do so? Here, a monk thinks: "Such is form,[681] such the arising of form, such the disappearance of form; such is feeling, such the arising of feeling, such the disappearance of feeling; such is perception,[682] such the arising of perception, such the disappearance of perception; such are the mental formations,[683] [302] such the arising of the mental formations, such the disappearance of the mental formations; such is consciousness,[684] such the arising of consciousness, such the disappearance of consciousness.'

(INSIGHT)

'So he abides contemplating mind-objects as mind-objects internally...And he abides detached, not grasping at anything in the world. And that, monks, is how a monk abides contemplating mind-objects as mind-objects in respect of the five aggregates of grasping.'

(3. *The Six Internal and External Sense-Bases*)

15. 'Again, monks, a monk abides contemplating mind-objects as mind-objects in respect of the six internal and external sense-bases.[685] How does he do so? Here a monk knows the eye, knows sight-objects,[686] and he knows whatever fetter arises dependent on the two.[687] And he knows how an unarisen fetter comes to arise, and he knows how the abandonment of an arisen fetter comes about, and he knows how the non-arising of the abandoned fetter in the future will come about. He knows the ear and knows sounds...He knows the nose, and knows smells...He knows the tongue and knows tastes...He knows the body[688] and knows tangibles...He knows the mind and knows mind-objects, and he knows [303] whatever fetter arises dependent on the two. And he knows

how an unarisen fetter comes to arise, and he knows how the abandonment of an arisen fetter comes about, and he knows how the non-arising of the abandoned fetter in the future will come about.'

(INSIGHT)

'So he abides contemplating mind-objects as mind-objects internally...And he abides detached, not grasping at anything in the world. And that, monks, is how a monk abides contemplating mind-objects as mind-objects in respect of the six internal and external sense-bases.'

(4. *The Seven Factors of Enlightenment*)

16. 'Again, monks, a monk abides contemplating mind-objects as mind-objects in respect of the seven factors of enlightenment.[689] How does he do so? Here, monks, if the enlightenment-factor of mindfulness is present in himself, a monk knows that it is present. If the enlightenment-factor of mindfulness is absent in himself, he knows that it is absent. And he knows how the unarisen enlightenment-factor of mindfulness comes to arise, and he knows how the complete development of the enlightenment-factor of mindfulness comes about. If the enlightenment-factor of investigation-of-states[690] is present in himself...If the enlightenment-factor of energy[691] is present in himself...If the enlightenment-factor of delight[692] is present in himself...[304] If the enlightenment-factor of tranquillity[693] is present in himself...If the enlightenment-factor of concentration is present in himself...If the enlightenment-factor of equanimity is present in himself, a monk knows that it is present. If the enlightenment-factor of equanimity is absent in himself, he knows that it is absent. And he knows how the unarisen enlightenment-factor of equanimity comes to arise, and he knows how the complete development of the enlightenment-factor of equanimity comes about.'

(INSIGHT)

'So he abides contemplating mind-objects as mind-objects

internally...And he abides detached, not grasping at anything in the world. And that, monks, is how a monk abides contemplating mind-objects as mind-objects in respect of the seven factors of enlightenment.'

(5. *The Four Noble Truths*)

17. 'Again, monks, a monk abides contemplating mind-objects as mind-objects in respect of the Four Noble Truths. How does he do so? Here, a monk knows as it really is: "This is suffering"; he knows as it really is: "This is the origin of suffering"; he knows as it really is: "This is the cessation of suffering"; he knows as it really is: "This is the way of practice leading to the cessation of suffering."

18. [694]'And what, monks, is the Noble Truth of Suffering? Birth is suffering, ageing is suffering, death is suffering, sorrow, lamentation, pain, sadness and distress are suffering. Being attached to the unloved is suffering, being separated from the loved is suffering, not getting what one wants is suffering. In short, the five aggregates of grasping[695] are suffering.

'And what, monks, is birth? In whatever beings, of whatever group of beings, there is birth, coming-to-be, coming forth, the appearance of the aggregates, the acquisition of the sense-bases,[696] that, monks, is called birth.

'And what is ageing? In whatever beings, of whatever group of beings, there is ageing, decrepitude, broken teeth, grey hair, wrinkled skin, shrinking with age, decay of the sense-faculties, that, monks, is called ageing.

'And what is death? In whatever beings, of whatever group of beings, there is a passing-away, a removal, a cutting-off, a disappearance, a death, a dying, an ending, a cutting-off of the aggregates, a discarding of the body, that, monks, is called death.

'And what is sorrow? Whenever, by any kind of misfortune, [306] anyone is affected by something of a painful nature, sorrow, mourning, distress, inward grief, inward woe, that, monks, is called sorrow.

'And what is lamentation? Whenever, by any kind of misfortune, anyone is affected by something of a painful nature and there is crying out, lamenting, making much noise for grief, making great lamentation, that, monks, is called lamentation.

'And what is pain? Whatever bodily painful feeling, bodily unpleasant feeling, painful or unpleasant feeling results from bodily contact, that, monks, is called pain.

'And what is sadness?[697] Whatever mental painful feeling, mental unpleasant feeling, painful or unpleasant sensation results from mental contact, that, monks, is called sadness.

'And what is distress? Whenever, by any kind of misfortune, anyone is affected by something of a painful nature, distress, great distress, affliction with distress, with great distress, that, monks, is called distress.[698]

'And what, monks, is being attached to the unloved? Here, whoever has unwanted, disliked, unpleasant sight-objects, sounds, smells, tastes, tangibles or mind-objects, or whoever encounters ill-wishers, wishers of harm, of discomfort, of insecurity, with whom they have concourse, intercourse, connection, union, that, monks, is called being attached to the unloved.

'And what is being separated from the loved? Here, whoever has what is wanted, liked, pleasant sight-objects, sounds, smells, tastes, tangibles or mind-objects, or whoever encounters well-wishers, wishers of good, of comfort, of security, mother or father or brother or sister or younger kinsmen or friends or colleagues or blood-relations, and then is deprived of such concourse, intercourse, connection, or union, that, monks, is called being separated from the loved. [307]

'And what is not getting what one wants? In beings subject to birth, monks, this wish arises: "Oh that we were not subject to birth, that we might not come to birth!" But this cannot be gained by wishing. That is not getting what one wants. In beings subject to ageing, to disease,[699] to death, to sorrow, lamentation, pain, sadness and distress this wish arises: "Oh that we were not subject to ageing...distress, that we might not come to these things!" But this cannot be gained by wishing. That is not getting what one wants.

'And how, monks, in short, are the five aggregates of grasping suffering? They are as follows: the aggregate of grasping that is form, the aggregate of grasping that is feeling, the aggregate of grasping that is perception, the aggregate of grasping that is the mental formations, the aggregate of grasping that is consciousness,[700] These are, in short, the five aggregates of grasping that are suffering. And that, monks, is called the Noble Truth of Suffering. [308]

19. 'And what, monks, is the Noble Truth of the Origin of Suffering? It is that craving[701] which gives rise to rebirth,[702] bound up with pleasure and lust, finding fresh delight now here, now there: that is to say sensual craving, craving for existence, and craving for non-existence.[703]

'And where does this craving arise and establish itself? Wherever in the world there is anything agreeable and pleasurable, there this craving arises and establishes itself.

'And what is there in the world that is agreeable and pleasurable? The eye in the world is agreeable and pleasurable, the ear..., the nose..., the tongue..., the body..., the mind in the world is agreeable and pleasurable, and there this craving arises and establishes itself. Sights, sounds, smells, tastes, tangibles, mind-objects in the world are agreeable and pleasurable, and there this craving arises and establishes itself.

'Eye-consciousness, ear-consciousness, nose-consciousness, tongue-consciousness, body-consciousness, mind-consciousness in the world is agreeable and pleasurable, and there this craving arises and establishes itself.

'Eye-contact,[704] ear-contact, nose-contact, [309] tongue-contact, body-contact, mind-contact in the world is agreeable and pleasurable, and there this craving arises and establishes itself.

'Feeling born of eye-contact, ear-contact, nose-contact, tongue-contact, body-contact, mind-contact in the world is agreeable and pleasurable, and there this craving arises and establishes itself.

'The perception of sights, of sounds, of smells, of tastes, of tangibles, of mind-objects in the world is agreeable and pleasurable, and there this craving arises and establishes itself.

'Volition in regard to sights, sounds, smells, tastes, tangibles, mind-objects in the world is agreeable and pleasurable, and there this craving arises and establishes itself.

'The craving for sights, sounds, smells, tastes, tangibles, mind-objects in the world is agreeable and pleasurable, and there this craving arises and establishes itself.

'Thinking[705] of sights, sounds, smells, tastes, tangibles, mind-objects in the world is agreeable and pleasurable, and there this craving arises and establishes itself.

'Pondering[706] on sights, sounds, smells, tastes, tangibles and mind-objects in the world is agreeable and pleasurable, and there this craving [310] arises and establishes itself. And that, monks, is called the Noble Truth of the Origin of Suffering.

20. 'And what, monks, is the Noble Truth of the Cessation of Suffering? It is the complete fading-away and extinction of this craving, its forsaking and abandonment, liberation from it, detachment from it.[707] And how does this craving come to be abandoned, how does its cessation come about?

'Wherever in the world there is anything agreeable and pleasurable, there its cessation comes about. And what is there in the world that is agreeable and pleasurable?

'The eye in the world is agreeable and pleasurable, the ear ..., the nose..., the tongue..., the body..., the mind in the world is agreeable and pleasurable, and there this craving comes to be abandoned, there its cessation comes about:

'Eye-consciousness, ear-consciousness, nose-consciousness, tongue-consciousness, body-consciousness, mind-consciousness in the world is agreeable and pleasurable, and there this craving comes to be abandoned, there its cessation comes about.

'Sights, sounds, smells, tastes, tangibles, mind-objects in the world are agreeable and pleasurable, and there this craving comes to be abandoned, there its cessation comes about.

'Eye-contact, ear-contact, nose-contact, tongue-contact, body-contact, mind-contact...;[311] the perception of sights, sounds, smells, tastes, tangibles, mind-objects...; volition in regard to sights, sounds, smells, tastes, tangibles, mind-objects...; craving for sights, sounds, smells, tastes, tangibles, mind-objects...; thinking of sights, sounds, smells, tastes, tangibles, mind-objects...; pondering on sights, sounds, smells, tastes, tangibles and mind-objects in the world is agreeable and pleasurable, and there this craving comes to an end, there its cessation comes about. And that, monks, is called the Noble Truth of the Cessation of Suffering.

21. 'And what, monks, is the Noble Truth of the Way of Practice Leading to the Cessation of Suffering? It is just this Noble Eightfold Path, namely: – Right View, Right Thought; Right Speech, Right Action, Right Livelihood; Right Effort Right Mindfulness, Right Concentration.

'And what, monks, is Right View?[708] [312] It is, monks, the knowledge of suffering, the knowledge of the origin of suffering, the knowledge of the cessation of suffering, and the knowledge of the way of practice leading to the cessation of suffering. This is called Right View.

'And what, monks, is Right Thought?[709] The thought of renunciation, the thought of non-ill-will, the thought of harmlessness. This, monks, is called Right Thought.

'And what, monks, is Right Speech? Refraining from lying, refraining from slander, refraining from harsh speech, refraining from frivolous speech. This is called Right Speech.

'And what, monks, is Right Action? Refraining from taking life, refraining from taking what is not given, refraining from sexual misconduct. This is called Right Action.

'And what, monks, is Right Livelihood? Here, monks, the Ariyan disciple, having given up wrong livelihood, keeps himself by right livelihood.

'And what, monks, is Right Effort? Here, monks, a monk rouses his will, makes an effort, stirs up energy, exerts his mind and strives to prevent the arising of unarisen evil unwholesome mental states. He rouses his will...and strives to overcome evil unwholesome mental states that have arisen. He rouses his will...and strives to produce unarisen wholesome mental states. He rouses his will, makes an effort, stirs up energy, exerts his mind [313] and strives to maintain wholesome mental states that have arisen, not to let them fade away, to bring them to greater growth, to the full perfection of development. This is called Right Effort.

'And what, monks, is Right Mindfulness? Here, monks, a monk abides contemplating body as body, ardent, clearly aware and mindful, having put aside hankering and fretting for the world; he abides contemplating feelings as feelings...; he abides contemplating mind as mind...; he abides contemplating mind-objects as mind-objects, ardent, clearly aware and mindful, having put aside hankering and fretting for the world. This is called Right Mindfulness.

'And what, monks, is Right Concentration? Here, a monk, detached from sense-desires, detached from unwholesome mental states, enters and remains in the first jhāna, which is with thinking and pondering, born of detachment, filled with delight and joy. And with the subsiding of thinking and pondering, by gaining inner tranquillity and oneness of mind, he enters and remains in the second jhāna, which is without thinking and pondering, born of concentration, filled with delight and joy. And with the fading away of delight, remaining imperturbable, mindful and clearly aware, he experiences in himself the joy of which the Noble Ones say: "Happy is he who dwells with equanimity and mindfulness", he enters the third jhāna. And, having given up pleasure and pain, and with the disappearance of former gladness and sadness, he enters and remains in the fourth jhāna, which is beyond pleasure and pain, and purified by equanimity and mindfulness. This is called Right Concentration. And that, monks, is called the way of practice leading to the cessation of suffering.'

(INSIGHT)

'So he abides contemplating mind-objects as mind-objects internally, [314] contemplating mind-objects as mind-objects externally, contemplating mind-objects as mind-objects both internally and externally. He abides contemplating arising phenomena in mind-objects, he abides contemplating vanishing-phenomena in mind-objects, he abides contemplating both arising and vanishing phenomena in mind-objects. Or else, mindfulness that "there are mind-objects" is present just to the extent necessary for knowledge and awareness. And he abides detached, not grasping at anything in the world. And that, monks, is how a monk abides contemplating mind-objects as mind-objects in respect of the Four Noble Truths.'

(CONCLUSION)

22. 'Whoever, monks, should practise these four foundations of mindfulness for just seven years may expect one of two results: either Arahantship in this life or, if there should be some substrate left, the state of a Non-Returner. Let alone seven years – whoever should practise them for just six years ..., five years..., four years...three years..., two years..., one year may expect one of two results...; let alone one year – whoever should practise them for just seven months..., six months..., five months..., four months..., three months..., two months..., [315] one month..., half a month may expect one of two results...; let alone half a month – whoever should practise these four foundations of mindfulness for just one week may expect one of two results: either Arahantship in this life or, if there should be some substrate left, the state of a Non-Returner.

'It was said: "There is, monks, this one way to the purification of beings, for the overcoming of sorrow and distress, for the disappearance of pain and sadness, for the gaining of the right path, for the realisation of Nibbāna: – that is to say the four foundations of mindfulness", and it is for this reason that it was said.'

Thus the Lord spoke, and the monks rejoiced and were delighted at his words.

23 *Pāyāsi Sutta: About Pāyāsi* Debate with a Sceptic

[316] 1. THUS HAVE I HEARD. Once the Venerable Kumāra-Kassapa[710] was touring round Kosala with a large company of about five hundred monks, and he came to stay at a town called Setavyā. He stayed to the north of Setavyā in the Siṁsapā Forest.[711] And at that time Prince Pāyāsi was living at Setavyā, a populous place, full of grass, timber, water and corn, which had been given to him by King Pasenadi of Kosala as a royal gift and with royal powers.[712]

2. And Prince Pāyāsi developed the following evil opinion: 'There is no other world, there are no spontaneously born beings, there is no fruit or result [317] of good or evil deeds.'[713] Meanwhile, the Brahmins and householders of Setavyā heard the news: 'The ascetic Kumāra-Kassapa, a disciple of the ascetic Gotama, is touring round Kosala with a large company of about five hundred monks; he has arrived at Setavyā and is staying to the north of Setavyā in the Siṁsapā Forest; and concerning the Reverend Kassapa a good report has been spread about: "He is learned, experienced, wise, well-informed, a fine speaker, able to give good replies, venerable, an Arahant." And it is good to see such Arahants.' And so the Brahmins and householders of Setavyā, leaving Setavyā by the north gate in large numbers, made for the Siṁsapā Forest.

3. And just then, Prince Pāyāsi had gone up to the verandah for his midday rest. Seeing all the Brahmins and householders making for the Siṁsapā Forest, he asked his steward why. [318] The steward said: 'Sir, it is the ascetic Kumāra-Kassapa, a disciple of the ascetic Gotama,. . . and concerning him a good report has been spread about. . . That is why they are going to see him.' 'Well then, steward, you go to the

Brahmins and householders of Setavyā and say: "Gentlemen, Prince Pāyāsi says: 'Please wait, the Prince will come to see the ascetic Kumāra-Kassapa.'" Already this ascetic Kumāra-Kassapa has been teaching these foolish and inexperienced Brahmins and householders of Setavyā that there is another world, that there are spontaneously born beings, and that there is fruit and result of good and evil deeds. But no such things exist.' 'Very good, sir', said the steward, and delivered the message.

4. Then Prince Pāyāsi, accompanied by the Brahmins and householders of Setavyā, went to the Siṁsapā Forest where the Venerable Kumāra-Kassapa was. Having exchanged courtesies with the Venerable Kumāra Kassapa, [319] he sat down to one side. And some of the Brahmins and householders saluted the Venerable Kumāra-Kassapa and then sat down to one side, while some first exchanged courtesies with him, some saluted him with joined palms, some announced their name and clan, and some silently sat down to one side.

5. Then Price Pāyāsi said to the Venerable Kumāra-Kassapa: 'Reverend Kassapa, I hold to this tenet and this view: There is no other world, there are no spontaneously born beings, there is no fruit or result of good or evil deeds.' 'Well, Prince, I have never seen or heard of such a tenet or view as you declare. And so, Prince, I will question you about it, and you shall reply as you think fit. What do you think, Prince? Are the sun and the moon in this world or another, are they gods or humans?'

'Reverend Kassapa, they are in another world, and they are gods, not humans.' 'In the same way, Prince, you should consider: "There is another world, there are spontaneously born beings, there is fruit and result of good and evil deeds."'

6. 'Whatever you may say about that, Reverend Kassapa, I still think there is no other world...' 'Have you any reasons for this assertion, Prince?' [320] 'I have, Reverend Kassapa.' 'How is that, Prince?'

'Reverend Kassapa, I have friends, colleagues and blood-relations who take life, take what is not given, commit sexual offences, tell lies, use abusive, harsh and frivolous speech, who are greedy, full of hatred and hold wrong views. Eventually they become ill, suffering, diseased. And when I am sure they will not recover, I go to them and say: "There are certain ascetics and Brahmins who declare and believe that those who take life,...hold wrong views will, after death at the breaking-up of the body, be born in a state of woe, an evil place, a place of punishment, in hell. Now you have done these things, and if what these ascetics and Brahmins say is true, that is where you will go. Now if, after death, you go to a state of woe,...come to me and declare that there is another world, there are spontaneously born beings, there is fruit and result of good and evil deeds. You, gentlemen, are trustworthy and dependable, and what you have seen shall be as if I had seen it myself, so it will be." But although they agreed, [321] they neither came to tell me, nor did they send a messenger. That, Reverend Kassapa, is my reason for maintaining: "There is no other world, there are no spontaneously born beings, there is no fruit or result of good or evil deeds."'

7. 'As to that, Prince, I will question you about it, and you shall reply as you think fit. What do you think, Prince? Suppose they were to bring a thief before you caught in the act, and say: "This man, Lord, is a thief caught in the act. Sentence him to any punishment you wish." And you might say: "Bind this man's arms tightly behind him with a strong rope, shave his head closely, and lead him to the rough sound of a drum through the streets and squares and out through the southern gate, and there cut off his head." And they, saying: "Very good" in assent, might...lead him out through the southern gate, and there cut off his head." Now if that thief were to say to the executioners: "Good executioners, in this town or village I have friends, colleagues and blood-relations, please wait till I have visited them", would he get his wish? [322] Or would they just cut off that talkative thief's head?' 'He would not get his wish, Reverend Kassapa. They would just cut off his head.'

'So, Prince, this thief could not get even his human executioners to wait while he visited his friends and relations. So how can your friends, colleagues and blood-relations who have committed all these misdeeds, having died and gone to a place of woe, prevail upon the warders of hell, saying: "Good warders of hell, please wait while we report to Prince Pāyāsi that there is another world, there are spontaneously born beings, and there is fruit and result of good and evil deeds"? Therefore, Prince, admit that there is another world...'

8. 'Whatever you may say about that, Reverend Kassapa, I still think there is no other world...' 'Have you any reason for this assertion, Prince?' 'I have, Reverend Kassapa.' 'What is that, Prince?'

'Reverend Kassapa, I have friends...who abstain from taking life, from taking what is not given, from committing sexual [323] offences, from telling lies or using abusive, harsh and frivolous speech, who are not greedy or full of hatred and who have right views.[714] Eventually they become ill...and when I am sure they will not recover, I go to them and say: "There are certain ascetics and Brahmins who declare and believe that those who abstain from taking life...and have right views will, after death at the breaking-up of the body, be born in a happy state, a heavenly world. Now you have refrained from doing these things, and if what these ascetics and Brahmins say is true, that is where you will go. Now if, after death, you go to a happy state, a heavenly world, come to me and declare that there is another world...You, gentlemen, are trustworthy and dependable, and what you have seen shall be as if I had seen it myself, so it will be." But although they agreed, they neither came to me, nor did they send a messenger. That, Reverend Kassapa, is my reason for maintaining: [324] "There is no other world..."'

9. 'Well then, Prince, I will give you a parable, because some wise people understand what is said by means of parables. Suppose a man had fallen head first into a cesspit, and you were to say to your men: "Pull that man out of the cesspit!" and they would say: "Very good", and do so. Then you would tell them to clean his body thoroughly of the filth with bamboo scrapers, and then to give him a triple shampoo with yellow loam. Then you would tell them to anoint his body with oil and then to clean him three times with fine soap-powder. Then you would tell them to dress his hair and beard, and to adorn him with fine garlands, ointments and clothes. [325] Finally you would tell them to lead him up to

your palace and let him indulge in the pleasures of the five senses, and they would do so. What do you think, Prince? Would that man, having been well washed, with his hair and beard dressed, adorned and garlanded, clothed in white, and having been conveyed up to the palace, enjoying and revelling in the pleasures of the five senses, want to be plunged once more into that cesspit?' 'No, Reverend Kassapa.' 'Why not?' 'Because that cesspit is unclean and considered so, evil-smelling, horrible, revolting, and generally considered to be so.'

'In just the same way, Prince, human beings are unclean, evil-smelling, horrible, revolting and generally considered to be so by the devas. So why should your friends...who have not committed any of the offences...(*as verse 8*), and who have after death been born in a happy state, a heavenly world, come back and say: "There is another world,...there is fruit [326] of good and evil deeds"? Therefore, Prince, admit that there is another world...'

10. 'Whatever you may say about that, Reverend Kassapa, I still think there is no other world...' 'Have you any reason for this assertion, Prince?' 'I have, Reverend Kassapa.' 'What is that, Prince?'

'Reverend Kassapa, I have friends who abstain...from telling lies, from strong drink and sloth-inducing drugs. Eventually they become ill..."There are certain ascetics and Brahmins who declare and believe that those who abstain from taking life...and sloth-producing drugs will...be born in a happy state, in a heavenly world, as companions of the Thirty-Three Gods..."[327] But although they agreed, they neither came to tell me, nor did they send a messenger. That, Reverend Kassapa, is my reason for maintaining: "There is no other world..."'

11. 'As to that, Prince, I will question you about it, and you shall answer as you think fit. That which is for human beings, Prince, a hundred years is for the Thirty-Three Gods one day and night. Thirty of such nights make a month, twelve such months a year, and a thousand such years are the life-span of the Thirty-Three Gods. Now suppose they were to think: "After we have indulged in the pleasures of the five senses for

two or three days we will go to Pāyāsi and tell him there is another world, there are spontaneously born beings, there is fruit and result of good and evil deeds", would they have done so?' 'No, Reverend Kassapa, because we should be long-since dead. But, Reverend Kassapa, who has told you that the Thirty-Three Gods exist, and that they are so long-lived? I don't [328] believe the Thirty-Three Gods exist or are so long-lived.'

'Prince, imagine a man who was blind from birth and could not see dark or light objects, or blue, yellow, red or crimson ones, could not see the smooth and the rough, could not see the stars and the moon. He might say: "There are no dark and light objects and nobody who can see them,...there is no sun or moon, and nobody who can see them. I am not aware of this thing, and therefore it does not exist." Would he be speaking rightly, Prince?' 'No, Reverend Kassapa. There are dark and light objects...,[329] there is a sun and a moon, and anyone who said: "I am not aware of this thing, I cannot see it, and therefore it does not exist" would not be speaking rightly.'

'Well, Prince, it appears that your reply is like that of the blind man when you ask how I know about the Thirty-Three Gods and their longevity. Prince, the other world cannot be seen the way you think, with the physical eye. Prince, those ascetics and Brahmins who seek in the jungle-thickets and the recesses of the forest for a resting-place that is quiet, with little noise – they stay there unwearied, ardent, restrained, purifying the divine eye,[715] and with that purified divine eye that exceeds the powers of human sight, they see both this world and the next, and spontaneously born beings. That, Prince, is how the other world can be seen, and not the way you think, with the physical eye. Therefore, Prince, admit that there is another world, that there are spontaneously born beings, and that there is fruit and result of good and evil deeds.'

12. 'Whatever you may say about that, Reverend Kassapa, [330] I still think there is no other world...' 'Have you any reason for this assertion, Prince?' 'I have, Reverend Kassapa.' 'What is that, Prince?'

'Well, Reverend Kassapa, I see here some ascetics and Brahmins who observe morality and are well-conducted, who want to live, do not want to die, who desire comfort and hate suffering. And it seems to me that if these good ascetics and Brahmins who are so moral and well-conducted know that after death they will be better off, then these good people would now take poison, take a knife and kill themselves, hang themselves or jump off a cliff. But though they have such knowledge, they still want to live, do not want to die, they desire comfort and hate suffering. And that, Reverend Kassapa, is my reason for maintaining: "There is no other world . . ."'

13. 'Well then, Prince, I will give you a parable, because some wise people understand what is said by means of parables. Once upon a time, Prince, a certain Brahmin had two wives. One had a son ten or twelve years old, while the other was pregnant and nearing her time when the Brahmin died. Then this youth said to his mother's co-wife: "Lady, whatever wealth and possessions, silver or gold, there may be, is all [331] mine. My father made me his heir." At this the Brahmin lady said to the youth: "Wait, young man, until I give birth. If the child is a boy, one portion will be his, and if it is a girl, she will become your servant." The youth repeated his words a second time, and received the same reply. When he repeated them a third time, the lady took a knife and, going into an inner room, cut open her belly, thinking: "If only I could find out whether it is a boy or a girl!" And thus she destroyed herself and the living embryo, and the wealth as well, just as fools do who seek their inheritance unwisely, heedless of hidden danger.

'In the same way you, Prince, will foolishly enter on hidden dangers by unwisely seeking for another [332] world, just as that Brahmin lady did in seeking her inheritance. But, Prince, those ascetics and Brahmins who observe morality and are well-conducted do not seek to hasten the ripening of that which is not yet ripe, but rather they wisely await its ripening. Their life is profitable to those ascetics and Brahmins, for the longer such moral and well-conducted ascetics and Brahmins remain alive, the greater the merit that they create; they practise for the welfare of the many, for the happiness of the many, out of compassion for the world, for the profit and benefit of devas and humans. Therefore, Prince, admit that there is another world...'

14. 'Whatever you may say about that, Reverend Kassapa, I still think there is no other world...' 'Have you any reason for this assertion, Prince?' 'I have, Reverend Kassapa.' 'What is that, Prince?'

'Reverend Kassapa, take the case that they bring a thief before me, caught in the act and say: "Here, Lord, is a thief caught in the act, sentence him to whatever punishment you wish." And I say: "Take this man and put him alive in a jar. Seal the mouth and close it with a damp skin, give it a thick covering of damp clay, [333] put it in an oven and light the fire." And they do so. When we are sure the man is dead, we remove the jar, break the clay, uncover the mouth, and watch carefully: "Maybe we can see his soul[716] escaping." But we do not see any soul escaping, and that is why, Reverend Kassapa, I believe there is no other world...'

15. 'As to that, Prince, I will question you about it, and you shall reply as you think fit. Do you admit that when you have gone for your midday rest you have seen pleasant visions of parks, forests, delightful country and lotus-ponds?' 'I do, Reverend Kassapa.' 'And at that time are you not watched over by hunchbacks, dwarfs, young girls and maidens?' 'I am, Reverend Kassapa.' 'And do they observe your soul entering or leaving your body?' [334] 'No, Reverend Kassapa.' 'So they do not see your soul entering or leaving your body even when you are alive. Therefore how could you see the soul of a dead man entering or leaving his body? Therefore, Prince, admit that there is another world...'

16. 'Whatever you may say about that, Reverend Kassapa, I still think there is no other world...' 'Have you any reason for this assertion, Prince?' 'I have, Reverend Kassapa.' 'What is that, Prince?'

'Reverend Kassapa, take the case that they bring a thief before me...and I say: "Weigh this man on the scales alive, then strangle him, and weigh him again." And they do so. As long as he was alive, he was lighter, softer and more flexible, but when he was dead he was heavier, stiffer[717] and more inflexible. And that, Reverend Kassapa, is my reason for maintaining that there is no other world...'

17. 'Well then, Prince, I will give you a parable... [335] Suppose a man weighed an iron ball that had been heated all day, blazing, burning fiercely, glowing. And suppose that after a time, when it had grown cold and gone out, he weighed it again. At which time would it be lighter, softer and more flexible: when it was hot, burning and glowing, or when it was cold and extinguished?' 'Reverend Kassapa, when that ball of iron is hot, burning and glowing with the elements of fire and air, then it is lighter, softer and more flexible. When, without those elements,[718] it has grown cold and gone out, it is heavier, stiffer and more inflexible.' 'Well then, Prince, it is just the same with the body. When it has life, heat and consciousness, it is lighter, softer and more flexible. But when it is deprived of life, heat and consciousness, it is heavier, stiffer and more inflexible. In the same way, Prince, you should consider: "There is another world..."'

18. 'Whatever you may say about that, Reverend Kassapa, I still think there is no other world...' 'Have you any reason for this assertion, Prince?' 'I have, Reverend Kassapa.' 'What is that, Prince?'

'Reverend Kassapa, take the case of a thief that they bring before me... [336] and I say: "Kill this man without wounding his cuticle, skin, flesh, sinews, bones or marrow",[719] and they do so. When he is half-dead, I say: "Now lay this man on his back, and perhaps we shall be able to see his soul emerging." They do so, but we cannot see his soul emerging. Then I say: "Turn him face downwards,... on his side,... on the other side,... stand him up,... stand him on his head,... thump him with your fists,... stone him,... hit him with sticks,... strike him with swords,... shake him this way and that, and perhaps we shall be able to see his soul emerging." And they do all these things, but although he has eyes he does not perceive objects or their spheres,[720] although he has ears he does not hear sounds..., although he has a nose he does not smell smells..., although he [337] has a tongue he does not taste tastes..., although he has a body he does not feel tangibles or their spheres. And that is why, Reverend Kassapa, I believe there is no other world...'

19. 'Well then, Prince, I will give you a parable...Once there was a trumpeter who took his trumpet[721] and went into the border country.[722] On coming to a village, he stood in the village centre, blew his trumpet three times and then, putting it down on the ground, sat down to one side. Then, Prince, those border folk thought: "Where does that sound come from that is so delightful, so sweet, so intoxicating, so compelling, so captivating?" They addressed the trumpeter and asked him about this. "Friends, this trumpet is where those delightful sounds come from." So then they laid the trumpet on its back, crying: "Speak, mister trumpet, speak!" But the trumpet never uttered a sound. Then they turned it face downwards,...on its side,...on its other side,...stood it up,...stood it on its head,...[338] thumped it with their fists,...stoned it,...beat it with sticks,...struck it with swords,...shook it this way and that, crying: "Speak, mister trumpet, speak!" But the trumpet never uttered a sound. The trumpeter thought: "What fools these border folk are! How stupidly they search for the sound of the trumpet!" And as they watched him, he took the trumpet, blew it three times, and went away. And those border folk thought: "It seems that when the trumpet is accompanied by a man, by effort, and by the wind, then it makes a sound. But when it is not accompanied by a man, by effort, and by the wind, then it makes no sound."

'In the same way, Prince, when this body has life, heat and consciousness, then it goes and comes back, stands and sits and lies down, sees things with its eyes, hears with its ears, smells with its nose, tastes with its tongue, feels with its body, and knows mental objects with its mind. But when it has no life, heat or consciousness, it does none of these things. In the same way, Prince, you should consider: "There is another world..."'

20. 'Whatever you may say about that, Reverend Kassapa, [339] I still think there is no other world...' 'Have you any reason for this assertion, Prince?' 'I have, Reverend Kassapa.' 'What is that, Prince?'

'Reverend Kassapa, take the case of a thief they bring before me...and I say: "Strip away this man's outer skin, and perhaps we shall be able to see his soul emerging." Then I tell them to strip away his inner skin, his flesh, sinews, bones, bone-marrow...but still we cannot see any soul emerging. And that is why, Reverend Kassapa, I believe there is no other world...'

21. 'Well then, Prince, I will give you a parable...Once there was a matted-haired fire-worshipper[723] who dwelt in the forest in a leaf-hut. And a certain tribe was on the move, and its leader stayed for one night near the fire-worshipper's dwelling, and then left. So the fire-worshipper thought [340] he would go to the site to see if he could find anything he could make use of. He got up early and went to the site, and there he saw a tiny delicate baby boy lying abandoned on his back. At the sight he thought: "It would not be right for me to look on and let a human being die. I had better take this child to my hermitage, take care of him, feed him and bring him up." So he did so. When the boy was ten or twelve, the hermit had some business to do in the neighbourhood. So he said to the boy: "I want to go to the neighbourhood, my son. You look after the fire and don't let it go out. If it *should* go out, here is an axe, here are some sticks, here are the fire-sticks, so you can relight the fire and look after it." Having thus instructed the boy, the hermit went into the neighbourhood. But the boy, being absorbed in his games, let the fire go out. Then he thought: "Father said: '...here is an axe...so you can relight the fire and look after it.' Now I'd better do so!" [341] So he chopped up the fire-sticks with the axe, thinking: "I expect I'll get a fire this way." But he got no fire. He cut the fire-sticks into two, into three, into four, into five, ten, a hundred pieces, he splintered them, he pounded them in a mortar, he winnowed them in a great wind, thinking: "I expect I'll get a fire this way." But he got no fire, and when the hermit came back, having finished his business, he said: "Son, why have you let the fire go out?" and the boy told him what had happened. The hermit thought: "How stupid this boy is, how senseless! What a thoughtless way to try to get a fire!" So, while the boy looked on, he took the fire-sticks and rekindled the fire, saying: "Son, that's the way [342] to rekindle a fire, not the stupid, senseless, thoughtless way you tried to do it!"

'In just the same way, Prince, you are looking foolishly, senselessly and unreasonably for another world. Prince, give up this evil viewpoint, give it up! Do not let it cause you misfortune and suffering for a long time!'

22. 'Even though you say this, Reverend Kassapa, still I cannot bear to give up this evil opinion. King Pasenadi of Kosala knows my opinions, and so do kings abroad. If I give it up, they will say: "What a fool Prince Pāyāsi is, how stupidly he grasps at wrong views!" I will stick to this view out of anger, contempt and spite!'

23. 'Well then, Prince, I will give you a parable... Once, Prince, a great caravan of a thousand carts was travelling from east to west. And wherever they went, they rapidly consumed all the grass, wood and greenstuff. Now this caravan had two leaders, each [343] in charge of five hundred carts. And they thought: "This is a great caravan of a thousand carts. Wherever we go we use up all the supplies. Perhaps we should divide the caravan into two groups of five hundred carts each", and they did so. Then one of the leaders collected plenty of grass, wood and water, and set off. After two or three days' journey he saw a dark red-eyed man coming towards him wearing a quiver and a wreath of white water-lilies, with his clothes and hair all wet, driving a donkey-chariot whose wheels were splashed with mud. On seeing this man, the leader said: "Where do you come from, sir?" "From such-and-such." "And where are you going?" "To so-and-so." "Has there been much rainfall in the jungle ahead?" "Oh yes, sir, there has been a great deal of rain in the jungle ahead of you, the roads are well watered and there is plenty of grass, [344] wood and water. Throw away the grass, wood and water you have already got, sir! You will make rapid progress with lightly-laden carts, so do not tire your draught-oxen!" The caravan-leader told the carters what the man had said: "Throw away the grass, wood and water...", and they did so. But at the first camping-place they did not find any grass, wood or water, nor at the second, the third, fourth, fifth, sixth or seventh, and thus they all came to ruin and destruction. And whatever there was of them, men and cattle, they were all gobbled up by that yakkha-spirit,[724] and only their bones remained.[725]

'And when the leader of the second caravan was sure the first caravan had gone forward far enough, he stocked up with plenty of grass, wood and water. Aftr two or three days' journey this leader saw a dark red-eyed man coming towards him. . . [345] who advised him to throw away his stocks of grass, wood and water. Then the leader said to the carters: "This man told us that we should throw away the grass, wood and water we already have. But he is not one of our friends and relatives, so why should we trust him? So do not throw away the grass, wood and water we have; let the caravan continue on its way with the goods we have brought, and do not throw any of them away!" The carters agreed and did as he said. And at the first camping-place they did not find any grass, [346] wood or water, nor at the second, the third, fourth, fifth, sixth or seventh, but there they saw the other caravan that had come to ruin and destruction, and they saw the bones of those men and cattle that had been gobbled up by the yakkha-spirit. Then the caravan leader said to the carters: "That caravan came to ruin and destruction through the folly of its leader. So now let us leave behind such of our goods as are of little value, and take whatever is of greater value from the other caravan." And they did so. And with that wise leader they passed safely through the jungle.

'In the same way you, Prince, will come to ruin and destruction if you foolishly and unwisely seek the other world in the wrong way. Those who think they can trust anything they hear are heading for ruin and destruction just like those carters. Prince, give up this evil viewpoint, give it up! Do not let it cause you misfortune and suffering for a long time!'

24. 'Even though you say this, Reverend Kassapa, still I cannot bear to give up this evil opinion. . . [347] If I give it up, they will say: "What a fool Prince Pāyāsi is. . ."'

25. 'Well then, Prince, I will give you a parable. . . Once there was a swineherd who was going from his own village to another. There he saw a heap of dry dung that had been thrown away, and he thought: "There's a lot of dry dung somebody's thrown away, that would be food for my pigs. I ought to carry it away. And he spread out his cloak, gathered up the dung in it, made it into a bundle and put it on his head, and went on. But on his way back there was a heavy shower of unseasonable rain, and he went on his way be-

spattered with oozing, dripping dung to his finger-tips, and still carrying his load of dung. Those who saw him said: "You must be mad! You must be crazy! Why do you go along carrying that load of dung that's oozing and dripping all over you down to your finger-tips?" "You're the ones that are mad! You're the ones that are crazy! [348] This stuff is food for my pigs." Prince, you speak just like the dung-carrier in my parable. Prince, give up this evil viewpoint, give it up! Do not let it cause you misfortune and suffering for a long time!'

26. 'Even though you say this, Reverend Kassapa, still I cannot bear to give up this evil opinion...If I give it up, they will say: "What a fool Prince Pāyāsi is..."'

27. 'Well then, Prince, I will give you a parable...Once there were two gamblers using nuts as dice. One of them, whenever he got the unlucky dice, swallowed it. The other noticed what he was doing, and said: "Well, my friend, you're the winner all right! Give me the dice and I will make an offering of them." "All right", said the first, and gave them to him. Then that one filled the dice with poison and then said: "Come on, let's have a game!" The other agreed, they played again, and once again the one player, whenever [349] he got the unlucky dice, swallowed it. The second watched him do so, and then uttered this verse:

> "The dice is smeared with burning stuff,
> Though the swallower doesn't know.
> Swallow, cheat, and swallow well –
> Bitter it will be like hell!"

Prince, you speak just like the gambler in my parable. Prince, give up this evil viewpoint, give it up! Do not let it cause you misfortune and suffering for a long time!'

28. 'Even though you say this, Reverend Kassapa, still I cannot bear to give up this evil opinion...If I give it up, they will say: "What a fool Prince Pāyāsi is..."'

29. 'Well then, Prince, I will give you a parable...Once the inhabitants of a certain neighbourhood migrated. And one man said to his friend: "Come along, let's go to that neighbourhood, we might find something valuable!" His friend agreed, so they went to that district, and came to a village

street. [350] And there they saw a pile of hemp that had been thrown away, and one said: "Here's some hemp. You make a bundle, I'll make a bundle, and we'll both carry it off." The other agreed, and they did so. Then, coming to another village street, they found some hemp-thread, and one said: "This pile of hemp-thread is just what we wanted the hemp for. Let's each throw away our bundle of hemp, and we'll go on with a load of hemp-thread each." "I've brought this bundle of hemp a long way and it's well tied up. That will do for me – you do as you like!" So his companion threw away the hemp and took the hemp-thread.

'Coming to another village street, they found some hemp-cloth, and one said: "This pile of hemp-cloth is just what we wanted the hemp or hemp-thread for. You throw away your load of hemp and I'll throw away my load of hemp-thread, and we'll go on with a load of hemp-cloth each." But the other replied as before, so the one companion threw away the hemp-thread and took the hemp-cloth. [351] In another village they saw a pile of flax..., in another, linen-thread..., in another, linen-cloth..., in another, cotton..., in another, cotton-thread..., in another, cotton-cloth..., in another, iron..., in another, copper..., in another, tin..., in another, lead..., in another, silver..., in another, gold. Then one said: "This pile of gold is just what we wanted the hemp, hemp-thread, hemp-cloth, flax, linen-thread, linen-cloth, cotton, cotton-thread, cotton-cloth, iron, copper, tin, lead, silver for. You throw away your load of hemp and I'll throw away my load of silver, and we'll both go on with a load of gold each." "I've brought this load of hemp a long way and it's well tied up. That will do for me – you do as you like!" And this companion threw away the load of silver and took the load of gold.

'Then they came back to their own village. And there the one who brought a load of hemp gave no pleasure to his parents, nor to his wife and children, nor to his friends and colleagues, and he did not even get any joy or [352] happiness from it himself. But the one who came back with a load of gold pleased his parents, his wife and children, his friends and colleagues, and he derived joy and happiness from it himself as well.

'Prince, you speak just like the hemp-bearer in my parable. Prince, give up this evil view, give it up! Do not let it cause you misfortune and suffering for a long time!'

30. 'I was pleased and delighted with the Reverend Kassapa's first parable, and I wanted to hear his quick-witted replies to questions, because I thought he was a worthy opponent.[726] Excellent, Reverend Kassapa, excellent! It is as if someone were to set up what had been knocked down, or to point out the way to one who had got lost, or to bring an oil-lamp into a dark place, so that those with eyes could see what was there. Just so has the Reverend Kassapa expounded the Dhamma in various ways. And I, Reverend Kassapa, go for refuge to the Blessed Lord, to the Dhamma, and to the Sangha. May the Reverend Kassapa accept me from this day forth as a lay-follower as long as life shall last! And, Reverend Kassapa, I want to make a great sacrifice. Instruct me, Reverend Kassapa, how this may be to my lasting benefit and happiness.'

31. 'Prince, when a sacrifice is made at which oxen are slain, or goats, fowl or pigs, or various creatures are slaughtered,[727] and the participants [353] have wrong view, wrong thought, wrong speech, wrong action, wrong livelihood, wrong effort, wrong mindfulness and wrong concentration, then that sacrifice is of no great fruit or profit, it is not very brilliant and has no great radiance. Suppose, Prince, a farmer went into the forest with plough and seed, and there, in an untilled place with poor soil from which the stumps had not been uprooted, were to sow seeds that were broken, rotting, ruined by wind and heat, stale, and not properly embedded in the soil, and the rain-god did not send proper showers at the right time – would those seeds germinate, develop and increase, and would the farmer get an abundant crop?' 'No, Reverend Kassapa.'

'Well then, Prince, it is the same with a sacrifice at which oxen are slain,...where the participants have wrong view, ...wrong concentration. But when none of these creatures are put to death, and the participants have right view, right thought, right speech, right action, right livelihood, right effort, right mindfulness, right concentration, then that sacrifice is of great fruit and profit, it is brilliant and of great radiance. Suppose, Prince, a farmer went into the forest with plough and seed, and there, in a well-tilled place with good soil from which the stumps had been uprooted, were to sow seeds [354] that were not broken, rotting, ruined by wind and heat, or stale, and were firmly embedded in the soil, and the rain-god were to send proper showers at the right time – would those seeds germinate, develop and increase, and would the farmer get an abundant crop?' 'He would, Reverend Kassapa.'

'In the same way, Prince, at a sacrifice at which no oxen are slain,...where the participants have right view,...right concentration, then that sacrifice is of great fruit and profit, it is brilliant and of great radiance.'

32. Then Prince Pāyāsi established a charity for ascetics and Brahmins, wayfarers, beggars and the needy. And there such food was given out as broken rice with sour gruel, and also rough clothing with ball-fringes.[728] And a young Brahmin called Uttara was put in charge of the distribution.[729] Referring to it, he said: 'Through this charity I have been associated with Prince Pāyāsi in this world, but not in the next.'

And Prince Pāyāsi heard of his words, [355] so he sent for him and asked him if he had said that. 'Yes, Lord.' 'But why did you say such a thing? Friend Uttara, don't we who wish to gain merit expect a reward for our charity?'

'But, Lord, the food you give – broken rice with sour gruel – you would not care to touch it with your foot, much less eat it! And the rough clothes with ball-fringes – you would not care to set foot on them, much less wear them! Lord, you are kind and gentle to us, so how can we reconcile such kindness and gentleness with unkindness and roughness?' 'Well then, Uttara, you arrange to supply food as I eat and clothes such as I wear.' 'Very good, Lord', said Uttara, and he did so.[730] [356]

And Prince Pāyāsi, because he had established his charity grudgingly, not with his own hands, and without proper concern, like something casually tossed aside, was reborn after his death, at the breaking-up of the body, in the company of the Four Great Kings, in the empty Serīsaka mansion. But Uttara, who had given the charity ungrudgingly, with his own hands and with proper concern, not as something tossed aside, was reborn after death, at the breaking-up of the body, in a good place, a heavenly realm, in the company of the Thirty-Three Gods.

33. Now at that time the Venerable Gavampati[731] was accustomed to go to the empty Serīsaka mansion for his midday rest. And Pāyāsi of the devas went to the Venerable Gavampati, saluted him, and stood to one side. And the venerable Gavampati said to him, as he stood there: 'Who are you, friend?' 'Lord, I am Prince Pāyāsi.' 'Friend, are you not the one who used to say: "There is no other world, there are no spontaneously born beings, there is no fruit or result of good or evil deeds"?' 'Yes, Lord, I am the one who used to say that, but I [357] was converted from that evil view by the Noble Kumāra-Kassapa.' 'And where has the young Brahmin Uttara, who was in charge of the distribution of your charity, been reborn?'

'Lord, he who gave the charity ungrudgingly...was reborn in the company of the Thirty-Three Gods, but I, who gave grudgingly,...have been reborn here in the empty Serīsaka mansion. Lord, please, when you return to earth, tell people to give ungrudgingly...and inform them of the way in which Prince Pāyāsi and the young Brahmin Uttara have been reborn.'

34. And so the Venerable Gavampati, on his return to earth, declared: 'You should give ungrudgingly, with your own hands, with proper concern, not carelessly. Prince Pāyāsi did not do this, and at death, at the breaking-up of the body, he was reborn in the company of the Four Great Kings in the empty Serīsaka mansion, whereas the administrator of his charity, the young Brahmin Uttara, who gave ungrudgingly, with his own hands, with proper concern and not carelessly, was reborn in the company of the Thirty-Three Gods.'

Division Three
The Pāṭika Division

24 *Pāṭika Sutta: About Pāṭikaputta* The Charlatan

[1] 1.1 THUS HAVE I HEARD.[732] Once the Lord was staying among the Mallas. Anupiya is the name of a Malla town, and the Lord, having dressed in the early morning and taken his robe and bowl, went to Anupiya for alms. Then he thought: 'It is too early for me to go into Anupiya for alms. Suppose I were to visit the hermitage[733] of the wanderer Bhaggava-gotta?' And he did so. [2]

1.2. And the wanderer Bhaggava-gotta said: 'Come, Blessed Lord, welcome, Blessed Lord! At last the Blessed Lord has gone out of his way to come here. Be seated, Lord, a seat is prepared.' The Lord sat down on the prepared seat, and Bhaggava took a low stool and sat down to one side. Then he said: 'Lord, a few days ago Sunakkhatta the Licchavi[734] came to me and said: "Bhaggava, I have left the Blessed Lord. I am no longer under his rule." Is that really so, Lord?' 'It is true, Bhaggava.[735]

1.3. 'A few days ago, Sunakkhatta came to me, saluted me, sat down to one side, and said: "Lord, I am leaving the Blessed Lord, I am no longer under the Lord's rule." So I said to him: "Well, Sunakkhatta, did I ever say to you: 'Come, Sunakkhatta, be under my rule'?" "No, Lord." [3] "Or did you ever say to me: 'Lord, I will be under your rule'?" "No, Lord." "So, Sunakkhatta, if I did not say that to you and you did not say that to me – you foolish man, who are you and what are you giving up? Consider, foolish man, how far the fault is yours."

1.4. '"Well, Lord, you have not performed any miracles."[736] "And did I ever say to you: 'Come under my rule, Sunakkhatta, and I will perform miracles for you'?" "No, Lord." "Or did you ever say to me: 'Lord, I will be under your rule if you will perform miracles for me'?" "No, Lord." "Then it appears, Sunakkhatta, that I made no such promises, and you made no such conditions. Such being the case, you foolish man, who are you and what are you giving up?

'"What do you think, Sunakkhatta? Whether miracles are performed or not – is it the purpose of my teaching Dhamma to lead whoever practises it[737] to the total destruction of suffering?" [4] "It is, Lord." "So, Sunakkhatta, whether miracles are performed or not, the purpose of my teaching Dhamma is to lead whoever practises it to the total destruction of suffering. Then what purpose would the performance of miracles serve? Consider, you foolish man, how far the fault is yours."

1.5. '"Well, Lord, you do not teach the beginning of things." "And did I ever say to you: 'Come under my rule, Sunakkhatta, and I will teach you the beginning of things'?" "No, Lord." ...Such being the case, you foolish man, who are you and what are you giving up? [5]

1.6. '"Sunakkhatta, you have in many ways spoken in praise of me among the Vajjians, saying: 'This Blessed Lord is an Arahant, a fully-enlightened Buddha, endowed with wisdom and conduct, the Well-Farer, Knower of the worlds, incomparable Trainer of men to be tamed, Teacher of gods and humans, the Buddha, the Blessed Lord.' You have in many ways spoken in praise of the Dhamma, saying: 'Well-proclaimed by the Blessed Lord is the Dhamma, visible here and now, timeless, inviting inspection, leading onward, to be realised by the wise, each one for himself.' You have in many ways spoken in praise of the order of monks, saying: 'Well-trained is the order of the Lord's disciples, trained in uprightness, methodically-trained, excellently-trained is the order of the Lord's disciples, that is, the four pairs of men, the eight classes of individuals. This is the order of the Lord's disciples, worthy of respect, worthy of homage, worthy of gifts, worthy of salutation, an unsurpassed field in the world for merit.'

'"In these ways you have spoken in praise of me, of the Dhamma, and of the order among the Vajjians. And I say to you, I declare to you, Sunakkhatta, there will be those who will say: 'Sunakkhatta the Licchavi was unable to maintain the holy life under the ascetic Gotama, and being thus unable he abandoned the training and reverted to a base life.'[738] That, Sunakkhatta, is what they will say." [6] And, Bhaggava, at my words Sunakkhatta left this Dhamma and discipline like one condemned to hell.

1.7. 'Once, Bhaggava, I was staying among the Khulus,[739] at a place called Uttarakā, a town of theirs. In the early morning I went with robe and bowl into Uttarakā for alms, with Sunakkhatta as my attendant. And at that time the naked ascetic Korakkhattiya the "dog-man"[740] was going round on all fours, sprawling on the ground, and chewing and eating his food with his mouth alone. Seeing him, Sunakkhatta thought: "Now that is a real Arahant ascetic, who goes round on all fours, sprawling on the ground, and chewing and eating his food with his mouth alone." And I, knowing his thought in my own mind, said to him: "You foolish man, do you claim to be a follower of the Sakyan?" "Lord, what do you mean by this question?" [7] "Sunakkhatta, did you not, on seeing that naked ascetic going around on all fours, think: 'Now that is a real Arahant ascetic, who goes round on all fours, sprawling on the ground, and chewing and eating his food with his mouth alone'?" "I did, Lord. Does the Blessed Lord begrudge others their Arahantship?" "I do not begrudge others their Arahantship, you foolish man! It is only in you that this evil view has arisen. Cast it aside lest it should be to your harm and sorrow for a long time! This naked ascetic Korakkhattiya, whom you regard as a true Arahant, will die in seven days from indigestion,[741] and when he is dead he will reappear among the Kālakañja asuras, who are the very lowest grade of asuras.[742] And when he is dead he will be cast aside on a heap of *bīraṇa*-grass in the charnel-ground. If you want to, Sunakkhatta, you can go to him and ask him if he knows his fate. And it may be that he will tell you: 'Friend Sunakkhatta, I know my fate. I have been reborn among the Kālakañja asuras, the very lowest grade of asuras.'"

1.8. 'Then Sunakkhatta went to Korakkhattiya and told him what I had prophesied, [8] adding: "Therefore, friend Korakkhattiya, be very careful what you eat and drink, so that the ascetic Gotama's words may be proved wrong!" And Sunakkhatta was so sure that the Tathāgata's words would be proved wrong that he counted up the seven days one by one. But on the seventh day Korakkhattiya died of indigestion, and when he was dead he reappeared among the Kālakañja asuras, and his body was cast aside on a heap of *bīraṇa*-grass in the charnel-ground.

1.9. 'And Sunakkhatta heard of this, so he went to the heap of *bīraṇa*-grass in the charnel-ground where Korakkhattiya was lying, struck the body three times with his hand, and said: "Friend Korakkhattiya, do you know your fate?" And Korakkhattiya sat up and rubbed his back with his hand, and said: "Friend Sunakkhatta, I know my fate. I have been reborn among the Kālakañja asuras, the very lowest grade of asuras." And with that, he fell back again.

1.10. 'Then Sunakkhatta came to me, saluted me, and sat down to one side. And I said to him: "Well, Sunakkhatta, what do you think? Has what I told you about the 'dog-man' Korakkhattiya come true or not?" "It has come about the way you said, Lord, and not otherwise." [9] "Well, what do you think, Sunakkhatta? Has a miracle been performed or not?" "Certainly, Lord, this being so, a miracle has been performed, and not otherwise." "Well then, you foolish man, do you still say to me, after I have performed such a miracle: 'Well, Lord, you have not performed any miracles'? Consider, you foolish man, how far the fault is yours." And at my words Sunakkhatta left this Dhamma and discipline like one condemned to hell.

1.11. 'Once, Bhaggava, I was staying at Vesālī, at the Gabled Hall in the Great Forest. And at that time there was a naked ascetic living in Vesālī called Kaḷāramuṭṭhaka[743] who enjoyed great gains and fame in the Vajjian capital. He had undertaken seven rules of practice: "As long as I live I will be a naked ascetic and will not put on any clothes; as long as I live I will remain chaste and abstain from sexual intercourse; as long as I live I will subsist on strong drink and meat, abstaining from boiled rice and sour milk; as long as I live I will never go beyond the Udena shrine to the east of Vesālī, the Gotamaka shrine to the south, the Sattamba shrine [10] to the west, nor the Bahuputta shrine to the north."[744] And it was through having undertaken these seven rules that he enjoyed the greatest gains and fame of all in the Vajjian capital.

1.12. 'Now Sunakkhatta went to see Kaḷāramuṭṭhaka and asked him a question which he could not answer, and because he could not answer it he showed signs of anger, rage and petulance. But Sunakkhatta thought: "I might cause this real Arahant ascetic offence. I don't want anything to happen that would be to my lasting harm and misfortune!"

1.13. 'Then Sunakkhatta came to me, saluted me, and sat down to one side. I said to him: "You foolish man, do you claim to be a follower of the Sakyan?" "Lord, what do you mean by this question?" "Sunakkhatta, did you not go to see Kaḷāramuṭṭhaka and ask him a question he could not answer, and did he not thereupon show signs of anger, rage and petulance? And did you not think: 'I might cause this real Arahant ascetic offence. I don't want anything to happen that would be to my lasting harm and misfortune'?" "I did, Lord. Does the Blessed Lord begrudge others their Arahantship?" [11] "I do not begrudge others their Arahantship, you foolish man. It is only in you that this evil view has arisen. Cast it aside lest it should be to your harm and sorrow for a long time! This naked ascetic Kaḷāramuṭṭhaka, whom you regard as a true Arahant, will before long be living clothed and married, subsisting on boiled rice and sour milk. He will go beyond all the shrines of Vesālī, and will die having entirely lost his reputation." And indeed all this came about.

1.14. 'Then Sunakkhatta, having heard what had happened, came to me. . . And I said: "Well, Sunakkhatta, what do you think? Has what I told you about Kaḷāramuṭṭhaka come about, or not?. . . Has a miracle been performed or not?". . . [12] And at my words Sunakkhatta left this Dhamma and discipline like one condemned to hell.

1.15. 'Once, Bhaggava, I was staying at Vesālī in the Gabled Hall in the Great Forest. And at that time there was a naked ascetic living in Vesālī called Pāṭikaputta, who enjoyed great gains and fame in the Vajjian capital. And he made this declaration in the assembly of Vesālī: "The ascetic Gotama claims to be a man of wisdom, and I make the same claim. It is right that a man of wisdom should show it by performing miracles. If the ascetic Gotama will come half-way to meet me, I will do likewise. Then we could both work miracles, and if the ascetic Gotama performs one miracle, I will perform two. If he performs two, I will perform [13] four. And if he performs four, I will perform eight. However many miracles the ascetic Gotama performs, I will perform twice as many!"

1.16. 'Then Sunakkhatta came to me, saluted me, sat down to one side, and told me what Pāṭikaputta had said. I said: "Sunakkhatta, that naked ascetic Pāṭikaputta is not capable of meeting me face to face unless he takes back his words, abandons that thought, and gives up that view. And if he thinks otherwise, his head will split in pieces."[745]

1.17. '"Lord, let the Blessed Lord have a care what he says, let the Well-Farer have a care what he says!" [14] "What do you mean by saying that to me?" "Lord, the Blessed Lord might make an absolute statement about Pāṭikaputta's coming. But he might come in some altered shape, and thus falsify the Blessed Lord's words!"

1.18. '"But, Sunakkhatta, would the Tathāgata make any statement that was ambiguous?" "Lord, does the Blessed Lord know by his own mind what would happen to Pāṭikaputta? Or has some deva told the Tathāgata?" "Sunakkhatta, I know it by my own mind, and I have also been told by a deva. [15] For Ajita, the general of the Licchavis, died the other day and has been reborn in the company of the Thirty-Three Gods. He came to see me and told me: 'Lord, Pāṭikaputta the naked ascetic is an impudent liar! He declared in the Vajjian capital: "Ajita, the general of the Licchavis, has been reborn in the great hell!" But I have not been reborn in the great hell, but in the company of the Thirty-Three Gods. He is an impudent liar...' Thus, Sunakkhatta, I know what I have said by my own mind, but I have also been told by a deva. And now, Sunakkhatta, I will go into Vesālī for alms. On my return, after I have eaten, I will go for my midday rest to Pāṭikaputta's park. You may tell him whatever you wish." [16]

1.19. 'Then, having dressed, I took my robe and bowl and went into Vesālī for alms. On my return I went to Pāṭikaputta's park for my midday rest. Meanwhile Sunakkhatta rushed into Vesālī and declared to all the prominent Licchavis: "Friends, the Blessed Lord has gone into Vesālī for alms, and after that he has gone for his midday rest to Pāṭikaputta's park. Come along, friends, come along! the two great ascetics are going to work miracles!" And all the prominent Licchavis thought: "The two great ascetics are going to work miracles! Let us go along!" And he went to the distinguished and wealthy Brahmins and householders, and to the ascetics and Brahmins of various schools, and told them the same thing, and they too thought: "Let us go along!" [17] And so all these people came along to Pāṭikaputta's park, hundreds and thousands of them.

1.20. 'And Pāṭikaputta heard that all these people had come to his park, and that the ascetic Gotama had gone there for his midday rest. And at the news he was overcome with fear and trembling, and his hair stood on end. And thus terrified and trembling, his hair standing on end, he made for the Tinduka lodging of the wanderers.[746] When the assembled company heard that he had gone to the Tinduka lodging, they instructed a man to go there to Pāṭikaputta and say to him: "Friend Pāṭikaputta, come along! All these people have come to your park, and the ascetic Gotama has gone there for his midday rest. Because you declared to the assembly at Vesālī: 'The ascetic Gotama claims to be a man of wisdom, and I make the same claim...(*as verse 15*). [18] However many miracles he performs, I will perform twice as many!' So now come halfway: the ascetic Gotama has already come half-way to meet you, and is sitting for his midday rest in Your Reverence's park."

1.21. 'The man went and delivered the message, and on hearing it Pāṭikaputta said: "I'm coming, friend, [19] coming!" but, wriggle as he might, he could not get up from his seat. Then the man said: "What's the matter with you, friend Pāṭikaputta? Is your bottom stuck to the seat, or is the seat stuck to your bottom? You keep saying: 'I'm coming, friend, I'm coming!', but you only wriggle and can't get up from your seat." And even at these words, Pāṭikaputta still wriggled about, but could not rise.

1.22. 'And when that man realised that Pāṭikaputta could not help himself, he went back to the assembly and reported the situation. And then I said to them: "Pāṭikaputta the naked ascetic is not capable of meeting me face to face unless he takes back his words, abandons that thought, and gives up that view. And if he thinks otherwise, his head will split in pieces."'

[*End of first recitation-section*]

2.1. 'Then, Bhaggava, one of the ministers of the Licchavis rose from his seat and said: "Well, gentlemen, just wait a little till I [20] I have been to see whether I can bring Pāṭikaputta to the assembly." So he went to the Tinduka lodging and said to Pāṭikaputta: "Come along, Pāṭikaputta, it is best for you to come. All these people have come to your park and the ascetic Gotama has gone there for his midday rest. If you come, we will make you the winner and let the ascetic Gotama be defeated."

2.2. 'And Pāṭikaputta said: "I'm coming, friend, I'm coming", but wriggle as he might, he [21] could not get up from his seat...

2.3. 'So the minister returned to the assembly and reported on the situation. Then I said: "Pāṭikaputta is not capable of meeting me...Even if the good Licchavis were to think: 'Let us bind him with thongs and try to drag him with yoked oxen!' he would burst the thongs. He is not capable of meeting me face to face..."[22]

2.4. 'Then Jāliya, a pupil of the wooden-bowl ascetic,[747] rose from his seat..., went to the Tinduka lodging and said to Pāṭikaputta: "Come along, Pāṭikaputta,...if you come, we will make you the winner and let the ascetic Gotama be defeated." [23]

2.5. 'And Pāṭikaputta said: "I'm coming, friend, I'm coming!" but wriggle as he might, he could not get up from his seat...

2.6. 'Then, when Jāliya realised the situation, he said: "Pāṭikaputta, once long ago the lion, king of beasts, thought: 'Suppose I were to make my lair near a certain jungle. Then I could emerge in the evening, yawn, survey the four quarters, roar my lion's roar three times, and then make for the cattle-pasture. I could then pick out the very best of the herd for my kill and, having had a good feast of tender meat, return to my lair.' And he did accordingly. [24]

2.7. '"Now there was an old jackal who had grown fat on the lion's leavings, and he was proud and strong. And he thought: 'What difference is there between me and the lion, king of beasts? Suppose I were to make my lair near the jungle...' So he chose a lair accordingly and emerging in the evening, he surveyed the four quarters, and then thought: 'Now I will roar a lion's roar three times', – and he gave out the howl of his kind, a jackal howl. For what has the wretched howl of a jackal in common with a lion's roar? In just the same way, Pāṭikaputta, you live off the achievements of the Well-Farer and feed on the Well-Farer's leavings, imagining you can set yourself up beside the Tathāgatas, Arahants and fully-enlightened Buddhas. But what have wretched Pāṭikaputtas in common with them?"

2.8. 'Then, being unable even with the aid of this parable to get Pāṭikaputta to rise from his seat, Jāliya uttered this verse: [25]

"Thinking himself a lion, the jackal says:
'I'm the king of beasts', and tries to roar
A lion's roar, but only howls instead.
Lion is lion and jackal jackal still.

In just the same way, Pāṭikaputta, you are living off the achievements of the Well-Farer..."

2.9. 'And, being unable even with the aid of this parable to get Pāṭikaputta to rise from his seat, Jāliya uttered this verse:

"Following another's tracks, and fed
On scraps, his jackal-nature he forgets,
Thinking: 'I'm a tiger', tries to roar
A mighty roar, but only howls instead.
Lion is lion and jackal's jackal still.

In just the same way, Pāṭikaputta, you are living off the achievements of the Well-Farer..."

2.10. 'And, being unable even with this [26] parable to get Pāṭikaputta to rise from his seat, Jāliya uttered this verse:

"Gorged on frogs and mice from threshing-floors,
And corpses cast aside in charnel-grounds,
In lonely forests wild the jackal thinks:
'I'm the king of beasts', and tries to roar
A lion's roar, but only howls instead.
Lion is lion and jackal's jackal still.

In just the same way, Pāṭikaputta, you are living off the achievements of the Well-Farer, feeding on the Well-Farer's leavings, imagine you can set yourself up beside the Tathāgatas, Arahants and full-enlightened Buddhas. But what have wretched Pāṭikaputtas in common with them?"

2.11. 'Then, being unable even with this parable to get Pāṭikaputta to rise from his seat, Jāliya returned to the assembly and reported on the situation.

2.12. 'Then I said: "Pāṭikaputtas is not capable of meeting me face to face unless he takes back his words, abandons that thought and gives up that view...Even if the good Licchavis were to think: 'Let us bind him with thongs and try to drag him here with yoked oxen', [27] he would burst the thongs. He is not capable of meeting me face to face...If he thinks otherwise, his head will split in pieces."

2.13. 'Then, Bhaggava, I instructed, inspired, fired and delighted that assembly with a talk on Dhamma. And having thereby delivered that company from the great bondage,[748] thus rescuing eighty-four thousand beings from the great path of peril, I entered into the fire-element[749] and rose into the air to the height of seven palm-trees, and projecting a beam for the height of another seven so that it blazed and shed fragrance, I then reappeared in the Gabled Hall in the Great Forest.[750]

'And there Sunakkhatta came to me, saluted me and sat down to one side. I said: "What do you think, Sunakkhatta? Has what I told you about Pāṭikaputta come about, or not?" "It has, Lord." "And has a miracle been performed, or not?" "It has, Lord." "Well then, you foolish man, do you still say to me after I have performed such a [28] miracle: 'Well, Lord, you have not performed any miracles'? Consider, you foolish man, how far the fault is yours." And, Bhaggava, at my words Sunakkhatta left this Dhamma and discipline like one condemned to hell.

2.14. 'Bhaggava, I know the first beginning of things,[751] and I know not only that, but what surpasses it in value.[752] And I am not under the sway of what I know, and not being under its sway I have come to know for myself that quenching,[753] by the realisation of which the Tathāgata cannot fall into perilous paths.[754] There are, Bhaggava, some ascetics and Brahmins who declare as their doctrine that all things began with the creation by a god,[755] or Brahmā. I have gone to them and said: "Reverend sirs, is it true that you declare that all things began with the creation by a god, or Brahmā?" "Yes", they replied. Then I asked: "In that case, how do the reverend teachers declare that this came about?" But they could not give an answer, and so they asked me in return. And I replied:

2.15.–17. ' "There comes a time, friends, sooner or later after a long period, when this world contracts... *Beings are born in the Ābhassara Brahmā world and stay there a long time. When this world expands, one being falls from there and arises in an empty Brahmā palace. He longs for company, other beings appear, and he and they believe he created them* (*Sutta 1, verses 2.2–6*). [29–30] That, Reverend Sirs, is how it comes about that you teach that all things began with the creation by a god, or Brahmā." And they said: "We have heard this, Reverend Gotama, as you have explained." But I know the first beginning of things... and not being under the sway of what I know I have come to know that quenching by the realisation of which the Tathāgata cannot fall into perilous ways.

2.18. 'There are some ascetics and Brahmins who declare that the beginning of things was due to corruption by pleasure. I went to them and asked them if this was their view. "Yes", they replied. [31] I asked them how this came about, and when they could not explain, I said: "There are, friends, certain devas called Corrupted by Pleasure. They spend an excessive amount of time addicted to merriment... *their mindfulness lapses, and they fall away* (*Sutta 1, verses 2.7–9*). That, [32] Reverend Sirs, is how it comes about that you teach that the beginning of things was due to corruption by pleasure." And they said: "We have heard this, Reverend Gotama, as you have explained."

2.19. 'There are some ascetics and Brahmins who declare that the beginning of things was due to corruption of mind. I went to them and asked them if this was their view. "Yes", they replied. I asked them how this came about, and when they could not explain, I said: "There are, friends, certain devas called Corrupted in Mind. They spend an excessive amount of time regarding each other with envy... *their minds become corrupted, and they fall away* (*Sutta 1, verses 2.10–13*). [33] That, Reverend Sirs, is how it comes about that you teach that the beginning of things was due to corruption of mind." And they said: "We have heard this, Reverend Gotama, as you have explained."

2.20. 'There are, Bhaggava, some ascetics and Brahmins who declare that the beginning of things was due to chance. I went to them and asked them if this was their view. "Yes", they replied. I asked them how this came about, and when they could not explain, I said: "There are, friends, certain devas called Unconscious. As soon as a perception arises in them, those devas fall from that realm... *remembering nothing* (*Sutta, 1, verse 2.31*) they think: 'Now from non-being I have been brought to being.' [34] That, Reverend Sirs, is how it comes about that you teach that the beginning of things was due to chance." And they said: "We have heard this, Reverend Gotama, as you have explained." But I know the first beginning of things, and I know not only that, but what surpasses it in value. And I am not under the sway of what I know, and not being under its sway I have come to know for myself that quenching, by the realisation of which the Tathāgata cannot fall into perilous paths.

2.21. 'And I, Bhaggava, who teach this and declare this am wrongly, vainly, lyingly and falsely accused by some ascetics and Brahmins who say: "The ascetic Gotama is on the wrong track,[756] and so are his monks. He has declared that whoever has attained to the stage of deliverance called 'the Beautiful'[757] finds everything repulsive." But I do not say this. What I say is that whenever anyone has attained to the stage of deliverance called "the Beautiful", he knows that it is beautiful.'

'Indeed, Lord, they are on the wrong track themselves who accuse the Lord and his monks of error. I am so delighted with the Lord [35] that I think the Lord is able to teach me to attain and remain in the deliverance called "the Beautiful".'

'It is hard for you, Bhaggava, holding different views, being of different inclinations and subject to different influences, following a different discipline and having had a different teacher, to attain and remain in the deliverance called "the Beautiful". You must strive hard, putting your trust in me, Bhaggava.'

'Lord, even if it is hard for me to attain and remain in the deliverance called "the Beautiful", still I will place my trust in the Lord.'[758]

Thus the Lord spoke, and Bhaggava the wanderer was delighted and rejoiced at the Lord's words.

25 *Udumbarika-Sīhanāda Sutta: The Great Lion's Roar to the Udumbarikans*

[36] 1. THUS HAVE I HEARD. Once the Lord was staying in Rājagaha at the Vultures' Peak. And at that time the wanderer Nigrodha[759] was staying at the Udumbarikā lodging[760] for wanderers, with a large company of some three thousand wanderers. And one morning early, the householder Sandhāna came to Rājagaha in order to see the Lord. Then he thought: 'It is not the proper time to see the Blessed Lord, he is in retreat; it is not the proper time to see the meditating monks, they are in retreat. Perhaps I should go to the Udumbarikā lodging for wanderers and call on Nigrodha.' And he did so.

2. And just then Nigrodha was sitting in the midst of a large crowd of wanderers who were all shouting and screaming and making a great clamour, and indulging in various kinds of unedifying conversation[761] about kings, [37] robbers, ministers, armies, dangers, war, food, drink, clothes, beds, garlands, perfumes, relatives, carriages, villages, towns and cities, countries, women, heroes, street- and well-gossip, talk of the departed, desultory chat, speculation about land and sea, talk of being and non-being.

3. Then Nigrodha saw Sandhāna approaching from a distance, and he called his followers to order, saying: 'Be quiet, gentlemen, don't make a noise, gentlemen! The householder Sandhāna, a follower of the ascetic Gotama, is approaching. He is one of the number of white-robed householder followers of the ascetic Gotama in Rājagaha. And these good folk are fond of quiet, they are taught to be quiet and speak in praise of quiet. If he sees that this company is quiet, he will most likely want to come and visit us.' At this the wanderers fell silent.

4. Then Sandhāna approached Nigrodha and exchanged

courtesies with him, and then sat down to one side. Then he said: 'Reverend sirs, the way the wanderers of another faith conduct themselves when they come together is one thing: [38] they make a great clamour and indulge in all manner of unedifying conversation...The Blessed Lord's way is different: he seeks a lodging in the forest, in the depths of the jungle, free from noise, with little sound, far from the madding crowd, undisturbed by men, well fitted for seclusion.'

5. Then Nigrodha replied: 'Well now, householder, do you know whom the ascetic Gotama talks to? Whom does he converse with? From whom does he get his lucidity of wisdom? The ascetic Gotama's wisdom is destroyed by the solitary life, he is unused to assemblies, he is no good at conversation, he is right out of touch. Just as bison[762] circling around keep to the fringes, so it is with the ascetic Gotama. In fact, householder, if the ascetic Gotama were to come to this assembly, we would baffle him with a single question, we would knock him over like an empty pot.'

6. Now the Lord, with his divine-ear-faculty, purified and surpassing human range, heard this exchange between Sandhāna and Nigrodha. And, descending from the Vultures' Peak, he came to the Peacocks' Feeding Ground beside the Sumāgadhā Tank, and [39] walked up and down there in the open air. Then Nigrodha caught sight of him, and he called his company to order, saying: 'Gentlemen, he quiet, be less noisy! The ascetic Gotama is walking up and down beside the Sumāgadhā Tank. He is fond of quiet, he speaks in praise of quiet. If he sees that this company is quiet, he will most likely want to come and visit us. If he does so, we will put this question to him: "Lord, what is this doctrine in which the Blessed Lord trains his disciples, and which those disciples whom he has so trained as to benefit from it recognise as their principal support, and the perfection of the holy life?"' At this, the wanderers were silent.

7. Then the Lord approached Nigrodha, and Nigrodha said: 'Come, Blessed Lord, welcome, Blessed Lord! At last the Blessed Lord has gone out of his way to come here. Be seated, Lord, a seat is prepared.' The Lord sat down on the prepared seat, and Nigrodha took a low stool and sat down to one side. Then

the Lord said to him: 'Nigrodha, what was the subject of your conversation just now? What talk have I interrupted?' Nigrodha replied: 'Lord, we saw the Blessed Lord walking up and down at the Peacocks' Feeding Ground by the Sumāgadhā Tank, [40] and we thought: "If the ascetic Gotama were to come here we could ask him this question: Lord, what is this doctrine in which the Blessed Lord trains his disciples, and which those disciples whom he has so trained as to benefit from it recognise as their principal support, and the perfection of the holy life?"'

'Nigrodha, it is hard for you, holding different views, being of different inclinations and subject to different influences, following a different teacher, to understand the doctrine which I teach my disciples...Come on then, Nigrodha, ask me about your own teaching, about your extreme austerity. How are the conditions of austerity and self-mortification fulfilled, and how are they not fulfilled?'

At this the wanderers made a great commotion and noise, exclaiming: 'It is wonderful, it is marvellous how great are the powers of the ascetic Gotama in holding back with his own theories and in inviting others to discuss theirs!'

8. Silencing them, Nigrodha said: 'Lord, we teach the higher austerities, we regard them as essential, we adhere to them. Such being the case, what constitutes their fulfilment or non-fulfilment?'

'Suppose, Nigrodha, a self-mortifier goes naked, uses no polite restraints, licks his hands, does not come or stand still when requested. [41] He does not accept food out of the pot or pan...(*as Sutta 8, verse 14*). He wears coarse hemp or mixed material, shrouds from corpses, rags from the dust-heap...He is a plucker-out of hair and beard, devoted [42] to this practice; he is a covered-thorn man, making his bed on them, sleeping alone in a garment of wet mud, living in the open air, accepting whatever seat is offered, one who drinks no water and is addicted to the practice, or he dwells intent on the practice of going to bathe three times before evening. What do you think, Nigrodha, is the higher austerity thereby fulfilled, or not?' 'Indeed, Lord, it is fulfilled.' 'But, Nigrodha, I maintain that this higher austerity can be faulted in various ways.'

9. 'In what way, Lord, do you maintain that it can be faulted?' 'Take the case, Nigrodha, of a self-mortifier who practises a certain austerity. As a result, he is pleased and satisfied at having attained his end. And this is a fault in that self-mortifier. Or else in so doing he elevates himself and disparages others. And this is a fault in that self-mortifier. Or else he has become intoxicated with conceit, infatuated and therefore careless. And this [43] is a fault in that self-mortifier.

10. 'Again, a self-mortifier practises a certain austerity, and this brings him gains, honours and fame. As a result, he is pleased and satisfied at having attained his end...Or else he elevates himself and disparages others...Or else he becomes intoxicated with conceit, infatuated and therefore careless. And this is a fault in that self-mortifier. Again, a self-mortifier practises a certain austerity, and he divides his food into two heaps, saying: "This suits me, that doesn't suit me!" And what does not suit him he eagerly rejects, while what suits him he eats up greedily, recklessly and passionately, not seeing the peril, with no thought for the consequences. And this is a fault in that self-mortifier. [44] Again, a self-mortifier practises a certain austerity for the sake of gains, honours and fame, thinking: "Kings and their ministers will honour me, Khattiyas and Brahmins and householders, and religious teachers." And this is a fault in that self-mortifier.

11. 'Again, a self-mortifier disparages some ascetic or Brahmin, saying: "See how he lives in abundance, eating all sorts of things! Whether propagated from roots, from stems, from joings, from cuttings or fifthly from seeds,[763] he chews them all up with that thunderbolt of a jaw of his, and they call him an ascetic!" And this is a fault in that self-mortifier. Or he sees another ascetic or Brahmin being made much of by families, being honoured and respected and worshipped, and he thinks: "They make much of that rich-liver, they honour him, respect him and worship him, whereas I who am a *real* ascetic and self-mortifier get no such treatment!" Thus he is envious and jealous because of those householders. And this is a fault in that self-mortifier.

'Again, a self-mortifier sits in a prominent position. And this is a fault in that self-mortifier. Or he goes round ostentatiously[764] among the families, as if to say: "See, this is my way of renunciation!" And this is a fault in that self-mortifier. [45] Or he behaves in an underhand way. On being asked: "Do you approve of this?" although he does not approve he says: "I do", or although he does approve he says: "I do not." In this way he becomes a conscious liar. And this is a fault in that self-mortifier.

12. 'Again, a self-mortifier, when the Tathāgata or a disciple of the Tathāgata presents the Dhamma in a way that should command his assent, withholds that assent. And this is a fault in that self-mortifier. Or he is angry and bad-tempered. And this is a fault in that self-mortifier. Or he is mean and spiteful, envious and jealous, crafty and deceitful, obstinate and proud, with evil desires and under their sway, with wrong views and given to extremist opinions; he is tainted with worldliness, holding on firmly, unwilling to give up. And this is a fault in that self-mortifier. What do you think, Nigrodha? Are these things faults in the higher austerity, or not?' 'Certainly they are, Lord. It could happen that a single self-mortifier was possessed of all these faults, not to speak of just one or the other.'

13.–14. 'Now, Nigrodha, take the case of a certain self-mortifier who practises a certain austerity. As a result, he is not pleased and satisfied at having attained his end. This being so, [46] in this respect he is purified. Again, he does not elevate himself and disparage others...(*similarly with all examples in 10–11*). [47] Thus he does not become a conscious liar. In this respect he is purified.

15. 'Again, a self-mortifier, when the Tathāgata or a disciple of the Tathāgata presents the Dhamma in a way that should command his assent, gives his assent. In this respect he is purified. And he is not angry or bad-tempered. In this respect he is purified. And he is not mean and spiteful, envious and jealous, crafty and deceitful, obstinate and [48] proud, he is without evil desires and not under their sway, without wrong views and not given to extremist opinions, he is not tainted with worldliness, does not hold on firmly and is not unwilling to give up. In this respect he is purified. What do you think, Nigrodha? Is the higher austerity purified by these things, or

not?' 'Certainly it is, Lord, it attains its peak there, penetrating to the pith.' 'No, Nigrodha, it does not attain its peak there, penetrating to the pith. It has only reached the outer bark.'[765]

16. 'Well then, Lord, how does austerity attain its peak, penetrating to the pith? It would be good if the Blessed Lord were to cause my austerity to attain its peak, to penetrate to the pith.'

'Nigrodha, take the case of a self-mortifier who observes the fourfold restraint. And what is this? Here, a self-mortifier does not harm a living being, does not cause a living being to be harmed, does not approve of such harming; [49] he does not take what is not given, or cause it to be taken, or approve of such taking; he does not tell a lie, or cause a lie to be told, or approve of such lying; he does not crave for sense-pleasures,[766] cause others to do so, or approve of such craving. In this way, a self-mortifier observes the fourfold restraint. And through this restraint, through making this his austerity, he takes an upward course and does not fall back into lower things.

'Then he finds a solitary lodging, at the root of a forest tree, in a mountain cave or gorge, a charnel-ground, a jungle-thicket, or in the open air on a heap of straw. Then, having eaten after his return from the alms-round, he sits down cross-legged, holding his body erect, having established mindfulness before him.[767] Abandoning hankering for the world, he dwells with a mind freed from such hankering, and his mind is purified of it. Abandoning ill-will and hatred, he dwells with a mind freed from them, and by compassionate love for the welfare of all living beings, his mind is purified of them. Abandoning sloth-and-torpor, . . . by the perception of light,[768] mindful and clearly aware, his mind is purified of sloth-and-torpor. Abandoning worry-and-flurry, . . . and with an inwardly calmed heart his mind[769] is purified of worry-and-flurry. Abandoning doubt, he dwells with doubt left behind, without uncertainty as to what things are wholesome, his mind purified of doubt.

17. 'Having abandoned these five hindrances, and in order to weaken by insight the defilements[770] of mind, he dwells, letting his mind, filled with loving-kindness, pervade one quarter, then a second, then a third, then a fourth. And so he continues to pervade the whole wide world, above, below,

across and everywhere with a mind filled with loving-kindness, extensive, [50] developed,[771] measureless, free from hatred and ill-will. And he dwells, letting his mind, filled with compassion,...with sympathetic joy,...with equanimity, pervade one quarter,...extensive, developed, measureless, free from hatred and ill-will. What do you think, Nigrodha? Is the higher austerity purified by these things, or not?' 'Certainly it is, Lord. It attains its peak there, penetrating to the pith.' 'No, Nigrodha, it does not attain its peak there. It has only penetrated to the inner bark.'[772]

18. 'Well then, Lord, how does austerity attain its peak, penetrating to the pith? It would be good if the Blessed Lord were to cause my austerity to attain its peak, to penetrate to the pith.'

'Nigrodha, take the case of a self-mortifier who observes the fourfold restraint...(*as verses 16–17*), free from hatred and ill-will. He recalls various past lives...There my name was so-and-so,...my caste was so-and-so...(*as Sutta 1, verse 1.31*). I experienced such-and-such pleasant and painful conditions ...Having passed from there, I arose there...[51] Thus he remembers various past lives, their conditions and details. What do you think, Nigrodha? Is the higher austerity purified by these things, or not?' 'Certainly it is, Lord. It attains its peak there, penetrating to the pith.' 'No, Nigrodha, it only reaches the fibres surrounding the pith.'[773]

19. 'Well then, Lord, how does austerity reach its peak, penetrating to the pith? It would be good if the Blessed Lord were to cause my austerity to attain its peak, to penetrate to the pith.'

'Well, Nigrodha, take the case of a self-mortifier who observes the fourfold restraint..., free from hatred and ill-will... Thus he [52] remembers various past lives, their conditions and details. And then, with the purified divine eye, he sees beings passing away and arising: base and noble, well favoured and ill-favoured, to happy and unhappy destinations as kamma directs them. What do you think, Nigrodha? Is the higher austerity purified by these things, or not?' 'Certainly it is, Lord. It attains its peak there, penetrating to the pith.'[774]

'So indeed it is, Nigrodha, that austerity is so purified as to reach its peak and penetrate to the pith. And so, Nigrodha, when you ask: "What, Lord, is this doctrine in which the Blessed Lord trains his disciples, and which those disciples whom he has so trained as to benefit from it recognise as their principal support, and the perfection of the holy life?" I say that it is by something more far-reaching and excellent that I train them, through which they...recognise as their principal support, and the perfection of the holy life.'

At this the wanderers made a great commotion and noise, exclaiming: 'We and our teacher are ruined! We know of nothing higher or more far-reaching than our teaching!' [53]

20. And when the householder Sandhāna realised: 'These wanderers of other views are actually listening and attending to the Lord's words, and inclining their minds to the higher wisdom, he said to Nigrodha: 'Reverend Nigrodha, you said to me: "Come now, householder, do you know whom the ascetic Gotama talks to?...His wisdom is destroyed by the solitary life, he is no good at conversation, he is right out of touch..." So now that the Blessed Lord has come here, why don't you baffle him with a single question and knock him over like an empty pot?' And at these words Nigrodha was silent and upset, his shoulders drooped, he hung his head and sat there downcast and bewildered.

21. Seeing the state he was in, the Lord said: 'Is it true, Nigrodha, that you said that?' [54] 'Lord, it is true that I said that, foolishly, mistakenly, and wickedly.' 'What do you think, Nigrodha? Have you ever heard it said by wanderers who were aged, venerable, the teachers of teachers, that those who in the past were Arahants, fully-enlightened Buddhas used to talk, when they came together, by shouting and screaming and making a great clamour, and indulging in unedifying conversation...the way you and your teachers do? Or did they not say rather that those Blessed Ones sought lodging in the forest, in the depths of the jungle, free from noise, with little sound, far from the madding crowd, undisturbed by men, well-fitted for seclusion, just as I do now?' 'Lord, I have heard it said that those who were Arahants, fully-enlightened Buddhas did not indulge in loud talk...but sought lodging in the forest,...just as the Blessed Lord does now.'

'Nigrodha, you are an intelligent man of mature years. Did it never occur to you to think: "The Blessed Lord is enlightened and teaches a doctrine of enlightenment, he is self-restrained and teaches a doctrine of self-restraint, he is calm and teaches a doctrine of calm. He has gone beyond [55] and teaches a doctrine of going beyond, he has gained Nibbāna and teaches a doctrine for the gaining of Nibbāna"?'

22. At this, Nigrodha said to the Lord: 'Transgression overcame me, Lord! Foolish, blind and evil as I was, that I spoke thus of the Lord. May the Lord accept my confession of this fault, that I may restrain myself in future!'[775] 'Indeed, Nigrodha, transgression overcame you when, through folly, blindness and evil you spoke thus of me. But since you recognise the nature of your transgression and make amends as is right, we accept your confession. For, Nigrodha, it is a mark of progress in the discipline of the Noble Ones, if anyone recognises the nature of his transgression and makes amends as is right, restraining himself for the future.

'But, Nigrodha, I tell you this: Let an intelligent man come to me who is sincere, honest and straightforward, and I will instruct him, I will teach him Dhamma. If he practises what he is taught, then within seven years he will attain in this life to that unequalled holy life and goal, for the sake of which young men of good family go forth from the household life into homelessness, by his own knowledge and realisation, and he will abide therein. Let alone seven years – in six years, five, four, three, two years, one year,...seven months, six months, [56] five, four, three, two months, one month, half a month. Let alone half a month – in seven days he can gain that goal.[776]

23. 'Nigrodha, you may think: "The ascetic Gotama says this in order to get disciples." But you should not regard it like that. Let him who is your teacher remain your teacher.[777] Or you may think: "He wants us to abandon our rules." But you should not regard it like that. Let your rules remain as they are. Or you may think: "He wants us to abandon our way of life." But you should not regard it like that. Let your way of life remain as it was. Or you may think: "He wants to establish us in the doing of things that according to our

teaching are wrong, and are so considered among us." But you should not regard it like that. Let those things you consider wrong continue to be so considered. Or you may think: "He wants to draw us away from things that according to our teaching are good, and are so considered among us." But you should not regard it like that. Let whatever you consider right continue to be so considered. Nigrodha, I do not speak for any of these reasons...[57]

'There are, Nigrodha, unwholesome things that have not been abandoned, tainted, conducive to rebirth,[778] fearful, productive of painful results in the future, associated with birth, decay and death. It is for the abandonment of these things that I teach Dhamma. If you practise accordingly, these tainted things will be abandoned, and the things that make for purification will develop and grow, and you will all attain to and dwell, in this very life, by your own insight and realisation, in the fullness of perfected wisdom.'

24. At these words the wanderers sat silent and upset, their shoulders drooped, they hung their heads and sat there downcast and bewildered, so possessed were their minds by Māra.[779] Then the Lord said: 'Every one of these foolish men is possessed by the evil one, so that not a single one of them thinks: "Let us now follow the holy life proclaimed by the ascetic Gotama, that we may learn it – for what do seven days matter?"'

Then the Lord, having uttered his lion's roar in the Udumbarikā park, rose up in the air and alighted on the Vultures' Peak. And the householder Sandhāna also returned to Rājagaha.[780]

26 *Cakkavatti-Sīhanāda Sutta: The Lion's Roar on the Turning of the Wheel*

[58] 1. THUS HAVE I HEARD.[781] Once the Lord was staying among the Magadhans at Mātulā. Then he said: 'Monks!' 'Lord', they replied, and the Lord said:

'Monks, be islands unto yourselves, be a refuge unto yourselves with no other refuge. Let the Dhamma be your island, let the Dhamma be your refuge, with no other refuge.[782] And how does a monk dwell as an island unto himself, as a refuge unto himself with no other refuge, with the Dhamma as his island, with the Dhamma as his refuge, with no other refuge? Here, a monk abides contemplating body as body,[783] ardent, clearly aware and mindful, having put aside hankering and fretting for the world, he abides contemplating feelings as feelings,...he abides contemplating mind as mind,...he abides contemplating mind-objects as mind-objects, ardent, clearly aware and mindful, having put aside hankering and fretting for the world.

'Keep to your own preserves,[784] monks, to your ancestral haunts.[785] If you do so, then Māra will find no lodgement, no foothold. It is just by the building-up of wholesome states that this merit increases.

[59] 2. 'Once, monks, there was a wheel-turning monarch named Daḷhanemi, a righteous monarch of the law, conqueror of the four quarters, who had established the security of his realm and was possessed of the seven treasures. These are: the Wheel Treasure, the Elephant Treasure, the Horse Treasure, the Jewel Treasure, the Woman Treasure, the Householder Treasurer, and, as seventh, the Counsellor Treasure. He has more than a thousand sons who are heroes, of heroic stature, conquerors of the hostile army. He dwells having conquered

this sea-girt land without stick or sword, by the law (*as Sutta 3, verse 1.5*).

3. 'And, after many hundreds and thousands of years, King Daḷhanemi said to a certain man: "My good man, whenever you see that the sacred Wheel-Treasure has slipped from its position, report it to me." "Yes, sire", the man replied. And after many hundreds and thousands of years the man saw that the sacred Wheel-Treasure had slipped from its position. Seeing this, he reported the fact to the King. Then King Daḷhanemi sent for his eldest son, the crown prince, and said: "My son, the sacred Wheel-Treasure has slipped from its position. And I have heard say that when this happens to a wheel-turning monarch, he has not much longer to live. I have had my fill [60] of human pleasures, now is the time to seek heavenly pleasures. You, my son, take over control of this ocean-bounded land. I will shave off my hair and beard, don yellow robes, and go forth from the household life into homelessness." And, having installed his eldest son in due form as king, King Daḷhanemi shaved off his hair and beard, donned yellow robes, and went forth from the household life into homelessness. And, seven days after the royal sage had gone forth, the sacred Wheel-Treasure vanished.

4. 'Then a certain man came to the anointed Khattiya King and said: "Sire, you should know that the sacred Wheel-Treasure has disappeared." At this the King was grieved and felt sad. He went to the royal sage and told him the news. And the royal sage said to him: "My son, you should not grieve or feel sad at the disappearance of the Wheel-Treasure. The Wheel-Treasure is not an heirloom from your fathers. But now, my son, you must turn yourself into an Ariyan wheel-turner.[786] And then it may come about that, if you perform the duties of an Ariyan wheel-turning monarch, on the fast-day of the fifteenth,[787] when you have washed your head and gone up to the verandah on top of your palace for the fast-day, the sacred Wheel-Treasure will appear to you, thousand-spoked, complete with felloe, hub and all appurtenances."

[61] 5. '"But what, sire, is the duty of an Ariyan wheel-turning monarch?" "It is this, my son: Yourself depending on the Dhamma, honouring it, revering it, cherishing it, doing hom-

age to it and venerating it, having the Dhamma as your badge and banner, acknowledging the Dhamma as your master, you should establish guard, ward and protection according to Dhamma for your own household, your troops, your nobles and vassals, for Brahmins and householders, town and country folk, ascetics and Brahmins, for beasts and birds.[788] Let no crime[789] prevail in your kingdom, and to those who are in need, give property. And whatever ascetics and Brahmins in your kingdom have renounced the life of sensual infatuation and are devoted to forbearance and gentleness, each one taming himself, each one calming himself and each one striving for the end of craving, from time to time you should go to them and consult them as to what is wholesome and what is unwholesome, what is blameworthy and what is blameless, what is to be followed and what is not to be followed, and what action will in the long run lead to harm and sorrow, and what to welfare and happiness. Having listened to them, you should avoid evil and do what is good.[790] That, my son, is the duty of an Ariyan wheel-turning monarch.'

'"Yes, sire", said the King, and he performed the duties of an Ariyan wheel-turning monarch. And as he did so, on the fast-day of the fifteenth, when he had washed his head and gone up to the verandah on top of his palace for the fast-day, the sacred Wheel-Treasure appeared to him, thousand-spoked, complete with felloe, hub and all appurtenances. Then the King thought: "I have heard that when a duly anointed [62] Khattiya king sees such a wheel on the fast-day of the fifteenth, he will become a wheel-turning monarch. May I become such a monarch!"[791]

6. 'Then, rising from his seat, covering one shoulder with his robe, the King took a gold vessel in his left hand, sprinkled the Wheel with his right hand, and said: "May the noble Wheel-Treasure turn, may the noble Wheel-Treasure conquer!" The Wheel turned to the east, and the King followed it with his fourfold army. And in whatever country the Wheel stopped, the King took up residence with his fourfold army. And those who opposed him in the eastern region came and said: "Come, Your Majesty, welcome! We are yours, Your Majesty. Rule us, Your Majesty." And the King said: "Do not take life.

Do not take what is not given. Do not commit sexual misconduct. Do not tell lies. Do not drink strong drink. Be moderate in eating."[792] And those who had opposed him in the eastern region became his subjects.

7. 'Then the Wheel turned south, west, and north...(*as verse 6*). Then the Wheel-Treasure, having conquered the lands from sea to sea, returned to the royal capital and stopped before the King's palace as he was trying a case, as if to adorn the royal palace.

8. 'And a second wheel-turning monarch did likewise, and a third, a fourth, a fifth, a sixth, and a seventh king also...told a man to see if the Wheel had slipped from its position (*as verse 3*). [64] And seven days after the royal sage had gone forth the Wheel disappeared.

9. 'Then a man came to the King and said: "Sire, you should know that the sacred Wheel-Treasure has disappeared." At this the King was grieved and felt sad. But he did not go to the royal sage and ask him about the duties of a wheel-turning monarch. Instead, he ruled the people according to his own ideas, and, being so ruled, the people did not prosper so well as they had done under the previous kings who had performed the duties of a wheel-turning monarch. Then the ministers, counsellors, treasury officials, guards and doorkeepers, and the chanters of mantras came to the King and said: [65] "Sire, as long as you rule the people according to your own ideas, and differently from the way they were ruled before under previous wheel-turning monarchs, the people do not prosper so well. Sire, there are ministers...in your realm, including ourselves, who have preserved the knowledge of how a wheel-turning monarch should rule. Ask us, Your Majesty, and we will tell you!"

10. 'Then the King ordered all the ministers and others to come together, and he consulted them. And they explained to him the duties of a wheel-turning monarch. And, having listened to them, the King established guard and protection, but he did not give property to the needy, and as a result poverty became rife. With the spread of poverty, a man took what was not given, thus committing what was called theft. They arrested him, and brought him before the King, saying:

"Your Majesty, this man took what was not given, which we call theft." The King said to him: "Is it true that you took what was not given – which is called theft?" "It is, Your Majesty." "Why?" "Your Majesty, I have nothing to live on." [66] Then the King gave the man some property, saying: "With this, my good man, you can keep yourself, support your mother and father, keep a wife and children, carry on a business and make gifts to ascetics and Brahmins, which will promote your spiritual welfare and lead to a happy rebirth with pleasant result in the heavenly sphere." "Very good, Your Majesty", replied the man.

11. 'And exactly the same thing happened with another man.

12. 'Then people heard that the King was giving away property to those who took what was not given, and they thought: "Suppose we were to do likewise!" And then another man took what was not given, and they brought him before the King. [67] The King asked him why he had done this, and he replied: "Your Majesty, I have nothing to live on." Then the King thought: "If I give property to everybody who takes what is not given, this theft will increase more and more. I had better make an end of him, finish him off once for all, and cut his head off." So he commanded his men: "Bind this man's arms tightly behind him with a strong rope, shave his head closely, and lead him to the rough sound of a drum through the streets and squares and out through the southern gate, and there finish by inflicting the capital penalty and cutting off his head!" And they did so.

13. 'Hearing about this, people thought: "Now let us get sharp swords made for us, and then we can take from anybody what is not given [which is called theft], [68] we will make an end of them, finish them off once for all and cut off their heads." So, having procured some sharp swords, they launched murderous assaults on villages, towns and cities, and went in for highway-robbery, killing their victims by cutting off their heads.

14. 'Thus, from the not giving of property to the needy, poverty became rife, from the growth of poverty, the taking of what was not given increased, from the increase of theft, the

use of weapons increased, from the increased use of weapons, the taking of life increased – and from the increase in the taking of life, people's life-span decreased, their beauty decreased, and as a result of this decrease of life-span and beauty, the children of those whose life-span had been eighty thousand years lived for only forty thousand.

'And a man of the generation that lived for forty thousand years took what was not given. He was brought before the King, who asked him: "Is it true that you took what was not given – what is called theft?" "No, Your Majesty", he replied, thus telling a deliberate lie.

15. 'Thus, from the not giving of property to the needy,... the taking of life increased, and from the taking of life, lying increased, [69] from the increase in lying, people's life-span decreased, their beauty decreased, and as a result, the children of those whose life-span had been forty thousand years lived for only twenty thousand.

'And a man of the generation that lived for twenty thousand years took what was not given. Another man denounced him to the King, saying: "Sire, such-and-such a man has taken what was not given", thus speaking evil of another.[793]

16. 'Thus, from the not giving of property to the needy,... the speaking evil of others increased, and in consequence, people's life-span decreased, their beauty decreased, and as a result, the children of those whose life-span had been twenty thousand years lived only for ten thousand.

'And of the generation that lived for ten thousand years, some were beautiful, and some were ugly. And those who were ugly, being envious of those who were beautiful, committed adultery with others' wives.

17. 'Thus, from the not giving of property to the needy,... sexual misconduct increased, and in consequence people's life-span decreased, their beauty decreased, and as a result, the children of those whose life-span had been ten thousand years lived for only five thousand.

'And among the generation whose life-span was five thousand years, two things increased: harsh speech and idle chatter, in consequence of which people's life-span decreased, their beauty decreased, and as a result, the children of those whose life-span had been five thousand years [70] lived, some for two-and-a-half thousand years, and some for only two thousand.

'And among the generation whose life-span was two-and-a-half thousand years, covetousness and hatred increased, and in consequence people's life-span decreased, their beauty decreased, and as a result, the children of those whose life-span had been two-and-a-half thousand years lived for only a thousand.

'Among the generation whose life-span was a thousand years, false opinions[794] increased...and as a result, the children of those whose life-span had been a thousand years lived for only five hundred.

'And among the generation whose life-span was five hundred years, three things increased: incest, excessive greed and deviant practices[795]...and as a result, the children of those whose life-span had been five hundred years lived, some for two hundred and fifty years, some for only two hundred.

'And among those whose life-span was two hundred and fifty years, these things increased: lack of respect for mother and father, for ascetics and Brahmins, and for the head of the clan.

18. 'Thus, from the not giving of property to the needy,... [71] lack of respect for mother and father, for ascetics and Brahmins, and for the head of the clan increased, and in consequence people's life-span and beauty decreased, and the children of those whose life-span had been two-and-a-half centuries lived for only a hundred years.

19. 'Monks, a time will come when the children of these people will have a life-span of ten years. And with them, girls will be marriageable at five years old. And with them, these flavours will disappear: ghee, butter, sesame-oil, molasses and salt. Among them, *kudrūsa*-grain[796] will be the chief food, just as rice and curry are today. And with them, the ten courses of moral conduct will completely disappear, and the ten courses of evil will prevail exceedingly: for those of a ten-year life-span there will be no word for "moral",[797] so how can there be anyone who acts in a moral way? Those people who have [72] no respect for mother or father, for ascetics and Brahmins,

for the head of the clan, will be the ones who enjoy honour and prestige. Just as it is now the people who show respect for mother and father, for ascetics and Brahmins, for the head of the clan, who are praised and honoured, so it will be with those who do the opposite.

20. 'Among those of a ten-year life-span no account will be taken of mother or aunt, of mother's sister-in-law, of teacher's wife or of one's father's wives and so on – all will be promiscuous in the world like goats and sheep, fowl and pigs, dogs and jackals. Among them, fierce enmity will prevail one for another, fierce hatred, fierce anger and thoughts of killing, mother against child and child against mother, father against child and child against father, brother against brother, brother against sister, just as the hunter feels hatred for the beast he stalks... [73]

21. 'And for those of a ten-year life-span, there will come to be a "sword-interval"[798] of seven days, during which they will mistake one another for wild beasts. Sharp swords will appear in their hands and, thinking: "There is a wild beast!" they will take each other's lives with those swords. But there will be some beings who will think: "Let us not kill or be killed by anyone! Let us make for some grassy thickets or jungle-recesses or clumps of trees, for rivers hard to ford or inaccessible mountains, and live on roots and fruits of the forest." And this they will do for seven days. Then, at the end of the seven days, they will emerge from their hiding-places and rejoice together of one accord, saying: "Good beings, I see that you are alive!" And then the thought will occur to those beings: "It is only because we became addicted to evil ways that we suffered this loss of our kindred, so let us now do good! What good things can we do? Let us abstain from the taking of life – that will be a good practice." And so they will abstain from the taking of life, and, having undertaken this good thing, will practise it. And through having undertaken such wholesome things, they will increase in life-span and beauty. [74] And the children of those whose life-span was ten years will live for twenty years.

22. 'Then it will occur to those beings: "It is through having taken to wholesome practices that we have increased in life-span and beauty, so let us perform still more wholesome

practices. Let us refrain from taking what is not given, from sexual misconduct, from lying speech, from slander, from harsh speech, from idle chatter, from covetousness, from ill-will, from wrong views; let us abstain from three things: incest, excessive greed, and deviant practices; let us respect our mothers and fathers, ascetics and Brahmins, and the head of the clan, and let us persevere in these wholesome actions."

'And so they will do these things, and on account of this they will increase in life-span and in beauty. The children of those whose life-span is twenty years will live to be forty, their children will live to be eighty, their children to be a hundred and sixty, their children to be three hundred and twenty, their children to be six hundred and forty; the children of those whose life-span is six hundred and forty years will live for two thousand years, their children for four thousand, their children for eight thousand, and their children for twenty thousand. The children of those whose life-span is twenty thousand years will [75] live to be forty thousand, and their children will attain to eighty thousand years.

23. 'Among the people with an eighty thousand-year life-span, girls will become marriageable at five hundred. And such people will know only three kinds of disease: greed, fasting, and old age.[799] And in the time of those people this continent of Jambudīpa will be powerful and prosperous, and villages, towns and cities will be but a cock's flight one from the next.[800] This Jambudīpa, like Avīci,[801] will be as thick with people as the jungle is thick with reeds and rushes. At that time the Vārāṇasi[802] of today will be a royal city called Ketumatī, powerful and prosperous, crowded with people and well-supplied. In Jambudīpa there will be eighty-four thousand cities headed by Ketumatī as the royal capital.

24. 'And in the time of the people with an eighty thousand-year life-span, there will arise in the capital city of Ketumatī a king called Sankha, a wheel-turning monarch, a righteous monarch of the law, conqueror of the four quarters. . .(*as verse 2*).

25. 'And in that time of the people with an eighty thousand-year life-span, [76] there will arise in the world a Blessed Lord, an Arahant fully-enlightened Buddha named Metteyya,[803] endowed with wisdom and conduct, a Well-Farer, Knower of the worlds, incomparable Trainer of men to be tamed, Teacher of

gods and humans, enlightened and blessed, just as I am now. He will thoroughly know by his own super-knowledge, and proclaim, this universe with its devas and māras and Brahmās, its ascetics and Brahmins, and this generation with its princes and people, just as I do now. He will teach the Dhamma, lovely in its beginning, lovely in its middle, lovely in its ending, in the spirit and in the letter, and proclaim, just as I do now, the holy life in its fullness and purity. He will be attended by a company of thousands of monks, just as I am attended by a company of hundreds.

26. 'Then King Sankha will re-erect the palace once built by King Mahā-Panāda[804] and, having lived in it, will give it up and present it to the ascetics and Brahmins, the beggars, the wayfarers, the destitute. Then, shaving off hair and beard, he will don yellow robes and go forth from the household life into homelessness under the supreme Buddha Metteyya. Having gone forth, he will remain alone, in seclusion, ardent, eager and resolute, and before long he will have attained in this very life, by his own super-knowledge and resolution, [77] that unequalled goal of the holy life, for the sake of which young men of good family go forth from the household life into homelessness, and will abide therein.

27. 'Monks, be islands unto yourselves, be a refuge unto yourselves with no other refuge. Let the Dhamma be your island, let the Dhamma be your refuge with no other refuge. And how does a monk dwell as an island unto himself...? Here, a monk abides contemplating body as body, ardent, clearly aware and mindful, having put aside hankering and fretting for the world, he abides contemplating feelings as feelings,...he abides contemplating mind as mind,...he abides contemplating mind-objects as mind-objects, ardent, clearly aware and mindful, having put aside hankering and fretting for the world.

28. 'Keep to your own preserves, monks, to your ancestral haunts. If you do so, your life-span will increase, your beauty will increase, your happiness will increase, your wealth will increase, your power will increase.

'And what is length of life for a monk? Here, a monk develops the road to power which is concentration of intention accompanied by effort of will, the road to power which is concentration of energy..., the road to power which is concentration of consciousness..., the road to power which is concentration of investigation accompanied by effort of will.[805] By frequently practising these four roads to power he can, if he wishes, live for a full century,[806] or the remaining part of a century. That is what I call length of life for a monk.

'And what is beauty for a monk? Here, a monk practises right conduct, is restrained according to the discipline, [78] is perfect in behaviour and habits, sees danger in the slightest fault, and trains in the rules of training he has undertaken. That is beauty for a monk.

'And what is happiness for a monk? Here, a monk, detached from sense-desires...enters the first jhāna,...(*as Sutta 22, verse 21*), the second, third, fourth jhāna,...purified by equanimity and mindfulness. That is happiness for a monk.

'And what is wealth for a monk? Here, a monk, with his heart filled with loving-kindness, dwells suffusing one quarter, the second, the third, the fourth. Thus he dwells suffusing the whole world, upwards, downwards, across – everywhere, always with a mind filled with loving-kindness, abundant, unbounded, without hate or ill-will. Then, with his heart filled with compassion,...with his heart filled with sympathetic joy,...with his heart filled with equanimity,...he dwells suffusing the whole world, upwards, downwards, across, everywhere, always with a mind filled with equanimity, abundant, unbounded, without hate or ill-will.[807] That is wealth for a monk.

'And what is power for a monk? Here, a monk, by the destruction of the corruptions, enters into and abides in that corruptionless liberation of heart and liberation by wisdom which he has attained, in this very life, by his own super-knowledge and realisation. That is power for a monk.

'Monks, I do not consider any power[808] so hard to conquer as the power of Māra. [79] It is just by this building-up of wholesome states that this merit increases.'[809]

Thus the Lord spoke, and the monks were delighted and rejoiced at his words.

27 *Aggañña Sutta: On Knowledge of Beginnings*

[80] 1. THUS HAVE I HEARD.[810] Once the Lord was staying at Sāvatthi, at the mansion of Migāra's mother[811] in the East Park. And at that time Vāseṭṭha and Bhāradvāja[812] were living among the monks, hoping to become monks themselves. And in the evening, the Lord rose from his secluded meditation and came out of the mansion, and started walking up and down in its shade.

2. Vāseṭṭha noticed this, and he said to Bhāradvāja: 'Friend Bhāradvāja, the Lord has come out and is walking up and down. Let us approach him. We might be fortunate enough to hear a talk on Dhamma from the Lord himself.' 'Yes, indeed', said Bhāradvāja, so they went up to the Lord, saluted him, and fell into step with him.

3. Then the Lord said to Vāseṭṭha: [81] 'Vāseṭṭha,[813] you two are Brahmins born and bred, and you have gone forth from the household life into homelessness from Brahmin families. Do not the Brahmins revile and abuse you?' 'Indeed, Lord, the Brahmins do revile and abuse us. They don't hold back with their usual flood of reproaches.' 'Well, Vāseṭṭha, what kind of reproaches do they fling at you?' 'Lord, what the Brahmins say is this: "The Brahmin caste[814] is the highest caste, other castes are base; the Brahmin caste is fair, other castes are dark; Brahmins are purified, non-Brahmins are not, the Brahmins are the true children of Brahmā,[815] born from his mouth, born of Brahmā, created by Brahmā, heirs of Brahmā. And you, you have deserted the highest class and gone over to the base class of shaveling petty ascetics, servants, dark fellows born of Brahmā's foot![816] It's not right, it's not proper for you to mix with such people!" That is the way the Brahmins abuse us, Lord.'

4. 'Then, Vāseṭṭha, the Brahmins have forgotten their ancient tradition when they say that. Because we can see Brahmin women, the wives of Brahmins, who menstruate and become pregnant, [82] have babies and give suck. And yet these womb-born Brahmins talk about being born from Brahmā's mouth...These Brahmins misrepresent Brahmā, tell lies and earn much demerit.

5. 'There are, Vāseṭṭha, these four castes: the Khattiyas, the Brahmins, the merchants and the artisans.[817] And sometimes a Khattiya takes life, takes what is not given, commits sexual misconduct, tells lies, indulges in slander, harsh speech or idle chatter, is grasping, malicious, or of wrong views. Thus such things as are immoral and considered so, blameworthy and considered so, to be avoided and considered so, ways unbefitting an Ariyan and considered so, black with black result[818] and blamed by the wise, are sometimes to be found among the Khattiyas, and the same applies to Brahmins, merchants and artisans.

6. 'Sometimes, too, a Khattiya refrains from taking life,...is not grasping, malicious, or of wrong views. Thus such things as are moral and considered so, blameless and considered so, to be followed and considered so, ways befitting an Ariyan and considered so, bright with bright results and praised by the wise, are sometimes to be found among the Khattiyas, and [83] likewise among Brahmins, merchants and artisans.

7. 'Now since both dark and bright qualities, which are blamed and praised by the wise, are scattered indiscriminately among the four castes, the wise do not recognise the claim about the Brahmin caste being the highest. Why is that? Because, Vāseṭṭha, anyone from the four castes who becomes a monk, an Arahant who has destroyed the corruptions, who has lived the life, done what had to be done, laid down the burden,[819] reached the highest goal, destroyed the fetter of becoming, and become emancipated through super-knowledge – he is proclaimed supreme by virtue of Dhamma and not of non-Dhamma.

Dhamma's the best thing for people
In this life and the next as well.

8. 'This illustration will make clear to you how Dhamma is best in this world and in the next. King Pasenadi of Kosala knows: "The ascetic Gotama has gone forth from the neighbouring clan of the Sakyans." Now the Sakyans are vassals of the King of Kosala. They offer him humble service and salute him, rise and do him homage and pay him fitting service. And, just as the Sakyans offer the King humble service..., [84] so likewise does the King offer humble service to the Tathāgata,[820] thinking: "If the ascetic Gotama is well-born, I am ill-born; if the ascetic Gotama is strong, I am weak; if the ascetic Gotama is pleasant to look at, I am ill-favoured; if the ascetic Gotama is influential, I am of little influence." Now it is because of honouring the Dhamma, making much of the Dhamma, esteeming the Dhamma, doing reverent homage to the Dhamma that King Pasenadi does humble service to the Tathāgata and pays him fitting service:

> Dhamma's the best thing for people
> In this life and the next as well.

9. 'Vāseṭṭha, all of you, though of different birth, name, clan and family, who have gone forth from the household life into homelessness, if you are asked who you are, should reply: "We are ascetics, followers of the Sakyan."[821] He whose faith in the Tathāgata is settled, rooted, established, solid, unshakeable by any ascetic or Brahmin, any deva or māra or Brahmā or anyone in the world, can truly say: "I am a true son of Blessed Lord, born of his mouth, born of Dhamma, created by Dhamma, an heir of Dhamma." Why is that? Because, Vāseṭṭha, this designates the Tathāgata: "The Body of Dhamma",[822] that is, "The Body of Brahmā",[823] or "Become Dhamma", that is, "Become Brahmā".[824]

10. 'There comes a time, Vāseṭṭha, when, sooner or later after a long period, this world contracts.[825] At a time of contraction, beings are mostly born in the Ābhassara Brahmā world. And there they dwell, mind-made, feeding on delight, self-luminous, moving through the air, glorious – and they stay like that for a very long time. But sooner or later, after a very long period, this world begins to expand again. At a time of expansion, the beings from the Ābhassara Brahmā world, [85] having passed away from there, are mostly reborn in this

world. Here they dwell, mind-made, feeding on delight, self-luminous, moving through the air, glorious[826] – and they stay like that for a very long time.

11. 'At that period, Vāseṭṭha, there was just one mass of water, and all was darkness, blinding darkness. Neither moon nor sun appeared, no constellations or stars appeared, night and day were not distinguished, nor months and fortnights, no years or seasons, and no male and female, beings being reckoned just as beings.[827] And sooner or later, after a very long period of time, savoury earth[828] spread itself over the waters where those beings were. It looked just like the skin that forms itself over hot milk as it cools. It was endowed with colour, smell and taste. It was the colour of fine ghee or butter, and it was very sweet, like pure wild honey.

12. 'Then some being of a greedy nature said: "I say, what can this be?" and tasted the savoury earth on its finger. In so doing, it became taken with the flavour, and craving arose in it.[829] Then other beings, taking their cue from that one, also tasted the stuff with their fingers. They too were taken with the flavour, and craving arose in them. So they set to with their hands, breaking off pieces of the stuff in order to eat it. And [86] the result of this was that their self-luminance disappeared. And as a result of the disappearance of their self-luminance, the moon and the sun appeared, night and day were distinguished, months and fortnights appeared, and the year and its seasons. To that extent the world re-evolved.

13. 'And those beings continued for a very long time feasting on this savoury earth, feeding on it and being nourished by it. And as they did so, their bodies became coarser,[830] and a difference in looks developed among them. Some beings became good-looking, others ugly. And the good-looking ones despised the others, saying: "We are better-looking than they are." And because they became arrogant and conceited about their looks, the savoury earth disappeared. At this they came together and lamented, crying: "Oh that flavour! Oh that flavour!" And so nowadays when people say: "Oh that flavour!" when they get something nice, they are repeating an ancient saying without realising it.

14. 'And then, when the savoury earth had disappeared, [87] a fungus[831] cropped up, in the manner of a mushroom. It was

of a good colour, smell, and taste. It was the colour of fine ghee or butter, and it was very sweet, like pure wild honey. And those beings set to and ate the fungus. And this lasted for a very long time. And as they continued to feed on the fungus, so their bodies became coarser still, and the difference in their looks increased still more. And the good-looking ones despised the others... And because they became arrogant and conceited about their looks, the sweet fungus disappeared. Next, creepers appeared, shooting up like bamboo..., and they too were very sweet, like pure wild honey.

15. 'And those beings set to and fed on those creepers. And as they did so, their bodies became even coarser, and the difference in their looks increased still more... [88] And they became still more arrogant, and so the creepers disappeared too. At this they came together and lamented, crying: "Alas, our creeper's gone! What have we lost!" And so now today when people, on being asked why they are upset, say: "Oh, what have we lost!" they are repeating an ancient saying without realising it.

16. 'And then, after the creepers had disappeared, rice appeared in open spaces,[832] free from powder and from husks, fragrant and clean-grained.[833] And what they had taken in the evening for supper had grown again and was ripe in the morning, and what they had taken in the morning for breakfast was ripe again by evening, with no sign of reaping. And these beings set to and fed on this rice, and this lasted for a very long time. And as they did so, their bodies became coarser still, and the difference in their looks became even greater. And the females developed female sex-organs,[834] and the males developed male organs. And the women became excessively preoccupied with men, and the men with women. Owing to this excessive preoccupation with each other, passion was aroused, and their bodies burnt with lust. And later, because of this burning, they indulged in sexual activity.[835] But those who saw them indulging threw dust, ashes or [89] cow-dung at them, crying: "Die, you filthy beast! How can one being do such things to another!" Just as today, in some districts, when a daughter-in-law is led out, some people throw dirt at her, some ashes, and some cow-dung, without realising that they are repeating an ancient observance. What

was considered bad form in those days is now considered good form.[836]

17. 'And those beings who in those days indulged in sex were not allowed into a village or town for one or two months. Accordingly those who indulged for an excessively long period in such immoral practices began to build themselves dwellings so as to indulge under cover.[837]

'Now it occurred to one of those beings who was inclined to laziness: "Well now, why should I be bothered to gather rice in the evening for supper and in the morning for breakfast? Why shouldn't I gather it all at once for both meals?" And he did so. Then another one came to him and said: "Come on, let's go rice-gathering." "No need, my friend, I've gathered enough for both meals." Then the other, following his example, gathered enough rice for two days at a time, saying: "That should be about enough." Then another being came and said [90] to that second one: "Come on, let's go rice-gathering." "No need, my friend, I've gathered enough for two days." (*The same for 4, then 8, days*). However, when those beings made a store of rice and lived on that, husk-powder and husk began to envelop the grain, and where it was reaped it did not grow again, and the cut place showed, and the rice grew in separate clusters.

18. 'And then those beings came together lamenting: "Wicked ways have become rife among us: at first we were mind-made, feeding on delight... (*all events repeated down to the latest development, each fresh change being said to be due to* 'wicked and unwholesome ways')... [91] [92] and the rice grows in separate clusters. So now let us divide up the rice into fields with boundaries." So they did so.

19. 'Then, Vāseṭṭha, one greedy-natured being, while watching over his own plot, took another plot that was not given to him, and enjoyed the fruits of it. So they seized hold of him and said: "You've done a wicked thing, taking another's plot like that! Don't ever do such a thing again!" "I won't", he said, but he did the same thing a second and a third time. Again he was seized and rebuked, and some hit him with their fists, some with stones, and some with sticks. And in this way, Vāseṭṭha, taking what was not given, and censuring, and lying, and punishment, took their origin.

20. 'Then those beings came together and lamented the arising of these evil things among them: taking what was not given, censuring, lying and punishment. And they thought: "Suppose we were to appoint a certain being who would show anger where anger was due, censure those who deserved it, and banish those who deserved banishment! And in return, we would grant him a share of the rice." [93] So they went to the one among them who was the handsomest, the best-looking, the most pleasant and capable, and asked him to do this for them in return for a share of the rice, and he agreed.

21. '"The People's Choice" is the meaning of Mahā-Sammata,[838] which is the first regular title[839] to be introduced. "Lord Of The Fields" is the meaning of Khattiya,[840] the second such title. And "He Gladdens Others With Dhamma" is the meaning of Rājā,[841] the third title to be introduced. This, then, Vāseṭṭha, is the origin of the class of Khattiyas, in accordance with the ancient titles that were introduced for them. They originated among these very same beings, like ourselves, no different, and in accordance with Dhamma, not otherwise.

Dhamma's the best thing for people
In this life and the next as well.

22. 'Then some of these beings thought: "Evil things have appeared among beings, such as taking what is not given, censuring, lying, punishment and banishment. We ought to put aside evil and unwholesome things." And they did [94] so. "They Put Aside[842] Evil And Uwholesome Things" is the meaning of Brahmin,[843] which is the first regular title to be introduced for such people. They made leaf-huts in forest places and meditated in them. With the smoking fire gone out, with pestle cast aside, gathering alms for their evening and morning meals, they went away to a village, town or royal city to seek their food, and then they returned to their leaf-huts to meditate. People saw this and noted how they meditated. "They Meditate"[844] is the meaning of Jhāyaka,[845] which is the second regular title to be introduced.

23. 'However, some of those beings, not being able to meditate in leaf-huts, settled around towns and villages and compiled books.[846] People saw them doing this and not meditating.

"Now These Do Not Meditate"[847] is the meaning of Ajjhāyaka,[848] which is the third regular title to be introduced. At that time it was regarded as a low designation, but now it is the higher. This, then, Vāseṭṭha, is the origin of the class of Brahmins in accordance with the ancient titles that were introduced for them. [95] Their origin was from among these very same beings, like themselves, no different, and in accordance with Dhamma, not otherwise.

Dhamma's the best thing for people
In this life and the next as well.

24. 'And then, Vāseṭṭha, some of those beings, having paired off,[849] adopted various trades, and this "Various"[850] is the meaning of Vessa, which came to be the regular title for such people. This, then, is the origin of the class of Vessas, in accordance with the ancient titles that were introduced for them. Their origin was from among these very same beings...

25. 'And then, Vāseṭṭha, those beings that remained went in for hunting. "They Are Base Who Live By The Chase", and that is the meaning of Sudda,[851] which came to be the regular title for such people. This, then, is the origin of the class of Suddas[852] in accordance with the ancient titles that were introduced for them. Their origin was from among these very same beings...

26. 'And then, Vāseṭṭha, it came about that some Khattiya, dissatisfied with his own Dhamma,[853] went forth from the household life into homelessness, thinking: "I will become an ascetic." And a Brahmin did likewise, a Vessa did [96] likewise, and so did a Sudda. And from these four classes the class of ascetics came into existence. Their origin was from among these very same beings, like themselves, no different, and in accordance with Dhamma, not otherwise.

Dhamma's the best thing for people
In this life and the next as well.

27. 'And, Vāseṭṭha, a Khattiya who has led a bad life in body, speech and thought, and who has wrong view will, in consequence of such wrong views and deeds, at the breaking-up of the body after death, be reborn in a state of loss, an ill fate, the downfall, the hell-state. So too will a Brahmin, a Vessa or a Sudda.

28. 'Likewise, a Khattiya who has led a good life in body, speech and thought, and who has right view will, in consequence of such right view and deeds, at the breaking-up of the body after death, be reborn in a good destiny, in a heaven-state. So too will a Brahmin, a Vessa or a Sudda.

29. 'And a Khattiya who has performed deeds of both kinds in body, speech and thought, and whose view is mixed will, in consequence of such mixed views and deeds, at the breaking-up of the body after death, experience both pleasure and pain. So too will a Brahmin, [97] a Vessa or a Sudda.

30. 'And a Khattiya who is restrained in body, speech and thought, and who has developed the seven requisites of enlightenment,[854] will attain to Parinibbāna[855] in this very life. So too will a Brahmin, a Vessa or a Sudda.

31. 'And, Vāseṭṭha, whoever of these four castes, as a monk, becomes an Arahant who has destroyed the corruptions, done what had to be done, laid down the burden, attained to the highest goal, completely destroyed the fetter of becoming, and become liberated by the highest insight, he is declared to be chief among them in accordance with Dhamma, and not otherwise.

> Dhamma's the best thing for people
> In this life and the next as well.

32. 'Vāseṭṭha, it was Brahmā Sanankumāra who spoke this verse:

> "The Khattiya's best among those who value clan;
> He with knowledge and conduct is best of gods and
> men."

This verse was rightly sung, not wrongly, rightly spoken, not wrongly, connected with profit, not unconnected. I too say, Vāseṭṭha:

> [98] "The Khattiya's best among those who value
> clan;
> He with knowledge and conduct is best of gods and
> men."'

Thus the Lord spoke, and Vāseṭṭha and Bhāradvāja were delighted and rejoiced at his words.

28 *Sampasādanīya Sutta: Serene Faith*

[99] 1. THUS HAVE I HEARD. Once the Lord was styaing at Nālandā in Pāvārika's mango-grove. And the Venerable Sāriputta came to see the Lord, saluted him, sat down to one side, and said:[856] 'It is clear to me, Lord, that there never has been, never will be and is not now another ascetic or Brahmin who is better or more enlightened than the Lord.'

'You have spoken boldly with a bull's voice, Sāriputta, you have roared the lion's roar of certainty. How is this? Have all the Arahant Buddhas of the past appeared to you, and were the minds of all those Lords open to you, so as to say: "These Lords were of such virtue, such was their teaching, [100] such their wisdom, such their way, such their liberation"?' 'No, Lord.' 'And have you perceived all the Arahant Buddhas who will appear in the future?' 'No, Lord.' 'Well then, Sāriputta, you know me as the Arahant Buddha, and do you know: "The Lord is of such virtue, such his teaching, such his wisdom, such his way, such his liberation"?' 'No, Lord.' 'So, Sāriputta, you do not have knowledge of the minds of the Buddhas of the past, the future or the present. Then, Sāriputta,have you not spoken boldly with a bull's voice and roared the lion's roar of certainty with your declaration?'

2. 'Lord, the minds of the Arahant Buddhas of the past, future and present are not open to me. But I know the drift of the Dhamma. Lord, it is as if there were a [101] royal frontier city, with mighty bastions and a mighty encircling wall in which was a single gate, at which was a gatekeeper, wise, skilled and clever, who kept out strangers and let in those he knew. And he, constantly patrolling and following along a path, might not see the joins and clefts in the bastion, even

such as a cat might creep through. But whatever larger creatures entered or left the city, must all go through this very gate. And it seems to me, Lord, that the drift of the Dhamma is the same. All those Arahant Buddhas of the past attained to supreme enlightenment by abandoning the five hindrances, defilements of mind which weaken understanding, having firmly established the four foundations of mindfulness in their minds, and realised the seven factors of enlightenment as they really are. All the Arahant Buddhas of the future will do likewise, and you, Lord, who are now the Arahant, fully-enlightened Buddha, have done the same.

'So I came once [102] to the Blessed Lord to listen to Dhamma. And the Blessed Lord taught me Dhamma most excellently and perfectly, contrasting the dark with the light. And as he did so, I gained insight into that Dhamma, and from among the various things I established one in particular, which was serene confidence[857] in the Teacher, that the Blessed Lord is a fully-enlightened Buddha, that the Dhamma is well taught by the Blessed Lord, and that the order of monks is well-trained.

3. 'Also, lord, the Blessed Lord's way of teaching Dhamma in regard to the wholesome factors is unsurpassed, that is to say: the four foundations of mindfulness, the four right efforts, the four roads to power, the five spiritual faculties, the five mental powers, the seven factors of enlightenment, the Noble Eightfold Path.[858] By these a monk, through the destruction of the corruptions, can in this very life, by his own super-knowledge, realise and attain the corruption-free liberation of heart and liberation by wisdom, and abide therein. This is the unsurpassed teaching in regard to the wholesome factors. This the Blessed Lord fully comprehends, and beyond it lies nothing further to be comprehended; and in such understanding there is no other ascetic or Brahmin who is greater or more enlightened than the Blessed Lord, as regards the wholesome factors.

4. 'Also unsurpassed is the Blessed Lord's way of teaching Dhamma in regard to the elucidation of the sense-spheres: there are the six internal and external sense-bases:[859] eye and visible objects, ear and sounds, nose and smells, tongue and tastes, body and tactiles, mind and mind-objects. This is the unsurpassed teaching in regard to the sense-spheres...

5. 'Also unsurpassed is the Blessed Lord's way of teaching Dhamma in regard to the modes of rebirth in four ways: thus, one descends into the mother's womb unknowing,[860] stays there unknowing, and leaves it unknowing. That is the first way. Or, one enters the womb knowing, stays there unknowing, and leaves it unknowing. That is the second way. Or, one enters the womb knowing, stays there knowing, and leaves it unknowing. That is the third way. Or, one enters the womb knowing, stays there knowing, and leaves it knowing. That is the fourth way. This is the unsurpassed teaching in regard to the modes of rebirth...

6. 'Also unsurpassed is the Blessed Lord's way of teaching Dhamma in regard to the telling of thoughts[861] in four ways. Thus, one tells by a visible sign, saying: "This is what you think, this is in your mind, your thought is like this." And however much one declares, it is so and not otherwise. That is the first way. Or, one tells not by a visible sign, but through hearing a sound made by humans, non-humans,[862] or devas ...That is the second way. Or one tells not by a sound uttered, [104] but by applying one's mind and attending to something conveyed by sound...That is the third way. Or one tells, not by any of these means, when one has attained a state of mental concentration without thinking and pondering,[863] by divining another's thoughts in one's mind, and one says: "As far as so-and-so's mind-force is directed, so his thoughts will turn to that thing." And however much one declares, it is so and not otherwise. That is the fourth way. This is the unsurpassed teaching in regard to the telling of thoughts in four ways...

7. 'Also unsurpassed is the Blessed Lord's way of teaching Dhamma in regard to the attainment of vision,[864] in four ways. Here, some ascetic or Brahmin, by means of ardour, endeavour, application, vigilance and due attention, reaches such a level of concentration that he considers just this body – upwards from the soles of the feet and downwards from the crown of the head, enclosed by the skin and full of manifold impurities: "In this body there are head-hairs, body-hairs, nails, teeth, skin, flesh, sinews, bones, bone-marrow, kidneys, heart, liver, pleura, spleen, lungs, mesentery, bowels, stomach,

excrement, bile, phlegm, pus, blood, sweat, fat, tears, tallow, saliva, snot, synovic fluid, urine." (*as Sutta 22, verse 5*) That is the first attainment of vision. Again, having done this and gone further, [105] he contemplates the bones covered with skin, flesh and blood. This is the second attainment. Again, having done this and gone further, he comes to know the unbroken stream of human consciousness as established both in this world and in the next.[865] That is the third attainment. Again, having done this and gone still further, he comes to know the unbroken stream of human consciousness that is not established either in this world or in the next.[866] That is the fourth attainment of vision. This is the unsurpassed teaching in regard to the attainments of vision...

8. 'Also unsurpassed is the Blessed Lord's way of teaching Dhamma in regard to the designation of individuals.[867] There are these seven types: the Both-Ways-Liberated,[868] the Wisdom-Liberated,[869] the Body-Witness,[870] the Vision-Attainer,[871] the Faith-Liberated,[872] the Dhamma-Devotee,[873] the Faith-Devotee.[874] This is the unsurpassed teaching in regard to the designation of individuals...

9. 'Also unsurpassed is the Blessed Lord's way of teaching Dhamma in regard to the [106] exertions.[875] There are these seven factors of enlightenment: mindfulness, investigation of states, energy, delight, tranquillity, concentration and equanimity. This is the unsurpassed teaching in regard to the exertions...

10. 'Also unsurpassed in the Blessed Lord's way of teaching Dhamma in regard to the modes of progress,[876] which are four: painful progress with slow comprehension, painful progress with quick comprehension, pleasant progress with slow comprehension, pleasant progress with quick comprehension. In the case of painful progress with slow comprehension, progress is considered poor on account of both painfulness and slowness. In the case of painful progress with quick comprehension, progress is considered poor on account of painfulness. In the case of pleasant progress with slow comprehension, progress is considered poor on account of slowness. In the case of pleasant progress with quick comprehension, progress is considered excellent on account of both pleasant-

ness and quick comprehension. This is the unsurpassed teaching in regard to the modes of progress...

11. 'Also unsurpassed is the Blessed Lord's way of teaching Dhamma in regard to proper conduct in speech: how one should avoid not only any speech involving lying, but also speech that is divisive[877] or sneeringly triumphant,[878] but should use wise words, words to be treasured, words in season. This is the unsurpassed teaching in regard to proper conduct in speech...

12. 'Also unsurpassed is the Blessed Lord's way of teaching Dhamma in regard to a person's proper ethical conduct. One should be truthful and faithful, not using deception, patter, hinting or belittling,[879] not [107] always on the make for further gains, but with sense-doors guarded, abstemious, a peacemaker, given to watchfulness, active, strenuous in effort, a meditator,[880] mindful, of fitting conversation, steady-going,[881] resolute[882] and sensible,[883] not hankering after sense-pleasures but mindful and prudent. This is the unsurpassed teaching in regard to a person's proper ethical conduct...

13. 'Also unsurpassed is the Blessed Lord's way of teaching Dhamma in regard to modes of receptivity to instruction, of which there are four: The Blessed Lord knows by his own skilled observation:[884] "That one will, by following instructions, by the complete destruction of three fetters, become a Stream-Winner, no more subject to rebirth in lower worlds, firmly established, destined for full enlightenment"; "that one will, by following instructions, by the complete destruction of three fetters and the reduction of greed, hatred and delusion, become a Once-Returner, and having returned once more to this world, will put an end to suffering"; "that one will, by following instructions, by the complete destruction of the five lower fetters, be spontaneously reborn,[885] and there will reach Nibbāna without returning from that world"; "that one will, by following instructions, by the destruction of the corruptions, gain in this very life the deliverance of mind, the deliverance through wisdom which is uncorrupted, and which one has understood and realised by one's own super-knowledge." This is the unsurpassed teaching in regard to the modes of receptivity to instruction...[108]

14. 'Also unsurpassed is the Blessed Lord's way of teaching Dhamma in regard to the knowledge of the liberation of others. The Blessed Lord knows, by his own skilled observation: "That one will, by the complete destruction of three fetters, become a Stream-Winner...; then with the reduction of greed, hatred and delusion, become a Once-Returner...; by the complete destruction of the five lower fetters, be spontaneously reborn...; by the destruction of the corruptions, gain in this very life the deliverance of mind, the deliverance through wisdom which is uncorrupted..."

15. 'Also unsurpassed is the Blessed Lord's way of teaching Dhamma in regard to the doctrine of Eternalism.[886] There are three such theories: (1) Here, some ascetic or Brahmin, by means of ardour, endeavour,...recalls various past existences ...up to several hundred thousand births...(*as Sutta 1, verse 1.31*). [109] In this way he remembers the details of his various past lives, and he says: "I know the past, whether the universe was expanding or contracting,[887] but I do not know the future, whether it will expand or contract. The self and the world are eternal, barren, steady as a mountain-peak, rooted like a pillar. Beings run on, transmigrate, pass away and rearise, yet these persist eternally." (2) Again, some ascetic or Brahmin recalls various existences...(*as (1), but* "up to twenty aeons..."). [110] (3) Again, some ascetic or Brahmin recalls various existence...(*as (1), but* "up to ten, twenty, thirty, forty aeons..."). This is the unsurpassed teaching in regard to the doctrine of Eternalism...

16. 'Also unsurpassed is the Blessed Lord's way of teaching Dhamma in regard to past lives. Here, some ascetic or Brahmin...recalls various past existences – one birth, two births, three, four, five, ten, twenty, thirty, forty, fifty, a hundred, a thousand, a hundred thousand lives, many aeons of contraction, [111] of expansion, of contraction and expansion: "Then I was called so-and-so, this was my clan, my caste, I ate this, had these happy and unhappy experiences, lived for so long. And when I passed away from there I was reborn in such-and-such other circumstances. Passing away from there, I was reborn here." In this way he remembers the details of his various past lives. There are devas whose life-span is not to be

reckoned by counting or computation,[888] yet whatever existence[889] they have previously experienced, whether in the World of Form or in the Formless World, whether conscious, unconscious or neither-conscious-nor-unconscious, they remember the details of those past lives. This is the unsurpassed teaching in regard to remembrance of past lives...

17. 'Also unsurpassed is the Blessed Lord's way of teaching Dhamma in regard to knowledge of the death and rebirth of beings. Here, some ascetic or Brahmin...attains to such concentration of mind that he sees with the divine eye, purified and surpassing that of humans, beings passing away and arising: base and noble, well-favoured and ill-favoured, to happy and unhappy destinations as kamma directs them, and he knows: "These beings, on account of misconduct of body, speech or thought or disparaging the Noble Ones, have wrong view and will suffer the kammic fate of wrong view. At the breaking-up of the body after death they are reborn in a lower world, a bad destination, a state of suffering, hell. But these beings, on account of good conduct of body, speech or thought, of praising the Noble Ones, have right view and will reap the kammic reward of right view. At the breaking-up of the body [112] after death they are reborn in a good destination, a heavenly world." Thus with the divine eye, purified and surpassing that of humans, he sees beings passing away and re-arising...This is the unsurpassed teaching in regard to knowledge of the death and birth of beings...

18. 'Also unsurpassed is the Blessed Lord's way of teaching Dhamma in regard to the supernormal powers. These are of two kinds. There is the kind that is bound up with the corruptions and with attachment,[890] which is called "un-Ariyan", and there is the kind that is free of the corruptions and not bound up with attachment, which is called "Ariyan". What is the "un-Ariyan" supernormal power? Here some ascetic or Brahmin enjoys various supernormal powers: being one, he becomes many – being many, he becomes one; he appears and disappears; he passes through fences, walls and mountains unhindered as if through air; he sinks into the ground and emerges from it as if it were water; he walks on the water without breaking the surface as if on land; he flies cross-

legged through the sky like a bird with wings; he even touches and strokes with his hand the sun and moon, mighty and powerful as they are; and he travels in the body as far as the Brahmā world. That is the "un-Ariyan" supernormal power. And what is the "Ariyan" supernormal power? Here a monk, if he wishes: "Let me abide with the disgusting[891] not feeling disgust", can so abide, and if he wishes: "Let me [113] abide with the non-disgusting feeling disgust", he can so abide, *also feeling either disgust or non-disgust in the presence of both*...or: "Ignoring both the disgusting and the non-disgusting may I abide in equanimity, mindful and clearly aware", he can so abide. That is the "Ariyan" supernormal power, that is free of the corruptions and not bound up with attachment. This is the unsurpassed teaching in regard to the supernormal powers. This the Blessed Lord fully comprehends, and beyond it lies nothing further to be comprehended; and in such understanding there is no other ascetic or Brahmin who is greater or more enlightened than the Blessed Lord, as regards the supernormal powers.

19. 'Whatever, Lord, it is possible for a clansman endowed with confidence to achieve by putting forth effort and by persistence, by human effort, human exertion and human endurance,[892] that the Blessed Lord has achieved. For the Blessed Lord gives himself up neither to the pleasures of the senses, which are base, vulgar, for worldlings and not for the Noble, and unprofitable, nor to self-torment, which is painful, ignoble and unprofitable.[893] The Blessed Lord is able, here and now,[894] to enjoy the surpassing[895] happiness of dwelling in the four jhānas.

'Lord, if I were asked: "Well now, friend Sāriputta, have there ever been in the past any ascetics and Brahmins more exalted in enlightenment than the Blessed Lord?" I should say: "No." If asked: "Will there be any such in the future?" I should say: "No." [114] If asked: "Is there any such at present?" I should say: "No." Again, if I were asked: "Have there been any such in the past equal in enlightenment to the Blessed Lord?" I should say: "Yes." If asked: "Will there be any such in the future?" I should say: "Yes." But if I were asked: "Are there any such at present equal in enlightenment to the Blessed Lord?" I should say: "No." And if I were then asked: "Venerable Sāriputta, why do you accord this highest recognition to one and not the other?" I should say: "I have heard and received it from the Blessed Lord's own lips: 'There have been in the past, and there will be in the future, Arahant Buddhas equal in enlightenment to myself.' I have also heard and received it from the Blessed Lord's own lips that it is not possible, it cannot be that in one and the same world-system two Arahant supreme Buddhas should arise simultaneously.[896] No such situation can exist."

'Lord, if I were [115] to reply thus to such questions, would I be speaking in conformity with the Blessed Lord's word, and not misrepresenting him by departing from the truth? Would I be explaining Dhamma correctly, so that no fellow-follower of the Dhamma could contest it or find occasion for censure?'

'Certainly, Sāriputta, if you answered like this you would not misrepresent me, you would be explaining Dhamma correctly and not laying yourself open to censure.'

20. At this, the Venerable Udāyi said to the Lord: 'It is wonderful, Lord, it is marvellous how content the Blessed Lord is, how satisfied and restrained,[897] when being endowed with such power and influence he does not make a display of himself! If the wanderers professing other doctrines were able to discern in themselves even one of such qualities, they would proclaim it with a banner! It is wonderful...that the Blessed Lord does not make display of himself!'

'Well then, Udāyi, just observe: so it is. If such wanderers were able to discern in themselves even one of such qualities, they would proclaim it with a banner. But the Tathāgata is content,...he does not make a display of himself.' [116]

21. Then the Lord said to Sāriputta: 'And therefore you, Sāriputta, should frequently speak about this matter to monks and nuns, to male and female lay-followers. And any foolish people who have doubts or queries about the Tathāgata will, by listening to such talk, have their doubts and queries resolved.'

This was how the Venerable Sāriputta proclaimed his confidence in the Lord. And so one name for this exposition is 'The Serene Faith'.

29 *Pāsādika Sutta: The Delightful Discourse*

[117] 1. THUS HAVE I HEARD. Once the Lord was staying among the Sakyans, at the [School] building[898] in the mango-grove belonging to the Vedhañña family.[899] At that time the Nigaṇṭha Nātaputta had just died at Pāvā.[900] And at his death the Nigaṇṭhas were split into two parties, quarrelling and disputing, fighting and attacking each other with wordy warfare: 'You don't understand this doctrine and discipline – I do!' 'How could *you* understand this doctrine and discipline?' 'Your way is all wrong – mine is right!' 'I am consistent – you aren't!' 'You said last what you should have said first, and you said first what you should have said last!' 'What you took so long to think up has been refuted!' 'Your argument has been overthrown, you're defeated!' 'Go on, save your doctrine – get out of that if you can!' You would have thought the Nigaṇṭhas, Nātaputta's disciples, were bent on killing each other. Even the white-robed lay [118] followers were disgusted, displeased and repelled when they saw that their doctrine and discipline was so ill-proclaimed, so unedifyingly displayed, and so ineffectual in calming the passions, having been proclaimed by one not fully enlightened, and now with its support gone, without an arbiter.[901]

2. Now the novice Cunda, who had spent the Rains at Pāvā, came to Sāmagāma to see the Venerable Ānanda. Saluting him, he sat down to one side and said: 'Sir, the Nigaṇṭha Nātaputta has just died at Pāvā.' And he related what had happened. The Venerable Ānanda said: 'Cunda, that is something that ought to be reported to the Blessed Lord. Let us go and tell him.' 'Very good, sir', said Cunda.

3. So they went to the Lord and told him. He said: 'Cunda,

here is a doctrine and discipline that is ill-proclaimed, [119] unedifyingly displayed and ineffectual in calming the passions because its proclaimer was not fully enlightened.

4. 'Such being the case, Cunda, a disciple cannot live according to that doctrine and maintain proper conduct, nor live by it, but deviates from it. To him one might say: "Friend, this is what you have received,[902] and you have your opportunity.[903] Your teacher is not fully enlightened...You cannot live according to that doctrine..., but deviate from it." In this case, Cunda, the teacher is to blame, the doctrine is to blame, but the pupil is praiseworthy. And if anyone were to say to that pupil: "Come now, reverend sir, and practise according to the doctrine proclaimed and given out by your teacher" – then the one who urged this, the thing urged and the one who so practised would all gain much demerit.[904] Why? Because the doctrine is ill-proclaimed...

5. 'But here, Cunda, is a teacher who is not fully enlightened...and a disciple lives according to that doctrine, and conforms to it. One might say to him: "Friend, what you have received is no good,[905] your opportunity is a poor one;[906] your teacher is not fully [120] enlightened, his teaching is ill-proclaimed,...but yet you continue to live according to it..." In this case the teacher, the doctrine and the disciple are all to blame. And if anyone were to say: "Well, reverend sir, by following that system you will be successful", the one who so recommended it, that which was recommended, and the one who, on hearing such recommendation, should make still greater efforts, would all gain much demerit. Why? Because the doctrine is ill-proclaimed...

6. 'But here now is a teacher who is fully enlightened: his doctrine is well-proclaimed, edifyingly displayed, effectual in calming the passions because of that enlightened teacher, but the disciple does not live up to the doctrine..., but deviates from it. In that case one might say to him: "Friend, you have failed, you have missed your opportunity;[907] your teacher is fully enlightened, his doctrine is well-proclaimed,...but you do not follow it, you deviate from it." In this case the teacher and the doctrine are praiseworthy, but the pupil is to blame. And if anyone were to say: "Well, reverend sir, you should follow the teaching proclaimed by your teacher", then the one

who urged this, that which was urged and the one who so practised would all gain much merit. Why? Because the doctrine is well-proclaimed...[121]

7. 'But now, Cunda, here is a teacher who is fully enlightened, his doctrine is well-proclaimed,...and the disciple, having taken it up, follows it, practising it properly and keeping to it. Someone might say to him: "Friend, what you have received is good, here is your opportunity,[908]...and you are following the doctrine of your teacher." In this case the teacher and the doctrine are praiseworthy, and the pupil is also praiseworthy. And if anyone were to say to such a disciple: "Well reverend sir, by following that system you will be successful", then the one who thus commended it, and that which was commended, and the one who, on hearing such commendation, should make still greater efforts, would all gain much merit. Why? Because that is so when the doctrine and discipline are well-proclaimed, edifyingly displayed and effectual in calming the passions because of the fully-enlightened Teacher and supreme Buddha.

8. 'But now, Cunda, suppose a Teacher has arisen in the world, an Arahant, fully-enlightened Buddha, and his doctrine is well-proclaimed,...effectual in calming the passions because of that Teacher. But his disciples have not fully mastered that true Dhamma, the full purity of the holy life has not become clear and evident to them in the logic of its unfolding,[909] and has not been sufficiently grounded among them,[910] [122] being still in course of being well-proclaimed among humans at the time of the Teacher's passing from among them.[911] That way, Cunda, the Teacher's death would be a sad thing for his disciples. Why? They would think: "Our Teacher arose in the world for us, an Arahant, fully-enlightened Buddha, whose doctrine was well-proclaimed,...but we did not fully master the true Dhamma...as long as it was well-proclaimed among humans, and now our Teacher has passed away from among us!" That way, the Teacher's death would be a sad thing for his disciples.

9. 'But suppose a Teacher has arisen in the world,...and his disciples have fully mastered the true Dhamma, the full purity of the holy life has become clear and evident to them in the logic of its unfolding, and has been sufficiently grounded

among them while being thus well-proclaimed among humans by the time of the Teacher's passing from them. That way, the Teacher's death would not be a sad thing for his disciples. Why? They would think: "Our Teacher arose in the world for us...and we have fully mastered the true Dhamma...while it was thus proclaimed among humans, [123] and now our Teacher has passed away from among us." That way, the Teacher's death would not be a sad thing for his disciples.

10. 'But, Cunda, if the holy life[912] is so circumstanced, and there is no teacher who is senior, of long standing, long-ordained, mature and advanced in seniority, then in such a case the holy life will be imperfect. But if such a teacher exists, then the holy life can be perfected in such a case.

11. 'If in such a case there is such a senior teacher, but if there are no senior disciples among the monks, who are experienced, trained, skilled, who have attained peace from bondage,[913] who are able to proclaim the true Dhamma, able to refute any opposing doctrines that may arise by means of the true Dhamma, and, having done so, give a grounded exposition of Dhamma, then the holy life is not perfected.[914]

12. 'In such cases, if there are such senior teachers, and such senior disciples, but there are no monks of middle standing with these qualities,...or [despite the presence of these] no junior monks with these qualities,...no senior disciples among the nuns,...[124] no middle-ranking or junior nuns,...no white-robed lay followers, male or female, celibate or otherwise,[915] or if the teaching does not prosper and flourish, is not widespread, widely known, proclaimed far and wide,...or [even if these conditions are fulfilled] has not gained the first place in public support, then the holy life is not perfected.

13. 'If, however, all these conditions are fulfilled, then [125] the holy life is perfected.

14. 'But, Cunda, I have now arisen in the world as an Arahant, fully-enlightened Buddha, the Dhamma is well-proclaimed,...my disciples are proficient in the true Dhamma, ...the full purity of the holy life has become clear and evident to them in the logic of its unfolding...But now I am an aged teacher of long standing, who went forth a long time ago, and my life is coming to its close.

15. 'However, there are senior teachers among the monks, who are experienced, trained, skilled, who have attained peace from bondage, able to proclaim the true Dhamma, able to refute by means of the Dhamma any opposing doctrines that may arise and, having done so, give a grounded exposition of Dhamma. And there are middle-ranking monks who are disciplined and experienced, there are novices who are disciples, there are senior, middle-ranking and novice nuns who are disciples, there are white-robed lay followers, male and female, celibate and [126] non-celibate, and the holy life I proclaim prospers and flourishes, is widespread, widely-known, proclaimed far and wide, well-proclaimed among humans.

16. 'Among all the teachers now existing in the world, Cunda, I see none who has attained to such a position of fame and following as I have. Of all the orders and groups in the world, I see none as famous and well-followed as my Sangha of monks. If anyone were to refer to any holy way of life as being fully successful and perfect, with nothing lacking and nothing superfluous, well-proclaimed in the perfection of its purity, it is this holy life they would be describing. It was Uddaka Rāmaputta[916] who used to say: "He sees, but does not see." What is it that, seeing, one does not see? You can see the blade of a well-sharpened razor, but not its edge. That is what he meant by saying: "He sees, but does not see." He spoke in reference to a low, vulgar, worldly ignoble thing of no spiritual significance,[917] a mere razor.

'But if one were to use that expression properly: [127] "He sees, but does not see", it would be like this. What he sees is a holy way of life which is fully successful and perfect, with nothing lacking and nothing superfluous, well-proclaimed in the perfection of its purity. If he were to deduct anything from it, thinking: "In this way it will be purer", he does not see it. And if he were to add anything to it, thinking: "In this way it will be more complete", then he does not see it.[918] That is the meaning of the saying: "He sees, but does not see." Therefore, Cunda, if anyone were to refer to any holy way of life as being fully successful and perfect,...it is this holy life that they would be describing.

17. 'Therefore, Cunda, all you to whom I have taught these

truths that I have realised by super-knowledge, should come together and recite them, setting meaning beside meaning and expression beside expression, without dissension, in order that this holy life may continue and be established for a long time for the profit and happiness of the many out of compassion for the world and for the benefit, profit and happiness of devas and humans.[919] And what are the things that you should recite together? They are: the four foundations of mindfulness, the four right efforts, the four roads to power, the five spiritual faculties, the five mental powers, the seven [128] factors of enlightenment, the Noble Eightfold Path. These are the things you should recite together.

18. 'And thus you must train yourselves, being assembled in harmony and without dissension. If a fellow in the holy life quotes Dhamma in the assembly, and if you think he has either misunderstood the sense or expressed it wrongly, you should neither applaud nor reject it, but should say to him: "Friend, if you mean such-and-such, you should put it either like this or like that: which is the more appropriate?" or: "If you say such-and-such, you mean either this or that: which is the more appropriate?" If he replies: "This meaning is better expressed like this than like that", or: "The sense of this expression is this rather than that", then his words should be neither rejected nor disparaged, but you should explain to him carefully the correct meaning and expression.

19. 'Again, Cunda, if a fellow in the holy life quotes Dhamma in the assembly, and if you think he has misunderstood the sense though he has expressed it [129] correctly, you should neither applaud nor reject it, but should say to him: "Friend, these words can mean either this or that: which sense is the more appropriate?" And if he replies: "They mean this", then his words should be neither rejected nor disparaged, but you should explain to him carefully the correct meaning.

20. 'And similarly, if you think he has got the right meaning but expressed it wrongly,...you should explain to him carefully the correct meaning and expression.

21. 'But, Cunda, if you think he has got the right meaning and expressed it correctly,...you should say: "Good!"[920] and should applaud and congratulate him, saying: "We are lucky,

we are most fortunate to find in you, friend, a companion in the holy life who is so well-versed in both the meaning and the expression!"

22. 'Cunda, I do not teach you a Dhamma for restraining the corruptions that arise in the present life alone.[921] [130] I do not teach a Dhamma merely for their destruction in future lives, but one for their restraining in this life as well as for their destruction in future lives. Accordingly, Cunda, let the robe I have allowed you be simply for warding off the cold, for warding off the heat, for warding off the touch of gadfly, mosquito, wind, sun and creeping things, just so as to protect your modesty.[922] Let the alms-food I have allowed you be just enough for the support and sustenance of the body, for keeping it unimpaired for the furtherance of the holy life, with the thought: "Thus I shall eliminate the former feeling[923] without giving rise to a new one – in that way I shall live without fault and in comfort." Let the lodging I have allowed you be simply for warding off the cold, for warding off the heat, for warding off the touch of gadfly, mosquito, wind, sun and creeping things, just for allaying the perils of the seasons and for the enjoyment of seclusion. Let the provision of medicines and necessities for the treatment of sickness that I have allowed you be just for warding off feelings of sickness that have arisen, and for the maintenance of health.[924]

23. 'It may be, Cunda, that wanderers of other sects might say: "The ascetics who follow the Sakyan are addicted to a life of devotion to pleasure."[925] If so, they should be asked: "What kind of a life of devotion to pleasure, friend? For such a life can take many different forms." There are, Cunda, four kinds of life devoted to pleasure which are low, vulgar, worldly, ignoble and not conducive to welfare,[926] not leading to disenchantment, to dispassion, to cessation, to tranquillity, to realisation, to enlightenment, to Nibbāna. What are they? Firstly, a foolish person[927] takes pleasure and delight in killing living beings. Secondly, [131] someone takes pleasure and delight in taking that which is not given. Thirdly, someone takes pleasure and delight in telling lies. Fourthly, someone gives himself up to the indulgence in and enjoyment of the pleasures of the five senses. These are the four kinds of life devoted to

pleasure which are low, vulgar,...not leading to disenchantment,...to enlightenment, to Nibbāna.

24. 'And it may be that those of other sects might say: "Are the followers of the Sakyan given to these four forms of pleasure-seeking?" They should be told: "No!" for they would not be speaking correctly about you, they would be slandering you with false and untrue statements.

'There are, Cunda, these four kinds of life devoted to pleasure which are entirely conducive[928] to disenchantment, to dispassion, to cessation, to tranquillity, to realisation, to enlightenment, to Nibbāna. What are they? Firstly, a monk, detached from all sense-desires,[929] detached from unwholesome mental states, enters and remains in the first jhāna, which is with thinking and pondering, born of detachment, filled with delight and happiness. And with the subsiding of thinking and pondering, by gaining inner tranquillity and oneness of mind, he enters and remains in the second jhāna, which is without thinking and pondering, born of concentration, filled with delight and happiness. Again, with the fading of delight, remaining imperturbable, mindful and clearly aware, he experiences in himself that joy of which the Noble Ones say: "Happy is he who dwells with equanimity and mindfulness", he enters and remains in the third jhāna. Again, having given up pleasure [132] and pain, and with the disappearance of former gladness and sadness, he enters and remains in the fourth jhāna, which is beyond pleasure and pain, and purified by equanimity and mindfulness.

'These are the four kinds of life devoted to pleasure which are entirely conducive to disenchantment, to dispassion, to cessation, to tranquillity, to realisation, to enlightenment, to Nibbāna. So if wanderers from other sects should say that the followers of the Sakyan are addicted to these four forms of pleasure-seeking, they should be told: "Yes", for they would be speaking correctly about you, they would not be slandering you with false or untrue statements.

25. 'Then such wanderers might ask: "Well then, those who are given to these four forms of pleasure-seeking – how many fruits, how many benefits can they expect?" And you should reply: "They can expect four fruits, four benefits. What are

they? The first is when a monk by the destruction of three fetters has become a Stream-Winner, no more subject to rebirth in lower worlds, firmly established, destined for full enlightenment; the second is when a monk by the complete destruction of three fetters and the reduction of greed, hatred and delusion, has become a Once-Returner, and having returned once more to this world, will put an end to suffering; the third is when a monk, by the complete destruction of the five lower fetters, has been spontaneously reborn, and there will reach Nibbāna without returning from that world. The fourth is when a monk, by the destruction of the corruptions in this very life has, by his own knowledge and realisation, attained to Arahantship, to the deliverance of heart and through wisdom. Such are the four fruits and the four benefits that one given to these four forms of pleasure-seeking can expect."

26. 'Then such wanderers [133] might say: "The doctrines of the Sakyan's followers are not well-founded." They should be told: "Friend, the Lord who knows and sees has taught and proclaimed to his disciples principles which are not to be transgressed as long as life shall last. Just like a locking-post[930] or an iron post which is deep-based, well-planted and unshakeable, immovable are these doctrines he has taught. And any monk who is an Arahant, whose corruptions are destroyed, who has lived the life, done what was to be done, laid down the burden, gained the true goal, who has completely destroyed the fetter of becoming, and is liberated by supreme insight, is incapable of doing nine things: (1) He is incapable of deliberately taking the life of a living being; (2) he is incapable of taking what is not given so as to constitute theft; (3) he is incapable of sexual intercourse; (4) he is incapable of telling a deliberate lie; (5) he is incapable of storing up goods for sensual indulgence as he did formerly in the household life; (6) he is incapable of acting wrongly through attachment; (7) he is incapable of acting wrongly through hatred; (8) he is incapable of acting wrongly through folly; (9) he is incapable of acting wrongly through fear. These are the nine things which an Arahant, whose corruptions are destroyed, cannot do..." [134]

27. 'Or such wanderers might say: "As regards past times,

the ascetic Gotama displays boundless knowledge and insight, but not about the future, as to what it will be and how it will be." That would be to suppose that knowledge and insight about one thing are to be produced by knowledge and insight about something else, as fools imagine. As regards the past, the Tathāgata has knowledge of past lives. He can remember as far back as he wishes. As for the future, this knowledge, born of enlightenment, arises in him: "This is the last birth, there will be no more becoming."

28. 'If "the past" refers to what is not factual, to fables,[931] to what is not of advantage, the Tathāgata makes no reply. If it refers to what is factual, not fabulous, but which is not of advantage, the Tathāgata makes no reply. But if "the past" refers to what is factual, not fabulous, and which is of advantage, then the Tathāgata knows the right time to reply. The same applies to the future and the present. [135] Therefore, Cunda, the Tathāgata is called the one who declares the time, the fact, the advantage, the Dhamma and the discipline. That is why he is called *Tathāgata*.[932]

29. 'Cunda, whatever in this world with its devas and māras and Brahmās, with its ascetics and Brahmins, its princes and people, is seen by people, heard, sensed,[933] cognised, whatever was ever achieved, sought after or mentally pondered upon – all that has been fully understood by the Tathāgata. That is why he is called *Tathāgata*. Between the night in which the Tathāgata gains supreme enlightenment, Cunda, and the night in which he attains the Nibbāna-element without remainder,[934] whatever he proclaims, says or explains is so and not otherwise. That is why he is called *Tathāgata*. And of this world with its devas and māras and Brahmās, with its ascetics and Brahmins, its princes and people, the Tathāgata is the unvanquished conqueror, the seer and ruler of all. That is why he is called *Tathāgata*.

30. 'Or such wanderers might say: "Does the Tathāgata exist after death?"[935] "Is that true, and any other view foolish?" They should be told: "Friend, this has not been revealed by the [136] Lord." . . . "Does the Tathāgata not exist after death?" . . . "Does he both exist and not exist after death?" . . . "Does he neither

exist nor not exist after death?" They should be told: "Friend, this has not been revealed by the Lord."

31. 'Then they may say: "Why has the ascetic Gotama not revealed this?" They should be told: "Friend, this is not conducive to welfare or to the Dhamma, or to the higher holy life, or to disenchantment, dispassion, cessation, tranquillity, realisation, enlightenment, Nibbāna. That is why the Lord has not revealed it."

32. 'Or they may say: "Well, friend, what *has* the ascetic Gotama revealed?" They should be told: "'This is suffering' has been declared by the Lord; 'This is the arising of suffering'...'This is the cessation of suffering'...'This is the path leading to the cessation of suffering' has been declared by the Lord." [137]

33. 'Then they may say: "Why has this been declared by the ascetic Gotama?" They should be told: "Friend, this is conducive to welfare, to Dhamma, to the higher holy life, to perfect disenchantment,[936] to dispassion, to cessation, to tranquillity, to realisation, to enlightenment, to Nibbāna. That is why the Lord has revealed it."

34. 'Cunda, those bases of speculation about the beginnings of things which I have explained to you as they should be explained, should I now explain to you as they should not be explained?[937] And likewise about the future? What are the speculations about the past...? There are ascetics and Brahmins who say and believe: "The self and the world are eternal. This is true and any other view is erroneous." "The self and the world are not eternal."..."The self and the world are both eternal and not eternal."..."The self and the world are neither eternal nor not eternal."..."The self and the world are self-created."..."They are created by another."..."They are both self-created and created by another."...[138] "They are neither self-created nor created by another, but have arisen by chance." And similarly with regard to pleasure and pain.

35.–36. 'Now, Cunda, I go to those ascetics and Brahmins who hold any of these views and if, being asked, they confirm that they do hold such views, I do not admit their claims. Why not? Because, Cunda, different beings hold different opinions on such matters. Nor do I consider such theories equal to my own, still less superior. I am their superior in regard to the higher exposition. [139] As for those bases of speculation about the beginning of things which I have explained to you as they should be explained, why should I now explain them to you as they should not be explained?

37. 'And what about those speculators about the future? There are some ascetics and Brahmins who say: "The self after death is material and healthy"; "...immaterial"; "...both"; "...neither"; [140] "The self is conscious after death"; "...unconscious"; "...both"; "...neither"; "The self perishes, is destroyed, ceases to be after death. This is true and any other view is erroneous."

38.–39. 'Now, Cunda, I go to those ascetics and Brahmins who hold any of these views and if, being asked, they confirm that they do hold such views, I do not admit their claims. Why not? Because, Cunda, different beings hold different opinions on such matters. Nor do I consider such theories equal to my own, still less superior. I am their superior in regard to the higher exposition. As for those bases of speculation about the future which I have explained to you as [141] they should be explained, why should I now explain them to you as they should not be explained?

40. 'And, Cunda, for the destruction of all such views about the past and the future, for transcending them, I have taught and laid down the four foundations of mindfulness. What are the four? Here, Cunda, a monk dwells contemplating body as body, ardent, clearly aware and mindful, having put aside hankering and fretting for the world. He dwells contemplating feelings as feelings,...mind as mind...; he dwells contemplating mind-objects as mind-objects, ardent, clearly aware and mindful, having put aside hankering and fretting for the world. That is how, Cunda, for the destruction of such views about the past and the future, and for transcending them, I have taught and laid down the four foundations of mindfulness.'

41. During this time the Venerable Upavāna[938] was standing behind the Lord, fanning him. And he said: 'It is wonderful, Lord, it is marvellous! Lord, this exposition of Dhamma is

delightful – highly delightful! Lord, what is the name of this discourse?' 'Well, Upavāna, you can remember it as "The Delightful Discourse."'

Thus the Lord spoke, and the Venerable Upavāna rejoiced and was delighted with his words.

30 *Lakkhaṇa Sutta: The Marks of a Great Man*

[142] 1.1. THUS HAVE I HEARD.[939] Once the Lord was staying at Sāvatthi, in Jetavana, Anāthapiṇḍika's park. 'Monks!' he said, and the monks replied: 'Lord.' The Lord said: 'There are, monks, these thirty-two marks peculiar to a Great Man,[940] and for that Great Man who possesses them, only two careers are open. If he lives the household life, he will become a ruler, a wheel-turning righteous monarch of the law, conqueror of the four quarters, who has established the security of his realm and is possessed of the seven treasures. These are: the Wheel Treasure, the Elephant Treasure, the Horse Treasure, the Jewel Treasure, the Woman Treasure, the Householder Treasure, and, as seventh, the Counsellor Treasure. He has more than a thousand sons who are heroes, of heroic stature, conquerors of the hostile army. He dwells having conquered this sea-girt land without stick or sword, by the law. But if he goes forth from the household life into homelessness, he will become an Arahant, a fully-enlightened Buddha, who has drawn back the veil from the world.

1.2. 'And what are these thirty-two marks? [143] (1) He has feet with level tread.[941] This is one of the marks of a Great Man. (2) On the soles of his feet are wheels with a thousand spokes, complete with felloe and hub. (3) He has projecting heels. (4) He has long fingers and toes.[942] (5) He has soft and tender hands and feet. (6) His hands and feet are net-like.[943] (7) He has high-raised ankles.[944] (8) His legs are like an antelope's. (9) Standing and without bending, he can touch and rub his knees with either hand. (10) His male organs are enclosed in a sheath. (11) His complexion is bright, the colour of gold. (12) His skin is delicate and so smooth that no dust can adhere to his body. [144] (13) His body-hairs are separate, one to each pore. (14) His body-hairs grow upwards, each one bluish-black like collyrium,[945] curling in rings to the right. (15) His body is divinely straight.[946] (16) He has the seven convex surfaces.[947] (17) The front part of his body is like a lion's. (18) There is no hollow between his shoulders. (19) He is proportioned like a banyan-tree: the height of his body is the same as the span of his outstretched arms, and conversely. (20) His bust is evenly rounded. (21) He has a perfect sense of taste.[948] (22) He has jaws like a lion's. (23) He has forty teeth. (24) His teeth are even. (25) There are no spaces between his teeth. (26) His canine teeth are very bright. (27) His tongue is very long. (28) He has a Brahmā-like voice, like that of the *karavīka*-bird. (29) His eyes are deep blue. (30) He has eyelashes like a cow's. (31) The hair[949] between his eyes is white and soft like cotton-down. [145] (32) His head is like a royal turban.[950] This is one of the marks of a Great Man.

1.3. 'These, monks, are the thirty-two marks peculiar to a Great Man, and for that Great Man who possesses them only two courses are open...And sages of other communions[951] know these thirty-two marks, but they do not know the karmic reasons for the gaining of them.

1.4. 'Monks, in whatever former life, former existence or dwelling-place the Tathāgata, being born a human being, undertook mighty deeds to good purpose, unwavering in good conduct of body, speech and thought, in generosity, self-discipline, observance of the fast-day, in honouring parents, ascetics and Brahmins and the head of the clan, and in other highly meritorious [146] acts; by performing that kamma, heaping it up, lavishly and abundantly, at the breaking-up of the body after death he was reborn in a happy state, in a heavenly world, where he was endowed beyond other devas in ten respects: in length of heavenly life, beauty, happiness, splendour, influence, and in heavenly sights, sounds, smells, tastes and contacts. Falling away from there and coming to be reborn here on earth, he acquired this mark of the Great Man: (1) feet with level tread, so that he places his foot evenly on the ground, lifts it evenly, and touches the ground evenly with the entire sole.

1.5. 'Being endowed with this mark, if he keeps to the household life, he will become a wheel-turning monarch...Conquering without stick or sword, but by justice, he rules over this earth as far as its ocean-boundaries, a land open, uninfested by brigands, free from jungle, powerful, prosperous, happy and free from perils. As a ruler, how does he benefit? He cannot be impeded by any human foe with ill-intent. That is his benefit as a ruler. And if he goes forth into homelessness, he will become a fully-enlightened Buddha...As such, how does he benefit? He cannot be impeded by any enemy or adversary from within or without, from greed, hatred or delusion, nor by any ascetic [147] or Brahmin, any deva, māra or Brahmā, or any being in the world. That is his benefit as a Buddha.' This was what the Lord declared.

1.6. About this it was said:

'Truthful, righteous, tamed and stilled,
Pure and virtuous, keeping fasts,
Generous, harming none, at peace
He undertook this mighty task,
And at his end to heaven went,
To dwell in joy and happiness.
Returned from there to earth, his feet
With level tread did touch the ground.
Assembled augurs then declared:
"For him who level treads the ground,
No obstacles can bar his path,
If he leads the household life,
Or if he leaves the world behind:
This the mark does clearly show.
If a layman, no adversary,
No foe can stand before him.
No human power exists that can
Deprive him of his kamma's fruit.
Or if the homeless life's his choice:
On renunciation bent, and clear
Of vision – chief of men he'll be,
Peerless, never more reborn:
This the law shall be for him."'

1.7. 'Monks, in whatever former life...the Tathāgata, being born a human being, [148] lived for the happiness of the many, as a dispeller of fright and terror, provider of lawful protection and shelter, and supplying all necessities, by performing that kamma,...was reborn in a happy state, a heavenly world... Falling away from there and coming to be reborn here on earth, he acquired this mark of the Great Man: (2) on the soles of his feet are wheels of a thousand spokes, complete with felloe and hub.

1.8. 'Being endowed with this mark, if he keeps to the household life, he will become a wheel-turning monarch...As a ruler, how does he benefit? He has a great retinue: he is surrounded by Brahmin householders, citizens and villagers, treasurers, guards, doorkeepers, ministers, tributary kings, tenants-in-chief, and pages. That is his benefit as a ruler. And if he goes forth into homelessness, he will become a fully-enlightened Buddha...As such, how does he benefit? He has a large retinue: he is surrounded by monks, nuns, male and female lay-followers, devas and humans, asuras,[952] nāgas and gandhabbas.[953] That is his benefit as a Buddha.' This was what the Lord declared.

1.9. About this it was said:

'In times gone by, in former births
As man, to many doing good,
Dispelling fright and panic fear,
Eager to guard and give defence,
He undertook this mighty task, [149]
And at his end to heaven went,
To dwell in joy and happiness.
Returned from there to earth, his feet
Are found to bear the mark of wheels,
Each a thousand-spoked, complete.
Assembled augurs then declared,
Seeing these many marks of merit:
"Great will be his following,
All his foes he will subdue.
This is the wheel-marks clearly show.
If he does not renounce the world,
He'll turn the Wheel, and rule the earth.

The nobles will his vassals be,
All in attendance on his power.
But if the homeless life's his choice:
On renunciation bent, and clear
Of vision – men and devas
asuras, sakkas, rakkhasas,[954]
gandhabbas, nāgas, garuḍas,
Four-foot beasts will serve him too,
Unrivalled, by devas and by men
Alike revered in all his glory."'

1.10. 'Monks, in whatever former life...the Tathāgata, being born a human being, rejecting the taking of life and abstaining from it, and laying aside stick and sword, dwelt, kind and compassionate, having friendship and sympathy for all living beings, by performing that kamma,...was reborn in a happy state...Falling away from there and coming to be reborn on earth, he acquired these three marks of the Great [150] Man: (3) projecting heels, (4) long fingers and toes, and (15) a divinely straight body.

1.11. 'Being endowed with these marks, if he keeps to the household life,...as a ruler, how does he benefit? He is long-lived, long-enduring, attaining a great age, and during that time no human foe can possibly take his life...As a Buddha, how does he benefit? He is long-lived...; no foe, whether an ascetic or Brahmin, a deva, māra or Brahmā, or anyone in the world can possibly take his life. That is his benefit as a Buddha.' This was what the Lord declared.

1.12. About this it was said:

'Knowing well their dread of death,
Beings he forbore to kill.
This goodness earnt him heavenly birth,
Where he rejoiced in merit's fruit.
Returning thence to earth he bore
On his person these three marks:
His heels are full and very long,
Brahmā like he's straight of form,
Fair to see, and shapely-limbed,
His fingers tender, soft and long. [151]
By these three marks of excellence

It's known the youth will be long-lived.
"Long he'll live in household life
Longer still as homeless one
Practising the noble powers:
So the three marks indicate."'

1.13. 'Monks, in whatever former life...the Tathāgata became a giver of fine food, delicious and tasty, hard and soft, and of drinks, by performing that kamma,...he was reborn in a heavenly world...Falling away from there and being reborn here on earth, he acquired this mark of the Great Man: (16) the seven convex surfaces, on both hands, both feet, both shoulders and his trunk.

1.14 'Being endowed with this mark,...as a ruler, how does he benefit? He receives fine food and drinks...As a Buddha, likewise.' [152] This is what the Lord said.

1.15. About this it was said:

'Dispenser of delicious foods
And finest-tasting drinks he was.
This goodness brought him happy birth,
And long he dwelt in Nandana.[955]
To earth returned, the seven signs
On gently-swelling limbs he bore.
Assembled augurs then declared,
Fine food and drink he would enjoy:
Not merely in the household life –
For though he should renounce the world
And cut the bonds of worldly living,
Delicious food he'd still receive!'

1.16. 'Monks, in whatever former life...the Tathāgata made himself beloved through the four bases of sympathy:[956] generosity, pleasing speech, beneficial conduct and impartiality, ...on returning to this earth he acquired these two [153] marks of the Great Man: (5) soft and tender hands and feet, and (6) net-like hands and feet.

1.17. 'Being endowed with these two marks,...as a ruler, how does he benefit? All his retinue are well-disposed to him:

Brahmin householders, citizens and villagers, treasurers, guards, doorkeepers, . . . pages. As a Buddha, how does he benefit? All his followers are well-disposed to him: monks, nuns, male and female lay-folowers, devas and humans, asuras, nāgas, gandhabbas. That is his benefit as a Buddha.' This is what the Lord said.

1.18. About this it was said:

'Through giving and through helpful acts,
Pleasing speech and evenness
Of mind, of benefit to all,
He at death to heaven went.
When he thence returned to earth,
His hands and feet were soft and tender,
His toes and fingers netwise spread.
Very fair he was to see:
Thus the infant was endowed. [154]
"He'll be ruler of the people,
Surrounded by a faithful flock.
Fair of speech, to good deeds given,
In conduct virtuous and wise.
But if the joys of sense he spurns,
A Conqueror, he will teach the path,
And, delighted by his words,
All those who hear will follow him
In Dhamma's great and lesser ways!"'

1.19. 'Monks, in whatever former life . . . the Tathāgata became a speaker to the people about their welfare, about Dhamma, explaining this to people and being a bearer of welfare and happiness to beings, a dispenser of Dhamma, . . . on returning to this earth he acquired these two marks of the Great Man: (7) high-raised ankles, and (14) upward-growing body-hairs.

1.20. 'Being endowed with these marks, . . . as a ruler, how does he benefit? He becomes the chief, foremost, highest, supreme among the unrenounced[957] . . . As a Buddha, he becomes the chief, foremost, highest, supreme among all beings. That is his benefit as a Buddha.' This was what the Lord declared.

1.21. About this it was said: [155]

'One time he spoke of all that's good,
Preaching loud to all mankind,
Bringing blessings to all beings,
Liberal dispenser of the law.
For such conduct and such deeds,
Heavenly birth was his reward.
Here returned, two marks were his,
Marks of happiness supreme:
Upward-growing body-hairs,
Ankles high above the foot,
Built up beneath the flesh and skin,
Well-formed above, and beautiful.
"If he leads the household life,
The greatest riches will be his,
No greater man will be found:
As Jambudīpa's Lord he'll rule. [156]
If, supremely strong, he leaves the world,
He will be the chief of beings,
No man greater will be found:
As Lord of all the world he'll rule."'

1.22. 'Monks, in whatever former life...the Tathāgata became a skilled exponent of a craft, a science, a way of conduct or action, thinking: "What can I learn quickly and acquire, quickly practise, without undue weariness?"...on returning to earth, he acquires this mark of the Great Man: (8) legs like an antelope's.

1.23. 'Being endowed with this mark,...as a ruler he quickly acquires whatever things befit a ruler, the things that pertain to a ruler, delight him and are appropriate to him. As a Buddha, likewise.' This was what the Lord declared.

1.24. About that it was said:

'Arts and sciences, ways and deeds:
"Let me learn with ease", he says. [157]
Skills that harm no living thing
Fast he learnt, with little toil.
From such deeds, skilled and sweet,

Graceful and fair his limbs will be,
While fairly set in spiral curves
From tender skin the hairs stand up.
Antelope-legged is such a man:
Wealth, they say, will soon be his.
"Each single hairlet brings him luck,
If he maintains the household life.
But should he choose to leave the world
On renunciation set,
Clear-eyed, all things he'll quickly find
Befitting such a lofty course."'

1.25. 'Monks, in whatever former life...the Tathāgata approached an ascetic or Brahmin and asked: "Sir, what is the good, what is the bad? What is blameworthy, what is not? What course is to be followed, what is not? What, if I do it, will be to my lasting sorrow and harm, what to my lasting happiness?"[958]...on returning to this earth, he acquired this mark of the Great Man: [158] (12) his skin is so delicate and smooth that no dust can adhere to his body.

1.26. 'Being endowed with this mark,...as a ruler he will be very wise, and among the unrenounced there will be none equal or superior to him in wisdom...As a Buddha he will have great wisdom, extensive wisdom, joyous wisdom, swift wisdom, penetrative wisdom, discerning wisdom,[959] and among all beings there will be none equal to him or superior to him in wisdom.' This was what the Lord declared.

1.27. About this it was said:

'In former days, in former births,
Eager to know, a questioner,
He waited on the homeless ones:
Keen to learn the truth, he would
Heed their words about life's goal.
The fruit of this, when born again
As man, his skin was soft and tender.
Assembled augurs thus declared:
"Subtle meanings he'll discern.
If he does not leave the world,
He'll be a wheel-revolving king

Wise to know all subtleties,
Equalled or surpassed by none. [159]
But should he choose to leave the world
On renunciation set,
Highest wisdom will be his,
Enlightenment supreme and vast."'

1.28. 'Monks, in whatever former life...the Tathāgata lived without anger, perfectly unruffled, and even after many words had been uttered was not abusive, or agitated, or wrathful, or aggressive, displaying neither anger nor hatred nor resentment, but was in the habit of giving away fine, soft rugs, cloaks, fine linen, cotton, silk and woollen stuffs,...on returning to this earth, he acquired this mark of the Great Man: (11) a bright complexion, the colour of gold.

1.29. 'Being endowed with this mark,...as a ruler he will receive such fine stuffs,...as a Buddha, likewise.' This was what the Lord declared.

1.30. About this it was said:

'Established in goodwill, he gave
Gifts of clothing, soft and fine. [160]
In former lives he thus dispensed
As the rain-god pours down showers.
This goodness brought him heavenly birth.
Where he rejoiced in merit's fruit.
That time past, like fine-wrought gold
His body is, more fair than all
The gods he seems, great Indra's like.
'If he lives the household life,
He'll regulate this wicked world,
And, for what he's done, receive
Clothes of finest quality,
Rugs and coverlets of the best.
And should he choose to leave the world,
Such things likewise he'll receive:
Virtue's fruit can not be lost."'

1.31. 'Monks, in whatever former life...the Tathāgata reunited those long-lost with relatives, friends and companions who had missed them, reunited mother with child and child with mother, father [161] with child and child with father, brother with brother, brother with sister and sister with brother, making them one again with great rejoicing,...on returning to earth he acquired this mark of the Great Man: (10) his male organs are enclosed in a sheath.

1.32. 'Being endowed with this mark,...as a ruler he will have numerous sons, more than a thousand sons, powerfully built heroes, crushers of the enemy host. As a Buddha, likewise.' This was what the Lord declared.

1.33. About this it was said:

'In former days, in former births,
Long-lost friends and relatives,
Companions too, he brought together,
Thus uniting them in joy.
This good deed brought heavenly birth,
Bliss and joy were his reward.
When he thence returned to earth,
Sheath-enclosed his organs were. [162]
"Numerous children such will have,
More than a thousand sons are his,
Hero-champions, conquerors,
And filial too, the layman's joy.
But if he leaves the world, still more
With children he will be endowed:
Those who depend upon his word.
And so, renounced or not, this sign
Such benefits as this portends."'

[*End of first recitation-section*]

2.1. 'Monks, in whatever former life...the Tathāgata, considering the welfare of people, knew the nature of each, knew each one himself, and knew how each one differed: "This one deserves such-and-such, that one deserves so-and-so", so he distinguished them,...on returning to earth he acquired these two marks of the Great Man: (19) he is proportioned like a banyan-tree, and (9) standing, without bending, he can touch and rub his knees with both hands.

2.2. 'Being endowed with these marks,...as a ruler [163] he will be rich, of great wealth and resources, having a full treasury of gold and silver, all sorts of goods, and his granary will be full of corn. As a Buddha he will be wealthy and rich, and these will be his treasures: faith, morality, moral shame,[960] moral dread,[961] learning, renunciation[962] and wisdom.' This was what the Lord declared:

2.3. About this it was said:

'Weighing in the balance, noting,
Seeking people's benefit,
Seeing: "This one that deserves,
And that one this", he judged them.
Now he can unbending stand
And touch his knees with both his hands,
And his tree-like girth and height
Is the fruit of virtuous deeds.
Those who read the marks and signs,
Experts in such lore declare:
"Things that suit the household life
As a child he'll get in plenty, [164]
Much worldly wealth as this world's lord,
As befits a layman, shall be his.
But should he worldly wealth renounce,
He'll gain the wealth that's unsurpassed."'

2.4. 'Monks, in whatever former life the Tathāgata...desired the welfare of the many, their advantage, comfort, freedom from bondage, thinking how they might increase in faith, morality, learning, renunciation, in Dhamma, in wisdom, in wealth and possessions, in bipeds and quadrupeds, in wives and children, in servants, workers and helpers, in relatives, friends and acquaintances,...on returning to earth he acquired these three marks of the Great Man: (17) the front part of his body is like a lion's, (18) there is no hollow between his shoulders, and (20) his bust is evenly rounded.

2.5. 'Being endowed with these marks,...as a ruler [165] he cannot lose anything: wealth and possessions, bipeds and quadrupeds, wives and children losing nothing, he will succeed in all things. As a Buddha he cannot lose anything: faith, morality, learning, renunciation or wisdom – losing nothing, he will succeed in all things.' This was what the Lord declared.

2.6. About this it was said:

'Faith, morality, learning, wisdom,
Restraint and justice, much good else,
Wealth, possessions, wives and sons,
Flocks, kin, friends, colleagues,
Strength, good looks and happiness:
These things he wished for others
That they might keep and never lose.
"So, lion-fronted, he was born,
Not hollow-backed, and round before.
Through past good kamma well stored up,
With such birth-marks spared all loss,
In household life he's rich in goods,
In wife and sons and quadrupeds,
Or if renounced, possessing naught,
Supreme enlightenment is his,
Where no failure enters in."' [166]

2.7. 'Monks, in whatever former life the Tathāgata...was one who avoided harming beings by hand, by stones, stick or sword,...on returning to earth he acquired this mark of the Great Man: (21) he has a perfect sense of taste. Whatever he touches with the tip of his tongue he tastes in his throat, and the taste is dispersed everywhere.

2.8. 'Being endowed with this mark,...as a ruler he will suffer little distress or sickness, his digestion will be good, being neither too cold nor too hot.[963] As a Buddha likewise, he is also equable and tolerant of exertion.' This was what the Lord declared.

2.9. About this it was said:

'Harming none by hand, stick, stone,
Causing death to none by sword,
Harmless, threatening none with bonds,

With happy birth he gained the fruit
Of these good deeds, and then reborn, [167]
Erect his taste-buds, and well-set.[964]
Those who know the marks declare:
"Great happiness will be his lot
As layman or as wanderer:
That's the meaning of this sign."'

2.10. 'Monks, in whatever former life the Tathāgata . . . was accustomed to look at people not askance, obliquely or furtively,[965] but directly, openly and straight-forwardly, and with a kindly glance, . . . on returning to earth he acquired these two marks of the Great Man: (29) deep blue eyes, and (30) eyelashes like a cow's.

2.11. 'Being endowed with these marks, . . . as a ruler, he will be looked upon with love by the common people; he will be popular and loved by Brahmin householders [168] citizens and villagers, treaturers, guards, doorkeepers, . . . pages. As a Buddha, he will be popular with and loved by monks, nuns, male and female lay-followers, devas and humans, asuras, nāgas and gandhabbas.' This was what the Lord declared.

2.12. About this it was said:

'Not looking askance, obliquely, or
Turning aside his glance, he looks
Direct and openly at folk
With candour and with kindly eye.
In happy place reborn, he there
Enjoys the fruits of his good deeds.
Reborn here, his lashes are
Like a cow's; his eyes are blue.
Those who know such things declare
(Interpreting the marks with skill),
"A child with such fine eyes will be
One who's looked upon with joy.
If a layman, thus he'll be
Pleasing to the sight of all. [169]
If ascetic he becomes,
Then loved as healer of folk's woes."'

2.13. 'Monks, in whatever former life the Tathāgata...became the foremost in skilled behaviour, a leader in right action of body, speech and thought, in generosity, virtuous conduct, observance of fasts, in honouring father and mother, ascetics and Brahmins and the head of the clan, and in various other proper activities,...on returning to earth he acquired this mark of the Great Man: (32) a head like a royal turban.

2.14. 'Being endowed with this mark,...as a ruler he will receive the loyalty of Brahmin householders, citizens...As a Buddha he will receive the loyalty of monks, nuns...' This was what the Lord declared.

2.15. About this it was said:

'He led the way in conduct then,
Intent on living righteously.
Thus folk were loyal to him here,
And heavenly reward was his. [170]
And after that reward was done,
He reappeared with turbaned head.
Those who know the signs declared:
"He will be the first of men,
All will serve him in this life
Just as was the case before.
If a nobleman of wealth,
He'll gain the service of his folk,
But should he leave the world, this man
Of doctrine will a master be,
And all the folk will flock to hear
The teaching that he will proclaim."'

2.16. 'Monks, is whatever former life the Tathāgata,...rejecting false speech, put away lies and became a truth-speaker, wedded to the truth, reliable, consistent, not deceiving the world,...on returning to earth he acquired these two marks of the Great Man: (13) his body-hairs separate, one to each pore, and (31) the hair between his brows white and soft like cotton-down.

2.17. 'Being endowed with these marks,...as a ruler he will be obeyed by Brahmin householders...[171] As a Buddha he will be obeyed by monks...' This was what the Lord declared.

2.18. About this it was said:

'True to his promise in past births,
Sincere of speech, he shunned all lies.
Breaker of his word to none,
He pleased by truth and honesty.
White and bright and soft as down
The hair appeared between his brows,
And from one pore no two hairs grew,
But each one separate appeared.
Assembled augurs thus declared
(Having read the marks with skill):
"With such a mark between the brows,
And such hairs, he'll be obeyed
By all, and if a layman still,
They'll respect him for past deeds;
If renounced, possessionless,
As Buddha they will worship him."'

2.19. 'Monks, in whatever former life the Tathāgata,...rejecting slander, abstained from it, not repeating there what he had heard here to the detriment of these, or repeating what he had heard there to the detriment of those...[172] Thus he was a reconciler of those at variance and an encourager of those at one, rejoicing in peace, loving it, delighting in it, one who spoke up for peace (*as Sutta 1, verse 1.9*). On returning to earth he acquired these two marks of the Great Man: (23) forty teeth, and (25) no spaces between the teeth.

2.20. 'Being endowed with these marks,...as a ruler, his followers: Brahmin householders, citizens...will not be divided among themselves. Likewise as a Buddha, his followers: monks, nuns...will not be divided among themselves.' This was what the Lord declared.

2.21. About this it was said:

'He's no speaker of wicked words
That cause dissension or increase it,
Prolonging strife and bitterness,

Leading to good friendship's end.
What he spoke was all for peace,
And relinking severed bonds. [173]
His power he used to end all strife,
Harmony was his delight.
In happy realm reborn, he there
Enjoyed the fruits of his good deeds.
Returned to earth, his teeth grew close,
Forty of them, firmly set.
"If a nobleman of wealth,
Gentle will his subjects be;
If a recluse, free from taint,
Well set-up his flock will be."'[966]

2.22. 'Monks, in whatever former life the Tathāgata,...rejecting harsh speech, abstained from it, spoke what was blameless, pleasing to the ear, agreeable, reaching the heart, urbane, pleasing and attractive to the multitude,...on returning to earth he acquired these two marks of the Great Man: (27) his tongue was very long, and (28) he had a Brahmā-like voice, like the *karavīka*-bird.

2.23. 'Being endowed with these marks,...as a ruler he will have a persuasive[967] voice: all...Brahmin householders, citizens...will take his words to heart. As a Buddha, too, [174] he will have a persuasive voice: all...monks, nuns...will take his words to heart.' This was what the Lord declared.

2.24. About this it was said:

'He's no speaker of abuse,
Harsh and painful, hurting folk,
His voice is gentle, kind and sweet,
Appealing to the hearts of folk
And delightful to their ears.
In happy realm reborn, he there
Enjoyed the fruits of his good deeds.
Having tasted this reward,
With Brahmā-voice endowed, to earth
He returned, and long his tongue.
"And what he says will carry weight.
If layman, he will prosper much.

But if this man should leave the world, [175]
Folk will take his words to heart,
And set great store by all he says."'

2.25. 'Monks, in whatever former life the Tathāgata,...rejecting idle chatter, spoke at the right time, what was correct and to the point, of Dhamma and discipline, and what was bound up with profit,...on returning to earth he acquired this mark of the Great Man: (22) jaws like a lion's.

2.26. 'Being endowed with this mark,...as a ruler he cannot be overcome by any human foe or opponent. As a Buddha he cannot be overcome by any foe or hostile thing from within or without, by lust, hatred or delusion, by any ascetic or Brahmin, deva, māra, Brahmā or anything in the world.' This was what the Lord declared.

2.27. About this it was said:

'No idle talk or foolishness,
Fruit of scatterbrain was his.
Harmful things he put aside,
Speaking only all men's good. [176]
And so at death he went to heaven
To taste the fruit of deeds well done.
Returned to earth once more, his jaw
Resembled that of him that's lord
Of all twice-two-footed things.
"He will be a king unbeaten,
Lord of men, of mighty power,
Like the Lord of threefold heaven,[968]
Like the greatest of the gods.
gandhabbas, sakkas, asuras
Will strive in vain to cast him down.
As layman thus he'll be throughout
All the quarters of the world."'[969]

2.28. 'Monks, in whatever former life the Tathāgata,...rejecting wrong livelihood, lived by right livelihood, refraining from cheating with false weights and measures, from bribery and corruption, deception and insincerity, from wounding, killing, imprisoning, lighway robbery, and taking goods by force.[970] [177] On returning to earth he acquired these two marks of the Great Man: (24) even teeth, and (26) very bright canine teeth.

2.29. 'Being endowed with these marks, if he keeps to the household life he will be a wheel-turning monarch...As a ruler, his followers...Brahmin householders...will be pure.

2.30. 'But if he goes forth from the household life into homelessness,...as a Buddha, his followers...monks, nuns...will be pure.' This was what the Lord declared.

2.31. About this it was said:

'Wrongful living he gave up
And took a pure and righteous course. [178]
Harmful things he cast aside,
Working only for folk's good.
Heaven brings him sweet reward
For deeds he's done that earn the praise
Of those who're wise and skilled:
He shares in all delights and joys
Like the lord of threefold heaven.
Falling thence to human state,
As residue of virtue's fruit,
He gains evenness of teeth,
Purity and brightness too.
Assembled augurs thus declared
He'll be the wisest of mankind,
"And pure his followers will be,
Whose even teeth like birds' plumes shine.
As king his pure retainers will
Bow to his, their lord's, command. [179]
Not oppressed by force, they will
Strive for general weal and joy.
But if he dwells, a wanderer,
Free from evil, all lust quenched,
Drawing back the veil;[971] with pain
And weariness all gone, he'll see
This world and the next, and there
Lay-folk and renounced, who flock
To cast aside, as he has taught,

Those impure, evil things he blames.
Thus his followers are pure,
For he drives out from their hearts
Evil and corrupting states.'"

31 *Sigālaka Sutta: To Sigālaka*[972] Advice to Lay People

[180] 1. THUS HAVE I HEARD. Once the Lord was staying at Rājagaha, at the Squirrels' Feeding Place in the Bamboo Grove. And at that time Sigālaka the householder's son, having got up early and gone out of Rājagaha, was paying homage, with wet clothes and hair and with joined palms, to the different directions: to the east, the south, the west, the north, the nadir and the zenith.

2. And the Lord, having risen early and dressed, took his robe and bowl and went to Rājagaha for alms. And seeing Sigālaka paying homage to the different directions, he said: 'Householder's son, why have you got up early to [181] pay homage to the different directions?' 'Lord, my father, when he was dying, told me to do so. And so, Lord, out of respect for my father's words, which I revere, honour and hold sacred, I have got up thus early to pay homage in this way to the six directions.' 'But, householder's son, that is not the right way to pay homage to the six directions according to the Ariyan discipline.' 'Well, Lord, how should one pay homage to the six directions according to the Ariyan discipline? It would be good if the Blessed Lord were to teach me the proper way to pay homage to the six directions according to the Ariyan discipline.' 'Then listen carefully, pay attention, and I will speak.' 'Yes, Lord', said Sigālaka, and the Lord said:

3. 'Young householder, it is by abandoning the four defilements of action,[973] by not doing evil from the four causes, by not following the six ways of wasting one's substance[974] – through avoiding these fourteen evil ways – that the Ariyan disciple covers the six directions, and by such practice becomes a conqueror of both worlds, so that all will go well with

him in this world and the next, and at the breaking-up of the body after death he will go to a good destiny, a heavenly world.

'What are the four defilements of action that are abandoned? Taking life is one, taking what is not given is one, sexual misconduct is one, lying speech is one. These are the four defilements of action that he abandons.' Thus the Lord spoke.

4. And the Well-Farer having spoken, the Teacher added:[975] [182]

'Taking life and stealing, lying,
Adultery, the wise reprove.

5. 'What are the four causes of evil from which he refrains? Evil action springs from attachment, it springs from ill-will, it springs from folly, it springs from fear. If the Ariyan disciple does not act out of attachment, ill-will, folly or fear, he will not do evil from any one of the four causes.' Thus the Lord spoke.

6. And the Well-Farer having spoken, the Teacher added:

'Desire and hatred, fear and folly:
He who breaks the law through these,
Loses all his fair repute
Like the moon at waning-time.

Desire and hatred, fear and folly,
He who never yields to these
Grows in goodness and repute
Like the moon at waxing-time.

7. 'And which are the six ways of wasting one's substance that he does not follow? Addiction to strong drink and sloth-producing drugs is one way of wasting one's substance, haunting the streets at unfitting times is one, attending fairs is one, being addicted to gambling is one, keeping bad company is one, habitual idleness is one.

8. 'There are these six dangers attached to addiction to strong drink and sloth-producing drugs: present waste of money, increased quarrelling, liability to sickness, loss of good name, [183] indecent exposure of one's person, and weakening of the intellect.

9. 'There are these six dangers attached to haunting the streets at unfitting times: one is defenceless and without protection, and so are one's wife and children, and so is one's property; one is suspected of crimes,[976] and false reports are pinned on one, and one encounters all sorts of unpleasantness.

10. 'There are these six dangers attached to frequenting fairs: [One is always thinking:] "Where is there dancing? Where is there singing? Where are they playing music? Where are they reciting? Where is there hand-clapping?[977] Where are the drums?"

11. 'There are these six dangers attached to gambling: the winner makes enemies, the loser bewails his loss, one wastes one's present wealth, one's word is not trusted in the assembly, one is despised by one's friends and companions, one is not in demand for marriage,[978] because a gambler cannot afford to maintain a wife.

12. 'There are these six dangers attached to keeping bad company: any gambler, any glutton, any drunkard, any cheat, any trickster, any bully is his friend, his companion. [184]

13. 'There are these six dangers attached to idleness: Thinking: "It's too cold", one does not work; thinking: "It's too hot", one does not work; thinking: "It's too early", one does not work; thinking: "It's too late", one does not work; thinking: "I'm too hungry", one does not work; thinking: "I'm too full", one does not work.' Thus the Lord spoke.

14. And the Well-Farer having spoken, the Teacher added:

'Some are drinking-mates, and some
Profess their friendship to your face,
But those who are your friends in need,
They alone are friends indeed.

Sleeping late, adultery,
Picking quarrels, doing harm,
Evil friends and stinginess,
These six things destroy a man.

He who goes with wicked friends
And spends his time in wicked deeds,

In this world and the next as well
That man will come to suffer woe.

Dicing, wenching, drinking too,
Dancing, singing, daylight sleep,
Untimely prowling, evil friends
And stinginess destroy a man.

He plays with dice and drinks strong drink
And goes with others' well-loved wives. [185]
He takes the lower, baser course,
And fades away like waning moon.

The drunkard, broke and destitute,
Ever thirsting as he drinks,
Like stone in water sinks in debt,
Soon bereft of all his kin.

He who spends his days in sleep,
And makes the night his waking-time,
Ever drunk and lecherous,
Cannot keep a decent home.

"Too cold! Too hot! Too late!" they cry,
Thus pushing all their work aside,
Till every chance they might have had
Of doing good has slipped away.

But he who reckons cold and heat
As less than straws, and like a man
Undertakes the task in hand,
His joy will never grow the less.[979]

15. 'Householder's son, there are these four types who can be seen as foes in friendly guise: the man who is all take is one, the great talker is one, the flatterer is one, and the fellow-spendthrift is one.

16. 'The man who is all take can be seen to be a false friend for four reasons: [186] he takes everything, he wants a lot for very little, what he must do he does out of fear, and he seeks his own ends.

17. 'The great talker can be seen to be a false friend for four

reasons: he talks of favours in the past, and in the future, he mouths empty phrases of goodwill, and when something needs to be done in the present, he pleads inability owing to some disaster.[980]

18. 'The flatterer can be seen to be a false friend for four reasons: he assents to bad actions, he dissents from good actions, he praises you to your face, and he disparages you behind your back.

19. 'The fellow-spendthrift can be seen to be a false friend for four reasons: he is a companion when you indulge in strong drink, when you haunt the streets at unfitting times, when you frequent fairs, and when you indulge in gambling.' Thus the Lord spoke.

20. And the Well-Farer having spoken, the Teacher added:

'The friend who seeks what he can get,
The friend who talks but empty words,
The friend who merely flatters you,
The friend who is a fellow-wastrel:
These four are really foes, not friends.
The wise man, recognising this,
Should hold himself aloof from them
As from some path of panic fear. [187]

21. 'Householder's son, there are these four types who can be seen to be loyal[981] friends: the friend who is a helper is one, the friend who is the same in happy and unhappy times is one, the friend who points out what is good for you is one, and the friend who is sympathetic is one.

22. 'The helpful friend can be seen to be a loyal friend in four ways: he looks after you when you are inattentive,[982] he looks after your possessions when you are inattentive, he is a refuge when you are afraid, and when some business is to be done he lets you have twice what you ask for.

23. 'The friend who is the same in happy and unhappy times can be seen to be a loyal friend in four ways: he tells you his secrets, he guards your secrets, he does not let you down in misfortune, he would even sacrifice his life for you.

24. 'The friend who points out what is good for you can be seen to be a loyal friend in four ways: he keeps you from

wrongdoing, he supports you in doing good, he informs you of what you did not know, and he points out the path to heaven.

25. 'The sympathetic friend can be seen to be a loyal friend in four ways: he does not rejoice at your misfortune, he rejoices at your good fortune, he stops others who speak against you, and he commends others who speak in praise of you.' Thus the Lord spoke.

26. And the Well-Farer having spoken thus, the Teacher added: [188]

'The friend who is a helper and
The friend in times both good and bad,
The friend who shows the way that's right,
The friend who's full of sympathy:
These four kinds of friends the wise
Should know at their true worth, and he
Should cherish them with care, just like
A mother with her dearest child.

The wise man trained and disciplined
Shines out like a beacon-fire.
He gathers wealth just as the bee
Gathers honey, and it grows
Like an ant-hill higher yet.
With wealth so gained the layman can
Devote it to his people's good.

He should divide his wealth in four
(This will most advantage bring).
One part he may enjoy at will,
Two parts he should put to work,
The fourth part he should set aside
As reserve in times of need.

27. 'And how, householder's son, does the Ariyan disciple protect the six directions? These six things are to be regarded as the six directions. The east denotes mother and father. [189] The south denotes teachers.[983] The west denotes wife and children. The north denotes friends and companions. The nadir denotes servants, workers and helpers. The zenith denotes ascetics and Brahmins.

28. 'There are five ways in which a son should minister to his mother and father as the eastern direction. [He should think:] "Having been supported by them, I will support them. I will perform their duties for them. I will keep up the family tradition. I will be worthy of my heritage. After my parents' deaths I will distribute gifts on their behalf."[984] And there are five ways in which the parents, so ministered to by their son as the eastern direction, will reciprocate: they will restrain him from evil, support him in doing good, teach him some skill, find him a suitable wife and, in due time, hand over his inheritance to him. In this way the eastern direction is covered, making it at peace and free from fear.

29. 'There are five ways in which pupils should minister to their teachers as the southern direction: by rising to greet them, by waiting on them, by being attentive, by serving them, by mastering the skills they teach. And there are five ways in which their teachers, thus ministered to by their pupils as the southern direction, will reciprocate: they will give thorough instruction, make sure they have grasped what they should have duly grasped, give them a thorough grounding in all skills, recommend them to their friends and colleagues, and provide them with security in all directions. [190] In this way the southern direction is covered, making it at peace and free from fear.

30. 'There are five ways in which a husband should minister to his wife as the western direction: by honouring her, by not disparaging her, by not being unfaithful to her, by giving authority to her, by providing her with adornments. And there are five ways in which a wife, thus ministered to by her husband as the western direction, will reciprocate: by properly organising her work, by being kind to the servants, by not being unfaithful, by protecting stores, and by being skilful and diligent in all she has to do. In this way the western direction is covered, making it at peace and free from fear.

31. 'There are five ways in which a man should minister to his friends and companions as the northern direction: by gifts, by kindly words, by looking after their welfare, by treating them like himself, and by keeping his word. And there are five ways in which friends and companions, thus ministered to by a man as the northern direction, will recipro-

cate: by looking after him when he is inattentive, by looking after his property when he is inattentive, by being a refuge when he is afraid, by not deserting him when he is in trouble, and by showing concern for his children. In this way the northern direction is covered, making it at peace and free from fear.

32. 'There are five ways in which a master[985] [191] should minister to his servants and workpeople as the nadir: by arranging their work according to their strength, by supplying them with food and wages, by looking after them when they are ill, by sharing special delicacies with them, and by letting them off work at the right time. And there are five ways in which servants and workpeople, thus ministered to by their master as the nadir, will reciprocate: they will get up before him, go to bed after him, take only what they are given, do their work properly, and be bearers of his praise and good repute. In this way the nadir is covered, making it at peace and free from fear.

33. 'There are five ways in which a man should minister to ascetics and Brahmins as the zenith: by kindness in bodily deed, speech and thought, by keeping open house for them, by supplying their bodily needs. And the ascetics and Brahmins, thus ministered to by him as the zenith, will reciprocate in six ways: they will restrain him from evil, encourage him to do good, be benevolently compassionate towards him, teach him what he has not heard, clarify what he has heard, and point out to him the way to heaven. In this way the zenith is covered, making it at peace and free from fear.' Thus the Lord spoke.

34. And the Well-Farer having spoken, the Teacher added:

'Mother, father are the east,
Teachers are the southward point, [192]
Wife and children are the west,
Friends and colleagues are the north.
Servants and workers are below,
Ascetics, Brahmins are above.
These directions all should be
Honoured by a clansman true.
He who's wise and disciplined,

Kindly and intelligent,
Humble, free from pride,
Such a one may honour gain.
Early rising, scorning sloth,
Unshaken by adversity,
Of faultless conduct, ready wit,
Such a one may honour gain.
Making friends, and keeping them,
Welcoming, no stingy host,
A guide, philosopher and friend,
Such a one may honour gain.
Giving gifts and kindly speech,
A life well-spent for others' good,
Even-handed in all things,
Impartial as each case demands:
These things make the world go round
Like the chariot's axle-pin.
If such things did not exist,
No mother from her son would get
Any honour and respect,
Nor father either, as their due.
But since these qualities are held
By the wise in high esteem, [193]
They are given prominence
And are rightly praised by all.'

35. At these words Sigālaka said to the Lord: 'Excellent, Reverend Gotama, excellent! It is as if someone were to set up what had been knocked down, or to point out the way to one who had got lost, or to bring an oil-lamp into a dark place, so that those with eyes could see what was there. Just so the Reverend Gotama has expounded the Dhamma in various ways, May the Reverend Gotama accept me as a lay-follower from this day forth as long as life shall last!'

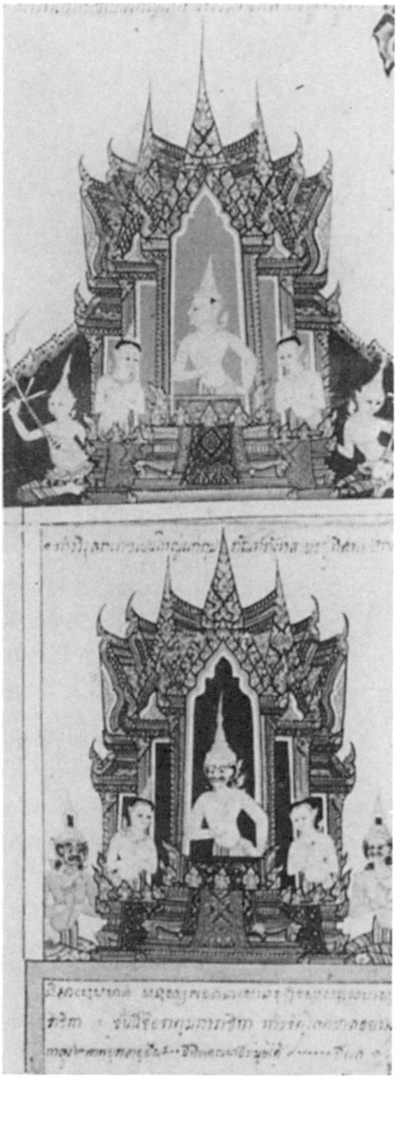

32 *Āṭānāṭiya Sutta: The Āṭānāṭā Protective Verses*

[194] 1. THUS HAVE I HEARD.[986] Once the Lord was staying at Rājagaha on Vultures' Peak. And the Four Great Kings,[987] with a great array of yakkhas, of gandhabbas, of kumbhaṇḍas and of nāgas,[988] having set up a guard, a defensive force, a watch over the four quarters,[989] as night was drawing to a close, went to see the Lord, lighting up the entire Vultures' Peak with their radiance, saluted him and sat down to one side. And some of the yakkhas saluted him and sat down to one side, some exchanged courtesies with him before sitting down, same saluted him with joined palms, some announced their name and clan, and some sat down in silence.[990]

2. Then sitting to one side, King Vessavaṇa[991] said to the Lord: 'Lord, there are some prominent yakkhas who have no faith in the Blessed Lord, and others who have faith; and likewise [195] there are yakkhas of middle and lower rank who have no faith in the Blessed Lord, and others who have faith. But, Lord, the majority of yakkhas have no faith in the Blessed Lord. Why is this? The Blessed Lord teaches a code of refraining from taking life, from taking what is not given, from sexual misconduct, from lying speech, and from strong drink and sloth-producing drugs. But the majority of the yakkhas do not refrain from these things, and to do so is distasteful and unpleasant to them. Now, Lord, there are disciples of the Blessed Lord who dwell in remote forest glades, where there is little noise or shouting, far from the madding crowd, hidden from people, suitable for retreat. And there are prominent yakkhas living there who have no faith in the word of the Blessed Lord. In order to give these folk confidence, may the Blessed Lord learn[992] the Āṭānāṭā protective verses, by means of which monks and nuns, male and female lay-followers may

dwell guarded, protected, unharmed and at their ease?' And the Lord consented by silence.

3. Then King Vessavaṇa, noting the Lord's consent, at once recited these Āṭānāṭā protective verses:

'Glory be to Vipassī,[993]
The splendid one of mighty vision.
Glory be to Sikhī too,
The compassionate to all.
Glory be to Vessabhū,
Bathed in pure asceticism.[994] [196]
To Kakusandha glory be,
Victor over Māra's host.
To Koṇāgamana glory too,
Brahmin fully perfect he.
Glory be to Kassapa,
Liberated every way,
Glory to Angīrasa,
To the Sakyas' radiant son,[995]
Teacher of the Dhamma he
That overcomes all suffering.
And they who from this world are freed,[996]
Seeing to the heart of things,
They who are so mild of speech,
Mighty and of wisdom too,
To him who helps both gods and men,
To Gotama they offer praise:
In wisdom trained, in conduct too,
Mighty and resourceful too.

4. 'The point from where the sun comes up,
Aditya's child, in mighty arc,
At whose arising shrouding night
Is dispelled and vanishes,
So that with the risen sun
There comes to be what folk call Day,
There too this moving watery mass,
The deep and mighty ocean swells,
This men know, and this they call
Ocean or The Swelling Sea. [197]
This quarter is the East, or First:[997]

That is how the people call it.
This quarter's guarded by a king,
Mighty in power and fame is he,
Lord of all the gandhabbas.
Dhataraṭṭha is his name,
Honoured by the gandhabbas.
Their songs and dances he enjoys.
He has many mighty sons,
Eighty, ten and one, they say,
And all with but a single name,
Called after Indra, lord of strength.
And when the Buddha greets their gaze,
Buddha, kinsman of the Sun,
From afar they offer homage
To the Lord of wisdom true:
"Hail, o man of noble race!
Hail to you, the first of men!
In kindness you have looked on us,
Who, though not human, honour you!
Often asked, do we revere
Gotama the Conqueror? –
We reply: 'We do revere
Gotama, great Conqueror,
In wisdom trained, in conduct too,
Buddha Gotama we hail!'"

5. 'Where they whom men call petas[998] dwell,
Abusive speakers, slanderers,
Murderous and greedy folk,
Thieves and cunning tricksters all, [198]
This quarter is the South, they say:
That is how the people call it.
This quarter's guarded by a king,
Mighty in power and fame is he,
Lord of all the kumbhaṇḍas,
And Virūḷhaka is his name.
Honoured by the kumbhaṇḍas,
Their songs and dances he enjoys...
(*continue as 4*).

6. 'The point at which the sun goes down,
Aditya's child, in mighty arc,
With whose setting day is done
And night, The Shrouder, as men say,
Comes again in daylight's place,
There too this moving watery mass,
The deep and mighty ocean swells,
This they know, and this men call
Ocean, or The Swelling Sea.
This quarter is the West, or Last:[999]
Such is how the people call it. [199]
This quarter's guarded by a king,
Mighty in power and fame is he,
Lord of all the nāga folk,
And Virūpakkha's his name.
Honoured by the nāga folk,
Their songs and dances he enjoys . . .
(*continue as 4*).

7. 'Where lovely Northern Kuru lies,
Under mighty Neru fair,
There men dwell, a happy race,[1000]
Possessionless, not owning wives.[1001]
They have no need to scatter seed,
They have no need to draw the plough:
Of itself the ripened crop
Presents itself for men to eat.
Free from powder and from husk,
Sweet of scent, the finest rice, [200]
Boiling on hot oven-stones,[1002]
Such the food that they enjoy.
The ox their single-seated mount,[1003]
Thus they ride about the land.
Using women as a mount,
Thus they ride about the land;[1004]
Using men to serve as mount,
Thus they ride about the land;
Using maidens as a mount,
Thus they ride about the land;

Using boys to serve as mount,
Thus they ride about the land.
And so, carried by such mounts,
All the region they traverse
In the service of their king.
Elephants they ride, and horses too,
Cars fit for gods they have as well.
Splendid palanquins are there
For the royal retinue.
Cities too they have, well-built,
Soaring up into the skies:
Āṭānāṭā, Kusināṭā,
Parakusināṭā,
Nāṭapuriya is theirs,
And Parakusitanāṭā. [201]
Kapīvanta's to the north,
Janogha, other cities too,
Navanavatiya, Ambara-
Ambaravatiya,[1005]
Āḷakamandā, city royal,
But where Kuvera dwells, their lord
Is called Visāṇā, whence the king
Bears the name Vessavaṇa.[1006]
Those who bear his missions are
Tatolā, Tattalā,
Tototalā, then
Tejasi, Tatojasi,
Sūra, Rājā, Ariṭṭha, Nemi.
There's the mighty water Dharaṇī,
Source of rain-clouds which pour down
When the rainy season comes.
Bhagalavati's there, the hall
That is the yakkhas' meeting-place,
Round it ever-fruiting trees
Full of many kinds of birds,
Where peacocks scream and herons cry,
And the cuckoo gently calls.
The *jīva*-bird who cries: "Live on!"[1007]
And he that sings: "Lift up your hearts!",[1008] [202]

The pheasant-cock, *kulīraka*,[1009]
The forest-crane, the rice-bird too,
And *mynah*-birds that mimic man,
And those whose name is "men on stilts".
And there for ever beauteous lies
Fair Kuvera's lotus-lake.
This quarter is the North, they say:
That is how the people call it.
This quarter's guarded by a king,
Mighty in power and fame is he,
Lord of all the yakkha folk,
And Kuvera is his name.
Honoured by the yakkha folk,
Their songs and dances he enjoys.
He has many mighty sons,
Eighty, ten and one, they say,
And all with but a single name,
Called after Indra, lord of strength.
And when the Buddha greets their gaze,
Buddha, kinsman of the Sun,
From afar they offer homage
To the Lord of wisdom true:
"Hail, o man of noble race!
Hail to you, the first of men!
In kindness you have looked on us,
Who, though not human, honour you!
Often asked, do we revere
Gotama the Conqueror? –
We reply: 'We do revere
Gotama, great Conqueror,
In wisdom trained, in conduct too,
Buddha Gotama we hail!'"' [203]

8. 'These, sir, are the Āṭānāṭā protective verses, by means of which monks and nuns, male and female lay-followers may dwell guarded, protected, unharmed and at ease. If any monk or nun, male or female lay-follower learns these verses well and has them off by heart, then if any non-human being, male or female yakkha or yakkha-offspring, or a chief attendant or

servant of the yakkhas, any male or female gandhabba,... kumbhaṇḍa,...nāga,...should approach that person with hostile intent while he or she is walking or starting to walk, standing or rising to stand, seated or sitting down, lying down or starting to lie down, that non-human being would not gain any honour or respect in village or town. Such a being would not gain a footing or a lodging in my royal city of Āḷakamandā, he would not be admitted to the yakkhas' assembly, nor would he be acceptable for taking or giving in marriage. And all the non-human beings, full of rage, would overwhelm him with abuse. Then they would bend down his head like an empty bowl, and they would split his skull into seven pieces.[1010]

9. 'There are, sir, some non-human beings who are fierce, wild and terrible. They heed neither the Great Kings, nor their officers, nor their attendants. They are said to be [204] in revolt against the Great Kings. Just as the bandit-chiefs whom the King of Magadha has overcome do not heed him, or his officers, or their attendants, so too do they behave. Now if any yakkha or yakkha-offspring,...gandhabba,...should approach any monk, nun, male or female lay-follower...with hostile intent, that person should alarm, call out and shout to those yakkhas, the great yakkhas, their commanders and commanders-in-chief, saying: "This yakkha has seized me, has hurt me, harmed me, injured me, and will not let me go!"

10. 'Which are the yakkhas, the great yakkhas, their commanders and commanders-in-chief? They are:

Inda, Soma, Varuṇa,
Bhāradvāja, Pajāpati,
Candana, Kāmaseṭṭha,
Kinnughaṇḍu and Nighaṇḍu,
Panāda, Opamañña,
Devasūta, Mātali,
Cittasena the gandhabba,
Naḷa, Rājā, Janesabha,
Sātāgira, Hemavata,
Puṇṇaka, Karatiya, Gula, [205]
Sīvaka, Mucalinda too,

Vessāmitta, Yugandhara,
Gopāla, Suppagedha too,
Hirī, Netti and Mandiya,
Pañcālacaṇḍa, Āḷavaka,
Pajunna, Sumana, Sumukha,
Dadimukha, Maṇi too,
Then Mānicara, Dīgha,
And, finally, Serissaka.[1011]

These are the yakkhas, great yakkhas, their commanders and commanders-in-chief who should be called upon in case of such an attack.

11. 'And these, sir, are the Āṭānāṭā protective verses by means of which monks and nuns, male and female lay-followers may dwell guarded, protected, unharmed and at ease. And now, sir, we must go: we have many duties, many things to do.' 'Do so, Kings, when you think fit.'

And the Four Great Kings stood up, saluted the Lord, passed by on his right side, and vanished. And the yakkhas stood up, and some saluted the Lord, passed by on his right, and vanished, some exchanged courtesies with the Lord, [206] some saluted him with joined palms, some announced their name and clan, some remained silent, and they all vanished.

12. And when the night was over, the Lord said to the monks: 'Monks, this night the Four Great Kings...came to see the Lord...(*repeat the whole of verses 1–11*).

13. 'Monks, you should learn these Āṭānāṭā protective verses, master them and remember them. They are for your benefit, and through them monks and nuns, male and female lay-followers may dwell guarded, protected, unharmed and at ease.'

Thus the Lord spoke. And the monks were delighted and rejoiced at his words.

33 *Sangīti Sutta: The Chanting Together*

[207] 1.1. THUS HAVE I HEARD. Once the Lord was touring in the Malla country with a large company of about five hundred monks. Arrived at Pāvā, the Mallas' capital, he stayed in the mango-grove of Cunda the smith.[1012]

1.2. Now at that time a new meeting-hall of the Mallas of Pāvā, called Ubbhaṭaka,[1013] had recently been built, and it had not yet been occupied by any ascetic or Brahmin, or indeed by any human being. Hearing that the Lord was staying in Cunda's mango-grove, the Mallas of Pāvā went to see him. Having saluted him, they sat down to one side and said: 'Lord, the Mallas of Pāvā have recently erected a new meeting-hall called Ubbhaṭaka, and it has not yet been occupied by any ascetic or Brahmin, or indeed by any human being. [208] May the Blessed Lord be the first to use it! Should he do so, that would be for the lasting good and happiness of the Mallas of Pāvā.' And the Lord consented by silence.

1.3. Noting his assent, the Mallas rose, saluted him, passed out to his right and went to the meeting-hall. They spread mats all round, arranged seats, put out a water-pot and an oil-lamp, and then, returning to the Lord, saluted him, sat down to one side and reported what they had done, saying: 'Whenever the Blessed Lord is ready.'

1.4. Then the Lord dressed, took his robe and bowl, and went to the meeting-hall with his monks. There he washed his feet, entered the hall and sat down against the central pillar, facing east. The monks, having washed their feet, entered the hall and sat down along the western wall facing east, [209] with the Lord in front of them. The Pāvā Mallas washed their feet, entered the hall, and sat down along the eastern wall facing west, with the Lord in front of them. Then the

Lord spoke to the Mallas on Dhamma till far into the night, instructing, inspiring, firing and delighting them. Then he dismissed them, saying: 'Vāseṭṭhas,[1014] the night has passed away.[1015] Now do as you think fit.' 'Very good, Lord', replied the Mallas. And they got up, saluted the Lord, and went out, passing him by on the right.

1.5. As soon as the Mallas had gone the Lord, surveying the monks sitting silently all about, said to the Venerable Sāriputta: 'The monks are free from sloth-and-torpor,[1016] Sāriputta. You think of a discourse on Dhamma to give to them. My back aches, I want to stretch it.' 'Very good, Lord', replied Sāriputta. Then the Lord, having folded his robe in four, lay down on his right side in the lion-posture,[1017] with one foot on the other, mindful and clearly aware, and bearing in mind the time to arise.

1.6. Now at that time the Nigaṇṭha Nātaputta [210] had just died at Pāvā. And at his death the Nigaṇṭhas were split into two parties, quarrelling and disputing...(*as Sutta 29, verse 1*). You would have thought they were bent on killing each other. Even the white-robed lay followers were disgusted when they saw that their doctrine and discipline was so ill-proclaimed,...having been proclaimed by one not fully-enlightened and now with its support gone, without an arbiter.

1.7. And the Venerable Sāriputta addressed the monks, referring to this situation, and said: 'So ill-proclaimed was their teaching and discipline, so unedifyingly displayed, and so ineffectual in calming the passions, having been proclaimed by one who was not fully enlightened. [211] But, friends, this Dhamma has been well proclaimed by the Lord, the fully-enlightened One. And so we should all recite it together[1018] without disagreement, so that this holy life may be enduring and established for a long time, thus to be for the welfare and happiness of the multitude, out of compassion for the world, for the benefit, welfare and happiness of devas and humans. And what is this Dhamma that has been well proclaimed by the Lord...?

'There is one thing that was perfectly proclaimed by the Lord who knows and sees, the fully-enlightened Buddha. So we should all recite together...for the benefit, welfare and happiness of devas and humans.

1.8. 'What is this one thing?[1019] (*eko dhammo*).

(1) 'All beings are maintained by nutriment (*āhāraṭṭhitikā*).

(2) 'All beings are maintained by conditions (*sankhāraṭṭhitikā*).'[1020] [212]

1.9. 'There are [sets of] two things that were perfectly proclaimed by the Lord...Which are they?

(1) 'Mind and body (*nāmañ ca rūpañ ca*).

(2) 'Ignorance and craving for existence (*avijjā ca bhavataṇhā ca*).

(3) 'Belief in [continued] existence and belief in non-existence (*bhava-diṭṭhi ca vibhava-diṭṭhi ca*).

(4) 'Lack of moral shame and lack of moral dread (*ahirikañ ca anottappañ ca*).

(5) 'Moral shame and moral dread (*hiri ca ottappañ ca*).

(6) 'Roughness and friendship with evil (*dovacassatā ca pāpamittatā ca*).

(7) 'Gentleness and friendship with good (*sovacassatā ca kalyāṇamittatā ca*).

(8) 'Skill in [knowing] offences and [the procedure for] rehabilitation from them (*āpatti-kusalatā ca āpatti-vuṭṭhāna-kusalatā ca*).

(9) 'Skill in entering and returning from [jhāna] (*samāpatti-kusalatā ca samāpatti-vuṭṭhāna-kusalatā ca*).[1021]

(10) 'Skill in [knowing] the [eighteen] elements[1022] and in paying attention to them (*dhātu-kusalatā ca manasikāra-kusalatā ca*).

(11) 'Skill in [knowing] the [twelve] sense-spheres (*āyatana-k.*) and dependent origination.

(12) 'Skill in [knowing] what are causes and what are not (*ṭhāna-k. ca aṭṭhāna-k.*) [213]

(13) 'Straightforwardness and modesty (*ajjavañ ca lajjavañ ca*).[1023]

(14) 'Patience and gentleness (*khanti ca soraccañ ca*).

(15) 'Gentle speech and politeness (*sākhalyañ ca paṭisanthāro ca*).

(16) 'Non-harming and purity (*avihiṁsā ca soceyyañ ca*).[1024]

(17) 'Lack of mindfulness[1025] and of clear awareness (*muṭṭhasaccañ ca asampajaññañ ca*).

(18) 'Mindfulness and clear awareness (*sati ca sampajaññañ ca*).

(19) 'Unguarded sense-doors and non-restraint in eating (*indriyesu aguttadvāratā ca bhojane amattaññutā ca*).

(20) 'Guarded sense-doors and restraint in eating (*...guttadvāratā...mattaññutā*).

(21) 'Powers of reflection[1026] and mental development (*paṭisankhāna-balañ ca bhāvanā-balañ ca*).

(22) 'Powers of mindfulness and concentration (*sati-balañ ca samādhi-balañ ca*).

(23) 'Calm and insight (*samatho ca vipassanā ca*).[1027]

(24) 'The sign of calm and grasping the sign (*samatha-nimittañ ca paggaha-nimittañ ca*).

(25) 'Exertion and non-distraction (*paggaho ca avikheppo ca*).

(26) 'Attainment of morality and [right] view (*sīla-sampadā ca diṭṭhi-sampadā ca*).

[214] (27) 'Failure of morality and view (*sīla-vipatti ca diṭṭhi-vipatti ca*).

(28) 'Purity of morality and view (*sīla-visuddhi ca diṭṭhi-visuddhi ca*).

(29) 'Purity of view and the effort to attain it (*diṭṭhi-visuddhi kho pana yathā diṭṭhissa ca padhānaṁ*).

(30) 'Being moved to a sense of urgency[1028] by what should move one, and the systematic effort of one so moved (*saṁvego ca saṁvejaniyesu ṭhānesu saṁviggassa ca yoniso padhānaṁ*).

(31) 'Not being content with wholesome acts and not shrinking from exertion (*asantutthitā ca kusalesu dhammesu appaṭivānitā ca padhānasmiṁ*).

(32) 'Knowledge and liberation (*vijjā ca vimutti ca*).

(33) 'Knowledge of the destruction [of the defilements] and of [their] non-recurrence (*khaye ñāṇaṁ anuppāde ñāṇaṁ*).

'These are the [sets of] two things that were perfectly proclaimed by the Lord...So we should all recite them together ...'

1.10. 'There are [sets of] three things...Which are they?

(1) 'Three unwholesome roots: of greed, hatred, delusion

(*lobho akusala-mūlaṁ, doso akusala-mūlaṁ, moho akusala-mūlaṁ*).

(2) 'Three wholesome roots: of non-greed, non-hatred non-delusion (*alobho* . . .).

(3) 'Three kinds of wrong conduct: in body, speech and thought (*kāya-duccaritaṁ, vacī-duccaritaṁ, mano-duccaritaṁ.*). [215]

(4) 'Three kinds of right conduct: in body, speech and thought (*kāya-sucaritaṁ* . . .).

(5) 'Three kinds of unwholesome thought (*akusala-vitakkā*): of sensuality, of enmity, of cruelty (*kāma-vitakko, vyāpāda-vitakko, vihiṁsa-vitakko*).

(6) 'Three kinds of wholesome thought: of renunciation (*nekkhamma-vitakko*), of non-enmity, of non-cruelty.

(7) 'Three kinds of unwholesome motivation (*sankappa*):[1029] through sensuality, enmity, cruelty.

(8) 'Three kinds of wholesome motivation: through renunciation (*nekkhamma*), non-enmity, non-cruelty.

(9) 'Three kinds of unwholesome perception (*saññā*): of sensuality, of enmity, of cruelty.

(10) 'Three kinds of wholesome perception: of renunciation, of non-enmity, of non-cruelty.

(11) 'Three unwholesome elements (*dhātuyo*): sensuality, enmity, cruelty.

(12) 'Three wholesome elements: renunciation, non-enmity, non-cruelty.

(13) 'Three more elements: the element of sense-desire,[1030] the element of form, the formless element (*kāma-dhātu, rūpa-dhātu, arūpa-dhātu*).

(14) 'Three more elements: the element of form, the formless element, the element of cessation[1031] (*rūpa-dhātu, arūpa-dhātu, nirodha-dhātu*).

(15) 'Three more elements: the low element, the middling element, the sublime element (*hīnā dhātu, majjhimā dhātu, paṇītā dhātu*). [216]

(16) 'Three kinds of craving: sensual craving, craving for becoming,[1032] craving for extinction[1033] (*kāma-taṇhā, bhava-taṇhā, vibhava-taṇhā*).

(17) 'Three more kinds of craving: craving for [the World of] Sense-Desires, for [the World of] Form, for the Formless [World] (*kāma-taṇhā, rūpa-taṇhā, arūpa-taṇhā*).

(18) 'Three more kinds of craving: for [the World of] Form, for the Formless [World], for cessation (*as for (14)*).

(19) 'Three fetters (*saṁyojanāni*): of personality-belief, of doubt, of attachment to rite and ritual (*sakkāya-diṭṭhi, vicikicchā, sīlabbata-parāmāso*).

(20) 'Three corruptions (*āsavā*): of sense-desire, of becoming, of ignorance (*kāmâsavo, bhavâsavo, avijjâsavo*).

(21) 'Three kinds of becoming: [in the World] of Sense-Desire, of Form, in the Formless World (*kāma-bhavo, rūpa-bhavo, arūpa-bhavo*).

(22) 'Three quests: for sense-desires, for becoming, for the holy life (*kāmesanā, bhavesanā, brahmacariyesanā*).

(23) 'Three forms of conceit: "I am better than...", "I am equal to...", "I am worse than..." (*"seyyo 'ham asmīti" vidhā, "sadiso 'ham asmīti" vidhā, "hīno 'ham asmīti" vidhā*).

(24) 'Three times: past, future, present (*atīto addhā, anāgato addhā, paccuppanno addhā*).

(25) 'Three "ends" (*antā*):[1034] personality, its arising, its cessation (*sakkāya anto, sakkāya-samudayo anto, sakkāya-nirodho anto*).

(26) 'Three feelings: pleasant, painful, neither (*sukhā vedanā, dukkhā vedanā, adukkham-asukhā vedanā*).

(27) 'Three kinds of suffering: as pain, as inherent in formations, as due to change (*dukkha-dukkhatā, sankhāra-dukkhatā, vipariṇāma-dukkhatā*). [217]

(28) 'Three accumulations: evil with fixed result,[1035] good with fixed result,[1036] indeterminate (*micchatta-niyato rāsi, sammatta-niyato rāsi, aniyato-rāsi*).

(29) 'Three obscurations (*tamā*):[1037] One hesitates (*kankhati*), vacillates (*vicikicchati*), is undecided (*nâdhimuccati*), is unsettled (*na sampasīdati*) about the past, the future, the present.

(30) 'Three things a Tathāgata has no need to guard against: A Tathāgata is perfectly pure in bodily conduct, in speech and in thought (*parisuddha-kāya-, -vacī-, -mano-samācāro*). There is no misdeed of body, speech or thought which he must conceal lest anyone should get to hear about it.

(31) 'Three obstacles:[1038] lust, hatred, delusion (*rāgo kiñcanaṁ, dosa kiñcanaṁ, moho kiñcanaṁ*).

(32) 'Three fires: lust, hatred, delusion (*rāgaggi, dosaggi, mohaggi*).

(33) 'Three more fires: the fire of those to be revered, of the householder, of those worthy of offerings[1039] (*āhuneyyaggi, gahapataggi, dakkhineyyaggi*).

(34) 'Threefold classification of matter: visible and resisting, invisible and resisting, invisible and unresisting[1040] (*sanidassana-sappaṭighaṁ rūpaṁ, anidassana-sappaṭighaṁ rūpaṁ, anidassana-appaṭighaṁ rūpaṁ*).

(35) 'Three kinds of karmic formation:[1041] meritorious, demeritorious, imperturbable[1042] (*puññâbhisankhāro, apuññâbhisankhāro, āneñjâbhisankhāro*). [218]

(36) 'Three persons: the learner, the non-learner, the one who is neither[1043] (*sekho puggalo, asekho puggalo, n'eva sekho nâsekho puggalo*).

(37) 'Three elders: an elder by birth, in Dhamma, by convention[1044] (*jāti-thero, dhamma-thero, sammuti-thero*).

(38) 'Three grounds based on merit: that of giving, of morality, of meditation (*dānamayaṁ puñña-kiriya-vatthu, sīlamayaṁ puñña-kiriya-vatthu, bhāvanāmaya puñña-kiriya-vatthu*).

(39) 'Three grounds for reproof: based on what has been seen, heard, suspected (*diṭṭhena, sutena, parisankāya*).

(40) 'Three kinds of rebirth in the Realm of Sense-Desire (*kāmupapattiyo*):[1045] There are beings who desire what presents itself to them (*paccuppaṭṭhita-kāmā*), and are in the grip of that desire, such as human beings, some devas, and some in states of woe. There are beings who desire what they have created (*nimmita-kāmā*),...such as the devas Who Rejoice in Their Own Creation (*Nimmānaratī*). There are beings who rejoice in the creations of others,...such as the devas Having Power over Others' Creation (*Paranimmita-vasavattī*).

(41) 'Three happy rebirths (*sukhupapattiyo*):[1046] There are beings who, having continually produced happiness now dwell in happiness, such as the devas of the Brahmā group. There are beings who are overflowing with happiness, drenched with it, full of it, immersed in it, so that they occasionally exclaim: "Oh what bliss!" such as the Radiant devas (*Ābhassarā*). There are beings...immersed in happiness, who, supremely blissful, [219] experience only perfect happiness, such as the Lustrous devas (*Subhakiṇṇā*).

(42) 'Three kinds of wisdom: of the learner, of the non-learner, of the one who is neither (*as (36)*).

(43) 'Three more kinds of wisdom: based on thought, on learning [hearing], on mental development [meditation] (*cintāmaya paññā, sutamayā paññā, bhāvanāmaya paññā*).

(44) 'Three armaments[1047] (*āvudhāni*): what one has learnt, detachment, wisdom (*sutâvudhaṁ, pavivekâvudhaṁ, paññâvudhaṁ*).

(45) 'Three faculties:[1048] of knowing that one will know the unknown, of highest knowledge, of the one who knows (*anaññātaṁ-ñassāmîtindriyaṁ, aññindriyaṁ, aññātā-v-indriyaṁ*).

(46) 'Three eyes: the fleshly eye, the divine eye,[1049] the eye of wisdom[1050] (*maṁsa-cakkhu, dibba-cakkhu, paññā-cakkhu*).

(47) 'Three kinds of training: in higher morality, higher thought, higher wisdom (*adhisīla-sikkhā, adhicitta-sikkhā, adhipaññā-sikkhā*).

(48) 'Three kinds of development: of the emotions,[1051] of mind, of wisdom (*kāya-bhāvana, citta-bhāvanā, paññā-bhāvanā*).

(49) 'Three "unsurpassables": of vision, of practice, of liberation (*dassanânuttariyaṁ, paṭipadânuttariyaṁ, vimuttânuttariyaṁ*).

(50) 'Three kinds of concentration: with thinking and pondering,[1052] with pondering without thinking, with neither (*savitakko savicāro samādhi, avitakko vicāra-matto samādhi, avitakko avicāro samādhi*).

(51) 'Three more kinds of concentration: on emptiness, the "signless", desireless (*suññato samādhi, animitto samādhi, appaṇihito samādhi*).

(52) 'Three purities: of body, speech, mind (*kāya-socceyyaṁ, vacī-socceyyaṁ, mano-socceyyaṁ*). [220]

(53) 'Three qualities of the sage:[1053] as to body, speech, mind (*kāya-moneyyaṁ, vacī-moneyyaṁ, mano-moneyyaṁ*).

(54) 'Three skills: in going forward,[1054] in going down, in means to progress (*āya-kosallaṁ, apāya-kosallaṁ, upāya-kosallaṁ*).

(55) 'Three intoxications: with health, with youth, with life (*ārogya-mado, yobbana-mado, jīvita-mado*).

(56) 'Three predominant influences: oneself, the world, the Dhamma (*attâdhipateyyaṁ, lokâdhipateyyaṁ, dhammâdhipateyyaṁ*).

(57) 'Three topics of discussion: Talk may be of the past:

"That's how it used to be"; of the future: "That's how it will be"; of the present: "That's how it is now."

(58) 'Three knowledges: of one's past lives, of the decease and rebirth of beings, of the destruction of the corruptions (*pubbenivāsânussati-ñāṇaṁ vijjā, sattānaṁ cutupapāte ñāṇaṁ vijjā, āsavānaṁ khaye ñāṇaṁ vijjā*).

(59) 'Three abidings: deva-abiding, Brahmā-abiding, the Ariyan abiding[1055] (*dibbo vihāro, Brahmā-vihāro, ariyo vihāro*).

(60) 'Three miracles:[1056] of psychic power, of telepathy, of instruction (*iddhi-pāṭihāriyaṁ, ādesanā-pāṭihāriyaṁ, anusāsani-pāṭihāriyaṁ*).

'These are the [sets of] three things...So we should all recite together...for the benefit, welfare and happiness of devas and humans.' [221]

1.11. 'There are [sets of] four things which were perfectly proclaimed by the Lord...

(1) 'Four foundations of mindfulness: Here a monk abides contemplating body as body, ardent, clearly aware and mindful, having put aside hankering and fretting for the world; he abides contemplating feelings as feelings...; he abides contemplating mind as mind...; he abides contemplating mind-objects as mind-objects, ardent, clearly aware and mindful, having put aside hankering and fretting for the world.

(2) 'Four great efforts (*sammappadhānā*): Here a monk rouses his will, makes an effort, stirs up energy, exerts his mind and strives to prevent the arising of unarisen evil unwholesome mental states. He rouses his will...and strives to overcome evil unwholesome mental states that have arisen. He rouses his will...and strives to produce unarisen wholesome mental states. He rouses his will...and strives to maintain wholesome mental states that have arisen, not to let them fade away, to bring them to greater growth, to the full perfection of development.

(3) 'Four roads to power (*iddhipādā*): Here a monk develops concentration of intention accompanied by effort of will, concentration of energy,...[222] concentration of consciousness, and concentration of investigation accompanied by effort of will.

(4) 'Four jhānas: Here a monk, detached from all sense-de-

sires, detached from unwholesome mental states, enters and remains in the first jhāna, which is with thinking and pondering, born of detachment, filled with delight and joy. And with the subsiding of thinking and pondering, by gaining inner tranquillity and oneness of mind, he enters and remains in the second jhāna, which is without thinking and pondering, born of concentration, filled with delight and joy. And with the fading away of delight, remaining imperturbable, mindful and clearly aware, he experiences in himself that joy of which the Noble Ones say: "Happy is he who dwells with equanimity and mindfulness", he enters and remains in the third jhāna. And, having given up pleasure and pain, and with the disappearance of former gladness and sadness, he enters and remains in the fourth jhāna which is beyond pleasure and pain, and purified by equanimity and mindfulness.

(5) 'Four concentrative meditations (*samādhi-bhāvanā*). This meditation, when developed and expanded, leads to (a) happiness here and now (*diṭṭhadhamma-sukha*), (b) gaining knowledge-and-vision (*ñāṇa-dassana-paṭilābha*), (c) mindfulness and clear awareness (*sati-sampajañña*), and (d) the destruction of the corruptions (*āsavānaṁ khaya*). (a) How does this practice lead to happiness here and now? Here, a monk practises the four jhānas. [223] (b) How does it lead to the gaining of knowledge-and-vision? Here, a monk attends to the perception of light (*ālokasaññaṁ manasikaroti*), he fixes his mind to the perception of day, by night as by day, by day as by night. In this way, with a mind clear and unclouded, he develops a state of mind that is full of brightness (*sappabhāsaṁ cittaṁ*). (c) How does it lead to mindfulness and clear awareness? Here, a monk knows feelings as they arise, remain and vanish; he knows perceptions as they arise, remain and vanish; he knows thoughts (*vitakkā*)[1057] as they arise, remain and vanish. (d) How does this practice lead to the destruction of the corruptions? Here, a monk abides in the contemplation of the rise and fall of the five aggregates of grasping (*pañc'upādāna-kkhandesu udayabbayânupassī*): "This is material form, this is its arising, this is its ceasing; these are feelings...; this is perception...; these are the mental formations...; this is consciousness, this is its arising, this is its ceasing."

(6) 'Four boundless states. Here, a monk, with a heart filled with loving-kindness, pervades first one quarter, then the second, the third and the fourth. Thus he stays, [224] spreading the thought of loving-kindness above, below and across, everywhere, always with a heart filled with loving-kindness, abundant, magnified, unbounded, without hatred or ill-will. And likewise with compassion, sympathetic joy, and equanimity.

(7) 'Four formless jhānas. Here, a monk, by passing entirely beyond bodily sensations, by the disappearance of all sense of resistance and by non-attraction to the perception of diversity, seeing that space is infinite, reaches and remains in the Sphere of Infinite Space. And by passing entirely beyond the Sphere of Infinite Space, seeing that consciousness is infinite, he reaches and remains in the Sphere of Infinite Consciousness. And by passing entirely beyond the Sphere of Infinite Consciousness, seeing that there is no thing, he reaches and remains in the Sphere of No-Thingness. And by passing entirely beyond the Sphere of No-Thingness, he reaches and remains in the Sphere of Neither-Perception-Nor-Non-Perception.

(8) 'Four supports[1058] (*apassenāni*): Here a monk judges that one thing is to be pursued, one thing endured, one thing avoided, one thing suppressed.

(9) 'Four Ariyan lineages (*ariya-vaṁsā*). Here, a monk (a) is content with any old robe, praises such contentment, and does not try to obtain robes improperly or unsuitably. He does not worry if he does not get a robe, and if he does, he is not full of greedy, blind desire, but makes use of it, aware of [such] dangers and wisely aware of its true purpose. Nor is he conceited about being thus content with any old robe, and he does not disparage others. And one who is thus skilful, not lax, clearly aware and mindful, [225] is known as a monk who is true to the ancient, original (*aggañña*) Ariyan lineage. Again, (b) a monk is content with any alms-food he may get... Again, (c) a monk is content with any old lodging-place... And again, (d) a monk, being fond of abandoning (*pahāna*), rejoices in abandoning, and being fond of developing (*bhāvanā*), rejoices in developing, is not therefore conceited...And

one who is thus skilful, not lax, clearly aware and mindful, is known as a monk who is true to the ancient, original Ariyan lineage.

(10) 'Four efforts: The effort of (a) restraint (*saṁvara-padhānaṁ*), (b) abandoning (*pahāna-p.*), (c) development (*bhāvanā-p.*), (d) preservation (*anurakkhaṇa-p.*). What is (a) the effort of restraint? Here, a monk, on seeing an object with the eye, does not grasp at the whole or its details, striving to restrain [226] what might cause evil, unwholesome states, such as hankering or sorrow, to flood in on him. Thus he watches over the sense of sight and guards it (*similarly with* sounds, smells, tastes, tactile sensations, thoughts). What is (b) the effort of abandoning? Here, a monk does not assent to a thought of lust, of hatred, of cruelty that has arisen, but abandons it, dispels it, destroys it, makes it disappear. What is (c) the effort of development? Here, a monk develops the enlightenment-factor of mindfulness, based on solitude, detachment, extinction,leading to maturity of surrender (*vossagga-pariṇāmiṁ*); he develops the enlightenment-factor of investigation of states, ...of energy,...of delight,...of tranquillity,...of concentration,...of equanimity, based on solitude, detachment, extinction, leading to maturity of surrender. What is (d) the effort of preservation? Here, a monk keeps firmly in his mind a favourable object of concentration which has arisen, such as a skeleton, or a corpse that is full of worms, blue-black, full of holes, bloated.

(11) 'Four knowledges: knowledge of Dhamma, of what is consonant with it (*anvaye ñāṇaṁ*), knowledge of others' minds[1059] (*paricce ñāṇaṁ*), conventional knowledge[1060] (*sammuti-ñāṇaṃ*).

(12) [227] 'Four more knowledges: knowledge of suffering, its origin, its cessation, the path.

(13) 'Four factors of Stream-Attainment (*sotâpattiyangāni*): association with good people (*sappurisa-saṁseva*), hearing the true Dhamma, thorough attention (*yoniso manasikāra*), practice of the Dhamma in its entirety (*dhammânudhamma-paṭipatti*).

(14) 'Four characteristics of a Stream-Winner: Here, the Ariyan disciple is possessed of unwavering confidence in the

Buddha, thus: "This Blessed Lord is an Arahant, a fully-enlightened Buddha, endowed with wisdom and conduct, the Well-Farer, Knower of the worlds, incomparable Trainer of men to be tamed, Teachers of gods and humans, enlightened and blessed." (b) He is possessed of unwavering confidence in the Dhamma, thus: "Well-proclaimed by the Lord is the Dhamma, visible here and now, timeless, inviting inspection, leading onward, to be comprehended by the wise each one for himself." (c) He is possessed of unwavering confidence in the Sangha, thus: "Well-directed is the Sangha of the Lord's disciples, of upright conduct, on the right path, on the perfect path; that is to say the four pairs of persons, the eight kinds of men. The Sangha of the Lord's disciples is worthy of offerings, worthy of hospitality, worthy of gifts, worthy of veneration, an unsurpassed field of merit in the world." And (d) he is possessed of morality dear to the Noble Ones, unbroken, without defect, unspotted, without inconsistency, liberating, praised by the wise, uncorrupted, and conducive to concentration.

(15) 'Four fruits of the ascetic life: the fruits of Stream-Entry, of the Once-Returner, of the Non-Returner, of Arahantship. [228]

(16) 'Four elements: the elements of "earth", "water", "fire", "air" (*paṭhavī-, āpo-, tejo-, vāyo-dhātu*).

(17) 'Four nutriments (*āhārā*): "material"[1061] (*kabalinkāra*) food, gross or subtle;[1062] contact as second; mental volition (*manosañcetanā*)[1063] as third; consciousness as fourth.

(18) 'Four stations of consciousness (*viññāṇa-ṭṭhitiyo*): Consciousness gains a footing either (a) in relation to materiality, with materiality as object and basis, as a place of enjoyment, or similarly in regard to (b) feelings, (c) perceptions or (d) mental formations, and there it grows, increases and flourishes.

(19) 'Four ways of going wrong (*agata-gamanāni*): One goes wrong through desire (*chanda*),[1064] hatred, delusion, fear.

(20) 'Four arousals of craving: Craving arises in a monk because of robes, alms, lodging, being and non-being[1065] (*iti-bhavâbhava-hetu*).

(21) 'Four kinds of progress: (a) painful progress with slow comprehension, (b) painful progress with quick comprehension, (c) pleasant progress with slow comprehension, (d) pleasant progress with quick comprehension.[1066] [229]

(22) 'Four more kinds of progress: progress with impatience (*akkhamā paṭipadā*), (b) patient progress (*khamā p.*), (c) controlled progress (*damā p.*), (d) calm progress (*samā paṭipadā*).[1067]

(23) 'Four ways of Dhamma:[1068] (a) without hankering, (b) without enmity, (c) with right mindfulness, (d) with right concentration.

(24) 'Four ways of undertaking Dhamma: There is the way that is (a) painful in the present and brings painful future results (*dukkha-vipākaṁ*), (b) painful in the present and brings pleasant future results (*sukha-vipākaṁ*), (c) pleasant in the present and brings painful future results, and (d) pleasant in the present and brings pleasant future results.

(25) 'Four divisions of Dhamma: morality, concentration, wisdom, liberation.

(26) 'Four powers:[1069] energy, mindfulness, concentration, wisdom.

(27) 'Four kinds of resolve (*adhiṭṭhānāni*): [to gain] (a) wisdom, (b) truth (*sacca*),[1070] (c) relinquishment (*cāga*), (d) tranquillity (*upasama*).[1071]

(28) 'Four ways of answering questions: the question (a) to be answered directly (*ekaṁsa-vyākaraṇiyo pañho*), (b) requiring an explanation (*vibhajja-v. p.*), (c) requiring a counter-question (*paṭipucchā-v. p.*), (d) to be set aside (*ṭhāpanīyo pañha*). [230]

(29) 'Four kinds of kamma: There is (a) black kamma with black result (*kaṇha-vipākaṁ*), (b) bright kamma with bright result (*sukka-v.*), (c) black-and-bright kamma with black-and-bright result (*kaṇha-sukka v.*), (d) kamma that is neither black nor bright (*akaṇham-asukkaṁ*), with neither black nor bright result, leading to the destruction of kamma.[1072]

(30) 'Four things to be realised by seeing (*sacchikaraṇīyā dhammā*):[1073] (a) former lives, to be realised by recollection (*satiyā*),[1074] (b) passing-away and rearising to be realised by the [divine] eye,[1075] (c) the eight deliverances, to be realised

with the mental body (*kāyena*),[1076] (d) the destruction of the corruptions, to be realised by wisdom.

(31) 'Four floods (*oghā*): sensuality, becoming, [wrong] views, ignorance.

(32) 'Four yokes (*yogā*)[1077] (= *(31)*).

(33) 'Four "unyokings" (*visaṁyogā*): from sensuality, becoming, views, ignorance.

(34) 'Four ties (*ganthā*):[1078] the "body-tie"[1079] (*kāya-gantha*) of hankering (*abhijjhā*), ill-will (*vyāpāda*), attachment to rite and ritual (*sīlabbata-parāmāsa*), dogmatic fanaticism (*idaṁ-saccâbhinivesa*).

(35) 'Four clingings (*upādānāni*): to sensuality, to views (*diṭṭhi*), to rules and ritual (*sīlabbata-pārāmāsa*), to ego-belief (*attavāda*).

(36) 'Four kinds of generation:[1080] from an egg, from a womb, from moisture,[1081] spontaneous rebirth (*opapātika-yoni*).[1082] [231]

(37) 'Four ways of descent into the womb: (a) One descends into the mother's womb unknowing, stays there unknowing, and leaves it unknowing; (b) one enters the womb knowing, stays there unknowing, and leaves it unknowing; (c) one enters the womb knowing, stays there knowing, and leaves it unknowing; (d) one enters the womb knowing, stays there knowing, and leaves it knowing (*as Sutta 28, verse 5*).

(38) 'Four ways of getting a new personality (*attabhāva-paṭilābhā*):[1083] There is an acquisition of personality that is brought about by (a) one's own volition, not another's, (b) another's volition, not one's own, (c) both, (d) neither.

(39) 'Four purifications of offerings (*dakkhiṇā-visuddhiyo*): there is the offering purified (a) by the giver but not by the recipient, (b) by the recipient but not by the giver, (c) by neither, [232] (d) by both.

(40) 'Four bases of sympathy (*saṁgaha-vatthūni*): generosity, pleasing speech, beneficial conduct and impartiality.

(41) 'Four un-Ariyan modes of speech: lying, slander, abuse, idle gossip.

(42) 'Four Ariyan modes of speech: refraining from lying, slander, abuse, idle gossip.

(43) 'Four more un-Ariyan modes of speech: claiming to

have seen, heard, sensed (*muta*),[1084] known what one has not seen, heard, sensed, known.

(44) 'Four more Ariyan modes of speech: stating that one has not seen, heard, sensed, known what one has not seen, heard sensed, known.

(45) 'Four more un-Ariyan modes of speech: claiming not to have seen, heard, sensed, known what one has seen, heard, sensed, known.

(46) 'Four more Ariyan modes of speech: stating that one has seen, heard, sensed, known what one has seen, heard, sensed, known.

(47) 'Four persons: Here a certain man (a) torments himself (*attan-tapo hoti*), is given to self-tormenting, (b) torments others (*paran-tapo hoti*),...(c) torments himself and others,...(d) torments neither himself nor others...Thereby [233] he dwells in this life without craving, released (*nibbuto*), cool, enjoying bliss, become as Brahmā (*brahma-bhūtena*).[1085]

(48) 'Four more persons: Here a man's life benefits (a) himself but not others, (b) others but not himself,[1086] (c) neither, (d) both.

(49) 'Four more persons: (a) living in darkness and bound for darkness (*tamo tamaparâyana*), (c) living in darkness and bound for the light (*tamo jotiparâyana*), (c) living in the light and bound for darkness, (d) living in the light and bound for the light.

(50) 'Four more persons: (a) the unshakeable ascetic (*samaṇam-acalo*), (b) the "blue-lotus" ascetic, (c) the "white-lotus" ascetic, (d) the subtly-perfect ascetic (*samaṇa-sukhumālo*).[1087]

'These are the [sets of] four things which were perfectly proclaimed by the Lord...So we should all recite them together...for the benefit, welfare and happiness of devas and humans.

[*End of first recitation-section*]

2.1. 'There are [sets of] five things perfectly proclaimed...

(1) 'Five aggregates: body, feelings, perceptions, mental formations, consciousness.

(2) 'Five aggregates of grasping (*pancûpādāna-kkhandhā*) (*as (1)*). [234]

(3) 'Five strands of sense-desire (*pañca kāma-guṇā*): a sight seen by the eye, a sound heard by the ear, a smell smelt by the nose, a flavour tasted by the tongue, a tangible object felt by the body as being desirable, attractive, nice, charming, associated with lust and arousing passion.

(4) 'Five [post-mortem] destinies (*gatiyo*): hell (*nirayo*),[1088] animal-rebirth (*tiracchāna-yoni*),[1089] the realm of hungry ghosts (*petā*), humankind, the deva world.

(5) 'Five kinds of begrudging (*macchariyāni*):[1090] as to dwelling-place, families,[1091] gains, beauty (*vaṇṇa*), Dhamma.

(6) 'Five hindrances: sensuality (*kāmacchanda*), ill-will (*vyāpāda*), sloth-and-torpor (*thīna-middha*), worry-and-flurry (*uddhacca-kukkucca*), sceptical doubt (*vicikicchā*).

(7) 'Five lower fetters: personality-belief (*sakkāya-diṭṭhi*), doubt, attachment to rite and ritual (*sīlabbata-parāmāsa*), sensuality, ill-will.

(8) 'Five higher fetters: craving for the world of form (*rūpa-rāga*), craving for the formless world (*arūpa-rāga*), conceit (*māna*), restlessness (*uddhacca*), ignorance. [235]

(9) 'Five rules of training (*sikkhāpadāni*): refraining from taking life, taking what is not given, sexual misconduct, lying speech, strong drink and sloth-producing drugs (*surā-meraya-majja-pamādaṭṭhānā*).

(10) 'Five impossible things: An Arahant is incapable of (a) deliberately taking the life of a living being; (b) taking what is not given so as to constitute theft; (c) sexual intercourse; (d) telling a deliberate lie; (e) storing up goods for sensual indulgence as he did formerly in the household life (*as Sutta 29, verse 26*).

(11) 'Five kinds of loss (*vyasanāni*): Loss of relatives, wealth, health, morality, [right] view. No beings fall into an evil state, a hell-state...after death because of loss or relatives, wealth or health; but beings do fall into such states by loss of morality and right view.

(12) 'Five kinds of gain (*sampadā*): Gain of relatives, wealth, health, morality, [right] view. No beings arise in a happy, heavenly state after death because of the gain of relatives,

wealth or health; but beings are reborn in such states because of gains in morality and right view.

(13) 'Five dangers to the immoral through lapsing from morality: (*as Sutta 16, verse 1.23*). [236]

(14) 'Five benefits to the moral through preserving morality: (*as Sutta 16, verse 1.24*).

(15) 'Five points to be borne in mind by a monk wishing to rebuke another: (a) I will speak at the proper time, not the wrong time, (b) I will state the truth, not what is false, (c) I will speak gently, not roughly, (d) I will speak for his good, [237] not for his harm, (e) I will speak with love in my heart, not with enmity.

(16) 'Five factors of endeavour: Here, a monk (a) has faith, trusting in the enlightenment of the Tathāgata: "Thus this Blessed Lord is an Arahant, a fully-enlightened Buddha..." (*as Sutta 3, verse 1.2*), (b) is in good health, suffers little distress or sickness, having a good digestion that is neither too cool nor too hot but of a middling temperature suitable for exertion, (c) is not fraudulent or deceitful, showing himself as he really is to his teacher or to the wise among his companions in the holy life, (d) keeps his energy constantly stirred up for abandoning unwholesome states and arousing wholesome states, and is steadfast, firm in advancing and persisting in wholesome states, (e) is a man of wisdom, endowed with wisdom concerning rising and cessation, with the Ariyan penetration that leads to the complete destruction of suffering.

(17) 'Five Pure Abodes (*suddhâvāsā*):[1092] Aviha,[1093] Unworried (*Atappā*), Clearly Visible (*Sudassā*), Clear-Sighted (*Sudassī*), Peerless (*Akaniṭṭhā*).

(18) 'Five kinds of Non-Returner (*anāgāmī*):[1094] the "less-than-half-timer", the "more-than-half-timer", the "gainer without exertion", the "gainer with exertion", "he who goes upstream to the highest".

(19) 'Five mental blockages (*ceto-khīlā*): Here, a monk has [238] doubts and hesitations (a) about the Teacher, is dissatisfied and cannot settle in his mind. Thus his mind is not inclined towards ardour, devotion, persistence and effort; (b) about the Dhamma...; (c) about the Sangha...; (d) about the training ...; (e) he is angry and displeased with his fellows in

the holy life, he feels depressed and negative towards them. Thus his mind is not inclined towards ardour, devotion, persistence and effort.

(20) 'Five mental bondages (*cetaso vinibandhā*):[1095] Here, a monk has not got rid of the passion, desire, love, thirst (*pipāsa*),[1096] fever, craving (*taṇhā*) (a) for sense-desires (*kāme*): thus his mind is not inclined towards ardour, devotion, persistence and effort; (b) for the body (*kāye*),...(c) for physical objects (*rūpe*),...or (d) having eaten as much as his belly will hold, he abandons himself to the pleasure of lying down, of contact, of sloth; or (e) [239] he practises the holy life for the sake of becoming a member of some body of devas (*deva-nikāya*), thinking: "By means of these rites or this discipline, this austerity or this holy life I shall become one of the devas, great or small." Thus his mind is not inclined towards ardour, devotion, persistence and effort.

(21) 'Five faculties (*indriyāni*): the faculty of eye, ear, nose, tongue, body.

(22) 'Five more faculties: pleasant [bodily] feeling (*sukha*), pain (*dukkha*), gladness (*somanassa*), sadness (*domanassa*), indifferent feeling (*upekhā*).

(23) 'Five more faculties: faith (*saddhā*), energy, mindfulness, concentration, wisdom.

(24) 'Five elements making for deliverance (*nissaraṇīyā dhātuyo*): (a) Here, when a monk considers sense-desires, his mind does not leap forward and take satisfaction in them, fix on them or make free with them,[1097] but when he considers renunciation it does leap forward, take satisfaction in it, fix on it, and make free with it. And he gets this thought [240] well-set, well-developed, well raised up, well freed and disconnected from sense-desires. And thus he is freed from the corruptions (*āsavā*), the vexations and fevers that arise from sense-desires, and he does not feel that [sensual] feeling. This is called the deliverance from sense-desires. And the same applies to (b) ill-will, (c) cruelty, (d) forms (*rūpa*),[1098] (e) personality (*sakkāya*). [241]

(25) 'Five bases of deliverance (*vimuttâyatanāni*): Here, (a) the Teacher or a respected fellow-disciple teaches a monk Dhamma. And as he receives the teaching, he gains a grasp of

both the spirit and the letter of the teaching. At this, joy arises in him, and from this joy, delight (*pīti*); and by this delight his senses are calmed, he feels happiness (*sukhaṁ*) as a result, and with this happiness his mind is established;[1099] (b) he has not heard it thus, but in the course of teaching Dhamma to others he has learnt it by heart as he has heard it; or (c) as he is chanting the Dhamma...; or (d) [242]...when he applies his mind to the Dhamma, thinks and ponders over it and concentrates his attention on it (*anupekkhati*); or (e) when he has properly grasped some concentration-sign (*samādhi-nimittaṁ*), has well considered it, applied his mind to it (*supadhāritaṁ*), and has well penetrated it with wisdom (*suppaṭividdhaṁ paññāya*). At this, joy arises in him, and from this joy, delight; and by this delight his senses are calmed, [243] he feels happiness as a result, and with this happiness his mind is established.

(26) 'Five perceptions making for maturity of liberation: the perception of impermanence (*anicca-saññā*), of suffering in impermanence (*anicce dukkha-saññā*), of impersonality in suffering (*dukkhe anatta-saññā*), of abandoning (*pahāna-saññā*), of dispassion (*virāga-saññā*).

'These are the [sets of] five things which were perfectly proclaimed by the Lord...'

2.2. 'There are [sets of] six things which were perfectly proclaimed by the Lord...

(1) 'Six internal sense-spheres (*ajjhattikāni āyatanāni*): eye-, ear-, nose-, tongue-, body-(*kāyâyatanaṁ*), mind-sense-sphere (*manâyatanaṁ*).

(2) 'Six external sense-spheres (*bahirāni āyatanāni*): sight-object (*rūpâyatanaṁ*), sound-, smell-, taste-, tangible object (*phoṭṭabbâyatanaṁ*), mind-object (*dhammâyatanaṁ*).

(3) 'Six groups of consciousness (*viññāṇa-kāyā*): eye-consciousness, ear-, nose-, tongue-, body-, mind-consciousness.

(4) 'Six groups of contact (*phassa-kāyā*): eye-, ear-, nose-, tongue-, body-, mind-contact (*mano-samphasso*).

(5) 'Six groups of feeling (*vedanā-kāyā*): feeling based on eye-contact (*cakkhu-samphassajā vedanā*), [244] on ear-, nose-, tongue-, body-, mind-contact.

(6) 'Six groups of perception (*saññā-kāyā*): perception of sights (*rūpa-saññā*), of sounds, of smells, of tastes, of touches, of mind-objects (*dhamma-saññā*).

(7) 'Six groups of volition (*sañcetanā-kāyā*): volition based on sights, sounds, smells, tastes, touches, mind-objects.

(8) 'Six groups of craving (*taṇhā-kāyā*): craving for sights, sounds, smells, tastes, touches, mind-objects.

(9) 'Six kinds of disrespect (*agāravā*): Here, a monks behaves disrespectfully and discourteously towards the Teacher, the Dhamma, the Sangha, the training, in respect of earnestness (*appamāde*), of hospitality (*paṭisanthāre*).

(10) 'Six kinds of respect (*gāravā*): Here, a monk behaves respectfully...(*as (9)*).

(11) 'Six pleasurable investigations (*somanassûpavicārā*):[1100] When, on seeing a sight-object with the eye, on hearing..., smelling..., tasting..., touching..., knowing a mind-object with the mind, one investigates a corresponding object productive of pleasure. [245]

(12) 'Six unpleasurable investigations: (*as (11) but:* productive of displeasure).

(13) 'Six indifferent investigations: (*as (11) but:* productive of indifference (*upekhā*).

(14) 'Six things conducive to communal living (*sārāṇīyā dhammā*):[1101] As long as monks both in public and in private show loving-kindness to their fellows in acts of body, speech and thought,...share with their virtuous fellows whatever they receive as a rightful gift, including the contents of their alms-bowls, which they do not keep to themselves,...keep consistently, unbroken and unaltered those rules of conduct that are spotless, leading to liberation, praised by the wise, unstained and conducive to concentration, and persist therein with their fellows both in public and in private,...continue in that noble view that leads to liberation, to the utter destruction of suffering, remaining in such awareness with their fellows both in public and in private (*as Sutta 16, verse 1.11*). [246]

(15) 'Six roots of contention (*vivāda-mūlāni*): Here, (a) a monk is angry and bears ill-will, he is disrespectful and discourteous to the Teacher, the Dhamma and the Sangha, and does not

finish his training. He stirs up contention within the Sangha, which brings woe and sorrow to many, with evil consequences, misfortune and sorrow for devas and humans. If, friends, you should discover such a root of contention among yourselves or among others, you should strive to get rid of just that root of contention. If you find no such root of contention..., then you should work to prevent its overcoming you in future. Or (b) a monk is deceitful and malicious (*makkhī hoti paḷāsī*)..., (c) a monk is envious and mean..., (d) a monk is cunning and deceitful..., (e) a monk is full of evil desires and wrong views..., (f) a monk is opinionated (*sandiṭṭhi-parāmāsī*), obstinate and tenacious. [247] If, friends, you should discover such a root of contention among yourselves or among others, you should strive to get rid of just that root of contention. If you find no such root of contention..., then you should work to prevent its overcoming you in future.

(16) 'Six elements: the earth-, water-, fire-, air-, space-element (*ākāsa-dhātu*), the consciousness-element (*viññāṇa-dhātu*).[1102]

(17) 'Six elements making for deliverance (*nissaraṇīyā-dhātuyo*): Here, a monk might say: (a) "I have developed the emancipation of the heart (*ceto-vimutti*) by loving-kindness (*mettā*), [248] expanded it, made it a vehicle and a base, established, worked well on it, set it well in train. And yet ill-will still grips my heart." He should be told: "No! do not say that! Do not misrepresent the Blessed Lord, it is not right to slander him thus, for he would not have said such a thing! Your words are unfounded and impossible. If you develop the emancipation of the heart through loving-kindness, ill-will has no chance to envelop your heart. This emancipation through loving-kindness is the cure for ill-will." Or (b) he might say: "I have developed the emancipation of the heart through compassion (*karuṇā*), and yet cruelty still grips my heart..." Or (c) he might say: "I have developed the emancipation of the heart through sympathetic joy (*muditā*), and yet aversion (*arati*) still grips my heart..." [249] Or (d) he might say: "I have developed the emancipationof the heart through equanimity (*upekhā*), and yet lust (*rāgo*) grips my heart." Or

(e) he might say: "I have developed the signless emancipation of the heart (*animittā ceto-vimutti*),[1103] and yet my heart still hankers after signs (*nimittânusāri hoti*)..." Or (f) he might say: "The idea 'I am' is repellent to me, I pay no heed to the idea: 'I am this.' Yet doubts, uncertainties and problems still grip my heart..." [250] (*Reply to each in similar terms to (a)*).

(18) 'Six unsurpassed things (*anuttariyāni*):[1104] [certain] sights, things heard, gains, trainings, forms of service (*pari-cāriyânuttariyaṁ*), objects of recollection.

(19) 'Six subjects of recollection (*anussati-ṭṭhānāni*): the Buddha, the Dhamma, the Sangha, morality, renunciation, the devas.

(20) 'Six stable states (*satata-vihārā*):[1105] On seeing an object with the eye, hearing a sound..., smelling a smell..., tasting a flavour..., touching a tangible object...or cognising a mental object with the mind, one is neither pleased (*sumano*) nor displeased (*dummano*), but remains equable (*upekhako*), mindful and clearly aware.

(21) 'Six "species" (*ābhijātiyo*): Here, (a) one born in dark conditions [251] lives a dark life, (b) one born in dark conditions lives a bright life, (c) one born in dark conditions attains Nibbāna, which is neither dark nor bright, (d) one born in bright conditions lives a dark life, (e) one born in bright conditions leads a bright life, (f) one born in bright conditions attains Nibbāna which is neither dark nor bright.

(22) 'Six perceptions conducive to penetration (*nibbedha-bhāgiya-saññā*): the perception of impermanence, of suffering in impermanence, of impersonality in suffering, of abandoning, of dispassion (*as Sutta 33, verse 2.1 (26)*) and the perception of cessation (*nirodha-saññā*).

'These are the [sets of] six things which were perfectly proclaimed by the Lord...'

2.3. 'There are [sets of] seven things which have been perfectly proclaimed by the Lord...

(1) 'Seven Ariyan treasures (*ariya-dhanāni*): faith, morality, moral shame (*hiri*), moral dread (*ottappa*), learning (*suta*), renunciation (*cāga*), wisdom.

(2) 'Seven factors of enlightenment (*sambojjhangā*): mindfulness, [252] investigation of phenomena, energy, delight (*pīti*), tranquillity, concentration, equanimity.

(3) 'Seven requisites of concentration:[1106] right view, thought, speech, action, livelihood, effort, mindfulness.

(4) 'Seven wrong practices (*asaddhammā*): Here, a monk lacks faith, lacks moral shame, lacks moral dread, has little learning, is slack (*kusīto*), is unmindful (*muṭṭhassati*), lacks wisdom.

(5) 'Seven right practices (*saddhammā*): Here, a monk has faith, moral shame and moral dread, has much learning, has aroused vigour (*āraddha-viriyo*), has established mindfulness (*upaṭṭhita-sati hoti*), possesses wisdom.

(6) 'Seven qualities of the true man (*sappurisa-dhammā*):[1107] Here, a monk is a knower of the Dhamma, of meanings (*atthaññū*), of self (*attaññū*),[1108] of moderation (*mattaññū*), of the right time, of groups (*parisaññū*), of persons.

(7) 'Seven grounds for commendation (*niddasa-vatthūni*),[1109] Here, a monk is keenly anxious (a) to undertake the training, and wants to persist in this, (b) to make a close study of the Dhamma, (c) to get rid of desires, (d) to find solitude, (e) to arouse energy, (f) to develop mindfulness and discrimination (*sati-nepakke*), [253] (g) to develop penetrative insight.[1110]

(8) 'Seven perceptions: perception of impermanence, of not-self, of foulness (*asubhasaññā*), of danger, of abandonment, of dispassion, of cessation.

(9) 'Seven powers (*balāni*): of faith, energy, moral shame, moral dread, mindfulness, concentration, wisdom.

(10) 'Seven stations of consciousness: Beings (a) different in body and different in perception; (b) different in body and alike in perception; (c) alike in body and different in perception; (d) alike in body and alike in perception; (e) who have attained to the Sphere of Infinite Space; (f)...of Infinite Consciousness; (g)...of No-Thingness (*as Sutta 15, verse 33*).

(11) 'Seven persons worthy of offerings: The Both-Ways-Liberated [254], the Wisdom-Liberated, the Body-Witness, the Vision-Attainer, the Faith-Liberated, the Dhamma-Devotee, the Faith-Devotee (*as Sutta 28, verse 8*).

(12) 'Seven latent proclivities (*anusayā*): sensuous greed (*kāma-rāga*), resentment (*paṭigha*), views, doubt, conceit, craving for becoming (*bhava-rāga*), ignorance.

(13) 'Seven fetters (*saṁyojanāni*): complaisance (*anunaya*),[1111] resentment (*then as (12)*).

(14) 'Seven rules for the pacification and settlement of disputed questions that have been raised:[1112] (a) proceedings face-to-face, (b) recollection (*sati*), (c) mental derangement, (d) confession, (e) majority verdict, (f) habitual bad character, (g) "covering over with grass".

'These are the [sets of] seven things which were perfectly proclaimed by the Lord...So we should all recite them together...for the benefit, welfare and happiness of devas and humans.'

[*End of second recitation-section*]

3.1. 'There are [sets of] eight things perfectly proclaimed by the Lord...

(1) 'Eight wrong factors (*micchattā*): wrong view...(*the reverse of (2) below*). [255]

(2) 'Eight right factors (*sammattā*): right view, right thought, right speech, right action, right livelihood, right effort, right mindfulness, right concentration.

(3) 'Eight persons worthy of offerings:[1113] the Stream-Winner and one who has practised to gain the fruit of Stream-Entry, the Once-Returner..., the Non-Returner..., the Arahant and one who has worked to gain the fruit of Arahantship.

(4) 'Eight occasions of indolence (*kusīta-vatthūni*): Here, a monk (a) has a job to do. He thinks: "I've got this job to do, but it will make me tired. I'll have a rest." So he lies down and does not stir up enough energy to complete the uncompleted, to accomplish the unaccomplished, to realise the unrealised. Or (b) he has done some work, and thinks: "I've done this work, now I'm tired. I'll have a rest." So he lies down...Or (c) he has to go on a journey, and thinks: "I have to go on this journey. It will make me tired..." Or (d) he has been on a journey...Or (e) he goes on the alms-round in a village or

town and does not get his fill of food, whether coarse or fine, and he thinks: "I've gone for alms...[256]...my body is tired and useless..." Or (f) he goes on the alms-round...and gets his fill...He thinks: "I've gone for alms...and my body is heavy and useless as if I were pregnant..."[1114]...Or (g) he has developed some slight indisposition, and he thinks: "I'd better have a rest..." Or (h) he is recuperating, having not long recovered from an illness, and he thinks: "My body is weak and useless. I'll have a rest." So he lies down and does not stir up enough energy to complete the uncompleted, to accomplish the unaccomplished, to realise the unrealised.

(5) 'Eight occasions for making an effort (*ārabbha-vatthūni*): Here, a monk (a) has a job to do. He thinks: "I've got this job to do, but in doing it I won't find it easy to pay attention to the teaching of the Buddhas. So I will stir up sufficient energy to complete the uncompleted, to accomplish the unaccomplished, to realise the unrealised." Or (b) he has [257] done some work, and thinks: "Well, I did the job, but because of it I wasn't able to pay sufficient attention to the teaching of the Buddhas. So I will stir up sufficient energy..." Or (c) he has to go on a journey...Or (d) he has been on a journey. He thinks: "I've been on this journey, but because of it I wasn't able to pay sufficient attention..." Or (e) he goes for alms...without getting his fill...And he thinks: "So my body is light and fit. I'll stir up energy..." Or (f) he goes for alms...and gets his fill...And he thinks: "So my body is strong and fit. I'll stir up energy..." Or (g) he has some slight indisposition... and he thinks: "This indisposition might get worse, so I'll stir up energy..." Or [258] (h) he is recuperating...and he thinks: "...it might be that the illness will recur. So I'll stir up energy..." Thus he stirs up sufficient energy to complete the uncompleted, to accomplish the unaccomplished, to realise the unrealised.

(6) 'Eight bases for giving: One gives (a) as occasion offers (*āsajja*), (b) from fear, (c) thinking: "He gave me something", (d) thinking: "He will give me something", (e) thinking: "It is good to give", (f) thinking: "I am cooking something, they are not. It would not be right not to give something to those who are not cooking", (g) thinking: "If I make this gift I shall

acquire a good reputation", (h) in order to adorn and prepare one's heart.[1115]

(7) 'Eight kinds of rebirth due to generosity: Here, someone gives an ascetic or Brahmin food, drink, clothes, transport (*yānaṁ*), garlands, perfumes and ointments, sleeping accommodation, a dwelling, or lights, and he hopes to receive a return for his gifts. He sees a rich Khattiya or Brahmin or householder living in full enjoyment of the pleasures of the five senses, and he thinks: "If only when I die I may be reborn as one of these rich people!" He sets his heart on this thought, fixes it and develops it (*bhāveti*).[1116] And this thought, being launched (*vimuttaṁ*) at such a low level (*hīne*), and not developed to a higher level (*uttariṁ abhāvitaṁ*), leads to rebirth right there. [259] But I say this of a moral person, not of an immoral one. The mental aspiration of a moral person is effective through its purity.[1117] Or (b) he gives such gifts and, having heard that the devas in the realm of the Four Great Kings live long, are good-looking and lead a happy life, he thinks: "If only I could be reborn there!" Or he similarly aspires to rebirth in the heavens of (c) the Thirty-Three Gods, (d) the Yāma devas, (e) the Tusita devas, (f) the Nimmānarati devas, (g) the Paranimmita-vasavatti devas. And this thought leads to rebirth right there...The mental aspiration of a moral person is effective through its purity. Or (h) he similarly aspires to rebirth in the world of Brahmā...But [260] I say this of a moral person, not an immoral one, one freed from passion (*vītarāgassa*), not one still swayed by passion.[1118] The mental aspiration of [such] a moral person is effective through liberation from passion.

(8) 'Eight assemblies: the assembly of Khattiyas, Brahmins, householders, ascetics, devas of the Realm of the Four Great Kings, of the Thirty-Three Gods, of māras, of Brahmās (*as Sutta 16, verse 3.21*).

(9) 'Eight worldly conditions (*loka-dhammā*): gain and loss, fame and shame (*yaso ca ayaso ca*), blame and praise, happiness and miserry.

(10) 'Eight stages of mastery: (a) perceiving forms internally, one sees external forms, limited and beautiful or ugly; (b) *(as (a) but)* unlimited; (c) not perceiving forms internally, one sees

external forms, limited...; (d) (*as (c) but*) unlimited; not perceiving forms internally, one perceives forms that are (e) blue, [261] (f) yellow, (g) red, (h) white (*as Sutta 16, verse 3.25–32*).

(11) 'Eight liberations: (a) possessing form, one sees forms; (b) not perceiving material forms in oneself, one sees them outside; (c) thinking: "It is beautiful", one becomes intent on it; one enters (d) the Sphere of Infinite Space; (e)...the Sphere of Infinite Consciousness; (f)...the Sphere of No-Thingness; (g)...the Sphere of Neither-Perception-Nor-Non-Perception; (h)...the Cessation of Perception and Feeling (*as Sutta 15, verse 35*). [262]

"These are the [sets of] eight things...'

3.2. 'There are [sets of] nine things...

(1) 'Nine causes of malice (*āghāta-vatthūni*): Malice is stirred up by the thought: (a) "He has done me an injury", (b) "He is doing me an injury", (c) "He will do me an injury", (d)–(f) "He has done, is doing, will do an injury to someone who is dear and pleasant to me", (g)–(i) "he has done, is doing, will do a favour to someone who is hateful and unpleasant to me."

(2) 'Nine ways of overcoming malice (*āghāta-paṭivinayā*): Malice is overcome by the thought: (a)–(i) "He has done me an injury..." (*as (1)*). [263] "What good would it do [to harbour malice]?"

(3) 'Nine abodes of beings (a) Beings different in body and different in perception, (b) beings different in body and alike in perception, (c) beings alike in body and different in perception, (d) beings alike in body and alike in perception, (e) the Realm of Unconscious Beings, (f) the Realm of Neither-Perception-Nor-Non-Perception, (g) beings who have attained to the Sphere of Infinite Space, (h) beings who have attained to the Sphere of Infinite Consciousness, (i) beings who have attained to the Sphere of No-Thingness (*as Sutta 15, verse 33*).

(4) 'Nine unfortunate, inopportune times for leading the holy life (*akkhaṇā asamayā brahmacariya-vāsāya*): [264] (a) A Tathāgata has been born in the world, Arahant, fully-enlightened Buddha, and the Dhamma is taught which leads to calm and perfect Nibbāna, which leads to enlightenment as taught by the Well-Farer, and this person is born in a hell-state (*nira-*

yaṁ),[1119]...(b)...among the animals, (c)...among the petas, (d)...among the asuras, (e)...in a long-lived group of devas,[1120] or (f) he is born in the border regions among foolish barbarians where there is no access for monks and nuns, or male and female lay-followers, or (g) he is born in the Middle Country,[1121] but he has wrong views and distorted vision, thinking: "There is no giving, offering or sacrificing, there is no fruit or result of good or bad deeds; there is not this world and the next world; [265] there are no parents and there is no spontaneous rebirth; there are no ascetics and Brahmins in the world who, having attained to the highest and realised for themselves the highest knowledge about this world and the next, proclaim it";[1122] or (h)...he is born in the Middle Country but lacks wisdom and is stupid, or is deaf and dumb and cannot tell whether something has been well said or ill said; or else...(i) no Tathāgata has arisen...and this person is born in the Middle Country and is intelligent, not stupid, and not deaf or dumb, and well able to tell whether something has been well said or ill said.

(5) 'Nine successive abidings: [the jhānas and Spheres of Infinite Space, Infinite Consciousness, No-Thingness, Neither-Perception-Nor-Non-Perception, and Cessation of Perception and Feeling]. [266]

(6) 'Nine successive cessations (*anupubba-nirodhā*): By the attainment of the first jhāna, perceptions of sensuality (*kāma-saññā*) cease; by the attainment of the second jhāna, thinking and pondering cease; by the attainment of the third jhāna, delight (*pīti*) ceases; by the attainment of the fourth jhāna, in- and out-breathing ceases;[1123] by the attainment of the Sphere of Infinite Space, the perception of materiality ceases, by the attainment of the Sphere of Infinite Consciousness, the perception of the Sphere of Infinite Space ceases; by the attainment of the Sphere of No-Thingness, the perception of the Sphere of Infinite Consciousness ceases; by the attainment of the Sphere of Neither-Perception-Nor-Non-Perception, the perception of the Sphere of No-Thingness ceases; by the attainment of the Cessation-of-Perception-and-Feeling, perception and feeling cease.

'These are the [sets of] nine things...'

3.3. 'There are [sets of] ten things perfectly proclaimed by the Lord...

(1) 'Ten things that give protection (*nātha-karaṇa-dhammā*):[1124] Here a monk (a) is moral, he lives restrained according to the restraint of the discipline, persisting in right behaviour, seeing danger in the slightest fault, he keeps to the rules of training; [267] (b) he has learnt much, and bears in mind and retains what he has learnt. In these teachings, beautiful in the beginning, the middle and the ending, which in spirit and in letter proclaim the absolutely perfected and purified holy life, he is deeply learned, he remembers them, recites them, recites them, reflects on them and penetrates them with vision; (c) he is a friend, associate and intimate of good people; (d) he is affable, endowed with gentleness and patience, quick to grasp instruction; (e) whatever various jobs there are to be done for his fellow-monks, he is skilful, not lax, using foresight in carrying them out, and is good at doing and planning; (f) he loves the Dhamma and delights in hearing it, he is especially fond of the advanced doctrine and discipline (*abhidhamme abhivinaye*);[1125] [268] (g) he is content with any kind of requisites: robes, alms-food, lodging, medicines in case of illness; (h) he ever strives to arouse energy, to get rid of unwholesome states, to establish wholesome states, untiringly and energetically striving to keep such good states and never shaking off the burden; (i) he is mindful, with a great capacity for clearly recalling things done and said long ago;[1126] (j) he is wise, with wise perception of arising and passing away, that Ariyan perception that leads to the complete destruction of suffering.

(2) 'Ten objects for the attainment of absorption (*kasiṇâyatanāni*):[1127] He perceives the Earth-Kasiṇa, the Water-Kasiṇa, the Fire-Kasiṇa, the Wind-Kasiṇa, the Blue Kasiṇa, the Yellow Kasiṇa, the Red Kasiṇa, the White Kasiṇa, the Space-Kasiṇa, the Consciousness Kasiṇa,[1128] above, below, on all sides, undivided, unbounded.

[269] (3) 'Ten unwholesome courses of action (*akusala-kammapathā*): taking life, taking what is not given, sexual misconduct, lying speech, slander, rude speech, idle chatter, greed, malevolence, wrong view.

(4) 'Ten wholesome courses of action: avoidance of taking life...(*and so on, as (3) above*).

(5) 'Ten Ariyan dispositions (*ariya-vāsā*): Here a monk (a) has got rid of five factors, (b) possesses six factors, (c) has established one guard, (d) observes the four supports, (e) has got rid of individual beliefs,[1129] (f) has quite abandoned quest, (g) is pure of motive, (h) has tranquillised his emotions,[1130] is well liberated (i) in heart, and (j) by wisdom. How has he got rid of five factors? Here, he has got rid of sensuality, ill-will, sloth-and-torpor, worry-and-flurry, and doubt; (b) what six factors does he possess? On seeing an object with the eye, hearing a sound..., smelling a smell..., tasting a flavour..., touching a tangible object..., or cognising a mental object with the mind, he is neither pleased nor displeased, but remains equable, mindful and clearly aware; (c) how has he established the one guard? By guarding his mind with mindfulness; (d) what are the four supports? He judges that one thing is to be pursued, one thing endured, one thing avoided, one thing suppressed (*as verse 1.11 (8)*); (e) how has he got rid of individual beliefs (*panunna-pacceka-sacco*)? Whatever individual beliefs are held by the majority of ascetics and Brahmins he has dismissed, abandoned, rejected, let go; (f) how is he one who has quite abandoned quests? He has abandoned the quest for sense-desires, for rebirth, for the holy life;[1131] (g) how is he pure of motive? He has abandoned thoughts of sensuality, ill-will, cruelty; (h) how is he one who has tranquillised his emotions (*passaddha-kāya-sankhāro hoti*)? Because, having given up pleasure and pain with the disappearance of former gladness and sadness, he enters into a state beyond pleasure and pain which is purified by equanimity, and this is the fourth jhāna; (i) how is he well emancipated in heart? He is liberated from the thought of greed, hatred and delusion; (j) how is he well liberated by wisdom? He understands: "For me greed, hatred and delusion are abandoned, cut off at the root, like a palm-tree stump, destroyed and incapable of growing again." [271]

(6) 'Ten qualities of the non-learner (*asekha*):[1132] The non-learner's right view, right thought; right speech, right action, right livelihood; right effort, right mindfulness, right concen-

tration; right knowledge (*sammā-ñāṇam*), right liberation (*sammāvimutti*).

'These are the [sets of] ten things which have been perfectly set forth by the Lord who knows and sees, the fully-enlightened Buddha. So we should all recite them together without disagreement, so that this holy life may be long-lasting and established for a long time to come, thus to be for the welfare and happiness of the multitude, out of compassion for the world, for the benefit, welfare and happiness of devas and humans.'

3.4. And when the Lord had stood up, he said to the Venerable Sāriputta: 'Good, good, Sāriputta! Well indeed have you proclaimed the way of chanting together for the monks!'

These things were said by the Venerable Sāriputta, and the Teacher confirmed them. The monks were delighted and rejoiced at the Venerable Sāriputta's words.

34 *Dasuttara Sutta: Expanding Decades*

[272] 1.1. THUS HAVE I HEARD.[1133] Once the Lord was staying at Campā beside the Gaggarā lotus-pond, with a large company of some five hundred monks. Then the Venerable Sāriputta addressed the monks: 'Friends, monks!' 'Friend!' replied the monks. And the Venerable Sāriputta said:

'In growing groups from one to ten I'll teach
Dhamma for the gaining of Nibbāna,
That you may make an end of suffering,
And be free from all the ties that bind.

1.2. 'There is friends, (1) one thing that greatly helps (*bahu-kāro*), (2) one thing to be developed (*bhāvetabbo*), (3) one thing to be thoroughly known (*pariññeyyo*), (4) one thing to be abandoned (*pahātabbo*), (5) one thing that conduces to diminution[1134] (*hāna-bhāgiyo*), (6) one thing that conduces to distinction (*visesa-bhāgiyo*), (7) one thing hard to penetrate (*dup-paṭivijjho*), (8) one thing to be made to arise (*uppādetabbo*), (9) one thing to be thoroughly learnt (*abhiññeyyo*), and (10) one thing to be realised (*sacchikātabbo*).

(1) 'Which one thing greatly helps? Tirelessness in wholesome states (*appamādo kusalesu dhammesu*).

(2) 'Which one thing is to be developed? Mindfulness with regard to the body, accompanied by pleasure (*kāya-gata sati sāta-sahagatā*).

(3) 'Which one thing is to be thoroughly known? Contact as a condition of the corruptions and of grasping[1135] (*phasso sâsavo upādāniyo*). [273]

(4) 'Which one thing is to be abandoned? Ego-conceit (*asmi-māna*).[1136]

(5) 'Which one thing conduces to diminution? Unwise attention (*ayoniso manasikāro*).

(6) 'Which one things conduces to distinction? Wise attention (*yoniso manasikāro*).

(7) 'Which one thing is hard to penetrate? Uninterrupted mental concentration[1137] (*ānantariko ceto-samādhi*).

(8) 'Which one thing is to be made to arise? Unshakeable knowledge (*akuppaṁ ñāṇaṁ*).

(9) 'Which one thing is to be thoroughly learnt? All beings are maintained by nutriment (*as Sutta 33, verse 1.8 (1)*).

(10) 'Which one thing is to be realised? Unshakeable deliverance of mind (*akuppā ceto-vimutti*).

'That makes ten things that are real and true, so and not otherwise, unerringly and perfectly realised by the Tathāgata.'

1.3. 'Two things greatly help, two things are to be developed ...((1)–(10) *as above*).

(1) 'Which two things greatly help? Mindfulness and clear awareness (*as Sutta 33, verse 1.9 (18)*).

(2) 'Which two things are to be developed? Calm and insight (*as Sutta 33, verse 1.9 (23)*).

(3) 'Which two things are to be thoroughly known? Mind and body (*as Sutta 33, verse 1.9 (1)*). [274]

(4) 'Which two things are to be abandoned? Ignorance and craving for existence (*as Sutta 33, verse 1.9 (2)*).

(5) 'Which two things conduce to diminution? Roughness and friendship with evil (*as Sutta 33, verse 1.9 (6)*).

(6) 'Which two things conduce to distinction? Gentleness and friendship with good (*as Sutta 33, verse 1.9 (7)*).

(7) 'Which two things are hard to penetrate? That which is the root, the condition of the defilement of beings, and that which is the root, the condition of the purification of beings (*yo ca hetu yo ca paccayo sattānaṁ saṁkilesāya,...sattānaṁ visuddhiyā*).

(8) 'Which two things are to be made to arise? Knowledge of the destruction [of the defilements] and of [their] non-recurrence (*as Sutta 33, verse 1.9 (33)*).

(9) 'Which two things are to be thoroughly learnt? Two elements, the conditioned and the unconditioned[1138] (*sankhatā ca dhātu asankhatā ca dhātu*).

(10) 'Which two things are to be realised? Knowledge and liberation (*as Sutta 33, verse 1.9 (32)*).

'That makes twenty things that are real and true, so and not otherwise, unerringly and perfectly realised by the Tathāgata.'

1.4. 'Three things greatly help, three things are to be developed . . .

(1) 'Which three things greatly help? Association with good people, hearing the true Dhamma, practice of the Dhamma in its entirety (*as Sutta 33, verse 1.11 (13)*).

(2) 'Which three things are to be developed? Three kinds of concentration (*as Sutta 33, verse 1.10 (50)*). [275]

(3) 'Which three things are to be thoroughly known? Three feelings (*as Sutta 33, verse 1.10 (26)*).

(4) 'Which three things are to be abandoned? Three kinds of craving (*as Sutta 33, verse 1.10 (16)*).

(5) 'Which three things conduce to diminution? Three unwholesome roots (*as Sutta 33, verse 1.10 (1)*).

(6) 'Which three things conduce to distinction? Three wholesome roots (*as Sutta 33, verse 1.10 (2)*).

(7) 'Which three things are hard to penetrate? Three elements making for deliverance (*nissāraṇīyā dhātuyo*): (a) deliverance from sensuality (*kāmā*), that is, renunciation (*nekkhammaṁ*), (b) deliverance from material forms (*rūpā*), that is, the immaterial (*āruppaṁ*), (c) whatever has become, is compounded, is conditionally arisen – the deliverance from that is cessation (*nirodho*).

(8) 'Which three things are to be made to arise? Three knowledges (*ñāṇāni*) of past, future, present.

(9) 'Which three things are to be thoroughly learnt? Three elements (*as Sutta 33, verse 1.10 (13)*).

(10) 'Which three things are to be realised? Three knowledges (*vijjā: as Sutta 33, verse 1.10 (58)*). [276]

'That makes thirty things that are real and true, so and not otherwise, unerringly and perfectly realised by the Tathāgata.'

1.5. 'Four things greatly help, four things are to be developed . . .

(1) 'Which four things greatly help? Four "wheels"[1139] (*cakkāni*): (a) a favourable place of residence (*paṭirūpa-desa-vāso*), (b) association with good people (*sappurisûpassayo*), (c) perfect

development of one's personality (*atta-sammā-paṇidhi*), past meritorious actions (*pubbe-kata-puññatā*).

(2) 'Which four things are to be developed? Four foundations of mindfulness (*as Sutta 33, verse 1.11 (1)*).

(3) 'Which four things are to be thoroughly known? Four nutriments (*as Sutta 33, verse 1.11 (17)*).

(4) 'Which four things are to be abandoned? Four floods (*as Sutta 33, verse 1.11 (31)*).

(5) 'Which four things conduce to diminution? Four yokes (*as Sutta 33, verse 1.11 (32)*).

(6) 'Which four things conduce to distinction? Four "unyokings" (*as Sutta 33, verse 1.11 (33)*). [277]

(7) 'Which four things are hard to penetrate? Four concentrations: (a) conducing to decline (*hāna-bhāgiyo*), (b) conducing to stasis (*ṭhiti-bhāgiyo*), (c) conducive to distinction (*visesabhāgiyo*), (d) conducive to penetration (*nibbedha-bhāgiyo*).

(8) 'Which four things are to be made to arise? Four knowledges (*as Sutta 33, verse 1.11 (11)*).

(9) 'Which four things are to be thoroughly learnt? Four Noble Truths (*as Sutta 33, verse 1.11 (12)*).

(10) 'Which four things are to be realised? Four fruits of the ascetic life (*as Sutta 33, verse 1.11 (15)*).

'That makes forty things that are real and true, so and not otherwise, unerringly and perfectly realised by the Tathāgata.'

1.6. 'Five things greatly help, five things are to be developed...

(1) 'Which five things greatly help? Five factors of endeavour (*as Sutta 33, verse 2.1 (16)*).

(2) 'Which five things are to be developed? Fivefold perfect concentration:[1140] (a) suffusion with delight (*pīti*), (b) suffusion with happiness (*sukha*), [278] (c) suffusion with will[1141] (*ceto*), (d) suffusion with light[1142] (*āloka*), (e) the "reviewing" sign[1143] (*paccavekkhaṇa-nimitta*).

(3) 'Which five things are to be thoroughly known? Five aggregates of grasping (*as Sutta 33, verse 2.1 (2)*).

(4) 'Which five things are to be abandoned? Five hindrances (*as Sutta 33, verse 2.1 (6)*).

(5) 'Which five things conduce to diminution? Five mental blockages (*as Sutta 33, verse 2.1 (19)*).

(6) 'Which five things conduce to distinction? Five faculties (*as Sutta 33, verse 2.1 (23)*).

(7) 'Which five things are hard to penetrate? Five elements making for deliverance (*as Sutta 33, verse 2.1 (24)*).

(8) 'Which five things are to be made to arise? The fivefold knowledge of right concentration (*pañcañāṇiko sammā samādhi*): the knowledge that arises within one that: (a) "This concentration is both present happiness and productive of future resultant happiness" (*āyatiñ ca sukha-vipāko*), (b) "This concentration is Ariyan and free from worldliness" [279] (*nirāmiso*),[1144] (c) "This concentration is not practised by the unworthy" (*akāpurisa-sevito*),[1145] (d) "This concentration is calm and perfect, has attained tranquillisation, has attained unification, and is not instigated,[1146] it cannot be denied[1147] or prevented",[1148] (e) "I myself attain this concentration with mindfulness, and emerge from it with mindfulness."

(9) 'Which five things are to be thoroughly learnt? Five bases of deliverance (*as Sutta 33, verse 2.1 (25)*).

(10) 'Which five things are to be realised? Five branches of Dhamma (*as Sutta 33, verse 1.11 (25)*) plus knowledge and vision of liberation (*vimutti-ñāṇa-dassana-kkhandho*).

'That makes fifty things that are real and true, and not otherwise, unerringly and perfectly realised by the Tathgāta.'

1.7. 'Six things greatly help, six things are to be developed...

(1) 'Which six things greatly help? Six things to be remembered (*as Sutta 33, verse 2.2 (14)*). [280]

(2) 'Which six things are to be developed? Six subjects of recollection (*as Sutta 33, verse 2.2 (19)*).

(3) 'Which six things are to be thoroughly known? Six internal sense-spheres (*as Sutta 33, verse 2.2 (1)*).

(4) 'Which six things are to be abandoned? Six groups of craving (*as Sutta 33, verse 2.2 (8)*).

(5) 'Which six things conduce to diminution? Six kinds of disrespect (*as Sutta 33, verse 2.2 (9)*).

(6) 'Which six things conduce to distinction? Six kinds of respect (*as Sutta 33, verse 2.2 (10)*).

(7) 'Which six things are hard to penetrate? Six elements making for deliverance (*as Sutta 33, verse 2.2 (17)*). [281]

(8) 'Which six things are to be made to arise? Six stable states (*as Sutta 33, verse 2.2 (20)*).

(9) 'Which six things are to be thoroughly known? Six unsurpassed things (*as Sutta 33, verse 2.2 (18)*).

(10) 'Which six things are to be realised? Six super-knowledges (*abhiññā*): Here, a monk applies and bends his mind to, and enjoys, different supernormal powers (*iddhī*): (a) Being one, he becomes many (*as Sutta 2, verse 87*); (b) with the divine ear he hears sounds both divine and human (*as Sutta 2, verse 89*); (c) he knows and distinguishes the minds of other beings (*as Sutta 2, verse 91*); (d) he remembers past existences (*as Sutta 2, verse 93*); (e) with the divine eye...he sees beings passing away and arising (*as Sutta 2, verse 95*); (f) he abides, in this life, by his own super-knowledge and realisation, in the attainment of the corruptionless liberation of heart and liberation through wisdom.

'That makes sixty things that are real and true, so and not otherwise, unerringly and perfectly realised by the Tathāgata.'

1.8. 'Seven things help greatly, seven things are to be developed ...

(1) 'Which seven things greatly help? Seven treasures (*as Sutta 33, verse 2.3 (1)*).

(2) 'Which seven things are to be developed? Seven factors of enlightenment (*as Sutta 33, verse 2.3 (2)*).

(3) 'Which seven things are to be thoroughly known? Seven stations of consciousness (*as Sutta 33, verse 2.3 (10)*).

(4) 'Which seven things are to be abandoned? Seven latent proclivities (*as Sutta 33, verse 2.3 (12)*).

(5) 'Which seven things conduce to diminution? Seven wrong practices (*as Sutta 33, verse 2.3 (4)*).

(6) 'Which seven things conduce to distinction? Seven right practices (*as Sutta 33, verse 2.3 (5)*). [283]

(7) 'Which seven things are hard to penetrate? Seven qualities of the true man (*as Sutta 33, verse 2.3 (6)*).

(8) 'Which seven things are to be made to arise? Seven perceptions (*as Sutta 33, verse 2.3 (8)*).

(9) 'Which seven things are to be thoroughly learnt? Seven grounds for commendation (*as Sutta 33, verse 2.3 (7)*).

(10) 'Which seven things are to be learnt? Seven powers of an Arahant[1149] (*khīṇāsava-balāni*). Here, for a monk who has destroyed the corruptions, (a) the impermanence of all compounded things is well seen, as it really is, by perfect insight. This is one way whereby he recognises that for him the corruptions are destroyed; (b)... sense-desires are well seen as being like a pit of glowing embers...; (c)... his heart (*cittaṁ*) is bent on and inclined towards detachment (*viveka*), slopes towards detachment and detachment is its object; rejoicing in renunciation (*nekkhammâbhirataṁ*), his heart is totally unreceptive to all things pertaining to the corruptions...; (d)... the four foundations of mindfulness have been well and truly developed...; [284] (e)... the five faculties[1150] have been well developed...; (f)... the seven factors of enlightenment[1151] have been been well developed...; (g) the Noble Eightfold Path has been well and truly developed... This is one of the powers whereby he recognises that for him the corruptions are destroyed.

'That makes seventy things that are real and true, so and not otherwise, unerringly and perfectly realised by the Tathāgata.'

[*End of first recitation-section*]

2.1. 'Eight things greatly help, eight things are to be developed ...

(1) 'Which eight things greatly help? Eight causes, eight conditions conduce to wisdom in the fundamentals of the holy life, to gaining what has not been gained and to increasing, expanding and developing what has been gained. Here, (a) one lives close to the Teacher or to a fellow-monk with the standing of a teacher, being thus strongly established in moral shame and moral dread, in love and veneration... [285] He who is so placed (b) from time to time goes to his teacher, asks and interrogates him: "How is that, Lord? What does this mean?" Thus his venerable teachers can reveal what is hidden and clarify obscurities, in this way helping him to solve his problems. (c) Then, having heard Dhamma from them, he achieves withdrawal (*vūpakāsa*),[1152] of body and mind. (d) Further, a monk is moral, he lives restrained according to the restraint of the discipline,

persisting in right behaviour, seeing danger in the slightest fault, and keeping to the rules of training. Also, (e) a monk, having learnt much, remembers and bears in mind what he has learnt, and those things that are beautiful in the beginning, in the middle and in the ending, which in spirit and letter proclaim the absolutely perfected and purified holy life, he remembers and reflects on, and penetrates them with vision. Again, (f) a monk, having stirred up energy, continues to dispel unwholesome states, striving strongly and firmly, and not casting off the yoke of the wholesome. [286] Again, (g) a monk is mindful, with the highest mindfulness and discrimination, remembering and bearing in mind what has been done or said in the past. Also, (h) a monk continually contemplates the rise and fall of the five aggregates of grasping, thinking: "Such is material form, its arising and passing; such are feelings, such are perceptions, such are the mental formations, such is consciousness, its arising and passing."

(2) 'Which eight things are to be developed? The Noble Eightfold Path: Right View...Right Concentration.

(3) 'Which eight things are to be thoroughly known? Eight worldly conditions (*as Sutta 33, verse 3.1 (9)*).

(4) 'Which eight things are to be abandoned? Eight wrong factors (*as Sutta 33, verse 3.1 (1)*). [287]

(5) 'Which eight things conduce to diminution? Eight occasions of indolence (*as Sutta 33, verse 3.1 (4)*).

(6) 'Which eight things conduce to distinction? Eight occasions for making an effort (*as Sutta 33, verse 3.1 (5)*).

(7) 'Which eight things are hard to penetrate? Eight unfortunate, inopportune times for leading the holy life (*as Sutta 33, verse 3.1 (4), omitting (d)*).

(8) 'Which eight things are to be made to arise? Eight thoughts of a Great Man (*Mahāpurisa-vitakkā*):[1153] "This Dhamma is (a) for one of few wants, not one of many wants; (b) for the contented, not for the discontented; (c) for the withdrawn, not for those delighting in company; (d) for the energetic, not for the lazy; (e) for one of established mindfulness, not for one of lax mindfulness; (f) for one of concentrated mind, not for one who is not concentrated; (g) for one who has wisdom, not for one lacking wisdom; (h) for one who delights in non-proliferation (*nippapañcârāmassa*),[1154] not for one who delights in proliferation."

(9) 'Which eight things are to be thoroughly learnt? Eight states of mastery (*as Sutta 33, verse 3.1 (10)*). [288]

(10) 'Which eight things are to be realised? Eight liberations (*as Sutta 33, verse 3.1 (11)*).

'That makes eighty things that are real and true, so and not otherwise, unerringly and perfectly realised by the Tathāgata.'

2.2. 'Nine things greatly help, nine things are to be developed . . .

(1) 'Which nine things greatly help? Nine conditions rooted in wise consideration (*yoniso-manasikāra-mūlakā dhammā*): When a monk practises wise consideration, (a) joy (*pāmojja*) arises in him, and (b) from his being joyful, delight (*pīti*) arises, and (c) from his feeling delight, his senses[1155] are calmed; (d) as a result of this calming he feels happiness (*sukha*), and (e) from his feeling happy, his mind becomes concentrated; (f) with his mind thus concentrated, he knows and sees things as they really are; (g) with his thus knowing and seeing things as they really are, he becomes disenchanted (*nibbindati*); (h) with disenchantment he becomes dispassionate (*virajjati*), and (i) by dispassion he is liberated.

(2) 'Which nine things are to be developed? Nine factors of the effort for perfect purity[1156] (*pārisuddhi-padhāniyangāni*): (a) the factor of effort for purity of morality, (b)...for purity of mind, (c)...for purity of view, (d)...of purification by overcoming doubt (*kankhā-vitaraṇa-visuddhi*),[1157] (e)...of purification by knowledge and vision of path and not-path (*maggâmagga-ñāṇa-dassana-visuddhi*), (f)...of purification by knowledge and vision of progress (*paṭipadā-ñāṇa-dassana-visuddhi*), (g)...of purification by knowledge and vision (*ñāṇa-dassana-visuddhi*), (h)...of purity of wisdom (*paññā-visuddhi*), (i)...of purity of deliverance (*vimutti-visuddhi*).

(3) 'Which nine things are to be thoroughly known? Nine abodes of beings (*as Sutta 33, verse 3.2 (3)*).

(4) 'Which nine things are to be abandoned? Nine things rooted in craving: [289] Craving conditions searching,...acquisition,...decision-making,...lustful desire,...attachment,... appropriation,...avarice,...guarding of possessions, and because of the guarding of possessions there arise the taking up

of stick and sword, quarrels,...lying and other evil unskilled states (*as Sutta 15, verse 9*).

(5) 'Which nine things conduce to diminution? Nine causes of malice (*as Sutta 33, verse 3.2 (1)*).

(6) 'Which nine things conduce to distinction? Nine ways of overcoming malice (*as Sutta 33, verse 3.2 (2)*).

(7) 'Which nine things are hard to penetrate? Nine differences (*nānattā*): Owing to difference of element (*dhātu*)[1158] there is difference of contact (*phassa*);[1159] owing to difference of contact there is difference of feeling; owing to difference of feeling there is difference of perception; owing to difference of perception there is difference of thought (*sankappa*); owing to difference of thought there is difference of intention (*chanda*); owing to difference of intention there is difference of obsession (*pariḷāha*); owing to difference of obsession there is difference of quest (*pariyesanā*); owing to difference of quest there is difference of what is gained (*lābha*).

(8) 'Which nine things are to be made to arise? Nine perceptions (*saññā*):[1160] of the foul (*asubha*), of death,[1161] of the loathsomeness of food (*āhāre paṭikkūla saññā*), of distaste for the whole world (*sabba-loke anabhirati-saññā*), of impermanence, of the suffering in impermanence, [290] of impersonality in suffering, of relinquishment (*pahāna*), of dispassion (*virāga*).

(9) 'Which nine things are to be thoroughly learnt? Nine successive abidings (*as Sutta 33, verse 3.2 (5)*).

(10) 'Which nine things are to be realised? Nine successive cessations (*as Sutta 33, verse 3.2 (6)*).

'That makes ninety things that are real and true so and not otherwise, unerringly and perfectly realised by the Tathāgata.'

2.3. 'Ten things (1) greatly help, (2) are to be developed, (3) are to be thoroughly known, (4) are to be abandoned, (5) conduce to diminution, (6) conduce to distinction, (7) are hard to penetrate, (8) are to be made to arise, (9) are to be thoroughly learnt, (10) are to be realised.

(1) 'Which ten things greatly help? Ten things that give protection (*as Sutta 33, verse 3.1 (1)*).

(2) 'Which ten things are to be developed? Ten objects for the attainment of absorption (*as Sutta 33, verse 3.3 (2)*).

(3) 'Which ten things are to be thoroughly known? Ten

sense-spheres (*āyatanāni*):[1162] eye and sight-object, ear and sound, nose and smell, tongue and taste, body and tactile object.

(4) 'Which ten things are to be abandoned? Ten wrong courses (*as Sutta 33, verse 3.1 (1)*) plus wrong knowledge (*micchā-ñāṇa*) and wrong liberation (*micchā-vimutti*).

(5) 'Which ten things conduce to diminution? Ten unwholesome courses of action (*as Sutta 33, verse 3.3 (3)*). [291]

(6) 'Which ten things conduce to distinction? Ten wholesome courses of action (*as Sutta 33, verse 3.3 (4)*).

(7) 'Which ten things are hard to penetrate? Ten Ariyan dispositions (*as Sutta 33, verse 3.3 (5)*).

(8) 'Which ten things are to be made to arise? Ten perceptions (*as verse 2.2 (8)*) and the perception of cessation (*nirodha-saññā*).

(9) 'Which ten things are to be thoroughly learnt? Ten causes of wearing-away (*nijjara-vatthūni*): By right view wrong view is worn away, and whatever evil and unwholesome states arise on the basis of wrong view are worn away too. And by right view many wholesome states are developed and perfected. By right thought wrong thought is worn away...By right speech wrong speech is worn away...By right action wrong action is worn away...By right livelihood wrong livelihood is worn away...By right effort wrong effort is worn away...By right mindfulness wrong mindfulness is worn away...By right concentration wrong concentration is worn away...By right knowledge[1163] wrong knowledge is worn away...By right liberation wrong liberation is worn away, and whatever evil and unwholesome states arise on the basis of wrong liberation are worn away too. And by right liberation many wholesome states are developed and perfected. [292]

(10) 'Which ten things are to be realised? Ten qualities of the non-learner (*as Sutta 33, verse 3.3 (6)*).

'That makes a hundred things that are real and true, so and not otherwise, unerringly and perfectly realised by the Tathāgata.'

So said the Venerable Sāriputta. And the monks were delighted and rejoiced at his words.

Bibliography
List of Abbreviations
Notes
Index

A Select Annotated Bibliography

Note: There is much confusion nowadays about dates of publication as given in bibliographies owing to the frequent reprinting of certain books. Here, the *original* date of publication is normally given. The sign + after this date means 'reprinted' (sometimes frequently); a date in brackets denotes the latest edition known to me, possibly with a different place of publication. Further, where the author is a Buddhist monk the prefix Ven. is used and the title Thera, etc., omitted after his name. This prevents the title being taken for a personal name as all too frequently happens! All or most of the books listed can be found in the library of the Buddhist Society in London.

GENERAL WORKS

G.F. Allen, *The Buddha's Philosophy*, London 1959. A useful, fairly elementary introduction.

A.L. Basham, *The Wonder that was India*, London 1967 +. A fascinating general work with much background information, including on Buddhism, technical appendices and also some brilliant translations of Indian poetry.

H. Bechert (ed.), *Die Sprache der ältesten buddhistischen Überlieferung/The Language of the Earliest Buddhist Tradition*, Göttingen 1980. Mainly for the specialist.

H. Bechert and R. Gombrich (eds.), *The World of Buddhism: Buddhist Monks and Nuns in Society and Culture*, London 1984. A beautifully illustrated book covering all branches of the Buddhist Sangha. Sadly, the information about Britain is out of date.

E.A. Brewster, *The Life of Gotama the Buddha, Compiled Exclu-*

sively from the Pali Canon, London 1926 + (1956). Makes no pretence to originality, but useful.

Michael Carrithers, *The Buddha* (Past Masters, Oxford 1983). A brief but remarkably fine introduction. The author has done extensive field-work with the meditating monks in the forests of Sri Lanka. Awarded the Christmas Humphreys Prize 1984.

S. Collins, *Selfless Persons. Imagery and Thought in Theravāda Buddhism*, Cambridge 1982. Required reading for all who are still bothered about *anattā*.

E. Conze, *Buddhist Thought in India*, London 1962. A brilliant survey – slightly biased against Theravāda. Like all Conze's works, absolutely reliable on facts but not always, perhaps, as regards opinions.

R.A. Gard (ed.), *Buddhism*, New York 1961. A good introduction to the different schools.

H. von Glasenapp, *Buddhism, a Non-Theistic Religion* (English transl.), London 1970. A much-needed work of clarification by a famous Indologist.

J.C. Holt, *Discipline: the Canonical Buddhism of the Vinayapiṭaka*, Delhi 1981. A useful work, unfortunately marred by some serious mistakes.

Christmas Humphreys, *Buddhism*, London 1949 +. The author was Founder-President, for 58 years, of the Buddhist Society. This book contains many inaccuracies, but as an introductory survey it is brilliant, and has drawn many into Buddhism.

K.N. Jayatilleke, *The Early Buddhist Theory of Knowledge*, London 1963. An important study, though criticised in some quarters.

K.N. Jayatilleke, *The Message of the Buddha*, London 1975. A posthumously published collection of radio talks, covering many important points in a more popular manner than the 1963 book.

R. Johansson, *The Psychology of Nirvana*, London 1969. Despite a possibly unfortunate title, a work of real value by a Swedish psychologist: an improvement on Mrs Rhys Davids's rather jejune 'psychological' studies.

N. Katz, *Buddhist Images of Perfection*, Delhi 1982. A comparative study of the Arahant, Bodhisattva and Mahāsiddha ideals.

N. Katz (ed.), *Buddhism and Western Philosophy*, Delhi 1981. 20 essays, of very varying quality and readability, by different scholars.

N. Katz (ed.), *Buddhism and Western Psychology*, New York 1983. A collection in many ways comparable to the above.

J. Kornfeld, *Living Buddhist Masters*, Santa Cruz 1977. Accounts of some living, and recently deceased, Theravāda meditation masters. Stimulating and valuable.

É. Lamotte, *Histoire du Bouddhisme indien*, i, Louvain 1958 + (1967). A work of great erudition by a Catholic scholar who devoted his life to the study of Buddhism.

T. Ling, *The Buddha's Philosophy of Man*, London 1981. Rhys Davids' versions of 10 Dīgha Nikāya Suttas modernised with introductory essays. Some errors in Pali.

G.P. Malalasekera, *Dictionary of Pali Proper Names*, 2 vols., London 1938 + (1974). A valuable tool. Takes concept of 'proper name' very widely. A partial substitute for articles not yet covered in the *Encyclopaedia of Buddhism*.

G.P. Malalasekera (ed.), *Encyclopaedia of Buddhism*, Colombo 1961-. (to date: A-*Hung-i*). Though only letters A-H have appeared.

Ven. Ñāṇananda, *Concept and Reality in Early Buddhist Thought*, Kandy (BPS) 1971. An important study of the conceptualizing process and its transcending.

K.R. Norman, *Pali Literature* (=*History of Indian Literature* vii, 2), Wiesbaden 1983. A useful survey with up-to-date bibliography.

Ven. Nyāṇaponika, *Abhidhamma Studies*, Colombo 1949 + (1965). By the veteran German scholar-monk, founder of the Buddhist Publication Society. An important contribution.

Ven. Nyāṇaponika, *The Heart of Buddhist Meditation*, London 1962 +. A classic.

Ven. Nyānapoṇika (ed.), *Pathways of Buddhist Thought*, London 1971. Selections from the famous 'Wheel' series.

Ven. Nyāṇatiloka, *Buddhist Dictionary*, Colombo 1950 + (1973). A valuable guide to Theravāda terms, with accurate definitions, by the Ven. Nyāṇaponika's teacher.

G.C. Pande, *Studies in the Origins of Buddhism*, Delhi 1957 + (1983). Useful for questions of chronology, etc., though some conclusions are dubious.

J.B. Pratt, *The Pilgrimage of Buddhism*, London 1928. Much has changed since this Buddhist travelogue was written by an American philosophy professor, but his impressions and reported conversations remain fascinating.

Ven. W. Rahula, *What the Buddha Taught*, Bedford 1959 + (1976). A classic introduction which has been translated into many languages.

Ven. W. Rahula, *Zen and the Taming of the Bull*, Bedford 1978. Collected essays. The author sees many 'Mahāyāna' features foreshadowed in Theravāda.

Ven. H. Saddhātissa, *Life of the Buddha*, London 1976. An attractive as well as authoritative account.

H.W. Schumann, *The Historical Buddha*, English translation by Maurice Walshe, London 1988.

F. Story, *Rebirth as Doctrine and Experience*. Foreword by Dr Ian Stevenson (BPS 1975). Contains well-researched case-histories of those remembering past lives.

S.J. Tambiah, *World Conqueror and World Renouncer*, Cam-1976. Buddhist Kingship.

B.J. Terwiel, *Monks and Magic*, London 1975. For this research, the author actually became a monk in Thailand – and was allowed to do so, though an 'unbeliever'.

E.J. Thomas, *Life of the Buddha as Legend and History*, London 1927 (1975). Still a valuable study despite its date.

E.J. Thomas, *History of Buddhist Thought*, London 1933 (1953). Dated but still useful.

C.S. Upasak, *Dictionary of Early Buddhist Monastic Terms*, Varanasi 1975. Useful.

A.K. Warder, *Indian Buddhism* (2nd ed.), Delhi 1980. A valuable original study, only marred by the author's eccentric translations of some terms.

A.K. Warder, *Pali Metre*, London 1967. Highly technical; stresses the importance of study of metres for dating texts: cf. note 10.

G. Welbon, *The Buddhist Nirvāṇa and Its Western Interpreters*, Chicago 1968. A useful account of the various interpretations – and misinterpretations.

The number of books on Buddhism at the present time is huge and growing. The above selection is bound to be arbitrary to a degree. In addition to the above, the 'Wheel' paperbacks (and occasional larger volumes) of the Buddhist Publication Society, Kandy, can be recommended to the serious student.

STUDY AIDS

R. Johannson, *Pali Buddhist Texts Explained to the Beginner*, Lund 1973 +. A very simple introduction to the Pali language, based on canonical passages; outline of grammar.

A.K. Warder, *Introduction to Pali*, London (PTS), 1963 + (1984 paperback). Based on the language of the Dīgha Nikāya.

R.C. Childers, *A Dictionary of the Pali Language*, London 1875 (Delhi 1979). A fine pioneer dictionary, using the European order of letters, based on traditional Sinhalese materials, i.e. not confined to the language of the Suttas. Nicely set out, with some long articles, though naturally dated. Some beginners find it more helpful than the PED.

T.W. Rhys Davids and W. Stede, *Pali-English Dictionary*, London (PTS) 1926 + (1959). The classical language. Words given in Indian alphabetical order. Typographically ill set out, articles cluttered with etymologies that probably merely confuse the student. Naturally a valuable work, but with undoubted shortcomings.

The Pali Text Society (founded 1881) has done and continues to do invaluable work. The Society's texts and translations from the Pali Canon are listed on page 51ff.

List of Abbreviations

A	Anguttara Nikāya (PTS page references, Pali edition)
AA	Anguttara Commentary
AN	Anguttara Nikāya (chapter and verse references, see p. 52)
Ap	Apadāna (= Kh N (xiii), see p. 53)
BB	Bhikkhu Bodhi, *The All-Embracing Net of Views: The Brahmajāla Sutta and its Commentaries* (BPS 1978)
BD	*Book of Discipline* (translation of the Vinaya by I.B. Horner, PTS 1938–66, see p. 51)
BDic	*Buddhist Dictionary* (Ven. Nyāṇatiloka, Colombo 1950 + (1973))
BPS	Buddhist Publication Society, Kandy, Sri Lanka
BT	*Buddhism in Translations* (Warren, New York 1896 + (1963))
D	Dīgha Nikāya (PTS page references, see p. 52)
DA	Dīgha Commentary (*Sumangalavilāsinī* by Buddhaghosa, see p. 50)
DAT	Dīgha Ṭīkā (Sub-Commentary, see p. 50–51)
Dhp	Dhammapada (= Kh N(ii), see p. 52)
Dhs	Dhammasangaṇī = Book 1 of the Abhidhamma
DN	Dīgha Nikāya (chapter and verse references, see p. 52)
DPPN	*Dictionary of Pali Proper Names* (G.P. Malalasekera, London 1938 + (1974))
EB	*Encyclopidia of Buddhism* (edited by G.P. Malalasekera, Columbo 1961, still in progress)
It	Itivuttaka (= Kh N(iv), see p. 53)
Ja	Jātaka (= Kh N(x), see p. 53)
Kh N	Khuddaka Nīkaya (see p. 52)

LDB — *Last Days of the Buddha* (Wheel Publication 67–69, BPS 1964, see n.363)
LEBT — *The Language of Early Buddhist Texts* (edited by H. Bechert, Göttingen 1980)
M — Majjhima Nikāya (PTS page references, Pali edition)
MA — Majjhima Commentary
MLS — *Middle Length Sayings* (translation of M by I.B. Horner, PTS 1954–59)
MN — Majjhima Nikāya (chapter and verse references, see p. 52)
PD — *Path of Discrimination* (translation of Pṭs by the Ven. Ñāṇamoli, PTS 1982)
PED — *Pali-English Dictionary* (PTS 1926 +)
PTC — *Pāli Tipiṭakaṁ Concordance* (PTS 1956, still in progress)
PTS — Pali Text Society, London
Pṭs — Paṭisambhidā Magga (= Kh N(xii), see p. 53)
RD — Rhys Davids (also his translation of D: *Dialogues of the Buddha*, see p. 52)
S — Saṁyutta Nikāya (PTS page references, Pali edition)
SA — Saṁyutta Commentary
SBB — Sacred Books of the Buddhists (a series continued by the PTS)
SN — Saṁyutta Nikāya (chapter and verse references, see p. 52)
Sn — Sutta Nipāta (= Kh N(v), see p. 53)
Thag — Theragāthā (= Kh N (viii), see p. 53)
Thig — Therīgāthā (= Kh N(ix), see p. 53)
Ud — Udāna (= Kh N(iii), see p. 53)
VM — *Visuddhimagga* (*The Path of Purification* by Buddhaghosa, translated by the Ven. Ñāṇamoli, BPS 1956 +, see p. 51)

Notes

INTRODUCTION

1 The Buddha's dates are doubtful. Lamotte (1958) took 566-486 B.C. as a working hypothesis, but recently many scholars have argued for a later dating, though with no exact consensus. Perhaps 'ca. 480-400' would be a reasonable guess. Lamotte's dating is not impossible, but the Sri Lankan tradition of 623-543 and other even earlier Oriental datings seem ruled out.

2 *Sutta*. There is no satisfactory English translation for this, and 'discourse' is used as a makeshift rendering. It is virtually synonymous with *suttanta*, favoured in volumes ii and iii by Rhys Davids and Carpenter. The literal meaning is 'thread', and the Sanskrit form is *sūtra*. Typically, a Sutta, which may be all or partly in verse, though prose is the norm, gives a discourse by the Buddha or one of his leading disciples, set within a slight narrative framework and always introduced by the words 'Thus have I heard', having supposedly been thus recited by the Ven. Ānanda at the First Council. Mahāyāna *sūtras* are normally much longer and more elaborate.

3 *Hīnayāna*. This term, meaning 'lesser vehicle or career', is sometimes used polemically by Mahāyāna writers for those Buddhists who do not accept their doctrines. Hence it has come in modern times to be applied to the Theravāda school, though it was originally applied to a now extinct school called the Sarvāstivādins. There is therefore no justification for applying it to the Buddhism of the south-east Asian countries using the Pali Canon.

4 *Sankhāra.* The various meanings of this word are well set out in BDic, the most important being that of 'formations' (the Ven. Nyāṇatiloka's word) in various senses. Here it means 'anything formed or compounded' in the most general sense. In the formula of dependent origination (q.v.) the term is rendered 'Karma-formations', and denotes the karmic patterns, good or bad, produced by past ignorance, which go to shape the character of the new individual. As one of the five groups of aggregates (*khandhas*) the *sankhāras* are 'mental formations', including some functions that are not karmic.

5 As, for instance, in the often quoted story of the thirty young men told to seek 'themselves' (*attānaṁ*) (Vinaya, Mahāvagga 14.3). Though the word used here is accusative singular, there is no justification for interpreting it as 'the Self'.

6 The difficulty of translating Pali (even when one thinks one knows the meaning!) is sometimes considerable. The structure of Pali somewhat resembles that of classical Latin, though with even greater complications and a particular propensity for participial constructions. The problem can be illustrated by a typical example. Sutta 28 opens:

> Evaṁ me sutaṁ. Ekaṁ samayaṁ Bhagavā Nāḷandāyaṁ viharati Pāvārikambavane. Atha kho āyasmā Sāriputto yena Bhagavā ten' upasaṁkami, upasaṁkamitvā Bhagavantaṁ abhivādetvā ekamantaṁ nisīdi. Ekamantaṁ nisinno kho āyasmā Sāriputto Bhagavantaṁ etad avoca...

> Literally:

> *Thus by-me [was] heard. One time Blessed-One at-Nāḷandā stays in-Pāvārika's-mango-grove. Then too Venerable Sāriputta where Blessed-One [was] there approached, having-approached Blessed-One having-saluted to-one-side sat-down. To-one-side having-sat-down too Venerable Sāriputta to-Blessed-One this said...*

We render this more economically:

> 'Thus have I heard. Once the Lord was staying at Nāḷandā in Pāvārika's mango-grove. And the Venerable Sāriputta came to see the Lord, saluted him, sat down to one side and said...'

It only remains to add that, as far as verse-passages are concerned, I have done my best. I have made no attempt to reproduce original metrical patterns. Here, too, taste has changed since the days of the earlier translators.

7 Sometimes there is doubt about the original form of a word. Thus in the Pali Canon, Gotama before his enlightenment is referred to as the *Bodhisatta*: a term much better known, with some doctrinal development, in its Sanskrit form of *Bodhisattva*, 'enlightenment-being'. But it has been suggested that the element *-satta* in Pali here stands not for *sattva* 'being' but for *sakta* 'intent on'. In this case *Bodhisatta* would mean 'one intent on enlightenment'. On philological grounds alone, at least, we cannot be sure which explanation is right.

8 This edition has its faults, being based on the somewhat fortuitous collection of manuscripts available at the time. Other and probably better editions exist, printed in Sri Lanka, Burma and Thailand. There is even one passage in Sutta 1 where the old translation by Gogerly (1846, reprinted in *Sept Suttas Palis* by P. Grimblot, Paris 1876) has a better reading than in the PTS edition.

9 The archaising, quasi-Biblical (in the old-fashioned sense) style adopted by Professor Rhys Davids and others may have been almost a necessity at the time, but is now not only irritating to many modern readers – it is often barely intelligible to them. Also, the early translators' technical terms have often been superseded. It must also be said that the Rhys Davids translation, the latter part of which was made by Mrs Rhys Davids, is often careless, with some curious omissions and inconsistencies. That said, tribute must be paid to the pioneering husband and wife team for the vast amount

of learning they jointly put into their work. Many of Rhys Davids's introductions to individual Suttas, for instance, are still a joy to read, and many of his interpretations have stood the test of time well – better indeed than most of those later developed by his wife.

10 The arguments of Rhys Davids, when, in 1899, he argued against those who unjustifiably disparaged the Sinhalese tradition (and who, much later, were to be joined by his own widow!), are echoed today by a leading specialist, A.K. Warder, who writes in the preface to vol. iii of the PTC (1963):

> The *Pāḷi*, as the only complete recension of the original canon extant, must play the central part in reconstructing such an original [i.e. 'as rehearsed by the Buddha's followers']. The possibility of establishing a substantial amount of such an original Buddhist Canon seems now vouched for by the comparisons made especially by É. Lamotte, in his most valuable *Histoire du Bouddhisme Indien* (Vol. I, Louvain, 1958), where the value of the basic Pāḷi texts on Buddhist doctrine – so often thrust aside in recent years as unauthentic Sinhalese perversions and fabrications probably less faithful to the original doctrine than even the Mahāyāna Sūtras – is reaffirmed by collation with whatever is available of the other recensions of the so-called 'Hīnayāna' Canon. A variety of methods now lie to hand for ascertaining the original Buddhist doctrine (presumably of the Buddha himself – who else?): (1) collation of the early canons, (2) collation of the *mātikā* [see n.1012], (3) the recorded history of the doctrinal peculiarities of the Buddhist schools, (4) comparison and contrast with non-Buddhist schools, (5) chronological distinctions among the texts on grounds of vocabulary and grammatical usages, (6) chronological distinctions among the texts on grounds of metrical usages.

It should be added here that A.K. Warder is himself the leading authority on point (6).

SUTTA 1

11 There is a separate translation of this Sutta by Bhikkhu Bodhi, *The All-Embracing Net of Views: The Brahmajāla Sutta and its Commentaries* (BPS 1978). This is most valuable for its introduction as well as the translated commentarial material. Beside the Rhys Davids translation (RD) there is also the somewhat abridged version by Mrs A.A.G. Bennett in *Long Discourses of the Buddha* (Bombay 1964, Suttas 1–16 only), and that by David Maurice in *The Lion's Roar* (London 1962), both of which I have occasionally found useful. I have also consulted the German partial translation (Suttas 1, 2, 3, 4, 5, 8, 9, 11, 13, 16, 21, 26, 27) by R.O. Franke (1913), and, as far as my limited knowledge of Thai would allow, the Thai translation (2nd ed., Bangkok 2521 (1978)). *Brahma-* in the title has the meaning of 'supreme'.

12 Nāḷandā, afterwards the seat of a famous Buddhist university, was about 12 km north of Rājagaha (modern Rajgir), the Magadhan capital.

13 A follower of Sañjaya Belaṭṭhaputta (see DN 2.31f.). Sāriputta and Moggallāna, the Buddha's most famous disciples, were originally followers of Sañjaya, and it was their defection, besides the loss of his gains, that angered Suppiya (DA).

14 Lit. 'That is not in us'.

15 DA points out that 'morality is inferior in comparison with higher qualities, for morality does not reach the excellence of concentration, nor concentration the excellence of wisdom.' Cf. verse 28.

16 *Puthujjana*: an 'ordinary person' who, not having broken through the first three fetters (personality-view, doubt, attachment to rites and rituals), has not yet 'entered the stream' and so started on the higher (supramundane) path.

17 The Buddha's usual way of referring to himself. See Introduction, p. 46.

18 These three sections on morality occur verbatim in all of the first 13 Suttas and may once have formed a separate 'tract' (RD).

19 This 'refrain' is repeated throughout.

20 *Brahmacariyā* is the supreme or holy life, i.e. celibacy. DA points out that it involves refraining from other forms of erotic behaviour besides intercourse.

21 *Atthavādī*: *attha* may also mean 'that which is profitable' (see next note).

22 *Atthasaṁhitaṁ*: here the meaning of *attha* as 'the profitable' is clear.

23 'At improper times' means between midday and the following dawn.

24 Verses 8–9 embrace the first four precepts undertaken by novices (*sāmaṇeras*). The elaboration of the different forms of wrong speech here (and elsewhere) reflects the importance of controlling the tongue. Curiously, there is no mention of abstaining from intoxicants, but instead a reference to 'damaging seeds and crops'. The next five items correspond to the novices' precepts 6–10.

25 The Buddha did, however, accept land from Anāthapiṇḍika and others for the Sangha.

26 *Sobha-nagarakaṁ*: 'of the city Sobha' (this was the city of the *gandhabbas* or heavenly musicians). RD thinks of a ballet with fairy scenes. BB renders it 'art exhibitions' – which surely gives the wrong impression for modern readers!

27 *Caṇḍālaṁ vaṁsaṁ dhopanaṁ*: rather obscure. The performers were presumably low-caste. DA thinks of an iron ball (used for juggling?).

28 Chess, with a board of 64 or 100 squares, originated in India. Though previously not unknown, it was popularised in Europe by the Crusaders.

29 Mental chess, played without a board.

30 Written in the air, or on one's back. Writing was known, but was not used by the Buddha or other teachers of the day.

31 A guessing game, not telepathy.

32 *Pallanka:* (whence, ultimately, our 'palanquin'), also means 'sitting cross-legged' (see n.519, 520).

33 *Tiracchāna-kathā*: lit. 'animal-talk'. As animals walk parallel to the earth, so this kind of talk does not lead upward (DA). See also n.244.

34 *Lokakkhāyikaṁ*: philosophical speculations of a materialist kind (DA).

35 *Iti-bhavâbhava-kathā*: also rendered 'profit and loss', but the philosophical sense (as in the Horner and Ñāṇamoli translations of MN 76) is preferable.

36 Also at MN 77, and SN 46.9.

37 For a detailed account of these practices, see VM 1.61–82.

38 *Angaṁ*: including soles as well as palms.

39 Knowing charms to be used by one dwelling in an earthen house.

40 *Kaṇṇika-lakkhaṇaṁ*: from *kaṇṇa* 'ear'. DA thinks it means either ear-rings or house-gables, both of which are incongruous here. I follow the Thai translation which, probably following an old tradition, has *tun* 'bamboo-rat' (see McFarland, *Thai-English Dictionary*, p. 371). Franke says 'an animal that is always mentioned with the hare', and considers that it must mean an animal with long ears.

41 *Raññaṁ* (gen. pl.): i.e. the joint leaders of a republican state.

42 *Viruddha-gabbha-karaṇaṁ*: Or perhaps 'reviving the foetus'.

43 It is the practice of medicine for gain that is here condemned.

44 These wrong views are summarised in verse 3.32ff.

45 I.e., producing nothing new.

46 *Saṁvaṭṭaṁ-vivaṭṭaṁ*: 'The PED definitions should be reversed' (BB). See VM 13.28ff.

47 *Takkī*: BB renders this 'rationalist', which is somewhat misleading.

48 This is part of the world of Form (*rūpaloka*) which escapes destruction. For this and other such 'locations' see Introduction, p. 37.

49 *Manomayā*: mentally created, not sexually generated.

They are devas. In another sense, all *dhammas* are said to be mind-made (Dhp. 1–2).

50 Not requiring material food, but nourished by the *jhāna* factor *pīti* 'delight' (n.81).

51 Brahmā is allotted a relatively humble position, and his creator-role explained away, in Buddhism. See also MN 49.8 (= MLS i, 391).

52 The life-span of beings is fixed in some realms, and variable in others. Merit (*puñña*) is karmically wholesome action, leading to a favourable rebirth.

53 *Khiḍḍapadosikā*: these devas and the next group are mentioned only here and in Suttas 20, 24. They illustrate the consequences of desire and aversion even in the (relatively) 'higher' worlds. Moral progress is virtually impossible outside the human state, so that they are actually fortunate to fall back to that state. Mindfulness (*sati*) is all-important. DA says the bodies of these devas are so delicate that if by forgetfulness they miss a single meal they will pass away from that place. Even if they eat immediately afterwards, it is too late!

54 *Manopadosikā*. DA says these dwell on the plane of the Four Great Kings (i.e. only just above the human realm). Interestingly, if only one of the devas gets angry while the other remains calm, this prevents the first from passing away, which would seem to illustrate the sentiment of Dhp. 5, 6. These devas are not essentially different from those mentioned in verses 1–2, though on a lower level.

55 *Citta*: more or less synonymous with *mano* 'mind', but often used much like 'heart' in English ('to know in one's heart', etc.).

56 *Antânantikā*: or 'Extensionists' (RD).

57 DA associates these various views with the higher jhānas (see Introduction, p. 42), obtained with the aid of the *kasiṇas* (coloured discs, etc., cf. VM chs. 4, 5). DA says: '(1) Without having extended the counterpart sign to the boundaries of the world-sphere, he abides perceiving the world as finite. (2) But he who has extended the *kasiṇa*-image to the boundaries of the world-sphere perceives the world to be infinite. (3) Not extending the

sign in the upward and downward directions, but extending it across, he perceives the world as finite in the upward and downward directions, and infinite across. (4) The rationalist doctrine should be understood by the method stated.' [This is unexplained, though the Sub-Commentary attempts an explanation: 'If the self were finite, its rebirth in distant places could not be recollected. And if it were infinite, one living in this world would be able to experience the happiness of the heavenly worlds and the suffering of the hells, etc. If one holds it to be both finite and infinite, one would incur the errors of both the previous positions. Therefore the self cannot be declared to be either finite or infinite.'] (Translated by BB, pp. 172, 171).

58 *Amarā-vikheppikā* can be interpreted as either 'eel-wriggling' (RD) or 'endless equivocation' (BB): *amarā* (lit. 'deathless') is the name of a slippery fish, perhaps an eel, which escapes capture by wriggling (DA). A deliberate pun may well be intended.

59 Either for the higher training or for a heavenly rebirth (DA). Cf. verse 1.5, where the former is certainly meant.

60 Due to moral shame and moral dread (*hiri-ottappa*) (DA), i.e. shame at doing what is wrong, and dread of it. These two qualities are called 'guardians of the world' (cf. Nyāṇaponika Thera, *Abhidhamma Studies*, 2nd. ed., Colombo 1965, p. 80). Thus it is recognised that the first three classes of 'eel-wrigglers' have a moral conscience. Their equivocation stems from lack of understanding, not of scruple.

61 The following views are attributed in DN 2.31f. to Sañjaya (see n.13).

62 The four 'alternatives' of Indian logic: a thing (*a*) is, (*b*) is not, (*c*) both is and is not, (*d*) neither is nor is not.

63 See n.185.

64 See also DN 9.25 and n.219.

65 Having attained a high absorption, and fearing the perils of conscious existence, they have wished for, and gained, an unconscious state. With the first stirring of perception, however, they fall away from that realm (DA).

66 The view of the Ājīvikas (DA): see DN 2.19–20 and nn.102–109 there. Cf. A.L. Basham, *History and Doctrine of the Ājīvikas,* (London 1951).

67 This is the view of the Jains. DA says the other views mentioned are based on various meditational experiences.

68 The Sub-Commentary (see BB, p. 190) is helpful here: (1) is based on experience of the unconscious realm (see n.65), (2) takes perception to be the self, (3) takes the material, or material and immaterial *dhammas* + perception to be the self, (4) is based on reasoning, (5–8) are to be understood as at n.57.

69 (1) is based on a subtle perception incapable of performing this function at death and rebirth-linking (see n.125). The rest as in n.68.

70 'Earth' (*paṭhavī*) or extension, 'water' (*āpo*) or cohesion, 'fire' (*tejo*) or temperature, 'air' (*vāyo*) or motion: the traditional names for the four qualities present, in varying proportions, in all matter.

71 In the Buddhist view, there is additionally required the presence of the *gandhabba* or 'being-to-be-born', i.e. the arising of a new 'continuity of consciousness' dependent on that of some being just deceased. Cf. MN 38.1–7. See p. 45.

72 *Dibba* (Skt. *divya*): derived from the same stem as *deva*: cf. Latin *divus.*

73 *Kāmâvacara*: belonging to the sensuous sphere (*kāmaloka*), the lowest of the three worlds.

74 *Kabalinkārâhāra* generally means 'material food'. Here it denotes the kind of nutriment on which the lower devas subsist.

75 DA says this one takes the divine form (*dibb'-atthabhāva*), i.e. the form of the devas of the sensuous sphere, for the self. The assumption is that this survives the break-up of the physical body for a period of time (of unspecified duration), 'annihilation' occurring at its cessation, and similarly with the remaining 'selves'. As BB points out (p. 32), 'Only the first form of annihilationism is materialistic; six admit that the doctrine can take on a spiritual garb.'

76 'Produced by the *jhāna*-mind' (DA).

77 The next four correspond to the 4th-7th 'liberations' (DN 15.35) or the four higher, 'formless' jhānas.

78 This is not, of course, the real Nibbāna of Buddhism (see Introduction, p. 27). DA says it means the subsiding of suffering (*dukkhavūpasama*) in this very individual form (subsiding being something far short of cessation). The New Sub-Commentary (quoted by BB, p. 197) adds: 'It is not the supreme fruit and not the unconditioned element (*asankhata-dhātu* = *nibbāna*), for these are beyond the domain of these theorists.'

79 The various jhānas are mistaken for Nibbāna.

80 *Vitakka-vicāra*: otherwise rendered 'initial and sustained thought', and the like. I am indebted to L.S. Cousins for the suggestion that I should adopt the Ven. Ñāṇamoli's original rendering 'thinking and pondering' (altered by the editor) in his MN translation (forthcoming). Cf. n.611.

81 *Pīti*: a difficult word to translate. Renderings vary from 'interest' through 'zest' to 'rapture'. It is classified not as a feeling (*vedanā*) but as part of the group of mental formations (*sankhārā*), i.e. as a mental reaction. BDic says: 'It may be described psychologically as "joyful interest"' – for which the simplest term would seem to be 'delight'.

82 *Sukha*: pleasant feeling, physical or mental (though for the latter the word *somanassa* exists). The difference between this and *pīti* may seem subtle but is important.

83 *Samādhi* here has its basic meaning of 'concentration'.

84 *Upekkhaka*.

85 *Sampajāna*: not 'self-possessed' as so many translators have repeated after RD.

86 *Phassa* is the 'contact' between sense-base and its object, e.g. eye and visible object. Such contact is the basis of feeling (*vedanā*).

87 Eye, ear, nose, tongue, body as base of the tactile sense, and mind (which is always the sixth sense in Buddhism).

88 This is the first, partial, exposition of dependent origination (*paṭicca-samuppāda*) in the Canon. See Introduction, p. 34, and Suttas 14, 15.

89 All that formerly bound him to the cycle of rebirth.

90 *Attha*: cf. nn. 21 and 22.

SUTTA 2

91 The royal physician. MN 55 (on meat-eating) is addressed to him. See n.417.

92 Reigned ca. 491–459 B.C. He had killed his father, the noble Bimbisāra, to gain the throne. See further n.365.

93 *Uposatha* (Skt. *upavasatha*): here denotes a Brahmin fast-day. Later, in Buddhism the fortnightly day of confession for monks.

94 *Kattika* : mid-October to mid-November.

95 Called after the white water-lily (*kumuda*) which blooms then.

96 'Our heart' is royal plural. Ajātasattu was troubled in conscience on account of his crime: see verse 99.

97 One who trains men (who are capable of being trained) as a charioteer trains horses.

98 The son who was eventually to kill him, only to be murdered in turn by *his* son. It evidently ran in the family (see DPPN).

99 A naked wanderer (DA). Such views as his, involving a denial of any reward or punishment for good and bad deeds, are regarded as especially pernicious.

100 Probably owing to his bad conscience. But the remark also suggests the enormous (and not always deserved) respect in which such wandering teachers were held.

101 'Makkhali of the Cow-Pen', leader of the Ājīvikas. See n.66.

102 *Hetu* means 'root' (e.g. greed, hatred or delusion); *paccaya* means 'condition'.

103 *Kamma*: but not quite in the Buddhist sense of 'volitional action'.

104 According to the five outward senses (cf. n.87).

105 Of thought, word and deed.

106 'Half-action', in thought only.

107 Basically, serpent-deities. See Introduction, p. 45.

108 *Nigaṇṭhi-gabbhā*: 'rebirths as a *Nigaṇṭha*'. See n.114.

109 Both the form (*paṭuvā, pavuṭā*?) and the meaning of this word are doubtful.

110 The Buddhist view of kamma is thus denied.

111 'Ajita of the Hairy Garment' (he wore a cloak of human hair): a materialist.

112 Cf. nn.49, 63.

113 Holder of an atomic theory.

114 The name given in the Pali Canon to Vardhamāna Mahāvīra (ca. 540–568 B.C.?), the leader of the Jains. He is several times referred to (unfavourably) in the Canon, e.g. at MN 56. *Nigaṇṭha* means 'free from bonds'. See next note and n.900.

115 *Sabba-vāri-vārito, sabba-vāri-yuto, sabba-vāri-dhuto, sabba-vāri-phuṭṭo* (with some variant readings). They do not represent the genuine Jain teaching but seem to parody it in punning form. The Jains do have a rule of restraint in regard to water, and *vāri* can mean 'water', 'restraint', or possibly 'sin', and some of the verbal forms are equally dubious. The reference to one 'free from bonds' and yet bound by these restraints (whatever they are) is a deliberate paradox. I am most grateful to K.R. Norman for his very helpful comments. Finally I settled for a slight variation on the Ven. Ñāṇamoli's rendering of the corresponding passage in MN 56.

116 Meritorious deeds (*puñña*) do not lead to enlightenment, but to (temporary) future happiness in this world or another. This is the usual aim of 'popular' Buddhism.

117 Māra, the personified tempter like the Biblical Satan (he appears in person in DN 16). Both Māra and Brahmā are subject to rebirth, and their 'office' is taken over by other beings according to their kamma.

118 *Deva* again, this time in the sense of 'devas by convention', i.e. kings.

119 *Parimukhaṁ satiṁ upaṭṭhapetvā*: probably means 'having firmly established mindfulness'. See n.637.

120 Cultivation of the perception of light is given as a standard way of overcoming the hindrance of sloth-and-torpor (*thīna-midha*). See VM 1.140.

121 The five hindrances are temporarily dispelled by the jhāna states.

122 This concludes the Buddha's answer to the first part of the question posed in verse 39.

123 *Uppala* (Skt. *utpala*), *paduma* (Skt. *padma*), *puṇḍarīka* are different kinds of lotus, usually of the colour mentioned.

124 *Upakilesa*: to be distinguished from *kilesa* 'defilement'. Perhaps the 10 'imperfections of insight' listed in VM 20.105ff. are meant; most of these are not defilements in themselves, but potential hindrances at a certain stage of insight meditation.

125 RD points out that this and other passages disprove the idea that consciousness (*viññāṇa*) transmigrates. For holding this belief Sāti was severely rebuked by the Buddha (MN 38). A new relinking consciousness (*paṭisandhi*) arises at conception, dependent on the old (see VM 17.164ff.).

126 *Veḷuriya*: from a metathetised form *veruliya* comes Greek *beryllos* 'beryl', whence German *Brille* 'spectacles' (originally of beryl).

127 Exactly like the physical body: cf. n.49. This mind-made body is what is mistaken for a soul or self.

128 *Iddhi* (Skt. *ṛddhi*, not, as often stated, *siddhi*): translated by RD as 'The Wondrous Gift' and glossed as 'well-being, prosperity'. With dawning recognition of ESP, it is no longer necessary to discount these powers. But despite his mention of them here, the Buddha disapproved of these practices (see DN 11.5).

129 DA has no useful comment on this, and modern commentators too are silent, but 'touching the sun and moon' probably refers to some psychic experience. In any case it is certainly not to be taken literally.

130 *Dibba-sota*: clairaudience (cf. n.72).

131 The following list of mental states is doubtless taken from DN 22.12, where it is more appropriate. For notes, see there.

132 The three villages are the three worlds of Sense-Desire, of Form, and the Formless World (DA).

133 *Dibba-cakkhu*: clairvoyance, not to be confused with the Dhamma-eye (verse 102). See n.140.

134 *Āsavā*: from *ā-savati* 'flows towards' (i.e. either 'into', or 'out' towards the observer). Variously translated 'biases', 'intoxicants', 'influxes', 'cankers' or 'Deadly Taints' (RD). A further corruption, that of wrong views

(*diṭṭhāsava*) is sometimes added. The destruction of the *āsavas* is equivalent to Arahantship.

135 *Nâparaṁ itthatāya*: lit. 'there is no more of "thusness"'. See DN 15.22.

136 All the preceding 'fruits' have led up to this, which alone, as RD points out, is exclusively Buddhist. There are 13 items or groups, and the list, in whole or with some omissions, recurs in every Sutta of Division 1. Summarised, they are: 1. The respect shown to a member of a religious order (verses 35–38); 2. The training in morality as in DN 1 (verses 43–62); 3. Confidence felt as a result of right action (verse 63); 4. The habit of guarding the sense-doors (verse 64); 5. Resulting mindfulness and clear awareness (verse 65); 6. Being content with little (verse 66); 7. Freedom from the five hindrances (verses 68–74); Resulting joy and peace (verse 75); 9. The four jhānas (verses 75–82); 10. Knowledge born of insight (verses 83–84); 11. The production of mental images (verses 85–86); 12. The five mundane forms of 'higher knowledge' (*abhiññā*) (verses 87–96); 13. The realisation of the Four Noble Truths, the destruction of the corruptions (= the sixth, supramundane, *abhiññā*), and the attainment of Arahantship (verses 97–98).

137 *Accayo*: often rendered (as by RD) 'sin', but this term with its theistic connotations is best avoided when translating Buddhist texts.

138 This is the formula used by bhikkhus when confessing transgressions.

139 *Khatâyaṁ bhikkhave rājā, upahatâyaṁ bhikkhave rājā*. RD went astray with his translation here: 'This king, brethren, was deeply affected, he was touched in heart.' Lit. 'uprooted and destroyed', the expression indicates that Ajātasattu was inhibited by his kamma from obtaining the results that would otherwise have accrued, since parricide is one of the evil acts 'with immediate result' (in the next world) that cannot be avoided. According to DA, he was unable to sleep until his visit to the Buddha.

140 The opening of the Dhamma-eye (*dhamma-cakkhu*) is a

term for 'entering the stream' and thus being set irrevocably on the path. As RD points out, it is superior to the divine eye (*dibba-cakkhu*: verse 95 and n.133), which is a superior kind of clairvoyance, and below the wisdom-eye (*paññā-cakkhu*), which is the wisdom of the Arahant.

SUTTA 3

141 A stock phrase, as at DN 4.1, 5.1, MN 95.1, etc. RD translates 'on a royal domain...as a royal gift (*rājadāyaṁ*), with power over it as if he were the king (*brahmadeyyaṁ*)'. *Brahmadeyyaṁ* = 'supreme gift', one which could not be revoked.

142 Another stock description, of a learned Brahmin.

143 For a full account of these (pre-Buddhist) marks, see DN 30. They are clearly important to the Brahmin as establishing 'the ascetic Gotama's' credentials.

144 See DN 17.

145 See DN 17.

146 *Loke vivattacchado*: a difficult expression. I follow DA. The 'veil' is that of ignorance, etc.

147 This division into four groups shows the earliest stage of the caste-system. In the Buddha's time and in his homeland, the Khattiyas ('Warrior-Nobles'), to whom he belonged, still formed the first caste, with the Brahmins taking second place, though the latter had already established themselves as the leading caste further west, and were clearly fighting for that position here. The Buddha himself often refers to a different fourfold grouping: Khattiyas, Brahmins, householders and ascetics.

148 *Sākasaṇḍa*. The word *sāka* can also mean 'herb' (RD), but here surely bears its other meaning of 'teak'. RD deliberately mistranslated as 'oak' for the sake of a somewhat feeble play on words. There is an actual play on *sakāhi* 'own (sisters)' just previously.

149 In conformity with the previous note, RD here translates 'hearts of oak' (!).

150 A curious threat that (as RD observes) never comes to anything, and is of course pre-Buddhist.

151 This yakkha, equated by DA with Indra, is ready, as in MN 35.14, to take the threat literally. Thus one of the old gods is seen as supporting the new religion. In later Mahāyāna texts we find a Bodhisattva of the same name. See D.L. Snellgrove, *Buddhist Himālaya* (Oxford 1957), p. 62, and I.B. Horner's note, MLS i, p. 185.

152 *Isi* (Sanskrit *ṛṣi*, anglicised as 'rishi'). Is he to be identified with Krishna (Skt. *Kṛṣṇa* = Pali *Kaṇha*)?

153 *Dakkhiṇa janapada*: anglicised as the Deccan.

154 According to DA, this was called the 'Ambaṭṭha spell'.

155 Bluff, according to DA: in reality the spell could only stop the discharge of the arrow.

156 *Brahmadaṇḍa*: 'extreme punishment' (in another sense at DN 16.6.4).

157 Here, and in the corresponding places in the other Suttas of this Division, the MSS abridge and say 'as in the Sāmaññaphala Sutta'. But 'refrains' differ, and it is not always quite clear how much of DN 2 is meant to be included.

158 *Apāya-mukhāni*: lit. 'outlets of loss' ('leakages', RD). Used in another sense, DN 31.3.

159 *Anabhisambhūṇamāno*: almost literally 'not up to it'.

160 A pole or yoke for carrying his possessions.

161 I.e. digging them up, which the first one did not do.

162 The sacred fire, or perhaps Aggi (Agni) the fire-god.

163 Ancient rishis associated with the Vedic hymns (cf. DN 13.13). For what follows, see also DN 27.22ff.

164 A frequent formula, belatedly explained by RD at DN 16.5.19. 'The Wanderers...lived with only one robe on, the one from the waist to the feet. When they set out for the village...they put on the second robe and...carried the third with them. At some convenient spot near the village they would put this also on, and enter – so to speak – in full canonicals.'

165 This passage recurs at DN 5.29, DN 14.11 and elsewhere. For the Dhamma-eye see DN 2.102 and n.140. The Pali phrase is *Yaṁ kiñci samudaya-dhammaṁ taṁ nirodha-dhammaṁ*.

166 Pokkharasāti did not apparently consult his wife, family and dependents. When Uruvela-Kassapa wanted to join

the Sangha, the Buddha bade him first consult his 500 followers (Mv 1.20.18). But there is of course a big difference between becoming a lay-follower and joining the Sangha.

SUTTA 4

167 Cf. MN 95.6.
168 The jhānas are here put, not under morality (*sīla*) but under wisdom (*paññā*) (RD). But their proper place is under concentration (*samādhi*), which is not specifically mentioned. See n.1127.
169 As RD remarks, Soṇadaṇḍa is 'represented as being a convert only to a limited extent'. Accordingly there is no mention in his case of the arising of the 'pure and spotless Dhamma-eye' as in the case of Pokkharasāti (DN 3.2.21) and others. Soṇadaṇḍa remained a *puthujjana*. See n.16.

SUTTA 5

170 Not the same place as that mentioned in DN 1.2, but one similar to it (DA).
171 His name means 'Sharp-tooth', and RD is almost certainly right in considering this an invented story. Apart from anything else, no Brahmin would have consulted the Buddha, of all people, about how to perform a sacrifice, which was supposed to be their speciality. But at SN 3.1.9 we have the presumably historical story of how King Pasenadi of Kosala planned a great sacrifice (though of only 500, not 700, bulls, etc.), with the Buddha's versified comments. From the commentary, though not the text, we hear that the King finally desisted from his intention. Perhaps the Buddha told the King this story on that occasion, and the incident was later tactfully transferred from the King of Kosala to an imaginary Brahmin 'with royal powers' living in the neighbouring kingdom of Magadha.
172 'Lord Broadacres' (RD).

173 *Purohitaṁ*. 'The king's head-priest (brahmanic), or domestic chaplain, acting at the same time as a sort of Prime Minister' (PED).

174 The Khattiyas, counsellors, Brahmins and householders.

175 Elephants, cavalry, chariots and infantry.

176 By knowing the workings of kamma: good fortune now is due to past kamma, and good deeds performed now will have similar results in the future (DA).

177 Cf. DN 3.20, and n.150.

178 In his important book *Five Stages of Greek Religion* (London, Watts & Co., 1935, p. 38) Gilbert Murray has a fine passage in praise of the Greek spirit. He writes:

> When really frightened the oracle generally fell back on some remedy full of pain and blood. The medieval plan of burning heretics alive had not yet been invented. But the history of uncivilized man, if it were written, would provide a vast list of victims, all of them innocent, who died or suffered to expiate some portent or *monstrum*...with which they had nothing whatever to do...The sins of the modern world in dealing with heretics and witches have perhaps been more gigantic than those of primitive men, but one can hardly rise from the record of these ancient observances without being haunted by the judgement of the Roman poet: 'Tantum religio potuit suadere malorum' ['To so many evils was religion able to persuade men'], and feeling with him that the lightening of this cloud, the taming of this blind dragon, must rank among the very greatest services that Hellenism wrought for mankind.

Murray seems only to think of human victims, and to be totally oblivious to the fact that Buddhism had, a century before Socrates, been much more radical in its abolition of cruelty to humans and animals, and with more lasting results, at least as far as India and neighbouring countries were concerned.

SUTTAS 6 & 7

179 This is his family-name or surname (*gotta*), as Gotama was the Buddha's. RD in a note on names explains that this is a polite form of address (remotely comparable to the now perhaps obsolescent English 'public school' use of surnames).

180 A very gifted young man, whose judgement was clearly respected by his seniors.

181 This was Nāgita's family-name (cf. n.179).

182 For more about Sunakkhatta, see DN 24.

183 A particular type of concentration.

184 The intolerably laboured repetition concerning a relatively unimportant matter is noteworthy, even in a style given to much repetition. This *may* be symptomatic of a late date for this Sutta.

185 *Opapātika*: here in the specific sense of Non-Returner (*anāgāmī*). See n.63.

186 *Jīvaṁ:* 'Life-principle'.

187 Cf. DN 1.3.10. Some MSS have: 'It is, friend'.

188 For some reason the last part of Sutta 6 is here repeated as a separate Sutta.

SUTTA 8

189 Alternative title to this Sutta, *Mahāsīhanāda Sutta*, is *Kassapa-Sīhanāda Sutta* (RD).

190 A public park in which the deer were safe from being hunted (DA).

191 *Tapaṁ*: severe forms of self-mortification as listed in verse 14. See Introduction, p. 23. This is to be distinguished from asceticism as such. However, the term 'penance' used by RD is wrong because the intention is quite different from the Christian idea of penance. Having used 'ascetic' for *samaṇa* (since the term 'recluse' favoured by some translators is inappropriate), I have fallen back on the cumbrous 'practiser of austerity' for the term *tapassī* used here. Fortunately this term occurs so much more rarely than *samaṇa* that little inconvenience results.

192 Cf. DN 2.95.

193 *Akusala*: lit. 'unskilled', i.e. unwholesome and productive of unfavourable karmic results.
194 Cf. DN 1.1.9.
195 In regard to bodily functions (DA). The whole list recurs, e.g. at MN 12.45.
196 *Thusodakaṁ*: 'rice-gruel', but the sense requires something fermented. RD's assertion to the contrary is not supported by the Sub-Commentary. Ñāṇamoli, at MN 12.45, renders it 'besotting drink'.
197 One who accepts alms from only one house.
198 One who takes only one portion.
199 Like Ajita Kesakambalī (DN 2.22).
200 *Apānaka*. Probably one who (like the Jains) does not drink cold water because of the living beings in it.
201 In order to wash away his sin: cf. the story of Sangārava (SN 7.2.11).
202 The passage: 'but if his morality...' recurs, first after 'twice a month', then after 'windfalls', and in conclusion. As RD points out, the Buddha is using the terms 'ascetic' and 'Brahmin' in his own sense, not Kassapa's.
203 See DN 25.

SUTTA 9

204 The principal queen of King Pasenadi of Kosala. She and the king were both devoted followers of the Buddha. The park had been given by the famous benefactor Anāthapiṇḍika.
205 *Abhisaññānirodha*. 'The prefix *abhi* qualifies not *saññā*, but the whole compound, which means "trance" [*sic!*]. It is an expression used, not by Buddhists, but by certain wanderers' (PED).
206 *Saññā* means primarily 'perception' as one of the five *khandhas*, but here approaches the meaning of 'consciousness' as such (see BDic). After some hesitation, I have retained the rendering 'perception' here.
207 DA says *athabbanikā* ('Atharva priests') can do this.
208 RD accidentally omits this passage.
209 *Sukusala*: an intensified form of *kusala* 'skilled'.
210 *Viveka-ja-pīti-sukha-sukhuma-sacca-saññā*: the regular

formula for the first jhāna but expanded with the words *sukhuma-sacca* 'subtle and true'.

211 *Saka-saññī hoti*: lit. 'becomes own-perceiving'. From the first jhāna on one has some control over one's perceptions.

212 *Abhisankhāreyyaṁ*. RD has 'fancying', with footnote: 'perhaps "perfecting" or "planning out"'. Mrs Bennett has 'manipulating'.

213 DA offers alternative explanations: 1. 'Perception' = 'jhāna-perception', 'Knowledge' = 'insight-knowledge' (*vipassanā-ñāṇaṁ*); 2. 'Perception' = 'insight-perception', 'Knowledge' = 'path-knowledge'; 3. 'Perception' = 'path-perception', 'Knowledge' = 'fruition-knowledge' (*phal-añāṇaṁ*). He then quotes an authority as saying 'Perception' is the perception of the fruition of Arahantship, and 'Knowledge' the immediately following 'reviewing-knowledge' (*paccavekkhaṇa-ñāṇaṁ*): cf. VM 1.32, 22.19 and BDic. But in fact 'reviewing-knowledge' is said also to occur at lower stages on the enlightenment path. It is, however, this 'reviewing-knowledge' which best seems to explain just how one is supposed to know that perception arises first and then knowledge.

214 RD quotes DA's comment that a village pig, even if bathed in perfumed water, garlanded and laid on the best bed, will still return to the dunghill. In the same way Poṭṭhapāda still returns to the idea of a 'self'.

215 *Paccesi* 'fall back on'.

216 Cf. DN 1.3.11.

217 Cf. DN 1.3.12.

218 Cf. DN 1.3.13. According to DA, this represents Poṭṭhapāda's real opinion.

219 These are the ten *avyākatāni* or so-called indeterminates (better: 'undeclared points') or questions which the Buddha refused to answer:

1–2. Is the world eternal or not?
3–4. Is the world infinite or not?
5–6. Is the soul (*jīvaṁ*) the same as the body or not?
7–10. Does the Tathāgata (a) exist, (b) not exist, (c) both exist and not exist, (d) neither exist nor not exist, after death?

All of these are vain speculations, not conducive to enlightenment, and as stated with reference to numbers 5 and 6 in DN 6, for one who 'thus knows and thus sees' it is not proper to speculate on such things: in other words, the questions will drop away as meaningless. The same ten questions are found in various parts of the Canon, notably at MN 63 (with the famous analogy of the man wounded by an arrow, who refuses treatment until he has received the answers to a long string of questions) and MN 72 (the fire that went out); and there is a whole section (*saṁyutta*) (44) in SN. It has been thought that these questions formed a sort of questionnaire among the 'wanderers' to determine a man's position. This is only possible if the word *Tathāgata* had a pre-Buddhist meaning, which may well be the case. See discussion by Ñāṇananda, *Concept and Reality*, 95ff.

220 *Atta-paṭilābha*. This is, of course, only an 'assumed' or 'presumed' self: 'the fleeting union of qualities that make up, for a time only, an unstable individuality' (RD). The word is glossed by DA as *attabhāva-paṭilābha* 'adoption (or assumption) of selfhood'. The three kinds of 'acquired self' correspond to the three realms of Sense-Desire, of Form and of No-Form. Cf. DN 33.1.11 (38) and AN 4.172.

221 Doubtless alluding to the well-known fact that higher states tend to appear very boring to the worldling who has not experienced them.

222 'This very one that you see'.

223 *Sankhaṁ gacchati*: lit. 'enters the reckoning'.

224 An important reference to the two truths referred to in DA as 'conventional speech' (*sammuti-kathā*) and 'ultimately true speech' (*paramattha-kathā*). See Introduction, p. 31f. It is important to be aware of the level of truth at which any statements are made. In MA (*ad* MN 5: Anangana Sutta), the following verse is quoted (source unknown):

> Two truths the Buddha, best of all who speak,
>   declared:
> Conventional and ultimate – no third can be.
> Terms agreed are true by usage of the world;

Words of ultimate significance are true
In terms of *dhammas*. Thus the Lord, a Teacher, he
Who's skilled in this world's speech, can use it, and not lie.

SUTTA 10

225 We may wonder slightly, as RD does, why this is included as a separate Sutta, consisting as it does of little more than the corresponding passages in DN 2. But repetitiveness was never regarded by the early redactors of the Canon as a bar to inclusion, and this was no doubt independently preserved as an account of Subha's conversion. RD points out that the three heads here are given as *sīla, samādhi* and *paññā*, which we render (somewhat differently from RD) as morality, concentration and wisdom. RD also states that the term *samādhi* is not found in any pre-Buddhist text. To his remarks on the subject should be added that its subsequent use in Hindu texts to denote the state of enlightenment is not in conformity with Buddhist usage, where the basic meaning of concentration is expanded to cover 'meditation' in general.

226 Chronology is of little account in this Nikāya. The Buddha's final passing is narrated in DN 16.

227 A Brahmin, whose name means 'man of Tudi'.

228 Like Todeyya, he is named after his birthplace in the Cetiya country.

229 *Sīlakkhandha*. This is also the name of the first of the three divisions of this Nikāya, but the other two do not conform to the same pattern.

SUTTA 11

230 Or Kevaṭṭa ('Fisher') as several manuscripts have it. RD admits that 'it may turn out to be the better of the two.'

231 *Iddhi-pāṭihāriya*: 'miracle of *iddhi*' (see n.128).

232 *Ādesanā-pāṭihāriya*. This is actual telepathy, not the

same as *manesika* 'mind-searching' or guessing another's thoughts mentioned in DN 1.1.14.

233 *Anusāsani-pāṭihāriya*. The Buddha's teaching can be called miraculous because it leads to the most wonderful results.

234 A charm for making oneself invisible.

235 Or *cintāmaṇī vijjā* (DA), the 'jewel of thought' charm which enabled one to know the thoughts of others. The sceptic, of course, does not have a really convincing way of explaining things away. Modern parallels suggest themselves.

236 Omitting DN 2.85–96, which deal with the powers disparagingly mentioned in verse 4ff.

237 For all these realms and their inhabitants (verses 68–81) see Introduction p. 38f.

238 *Devaputta* here denotes the ruler of a certain group of devas. In other contexts it simply means 'male deva'.

239 Mind and body, i.e. 'subject and object' (Neumann quoted by RD).

240 *Anidassanaṁ*: or 'invisible'. Ñāṇananda (n.242) renders it 'non-manifesting'.

241 This word (*pabhaṁ* or *pahaṁ*) has been variously interpreted. DA takes it in the sense of a ford, or a place to enter the water 'accessible from all sides', by means of which one can reach Nibbāna. There is an improbable suggestion that the meaning is 'rejecting', and Mrs Bennett translates the line: 'Where the consciousness that makes endless comparisons is entirely abandoned', which seems to involve a misunderstanding of *anidassanaṁ*. (But see next note). The same sequence also occurs at MN 49.11, rendered by I.B. Horner (MLS i, 392): 'Discriminative consciousness (= *viññāṇaṁ*) which cannot be characterised (= *anidassanaṁ*), which is unending, lucid in every respect (= *sabbato pabhaṁ*).' The two passages should be studied in conjunction. Cf. also AN 1.6: 'This mind (*citta*) is luminous, but is defiled by adventitious defilements.' See important discussion by Ñāṇananda, 57–63.

242 G.C. Pande (*Studies in the Origins of Buddhism*, 92, n.21) says: 'Buddha says that the question should not be asked in the manner in which it is done in the prose

quotation above, but thus – as in the metrical lines that follow. One may pertinently ask: "Why? what is wrong with the prose formulation?" The only answer would seem to be: "Nothing. But the verses have to be brought in!".

Ñāṇananda (*Concept and Reality*, 59) explains it thus: 'The last line of the verse stresses the fact that the four great elements do not find a footing – and that 'Name-and-Form' (comprehending them) can be cut-off completely – in that '*anidassana-viññāṇa*' (the 'non-manifestative consciousness') of the Arahant, by the cessation of his normal consciousness which rests on the data of sense-experience. This is a corrective to that monk's notion that the four elements can *cease altogether* somewhere – a notion which has its roots in the popular conception of self-existing material elements. The Buddha's reformulation of the original question and this concluding line are meant to combat this wrong notion.'

SUTTA 12

243 *Kusalaṁ dhammaṁ.*

244 *Nirayaṁ vā tiracchāna-yoniṁ vā.* The statement that those who hold 'wrong views' are liable to hell or an animal rebirth is off-putting to modern readers. It is doubtful whether either term originally meant what it was later taken to mean. See Introduction, p. 40f. 'A painful or beast-like rebirth' might express the meaning better. It should be realised, too, that the 'wrong view' referred to means one according to which there are no rewards and punishments for good and evil deeds – hence no operation of a moral law. This kind of view the Buddha always declared to be particularly reprehensible. Cf. n.801.

245 Those whose meritorious deeds (*puñña*) will lead to rebirth in a deva-world, life in which is exceedingly pleasant, but not, of course, everlasting. The mischief of Lohicca's evil view is precisely that it may hinder such a consummation.

246 *Dhammaṁ*: but not necessarily the Buddhist Dhamma.
247 The Buddha repeats Lohicca's own phrase.
248 *Naraka*: a synonym of *niraya*, hell (n.244).

SUTTA 13

249 Union with Brahmā was the ultimate goal for the Brahmins. See n.258.
250 The alternative reading, adopted by RD, is *Bavharijā*, but RD notes: 'If we adopt the other reading [i.e. *Brāhmacariyā*, as he omits to say] for the last in the list, then those priests who relied on liturgy, sacrifice or chant would be contrasted with those who had "gone forth" as *religieux*, either as *Tâpasas* or as *Bhikshus*.'
251 The ten rishi authors of the Vedic mantras. Cf. MN 95.12.
252 Cf. DN 11.80.
253 Cf. MN 95.13.
254 *Saparigaha*. The PED gives both 'married' and 'encumbered'. Both are implied.
255 *Vasavattī*: lit. 'powerful', but here meaning having power, or control, over oneself.
256 These (pre-Buddhist) 'Divine Abidings' (*Brahmavihāra*) are also called the Boundless States (*appamaññā*).
257 *Pamāṇa kataṁ* according to DA denotes the sensuous sphere (*kāmaloka*). Cf. SN 42.8 (= KS iv, p. 227). DA says: 'Like the mighty ocean, flooding a little creek, he even reaches up to Brahmā' (tr. Woodward, *loc. cit.*).
258 See also DN 27, MN 98 and Sn. 594ff. DA says Vāseṭṭha's first taking refuge was after the preaching of the Vāseṭṭha Sutta (MN 98), and this was the second occasion. He 'went forth' and, after the preaching of the Aggañña Sutta (DN 27) he received the higher ordination and attained Arahantship.

RD's comment (RD i, p. 299), 'It should be recollected that the argument here is only *argumentum ad hominem*. If you want union with Brahmâ – which you had much better not want – this is the way to attain it', ignores the outcome as reported by DA. The Buddha's words were indeed, as in other cases, *ad hominem*, and had, as in other cases, the result of leading the enquirer beyond his original premises.

On 'union with Brahma' see Introduction, p. 43. See also DN 19.61.

SUTTA 14

259 This Sutta, the *Mahâpadāna Sutta*, marks the beginning of a new division and a new atmosphere. The division is called 'great' probably merely because most of the Suttas in it include *mahā* 'great' in their titles. *Mahâpadāna* = *Mahā-apadāna*. *Apadāna* (which is also the title of a book of the Khuddaka Nikāya) means 'legend, life-story': here of the last seven Buddhas as exemplified by Vipassī, whereas in the Khuddhaka Nikāya the stories are those of Arahants. The Sutta as it stands is clearly a late one, though with some earlier elements.

260 A fortunate aeon is one in which one or more Buddhas are born: the present aeon is one of five Buddhas, four of whom have already appeared.

261 The *ficus religiosa*. Descendants of the original tree are preserved at Bodh Gayā and Anuradhapura (Sri Lanka).

262 Cf. MN 123.4.

263 Identical, except for the 'refrains', with MN 123.8-end (MLS iii, pp. 165–169).

264 *Dhammatā*: that which is in accordance with *Dhamma* as universal law.

265 This is said to be one of the hell-states (cf. n.244).

266 The Four Great Kings (DA) (cf. DN 11.69).

267 Again, the Four Great Kings.

268 Vārāṇasī (Benares).

269 A symbol of royalty.

270 All these things are symbolic, according to DA. Standing on the earth denotes the four 'roads to power' (*iddhipadāni*). Facing north denotes the multitude to be won over. The seven steps are the seven factors of enlightenment (*bojjhangā*). The sunshade denotes liberation. Looking round denotes unobstructed know-

ledge. The bull's voice denotes the turning of the wheel, and the declaration of his last birth the 'lion's roar' of Arahantship to be.

271 Thus this light appears twice, at the conception and the birth of the Bodhisatta.

272 These marks are treated *in extenso* in DN 30.14ff. See notes there.

273 Related to *vipassanā* 'insight' (also as a meditation practice: cf. n.287 and DN 22).

274 Bearing in mind that the life-span of human beings at this time was supposedly 80,000 years (1.7). What follows is told, with reference to the Buddha Gotama, in the introduction (*nidānakathā*) to the Jātakas. Cf. Warren, BT, pp. 56ff.

275 *Antepuraṁ*: lit. 'inner dwelling', generally means 'harem', and according to 1.38 Vipassī was in fact attended solely by women. DA says he dismissed them and sat alone grieving, 'as if pierced to the heart by this first dart.'

276 Reading *sīro* 'head'. RD follows different MSS which read *saro* 'voice'. Cf. 2.14.

277 *Pabbajita*: we might say, the nearest equivalent of a Buddhist monk. In the *Nidānakathā* (n.274), where all four signs are specifically said to be sent by the gods, this is rationalised: 'Now although there was no Buddha in the world, and the charioteer had no knowledge of either monks or their good qualities, yet by the power of the gods he was inspired to say, "Sire, this is one who has retired from the world"' (Warren's translation).

278 This can be either taken as 'universal law' or, with a slight anachronism (in implied agreement with n.277) as the Buddhist teaching. 'Well and truly' renders *sādhu*. 'Does good actions' renders *kusala-kiriyā* lit. 'doing skilful actions', which has a definitely Buddhist ring.

279 Conventional for 'a very large number'.

280 Vipassī is here called the Bodhisatta for the first time, having now 'gone forth'.

281 There is a play on words here: *jāyati ca* (there is birth), *jīyati ca* (there is decay), *mīyati ca* (there is dying): the

first two terms are linked by alliteration, the second and third by rhyme.

282 *Yoniso manasikāra*: *yoni* means 'womb', hence 'source, origin'. The phrase really means 'going back to the root of the matter' – here, with perfect penetration; for lesser mortals, to a corresponding degree.

283 The realisation of dependent origination (*paṭicca-samuppāda*): see Introduction, p. 34. Here and in DN 15, only links 3–12 of the usual series are given (cf. n.286).

284 *Bhava*: the process of 'coming-to-be'. It also corresponds to the first two links not given here, which represent the 'coming-to-be' process in a past life.

285 *Phassa*. See n.86.

286 DA explains that Vipassī's reflection went back only to the beginning of *this* life.

287 RD comments: 'As this is not a stock phrase...it doubtless contains a play on the name Vipassī.'

288 He became an Arahant.

289 *Atakkâvacaro*: beyond the sphere of logical thought' (cf. n.97). That can only be realised by insight, not by reasoning alone.

290 *Ālaya-rāma*: 'delighting in a basis' (i.e. something it can cling to).

291 *Ida-paccayatā*: 'being conditioned by this' (i.e. the fact that everything has some specific condition).

292 *Paṭicca-samuppāda* (n.283).

293 *Sankhārā*: may here be loosely paraphrased as 'the emotions'.

294 *Upadhi*: all factors conducive to clinging, and hence to rebirth.

295 In other versions he is called Brahmā Sahampati (a mysterious title), and is identified with the Supreme Brahmā (though in the Buddhist view his supremacy is distinctly relative: cf. DN 11).

296 *Bhavissanti dhammassa aññātāro ti*. The meaning is quite plain, but I.B. Horner, piously following the (second) thoughts of her teacher Mrs Rhys Davids, renders (MN 26 = MLS i, p. 212): '(but if) they are learners of *dhamma* they will grow', thus giving *bhavissanti* the pregnant sense of '(more) becoming' which Mrs Rhys

Davids arbitrarily read into it wherever possible. Mrs Bennett in her version makes a different mistake: 'would not be informed of the Truth', taking *aññātāro* as incorporating the negative prefix.

297 This is, of course, superior to all those mentioned in n.140.

298 *Sumedho*: the name of the Brahmin who, going forth under Buddha Dīpankara, was to become the Buddha Gotama.

299 *Pamuñcantu saddhaṁ*. This has been strangely misinterpreted, e.g. 'renounce your empty faith' (Mrs RD), and 'abandon blind beliefs' (Bennett), through a misreading of DA. The Sub-Commentary renders it: 'let them declare their faith'.

300 A half-brother of Vipassī.

301 Cf. n.172.

302 The heavenly world that alone was open to people before the appearance of a Buddha.

303 This is a profounder insight than that mentioned in verse 11.

304 The attainment of Nibbāna (the 'Deathless') is now open to people by following the Buddha's teaching.

305 The number is, of course, even more absurd than the previous 84,000. It is based on the statement that Vipassī had an 'assembly' of that number.

306 'Rose-Apple Land', i.e. India.

307 = Dhp. 184.

308 = Dhp. 183.

309 = Dhp. 185.

310 Cf. DN 3.1.1.

311 The realm where Non-Returners are reborn.

312 *Mārisa*: 'Sir'. They do not recognise him as the Lord.

313 As Non-Returners.

314 *Dhammadhātu*: 'the Dhamma-Element'.

315 *Papañca*. According to Ven. Ñāṇananda, *Concept and Reality* (BPS 1971) this means man's 'tendency towards proliferation in the realm of concepts'.

316 The round of rebirths.

317 Burmese and Thai texts add a statement that the Buddha was also told about these matters by devas: cf. 1.15.

SUTTA 15

318 See *The Great Discourse on Causation: The Mahānidāna Sutta and its Commentaries*, translated from the Pali by Bhikkhu Bodhi, (BPS 1984).

319 There was nowhere in the town for the Buddha to stay, so he stayed outside, in the jungle: hence the construction 'There is a market town' (DA).

320 *Guḷāguṇṭhika-jāta*: or 'matted like a bird's nest.'

321 *Saṁsāra*.

322 *Idapaccayā*. Cf. n.291.

323 The six sense-bases are omitted, for some reason, in this Sutta.

324 Cf. n.286.

325 The more literal rendering is: 'with *x* as condition, *y* comes to be.'

326 *Bhūtānaṁ*: 'beings', but the term is sometimes used in the sense of 'ghosts'. The Sub-Commentary identifies them with the Kumbhaṇḍas mentioned at DN 32.5 (q.v.).

327 *Pariyesanā*. Verses 9–18 constitute an excursus.

328 *Lābha*.

329 *Vinicchaya*.

330 *Chanda-rāga*.

331 *Ajjhosāna* (= *adhi-ava-sāna* 'being bent on something').

332 *Pariggaha*: 'possessiveness' (BB).

333 *Macchariya*.

334 *Ārakkha*: 'watch and ward' (RD), 'protection' (Bennett), 'safeguarding' (BB).

335 The two aspects of craving: 1. as primary craving, the basis of rebirth, and 2. craving-in-action (*samudācāra-taṇhā*) (DA). See RD's notes.

336 *Nāma-kāya*: the mental component of the pair *nāma-rūpa* 'name-and-form' or 'mind-and-body'. See next note.

337 *Rūpa-kāya*: the physical component of the pair *nāma-rūpa*. Both *rūpa* and *kāya* can on occasion be translated 'body', but there is a difference. *Rūpa* is body as material, especially visible, form, while *kāya* is body as aggregate, as in 'a body of material, a body of men'.

338 'We can trace' is inserted for clarity.

339 The same words as at DN 14.18: see n.281 there.

340 This confirm DA's statement mentioned in DN 14, n.286 (cf. n.324).

341 The four declarations are in Pali: 1. *'Rūpī me paritto attā'*, 2. *'Rūpī me ananto attā'*, 3. *Arūpī me paritto attā'*, 4. *'Arūpī me ananto attā'*. *Rūpī* is the adjective from *rūpa* (see n.337) and may mean 'material', though DA takes it as referring to the World of Form (*rūpaloka*) as experienced in the lower jhānas, *arūpī* then referring similarly to the Formless World of the higher jhānas. Cf. DN 1.3.1ff.

342 *Upakappessāmi*: glossed by DA as *sampādessāmi* 'I shall strive for, attain'.

343 Identifying the (supposed) self with the feeling-aggregate (*vedanā-kkhandha*).

344 Identifying the self with the body-aggregate.

345 Identifying the self with the aggregates of perception, mental formations and consciousness. Such are the commentarial explanations.

346 *Sankhata*: as opposed to the 'unconditioned element', which is Nibbāna.

347 The MSS appear to ascribe these answers to Ānanda himself rather than the hypothetical interlocutor.

348 I.e. this feeling.

349 He gains Nibbāna for himself (individually: *paccattaṁ*).

350 Cf. DN 1.2.27.

351 *Abhiññā*.

352 RD makes heavy weather of this in his note. These are the 'places' or 'states' in which conscious rebirth takes place. The stations also occur at AN 7.41 (not 39, 40, as stated by RD).

353 *Ayatanāni*: normally translated 'spheres', is here rendered 'realms' to avoid confusion with the 'spheres' of Infinite Space, etc., included among the seven 'stations'. Glossed as *nivāsanaṭṭhānāni* 'dwelling-places', they clearly differ from the station as being where *unconscious* (or not fully conscious) rebirth takes place.

354 Cf. DN 1.2.1.

355 *Paññā-vimutto*. Mrs RD's translation 'Freed-by-Reason'

is certainly misleading, even if learnedly supported by a reference to Kant's *Vernunft*! The usual rendering of *paññā* is 'wisdom', though Ñāṇamoli prefers 'understanding'. It is the true wisdom which is born of insight. The important point is the commentarial statement that this means: 'liberation without the aid of the following eight "liberations"'. It will be noticed that 'stations' 5–7 formally correspond to 'liberations' 4–6. The difference is that by the first way these 'stations' are seen through with insight and rejected, whereas by the second way they are *used* as means towards liberation.

356 These are really only relative 'liberations', since one has to pass through them successively to gain true freedom.

357 Referring, as in verse 23, to the World of Form. Jhāna is here induced by observing marks on one's own body.

358 Here, the *kasiṇa* (disc, etc., used as a meditation-object) is external to oneself.

359 By concentrating on the perfectly pure and bright colours of the *kasiṇa*.

360 *Saññā-vedayita-nirodha* or *nirodha-samāpatti*: a state of a kind of suspended animation, from which it is possible to break through to the state of Non-Returner or Arahant. For an illuminating account of this – to the ordinary person – mysterious state, see Nyāṇaponika, *Abhidhamma Studies* (2nd ed.), 113ff.

361 *Ceto-vimutti paññā-vimutti*: (cf. DN 6.12) 'liberation *of* the heart and *by* wisdom', i.e. in the two ways mentioned.

362 This again refers to the two ways mentioned. The various kinds of 'liberated one' are listed at DN 28.8.

SUTTA 16

363 With this Sutta, Mrs Bennett's volume of abridged translations comes to an end. Of greater value was *The Last Days of the Buddha*, translated by Sister Vajirā and revised by Francis Story, with notes by the Ven. Nyāṇaponika Mahāthera (Wheel Publication 67–69, BPS, Kandy 1964).

The Sutta is a composite one, many portions of which are found separately in other parts of the Canon, as listed by RD. No doubt it contains the basic facts about the Buddha's last days, but various late and more than dubious elements have been incorporated in it – a process which continued in the later Sanskrit versions (produced by the Sarvāstivādins and other schools), which are known to us mainly from the Chinese and Tibetan translations (though some Sanskrit fragments have been found). For E. Waldschmidt's (German) study of these, see A.K. Warder, *Indian Buddhism* (2nd ed., Delhi 1980). The Tibetan version is translated into English in W.W. Rockhill, *Life of the Buddha* (2nd ed., London 1907), pp. 123–147. It should perhaps be mentioned that the (expanded, Sanskrit-based) *Mahāparinirvāṇa Sūtra* is sometimes cited as evidence for the belief in a supreme self in Mahāyāna Buddhism. One Chinese version does indeed contain a passage to this effect, but this is a late interpolation, and is not representative of the general Mahāyāna position.

364 *Gijjhakūṭa*: a pleasant elevation above the stifling heat of Rājagaha. The name was taken up by Mahāyāna writers, who often located the Buddha's discourses there.

365 See also n.92. He is certainly a historical figure, unlike the 'King Ajātaśatru of Benares' of the *Bṛhadāranyaka Upaniṣad*, with whom he shared a taste for philosophical discussion with sages. RD points out that this is not his personal name but an official epithet. The literal meaning 'unborn foe' must then mean 'he against whom a foe (capable of conquering him) has not been born', though in view of his act of parricide it came to be taken as 'the unborn foe (i.e. while still in the womb) of his father' – with legendary elaboration. In Jain sources he is called Kūṇika or Koṇika. *Vedehiputta* means 'son of the Videha woman' (see next note). There is a long article on him in EB, where, however, RD's mistranslation at DN 2.102 (see n.139 there) is repeated.

366 The Vajjian confederacy, northward across the Ganges from Magadha, consisted of the Licchavis of Vesālī and the Vedehis (of Videha – to whom Ajātasattu's mother belonged), whose capital was Mithilā.

367 *Upalāpana*, which RD says must mean 'humbug, cajolery, diplomacy'.

368 *Aparihāniyā dhammā*: 'factors of non-decline'.

369 *Kammârāmā* etc.: 'fond of action, etc.' Here *kamma* obviously does not have the technical Buddhist meaning, and is glossed as 'things to be done'.

370 Stopping short of the goal of enlightenment, 'resting on their laurels'.

371 This is the Ambalaṭṭhikā mentioned in DN 1, not that in DN 5.1.

372 *Dhammanvaya*: 'the way the Dhamma goes'; *anvaya* also means 'lineage', and RD has 'the lineage of the faith', which is doubly inappropriate.

373 Most buildings being of wood, this was exceptional, hence its name.

374 As a Non-Returner (*anāgāmī*).

375 DA stresses that Buddhas can feel only physical, not mental weariness.

376 *Dhammâdāsa*: in which one can 'inspect' oneself.

377 'Has no doubt' (i.e. has, by 'entering the Stream', transcended doubt).

378 The eight are the one who has gained the state of Stream-Winner, and the one who has gained its 'fruition' (counted separately), and similarly for the three higher stages.

379 He, referring to the disciple and not (as RD) to the Sangha.

380 *Viññupassaṭṭhehi*: 'not deficient, undisturbed' (cf. PED), not (as RD) 'praised by the wise'.

381 For this and the next verse, see DN 22.1.

382 DA says mindfulness is stressed here because of the approaching encounter with the beautiful Ambapālī.

383 *Gaṇikā*. She was a rich and cultivated woman, with skills similar to those of a geisha.

384 *Nīla*: variously rendered as 'dark blue, blue-green', etc.

385 Men wore cosmetics of various colours.

386 *Sâhāraṁ*: lit. 'with its food', i.e. revenue.

387 A play on *amba* 'mango' and *ambakā* 'woman'. Her name means 'mango-guardian'.

388 A famous statement, implying that there is no 'esoteric' teaching in Buddhism, at least as originally taught by

the Founder. There is no contradiction with the parable of the *siṁsapā* leaves at SN 56.31.

389 *Pariharissāmi*: 'I will take care of'.

390 The idea that the Buddha died at the age of eighty has, for some reason, been considered implausible. We might as well query the fact that Wordsworth died shortly after his eightieth birthday, the year of his death, too, bearing the suspiciously 'round' figure of 1850! See n.400.

391 *Vegha-missakena*. The precise meaning of the expression seems to be unknown, but it remains a vivid image!

392 *Sabba-nimittānaṁ amanasikārā*: 'not attending to any signs', i.e. ideas.

393 I.e. mundane feelings (DA).

394 'The concentration attained during intensive insight-meditation' (AA, quoted in LDB).

395 *Dīpa* = Skt. *dvīpa* 'island' rather than Skt. *dīpa* 'lamp'. But we do not really know whether the Buddha pronounced the two words alike or not! In the absence of such knowledge, it is perhaps best not to be too dogmatic about the meaning. In any case, it is just 'oneself' that one has to have as one's 'island' (or lamp), not some 'great self' which the Buddha did not teach (cf. n.363, end).

396 *Tamatagge*. The meaning of this is rather obscure, to say the least. It seems to mean something like 'the highest', even if scholars cannot agree as to how this meaning is reached. See the long note (28) in LDB.

397 The 'Seven Mangoes' Shrine.

398 The 'Many Sons' Shrine, at which people used to pray for sons to an ancient banyan-tree.

399 *Iddhipādā*. See DN 18.22.

400 *Kappaṁ vā tiṭṭheyya kappâvasesaṁ vā*. This passage is much disputed. The usual meaning of *kappa* is 'aeon' (but see PED for other senses). DA, however, takes it to mean 'the full life-span' (i.e. in Gotama's day, 100 years: cf. DN 14.1.7). DA also takes *avasesa* to mean 'in excess' (the usual meaning being 'the remainder'). After some hesitation, and preferring the lesser 'miracle', I have translated the sense of *kappa* (as I take it) by 'a century'. This, of course, accords with DA. I have, however,

adopted the usual meaning of *avasesa* as making good sense. For the Buddha, the 'remainder' would have been twenty years. PTS translators of the parallel passages have differed in their interpretations. Whereas RD in DN preferred 'aeon', Woodward at SN 51.10 (followed reluctantly by Hare at AN 8.70!) has 'allotted span', and at Ud 6.1 he tersely remarks: 'Supposed by some to mean "the aeon or world-period"'. It may be noted that LDB has 'world-period', while Mrs Bennett discreetly omits the passage.

401 Māra (= 'Death') is the personified spirit of evil, the Tempter, very like the Biblical Satan. But like Brahmā, he is only the temporary incumbent of an 'office'.

402 *Sappāṭihāriyaṁ dhammaṁ*. RD renders this 'the wonder-working truth', to which the Ven. Nyāṇaponika (LDB, n.30) takes exception, pointing out that the adjective could be rendered (paraphrased) by 'convincing and liberating'. It must however be said that in DN 11.3 we find *anusāsani-pāṭihāriya* 'the miracle of instruction' (see n.233 there). In neither place does it imply a miracle in the 'vulgar' sense.

403 'As a warrior breaks his armour after the battle' (DA).

404 DA has an involved and dubious explanation. The point, surely, is that there is an imbalance in the powers of such a mighty deva (who, of course, is far from being enlightened!).

405 *Anupādisesāya nibbāna-dhātuya parinibbāyati*: 'enters the Nibbāna-element without the groups (of attachment) remaining'; or, in mundane parlance, 'dies'. See BDic under *Nibbāna*.

406 Or: 'assemblies of many hundreds of Khattiyas'.

407 *Abhibhū-ayatanāni* > *abhibhâyatanāni*. See MN 77 and articles in BDic and EB.

408 On one's own person.

409 The flower of the tree *Pterospermum acerifolium*.

410 The 'healing star', equated with Venus.

411 RD says (in part): 'I do not understand the connexion of ideas between this paragraph and the idea repeated with such tedious iteration in the preceding paragraphs.' I do not understand what he does not under-

stand. There seems to be no special contradiction of ideas. Whether a Buddha lives on for a century, or even an aeon, he must eventually die.

412 The five (spiritual) faculties are: faith (or confidence: *saddhā*), energy (*viriya*), mindfulness (*sati*), concentration (*samādhi*), and wisdom (*paññā*). Faith needs to be balanced with wisdom, and energy with concentration, but mindfulness is self-balancing (see VM 4.45–49).

413 The names of these powers are the same as those of the faculties listed above. The difference is that at Stream-Entry they become powers as being unshakeable by their opposites. This answers RD's query at ii, 129 (he has, incidentally reversed the order of the two groups there).

414 This group of 37 items constitutes the *Bodhipakkhiya-Dhammā* or 'Things pertaining to enlightenment' (cf. MN 77).

415 Buddhas, like elephants, apparently turn the whole body round to look back!

416 The usual triad of morality, concentration and wisdom, with the outcome, which is liberation.

417 I have chosen this ambiguous expression to translate the controversial term *sūkara-maddava* (*sūkara* = 'pig', *maddava* = 'mild, gentle, soft', also 'withered'). It could therefore mean either 'the tender parts of a pig' or 'what pigs enjoy' (cf. note 46 in LDB). What is quite clear is that the old commentators did not know for certain what it did mean. DA gives three possibilities: 1. The flesh of a wild pig, neither too young nor too old, which had come to hand without being killed, 2. soft boiled rice cooked with 'the five products of the cow', or 3. a kind of elixir of life (*rasāyana*) (cf. next note). Modern interpreters from RD onwards have favoured truffles as a plausible explanation, and some evidence for this has been adduced. Trevor Ling, in n.31 to his revision of the RD translation of this Sutta (*The Buddha's Philosophy of Man* (Everyman's Library, London 1981, p. 218), remarks: 'This explanation seems intended to avoid offence to vegetarian readers or hearers. Rhys Davids's statement that Buddhists "have been mostly vegeta-

rians, and are increasingly so", is difficult to accept.' Be that as it may (and in fact Eastern Theravāda Buddhists have rarely been vegetarians, though some are now, almost certainly under Western influence!), the question of vegetarianism has frequently been raised in the Buddhist field.

The standard Theravāda position is set out in the Jīvaka Sutta (MN 55), in which the Buddha tells Jīvaka that monks must not eat the meat of any animal concerning which they have seen, heard or suspect that it was specially killed for them. The Buddha rejected Devadatta's proposal to forbid meat-eating altogether to the monks. Living on alms as they did in the conditions of rural India at the time, they would either have gravely embarrassed those who offered them food, or starved if they had refused all meat. At the same time, under modern conditions, especially in the West, the question does arise as to whether the Sangha might not educate the laity into *offering* only vegetarian food. Many Western Buddhists (and not only Mahayanists) are in fact vegetarians today.

In many schools of Mahāyāna Buddhism, vegetarianism is the rule, and some writers have indulged in polemics against the Theravāda school on this score. This, whatever may be said, has not always been purely for reasons of compassion. Shinran Shōnin, the founder of the Shin School in Japan, abolished compulsory vegetarianism along with celibacy because he considered it a form of penitential practice.

418 The reference to an elixir noted above is interesting. É. Lamotte, *The Teaching of Vimalakīrti* (Engl. transl., PTS, London 1976), p. 313f., has an interesting and learned note in which he refers to deities mentioned in MN 36, who offered to insert a special divine essence into the Bodhisatta's pores to keep him alive, at the time of his extreme austerities. He compares the Buddha's last meal with the wondrous food served to the Bodhisattvas by Vimalakīrti, which takes seven days to digest, whereas the *sūkara-maddava* eaten by the Buddha can only be digested by the Tathāgata (or so we are told). The trou-

ble was, of course, that in fact even the Tathāgata failed to digest it! Cf. also SN 7.1.9.

419 'These verses were made by the elders who held the Council' (DA), and likewise at verses 38, 41.

420 The first teacher the future Buddha went to: see MN 26.

421 This ridiculous story is probably a late insertion.

422 The river Ānanda had previously mentioned (verse 22).

423 Or 'the recreation-ground (*upavattana*) belonging to the Mallas'.

424 Normally it is understood that devas are unenlightened, but DA here states – without further comment – that these are Non-Returners or even Arahants.

425 *Saṁvejanīyāni*: 'arousing *saṁvega*' ('sense of urgency': Ñāṇamoli in VM and Pṭs. translations).

426 Lumbini (now Rummindei in Nepal).

427 Uruvelā (now Buddha Gayā in Bihar).

428 The deer-park at Isipatana (modern Sarnāth) near Vārāṇasī (Benares).

429 Kusinārā.

430 This small passage seems arbitrarily inserted at this point. Cf. SN 35.127.

431 Lit. 'for your own good', but DA says 'for the highest purpose, Arahantship'. Cf. n.370.

432 *Āyasa* means 'of iron', but DA, not considering this good enough, glosses it as 'of gold': improbable even though, as Ven. Nyāṇaponika notes (LDB, n.53), there is some support in Sanskrit for this meaning.

433 Probably sandalwood or ochre paste.

434 A 'private Buddha' who, though enlightened, does not teach.

435 The word used is *vihāra* which in the context cannot mean 'monastery', and DA calls it a pavilion. The neutral rendering 'lodging' is safest.

436 *Kapisīsaṁ* lit. 'monkey's head'. Scarcely 'lintel' (RD): Ānanda would have to be fairly tall to lean on this! The definition in DA is rather obscure, but that quoted by Childers from the 12th-century *Abhidhānapadīpikā* (his main source) is 'the bolt or bar of a door' (*aggaḷathambo*), and *aggaḷa* is used in this sense at DN 3.1.8. But

Childers also quotes a Sanskrit meaning of 'coping of a wall'.

437 An Arahant. Ānanda is said to have become an Arahant just before the first Council, after the Buddha's passing.

438 This may seem like only one 'wonderful quality', but it is fourfold because equally applicable in regard to each of the four groups.

439 Kuvera's city: see DN 32.7.40.

440 Verses 17–18 are repeated practically verbatim in the next Sutta.

441 This is the family-name (cf., n.179).

442 *Aññā-pekho*: rendered by RD as 'from a desire for knowledge', which agrees with DA. But *aññā* is used for 'the highest knowledge', i.e. 'enlightenment', and we may assume a play on the two senses (mundane and supramundane) of 'enlightenment', equally possible in Pali and in English.

443 These are, of course, the Stream-Winner, Once-Returner, Non-Returner and Arahant.

444 The PTS text makes the verse run only to line 6, and this is followed by RD and in LDB. But in the addenda to the second edition of 1938, it is indicated that the verse continues as shown here (except, probably, for the line in parentheses), and omitting the name of Subhadda.

445 I.e. properly qualified. This passage also at DN 8.24.

446 Sentence added by the Elders at the Council (DA).

447 *Āvuso*.

448 *Bhante*. Rendered here as 'Lord', but in modern usage the normal form of address to monks, rendered 'Venerable Sir'. Western Buddhists should note that it is a *vocative*, i.e. used in direct address, and not as a kind of pronoun denoting 'the Venerable So-and-so'.

449 *Āyasmā*: the regular prefix as in 'the Venerable Ānanda', etc.

450 The Sangha did not take advantage of this permission, mainly because Ānanda had omitted to enquire which rules were to be regarded as 'minor'. It would not be appropriate to get involved here in modern debates on the subject.

451 *Brahmadaṇḍa*: used in a different sense at DN 3.1.23.

Channa had been Gotama's charioteer, and had since joined the Order, but showed a perverse spirit. The treatment imposed on him by the Buddha's orders brought him to his senses.

452 *Pasādā*: 'brightness, serenity of mind'. According to DA 'the least one' was Ānanda himself.

453 *Vayadhammā sankhārā. Appamādena sampādetha.* The words occurred previously at DN 16.3.51. RD's rendering of the latter two words, 'Work out your salvation with diligence' (adopted from Warren) has become too famous. Even Brewster, who normally follows RD, has changed it to 'Accomplish earnestly!', which is much better. Much has been made in some quarters of the fact that the Sarvāstivādin version (and therefore the Tibetan translation) omits these words. But the passage is even expanded in one Chinese version, which makes dubious any conclusions which may be drawn from the omission elsewhere. However, there does seem to have been an early corruption in the text, as in the parallel passage at SN 6.2.5.2 the order of the two sentences is reversed: *appamādena sampādetha vayadhammā sankhārā* (= S i, 158). The inference is that the words quoted were lost at an early stage in the Sarvāstivādin tradition. The SN passage probably reflects an intermediate stage in that process.

454 RD says 'No one, of course, can have known what actually did occur.' Since Anuruddha is said to have had highly developed psychic powers, we cannot be so sure.

455 Note that Ānanda, the junior, addresses Anuruddha as instructed by the Buddha, and Anuruddha replies similarly.

456 As in MN 26, etc., and playing the same role as in DN 14.3.2.

457 *Aniccā vata sankhārā uppāda-vaya-dhammino,*
Uppajitvā nirujjhanti, tesaṁ vupasamo sukho.
RD rightly calls this a 'celebrated verse'. Frequently quoted, it concludes DN 17.

458 One of the Buddha's most eminent disciples, not to be confused with the many other Kassapas. He had great

psychic powers and is said to have lived to be more than 120. He presided at the first Council.

459 Cf. n.66.

460 Not, of course, the same person as the Subhadda mentioned at 5.23–30.

461 *Sarīra*: bones (later interpreted as the indestructible substance supposed to be found in the ashes of Arahants).

462 Some trees are said to have the property of putting out fires. In Japan this is said of the gingko – despite considerable evidence to the contrary!

463 This seems to have been the original end of the Sutta.

464 These verses were, as Buddhaghosa (DA) obviously correctly says, added by the Sinhalese Elders.

SUTTA 17

465 As RD notes, this Sutta is an expansion of the conversation recorded at DN 16.5.17f. The same legend also occurs, with some variations (analysed by RD) in the Mahāsudassana Jātaka (No. 95). As in DN 5, the Buddha at the end identifies himself, Jātaka-fashion, with the leading character in the story. The whole thing is deliberately set in an atmosphere of fairy-tale splendour: cf. n.468.

466 'The Great King of Glory' (RD). RD is probably right in believing that the germ of the story (though not, I think, its Buddhist moral) lies in a sun-myth, a theory which in his day was unpopular because of having been overworked.

467 RD accidentally writes 'seven' instead of 'five'. The five kinds are given as drums with leather on one side, on both sides, completely covered in leather, cymbals (or bells) and wind.

468 Or perhaps 'feasted their senses', but hardly, I think, 'danced' (as RD: a ludicrous picture!): see PED under *paricarati*. RD quotes a passage from the Mahāyāna *Sukhāvativyūha*, a key text of the Pure Land school (as, e.g. Shin in Japan). The 'Land of Bliss' (Sukhāvatī) created by Amitābha Buddha for those who have faith in

him has features which appear to owe something to this description. But there the effect of the sound of the bells is: 'And when the men there hear that sound, reflection on Buddha arises in their body (*sic!*), reflection on the Law, reflection on the Assembly'.

469 Cf. n.93.

470 RD declares categorically: 'This is the disk of the sun', which may, originally, be correct. It symbolises both royal authority and the moral law.

471 Elephants, cavalry, chariots and infantry.

472 Lit. 'eat according to eating'. The exact meaning is doubtful. See also n.792.

473 *Attha-karaṇa-pamukhe*. 'As he was trying a case' omitted by RD.

474 This description may have something to do with the veneration accorded so-called 'white' elephants in Thailand.

475 See n.93. RD translates, cumbrously, 'Changes of the Moon'.

476 'With a crow-black head' (RD). But the term may refer to the shape not the colour.

477 'Thunder-Cloud', and so rendered by RD.

478 This is a stock description, as RD notes. The humour of the Buddha's employing such a description to the aged ascetic Ānanda should not pass unnoticed!

479 All such gifts are the result (*vipāka*) of past kamma.

480 The third clause omitted by RD.

481 *Iddhi*: quite distinct from those listed at DN 2.87 (and see n.128 there).

482 *Gahaṇi*: supposedly a special organ of digestion. But the medieval Sinhalese rendering quoted by RD (and Childers), 'the internal fire which promotes digestion', is not so far wrong.

483 *Dhanu*: 'bow'. Childers, but not PED, gives 'a measure of length' – the required meaning here.

484 RD notes the literal meaning: 'have garlands planted for all the people to put on' – being the only use for flowers at the time.

485 'All-maker' (or 'Factotum'), Skt. *Viśvakarman*. He has come down here a little from once being 'the great architect of the Universe'.

486 See DN 2.17 (end). Pūraṇa Kassapa denied that there was any merit in these.
487 The four Divine Abidings (*Brahmavihāras*): cf. DN 13.76ff. and n.256 there.
488 The conventional ('fairy-tale') nature of the repeated figure of 84,000 is obvious.
489 'Flag of Victory' (RD).
490 Subhaddā 'Queen of Glory' (RD). See also n.496.
491 RD has 'horns tipped with bronze'. The meaning is uncertain.
492 As adopted by the Buddha at his passing, and on other occasions. Cf. DN 16.4.40.
493 Cf. DN 16.4.37.
494 This would amount to more than four times the life-span under Buddha Vipassī (DN 14.7). RD accidentally has 48,000 in this verse.
495 The highest world attainable in a non-Buddha age.
496 These may be names (as taken by Woodward in the parallel passage at SN 32.96), or they may mean 'Khattiya lady' and 'young maiden' respectively. Anyway, what about Subhaddā?

SUTTA 18

497 Cf. DN 16.2.5ff and n.373.
498 Cf. DN 16.2.7. RD considers, probably rightly, that the DN 16 passage is the older. There, no mention was made of Magadhan devotees, and one purpose of this Sutta is to remedy that omission.
499 A curious remark, considering that Ānanda had been present at the Lord's 'report'.
500 Killed, of course, by his son Ajātasattu.
501 This rings true as a veiled criticism of Ajātasattu.
502 The Buddha did not, of course, claim the immediate kind (or indeed any kind) of omniscience, as other teachers did. But in view of his immediate response at DN 16.2.7, he seems to be making rather heavy weather of this.
503 Yakkhas are generally thought of as unpleasant creatures like demons or ogres. In fact they are curiously ambivalent (as Mrs Rhys Davids' term for them, 'fairy'

suggests). The matter is largely explained by King Vessavaṇa, who (as we know from this sutta too) is their ruler, at DN 32.2. But see also DN 23.23, and article *Yakkha* in DPPN.

504 Lit. 'Bull (i.e. hero) of the People'.

505 The 'Great King' of the North.

506 A Stream-Winner. The seven human births indicate the maximum number of births a Stream-Winner can take. Hence the 'desire' arising in him to go on to the next stage. But why should the Buddha be so surprised at his awareness of having gained such a 'specific attainment'? His answer seems to be entirely in keeping with the 'Mirror of Dhamma' test mentioned by the Buddha at DN 16.2.8.

507 The 'Great King' of the South. It is curious that a king should be sent as a messenger in this way.

508 The two reasons, as RD points out, are (1) the fact that Vessavaṇa had made a statement on this very subject, and (2) that he had been aware that the Buddha (whose mind he could read!) was pondering the same subject. This also conforms to the Buddha's statement at various places (e.g. DN 14.1.15) that he knows certain things both by his own knowledge and because devas have told him.

509 *Vassa*: the annual three-monthly retreat during the rainy season.

510 'Hall of Good Counsel' (RD).

511 For a fuller account of him and the other 'Great Kings' (who actually preside over the lowest of the heavens, only just above the human realm), see DN 32.

512 The asuras suffered a decline in India, compared with the Persian *ahura*. They are at war with the devas, and hence are sometimes termed by Western scholars 'titans'. Since humans can be reborn in either camp (see DN 24.1.7 for an example of one born among the asuras), it is natural that the devas should rejoice at the accession to their ranks through the Buddha's disciples.

513 They seem, as RD notes (to a later passage, DN 19.14) to have been the recorders of the proceedings at assemblies of the Thirty-Three Gods. They had to memorise

what was decided. RD draws the inference that this was also done at real assemblies in the India of the time.

514 Cf. DN 11.80.

515 *Vipāka*: not here, as usually, in the technical sense of 'result of kamma', but (a rare usage) 'outcome in general'.

516 'Ever virgin' (or 'ever young'). One of the five sons of Brahmā according to legend.

517 An indirect way of exalting the Buddha: Brahmā is so vastly superior to the Thirty-Three Gods, and yet he is inferior to the Buddha, and knows it.

518 The *añjali* gesture of veneration or greeting, still used in India and Buddhist countries – frequently mistaken by Westerners for a gesture of prayer (which, for Theravāda Buddhism at least, is inappropriate).

519 *Pallankena*: instrumental case of *pallanka* 'in a cross-legged position'.

520 *Pallanka* is also the couch on which one sits cross-legged. Cf. n.32.

521 Cf. DN 21.2 (and DN 19.1). DA says Brahmā adopted this form because all the devas loved Pañcasikha.

522 Phrase omitted by RD – though it is an important qualification!

523 For all of these groups, see Introduction, p. 38f.

524 Celestial musicians (cf. n.26). As attendants on the devas of the Realm of the Four Great Kings, they were the lowest grade of beings in the heavenly worlds. For a monk to be reborn among them was shameful: cf. DN 21.11ff. It should be noted that the *gandhabba* mentioned in MN 38 as being present at the time of conception is not the same. The term there means 'one about to be born': see I.B. Horner's note, MLS i, p. 321, n.6.

525 RD mistranslates: 'betook himself to one end [of the Hall]'.

526 Defined at Sutta 26.28. For further details see BDic.

527 *Sukha*: 'pleasant feeling (physical or mental)'.

528 *Somanassa*: 'pleasant mental feeling'. Here, a higher degree of *sukha*, not to be equated with *pīti* (see n.81).

529 *Sankhārā*: a multi-valent term (see n.293), for which see the excellent article in BDic. In his note to this passage,

RD wrestles with its meaning, and coins the unfortunate rendering 'Confections', which, still more unfortunately, was later taken up by Suzuki, on whom it is usually fathered.

530 See DN 22 for these.

531 Or 'physical forms external to himself' (RD).

532 A rare formulation of the factors of the Eightfold Path (see DN 33.2.3 (3)). Elsewhere, such a progressive explanation is denied: this points to a late formulation. See BDic under *Magga*, and EB under *Aṭṭhaṅgika-magga*.

533 *Sammā-ñāṇaṁ*.

534 *Sammā-vimutti*. These additional two steps are part of the supramundane path (MN 117).

535 DN 14.3.7.

536 These are the Non-Returners, who are presumably so far above Brahmā Sanankumāra that he cannot speak of them with knowledge!

SUTTA 19

537 Mention must be made of RD's brilliant introduction to this Sutta, which he analyses in terms of a play, showing its obvious links with the previous Sutta with reference to 'the episode told in Act I, Scenes 1 and 2', and so on. He stresses the humour and the propagandist technique employed, which consists in accepting and then outflanking the opponents' position rather than direct confrontation. While we may not be convinced that this Sutta goes back to the Buddha personally (but equally – are we sure that it does *not*, in some form?), this is indeed the method he uses in discussions with a variety of interlocutors. RD also analyses the differences between this Sutta and the version in the Sanskrit *Mahāvastu*, a product of the Lokuttaravāda school.

538 Referred to at DN 18.18, where Brahmā disguises himself as Pañcasikha, who now appears in person. He wore his hair in five knots or ringlets as he had done when he had died as a young boy.

539 The radiance of the devas is a standard feature: in the Deva Saṁyutta with which SN opens, we are intro-

duced to a succession of devas who 'light up the entire Jeta Grove with their effulgence'. Brahmā's radiance is much greater and in DN 14.1.17 we learn of the even greater radiance which appears at the conception and birth of a Bodhisatta.

540 As at DN 18.25. Cf. the 'eel-wriggler' mentioned at DN 1.2.24.

541 The 'path' here is really the practice, *paṭipadā*. The Noble Eightfold Path is the 'Middle Way' or 'Middle Practice', *majjhima-paṭipadā*.

542 *Sekhā*: learners who, having gained one of the first three paths, have yet to attain enlightenment.

543 Arahants.

544 'Crossed over the sea of doubt' (RD).

545 This repeated passage even includes the reference to Brahmā's adopting the form of Pañcasikha, even though it is Pañcasikha himself who is telling the tale.

546 *Purohita*: cf. n.173.

547 Govinda. RD notes: 'It is evident...that Govinda, literally "Lord of the Herds", was a title, not a name, and means Treasurer or Steward.' But people were often known by some designation other than their proper names, probably for taboo reasons. We may note how in Scotland the royal house of Stuart derived their name from the Steward who was originally the 'sty-ward'! Cf. n.365.

548 The name means 'Guardian of the Light'.

549 As RD remarks, the expression 'anoint' is noteworthy, suggesting that the office is of royal rank.

550 There is no note of any value in DA on this. Presumably the assembled nobles (Khattiyas).

551 *Sakaṭamukha*. This expression, which puzzled RD, has been explained as the (narrow) front of a cart, in reference to the tapering shape of India.

552 RD draws up a table showing the relationships and geographical distribution, which however, as he says, does not fit the story very well.

553 Not 'instructed...in government' (RD). The expression used is the same as that previously rendered 'administer'.

554 *Nahātaka*: lit. 'having bathed' (i.e. graduated).

555 Cf., *per contra*, DN 13.12ff.

556 This is also the way recommended by the Buddha in DN 13.

557 As RD indicates, he feels he must offer Brahmā something, but does not know what is right.

558 To the Buddhist, of course, Brahmā's realm is not really deathless. But in a pre-Buddhist age it was the highest goal one could aspire to.

559 *Purohita*: as at n.546. I have ventured to play on the two meanings of 'minister' in English: 'minister of religion' and 'government minister'. The Pali word approximates to a combination of the two.

560 Cf. n.558.

561 *Puthujjanas*: or 'worldlings'. See n.16.

562 *Mantāya*: apparently 'by mantra', but glossed in DA as 'wisdom'.

563 The delicious irony of this should not be missed. The suspicions of the six nobles, expressed in verses 48–49, were not without foundation so far as *ordinary* Brahmins were concerned. And cf., e.g. DN 4.26!

SUTTA 20

564 This is another curious document, doubtless an example of what RD calls 'a mnemonic doggrel as was found useful in other cases also by the early Buddhists, who had no books, and were compelled to carry their dictionaries and works of reference in their heads.' A Sanskrit version from Central Asia has been published, with English translation, by E. Waldschmidt in LEBT, pp. 149–162, and there are also Chinese and Tibetan versions, all of which are quite close to the Pali in general. RD considers the poem (if such we can call it) 'almost unreadable now', because 'the long list of strange names awakes no interest.' That was in 1910. Possibly modern readers who know their Tolkien may think otherwise. At any rate I have not felt it necessary to try to follow up all the allusions, some of which remain obscure or dubious.

565 RD has, wrongly, 'ten thousand world-systems'. The Sanskrit confirms the lower figure.

566 The realm where Non-Returners dwell before gaining final Nibbāna. The Sanskrit has deities (*devatā* – rendered 'goddesses' (!) by Waldschmidt) from the Brahmā world.

567 As RD remarks, 'the connexion of the various clauses of this stanza is obscure'. It is not clear where the Buddha's actual words are supposed to begin. The verse seems to have been badly joined to the introductory section.

568 Here begins the mnemonic 'doggrel'.

569 The name is the same as that of the ironically-named King Dhṛtarāṣṭra 'whose empire is firm' in the *Mahābhārata*. In verse 11 another Dhataraṭṭha, a Nāga king, is mentioned, and the name also occurs elsewhere. Cf. DN 19.1.36.

570 Indra's three-headed elephant. The nāgas were both snakes and elephants.

571 Birds, like Brahmins, are 'twice-born' – first laid as eggs, then hatched!

572 Cf. DN n.512. Indra, the champion of the gods, had defeated them.

573 This is the Pali form of Viṣṇu, and the Sanskrit text has indeed *Viṣṇu* here, though that great god came into his own only after the Buddha's time.

574 *Purindada*: 'the generous giver in former births' (RD), deliberately altered from *Purandara* (which the Sanskrit version has!) 'destroyer of cities'. RD thinks the change was made to distinguish Sakka from the Vedic god, but perhaps it is rather a change to make him more Buddhistically 'respectable'.

575 See DN 1.2.7ff.

576 The Nimmānarati and Paranimmitā devas: see Introduction, p. 42.

577 *Kaṇha*: 'black', but not connected with the Kaṇha mentioned in DN 3.1.23.

578 RD says: 'We have followed the traditional interpretation in ascribing these last four lines to Māra. They may quite as well, or better, be a statement by the author

himself.' I have had the courage of his convictions, and made it so.

SUTTA 21

579 Another Sutta with a mythological background, and some truly remarkable features, including the amazing conceit of having Pañcasikha the gandhabba attract the Buddha's attention by means of a *love-song*! But all this should not blind us to the fact that some deep matters are discussed in the body of the Sutta – just a little like those later Sūtras in which the Lord discussed the mysteries of the *Prajñāpāramitā* with Subhūti against a gorgeous mythological backdrop.

580 RD disbelieves in any original association of this cave and tree with the god Indra (who is, or is not exactly, identical with the Sakka we meet here). The cave was still inhabited at the time of the visit of the Chinese pilgrim Fa-hsien (ca. 405 C.E.), but by the time of Hsüan-tsang (ca. 630) it was deserted.

581 Sakka is the ruler of the Thirty-Three Gods, in a heaven which still belongs to the Realm of Sense-Desires (*kāmâvacara*), above that of the Four Great Kings but far below the Realm of Brahmā – actually quite a lowly position in the Buddhist scheme of things (see Introduction, p. 41). RD has a useful summary of information about him in the introduction to this Sutta, with a list of his titles and a discussion of the question of how far he can be identified with Indra.

582 The *vīṇā* is better known in the West today by its Indian name than it was in RD's time. RD mistakenly calls it a lyre, but it is definitely a kind of lute. The author of the article *beluva* in PED calls it a flute (and the mistake is repeated under *paṇḍu*, so is not, apparently, a misprint). It would surely have been beyond the powers of Pañcasikha, or of Krishna himself, to accompany his own song on the flute!

583 Jhāna, according to Sakka, but he would scarcely have known what kind of meditation the Tathāgata was practising!

584 *Pasādeyyāsi*: 'please, attract, charm'. Not the most appropriate term (RD has 'win over'), but suited to Pañcasikha's talents.

585 RD draws attention to similar things in the *Mahābhārata* and elsewhere in Indian literature, without commenting on the extreme oddity of its occurrence here!

586 The meaning of Suriyavaccasā (cf. DN 20.10).

587 Elephants do indeed suffer from the heat, and have to be kept cool.

588 This epithet omitted by Mrs Rhys Davids in her translation.

589 As we see below, this was supposedly composed just prior to Gotama's enlightenment, though this conflicts with the just previous mention of Arahants!

590 The Buddha refrains from rebuking Pañcasikha for his somewhat inappropriate song, and pays him a neat compliment. In the 'household life' Gotama must have heard many love-songs, even if we disregard all the legends of his upbringing.

591 A title or name of Indra, used politely as, e.g., Vāseṭṭhas in DN 16.5.19, etc.

592 This seems to conflict a little with DN 16.4.28ff.

593 *Devaputta*: either simply a male deva or the head of a group of devas.

594 Note the importance of this: the following Sutta is, of course, devoted entirely to this subject.

595 Higher than that of the Thirty-Three Gods (see n.581).

596 Another name for the Heaven of the Thirty-Three Gods.

597 There is considered to be an implied contract between monks and their lay supporters. In return for support, monks are supposed to do their best to gain enlightenment. Not to do so is a form of dishonesty.

598 Vāsava is yet another name for Sakka (see RD ii, p. 296f.).

599 *Sakyamuni*: a common term for the Buddha in Mahāyāna scriptures, but extremely rare in the Pali Canon.

600 In general it is considered almost impossible for inhabitants of the heaven-worlds to gain enlightenment – almost, but not quite, is the implication here!

601 *Mārisa*: 'Sir', not 'Lord'. Sakka does later go over to the

more respectful form of address.

602 *Issa-macchariya*. This is better than RD's 'envy and selfishness'.

603 *Piya-appiya*: 'dear and not-dear'.

604 *Chanda*: equated by DA with *taṇhā* 'craving'.

605 *Vitakka*. RD says (in part): 'The word is used, not with any fine shade of psychological meaning, but in its popular sense... "taking thought for"..., "being preoccupied about"'. See n.611.

606 *Papañca*: a difficult word. The meaning 'diversification' has been established by Bhikkhu Ñāṇananda, *Concept and Reality in Early Buddhist Thought* (Kandy, BPS 1971).

607 'How has that bhikkhu gone about...?' (RD).

608 *Somanassa*: cf. n.528.

609 *Domanassa*. *Somanassa-domanassa* are sometimes rendered 'gladness and sadness'.

610 *Upek(k)hā*.

611 *Vitakka-vicāra*. This refers to the second jhāna (cf. DN 2.75, 11). I have used the rendering mentioned at n.80, instead of the more usual 'initial and sustained application'. In a private communication, L.S. Cousins writes: 'The words simply do not mean this...Suttanta does not distinguish between access and absorption – hence the terms used do not have their momentary Abhidhamma sense. In the case of *vicāra* this is not even the Abhidhamma sense, since Dhs clearly explains *vicāra* as "investigating".'

612 *Pātimokkha*.

613 The same question as posed in DN 16.5.26 by Subhadda.

614 *Ejā*: glossed by DA as *calamaṭṭhena taṇhā*, which RD renders 'Craving, with respect to the thrill' (better, perhaps: 'trembling with desire'). '"Passion"', says RD, 'lacks etymological coincidence...but no other term is forceful enough'. Finding no better alternative, I have adopted it here.

615 Cf. the similar passage in 2.15, though the response of those questioned is different, if equally unsatisfactory.

616 *Na sampāyanti*: mysteriously rendered 'did not withdraw themselves' (RD).

617 See n.622.

618 *Ojā*: cf. n.418.

619 The idea that a god needs to return to the human state before gaining enlightenment seems to apply here, even though Sakka is, or is supposedly, a Stream-Winner.

620 *Akaniṭṭhā*, those in the highest heaven of all. See Introduction, p. 39.

621 The Gotama clan were supposed to be of solar descent.

622 It is not quite clear whether Sakka really became a Stream-Winner at this point, or earlier, when he made the claim (n.617). At the earlier point the Buddha made no direct comment, possibly knowing that this 'conversion' (RD), though it had not quite happened, was imminent.

According to DA (*ad* DN 22.1) Sakka had observed with terror the signs that his reign as king of the gods was approaching its end: hence his visit to the Buddha. For the length of life among the Thirty-Three Gods, see DN 23.11.

623 Or 'was invited' (RD, but described in a footnote as 'doubtful').

SUTTA 22

624 This is generally regarded as the most important Sutta in the entire Pali Canon. It recurs verbatim at MN 10 as the Satipaṭṭhāna Sutta, with the omission of verses 18–21. The text (or that of MN 10) has been separately translated a number of times, notably by Soma Thera as *The Way of Mindfulness* (2nd ed. Colombo 1949, 3rd ed. BPS 1967). The important book *The Heart of Buddhist Meditation* by Nyāṇaponika Mahāthera (Colombo 1954, London 1973 and later) is essentially based on this Sutta and contains a translation, not only of this but of other relevant texts from the Pali Canon and from Mahāyāna sources (especially Śāntideva's *Śikṣāsamuccaya*). The author's remark in the Introduction (p. 14) should also be noted: 'Among the Mahāyāna schools of the Far East, it is chiefly the Chinese Ch'an and Japanese Zen that are closest to the spirit of Satipaṭṭhāna. Notwithstanding the differences in method, aim and basic philosophical

conceptions, the connecting links with Satipaṭṭhāna are close and strong, and it is regrettable that they have hardly been stressed or noticed.' It should however be mentioned that since those words were written, the realisation has begun to dawn that Zen has much in common with Theravāda in general, and the Satipaṭṭhāna method in particular – somewhat to the surprise of some who have overstressed the 'uniqueness' of Zen. The cross-headings in this Sutta correspond closely to those used by the Ven. Ñāṇamoli for MN 10.

625 Or Kammāsadhamma. For explanation of the construction, see DN 15, n.319.

626 *Ekāyano maggo*. Sometimes translated 'the only way' or 'the one and only way' with, on occasion, a slightly triumphalist connotation. DA in fact offers a number of possibilities, thus showing that the old commentators were not entirely sure of the exact meaning. *Ekâyana* can be literally rendered 'one-going', which is ambiguous. Ñāṇamoli has 'a path that goes one way only'. In any case it should not be confused with the term sometimes found in Buddhist Sanskrit *ekayāna* 'one vehicle' or 'career'.

627 *Domanassa*: in this context usually translated 'grief', but cf. DN 21, n.609.

628 *Ñāya*: 'leading, guiding' (sometimes = 'logic'). Here = 'the right path'.

629 *Satipaṭṭhānā*. It is probably a compound of *sati* + *upaṭṭhāna* (lit. 'placing near'), as in the old Sanskrit version (*Smṛty-upasthāna Sūtra*). 'Foundations', though used by Nyānaponika and others, is really a makeshift translation. In any case, whatever the etymology, the meaning emerges clearly enough from the instructions that follow.

Sati (Skt. *smṛti*) originally meant 'memory' (and still, rarely, does in Pali). The rendering 'mindfulness' by RD was a brilliant one which is almost universally used (though 'recollection' or 'recollectedness' is occasionally found). The use of 'self-possession' by A.K. Warder in his otherwise excellent *Indian Buddhism* is regrettable. It should perhaps be mentioned that Buddhist Sanskrit *smṛti* is clearly used in a different sense from the Hindu *smṛti* 'oral tradition'.

630 *Bhikkhu*: but here used, according to DA, for anyone who does this practice.

631 *Kāye kāyânupassī viharati*: lit. 'contemplating the body in the body', and with similar repetitive formulations for the other three 'foundations'. 'Why is the word "body" used twice in the phrase: "Contemplating the body in the body"? For determining the object and isolating it.' (DA). Ñāṇamoli paraphrases: 'This means not confusing, during meditation, body with feeling, mind, etc. The body is contemplated just as body, feelings just as feelings, etc.'

632 I have tried to get away from the usual rendering 'coveting and grief' in order to bring out the true meaning. The theme is fully developed in verse 19.

633 *Vedanā* is feeling (physical or mental) in its most basic sense of 'sensation', pleasant, painful or neutral. It is regrettable that Warder (as n.629) has chosen 'emotion' for this word, which is precisely what it does not mean!

634 *Citta*: 'mind' or, metaphorically, 'heart'. See verse 12.

635 *Dhammā* (plural): one of the standard meanings of this term (see BDic).

636 Or 'an empty room'.

637 I.e. on the breath in front of him, as DA. Nyāṇaponika paraphrases 'keeping...his mindfulness alert'. Readers of F.L. Woodward's somewhat dated *Some Sayings of the Buddha* should note that there is no basis for his footnote 'Concentrating between the eyebrows'.

638 This is the probable meaning of *assasati, passasati*, though it is just possible that the terms should be reversed. Ñāṇamoli's footnote: 'The exercise described is one in mental observation not in bodily development or breath control as in Hatha-yoga' may be a necessary reminder to some.

639 Lit. 'He knows: "I breathe in a long breath"', etc. Pali regularly uses direct speech in such cases.

640 This is taken to mean 'the whole body of breath' (cf. n.337). '"Making known, making clear to myself the beginning, middle and end of the whole body of breathings in..."' (DA, transl. Soma Thera).

641 *Kāya-sankhāra.* This calming process may lead to the development of jhāna, but this is not the primary object here.

642 Internally means 'one's own body' and externally means 'someone else's body'.

643 *Samudaya-dhammā. Samudaya* is, perhaps significantly, the word used for the 'origin' of suffering in the Second Noble Truth. Awareness of how phenomena (body, etc.) come to be is meant. Ñāṇamoli has 'contemplating the body in its arising factors'.

644 *Vaya-dhammā*: cf. n.457. Ñāṇamoli has 'contemplating the body in its vanishing factors'.

645 Just holding the thought in mind without speculating, mind-wandering, etc.

646 *Sampajāna-kārī hoti*: 'Is acting in a clearly conscious way' (Horner). RD's rendering of 'self-possession' for *sampajañña* (adopted, even more ridiculously, for *sati* by Warder (n.629)) breaks down here.

647 *Paccavekkhati.* The same verb-stem is used in *paccavekkhaṇa-ñāṇa* 'reviewing-knowledge': see n.213.

648 These first five are given as a standard meditation for novices.

649 With the addition of 'brain' these 32 parts of the body are included as a meditation-subject: cf. VM 8.42ff.

650 *Phaseolus mungo*: sometimes sold in the West as 'mung beans'.

651 Cf. n.70.

652 An unpleasant image, heightened for the modern reader when the hygienic aspect is considered! It shows that there were no 'sacred cows' in the Buddha's day.

653 'Cemetery', favoured by some translators, conveys a totally false impression: it is a place of rotting corpses just thrown down – splendid for this kind of meditation!

654 Cf. n.633, also, for repetition, n.631.

655 *Sukhaṁ vedanaṁ*: this can be bodily or mental.

656 *Dukkhaṁ vedanaṁ:* this too can be bodily or mental.

657 *Adukkhamasukhaṁ vedanaṁ:* this is mental only. In all cases one is simply aware that a feeling is present.

658 *Sâmisaṁ sukham vedanaṁ. Sâmisa* = *sa-āmisa*: lit. 'with flesh', thus approximating to the sense of 'carnal'.

659 *Nirāmisaṁ sukhaṁ vedanaṁ:* 'non-carnal' or 'spiritual' (a word Buddhists tend to avoid owing to possibly misleading connotations). In MN 137 *sâmisa* and *nirāmisa* are referred to the 'household' life and to that of renunciation respectively.

660 He infers, or knows telepathically, the feelings of others, and then contemplates his own feelings and those of others alternately.

661 *Citta*: also rendered 'thought' or 'consciousness'. From what follows it is clear that various states of mind are meant. As with feelings, one is at this stage simply aware that certain states of mind are, or are not, present.

662 *Sankhittaṁ cittaṁ* (from the verb *sankhipati*: cf. *sankhittena* 'in brief'): a mind that is 'contracted' or 'shrunken' by sloth-and-torpor (verse 13) and the like.

663 *Vikhittaṁ cittaṁ*: a mind distracted by worry-and-flurry (verse 13).

664 *Mahaggataṁ*: 'grown great' through the lower or higher jhānas.

665 'Not grown great', not developed by the jhānas.

666 *Sa-uttaraṁ*: 'having (other mental states) surpassing it', is synonymous with the 'undeveloped' mind.

667 *An-uttaraṁ*: 'having no other states surpassing it', might seem to refer to transcendental consciousness, but is referred by DA to mundane states, therefore in effect synonymous with the 'developed' mind. In view of the tautology involved in the last two cases, one might wonder whether the commentarial explanation is correct. But see n.670.

668 *Samāhitaṁ*: having attained *samādhi*, i.e. jhānic absorption.

669 Not having attained such absorption, thus as in nn.665–6.

670 *Vimuttaṁ*. This is stated by DA to mean the mind that is temporarily 'freed' either by insight or by jhāna, which suppresses the defilements. Neither is, of course, true and permanent liberation. 'There is no occasion here for the liberations by cutting-off, final stilling (*paṭipassaddhi*) and final escape (*nissaraṇa*)': in other words, we are here dealing purely with the mundane world of the beginner in meditation.

671 As in n.660.

672 *Dhammā* (cf. n.635). The question is sometimes asked concerning the relation of the four foundations of mindfulness to the schema of the five aggregates (*khandhas*). The point is explained here by DA as follows: contemplation of body is concerned with the aggregate of materiality or form (*rūpakkhandha*); contemplation of feelings is concerned with the aggregate of feeling (*vedanākkhandha*); contemplation of mind is concerned with the aggregate of consciousness (*viññāṇa-kkhandha*); and contemplation of mind-objects concerns itself with the aggregates of perception and mental formations (*saññā-, sankhāra-kkhandha*).

673 *Kāma-cchanda*. The terminology is different from the first statement in verse 12, which refers to a lustful mind (*sarāgaṁ cittaṁ*), but there is little difference in meaning. Both refer to sensual desire in general, including but by no means confined to sexual desire. It arises, according to DA, from wrong reflection on an object that is agreeable to the senses. In verse 12 the exercise was simply to note the presence of such a state of mind, if it was present. Here one goes further, and investigates how such a state arises, and how it can be got rid of, etc.

674 DA lists six methods for getting rid of sensuality: (1) 'Right reflection' on an unpleasing (*asubha*) object; (2) Developing jhāna, whereby the hindrance is suppressed; (3) Guarding the senses; (4) Moderation in eating; (5) The support of 'good friends' (*kalyāṇa-mittatā*); (6) Helpful conversation (*sappāyakathā*).

675 *Vyāpāda*.

676 *Thīna-midha*. The principal cure for this is the 'perception of light'.

677 *Uddhacca-kukkucca*.

678 *Vicikicchā*. This includes doubt of the Buddha, the Dhamma, the Sangha, and also inability to distinguish that which is good from that which is not, etc. (cf. DN 1.2.24), i.e. both scepsis and vacillation.

679 The factors productive of the hindrances and of their disappearance. On these hindrances, see Nyāṇaponika Thera, *The Five Mental Hindrances*, Wheel Publ., BPS 1961.

680 *Pañc'upādāna-kkhandhā*: 'The 5 aspects in which the

Buddha has summed up all the physical and mental phenomena of existence, and which appear to the ignorant man as his Ego, or personality, to wit: (1) the Corporeality group (*rūpa-kkhandha*) [here called 'Form'], (2) the Feeling (*vedanā*°), (3) the Perception° (*saññā*°), (4) the Mental-Formation° (*sankhāra*°), (5) the Consciousness-group (*viññāṇa-kkhandha*)' (BDic).

681 *Rūpa*: cf. n.337. Briefly defined in SN 22.56 as 'The four Great Elements [cf. n.70] and corporeality depending on them.'

682 *Saññā*. Defined at SN 22.79 as 'distinguishing a thing by its marks'.

683 *Sankhāra-kkhandha*. The term *sankhāra* has various meanings and as many translations (cf. n.529). Here, it applies to the group of mental formations. Conventionally fifty in number, they embrace various factors including what we term the emotions (i.e. karmic reactions, wholesome or otherwise). The most important one is volition (*cetanā*), the basis of kamma.

684 *Viññāṇa*: which is subdivided according to the six senses, mind being the sixth.

685 For fuller details see BDic under *āyatana*. They consist, as appears from the following, of sense-base (e.g. eye, mind) and its object (sight-objects, mind-objects).

686 *Rūpe* (acc. pl. of *rūpa* in this specific sense): 'visible forms, sight-objects'.

687 Ten fetters are listed, which differ slightly from those given in connection with attaining to Stream-Entry, etc., being found in the Abhidhamma. They are: Sensuality, resentment (*paṭigha*), pride (*māna*), (wrong) views (*diṭṭhi*), doubt (*vicikicchā*), desire for becoming (*bhavarāga*), attachment to rites and rituals (*sīlabbata-parāmāsa*), jealousy (*issa*), avarice (*macchariya*) and ignorance.

688 Here 'body' is *kāya* in the specific sense of 'body-organ', i.e. the base of tactile contact. See BDic for further details.

689 Described in detail at, e.g. MN 118.

690 *Dhamma-vicaya*: sometimes taken to mean 'investigation of the Doctrine', but the meaning is rather 'investigation of bodily and mental phenomena'.

691 *Viriya*. This corresponds to Right Effort in the Noble Eightfold Path.

692 *Pīti*: a term variously translated. See n.81.

693 *Passaddhi*.

694 Verses 18–21 are not in the parallel version at MN 10.

695 Cf. n.680.

696 *Ayatanānaṁ paṭilābho*. According to the formula of dependent origination, these six sense-bases arise dependent on mind-and-body.

697 *Domanassa*. See n.627.

698 *Upāyāsa*: usually translated 'despair', which does not at all agree with the definition given here or in PED. 'Despair' means giving up hope, which is not stated here.

699 *Vyādhi*: omitted in most MSS from the definition at the beginning of this verse, though as disease is such an obvious cause of suffering and occurs in other contexts, the omission is probably accidental, perhaps reflecting a lapse in the tradition of the Dīgha reciters (*bhāṇakas*), such as is doubtless responsible for the omission of the six sense-bases in DN 15. See n.323 there.

700 Cf. n.680.

701 *Taṇhā*.

702 *Ponobhavikā*: lit. 'causing again-becoming'.

703 *Vibhava-taṇhā*. *Vibhava* means (1) 'power, success, wealth', and some translators have wrongly taken this meaning here; (2) 'ceasing to become', i.e. extinction. This is undoubtedly the meaning here. But the *vibhava* meant in this sense is not the higher 'cessation' of Nibbāna, but the materialists' 'extinction' at death (cf. the Freudian 'death-wish').

704 *Cakkhu-samphassa*: the making contact by the eye with its (sight-) object.

705 *Vitakka*: cf. n.611.

706 *Vicāra*: cf. n.611.

707 Interestingly, it is left to the commentary to point out that the positive meaning of this is Nibbāna.

708 *Sammā-diṭṭhi*. This, or 'Right Seeing' is the literal rendering ('Right Vision' would be an unwise rendering, because liable to be misleading!). *Diṭṭhi* here is a

singular, and denotes 'seeing things as they really are', whereas 'views' in the plural are always wrong. It should be noted that when not prefixed with the word *sammā, diṭṭhi* means 'speculative opinions', and the like, which are not based on 'seeing things as they really are'. The formal opposite of *sammā-diṭṭhi* is *micchā-diṭṭhi,* a term generally reserved for especially pernicious views (cf. n.245). *Sammā-diṭṭhi* and the rest are sometimes rendered 'Perfect View', and so on, but this only refers to the supramundane path as described in MN 117.

709 *Sammā-sankappa*: variously rendered as 'right aspiration, right motive', etc.

SUTTA 23

710 Known as 'Young Kassapa' to distinguish him from other Kassapas, such as Mahā-Kassapa or Kassapa the Great (DN 16.6.19). Described as 'the best preacher in the Sangha', he showed his debating skill in this battle of wits with Pāyāsi.

711 Not the same place as the Siṁsapā Grove where the Buddha gave the famous parable of the *siṁsapā* leaves (SN 56.31), which was in Kosambi. Cf. n.388.

712 A stock phrase, cf. n.141.

713 Cf. the views of Ajita Kesakambalī (n.111).

714 A purely conventional phrase: one wonders what Pāyāsi's idea of 'right view' was.

715 Cf. nn.133, 140.

716 *Jīvaṁ*: cf. DN 6 and 7.

717 *Patthīnataro*: from the same root as *thīna-middha* 'sloth and torpor', more lit. 'stiffness and sluggishness'.

718 Of course the elements have not completely vanished, as all four elements are always present. But they have ceased to predominate.

719 Corrected after Buddhadatta Thera, from RD's rendering 'stripping off cuticle and skin', which applies to verse 20.

720 *Āyatana* (n.685). This comes in here rather strangely.
721 *Sanka*: a conch-shell trumpet or 'chank'.
722 The border-country folk were regarded as stupid.
723 *Jaṭila*. Soon after his enlightenment, the Buddha had converted the three Kassapa brothers who were fire-worshippers.
724 Here the yakkha is definitely evil, but cf. n.503.
725 The story is also told in Jātaka 1, and a related one in Jātaka 2 (see I.B. Horner, *Ten Jataka Stories*, Bangkok 1974).
726 Pāyāsi, like Poṭṭhapāda (n.218), and many Indians to this day, enjoys a good argument for its own sake.
727 Cf. DN 5.
728 These were to weigh the garment down.
729 RD has blundered here with a mistranslation of *vyāvaṭa* (see PED).
730 RD thinks he did so at his own expense. We do not know one way or the other about this!
731 One of the Buddha's early converts. He went for his siesta to the lower heavens!

SUTTA 24

732 With this Sutta, the third and final division of the Nikāya starts. It is curious that this division is named after one of the poorest texts in the whole Nikāya, but this probably has little significance other than mnemonic. But the Sutta itself is misnamed, since its 'anti-hero' (if that dubious distinction does not rather belong to the wretched Sunakkhatta!) is actually referred to as Pāṭikaputta or 'Pāṭika's son', and his own name is unrecorded. Perhaps *Pāṭikasutta* stands, by a kind of haplology, for **Pāṭikaputtasutta*.
733 *Ārāma*: lit. 'pleasure', hence a pleasure-park. It came to be used for such parks as were presented to the Buddha, or to other 'ascetics and Brahmins'. Hence its modern sense of 'temple-complex, monastery-complex'.
734 First mentioned at DN 6.5. His name, most inappropriately, means 'born under a lucky star'.

735 His personal name was Channa, but the Buddha addresses him by his 'surname' (cf. n.179). His clan seem to have been potters.

736 Cf. DN 11.5, where the performance of 'miracles' is condemned by the Buddha (as it is here too, though the text goes on to contradict the Master's words). On the significance of this for dating the Sutta, RD's wise words should be noted (p. 3): 'We are not entitled on these facts to suppose that the Pāṭika Suttanta was either later or earlier than the Kevaddha... The editors may have been tolerant of whichever of the opposing views they did not share.' Those who seek to establish chronological criteria should bear such considerations in mind.

737 *Takkara*: 'the so-doer'.

738 *Hīnāy'āvatto*.

739 The name is doubtful. RD has 'Bumus'. I follow DA.

740 A dog-ascetic like Seniya in MN 57, who was told by the Buddha that if he persisted in this practice he would be reborn either in hell or 'in the company of dogs'.

741 *Alasakena*. RD has 'of epilepsy', for which there seems to be no evidence. The sub-commentary and Buddhadatta's dictionary suggest 'indigestion', which seems not unreasonable.

742 See n.512. The Kālakañjas, described as 'terrible to see', are mentioned in DN 20.12.

743 The form of this name is doubtful. RD has Kandaramasuka. Again, I follow DA.

744 For these, see DN 16.3.2 and notes there.

745 See DN 3.1.20 and n.150 there.

746 A home for wanderers which had been charitably donated near some Tinduka trees.

747 Cf. DN 6.15 and DN 7, which is named after him.

748 DA seems to imply that he brought them all to Arahantship: more modestly, one might settle for the 'opening of the Dhamma-eye' (see n.140).

749 *Tejo-dhātuṁ samāpajjitvā*: RD translates 'entered on jhāna by the method of flame' with no comment, and DA, more remarkably, is silent. Could this peculiarly unnecessary miracle have been inserted later?

750 All this despite the Buddha's expressed dislike of miracles. But see n.736.

751 *Aggañña*. See DN 27 for a full development of the theme of 'beginnings' – not, of course, in the sense of an absolute first cause, for which Buddhism has no use.

752 Or 'goes beyond it' – even to omniscience, says DA, not quite correctly.

753 *Nibbuti*: a term associated with Nibbāna, though actually from a different root.

754 *Anaya*: 'wrong leading', i.e. into suffering or trouble.

755 *Issara* (Skt. *Īśvara*): 'God as creator and ruler', now often the Christian God.

756 *Viparīto*: 'reversed, changed'.

757 Cf. DN 15.35.

758 RD says: 'Buddhaghosa judges that this was merely affected appreciation. But we are not told anything of the later history of this man.' DA does, however, add that the Buddha's words 'made an impression on him in the future'. Could it be that Bhaggava's allegedly dubious reaction is DA's coded way of expressing doubts about this Sutta? Not only is the main part inferior and contradictory, if humorous, but it concludes, first with an appendix (2.14ff.) on the beginning of things which is clumsily tacked on, doubtless in response to Sunakkhatta's remarks at 1.5 (which were adequately answered *there*), and then (2.21) with an even more irrelevant appendix to that appendix. Another curious feature is that it is probably the only Sutta in the Canon which consists almost entirely of a narrative (as opposed to a discourse) related by the Buddha to a third party (and, at that, an obscure character not owing him any allegiance).

SUTTA 25

759 His name means 'Banyan'. Cf. DN 8.23.

760 A park given by Queen Udumbarikā for wanderers, similar to that mentioned at DN 24, n.746.

761 Cf. DN 1.1.17, and DN 9.3.

762 *Go-kaṇṇa*. Dictionaries give 'a large species of deer', for

which 'bison' seems to be the correct rendering; RD, following DA, has 'a one-eyed cow'.

763 As at DN 1.1.11.

764 *Adassayamāno*: rendered by RD as 'furtively' ('not showing himself'), but DA considers the seemingly negative prefix *a-* 'a mere particle'. The Sub-Commentary declares that *ādassamāno* ('showing off') is the meaning. It makes little real difference, since either direct ostentation or mock-humility is intended.

765 For a fuller treatment of the pith-image, see MN 18.

766 Or: 'remain satisfied with what has been achieved.'

767 Cf. n.637.

768 Cf n.676.

769 'Heart' and 'mind' here both render *citta*.

770 *Upakkilesā*.

771 *Mahaggata*: cf. DN 22.12 and n.664 there.

772 The stages reached as at DN 2.93.

773 The stage reached as at DN 2.95. Cf. MN 29.

774 This is the stage reached at DN 2.97, though the wording is slightly discrepant.

775 Cf. DN 2.99ff.

776 As at DN 22.22.

777 The extreme tolerance of Buddhism is shown here. This can be quoted to those who, wishing to practise, e.g. Buddhist meditation, are worried about their prior allegiance to another faith. But see DN 29.4.

778 *Ponobhavika*: as at DN 22.19 and n.702 there.

779 Like Ānanda at DN 16.3.4ff.

780 DN says that the Buddha's words, though not successful at the time, were of benefit to the wanderers in the future.

SUTTA 26

781 We seem to be back in the 'fairy-tale' world of some previous Suttas, but with a difference. RD, in another brilliant introduction in which he develops his theory of Normalism (the belief, in contrast to Animism, in a certain rule, order, or law), fails to analyse the structure

of this fable (which is what, rather than a fairy-tale, it really is). The narrative part is framed by certain important remarks by the Buddha which, announced at the beginning, are repeated in elaborated form at the end (n.809).

782 Cf. DN 16.2.26 and n.395 there.

783 Cf. DN 22.1.

784 *Gocare*: lit. 'pastures'.

785 *Pettike visaye*: 'the range of your fathers'.

786 *Cakkavatti-vatte vattāhi*. RD points out the play on 'turning into a Wheel-Turner': *vatta* meaning both 'turning' and 'duty'.

787 Cf. DN 17.1.8.

788 A truly Buddhist touch! Asoka, who made some effort to live up to the ideal of a wheel-turning monarch, established animal hospitals.

789 *Adhamma-kāro*: 'non-Dhamma-doing'.

790 The word rendered 'good' is the same, *kusala*, as rendered just previously by 'wholesome'. The literal 'skilful' is also sometimes to be preferred. A case where variation in translation is desirable – but it should be indicated.

791 All as in DN 17.

792 But see n.472. Warder (as n.801) has 'rule (collect taxes) in moderation'.

793 Even though the charge was justified! But the denunciation was malicious.

794 *Micchā-diṭṭhi*: see n.708.

795 *Micchā-dhamma*. DA says 'men with men, women with women'.

796 Said by RD to be 'a kind of rye'. The dictionaries are less specific.

797 *Kusala* (see n.790). The real meaning is 'skilful' in regard to knowing the karmic consequences of one's actions – in other words not having *micchā-diṭṭhi* (see n.708).

798 RD's note is barely intelligible, or at least unhelpful: '*Satthantarakappa. Sattha* is sword; *antarakappa* is a period included in another period. Here the first period, the one included, is seven days. See Ledi Sadaw in the Buddhist Review, January 1916' – a journal not all

readers will have to hand. On *Antarakappa*, Childers (as often) is more helpful than PED: 'Each Asankheyya-kappa ["incalculable aeon"] contains twenty Antarakappas, an Antarakappa being the interval that elapses while the age of man increases from ten years to an asaṅkheyya, and then decreases again to ten years.' Clearly this immense period – which, in regard to the human life-span, is not canonical – is not meant here, but the reference to 'ten years' is relevant. DA distinguishes three kinds of *Antarakappa: Dubbhikkhantara-kappa, Rogantarakappa,* and *Satthantarakappa*, caused by greed, delusion and hatred respectively. RD ignores all this.

Cf. EB under *Antarakalpa*, where a parallel to this commentarial passage is cited from the 11th-century Sanskrit-Tibetan dictionary called *Mahāvyutpatti*. The article concludes: 'Yet, the context in which the term *satthantara-kappa* occurs in the *Dīgha Nikāya* (III, 73) seems to suggest that the word could also be used in a very general sense to mean a period which is not of the same duration as an *antarakappa*.' The context in fact suggests that this period of one week marks a turning-point which is the beginning of an Antarakappa in the sense mentioned by Childers.

799 There will be, it seems, no real disease at all: death will result only from excessive or inadequate nourishment or the inevitable onset of old age. Accidents also seem to be excluded.

800 This seems to be the meaning of a doubtful expression.

801 In the commentaries and later literature Avīci denotes the lowest of the hells (or 'purgatories', as RD and other translators have it, to indicate that no such hell is eternal). This, and a parallel passage at AN 3.56, is the only passage in the first four Nikāyas where it is mentioned, and 'hell' does not seem to be its meaning (RD renders it 'the Waveless Deep'), though its exact sense is doubtful. Warder, in his paraphrase of this Sutta (*Indian Buddhism*, 168) says parenthetically: '"like purgatory", the Buddha remarks ambiguously, thinking probably of his preference for seclusion.' The Buddhist hells grow steadily worse in the popular imagination, but most of

their horrors find little support in the Suttas (though see MN 129, 130). Cf. n.244 and Introduction, p. 40.

802 Benares.

803 The next Buddha, perhaps better known by the Sanskrit name Maitreya.

804 This had been drowned in the Ganges.

805 Cf. DN 16.3.3. and 18.22.

806 See n.400.

807 As DN 13.76, 78.

808 The word *bala* 'power' is repeated from just before.

809 As RD fails to mention (though it is surely significant), the conclusion (verses 27–28) repeats the Buddha's words in verse 1, the reference there to Māra being expanded after the first sentence of verse 28, Māra and his power being again alluded to before the last sentence of verse 1 is repeated. The fable shows the large-scale effect of keeping morality, and indicates how monks are to use this lesson.

SUTTA 27

810 This is a parallel fable to the previous Sutta, giving a slightly different account of 'origins', and including a devastating attack on the pretensions of the Brahmins. It has close links with Sutta 3, and RD refers to it in some detail in the introduction to that Sutta. He calls it a kind of Buddhist book of Genesis, which is fair enough if one pays attention to the differences. Here there is no creator god, and though we start (at verse 10) with something like the same state 'in the beginning', this is of course no absolute beginning but one of the eternally recurring 'fresh starts' in saṁsāra.

811 She was called Visākhā, and her 'mansion' was a comparatively splendid structure, though still small to the modern way of thinking.

812 See also DN 13.3.

813 Or *Vāseṭṭhā* (vocative plural) with some manuscripts, as a way of addressing the two.

814 Cf. DN 3.1.14, and also MN 84 and 93.

815 They are of course priests of Brahmā.

816 DN 3.1.14.

817 The Buddhists always place the Khattiyas first. This was their original position, and still applied in the area of the Buddha's ministry.

818 Cf. DN 33.11. (29), also MN 57.

819 *Ohita-bhāro.*

820 Cf. DN 2.35 for the respect accorded to ascetics in general.

821 *Sakyaputta*: 'Son of the Sakyans'.

822 *Dhamma-kāya*: a term which, as *Dharmakāya*, was destined to play a great role in Mahāyana Buddhism.

823 Brahmā here means 'the highest' but is used because the Buddha is speaking to Brahmins.

824 The Tathāgata, by his gaining of enlightenment by his own efforts, has become 'the highest'.

825 Cf. DN 1.2.2.

826 Though born on earth they are still devas, not human beings.

827 As devas from the Brahmā World they are sexless.

828 *Rasa-paṭhavī.* Note that all the various forms of food mentioned are vegetarian.

829 In terms of a 'Buddhist book of Genesis' this would correspond to the eating of the fruit – but not of knowledge.

830 Since these beings, however glorious, are unenlightened, they fall victim to craving (*taṇhā*) and thereby progressively lose their ethereal qualities.

831 *Bhūmi-pappaṭaka*: the exact meaning is unknown. RD has 'outgrowths'.

832 In land free from the jungle (DA).

833 This phrase may be a fragment of verse.

834 As noted above, these beings were previously sexless. DA says 'those who were women in a previous life.'

835 Hitherto they had been 'spontaneously born', a process assumed to continue (see n.849).

836 RD has gone wrong here, rendering this: 'That which was considered immoral...' The reference is not to the sexual activity, but to the throwing of dirt, etc. I have therefore transferred this sentence back from verse 17.

837 The dwellings were constructed not for concealment (as implied by RD) so much as for shelter.

838 Name of the first king of the solar race and ancestor, among others, of the Sakyan rulers (and hence of Gotama).

839 *Akkhara*: later meaning letter (of the syllabary): see n.30.

840 Associated with *khetta* 'field', an etymology which may not be altogether incorrect.

841 *Rājā*: cognate with Latin *rex, rēgis* 'king', is here linked with the root of *rāga* 'desire, lust'.

842 *Bāhenti.*

843 A wholly fanciful etymology, but one which throws a light on what was considered to be the ideal of a Brahmin.

844 *Jhāyanti*: from the same root as *jhāna*, a pre-Buddhist type of meditation.

845 'Meditator'.

846 *Ganthe*: to assume written books would be anachronistic. DA says compiling the Vedas and teaching them.

847 *Na dān' ime jhāyanti.*

848 *Ajjhāyaka*: 'repeater' is for *adhy-āyaka,* but could also be taken as *a-jhāyaka* 'non-meditator'.

849 'Adopting the sexual practice' (*methuna-dhamma*), thus implying that the others were celibate.

850 *Vissa*: 'various', hence, allegedly, *vessa* 'merchant'.

851 A play on *ludda* 'hunting', *khudda* 'mean fellow', *sudda* 'low grade' (RD's renderings). RD remarks: 'Our modern nobles would lift their eyebrows at so amazing a mixture of epithets'. Today many would agree with the sentiment expressed.

852 'Artisans'.

853 I have retained the word 'Dhamma' here (RD, as usual, has 'Norm'), though it is obviously not the Buddha's Dhamma – that is what he goes forth to seek!

854 See DN 22.16 and notes there.

855 Parinibbāna is the attainment of final Nibbāna, as in DN 16.

SUTTA 28

856 The first two verses are the same as DN 16.1.16ff, and the rest of the Sutta is a (doubtless later) expansion of that conversation.

857 Sāriputta was thus established in terms of the 'Mirror of Dhamma': DN 16.2.8ff.

858 The 37 *Bodhipakkhiya-Dhammā* or 'Requisites of Enlightenment', listed at Sutta 33.2.3(2). See BDic and EB for further details.

859 The six sense-organs (mind being the sixth) and their objects.

860 These refer (1) to ordinary human beings, (2) to the eighty 'Great Elders', (3) to the two chief disciples of a Buddha, to Pacceka-Buddhas and Bodhisattas, (4) to 'omniscient Bodhisattas', i.e. those in their last rebirth, when about to become Buddhas (DA).

861 Cf. DN 11.3, here elaborated.

862 By Yakkhas and the like (DA).

863 This implies having gained the second jhāna.

864 *Dassana-samāpatti*. The first two of these approximate to the contemplation described in VM 6.

865 *Viññāṇa-sota*: a rare expression which seems to equate with *bhavanga*, the (mainly) commentarial term for the 'life-continuum' (Ñāṇamoli). See BDic and EB under *Bhavanga*. In this case both worldings (*puthujjana*: n.16) and 'learners' (*sekhā*: n.542).

866 Arahants.

867 *Puggala-paññatti*: also the title of a book of the Abhidhamma, but here the reference is to the different classes of Arahants.

868 *Ubhato-bhāga-vimutto*: one who has gained liberation by both the jhānas and insight. This is the 'liberation of heart and through wisdom' frequently mentioned (e.g. DN 6.13). But only the second part, 'through wisdom', is complete and final liberation. See n.355.

869 *Paññā-vimutto*: one who has gained liberation through insight alone, without, or without necessarily having gone through the jhānas.

870 *Kāya-sakkhī*. For the somewhat scholastic (and doubtless late) definitions of this and the rest, see BDic under *Ariya-Puggala* (B), or VM 21. Also listed at MN 70.

871 *Diṭṭhi-ppatto.*

872 *Saddhā-vimutto.*

873 *Dhammânusārī.*

874 *Saddhânusārī.*

875 As RD remarks, it is most unusual to find these called *padhānas* or efforts.

876 These are detailed at AN 4.162.

877 *Vebhūtiyaṁ.*

878 *Sārambhajaṁ jayāpekkho*: angrily keen on victory.

879 As at DN 1.1.20.

880 Reading *jhāyī* with DA.

881 *Gatimā.*

882 *Dhitimā.*

883 *Mutimā.*

884 *Paccattaṁ yoniso manasikārā.*

885 As a Non-Returner: cf. n.374.

886 As DN 1.30ff.

887 As DN 1.2.2ff.

888 Beyond all calculation.

889 *Atta-bhāva*: cf. n.220.

890 *Sa-upadhika.*

891 *Paṭikkūla.*

892 Note the stress on 'human': the Buddha was still thought of as a man, in some sense. This contrasts with later developments in the Mahāyāna schools.

893 The two extremes to be avoided according to the Buddha's first sermon.

894 In this life.

895 *Abhicetasikānaṁ*: glossed as 'transcending thoughts of the sense-sphere' – not of course 'transcendental' in the sense of supramundane.

896 Cf. DN 19.14.

897 *Sallekhatā*: 'austerity'.

SUTTA 29

898 Described by RD as a technical college. Crafts were taught there.

899 The name means 'Archer'.

900 For the Nigaṇṭha Nātaputta see n.114. This raises a chronological problem, as the Jain leader is generally believed to have died after the Buddha, A.L. Basham (as n.66) thinks Makkhali Gosāla may be meant here.

901 *Paṭisaraṇaṁ* 'a resort'.

902, 903 The words here are *tassa te āvuso lābhā, tassa te suladdhaṁ* 'this, friend, is your gain (*lābhā*), this for you is well-gained (*su-laddhaṁ*)', i.e. a good opportunity, glossed by DA as 'human birth'.

904 *Apuññaṁ*.

905, 906 As at 902–3 but *alābhā* 'non-gain' and *dulladdhaṁ* 'ill-gained'.

907 Here the words are *alābhā, dulladdhaṁ* as in nn.905–6, but a different translation seemed appropriate. It seemed impossible to preserve the parallelism.

908 *Lābhā, suladdhaṁ*: as at nn.902–3.

909 *Āvikataṁ* (not in PED).

910 *Sappaṭihīrakata*: 'well-founded' (PED, where RD's curious rendering 'made a thing of saving grace' is quoted without comment).

911 *Antaradhānaṁ*: 'disappearance', perhaps a deliberately neutral term to cover both the *parinibbāna* of a Tathāgata and the death of an ordinary teacher.

912 *Brahmacariyā* (n.20).

913 *Yoga-kkhema*: 'Arahantship'. Note that *yoga* in early Buddhist terminology generally has the negative meaning of 'bondage', specifically as a synonym for the *āsavas*. Its positive religious connotations developed gradually, both within and without Buddhism. See DN 33.1.11 (32).

914 RD has accidentally translated 'made perfect' here, instead of the opposite!

915 *Kāma-bhogino*: 'enjoying sense-pleasures'. RD translates 'who are wealthy' and quotes DA as saying 'wealthy converts'. DA actually has *gihi-sotâpannā* which means 'householder-Stream-Winners' – i.e. not necessarily wealthy, but much more than mere 'converts'.

916 The second of Gotama's early teachers before he went off on his own to seek enlightenment. See MN 26, 36, etc.

917 *Anattha-saṁhitaṁ*: as at DN 9.28, where I have rendered it 'not conducive to the purpose.'

918 Some modern writers who have attempted to read their own ideas into Buddhism should take note!

919 This invitation to 'recite' may have inspired Suttas 33, 34! The groups which follow as at n.858.

920 *Sādhu*: which in some cases approximates in meaning to 'Amen'.

921 RD has here: 'A new doctrine, Cunda, do I teach...' But there is nothing new in what follows, which is merely the standard statement concerning the requisites, explained in relation to this life and the next. The correct reading is not *Navaṁ* 'new' but *na vo* 'not to you': confusion arose because the negative was not understood (another wrong reading is *namo*, which is also derived from *na vo*). The solution is found in the parallel with the second sentence: in both cases we have *na...yeva* 'not merely', which makes perfect sense. DA, indeed, has *na vo*.

922 *Hiri-kopīna-paṭicchādanatthaṁ*: a regular part of the formula accidentally omitted by RD. Ñāṇamoli has at MN 2.12 for *hiri-kopīna* 'that which disturbs conscience.'

923 Of hunger (DA).

924 For further details see VM 1.85ff.

925 This recalls the accusation made against Gotama by his five companions when he abandoned self-mortification.

926 This is yet another rendering of *anattha-saṁhita*: cf. n.917.

927 *Bālo*. This word is not used in connection with the other three categories, no doubt to show that 'taking pleasure in killing' is particularly foolish and reprehensible.

928 *Ekanta-nibbidāya*...The intensifier *ekanta*, added to the usual formula, makes it more emphatic.

929 As DN 17.2.3, etc.

930 *Inda-khīlo*: explained by Ñāṇamoli, *Minor Readings and Illustrator* (PTS 1960), p. 203 (commentary to Khuddaka-Pātha): 'the post made of heart-wood hammered in after digging out the earth to [a depth of] eight or ten hands in the middle of the threshold [of a city gateway], its purpose being to hold fast the [double] gates of a city.'

931 *Ataccham* (= *a-tath-yaṁ*): 'not true'.

932 The various meanings of *Tathāgata* are quoted in translation from DA by BB (see n.11).

933 *Mutaṁ*: 'sensed' is used for the three senses of smelling, tasting and touching.

934 Cf. n.405.
935 See DN 1.2.27ff.
936 As n.928.
937 These are some of the speculations dealt with in DN 1.
938 Cf. DN 16.5.4.

SUTTA 30

939 This Sutta may seem the most uninteresting and unedifying of the entire Nikāya. Yet, properly considered, it has its interest, first, as an example of the forms Buddhist propaganda was perhaps sometimes obliged to assume, and also from the point of view of iconography, as some of the marks came to be depicted in images of the Buddha: the great reclining Buddha-figure in Wat Pho in Bangkok is a well-known example. RD has a wide-ranging introduction tracing the possible origins of such marks, which clearly must have been important in the minds of influential Brahmins in the time of the Buddha (see, e.g. DN 3). However, later Brahmin tradition has preserved very little about them. Certainly, many of them seem quite arbitrary and even difficult to distinguish clearly. Nevertheless, there are more traces of their influence in later Buddhist writing (and, as observed, iconography) than RD is anxious to admit, and there are even 'eighty minor marks' mentioned in addition to the thirty-two major ones here listed. Both lists, major and minor, are found in the *Dharma-Saṁgraha* (ed. Kenjiu Kasawara and F. Max Müller, 1885, rep. Delhi 1981), carefully collated with the lists as they occur in the present Sutta and elsewhere. RD remarks that 'most of the marks are so absurd, considered as marks of any human, that they are probably mythological in origin, and three or four seem to be solar.' He adds that 'our Suttanta seems gravely ironical in the contrast it makes between the absurdity of the marks and the beauty of the ethical qualities they are supposed, in the Suttanta, to mean.' But it must be added that, however absurdly as regards the details, they are intended to show the relation between action

and karmic result, and they could have been used pedagogically to inculcate this lesson. Scholars are agreed on the fairly obvious fact that this is one of the latest texts in the Nikāya, and this is even hinted at in the commentary itself. The verses, ascribed to Ānanda, show an exceptionally wide variety of metres, but all of late types. It is possible that someone tried to give this unpromising material some literary grace by dexterous versification. I considered trying to reproduce the different metrical forms in translation, but decided this was beyond my powers. Perhaps some other translator will attempt this one day.

940 *Mahāpurisa*. Though a 'Great Man', endowed with very special qualities, the Buddha as born on earth is still a man. Cf. n.892.

941 This appears to mean flat feet! See RD's notes to DN 14.32.

942 Often taken, and shown iconographically, as having the fingers all of the same length, and the toes likewise.

943 Or reticulated.

944 Or with the ankle half-way up the calf.

945 Used as a cosmetic.

946 Like Brahmā.

947 The backs of the four limbs, the shoulders and the trunk are well-rounded (RD).

948 Explained below. It is hard to know how Pokkharasāti (DN 3) *observed* this!

949 Or a hairy mole.

950 *Uṇhīsa* (Skt. *uṣṇīṣa*), represented iconographically by a protuberance on the top of the head. Incidentally, the elongated ear-lobes commonly seen in Buddha-images do not figure in the list.

951 This provides the excuse for listing them here.

952 See n.512.

953 See n.524.

954 A class of man-eating demons.

955 'Place of delight', a term for the heavenly realms.

956 *Sangaha-vatthū*.

957 As at DN 29.13.

958 Cf. DN 26.5.

959 As at MN 111.2 and elsewhere. Explained at PD 21.20.
960 *Hiri.*
961 *Ottappa.*
962 *Cāga.*
963 See n.482.
964 In the throat.
965 Following DA's interpretation.
966 *Anugata* (exact meaning doubtful).
967 *Ādeyya*: lit. 'to be taken up', i.e. acceptable.
968 See n.596.
969 As RD remarks, the absence of the 'Buddhological complement' is quite remarkable. DA has no comment on the last few lines, which seem to be corrupt.
970 Cf. DN 1.1.10.
971 Cf. n.146.

SUTTA 31

972 Alternatively called (as by RD) *Sigālovāda Suttanta* 'The Sigāla Homily'.
973 *Kamma-kilesa.*
974 *Apāya-mukhāni*: cf. n.158.
975 The expression is awkward in English, suggesting that the Well-Farer and the Teacher are two different persons, which is of course nonsense. Contrast this formula with that used before the verse-passages in DN 30, where the verses are ascribed to Ānanda.
976 Crimes committed by others are laid at one's door.
977 Cf. DN 1.1.13.
978 Because a gambler cannot support a wife properly.
979 Cf. Thag 74.
980 If you want a cart, he has just lost a wheel, and so on.
981 *Suhadā*: 'good-hearted', or 'sound at heart' (RD).
982 If you are drunk, etc. (DA!).
983 A pun on *dakkhiṇa* 'right hand, south', and *dakkhiṇā* 'fee or offering to teacher'.
984 The last is omitted by RD.
985 *Ayiraka*: a metathetised form for *ariyaka* 'nobleman, master'.

SUTTA 32

986 This is a *paritta* (Sinhalese *pirit*), a set of protective verses (strangely called a 'ward-rune' by RD). The purist may be shocked to find this not only in 'popular Buddhism' but actually enshrined in the Canon; but Mrs Rhys Davids offers a spirited defence of such things in the introduction to her translation of this Sutta. She quotes the list of canonical *parittas*, and a similar list also occurs at VM 13.31: the Ratana Sutta (Sn 222ff., Khp 6), Khandha Paritta (AN 4.67), Dhajagga Paritta (SN 11.1.3), and Mora Paritta (Ja 159), beside the present Sutta. These are said to be efficacious through ten thousand million world-systems. DA, however, advises the use of the Metta Sutta in the first place, then the Dhajagga and Ratana Suttas. Only if, after a week, these do not work, should the Āṭānāṭiya be resorted to – which would be of no use in the kind of emergency envisaged in the text! But the mention of the Metta Sutta is interesting because the Khandha Sutta (delivered after a monk had died of a snake-bite) enjoins the practice of loving-kindness to all beings as a form of self-protection. Like certain truthful declarations, this can have powerful effects. See Piyadassi Thera, *The Book of Protection* (BPS 1975).

A Tibetan version of this Sutta exists, and a fragment of a Sanskrit version has been found in Central Asia, but this differs considerably from the Pali. It is quoted with translation by K. Saha, *Buddhism in Central Asia* (Calcutta 1970), 47–49. This includes a reference to 'Āṭānāṭi the much renowned', and 'the heart of Āṭānāṭi furthering all acts . . .' as if this were a person, though according to our text and DA, Āṭānāṭā is a town.

This Sutta is much used on special occasions in the countries of Theravāda Buddhism. Thus in Thailand it is chanted at the New Year, together with the Mahāsamaya Sutta (DN 20, with which it has much in common) and the Dhammacakkappavattana Sutta (SN 56.12.2, the Buddha's first sermon). The Thai version also includes a non-canonical introductory portion containing verses of homage to twenty-one Buddhas earlier than Vipassī, going right back to Dīpankara, under whom the future Buddha Gotama first went forth, and to three even earlier Buddhas before him. See also K.R. Norman, *Pali Literature* (Wiesbaden 1983), 173ff.

987 Cf. DN 18.11.

988 See Introduction p. 45. The four groups mentioned are those of their respective followers.

989 Defence of the four quarters is the special charge of the Four Great Kings. We may, however, note by way of contrast the 'protection of the four quarters', and the associations of those quarters, in DN 31.

990 As at DN 4.9 and elsewhere, indicating the various degrees of commitment or otherwise those concerned felt towards the Buddha. In the case of the yakkhas, the position is explained in verse 2.

991 The Great King of the North (cf. DN 18.11ff.).

992 DA carefully explains that the Buddha did not really need to *learn* it, but went through the motions for pedagogical reasons.

993 The canonical text begins with Vipassī, seven Buddhas and ninety-one aeons back from Buddha Gotama. The Thai introductory portion, going back further, is certainly of later origin.

994 This is more literal than RD's 'ascetic, wholly pure'.

995 The term *angīrasa* 'radiant' applies to all the Buddhas mentioned.

996 DA is clearly unsure whether Buddhas only, or all Arahants are meant.

997 *Purima* means both 'first' (or 'former') and 'east'.

998 These are often called 'hungry ghosts'. A whole book of the Khuddhaka Nikāya, the Petavatthu, is devoted to them. The next three lines refer to their character in life, which resulted in their present miserable state. They are in the south because they were led out to execution through the south gate of the town (as DN 23.7).

999 *Pacchima* means both 'last' (or 'later') and 'west'.

1000 It may seem strange to us that this mythical ideal land (thought of as still existing, though almost inaccessible) should be located in the north, of all directions, but in the tropics this is quite natural. Later, with the growth of geographical knowledge, the region was relocated in the Antipodes. The whole mythology is, of course, pre-Buddhist.

1001 The inhabitants of this region, though obviously not enlightened, have high moral standards.

1002 *Tuṇḍikīre*: so explained by DA (the now familiar 'tandoori'?).

1003 Not clearly explained by DA.

1004 DA's only relevant comment is that 'right-thinking people cannot do this'. This trait, which rather spoils the otherwise idyllic picture, remains an unexplained curiosity.

1005 DA insists that Ambara-Ambaravatiya is one name.

1006 He thus has two names, Kuvera and Vessavaṇa.

1007 *Jīva* means 'live!' A sort of pheasant or partridge.

1008 This bird calls '*Uṭṭhehi citte!*' 'Lift up your hearts!'

1009 Doubtful: the usual meaning of this word is 'crab'.

1010 As at DN 3.1.20.

1011 A strangely heterogeneous list, including famous gods and sages – clearly designed to show the Buddha's influence. RD gives full references.

SUTTA 33

1012 This is undoubtedly a late Sutta. RD with characteristic caution says of this and DN 34: 'They contain here and there matter which suggests that they took their present shape at a later date than the bulk of the rest of the Dīgha'. It is associated, like DN 29, with the time immediately following the death of the Nigaṇṭha Nātaputta, the Jain leader, and it is located 'in the mango-grove of Cunda the smith', known to us from DN 16.4.14ff. If we compare DN 29, we find that that discourse is addressed to 'the novice Cunda', who is quite a different character – but we may wonder whether the two have not become confused. Part of the inspiration of DN 34 may have come from the Buddha's words at DN 29.17. Could the whole Sutta have been expanded from that nucleus? In any case the method of listing items in expanding numerical groups was used (whether earlier or later) on a large scale in the Anguttara Nikāya, and in fact quite a number of entries in the lists in this Sutta appear there too.

Such numerical listing has also been compared by different writers from RD onwards to the so-called 'matrices' (*mātikā*) of the Abhidhamma – partly with the implication that this type of presentation always represents a stratum considerably later than the Buddha's time. In fact we do not know to what extent the Buddha himself resorted to the obvious pedagogic device of teaching 'by numbers'. In any case, when such numerical lists were in existence, they readily lent themselves to expansion, and it is likely that the material of this Sutta dates from a variety of periods, and because some of it is obviously late, this does not mean that other parts are not early. There are in existence Tibetan and other versions. It should perhaps be stressed that, arid as this type of Sutta may appear to many today, it is from the monastic point of view valuable for use in chanting (its ostensible – and probably real – original object), incorporating as it does not only the major doctrinal categories in brief, but many points on behaviour and discipline which monks should constantly bear in mind.

N.B. Since the lists in this and DN 34 consist largely of technical terms, the Pali words have been given wherever confusion or doubt seemed possible.

1013 The lofty ('Thrown-aloft-er', RD).

1014 Cf. n.441. The Mallas of Pāvā were, of course, closely related to those of Kusinārā.

1015 Not 'lovely is the night' (an odd mistranslation of a stock phrase by RD).

1016 The third of the five hindrances (below, 2.1 (6)).

1017 As at DN 16.4.40.

1018 As proposed at DN 29.17 (see n.1012).

1019 Or really, like the parallel following groups, '(set of) one thing'.

1020 This second 'one thing' is not found in all texts, or in the AN parallel passage, perhaps owing to a misunderstanding of 'one thing'.

1021 The link here with (8) seems to be simply a play on words: *āpatti* 'offence', and *samāpatti* 'attainment'. Despite the divergence in meaning, the two verbs are from the same root.

1022 These are the six senses (mind as the sixth), their objects and corresponding consciousnesses, e.g. 'eye, sight-object, eye-consciousness', as in MN 115. See BDic under *Dhātu*.

1023 Note again the play on words: a useful mnemonic device.

1024 'Purity of fraternal love' is RD's rather loose paraphrase of DA.

1025 RD's 'absence of mind' may just do for this, but 'want of intelligence' is quite wrong for *asampajañña*, which is quite simply failure to comply with the injunction at DN 22.4 (see n.646 there).

1026 *Bala*: 'power' used here in an unusual sense.

1027 These are the two basic forms from which stems all Buddhist meditation.

1028 Ñāṇamoli's rendering of this difficult word.

1029 Or 'thought', as in the second step of the Noble Eightfold Path.

1030 Here, the World of Sense-Desire (*kāma-loka*).

1031 Note the overlap with the previous three, which represented the 'Three Worlds'. Here we have the two 'higher worlds' and the supramundane (*lokuttara*), referred to here as 'cessation' (as in the Third Noble Truth).

1032 Craving for continued existence.

1033 Craving, not for 'cessation' (n.1031) but for (materialistic) extinction. Only those in whom the Dhamma-eye (n.140) has opened can clearly see the vital distinction between these, though it can be more or less dimly intuited by reason and/or faith. See n.703.

1034 Lit. 'own body', this is the erroneous self-idea. The destruction of this fetter (with two other associated ones) constitutes the opening of the Dhamma-eye (n.1033) or 'Stream-Entry'.

1035 Certain crimes (as parricide, cf. DN 2.100) have a fixed result which cannot be avoided.

1036 When the first path-moment (or Stream-Entry, n.1034) has been gained, progress is inevitable, and retrogression to 'states of woe' impossible.

1037 RD reads *kankhā* 'doubts'.

1038 Lit. 'somethings', glossed by DA as 'obstacles'.

1039 I.e. religious teachers (cf. DN 31.29).

1040 This refers to 'very subtle matter'.

1041 'They compound co-existent states and (their) future fruition-states' (DA).

1042 This refers to rebirth in the Formless World.

1043 Cf. n.542.

1044 The last receives the courtesy title of 'elder' from juniors without being strictly entitled to it.

1045 These are all the realms from the hells up to the heaven of the Paranimmita-vasavatti devas. (See Introduction, p. 40).

1046 These are all in the World of Form.

1047 Ways in which one is 'guarded'.

1048 The higher faculties of the Stream-Winner, etc.

1049 Cf. n.140.

1050 That of the Stream-Winner.

1051 *Kāya* here means not (as RD) 'the psycho-physiological mechanism of sense', but 'mental (i.e. broadly 'emotional') body'.

1052 Different stages of jhāna. The distinction made between the first two seems to reflect the (later) Abhidhammic subdivision of the first jhāna into two.

1053 *Moneyya* is derived from *muni* 'sage' (or 'anchorite', RD).

1054 Note the play on words here: three derivatives of the root *i* 'to go'. *Āya* can also, in more mundane contexts, mean 'money-making' (as absurdly suggested for this passage in PED!). *Apāya* generally refers to 'states of woe' (evil rebirths), while *upāya* comes to mean 'skilful device', and as such is much used of the Bodhisattva in the Mahāyāna tradition.

1055 The second refers to the Brahmavihāras (DN 13), the third to Arahantship.

1056 Cf. DN 11.3 and nn.231–3.

1057 This is just the uprising of any thought that occurs.

1058 'Bases of Conduct' (RD).

1059 Telepathy.

1060 Knowledge in terms of conventional truth. Cf. n.224.

1061 Usually this means ordinary human food, but see n.1062.
1062 This refers to the food of the devas, sometimes also called *kabalinkāra* (cf. n.74). See BDic under *Āhāra*.
1063 This volition = kamma.
1064 *Chanda* is the most general word for 'desire, intention': see BDic.
1065 Cf. DN 1.1.17. DA's gloss here: 'oil, honey, ghee', etc., seems mysterious, and is not supported by the Sub-Commentary.
1066 See DN 28.10.
1067 By developing *samādhi*.
1068 *Dhamma-padāni*. Formally this is the plural of *Dhamma-pada*, the title of perhaps the most famous Buddhist scripture, but it is glossed as 'divisions of the Dhamma'.
1069 Omitting 'faith' as the first of this group, normally of five.
1070 Truth, i.e. realisation of 'things as they really are'.
1071 Not 'to master self' (RD).
1072 Kamma that leads to enlightenment, when no more kamma will be created.
1073 'Making present to the eye'.
1074 Here *sati* is perhaps being used in its older, occasional sense of 'memory' rather than mindfulness: see n.629.
1075 See n.140.
1076 Factors present in the 'mental group' at any given moment.
1077 See n.913.
1078 Which tie mind (*nāma*) and body (*rūpa*) together. *Gantha* also means 'book' in the later language (see n.846).
1079 *Kāya* here means *nāma-kāya* 'mental body'.
1080 *Yoniyo*: 'wombs'. Further details are given in MN 12.
1081 'As from rotting fish, etc.' (MN 12).
1082 Rebirth in the deva world (also as a Non-Returner).
1083 A new 'self' in another existence. Cf. n.220.
1084 See n.933.
1085 Cf. n.823.
1086 Like Upananda, whose conduct was not good, though he was still able to help others (DA).

1087 These curious designations are supposed to refer to the Stream-Winner, Once-Returner, Non-Returner, and Arahant respectively.

1088 Cf. n.244.

1089 Cf. n.244.

1090 Faults of begrudging in a monk.

1091 Begrudging others the support of a particular family.

1092 Realms inhabited by the Non-Returners, who attain to Nibbāna directly from there.

1093 The meaning of this name is perhaps 'not falling from prosperity' (see EB).

1094 For these scholastic distinctions see BDic or EB.

1095 See also MN 12.

1096 This, though here used metaphorically, is the word for 'thirst' in the literal sense. Here it means something less strong than *taṇhā*.

1097 *Vimuccati,* apparently meaning 'is liberated', but glossed by DA as *adhimuccati,* rendered by RD as 'choose'. The same verb is used in the next sentence with regard to renunciation. I have used 'make free' as a makeshift, free rendering, and suspect a textual corruption.

1098 *Rūpa* here perhaps means 'thing seen'.

1099 'By the *samādhi* of the fruit of Arahantship' (DA). In this context, it is perhaps worth noting that in Buddhism, as opposed to some non-Buddhist usage, *samādhi* by itself never means 'liberation' or 'enlightenment' (see n.225).

1100 'Investigations linked with pleasure' (DA).

1101 The meaning of *sārāṇīyā dhamma* is not quite certain. At DN 16.1.11, RN has 'conditions of welfare', which is a slip for the preceding *aparihāniyā dhammā.*

1102 The four primary elements (n.70) with the two additional ones sometimes found with them (as MN 140). For the first five in later Buddhism, cf. Lama Anagarika Govinda, *Foundations of Tibetan Mysticism* (London 1959), 183ff.

1103 Cf. VM 21.66.

1104 A miscellaneous collection of 'unsurpassed' things, the last, for example, being the recollection (not 'memory', RD!) of Buddha, Dhamma and Sangha.

1105 RD quaintly renders this 'chronic states'.

1106 As if the entire Eightfold Path simply led up to Right Concentration! (cf. n.1099). See DN 18.27.

1107 The ideal man (Buddha or Arahant).

1108 Naturally in the relative sense: there would be no justification for reading any notion of a 'Great Self' into this (basically pronominal) usage! Note the characteristic play on words: *attha, attā, mattā.*

1109 Reading *niddasa*. RD's 'bases of Arahantship' is pretty free.

1110 *Diṭṭhi-paṭivedhe*. RD's 'intuition of the truth' does not quite hit this off.

1111 Lit. 'going along with'.

1112 These form the final part (rules 221–227) of the Pātimokkha or code of discipline.

1113 As n.1039.

1114 RD has 'like a load of soaked beans', following DA, but the sense of 'pregnant' seems well established. Perhaps a case of prudishness on Buddhaghosa's part, echoed by Mrs Rhys Davids.

1115 In practising (not 'studying': RD) for calm and insight. Giving (RD has 'forgiving' – a misprint for 'for giving'!) softens the heart in both donor and recipient. DA quotes the verse also found at VM 9.39:

> A gift for taming the untamed,
> A gift for every kind of good;
> Through giving gifts they do unbend
> And condescend to kindly speech. (Ñāṇamoli's translation).

1116 'Expands' (RD). But this is the usual verb for 'developing' in meditation.

1117 'I.e. its being unmixed, single-minded' (RD). DA has no comment, but the idea of the power of such a 'pure-minded' aspiration is very similar to that regarding the efficacy of a 'declaration of truth'.

1118 Brahmā to the Buddha is not immortal and is not a creator-god. His wisdom, though considerable, is limited, and he can be boastful (see DN 11!), but he is free from sensual passions, and so must those be who are reborn in his realm (though the passions may have only been suppressed by jhāna – which is *cetovimutti* 'liberation of the heart' – and not necessarily by insight, which is *paññāvimutti* 'liberation by wisdom': cf. nn.355, 868). But those who are reborn there have not, says the Sub-Commentary, got rid of the desire for continued existence (*bhavataṇhā*: n.1032).

1119 As n.244.

1120 I.e. rebirth among those devas whose lives are so long that they miss the chance of human rebirth at a propitious time. Cf. n.888.

1121 The central, 'civilised' area of India (including the Gangetic basin) as opposed to other less favoured regions: cf. n.722.

1122 The words of Ajita Kesakambali (DN 2.23).

1123 I.e. becomes so subtle as to be imperceptible.

1124 *Dhammā* here clearly means 'things, factors', not 'doctrines' (RD).

1125 DA is doubtful whether *abhidhamma* here means 'the seven Pakaraṇas', i.e. the Abhidhamma Piṭaka as we know it, or not. The short answer is that if this text goes back to the Buddha's time (which is possible but far from certain), the word *abhidhamma* can only have the more general sense of 'higher teaching' or the like. Similar considerations apply to *abhivinaya*.

1126 Cf. n.1074.

1127 Not 'objects for self-hypnosis' (RD). The jhānas differ from hypnotic trance in that one has full control and is not suggestible. I am indebted to Dr Nick Ribush for this valuable clarification (cf. n.211).

1128 There is some confusion about the last two members of this list. Elsewhere we find *āloka* 'light' instead of consciousness (the latter is difficult to envisage as a *kasiṇa*). See VM 5.26 and n.5 there.

1129 Or 'sectarian opinions' (RD). Private aberrations of view.

1130 *Passaddha-kāya-sankhāro*, where *kāya* means the mental body.

1131 Cf. 1.10 (22). Getting involved in problems about 'self', etc.

1132 Cf. n.542.

SUTTA 34

1133 This is largely a rearrangement, under ten heads, of the material found in DN 33. As in 33, Sāriputta gives the systematic instruction, but it is noteworthy that the Buddha is not stated either to request him to do so, or to confirm what he has said. In fact 70 out of the 100 items in 34 are identical with 70 out of the 230 items in 33.

1134 Or 'decline': cf. n.368.

1135 Cf. n.86.

1136 RD's laconic note 'Rūpādisu' conveys, of course, nothing to the reader ignorant of Pali! The meaning is 'beginning with the body', i.e. the conceit: 'I am this body', etc.

1137 The arising of a 'path-moment' (Stream-Entry, etc.) after insight.

1138 The latter part of RD's mysterious-seeming note 7 (p. 251) actually belongs here. The 'unconditioned element' (*asankhata-dhātu*) is a term for Nibbāna.

1139 'Wheels' in the sense of means of progress (DA).

1140 This refers to the various jhāna states: (a) is the first two jhānas, and (b) the first three. (c) and (d), according to DA, refer to telepathic awareness of others' minds, and clairvoyance respectively (though this interpretation seems dubious). See nn.1141–2.

1141 *Ceto* here probably means 'will', rather than other people's minds (why should these be 'suffused'?).

1142 There is no apparent justification for identifying this 'light' with clairvoyance, as DA does. It probably implies absence of sloth-and-torpor.

1143 The 'reviewing consciousness' on emerging from jhāna, etc. See n.213.

1144 Cf. n.659.

1145 From *kā-purisa* 'unworthy person'.

1146 According to the Abhidhamma, volitional (karmic) acts are either 'instigated' or 'not instigated', i.e. spontaneous. The karmic effect of the latter is more powerful, for good or ill as the case may be.

1147 This seems to be the meaning here of *niggayha*.

1148 There is some doubt as to the correct reading, though the sense is fairly clear. RD simply quotes DA's comment *paccanīkadhamme gatattā*, meaning something like 'going into reverse', which confirms our rendering, at least as a paraphrase.

1149 *Khīṇāsava* 'one in whom the corruptions are exhausted' is a synonym for an Arahant. The seven powers mentioned here correspond to Nos 1, 2, 3, 4, 7, 9 and 10 of the list at PD 19.24–33 (= Pṭs ii, 173f.).

1150 One would expect, rather, the five powers, since these five 'faculties' (faith, etc. as 6 (vi)) become powers (i.e. unshakeable by their opposites) from First Path onwards. In fact the fuller list at PD 19 (n.1149) includes both 'faculties' *and* 'powers'.

1151 As (2) above.

1152 Rendered 'serenity' by RD, but see PED.

1153 These are given at AN 8.3.30 with the statement that the first seven were proposed by the Venerable Anuruddha, and the eighth added by the Buddha.

1154 For the meaning of *papañca* see n.606.

1155 *Kāyo* as 'mental body'. Cf. n.641.

1156 The first seven of these form the framework of VM, which in turn is based on the scheme of MN 24.

1157 Not 'escaping doubt' (whatever that may mean!): RD.

1158 The subject is elaborated at SN 14.1.1ff.

1159 This, as usual, means contact of sense-base with object, e.g. eye and thing seen.

1160 The term 'perception' is used in a very pregnant sense here, being virtually equivalent to 'realisation'.

1161 RD's remark that *saññā* here is 'concept rather than percept, or perception widely understood' does not quite hit the mark. See previous note.

1162 Here only the five outward senses and their objects are mentioned, omitting mind and mind-objects.

1163 As at DN 33.3.3 (6).

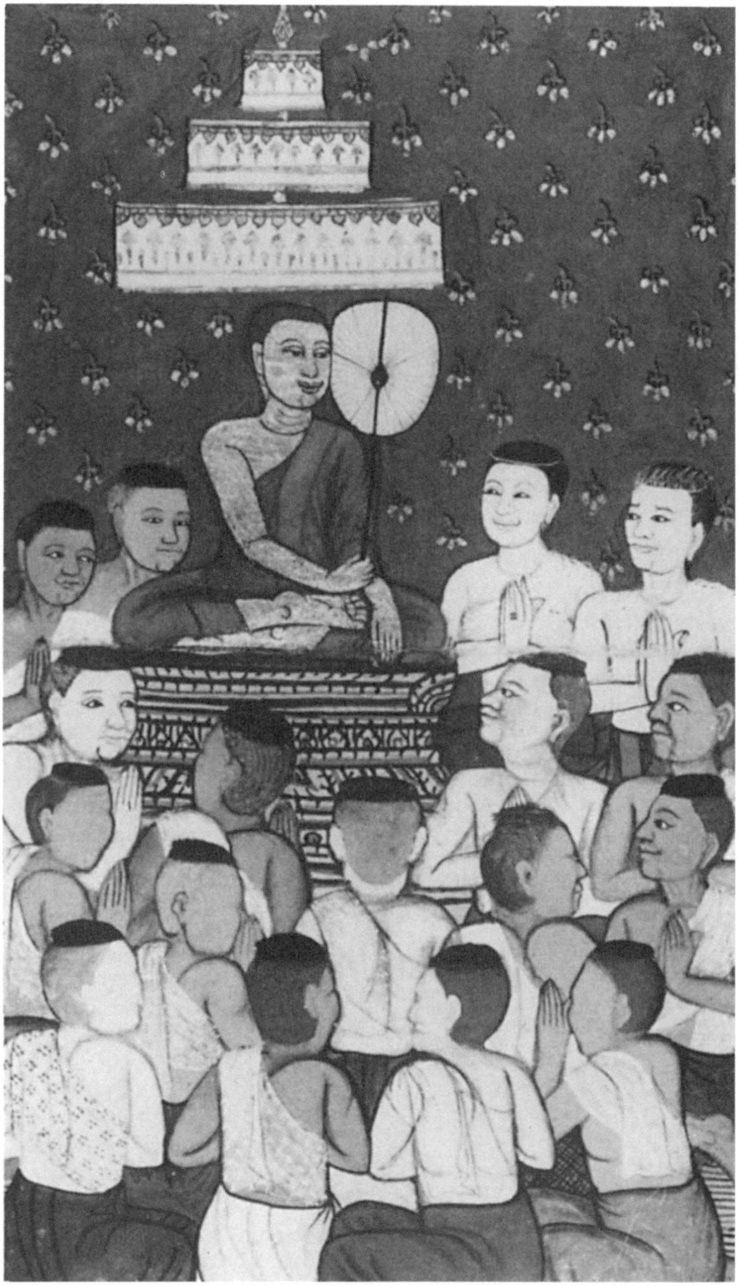

Index

This index includes significant references only. In particular it does not list all the minor mythological figures found in Suttas 20 and 32. Italicised figures refer to page of Introduction. Other entries are either Sutta and verse numbers or note numbers. Notes are mentioned in the serial order of the Suttas to which they refer.

Cross-references are normally given from Pali to main entries in English. However, in certain cases where a Pali word has more than one meaning, or where its meaning is doubtful, this is made the main entry, and English cross-references are made to it. Pali terms, except for a few (e.g. Dhamma) which may be regarded as anglicised, are given in italics. Titles of canonical scriptures are not italicised.

hulā dhammī kathā), 16.1.12 etc
Concentration (*samādhi*), 1.3.22, n.83, n.225, n.668, 33.1.10(50–51), 33.1.11(5), n.1067, n.1099
Concentration, Requisites of (seven) (*samādhi-parikkhārā*), 18.27, 33.2.3(3), n.1106
Connected with the goal (*attasaṁhitaṁ*)
Consciousness (*viññāṇa*), *34*, *36*, 1.2.13, 11.85, n.241, n.242, n.684, 33.2.2(3)
Consciousness, conditioning/conditioned by Mind-and-Body, 14.2.18f., 15.21, n.286
Consciousness, Stations of, see Stations of Consciousness
Consciousness, Relinking (*paṭisandhi-viññāṇa*), n.125
Consciousness-Element (*viññāṇa-dhātu*), 33.2.2(16)
Contact (*phassa*), 1.3.45ff., n.86, 14.2.18, 15.2, 33.2.2(4), 34.1.2(3), 34.2.2(7)
Controlled Perception (*sakasaññī*), 9.17, n.211; see also n.1127
Conversation, Unedifying, see *Tiracchāna-kathā*
Corpses, 22.7ff
Corrupted by Pleasure (*khiḍḍapadosikā*), 1.2.7, n.53, 24.2.18
Corrupted in Mind (*manopadosikā*), 1.2.10–12, n.53, 24.2.18
Corruptions (*āsavas*), 2.97, n.134, 26.28, 33.1.10(20)
Cosmology, *37*ff
Council, First, *47*, Second *47*
Counsellor-Treasure (*pariṇāyaka-ratana*), 17.1.17
Courses of Action (*kammapāthā*), Ten unwholesome 33.3.3(3), Ten wholesome 33.3.3(4)
Craving (*taṇhā*), *25*, *34*, 1.3.32ff., 14.2.20, 15.9, 15.18, n.335, 22.19, nn.701–703, n.830, 33.1.10(16–18), 34.1.4(4), 34.2.2(4)
Creator God, 1.2.3ff., 24.2.14
Criteria, Four (*mahā-padesā*) 16.4.7ff
Cross-legged position, see *Pallanka* (ii)
Cunda, (i) (novice), 29.2ff., n.1012; (ii) (smith), 16.4.13ff., 16.4.42, 33.1.1f., n.1012
Cundaka, 16.4.39ff

Dakkhina Janapada (Southern Country), the Deccan, 3.1.23, n.153
Daḷhanemi, King, 26.2ff
Dassana-samāpatti, see Vision, Attainment of
Dasuttara Sutta, 34.1ff
Dead man, Vipassi's sight of, 14.2.10
Deathless, Doors to (*amatassa dvārā*), 14.3.7 (stanza), 18.27, n.535
Delight (*pīti*), 1.3.21, n.81, 22.16, n.692, 33.2.1(25), 34.2.1(1)
Delightful Discourse (Pāsādika Sutta), 29.1ff., 29.41
Dependent Origination (*paṭicca-samuppāda*), *34*, n. 88, 14.2.18ff., nn. 283–286, 15.1ff